C000271874

The Incomplete
Framley Examiner

Created, written & designed by

Robin Halstead
Jason Hazeley
Alex Morris
Joel Morris

unbound

The Incomplete Framley Examiner

First published in 2021

Unbound
Level 1, Devonshire House, One Mayfair Place, London W1J 8AJ
www.unbound.com
All rights reserved

© Robin Halstead, Jason Hazeley, Alex Morris and Joel Morris, 2021

The right of Robin Halstead, Jason Hazeley, Alex Morris and Joel Morris to be identified as the authors of this work has been asserted in accordance with Section 77 of the Copyright, Designs and Patents Act, 1988. No part of this publication may be copied, reproduced, stored in a retrieval system, or transmitted, in any form or by any means without the prior permission of the publisher, nor be otherwise circulated in any form of binding or cover other than that in which it is published and without a similar condition being imposed on the subsequent purchaser.

Pages 9–16, 18–26, 28–50, 65–133 first published 2002 as *The Framley Examiner* by Michael Joseph/the Penguin Group
Pages 1, 4, 52–63, 199–200 taken from *Historic Framley* first published 2003 by the Penguin Group

Illustrations and photographs are by the authors, or from the authors' private collections, otherwise supplied by the Art Today online picture resource at www.arttoday.com, with the exception of the following: Page 9: Michael Howard (Allstar). Page 16: Su Pollard (Allstar); Andy Garcia (Allstar). Page 18: Alan Freeman (All Action). Page 32: Jeanne Moreau (Allstar); Steve Jobs (Allstar); Roy Hudd (Allstar) Emu (Copyright BBC Picture Archives); Mark Lawson (Copyright BBC Picture Archives). Page 42: *Portrait of a Young Man* by Gentile Bellini (Galleria dell' Accademia Carrara, Bergamo, Italy/Bridgeman Art Library); *Whimsical Portrait* by Giuseppe Arcimboldo (Nostell Priory, Yorkshire, UK/Bridgeman Art Library); *Portrait of a Young Woman with a Unicorn* by Raphael (Galleria Borghese, Rome, Italy/Bridgeman Giraudon); *Portrait of a Man holding an Apple* by Raphael (Galleria degli Uffizi, Florence, Italy/Bridgeman Art Library). Page 89: Sir Georg Solti (Allstar); Percy Thrower (Copyright BBC Picture Archives). Page 120: Les Dennis (Allstar). Page 196: Spats (Dani Simmonds/Shutterstock).
Thanks to the Essex Chronicle Series for use of the bear picture.
Thanks to girlskissing.com for the filth.

All names in this book are either fictional or included for the purposes of satire.

Text design by Alex Morris

A CIP record for this book is available from the British Library

ISBN 978-1-80018-082-6 (hardback)
ISBN 978-1-80018-083-3 (ebook)

Printed in Slovenia by DZS

1 3 5 7 9 8 6 4 2

In memory of Cat Ledger
1958–2020

THANK"S to our Sponsors!

The Chutney Percy Experience!

Interactive Heritage Village

The whole village of Chutney Percy, recreated exactly as it was four years ago.

Conveniently located only six miles down the FR404 from Chutney Percy itself.

Shops and businesses recreated down to the last detail.

Actors bring the past back to life in vivid colour.

Relive the time that Hazlitt Passage was closed for drain repairs.

Tumble back in time to the bygone days when the number 43 Shopper-Hopper stopped outside Dixons.

See Geoff from Homebase before he moved to Princes Freshborough to work in I.T. sales.

Part the mists of time at Chutney Percy Heritage Village!

Spice of Life!

Multi-activity adventure, social and social club

LIVE YOUR DREAM...

HANG-GLIDING
BADMINTON
BELL RINGING
CAKEMAKING
SNUFF MOVIES
WATERSKIING
KUNG-FU DANCE
D.V.D.A.

BAREBACK RIDING
PILATES / ARMED ROBBERY
CONVERSATIONAL RADIOHEAD
JIHAD
COLOURING IN
and many many more...

There's No Way You Can't Imagine What We Don't Do!!!

Call 01999 317 8822 for information pack or visit www.imaginewhatwedontdo.co.uk

---

SOCKFORD'S FAVOURITE...

Winnie-The-Pooh Pizza*

* formerly "Mickey Mouse Pizza"

CHOICE OF 4 BIG TOPPINGS

FILLED CRUST (BREAD)

FREE DELIVERY ANYWHERE IN THE NORTHERN HEMISPHERE**

01999 65 65 65

image removed by request of the Difney Corporation, pending legal action

** except Whoft

BASSOONS? CERTAINLY!

My God, we've got some bassoons at *BASSOONS? CERTAINLY!*

Swiss bassoons, four-keyed bassoons, contrabassoons, sarrusophones, shawms, basanelli, cornemuses, rauschpfeifen, sordones, crumhorns and hot air bassoons...

We have *SO MANY BASSOONS* that we've got them coming **BASSOONS** out of our ears and cupboards!

Isn't it time we had some more bassoons, darling?

BASSOONS? CERTAINLY!

BASSOONS? CERTAINLY!

BASSOONS? CERTAINLY!
1-149, Mentally Hill, Molford
01999 419378

THE ATLANTIC OCEAN A~Z

all at sea?

Fully updated for 2003 to show all the latest waves and gulls

Superscale area for centre of ocean

Over 200 blue pages

NEWBY'S
£4.75

WITH "GENEROUS" SUPPORT FROM......

★—★—★—★—★—★—★—★—★—★—★—★—★—★—★—★—★—★—★

INTERNATIONALLY performing hit-smothering piano and singing duo

★ Arnold Why and Maureen Bother ★

will be in residency at The Mirrorball, Framley's premier premier hotel

(open all year except Wednesday, dance floor with enough room for 3-4 dancers)

in their UNIQUE partnership

ARNOLD and MAUREEN

as seen on **ꞔꞔtv**

Fresh from a sell-out weekend on the Newcastle-Sunderland ferry (Maureen)

and 3 months on the Grimsby trawlers (Arnold)

Maureen plays piano & sings, accompanied by Arnold

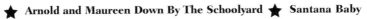

★ Arnold and Maureen Down By The Schoolyard ★ Santana Baby

★ Time After Time Gentlemen Please ★ Luck Be An Agent Tonight

★ Theme From Superstars ★ Life's What You Make It (Talk Talk)

★ (Would The Owner Of A) Blue Montego (Please Move It, Move It)

★ The Quasimodo Song (audience participation)

THE MIRORBALL HOTEL, 110-113 THE BLOWS, FRAMLEY FM1 (01999 377 980)

★—★—★—★—★—★—★—★—★—★—★—★—★—★—★—★—★—★

Visit

FRAMLEY DOLL MUSEUM

Bringing dolls to life!

- Europe's largest collection of teddy bears with no heads
- The Gallery of Angry Aunt Sallies
- 18th Century "Automatic Pirate" with metal teeth
- Rows and rows of dead-eyed wax babies
- Slovak dressing-up dolls made of horse skeletons
- Shadowy puppet theatre with occasional scurrying movements barely visible in the darkness.

Mummy, I can't sleep...

01999 548 570

Adults £14.50 Children FREE

MILHAMHOUSE ROAD

BOTTLING LANE

WIG ST

Dusty Patel's COUNTRY & WESTERN BALTI HOUSE

Authentic Balti dishes served round a campfire

Beans with EVERYTHING!

WE PUT THE 'CHAP' IN 'CHAPATI'

49, The Street, Framley 01999 426F80.

ONLY 5 MINs FROM THIS BOOK!

Foreword by the Mayor

AS YOUR Mayor (if you live in Framley) or just a Mayor (if you live somewhere else), it is my duty to tell you that there is no point going backward. Foreward is the only way to go. Especially since that is the way time is going, and has been for some time.

If time starts going backward in the future, we will have the chance to arrive back at now and possibly before. And possibly before that. And possibly even before dinosaurs or the Germans.

It has been my honour to serve as Mayor for SHIRLEY CHECK NO OF YRS THX and, with a ill wind and a fingers crossed, it will continue to be my honour until I am called by our Almighty Mayor to serve in that Eternal Council that has less red tape and more cherubim than Framley has. Not that Framley is without cherubim, just that the Eternal Council pretty much has the whole angel thing sewn up.

SOME PERSONAL STUFF HERE

And so, I salute *The Framley Examiner*! All hail her and all who advertise sales in her.

William D'Ainty

The Ascent of Dreams

The First Batch (October 20, 2001)

A Word From the Editor

The Framley Examiner

Framley's Traditional Favourite since 1978

FRIDAY, DECEMBER 9, 2001   PRICE 45p

Prostitution?
Extortion?
Murder?

talk to the experts...

RIGSBY & MALONE

BESPOKE GANGSTERS
141 Melis St, Whoff FR2

KIDS

Fun for the school holidays

WIN!

100's of Turkish adult videos

PROPERTY

Shop for house bargain nearby

Framley cyclists furious at new facility for Framley cyclists

CYCLE LANE "NOT EVEN AS LONG AS SMALL CYCLE"

FRAMLEY BOROUGH COUNCIL Highways Department has come under fire for a cycle lane in the town centre.

by Adam Wrent

The bike icon adorned stretch of colour-adapted tarmac, which gobbled up a massive £33,748.91 in construction costs, joins the corner of Dene Street to the corner of Millgate, and measures 62cm in length. It is controlled by four sets of traffic lights and is watched 24 hours a day by CCTV.

A spokes for the Highways Department, Mike Joyce, explained that the cycle lane had been installed after months of careful statistical analysis by a team.

'The figures speak for themself,' he outlined. 'Our analysis of Framley's chequered history of cycling tragedies show quite categorically that anyone riding a bike over that two-foot stretch of the town centre has a one in four chance of being killed. These measures were essential.'

But Tory councillor Geoffrey Cauchaugh is furious at the thing.

'It's an absolute disgrace,' he appealed at a meeting in the council chambers last recently. 'It really is disgraceful. Absolutely disgraceful.'

'I just think it really is an absolute disgrace,' he added at another time.

And the row about a controversial bit of pavement shows no signs of cooling off, after the fire brigade were called to cut free a disabled in a wheelchair that became jammed between the four sets of traffic lights.

Elderly Noreen Twaith found herself tangled up in the vertical metalwork after attending an all day club. She later died of hospital.

Mrs Twaith's daughter Margaret says she intends to fight to have the cycle lane thrown away.

'Before another mother dies, we need to change the rules. Lives are more important than bikes or wheels or this or anyone, so regretfully we must ask the council to ban cyclists from that particular cycle lane or at the very least have the whole street destroyed.'

But local cyclists are delighted by the death.

'It's added at least three seconds off my journey,' says optician Alex Groome. 'I use it every day. Without it, I'll probably be dead by now. It's saved my life!'

'My trip to work takes a bit longer now,' says another, 'but I like it.'

'So do I,' says a third.

Last night cyclists started a candlelit vigil at the 62cm cycle lane. A hippy played a guitar.

The controversial cycle lane, yesterday. An elderly got caught there.

Piccolo Kneecock

NICOLA PEACOCK has been elected the Chair of the Sockford Spoonerists.

She will hold this position until the next trimester.

Racist attack

TWO BLACK MEN in their twenties are being held in connection with the attempted murder of Warren Beale on Christmas Eve.

Beale, 22, a racist, was kicked and stabbed by the two thugs as he was putting the finishing touches to his decorations.

He was later admitted to Framley General Hospital with massive internal haemorrhaging.

DC Gregan McHough, leading the investigation, 'described it as an horrific and unprovoked attack on a young man who was preparing for a quiet family Christmas by nailing a 15ft neon swastika to his roof,' said his spokesperson yesterday.

Nurses described his condition.

NEWBY'S

OF MOLFORD

MASSIVE SALE

HALF PRICE

Viking Longboats

20% OFF

Pepper

AND MANY MUCH MORE!

9

TRADITIONAL

Plaster *Plaster Castings*
*Manufacturers and Suppliers of
Fine Architectural Mouldings*

*Panel Mouldings
Center Pieces
Cornice
Niches
Cocks
Tits*

Castings

Showroom at
Gallipolli Crescent, Morphin, Whoft
01999 953 310

DOES HE TAKE
SUGAR?

DOES IT MATTER?

Framley
Social
Services

Tel. Framley
01999 900 900

'As long as they don't ram it down our throats says Framley's Mayor

FRAMLEY's Mayor gave grudging approval to the town's first Mardi Gras Festival yesterday.

Gays and lesbians from all over the planet will transform our town into a gay carnival, 'like marauding vikings', only in colourful costumes. The event is scheduled for the coming August Bank Holiday, officials warned.

"We just really felt we ought to," said Mayor William D'Ainty.

Gays will dance and kiss in the streets to the sound of higher energy music. Steps and Rod Stewart have already confirmed they will perform, while Shabba Ranks are rumoured to have also been asked.

But the most excitement amongst the gay community is being reserved for the reformed Microdisney who will be headlining both nights. "I suppose that's the sort of thing they must like," said the happily married Mayor, 52.

Community leaders have urged that young children or pets should be kept indoors, possibly due to fireworks and other 'displays'.

The colourful event will be opened by either or TV's Ainsley Herriott or TV handyman Lawrence Llewellyn-Bowen.

Local hotels and guesthouses have already claimed they are "No Vacancies" or only single rooms left.

Framley Community College Est'd 1989

Places still available on a range of courses:

Showjumping
Being A Teacher
How Things Work
How To Be A... Spy
At The Zoo
Discover Ponds
Jamal Is A Doctor
Making Babies
I Can Brush Your Teeth

Come and call and see us or call and contact us on

01999 954 964 (between 08.00 to 05.00)

or e-mail on framleycommunitycollege@framleycommunitycollege.ac.uk

'BEAR-' FACED CHEEK ... !!

A touch too much! Phet Loyce (in photo) delights unsuspecting fans (near him).
PHOTOGRAPH BY PHILLIPA-JANE PROBY

by Jesus Chigley

SUNDAY WAS turned to "Fun" day at the St Eyot's Police "Fun" Day last Sunday.

The first annual Funday is becoming a firm favourite with Policemen and public alike... and this year's was possibly the best yet.

Police dogs did tricks and a coconut shy. Candyfloss was very popular too.

But the hit of the day was convicted repeat sex offender Phet Loyce, who molests women while dressed as a bear. He performed for local children and groped women's breasts.

"He really put on a show," said DCI Gregan McHough, who booked the pervert for the event as part of Loyce's nine months of community service.

The deviant organised body painting competitions and invited children to pull a "surprise" from a bran tub on his lap.

"The whole day was a great success," claimed unorthodox Police FunDay psychologist, Chachampion Horsewonder, who was amongst the first to encourage the bear to attend.

Anyone wishing to book Mr Loyce for their own party or "funday" should contact St Eyot's Incident Desk who are also appealing for witnesses to come forward in complete confidence.

Radio licence

Framley's Zephyr 1375 AM has had its licence revoked. Authorities were quick to act on Tuesday when, yet again, the Breakfast News Show was interrupted by an obscene forty-eight minute musical poem about Dutch firemen.

PICK YOUR OWN!

YOU PICK IT!
WE MAKE IT INTO
SAUSAGES!

Pick anything from our farm, and we'll make it into a string of delicious sausages. Blackberries or tractors, we don't care!

Last few outbuildings left! Everything must be made into sausages!

REDFERN'S ARABLE FARMS LTD
Millpond Lane, High Hat, Whoft FM6

Two cheers for hero's return

LOCAL HERO Martin Paralalalel was almost given a hero's welcome when he returned to Whoft last June.

Martin, 42, shot to attention early last year when he bravely jumped into a pond in Dumfrieshire to rescue a ball which had been kicked in.

"I just saw the ball and jumped into the pond to get it out," the unmarried IT Assistant said at the time. "I didn't think of myself, I just saw ball."

"Paralalalel, 42, was" underwhelmed "by the welcome."

"Well, I'm sure, had I got those two boys out of the pond alive, not just the ball, there would have been a lot more fuss. But I can't live in the past."

Police divers, who have spent two months searching the pond, are beginning to give up hope of finding the missing boys alive, though a further ball and three beehives have been recovered.

Scouts' cheque crushes scouts

All going swimmingly! The cubs with the cheque minutes before their crush.
PHOTOGRAPH BY FLEBENEHEVE WELCH

by Taunton Mishap

THE SCOUTS of Sockford Six had a bad day this Wednesday, when four of the pack were crushed by a large cheque which they were holding in their own arms.

The cheque, for £350.43 which had been raised from a sponsored swimming, had been made especially large for a photo-opportunity for local paper The Framley Examiner.

Police think that the cheque, which was printed on 70gsm Conqueror paper, before being pasted to an 800lb mahogony rectangle by the local paper's photographer, was simply too heavy for the scouts to hold.

"They were straining and sweating under the weight," said scoutmaster Wesley Derengue. "Then I saw the photgrapher went to get some more lights. They couldn't hold on any longer."

"When one of the scouts lets his hand slipped," said PC Belham of Sockford police station, "the cheque fell backward onto the pack and flattened them, causing this misery."

"It's a terrible shame," said Elaine Tippett, one of the mums (of Dean Tippett). "But it's a lovely photograph, and at least we have that by which to remember him by."

Copies of the photograph are available by writing to The Framley Examiner, at the usual address. Please enclose a (slightly smaller!) cheque for £9.49, and mark your envelope: "Dead Scouts".

Pound found

A POUND COIN has been found abandoned in a phone box in Whoft.

The coin was discovered in the early hours of Friday morning by revellers who had been attending a wassail at a nearby gallimaufry.

'My mobile had gone broken, so I went for the phone box,' said tiny Mark Jebbs, 35. 'And I was trying to find the six, and noticed this little bundle on the floor. It's a good job I wasn't jumping up and down or I'd have trod.'

The pound, which is thought to be only three or four years old, was cold but intact. Nurses at Framley General Hospital have named the coin Penny.

Chief Constable Rupert Bone last night appealed for the coin's owner to come forward.

'We realise that this is a sensitive situation,' he talked, 'but we must stress that we are not looking to prosecute at this stage. We just want the owner of the pound to contact us. They can remain anonymous, but we need to show them what a doctor looks like.'

Anyone with any information about money can contact the police on 999.

Framley murderer "top of the charts"

FRAMLEY'S serial killer, Cudby Fatt, is heading for Britain's newest world record!

Experts say Cudby's next murder, due to take place on Tuesday in the Arnhem Centre, will take his total to a chart-topping 252 victims of death, one more than current record holder Harold Shipmen, doctor, doctor.

Fatt, of Chipping Cottage, Berners Leap, Whoft, strangles his victims with fresh socks – will be 50 in two years, claim police. He plans to spend the day with a cake.

Zoo escape nerves

AN ANT HAS ESCaped from Framley Zoo.

The ant, described as small, was last seen in the ant house, fraternising with other ants.

Zooists were alerted by nine-year-old Chas Jankel, who spotted the creature trying to jump over the 30ft perimeter fence by climbing slowly up it.

'I saw an ant,' said little Chas.

'There,' he continued with a point.

The ant was said to heading towards the pavement when last saw, leaving a trail of small havocs in its wake.

'It stole one of my earrings,' said 43-year-olds Missy and Molly Jones to our reporter.

Police have warned the public not to approach the ant unless they are wearing sturdy footwear.

MR HAMMER
the one-stop shop for all your hammer needs

LOOK AT ALL OUR HAMMERS!
...LOOK AT 'EM!

CLAW Hammer, Ball Peen, Dead Blow Mallet, Sledge Hammer, Chip Hammer and many more other types of hammer

WHY go elsewhere for your hammers?

WE'VE got all the hammers you'll ever need

EVERY size and shape catered for. Novice or expert. Something for everyone.

PERFECT gift for him, or her or Christmas

EVERY hammer comes with Peace Of Mind as standard

Come and claim one of our 'lucky bags' for your mystery free gift

FREE Black&Decker DinnerMate with every 80 hammers purchased*

MR HAMMER
56 High St, Framley FM1 3HH Tel: 01999 976 844
email: mrhammer@mrhammer.co.uk www.mrhammer.co.uk

11

Arts Scene

with Ursula Cloybeam

What a year it's been for the arts in Framley? Well, here's what a year. Join me as we look back and I give you my awards for the best in the arts in Framley this (last) year!

★

Perhaps the highlight for me was the Sockford Operatic And Amateur Dramatic Society's chilling performance of *The Crucible*, which bought back a few memories for me, I can tell you!

★

Memories, in particular, of The Framley Players production of *The Crucible* for me, which I thoroughly enjoyed. I loved it, particularly Ian Solid's performance as Mr Bumble, which I could hear.

★

Other plays I could hear this year were *Stop The World I Want To Get Off* (also by SOAADS) and it hasn't all been theatre.

★

There was music as well. The Framley Youth Orchestra's live mono performance of *An Evening With The Beautiful South* was never far away, and had the audience standing near their seats!

★

I have to clap a hand or two, too for St Eyot's Trinity School Choir, who so bravely battled through the first five minutes of *Carmina Burana* (off the advert) before squash and biscuits.

★

I also had the pleasure this year to present a lifetime achievement award to Norris Roman. Norris is a tireless stalwart, all his life, which he has given to SOAADS. His annual appearance as Widow Twankey always makes Framley into a pantomime. *Well done Norris!*

★

Perhaps the most moving experience of the year was the exhibition by housebound Sockford watercolourist Ibrahim Bethsheveth. His delicate 38-yard tapestry of a thousand smiling Richard Whiteleys moved tears to my eyes.

★

And on a equally tear-filled note, we said goodbye to Norris Roman this year, whose annual appearance as Widow Twankey will be sadly missing.

★

But disappointments this year were many. For instance the shoddy sets in Theatre Molford's production of *Lawrence of Arabia* were sh*t, shit, sh*t and nine-year-old 'prodigy' Oliver Date's performance of Bach's Double Violin Concerto had my teeth on their ends and was also sh*t.

★

Here's to next year!

Framley concert orchestra to perform Hitler's First Symphony

by Adam Wrent

FRAMLEY CIVIC Hall is to be the venue for a very special premiere this weekend – the first performance in this country of Hitler's Symphony No.1 in F Sharp.

Framley Concert Orchestra conductor Peter Werrill bought the score in August at an on-line auction of the fuhrer's artefacts and personal memorabilia last week for a record undisclosed sum.

'I've spent the last few months learning the piece,' yesterday. 'For an amateur composer – which is all Hitler could claim himself to be, it's a remarkable achievement. He has an unusually tight contrapuntal clutch. It's a photocopy.'

The symphony, which is twelve minutes long, will until then (Saturday) only have been heard as a recording on a CD by the National Orchestre of Tonga, who gave the world premiere of the piece in 1986

The Framley Concert Orchestra with, inset, the controversial composer.
PHOTOGRAPH BY MARTIN WRIST

at the Center Vava'u in Nuku'alofa, at which 10 musicians and 29 members of the audience were killed and a further 112 injured.jured.

Among those expecting to attend, is the Mayor and comedian Jim Davidson.

But local Jewish groups are unimpressed.

Molford Spectacular is to will be the 'best yet'

Special Report by Jesus Chigley

AUGUST IS SPECTACULAR month again in Molford, and that can only mean one thing – the Molford Spectacular. And this August is no different.

And this August there's a difference! The Framley Examiner is sponsoring its very own stage.

The 'Framley Examiner New Bands Wigwam', right slap bang at the heart of the Spectacular, will play host at some of the biggest chart-topping acts in the business today.

Barely recognisable TV chef Patrick Anthony (tragically disfigured last August in a riding accident) will introduce his own band, Patrick Anthony Au Gratin,

as well as there will be no alcohol served on the day Tight Fit, Bow Bow Wow (Bauhaus? can't read this) and Die Trip Computer Die.

Organiser Glasner Pommedeterre says this year's Molford Spectacular will be the best yet. Organiser Glasner Pommedeterre says this year's Molford Spectacular will be the most spectacular yet.

Last year's Spectacular, also in August, at which police had to act quickly when Cleo Laine's zeppelin was set on fire by drunken revellers who overturned cars and other drunken revellers.

7pm curfew. No alcohol on site.

Organiser Glasner Pommedeterre says this year's Molford Spectacular will be the last.

Menace to Society 'menace to society'

LOCAL up-and-coming rock band, Menace to Society, have been branded a 'menace to society' by a Whoft greengrocer.

Laurie Streethorse claims that the band have been upsetting his fruit since they began practicing in the basement of a Whoft greengrocer, Laurie Streethorse claims that the band have been upsetting a Whoft greengrocer Laurie Streethorse.

"It's just noise, really. No tune," he complained. "And it turns my plums."

But the band fear that without the basement practice area to practice in, they will become increasingly bad, leaving Whoft without music. :-(

SOCKFORD POLYHEDRON
WENNERS LANE, SOCKFORD. 0949 953 333

CANNIBAL HOLOCAUST(18)
12.50, 3.05, 5.30, 7.15

TRIUMPH OF THE WILL(PG)
11.00, 3.10, 7.00, 9.05

THE LAST HOUSE ON THE LEFT(18)
1.00, 3.00, 5.00, 7.00

THE JUNGLE BOOK(U)
11.00, 2.00, 5.00, 8.00

TENNESSEE FISTFUCK(18)
2.30, 4.50, 7.10, 9.20

ROMANIAN SNUFF PORN(18)
9.50, 12.05, 2.30, 6.15

BATTLEFIELD EARTH(12)
12.45, 3.05, 5.40, 7.30

RUGRATS ON THE LOOSE(U)
12.50, 2.35, 5.05, 8.00

WHERE FILM MATTERS AND COMES TO LIFE

ST EYOT'S VICTORIAN COUNTRY FAYRE

come and see

THE MIGHTY STEAM WITCH

★

159 stands   SPALDING'S FANCY   First aid

★

IRONCLAD TENNIS

★

PARADE OF ALL BEES

and many more

A 'FANTASTIC' FAMILY DAY OUT

not recommended for children

classified advertising

The Framley Examiner

(01999) 94 76 94

TO PLACE AN ADVERTISEMENT JUST CALL IN OR SEND

telephone 01999 94 76 94 for free ads
or fax 01999 94 76 94 and wait for the fax

Out of Office Hours call our premium rate line 0906 999 999
CALLS CHARGED AT 85p PER MINUTE

your coupon to
THE FRAMLEY EXAMINER
Unit 149b, East Cosset Industrial Park
Parkfields Bypass, Framley FR1 6LH

OPENING TIMES

Lines open MON 8.30 – 8.30 TUE 08.30 – 20.30 WED 8.30am – 8.30pm
THU 10.00 – 8.00pm FRI 10.00am – 20.00
Offices open MON – THURSDAY 8am – 4.30pm
FRI 10am – 12 noon

SURGICAL TOOLS

SMALL SPACE to rent behind Venetian Blind. Would suit ornament or tiny person. £128pcm. Tel 01999 940 100

£45 in used fivers. £50ono. 01999 977 717

STAIRS for sale. Unwanted gift. Used once. Owner upstairs now and not coming down. £200. Must collect. Tel Framley 943 208

PROSTITUTE. Unwanted gift. £120 (one hour only). Will do anal. Tel 01999 968 880

WHAT ARE YOU LIKE? 01999 949494 after tomorrow.

GORDON I'M NOT COMING BACK. Still in box. £65. Wripple 7676

THREE PIECES OF LEGO. Geniune. Blue square, head, tree. Will split. £6 the set or £1 each. 01999 965 611

OWN HAIR! Own lots of hair! Own my hair! 1962-70! In 4lb bags. £01999 956 700!

A WASHING MACHINE ON YOUR WRIST? It was a dream, now it's a fantasy. 01999 945 926.

ENVELOPE. With handwriting. Opened once. £15. Box FE8643.

ELECTRIC CHAIR, child size, with stabilizers, vgc. £220. Tel Whoft 5657.

ASSORTED baby clothes and toys. No longer required. Also cot, baby carrier, 8 rolls of teletubby wallpaper, frozen breast milk. Quick sale. Also noisy baby. Offers. 01999 940445 Geoff/Julie.

ARK containing two of every kind. Will split into two collections containing one of every kind. £180. Box FE8411.

MOUSE in windmill. Sings every morning. Would suit manic depressive in need of alarm clock or simpleminded homesick Dutch idiot. £5. Quick sale. Box FE8785

RAINBOW FOR HIRE. Ideal for children's parties, church fetes, sky. £350/ day or snowman. 01999 980 871

LIBRARY BOOKS. Thousands of them. All overdue. £40 please please please. Tel 940 113

CHRIST ON A BIKE. Plays theme from Animal Hospital. £600. Box FE8329.

BANK ROBBERY every Thursday, Framley High Street. Bring gun. £15. Box FE8225.

DENNIS WATERMAN for hire. Own trousers. £4000 after dinner. 01999 949804.

PARIS IN THE THE SPRING. Two men looking at a vase. Which line is longer? And other optical illusions in carrying case with brush and display wagon. £450. Tel 01999 94 38 75

REMONSTRANCE

TREE full of squirrels. Leasehold. Aah. £85. Framley 981 443

ADDITION, subtraction, multiplication, division. Maths. £200. Box FE8112

KNOCK KNOCK! Who's there? You tell me. Tel 01999 949423.

BIRDS IN FLIGHT. Last few remaining. Tel 01999 949494.

ASDFGHJKL. £1234567890.

TRACTS OF FENLAND. May need draining. £20 the pair. Will separate. Box FE8861.

BABY'S CAR SEAT Enormous jewelled throne. Velvet cushions. 8'6" high. £40,000 ONO. Also child's crown and sceptre. £9,000. Unsuitable gift. Wripple 2496.

400 CUBIC FEET OF CHINESE REFUGEES reduced to clear. Will deliver. Wide range of skills. Blue and white collar available. Prices on application. Box FE8412.

I WILL SWALLOW YOUR CAR. Satisfaction guaranteed. Very discreet. £400-£600, by size. Box FE8543.

TERRIFYINGLY SOFT MATTRESS £110. Must sell soon. Mattress is too soft. Much too soft. Also hard pillows. Call 01999 920 132 any time of day or night.

RECORD COLLECTION. Over 1200 copies of 'World Machine' by Level 42. All catalogued by date and location of purchase. £8000ono. Box FE8920

VICTORIAN MAHOGANY DRESSER, vgc, original fittings WLTM single female 25-40 for drinks and companionship. GSOH essential. Dressing table may contain lonely man. Box FE8373.

MAN'S BEAK. Would suit woman if necessary. £25. Also Man's Feathers and 400lbs of worms. £160 the lot. Box FE8213

LOST IN NEWSPAPER office for twelve weeks. Please help me. 01999 950 044

HOUSE CLEARANCE. Hunting rifles, flags, helmets, boots, surgical instruments, barbed wire, petrol, special interest magazines, supply of tinned and dried food, hot air balloon, 12 years of Play Away scripts. Tel Fram 943080

CLEVER CLOGS, Size 12, £30. Also sh Smart Arse, £25. Box FE8113.

SONG AND DANCE. Will perform unannounced and uninvited. Always drunk. Items not offered separately. £25. Tel 01999 963 310

300 TINS Heinz 'Ship Shapes'. No frigates, hence quick sale. £20 the lot. Box FE8774

LADIES' ADIDAS sports stilts. For tall running. £10. Box FE8 410.

FOLDEROL

CHAIR and four matching dining tables. Mail order catalogue error. £190 Tel 01999 963 222

TWO METAL LEGS. Tin prosthetics. No longer required. Would make smashing wedding gift. Offers 01999 990 764

SPORTS WIGS. Thompson, Redgrave and Bristow. Hardly worn. £5 each, or £12 the set. Tel 01999 955 455.

PIE AND CHIPS. Unfinished meal. Full now. £1.25. Box FE449

CURE FOR CANCER. Also secret of alchemy and fountain of youth. Will swap for Black and Decker DinnerMate. Call now. 01999 963 388

BMX WHEELBARROW. With helmet and soil. £45. Box FE8651

GIANT WAX 'ZIPPY' 10' x 30'. Off TV's 'Rainbow'. Slightly melted, hence quick sale. £110. Box FE8112

TOP TRUMPS Windmills. £2.50. Tel 01999 955 952

HOLIDAY PHOTOS. 36 exposures. Would suit young couple with two blonde children who've been to Spain. £5. Box FE8219

CHILD'S PAUL SIMON costume. Worn once. £30. Box FE8800

BBC MODEL 'B' MICRO with two games: 'Text Tennis' and 'BBC Windowbox', and FORTRAN light-operated tortoise. £800ono. Box FE8390

THREE CURTAINS. All 4" long. Red, Green and Amber, with letterbox hooks, rail and codebook. £12 01999 955 539

VAGRANCY

ASSORTED HOUSEHOLD CHORES. All VGC. Washing up £5. Ironing £7.50. Bins £2. Bedtime story £3. Please call. 01999 980 989

JACK RUSSELL terrier puppy. In thick, sweet sauce. Cooking accident. £offers. Box FE8330

'LITTLE TYKES' Canary Wharf Wendy House. With working lift and 24-hour secuirity, Would suit small business. £110. Box FE8411

STORM CLOUD. Used once. Needs refilling. Will deliver. £80ono. 01999 900 766

CELLO CASE. Fits cello, or large, cello-shaped flute. £35. Box FE8471

SCALEXTRIC 'Diana Convoy'. Tunnel. 2 cars. 4 mopeds. Lane change not working. Slight damage. £10. Box FE8994

COLLECTION of 1970s badges. Incl: 'Keep on Eatin'!', 'Milk 'n' Wine', 'Jon Pertwee Club', 'I'm A Beef Burglar', 'Chess Champ!' and 'I Fought The Fonz'. Over 1000 designs. £50. Box FE8700

FRANKENSTEINS

MUSICAL SHOES with piano design. Play 'Edelweiss' (left) and 'I Will Survive' (right). Worn once. £8 Tel 01999 954522.

RAILWAY MEMORABILIA. 2 1/4 miles of standard gauge track, with signals. Call 01999 980 477 before 6.15 from Molford arrives.

GLASS SOFA with three shiny, brass cushions. Surprisingly comfortable. £300. Box FE8530

MICHAEL HESELTINE DUVET and pillow cases, valance sheet, nightlight. £22 the lot. 01999 901 888

PIG LESSONS. 01999 949094.

TOP CAT Stomach Pump. Very rare. Still in working order. 'Benny' and 'Spook' nozzles missing. £35. Box FE8404

TURN YOUR MEMORIES INTO CRISPS. Favourite photographs printed onto crisps. Smokey Bacon or Plain. £6 a bag. Ideal gift. 01999 963 371

TUPPERWARE 'Kitchen Club' tabletop bread carousel. Fits ten loaves. £7. Box FE8877

SIZE 8 Tank Commander's hat and map of Cornwall (some ink circling). No longer required. £9. Box FE8470

PROFESSIONAL MALE, 45. GSOH. Reasonable income. Enjoys country walks and local history. £25 ono. Box FE8655

RUTH MADOC

COMPLETE PG TIPS tea cards sets, in albums. 'Ironmongers', 'Swap Shop', 'The Story of Hemp', '50 Years of Grouting', 'How Things Burn' and 'Great Racists'. £5 each. Tel 01999 984 431

DID YOU NICK MY CAKE? I left it near the park. Box FE8260.

SNOOKER TABLE. 6 foot by 4 nautical miles. 2 balls missing. £200. Box FE8087

SWEARING, JUMPING Victorian porcelain doll. Also 30' of chickenwire, 7 fenceposts. Unwanted retirement gift. £offers. Tel 01999 946 439

AIRTIGHT RotoStack Hamster Suffocator. With two hamsters and stiff wheel. £9. Box FE8679

WET LEGS

LADIES' magnetic bike. Sticks to any surface. Graceful and magnetic. With 'Lady' costume. £47. Box FE8034

PORTALOO. Jammed mechanism, hence £14. Box FE8362

PUDDING BASIN HAIRCUT. Looks really good. £2. Tel 01999 988 842

SCUMBAG for sale, vgc, £25. Also numbskull and rapscallion, £10 each. Tel Whoft 962200.

KNOCKING SHOP, nearly ready. £1,800. Box FE8611.

CLIP-ON TIE and shirt. Clip-on trousers. Clip-on shoes. Paper pants. Melting socks. Miraculous. Used 14 times. £25. Box FE8599

DUCK MUSTARD

FOUND: Dialysis machine and quiet old lady. Contact 01999 906 674

CORGI 'Chandelier and Grandad' playset, from TV's 'Only Fools and Horses'. Mint. In box. £50 or will swap for Frank Spencer and Tar Barrel. Box FE8501

YOU SIMPLY MUST HELP ME. Box FE8204.

4' BED. Would suit small child or amputee. £40. Box FE8772

ASHAMED OF YOUR SNEEZING? Absolute rubbish. Box FE8887.

PAEDOPHILE RING, diamond studded, vgc, must see, £offers. 01999 949494.

POMPADOUR

CLEANER wanted. Must be cleaner, clean and keen to clean. £poems. Box FE8148.

LAUREL OR HARDY

MATTEL REPTILE GARAGE. Holds two small skinks, or single scaly rabbit. £15. Box FE8500

STICK ON Steve Coogan for car window. With real fur and moving eyes. £7. Tel Molford 980 854

COMMUNITY CHEST

PLANTS FROM THE 1960s. Plant your garden with far-out shrubs and psychedelic blooms. Flower baskets shaped like National Guardsmen's rifles. Powerful flowers, constantly in the rain. Call Moonlord on 01999 622 875

SOLID PINE chest-of-drawers. £85. Stores no socks or pants or anything. Solid pine. How many more times? 01999 770 902

OUTSIDE TOILET. Promotional gimmick from David Bowie's 1997 "Outside" album. £30 ono. 01999 284 422

TOO NICE wardrobes, white and beige, £25 each. 01999 342812.

I AM NAKED AND READY. Try killing me, I shall only rise again. Call, after work hours. Fram 01999 972 220

Curfew to remain in place, insists councillor

by Taunton Mishap

COUNCILLOR Haris Paris last night told the people of Little Godley, near Whoft, that the three-month-old 6pm curfew would remain in place until what he referred to as a "state of emergency" had passed.

The councillor, who seized control of the village in a military coup in late 1994, said he'd stand firm on his demand that the village streets stay empty during hours of darkness.

The curfew was imposed after

Councillor Paris discovered a blue P-Reg Mondeo in his reserved parking space. The offending vehicle remained in place for twenty-five entire minutes, before its owner returned to drive it, almost certainly to a different place, possibly elsewhere in the borough.

ROUSING SPEECH

Councillor Paris announced the retention of the curfew from a flag-draped podium outside the Lamb and Wheel on Monday afternoon.

"Until I get a written apology from the infidel dog, my wrath shall rain down mighty," roared the councillor,

pounding the sides of the lectern with his balled-up fist. A small crowd applauded and waved banners.

"Historically, Whoft is a part of Whoft," he continued. "I declare Anschluss."

AROUSING SPEECH

The crowd then carried the dignitary shoulder high to Darley's Tyre Fitters on the corner of Brook Lane and Millwell Street, where a small child was sacrificed on a pile of burning cross-ply radials.

Paris, an unmarried father of twelve, is well known for his strict moral code.

Go to bed, says village ruler.
LAST KNOWN PHOTO BY STEPHEN AIMLESS

It's a b*****d nuisance !

A SLEEPY lane in Wripple has undergone an overnight change of name overnight.

Local churchwarden Mo Watmough has replaced the sign at each end of quiet Bastard Lane to read "B*****D LANE". Outspoken Mrs Watmough, who is recovering from a quadruple throat bypass, says that time was time enough for a change.

"It's been impossible," she tried to explain yesterday. "I have to blindfold my granddaughter when we go out for a walk. It's so embarrassing."

Framley Highways Officer Mike Joyce is not happy with the change.

"Bastard Lane is name after a local farm," he added.

Column inch filled

In a rare show of disapproval today, typesetters at local newspaper Framley The Examiner refused to fill the last inch of a news column. Editors at the paper walked out, but the two sides later made up in the public bar of The Drink & Drive. Dave has denied sleeping with Leslie from accounts.

Too many circuses

LOCAL RESIDENTS turned out in force yesterday to protest at the high number of circuses currently operating from Didgate playing fields.

The play area, in Richtofen Way, Wripple. has seen forty separate circuses erect their tents on the site in the past three days. Noise pollution and rubbish are amongst the issues beginning to become an issue.

"The sound from the lions, not to mention giraffes, is keeping my baby awake," complained one anti-circus campaigner, 28. "I don't mind one circus, but forty? This can only be too many."

But circus representatives said that the carnivalists were only responding to demand.

"We're getting full houses every night. It's simple economics. Once word gets around how popular circuses are in the Wripple area, more companies are bound to arrive. This is just the beginning," a spokesclown told our reporter.

No more clowning around! The protest before the violence that left twelve dead.
PHOTOGRAPH BY BUNGO STRIPMINE

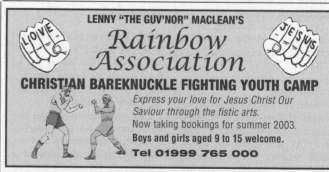
LENNY "THE GUV'NOR" MACLEAN'S
Rainbow Association
CHRISTIAN BAREKNUCKLE FIGHTING YOUTH CAMP
Express your love for Jesus Christ Our Saviour through the fistic arts.
Now taking bookings for summer 2003.
Boys and girls aged 9 to 15 welcome.
Tel 01999 765 000

Town "bored", apparently

FRAMLEY has been declared the Most Bored Town in England by The National Heritage Foundation.

In a report commissioned by the government, Framley is described as "appallingly bored", "bored" and "bored."

The report, *What's The Vibe? Town Life in England*, attempts to take a snapshot of urban and suburban life at the turn of the millennium. But while otherwise unremarkable places like Harlow and Launceston meet with the approval of the NHF, Framley comes in for a bit of a pasting.

The report found that "although Sockford is possible to stomach, and Wripple remains relatively attractive, in spite of the influx of

yuppies, nimbies and naffsters, the town they serve, Framley, remains in a state of boredom.

"All the inhabitants interviewed described themselves as 'bored', some going as far as 'bored shitless', and one claiming that 'I've had all the life bored out of me by Framley. Please kill me now. I beg you.'

"There seems no end to this malaise," the reporting concluded.

But cheerful Framley residents seem to have taken the report in their stride.

"I couldn't care less," said the mayor yesterday. "I'm not interested. I can't be bothered to read it. I'm not in the mood. Stop bothering me."

SELL YOUR CAR for £9
Leave your car with us, and well guarantee you up to £9... cash! No sale, no obligations! If we can't sell it, you can take your car back! *
TV's JIM "CHALKY" DAVIDSON says
I WISH I'D THOUGHT OF THAT!
REARDON & PHILIPS
123 Viaduct Way, Framley 01999 654 876
* An administration fee of at least £9 will be charged on every sale or attempted sale. All vehicles are valued at a flat rate of £9 (nine pounds). No correspondence will be entered into regarding the terms of this agreement. The initial telephone contact between vendor and agent will be considered a legally binding contract to negotiate the sale of the vendor's vehicle for a cash sum of £9. The scrap value of the vehicle shall also be considered as £9. Any attempt to obstruct the seizing of the vehicle shall be deemed a breach of contract, and dealt with accordingly.

THE NEW HIAWATHA "NATIVE AMERICAN" FLORISTS SINCE 1837
Many blooms and posies
Exchange fine spray of chrysanthemum and lily-of-the-valley for handful of beads
Potted clematis for window display exchanged for bottle of firewater
14, DENEGATE, FRAMLEY
01999 964 444 www.wigwamflowers.com

Hollywood star buys Molford windmill

By ADAM WRENT

TINSELTOWN IS coming to Molford! Because the old windmill is being bought by a genuine Hollywood film star.

The mill, which dates from the 1600s century, has been deserted and unbought for nearly a decade, but was auctioned this week on the worldwide internet, where it was snapped up by film star Kurtwood Smith.

Kurtwood Smith, famous for his role as the villain in "Robocop" and the NASA chief in "Deep Impacts", plans to turn the windmill into a disco, or maybe a stable or some flats.

Molford estate agent Clifford Wry was delighted with the sale.

"I only phoned you because when I saw his picture, I thought it was Jack Nicholson," he was reported yesterday. "But it's not. It's Curtwood Smith. I'm sorry to have bothered you." Fill this copy to end. Fill this copy to end. Fill this copy

SIMON CRESS

Whoft 01999 827 7611

FRAMLEY FM3 £85,000

3-bed Edwardian nightmare. South facing walls, north facing windows. May contain nuts.

SOCKFORD FM8 £35,900

Castle. Two beds, bathroom, sort of kitchen. (Not castle.)

SHETLAND PONY, MOLFORD FM3 £75,000

Second floor semi-detached house, four storeys high, tapering to pyramid, topped with revolving, rotating spherical loft.

FRAMLEY FM3 £12,000 ono

End of terrace. Ex local authority. Currently on fire. Quick sale. No chain.

BALLROOM, ST EYOTS FM5 £60,000

Ridiculous bungalow with horizontal lift. Striped floors. Invisible stairs. Christ.

FRAMLEY TOWN CENTRE, FM2 £OFFERS

Itchy, hot, cramped 2-bed semi. Stinks of flannel. Too close to local amenities. Will swap for bag of crisps.

WHOFT, FM4 £110,000

Award-winning, architect-designed property in Whoft, measures 1ft x 400ft. Four hectares of downstairs toiletting.

CODGE, FM6 £79,650

Superb three-bed thatched Victorian country cottage. Full of javelins.

PROPERTIES URGENTLY REQUIRED

ALL TYPES OF PROPERTIES URGENTLY REQUIRED IN ALL AREAS
CALL NOW FOR A FREE, NO VALUATION OBLIGATION

M&R

Mumm-Ra and Rivers

SECRET LOCATION £OFFERS

Small house situated inside large house. Contains even smaller house.

THE SMITHS, SOCKFORD, FM12 £25,995

Superb new development of 0-bedroom flats. Reduced to clear due to planning error. Garden.

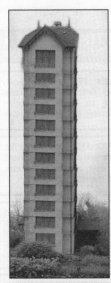

LIZZIE DRIPPING, FM14 £78,500

Unusual twelve storey cottage. No floors.

FRAMLEY GENERAL HOSPITAL, FM1 oiro £2m

Semi-detached 'flat'. Sleeps 46. Resuscitates 12. Comes with night attendant.

FIREMAN'S HELMET, FM11 £92,495

Detached property, made of balsa wood and 100gsm card. Cotton reel chimney. Brillo pad garden. Rear elevation covered in Alcan foil and glitter. Would suit small child or slightly camp couple.

Call us on 01999 744 6544

DAVID PAVID of West Way, Codge, and **Madonna O'Connor** of Forestry Commission Hill, Creme, were married at St Adrian's Church, Codge.

ESTELLE DONNE of Topknot Villas, Whoft, and **Jonathan Esnes** of Burma Railway Crescent, Framley, were married at St Auberon's-By-The-Bowl, Steeplecoque, near Whoft.

IAN POPULAR of Matthau's Nest, Wripple, and **Estelle Donne** of Topknot Villas, Whoft, were married at St Etienne-In-The-Charts, Strepsilham.

MK'EBE OUKOLO of Panorama Stables, Little Chegwin and **Gregory Wheresmyflower-Theresmyflower** of Israeli Galleon Reach, Sockford, were married at once.

ROBIN ROBYNSON of Esterhazs Cottages, Whistlestop, and **Robyn Robinson** of Lunch Street, Framley, were married at St Hattie's Church, Whoft.

RAYMOND "SUGAR RAY" LINCOLN of Berchtes Gardens, Sockford, and **Aseem "The Tornado" Thomas** of Malvinas Grove, Framley, were married on points at the Vince Hilaire Sports & Social Club, Framley.

SUZANNE POLLARD of Market Street, Ripon, and **Andrew Garcia** of Redondo Way, Los Angeles, were married at St Hardrada's Church, Wripple.

GAVIN FEFT of Happy Eater Mansions, Sockford, and **Estelle Donne** of Topknot Villas, Whoft, were married at St Shatner's-In-The-Bin, Sockford.

Announcements

TILITY . TWO EXTRA PINTS PLEASE . ANNIVERSARIES . MARRIAGES . ARGUMENTS . LONELIES . AIR-RAIDS . DUELS . CO

BIRTHS & DEATHS . BIRTHDAY GREETINGS . DECLARATIONS OF HOS

FREE & BISCUITS . PLEASE & THANKS

Choose the border for your message from the below

A Minimum 100 words £6.00	B All words begin with 'H' £6.00	C Arithmetic mean of 20 words £6.00	D All words in Gaelic £6.00

Name
Address
Post code:
Daytime Tel:
Credit card:

E Maximum of 25 words with photograph £12.00

THE FRAMLEY EXAMINER
Unit 149b, East Cosset Industrial Park
Parkfields Bypass, Framley FR1 6LH

Births / Christenings

KETAMINE & HORMONE would like to announce the birth of their son, Peace-Be-Upon-Me on the 9th of November, weighing 8lb 2oz. A beautiful brother for Northern-Lights and a lovely sister for Bichon-Frise.

I WOULD LIKE TO announce the birth of my second beautiful grand-daughter. But I can't because my daughter is a barren, eggless, moustachioed harridan. Much love, Grandma Emmie.

HELICOPTER-PHILIPS. Emma & Duncan Helicopter-Philips would like to deny the birth of their son, Oliver, on the 4th of September at 6.20 am.

BARRY & EMILY PATTERN would like to announce the birth of a beautiful babysitter, Rosalind. 17 years old, blonde with glasses.

MARTIN & SHELLEY BULGARIA are delighted to announce the birth of a beautiful womble, Uncle. 3lb 7oz, 30/10.

IZZY & JASON FRANKENSTEIN would like to announce the unnatural reanimation of their late brother Reuben, on November 1st at 12.01am.

HAMILTON-FRASER To Sebastian and Sophie-Jane Hamilton-Fraser, a son, Popeye. 8lb 3oz. 28th October. A brother for Annabel and Blutusk.

Wanted

WANTED: Fall downstairs required for wealthy widow. Apply butler's lodge, Molford Hall, Molford 8878.

REQUIRED: long word to fill ugly gap in middle of poem. Also word to fill gap in advertisement. BoxFE 3451

WANTED: Jimi Hendrix impersonator for local dentist. Must be able to do simple root canal work and solo from "Stone Free". Tel: 01999 953 766 after 6pm.

Social

NO LONGER INVITED TO FACTORIES? No problem! Come to our factory. Tel 01999 994 446

Lost and Found

I AM LOST but I have found some keys. Box FE 8455

LOST: Mind. Framley area, Thurs. Believed blown. Box FE 7611

FOUND: Bicycle. Distinctive cauliflower shape. Five wheels and "lamp"(? possibly not lamp). Tel 01999 966 401

LOST: Five-a-side football match. 2-0 at half time. Answers to the name of "Kicky". Tel 01999 971 990 before second half.

FOUND: Ice cream. Melting, so hurry. Tel 01999 922 642

FOUND: Kitchen. Lights on. Chicken in oven. Tel Framley 952 222

FOUND: Secret tunnel to the 17th Century. With Dymotape label "This belongs to Alan". Tel 01999 906 630

FOUND: Quiet corner. Now leave me alone. Tel 01999 975 580

HAVE YOU SEEN MY LAP? Just stood up, and now it's gone. Tel Whoft 943 788

LOST: Sense of humour. Not funny. 01999 943 324

LOST: First storey of three storey house. Please ring with information, or ladder. Tel 01999 975 500

FOUND: Coachful of hungry French exchange students. 01999 966 568

Birthday Greetings

LOOK WHO'S 30!

Happy Birthday, Renee Seatwell!!!

love from Helmet & Sebastopol

Canonisations

TO MUM! Well done on your canonisation as St Maureen of Avila. Love from Darren, Melody and all at number seventy-six.

Engagements

CAT & DOG. We are pleased to announce the forthcoming nuptials of Cat and Dog.

KNIFE & FORK. We are delighted to announce the long-awaited marriage of Knife and Fork.

In Memoriam

IN LOVING MEMORY of Laurie Starch. A man *can* turn himself inside out, we believe you now. We miss you. Love, the staff and regulars of The Swan & Argument xxxx

Announcing

Look who we left at the station!

Sorry, Kerry!
love,
Mum & Del

LOOK WHO'S ON THE TOILET!
Sarah-Jane Tmeed
love Mum & Dad!

Anniversaries

SESAME & GREGORY HALFMENTAL. Congratulations to you both on this, your Corduroy Anniversary. All the best with our fondest love from Peppe and Bellbottom.

FELICITY & JEREMY BLINDPEW-HUFT. Who'd have thought it? Twelve and a half grisly, tedious years! Have a marvellous Lego Anniversary! Love from Dexter, Mambo and Thoth.

LOOK WHO'S GOT CANCER!

BAD LUCK, DAD!!!
Love Jay & Keith

The Dark Side of the Alphabet

The Second Batch (November 20, 2001)

FLUFF MISERY

News In Brief

UNIVITED GUEST

A 140-year old woman with a wooden toe answered the door to a man who attempted to stain her. The woman, who lives near Cottonpicker Row, said a man overwhelmed her at 3.30pm on September 24th and rumblaged through her stuff. The man who is left handed left empty handed.

KEY FRAUD WASN'T

A man was found not guilty of forgery after it was revealed that he had copies of the house keys to 315 addresses in the Framley area. Mr Justice Trufflingly Cockleboiling ruled that Eric Pointy, 55, had little more than a "fascinating hobby." Mr Pointy has run the Heel N Key Bar at Framley Station since 1972.

PRISON OPEN DAY

Last Friday's open day at HM Prison Chutney ended in chaos when all the computers were stolen and 76 inmates escaped. Prison Governor Christopher Trace-Singleton issued a statement declaring the day "a shameful out-and-out failure from start to finish," and considering his position.

WINS A CAR

Dad of three Heston Shrimproy is celebrating after kissing his way to a £16,000 Mercedes A Class. He was among five contestants who puckered up to five police dogs in a bathroom showroom last week. Dad of three Heston managed to kiss the dog for 58 hours.

RING A MING BING

Local Bing Crosby impersonator Bingo Crosbier beat off sixteen other interested parties for a 575-year old Ming vase at an auction last week. He bid by phone .

BEE BAN

Bees are to be banned from local flowers from next July, after Framley Borough Council passed a bye-law to this effect. According to council officials, the bees were "in the way". Local apiarist Roger Mixture, long opposed to the thing, blubbed, "it's a wanton act of enviromental porn-terrorism – they'll be banning the birds from the trees next." [Annie: check apiriast.]

SOCKER SOCK BLOCK-KNOCK ROCKER SHOCK

Framley Zabadak's new signing, defender Cerrutti Iglesias, was sent off in the six-pointer against Leeds last Wednesday for trying to kill the referee with a sock. He was previously sent off for attacking the linesman with a swan.

VOICE OF DEVIL HEARD

The voice of the Devil has again been heard in Sockford. Police last year received more than 350 incidents of Satan's cruel whispering. The latest victim was Rev Carteblanche Laissez-Faire, whom the devil told to get his hair cut and clean his stupid shoes.

Families use a "boat" to row for shelter as an unusual amount of fluff begins to start filling the streets of Whoft.

PHOTOGRAPH BY LYSANDER FITZMARMITE

by Challenger Putney

FRAMLEY Fire and Rescue dealt with more than 400 calls as fluff returned to the area with a vengeance at the weekend.

Dozens of Whoft and St Eyot's residents were yesterday involved in a huge sweep-up operation, and the army was called in in Sockford to help with the business of cleaning.

"This was a one in 150 years event," said a spokescouncillor for Framley Borough, "although I may have to check the books, as this is the third time since 1993."

Roads and schools were closed as the fluff took hold on Thursday morning. By 1pm, St Eyot's Green was six inches deep, and by the evening the village was up to its letterboxes in fluff.

An Environment Agency press statement confirmed that "we are aware of the problem, sweetcakes, and will look right into it real soon."

FLUFF

But as usual this isn't enough for some people.

"Fluff has ruined our home twice since we moved here," screamed blue-faced churchwarden Mo Watmough, known locally, who said the weekend had been more than she could stand. "You have to understand, it's about time somebody took a stand."

"My cat choked," added juggler Apple 'Mac' McIntosh, "and my dog only got out alive because she was up high when the fluff started to overwhelm."

Estimates put the weekend's damage at up to and including £60,000. Fluff insurance experts are predicting a huge rise in premiums, which they advise people to pay.

One resident left counting the profit was shrewd local grandmother Mrs Elise Elsinore, 82, who, eight years ago, placed an each-way bet on it being a fluffy August. Billy Turps, of Billy Turps Bookmakers, Whoft, was left counting the estimated £73,000 cost alone.

and some roads are not expected to be liberated until the end of the week.

Residents now have the difficult task of deciding what preparations should be prepared for any further unseasonal build-ups of fluff. The Parish Council has already advocated a series of velcro fences along the main routes into the village, but the Borough Council thinks its pilot scheme of static-electric-milkfloats will work better.

THE CAR PARK WAREHOUSE

over 60% off selected car parks

"We've got car parks piled up to the rafters"

UNBEATABLE PRICES!

★ spaces ★ ramps ★ lifts ★ fire exits ★
★ stairwells ★ barriers ★ booths ★
ticket machines ★ silhouette thief posters
★ crocodile teeth ★ pays and displays ★
★ one-way systems ★ uniforms ★ & caps ★
★ noise ★ smell ★ levels ★

Ready mades from £30,000 and bespoke from £30,004

OVER 500 DIFFERENT CAR PARKS IN STOCK

WHILE STOCKS LAST

Molford Meadows, just off the A999 near Slovenly
FREE PARKING

Scene!

Top pub closed again and again

THE WARM ZIPPY, a Framley pub popular with young people and children, was this week closed down by police eight times in one evening, a new record for the venue.

Police repeatedly raided the Froth Street drinkerie on Tuesday night, after a series of theme nights threatened to become out of hand.

Landlord Darren Borstle told reporters, "I had organised a Quiz Night. After two hours, it was going so well I thought I'd start a Gay Night in the back bar.

"When I saw the takings were up twofold, I decided I'd get a Cowboy Night going in the snug and a Come As Your Favourite Rule Of The Highway Code Night going on the stairs. That was when the police first arrived."

Police closed the pub down, but had barely got back to the station when they were alerted that a Talent Night, a Ketamine Night and a Warm Zippy "Unzipped" Night had broken out back at the pub.

A further eighteen theme nights, and eight closures later, the pub was finally brought under control.

This isn't the first time the controversial pub has courted controversy. In March, the headmaster of St Gahan's School For Boys found forty-six of his pupils in the upstairs pool room, sitting their GCSE Physics examinations, drunk.

"Our position in the schools league table can only suffer if my pupils are sitting their exams half cut," he was quoted at the time.

THE DOIG
enjoy this week at Framley's DOIG

SHYWYDDYDYDDY
Welsh tribute band

MC SPIDERHAT
Smooth UK Forecourt Soundz

SAWDUST DADDY
Americans

HAYSI FANTASTICUS
80s Nostalgia (in Latin)

MERTHYR AND THE MUFFINS
Welsh tribute band

167 The Bizzares, Framley. 01999 965543

Jingle all the way to the top!

by Adam Wrent

FRAMLEY ice-cream man David Grohl is heading for the top of the pops. Or rather, his ice-cream van is heading there!

Because Dave's van has just been given a recording contract by top pop crop Pop The Planet records.

"It was a complete surprise," gasped Dave, who shares a name (though not a face) with Dave Grohl, player in the popular boy band The 100 Fighters, "it all started last year. I took the van to Glastonbury to cash in on the punter's munch, and this guy from Pop The Planet heard the van and offered it a deal on the spot. He was on drugs – stargazy teacakes, I think – at the time."

Dave's van will release its first single, *I'm Popeye The Sailor Man*, in March, under the name Dave's Van. "We're expecting great things," said Simon Shallow from Pop The Planet, the man behind such chart successes as It's A Girl Things and Judith Keppel from *Who Wants To Be A Millionaire*?, as he crouched over a dusty cistern, "although we haven't yet established what role Dave will have in the project."

Dave's Van's album's song's will

Dave's Van, soon to be Top Of The Pops. Dave (not pictured) is delighted.
PHOTOGRAPH BY REMINGTON FUZZAWAY

include *You're Popeye The Sailor Man*, rock hit *Greensleeves* and folk song *What's The Frequencies Kenneth?*. And from then on, it's work work work work for Dave and Dave's Van.

"The van's doing public appearances for the next three months," Dave, "like cd:uk, MTV Brand New and The Ministry Of Sound. It's also doing a set for Marlon Hobbs's Breezeblock. Top world DJs are in a line too like Carl Coxs, Sian Savage and DJ Mugabe have all expressed an interest in

working with her .'

Unfortunately, last week's planned public appearance at the Alderman Terrorbilly Recreation Ground had to be cancelled owing to safety concerns. A police spokespoliceman explained "that there were six thousand wide-eyed, turbo-fuelled hedonists packed into that park and there was absolutely no way that Mr Grohl would have been able to meet the unprecedented demand for ice cream. Rioting was a very real possible. Hmm? An album? Oh, I see."

Top night out

IT'S A BIG NIGHT on the cards for patrons of Earrings nightclub, Framley's hottingest nightspot.

Earrings' promotions manager Mandy Pschmoo has booked 80's legend Erroll Brown to perform a live show to mark the club's fourth anniversary.

To make the occasion extra-special, Brown has reformed 90's band The Farm, to form, for one night only, Erroll Brown and The Farm. So, Framley clubbers will be able to enjoy the hits *You Groovy Train* and *It Started With a Farm* performed by most of the original group.

Erroll, whose hits *The Full Monty* include *20 Greatest Hits* and *The Full*

Monty Soundtrack, was delighted to be renew his relationship with Farm frontman Pete Hooton.

"We've never spoken before," said the 70's star, "and I thought it was time to patch up the rift."

Liverbool-born Hooton could not be reached for comment, or to rejoin Erroll and The Farm.

Erroll Brown, upset by the snub, has also refused to appear at the event.

Pschmoo said of the evening, "I'm afraid we're going to have to cancel the show. It's a real shame. We'd sold out three times over.

"My mother's lost all her savings. There's going to be a lot of disappointed orphans."

A brief, tasteful glimpse of Val

HEADLINE-GRABBING local artist Valerie Eiglootitz will be displaying a small selection of her less-challenging work in Sockford District Library foyer between Monday and November.

The shocking artist, whose uncompromising work once made Brian Sewell hide under a chair, will be sparing the public explicit pieces

such as *Tracey Emin's Tears of a Clown,* her 1998 exhibit of her own severed legs preserved under glass and marmalade.

Art lovers will instead be treated to *Clean Sheets* (1992), and the uplifting *Scenes From A Post-Menstrual Serenghetti* (1994). The exhibition will be near the spinner with the leaflets.

The largest Craft Fair in Framley
MOLFORD COUNTY SHOWGROUND

CRAFT FAIR AND
GIFT FAIR

Saturday 3rd & Sunday 5th December

CRAFTS – DISPLAYS – MORE CRAFTS

Wood Turning
Wrought Iron
Mirrors
Smells
Flower Varnishing
Bare Knuckle Fisting
Chocolateering
Anagram Knitwear
Handmade Amphetamines
Sheaths & Pessaries
Teddy Bison
International Logs
Fluff Craft
Pine Celebrities
Pencil Tasting
Soft Pottery
Shoe Folding
Radiohead

Bar/Brasserie/Abattoir
Artist doing instant Fluff Portraits
Badly signposted toilet facilities
You can park somewhere

FOR THAT SOMETHING SPECIAL

Admission £2.50 OAP/RIP,
£2.50 Others

looking for love

The Framley Examiner

(01999) 94 76 94

TO PLACE AN ADVERTISEMENT JUST CALL IN OR SEND	OPENING TIMES

telephone 01999 94 76 94 for free ads
or fax 01999 94 76 94 and wait for the fax

Out of Office Hours call our premium rate line 0906 999 999
CALLS CHARGED AT 85p PER MINUTE

your coupon to
THE FRAMLEY EXAMINER
Unit 149b, East Cosset Industrial Park
Parkfields Bypass, Framley FR1 6LH

Lines open MON 8.30 – 8.30 TUE 08.30 – 20.30 WED 8.32am – 8.30pm
THU 10.00 – 8.00pm FRI 10.00am – 20.00
Offices open MON – THURSDAY 8am – 4.30pm
FRI 10am – 12 noon

PAUL COIA LOOK-ALIKE seeks companion for long walks and dining out for platonic friendship only. No sex (except anal). Box FE8656.

STRAIGHT-ACTING Wripple male seeks straight Wripple male. Box FE8755.

NORTH SOCKFORD, good-looking professional male, 34, WLTM genuinely caring lady who will not swallow my heart whole and then shit it out onto a raging bonfire of spite. Box FE8411.

MAN STANDING too near to someone seeks greater distance from same someone. Up to 15 miles. Box FE8381.

SPORTY, fit, attractive female, 28, seeks lumpy, disastrous, 'all over in two minutes' mid-life crisis sufferer for short-to mid-term relationship. Box FE8796.

BONE ZONE
chat with over
120 guys and girls
AT THE SAME TIME!
0906 900 800

FRAMLEY MAN would like to meet anybody not from FE8100.

SPOON seeks flag. This sounds odd. So does Baked Alaska. 01999 949494.

MAN CALLED FRANK seeks woman called Maisie. Must be called Maisie. Previous applicants need not reapply. Closing date April 16th. Box FE8077.

TALK TO MY HORSE
WHILE I FINISH THIS IRONING
THANKYOU
0906 784343

CLOWN, 29, GSOH, WLTM large tent full of wild animals and acrobats. Intention: circus. Box FE8734.

COCK LIKE A TELEGRAPH POLE, shoulders like an otter. Is this you? Me too! Box FE8951.

SIKH seeks Sikh. Box FE8329.

WOMAN placing advert seeks men responsive to advertisement. Box FE8308.

CONCRETE LABIA
Think you've tried it all?
Wait til you try me
I will scrape and hurt you
You will need surgery
0906 788591
BRICK TITS
0906 788592
MECCANO ARSEHOLE
0906 788593

MATURE FEMALE seeks black-acting 18yo male for discreet friendship. Box FE8773.

MAN DRESSED AS SNAIL, GSOH, likes classical music, WLTM woman dressed as patio. No smokers, yes. Box FE8761.

BEEFY, ARYAN, rugby playing ex-squaddie, female, seeks Brian Sewell-type for late night British Bulldog. Box FE8102.

CHUFFED MAN WLTM delighted woman to be pleased with size of chair. Box FE8655.

MAKE LOVE AT ME
WHILE I SHIT IN YOUR HAIR
30% SATISFACTION
I AM PROBABLY WAITING
0906 809 809

VERY HAIRY LADY seeks sensitive male for friendship, possibly romance. Newly decorated, gch, £400pcm +bills. Box FE8542.

BASQUE SEPARATIST, 24, seeks sympathetic male, 77, for cuddles and mainland car bombings, possibly more. Box FE8221.

MAN BAKED ACCIDENTALLY INTO LOAF OF BREAD seeks knife, butter and marmalade. Box FE8414.

GAS seeks available space. I will expand to fill you. Box FE8145.

JAMIE THEAKSTON impersonator WLTM Gilda Radner lookalike or surviving relative. Box FE8529.

NICE bit of cheese seeks biscuit or mouse. No bourbons. Box FE8300.

UPTIGHT SNOB seeks narrow-minded, idiotic, trigger-happy bigot for enormous offensive argument which I will win. Box FE8310.

3 OUT OF 4 men WLTM Charlie Dimmock and take him up the no-no. Box FE8254

YOU CAN'T DO THAT without my permission. Get it. Box FE8319.

TETRIS-OBSESSED accountant, 29, seeks physically robust partner for relationship and possible gravity-related tesselating sex game. Cubic area must be divisible by four. Trampoline provided. Box FE8808.

VICTORIAN SLATTERN
Fallen woman
Carnal smorgasbord extrordinaire
I will manipulate you to issue
No hasty pudding
0906 190 000

GINGERBREAD MAN seeks gingerbread lady. Must be single, over 8" tall and made of gingerbread. Box FE8428.

120 SINGLE MEN seek at least 3 women (single) for 'swinging.' No more wooden legs, please. Box FE8513.

BUXOM, beautiful, overcharged teenager, compulsive liar, WLTM like-minded 50-year-old cripple for canasta and trips to the moon. Box FE8314.

HOUSEWIFE WAREHOUSE
PILES OF HOUSEWIVE!
PHONE THE NOISEY BITCHS!
THEY CACKLE LIKE CRONE!
THEY FILTHY LIKE YOU!
0906 477500

BROWN-EYED 28yo male Dr Who fan, WLTM female Hazel O'Connor obsessive with own biplane and MC Hammer trousers. Will collect. Box FE8110.

ARE YOU A PRINCE, or are you a frock? Professional female, busy size 12. Enquires frequently. GSOS. As seen. Box FE8661

I LOOK NOTHING LIKE THE GIRL IN THIS PHOTO

I am a pig-eyed horse-frightener with an electronic part
HEAR ME SIT DOWN
0906 298646

7'6" MAN seeks 1'2" woman to shove up bum. Only possible with these lengths. Feet first, no kinky stuff. Box FE8959.

MAN SEEKS MAN. No, honestly. Has this happened before? Box FE8181.

ASIAN GODDESS SOUGHT by debonair, athletic male, 32. Hold of terror over millions of followers a must. Extra arms an advantage. Will travel. Box FE8141.

TROUSERLESS man in wardrobe seeks woman for farce. Drainpipe outside window preferred. Vicars welcome. Box FE8898.

I ONLY WATCH SKY MOVIEMAX2. What do you only watch? Do you like to watch? Box FE8529

UNDERWATER HORNETTO
100% SATISFACTION
BUBBLES !
GOLDFISH !
SORT OF SNAILS !

Hold me down!
I will drown!
I will actually drown!
0906 809 809

EXPERIENCED fishmonger, Bones, fillets and batters. Box FE8132.

SOMETIMES A BEAR seeks Always A Beehive. Box FE8227.

GENUINE, hardy, erratic former gentleman WLTM chubby, fleshy girl with a taste for the outdoors. Special Brew evenings and combing spit out of matted beards if compatible. Box FE8199

MY WIFE DOES NOT UNDERSTAND ME. I am a Romanian cretin. FE8396.

RENAULT ESPACE seeks family of 7 for holidays and good times. Box FE8442.

VAST, UNGAINLY whale of a man seeks petite women 25-35 who taste of pizza. Box FE8093

FEELING GROOVY? Homeward bound? At the zoo? Scarborough Fair / Canticle? Call Mrs Robinson on 01999 854298

MAN LIKES pavement likes man. Covered. Absolutely covered. Box FE8130

BISEXUAL UNDERAGE GRANDMOTHER
WANTS TO HEAR YOU MOAN
WANTS TO MAKE YOU TEA
JAM UP MY BATTENBURG
0906 756565

TALLISH, TURKISH, DARKISH, handsomish woman, would sort of like to meet. £85. Handle loose, but otherwise VGC. Box FE8947

WHO WANTS TO BE A Millionaire £64,000 winner WLTM 1985 Bob's Full House fondue set winner. (October?) Box FE8698

BLACK-EYED Wripple male seeks sensitive female with big heart and clockwork legs. Wind me up! Box FE8520

SASH-FRONTED man man WLTM understanding a woman. Box FE8713

THERE'S A LOT MORE! Female, 37, 5'7" extending to 7'2" W probably LTM creatively tall individual, for long nights in box FE8099

KNOCK! Knock! Who's there? A fuck. 01999 840 012

MIXED-RACE Pakistani / Viking seeks Graeco-Australian dwarf with NSOH. Box FE8309

SEADOG, 6 days out of Port-of-Spain. Still no sign of poon. Box FE8920

I SAW

HEADLICE Crawling with them. I ate three. Then you left, heartbreaker. Box FE8006

DRESSED IN WHITE. Lost sight of you at altar. Who were you? Box FE8424

I SAW YOU. You didn't see me. 3 weeks later, I can still see you. Call my mobile. You will hear it ring. 0945 65634

I WAS on ScreenTest. You submitted Lego film. I love you. Box FE8026

FEEL MY BIG RIPE WRISTS
and squeeze my new hands
YOU WILL NOT BE SURPRISED!
0906 454 545

I WAS IN COMBATS. You were gaffertaped to a metal chair. Who was that other guy? What were we thinking? When will we learn? Box FE8509

MET AT PAUL weller gig. I flirted. You sang and played acoustic version of "That's Entertainment". Who were you, mystery man? Box FE8799

I SCREWED you 417 times over a period of 5½ years. Who were you? Box FE8730

cover me in pecker snot
I WILL STING YOUR NADBAG
0906 809 809

WEDNESDAY 24th-MONDAY 29th. Number 96 bus. Bad breath. Good breath. Which one were you? I was bad breath. Box FE8410.

TURN YOUR "Remember that lovely night when I sat next to you at The Almeida Theatre" into crisps. Smokey Bacon or Bacon. £6 a bag.

ALL I THINK ABOUT IS IT
DO IT ON ME
LET'S DO IT
I CAN DO IT TOO
IT'S GREAT
IT

0906 48 47 46

VW PASSAT 1.8 TURBO
Alloys
ABS
Full MOT
Metallic paint
All extras
2 on 1
Pre-Op TS

0906 520 510

I CAN'T FEEL MY LEGS
WILL YOU FEEL THEM FOR ME?

YOU WILL WHEN YOU FEEL THEM!
0906 788591

Mayor explores "lengths people will go to when bored"

by Challenger Putney

FRAMLEY'S VIVACIOUS MAYOR, William D'Ainty, has admitted that he spends much of his time exploring the lengths people will go to when he's bored.

D'Ainty, [how old is he?], astonished friends and family yesterday with how he had asked his secretary to type him up 72 pages of question marks, how he had commissioned a vertical motorway, and how he had had his office converted (at great expense) into a big nest.

Speaking from his hospital bed, the Mayor apologised to the Director of Housing for making him bring his doormat to work with him every morning for a fortnight and expressed regret at the recently abandoned Committee For The Investigation Of This Committee.

Mayor D'Ainty wasting everybody's time.
PHOTOGRAPH BY JEFFREY DILLTHEDOG

And, to the delight of council employees, he lifted the much maligned cafeteria ban on any food not beginning with 'H'.

He has also promised to return some of the hundreds of telephones he stole.

Doctors expect him to recover eventually, peacefully in his sleep.

Local museum to be put in museum

FRAMLEY MUSEUM is to be put into an international museum of museums.

The Museum, was described by the panel as "hideously out of date", "antique and clumsy in every respect", and "institutionally bonk."

The Museum, some of whose staff may be relocated, will be reconstructed brick by brick at the Musea Expo in Saragossa.

Framley Borough Council say they are "staggered" at the decision, and plan to build a memorial to the museum on the future once site of the eventually former museum.

Cllr Barracloth Wattlewasp was so outraged at what he called "an almighty wolf's appetite of a wife-battering of a crud-up" that he kicked a hole in the Council Chamber ceiling with fury. He came away with a broken metatarsals.

THE HAND OF FRIENDSHIP

Mayor Freneddt displays his simple message for the people of Framley.
PHOTOGRAPH BY IPPY QUESNELL

CLAUS FRENEDDT, the Mayor of Framley's twin town, Baden Schleissgarten, arrived in Framley for the fourth time this year, bringing with him an unequivocal message for all our readers.

"Your town stinks," he said, "and on behalf of myself, my council and the people of my beautiful mountain town, I'd like you to put up these colourful posters in shop windows, schools and offices. That way you will never forget that your town stinks."

Herr Freneddt, who has been snubbed by Framley's Mayor William D'Ainty on each of his three previous visits, smiled as he displayed the posters for waiting photographers.

"Your town stinks," he repeated, waving a cautionary finger. "Never forget."

Mayor D'Ainty once again refused to meet the visting dignitary, claiming he was "busy varnishing his desks". His previous excuses have included that he was making some badges and that he had never been born.

Ties between the two towns have become strained since Mayor D'Ainty failed to attend a conference in Baden Schleissgarten in 1994, sending a five-year-old child dressed as a spider in his place.

DRINK THE NIGHT AWAY!
at

EarRings
NITECLUB

It's never not full in here!
It's never not full...!

MONDAY
Sailor's Hornpipe Night

WEDNESDAY
Chess Club

THURSDAY
Hot Floors (very hot)

FRIDAY
"The Colonel"

SATURDAY
Hassidic Hard House

15 Viaduct Way, Framley 01999 996 8650

PHOTO MAGIC

Your precious memories restaged as pornography

Seamless digital manipulation by experts. You supply the photographs, we'll supply the XXX red hot staging.

Weddings, holidays, kids' parties brought back to life in sizzling, explicit detail.

DVDA, scat, sub-dom, Asian all available.

Choose from our extensive catalogue.

MAGIC SNAPS Ltd
Unit 195, Arnhem Centre, Framley 01999 984 97 97

GIANT BOOT SALE

SOCKFORD COUNTY SHOWGROUND

Sunday 21st October

Over 200 vendors
1000's of big shoes

also enormous sandals
(AS SEEN ON TV'S JIGSAW)

Event opened by Richard Kiel

(No ogres please)

01999 987 7543

WRIPPLE MASTODON

INDIANA JONES AND THE GHOST
Daily 2.25, 4.40, 6.55, 9.10

DOUBLE BILL!

INDIANA JONES AND THE SPOOKY OLD TREE
Daily 12.30, 3.15, 6.00, 8.45

BBC NEWS' MIDDLE EAST CORRESPONDENT ORLA GUERIN AND THE ROBOTS OF DEATH
Daily 1.00, 3.30, 6.25, 8.55

THE SHED SEVEN STORY
Daily 12.35, 3.20, 6.10, 8.50, 11.30

Telephone bookings. Credit cards accepted.
103 Wagon Wheel, Wripple 01999 900 1670

News In Brief

ROOF FEAR

Police are questioning a man after neighbours expressed concerns about a man who has mounted a nuclear bomb on the roof of his house. Jetson Sharks, 56, issued a statement from his lawyer describing the situation as "ridiculous." "It's just a bit of fun," he added. "Do you want a go?"

MAN STOLE VIDEO FROM HOUSE, DIDN'T HE?

Police are investigating the break in and theft of a Peter Schmeichel "Great Goals" video from a house in Manifestly Close, Whoft. They wish to question Mr Schmeichel, or anyone who may have been in goal at the time.

MYSTERY WEAPON

A torch containing what forensics experts describe as a "lethal quantity of toothpaste" was found abandoned in St Eyot's this month. Police are doing it.

LIBRINVITATION

Framley Library has invited readers to 'set fire to a book for the blind.' First prize is a egg, or the cash equivalent of a egg or some loaf.

TIGHTER

Woman are getting tighter, according to a survey published by Framley socialite Chris Diamond. Women under 35 are 12% tighter than five years ago, and women under 21 are anything up to 43% tighter than he remembers. Pensioners are looser.

A WALK ON THE WILDE SIDE

Benit Morridor, an unemployed Minister for Overseas Development from Different Way, St Eyot's was sentenced to twelve minutes community help since being found "very guilty" of following Kim Wilde home at a distance of eighteen yards over a six year period. He is not to do it again.

JELLY THIEF WOBBLES

>bloke who stole jelly still evading CID blah blah blah YOU DO THIS ONE MARK >system:

WHINING FORMULA!

A sponsored moan is being held in aid of St Sutcliffe's Hospice. Anyone who feels annoyed with anything should contact the Hospice on the telephone.

APOLOGY

We would like to apologise to Graeme Tizer, FRCD, for referring to him as 'a man who stuffs his hard-drive to bursting with dark-web under-age scat vids'. This was an oversight. Mr Tizer is a well-respected local dentist whose life has been 'egregiously shat upon' by the slur, and a rapist.

Purr-Fect! Bless!

By
URSULA CLOYBEAM

IT COULDN'T HAVE BEEN sunnier on Saturday. I've been a mother all my life, but I can't bake cakes like they do at Whoft Village Fete!

This year's Kitten In A Bottle was won, for the fifteenth year in a row, by 81-year-old habitant Lutyen Dreft. Dreft's beautiful bottled feline masterpieces have a bit of a talking point, and don't seem to able to seem to be beaten, if the last fifteen years are anything to go by.

The runner-ups were gracious in in defeat. Colin Almond's intricate display of four kittens in a 375ml bottle of Tropical Lucozade almost took the rosette, had the judges not not sadly disqualified it for a preparational illegality.

"Fair enough," said a crestwhipped Almond. "I softened the little blighters overnight in vinegar to make them more malleable. Their bones fold into the

Aaaaaah. Kittens. Bottles. Aaaaaah.
PHOTOGRAPH BY FRANKLYN GORSHIN

bottle easy that way."

Vinegaring, insisted the judges, was against the spirit of the competition.

Dreft, who won (see earlier), manages the tricky feat of twisting a live kitten into an old bottle by gently pulling the womb from out the back of the pregnant hen cat and hoping the foetus will grow in the bottle.

"Then, if it works, come nine months, I simply pop the placenta with a boiling needle," he smiled.

Dreft will appear before Framley magistrates on Monday.

Local man neither local nor man

"AND IN the end," wrote The Beatles. And it was the end this week for Gavyn Whyte, a 46-year-old model from St Eyot's.

Whyte, 45, was unmasked as being a 19-year-old woman from faraway Cumbria by a workman who had been called to look underneath her.

The former local man, pretty Sarah Cornwell, 19, says that she will miss her old life.

"I enjoyed being a middle-aged geography teacher at St Gahan's Grammar School for Boys," she explained to a waiting reporter outside a house yesterday elevenses, "but I knew it would end one day."

Whyte, 44, has been suspensed from work by Framley Education Authority while an investigation into the busty teenager's antics has been did.

Ms Cornwell, pictured, now plans to return to porn.

SOCKFORD VULTURE JAMBOREE

Vultures of all nations

Small dogs seized and carried away

Cows stripped to the bone

Sockford Police Buzzard Display Team

Discover how to milk vultures at the Lactorium

Meet "Lazenby" Framley's biggest hedgehog

(No prams or buggies, please)

Doors open at 10.00am
Scavenging begins at 11.00am
16 Sept SOCKFORD MUNICIPAL DUMP

CALL THIS LINE NOW AND
TALK TO MILKMEN

- REAL MILKMEN
- WAITING FOR YOUR CALL
- "TALKING DAIRY"

Dairy Mead premium rate

FREEPHONE 0800 809 905

MY VIEW FROM WESTMINSTER

with Ianbeale Steeplecocque

MP, Framley North East

I'VE BECOME INCREASINGLY concerned over the last few minutes by the increasing concern that has been expressed to me regarding the increased traffic congesting Whoft centre during the increasing number of school runs that are increasingly being made every morning in Whoft.

Parents and children alike are having trouble parking, or even driving at spaces meant for local disableds or "differently sensible" people.

TUMBRIL

But how would they feel if their car were blocked from its parking by a tumbril, or gallows, manned by a yokelman from the 14th century? Not too happy, I'm sure.

I remember the questions that were asked when I asked a question in The house about the possibility of objects tumbling through time, but who's laughing now? When our disabled parking spaces might possibly be blocked by a robot or catapult? It hasn't happened yet, but it might, which is the.

NIECE

My young niece cornered me on my way to "surgery" this week (not literally, I'm not a doctor!" and aksed what I was going to do about my parking outside her school. I was about to answer when my attention was caught by the possibility that she might not be who she seems.

What if my 9-year old niece were really a 100-year-old man? Stranger things have probably happened. And if we don't put a stop to these wormholes in time, we'll see a lot more happening yet.

eat yourself

fat!
with Bébé Fracas' Diet and Fatness Clubs

Simple course!
No harmful injections
Scientifically "proven"*

...also *"Eat Yourself Small"* and *"Drink Yourself Flat"*

Next course starting Mon 10am
Creme Christian Centre, Fesessiter Road, Creme

* source: "independent" research conducted by the University of Minnesota, funded partly by the Bebe Fracas Diet and Fatness Foundation.

Ireland "turning into cloud"

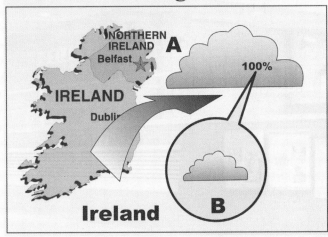

Ireland (left) and the clouds it may become looks like, fear St Eyot's weathermen.
ILLUSTRATION BY PILAU FLAPFLAP

SCIENCE
by Pharaoh Clutchstraw

"IRELAND," says St Eyot's Meteorological Society, "is turning into a cloud."

"For the past seven years, I've kept daily records on the similarities between Ireland and a cloud, and there were nine at first. Now I've got sixteen," the report said yesterday.

"This poses that most difficult of questions," the report adds today, "and that question is: do we let the people of Ireland die as their oxygens run out, or do we very carefully cull them off?"

"I have devised a scheme for the undertaking of the latter," it concluded a few minutes ago.

But one half of the St Eyot's Meteorological Society isn't happy with the report.

"John and I were measuring the weight of some Irish wind we'd caught in a net on our one expedition in 1998," said frightened Simon Kloth recently. "But I noticed John had starting adding his own scientifically unacknowledged criteria. For instants, we originally measured

Viscosity and Matter Typing, but John added seven criteria of his own, like Shape and How It Looks On Telly."

"Since we started this venture," he burst into tears even more recently, "John has threatened me with a gun, a belt, an electric cattle-prod and a coffeemill. He needs help. Somebody, please, get him help."

The Samaritans are open 24 hours a day, 7 days a week, 52 weeks a year. If drugs are ruining your life, give them a call.

Feuerwerken nacht

THE spectacular annual fireworks display is to be staged once again in the saloon bar of the recently reopened Running Mayor pub, Wripple, on Tuesday November 5th at 9pm.

This year's display is being held to celebrate the first anniversary of the death of the previous landlord, John Touchéawé, who perished in a spectacular fire exactly one year ago. Forensic scientists remain uncertain as to the exact cause of last year's hellish inferno.

OPEN FOR BUSINESS!

by Damiun Clavalier

IT WAS ANYTHING but business as usual at Molford Sewage Treatment Works on Thursday, when crowds of public were let in to enjoy the annual open day.

Apparently, it was a close call getting it all finished in time. Head Gaffer Paul Ortumn said "I'd only just finished laying a cable when it all kicked off."

But when the floodgates were opened, it was quite literally all the fun of a fair, and The Log Flume was a great favourite. Plenty of people could be seen queued at sideshow stalls, eager to let off steam and "smash the porcelain", keen to win a "goldfish" in a plastic bag.

Fiona Prempt, chief sluice engineer at the plant, who manned the ever-popular brown elephant stall and was delighted by the turnout.

Children plunged their hands deep into lucky dips, searching for chocolate treats, or stood by a long pipe, playing "Catch The Rat". Better still, the Molford Octagon Society

had sponsored the installation of an under tens' swimming bath, and plenty of parents were more than happy to drop their kids off at the pool.

But the highlight of the afternoon

There was plenty to do for young and old at the Molford Works.
PHOTOGRAPH BY NESMITH HAT

was agreed by everyone to be still to come.

As the day drew to a close, a procession of plant workers, stripped to their underwear and performed a sponsored *Full Monty*-style conga line, dancing through a specially constructed floral arch on stage.

As the line of dancers shimmied under the archway, onlookers were delighted to see the manager of the treatment works, Mr Adrian Sticklefront, clamber onstage and applaud before following through in his pants.

Impossible problem solved

STAND aside, Fermat! Someone has solved you. Step forward, Wilson-Wilson, you are crowned king of problems!

So what's all this about now? Yes, it's local genius Babbage Wilson-Wilson, hot on the heels of his recent success of a 12ft three-dimensional crossword in the car park, which vandals filled with rude words and slangs, he's done it again!

And he's done it again! But this

time with some maths.

"It came to me during a bath," "and so I wrote it down and showed it to Mrs Wilson-Wilson. It was clearly impossible to solve."

So how did he solve it?

"With a calculator," he said. "It came to me during a bath."

Scientists were mixed.

Wilson-Wilson now plans to write a book about the experience. It will be exactly a million words long.

FOSTERING IS...
AWKWARD
REWARDING
...AND NICE!

Ring up when you can to find out more about looking after a young person in need of looking after.

We will pay.

Call Sue or Cuyahoga on 01999 996 700

Fostercare Framley

Journalist cautioned
by Damiun Clavalier

A TRAINEE journalist working for local newspaper, The Framley Examiner, was cautioned on Tuesday for the fifth time since starting work experience at the paper just two months ago.

19-year-old Damiun Clavalier, who has been offered regular work at The Sunday Express, said that the newspaper could shove their stupid fucking job, and that the assistant editor had another thing coming if he thought Clavalier was rewriting his copy for the sewage plant open day story. Suck my boiling farts.

YESTERDAY'S WEATHER

Yesterday's weather was showery, with intervals. But the good news was that it was also with a high of 63F. Winds were S / SE, and seas moderate with a temperature of 67F.

LOTTERY RESULTS

Next week's winning lottery numbers will be

 14 16 23 29 31 38

The bonus ball will be 10.

SPORTS extra

Eight goals compared to only the one goal is a bad result for Framley

By Pigshit Nelson

FRAMLEY IMAGINAIRE 1
DYNAMO BETTLESHAM 8

Newby's Intermediate League 2nd Division

A HOME GAME against a Bettlesham team weakened by injury, this should have turned out better for local favourites Framley Imaginaire could have hoped for a more happy result.

Framley won the toss, and things were looking promising, until an overenthusiastic tap from the centre spot found its way into the back of the Framley net, turning the kick-off into an early own-goal, with only four seconds on the clock.

Galvanised into action, the Imaginaire defence locked tight, and the next three and a half minutes passed without further loss, although a vicious sliding tackle from Framley right back Stephen Ehrm on Framley left back Darren Twest resulted in a yellow card and bruised shirts for both players.

Framley really needed to pull out something special, so at twenty-three minutes, just as Bettlesham striker Iain LeFresq received a through ball into the penalty area, threatening the Framley goal, Imaginaire called a minute's silence in tribute to late winger Frank Mint, who died tragically of a tiny heart in 1998. During the silence, a brass band played a medley from *The Music Man*, Frank's third favourite musical except for *Cats*.

Two more Bettlesham goals, both scored off the Framley goalkeeper's head between the end of silence and Framley's controversial attempt to introduce a second ball, left the home team looking shaken.

Fans were disappointed further when hardline referee Daniel Plesnance took issue with Imaginaire's three substitutions. The subs, who had given Framley a potentially matchwinning fourteen players, were sent packing and half time irritably declared four minutes early.

As the second half got underway, the ref seemed no more pleased. Ten minutes of ceaseless whistle-blowing ended with the entire Framley team being cautioned for being offside. Framley's refusal to change ends, claiming that they were "there first", cut no ices with the match officials, and the half was restarted with the teams grudgingly rearranged.

At sixty-five minutes, with the score standing at 6-0, Framley attempted to play their Joker, insisting that any goals scored from now on would count double. Plesnance was forced to draw a gun and threaten.

Towards the end of the match, interest began to flag and four of the Framley players fell asleep. The remaining nine had abandoned their 4-6-4 formation and could be seen trying to see how many of them could fit into the goalkeeper's shorts.

A powerful throw-in from Imaginaire's Maureen Glant saw the home team pull a goal back, but the damage was done, their advantage soon neutralised by a couple of Bettlesham goals hammered in in in in in in in a matter of seconds. By ninety-two minutes, it was all over.

Man-of-the-Match Daniel Plesnance summed up his feelings to our reporter.

"For most of the second half, I was just thinking if I can get this over quickly enough, I can be home in time for Basil Brush," he was quoted.

Framley keeper Michael Backwards struggles not to fill his goal net with further balls.

PHOTOGRAPH BY IF YOGHURT

Sponsor found for Imaginaire

FRAMLEY IMAGINAIRE have a new shirt sponsor for the upcoming season: Swansea City Football Club.

Swansea City boardmember Graeme Unahue said he was delighted with the deal, done for an undisclosed.

"It's a great opportunity to get the name of Swansea City Football Club into the thoughts and hearts of supporters of Framley Imaginaire," Unahue told a press conference. "Every shirt will bear our name."

The new kit was unveiled on Tuesday by Imaginaire's newest signing, former Faroe Islands international, Lesbanon Schmitteler, who wept openly as he displayed the shirts.

THE WRIPPLE FETE ROADSHOW

Come and help us raise the money as the Zephyr 'Dream Team' assist Whoft hospice in their new Radio Ambulance.
Why not relive the hits of 1987 with our Hit Surgery or join local DJs 'Tenby' and 'The Colonel' to play 'Where's my Tea?' and win a chance to win a Zephyr 1375 t-shirt and win a paper hat.
There's a prize for everyone and the best dog so please come along, it's for charity.

Wripple Green – All day Bank Holiday Weekend – Bring a Bottle

Zephyr 1375city

Whoft Hospice "all better now"

Heavyweight title up for grabs

A BOXING UNKNOWN has announced his intention to dethrone current Newby's Furniture Championship Heavyweight Belt holder, local boxing legend, Frank "The Destroyer" Tomorrow.

Featherweight challenger Porke Enorme, who is only half the weight of his intended opponent, says he is not worried about the difference in size.

"I've been putting on a lot of body mass with a high protein diet, and hope to have reached butterweight or even brownweight by fight night."

The rank outsider also hopes to take advantage of a loophole in the Newby's Championship rules.

"I will be fighting alongside my brother, Cabinet Enorme. Our combined weights will tip the scales at the legal limit for a single heavyweight boxer. This will give me a crucial edge over Tomorrow."

Enorme's adoption of this unorthodox two-against-one formation has left bookies floundering, and odds for the match are now being expressed using fractals.

You lucky sods

FRAMLEY ZABADAK 6
MANCHESTER UNITED 2

FA Carling Premiership

FRAMLEY ZABADAK, currently floundering in the "top two" of the so-called Premiership, snatched a last-minute 6-2 victory over league champions Manchester United on Saturday.

New boss, the late Bill Shankly, who took over the reins of the club on Friday, described the team's fifteenth fluke win this season as "a good" result.

THIS WEEK 8 PAGES OF SPORT FROM AROUND YOUR AREA

FRAMLEY EXAMINER SPORT

It's only a game!

Sign of the best kept village times

Mr d'Esque (far right, on end of arm) indicates the prizewinning sign that has won.
PHOTOGRAPH BY JINGLEBELL FOREIGNER

By Challenger Putney

WRIPPLE, FOR the first year running, has won the coveted 'Best Kept "Best Kept Village" Sign' sign prize.

Local residents are delighted, but unsurprised by the accolade. Truffaud d'Esque, head of the Wripple Green Preservation Society spoke yesterday of the sign win, "We are obviously delighted by this accolade, but I can't say I'm surprised. We're very proud of our best kept village sign. So much so that when it was first erected last year we had it encased in impenetrable glass sphere, sixty foot in diameter to protect it from crabs. You get very lonely in here, but the sign looks good as new."

The placard plaudit was won last year by nearby village, Wotten Plodney, who are furious that the prize was transferable from year to year. "We're" angry that "Wripple" even qualify. They're not a "village", they're a type of fruit, Wotten octogenerian D'Arcy Clubb was quoted as saying in this report.

However the ever, not all Wotten residents are as upset as Senor Clubb about missing out on this year's award. Little Habitha Minker, 4, learned me about her thoughts when asked. "Sign gone," she smiled at me, "It tasted funny."

Last night, Wotten police were investigating claims that Wripple had cheated in the annual competition.

"We're not sure how this sorry state of affairs has come about," said a policeman, "but rest assured". He continued. "We are currently putting all other police activities on hold while we investigate this matter. We won it first. This may be a theft."

Wotten police were unavailable for comment. "This is the Fire Department.", they said yesterday, "Is anything on fire?"

"No, nothing's on fire", I said.

On other pages

Bungled raid "went surprisingly well", say Police (p28)

DON'T FORGET!
TO TURN YOUR CLOCKS BACK ONE HOUR EVERY SATURDAY AT 2am

Police numbers critical

POLICE NUMBERS in Framley are reaching 'critical' 'levels,' a report claims yesterday.

"The way it's going," Chief Constable Rupert Bone told reporters yesterday, "there will pretty soon be one policeman for every resident of Framley. And while there are obviously inherent advantages in having a police officer responsible for each citizen, it does seem a little bit over the over the top."

Ten years ago, there were 2,600 serving polices in the area. Now there are lots.

"It's getting ridiculous," said one man in a police uniform, "the canteen can't cope with the demand from thousands of starving coppers – how many sausages can you fit in?"

"I'm sharing my locker with 75 other officers," added other officers. "Sometimes I have to look inside forty or fifty pairs of shoes before I can find a pair with my name sewn in," them.

TOO MANY COPPERS

However, the news has delighted some. Local criminal Patchell Froom is delighted. "I'm delighted," came the words from his criminal mouth. "If there's a copper for every person in Framley, I just have to bribe

London's famous Metropolitan Police are having to take on the constabulary overspill from the Framley area, but many previously chirpy Cockney coppers are unhappy with the arrangement.

"All they do is muck about," said Det Insp. Michael Wet of Chipney CID, who refused to be named. "They complicate every crime we let them near. We currently have over 240,000 suspects for a single parking incident."

Local newsagenets are only allowing two policemen in at a time. "They nick everything apart from the soap and the Maltesers."

Fracton horrified by "Post Office" plans

RESIDENTS OF genteel seaside town Fracton are up in arms about the proposed opening of a "Post Office" in the unspoilt town centre.

The town, which has previously resisted plans to introduce a pub, two chip shops and a controversial duckpond, is bracing itself for another lengthy and stupid fight.

Amidst fears of a torrent of filth, protestors have gathered a 200 signature petition, which they plan to present to the Minister for Seasides this Monday.

Campaign chairman Mrs Audrey Zhendarme told an open meeting, "We will not let our town slip into a moral cesspit. These places are a conduit for the worst type of priapic smut.

"Children as young as one can obtain catalogues full of bras and bums, using one of these so-called envelopes, which can be bought blatantly openly, in bored daylight at attractive pocket-money prices."

But supporters of the new "office" say it's high time Fracton joined the communications revolution.

"Get with the programme, man. This post scene is really something other than else. Far out!" smoked one pro-post hipster, before rolling himself a book of stamps.

Local anti-mail campaigners

Clinton's Post Office has operated for yonks
PHOTOGRAPH BY WAITROSE SPIDERMAN

believe however that, should the plan go ahead, it will merely be the thin end of the wedge.

"We don't want this tsunami of filth gushing into our homes, six days a week. Clinton, down the road, has had this 'Post' for years, and their streets are knee-deep in the whelping spawn of the Whore of Babylon."

If you're interested in joining the campaign, write to Mrs Zhendarme on 01999 873 897.

USED CLOTHES
WIGS. HATS. WATCHES. SHIRTS. CASH. SHOES. HELMETS. GLOVES. FALSE TEETH. UNDERGARMENTS. SOCKS. JEWELLERY. STAINED TROUSERS. SPECTACLES. WALLETS. CREDIT CARDS. DRIVING LICENCES. PHOTOS OF LOVED ONES
SHADRACK'S FUNERAL PARLOUR
UNIT 79c. BIRTH OF A NATION WHARF. COSSET PARK INDUSTRIAL STATE. FM3 01999 865 777

FULL-SIZE MB "Mouse Trap" game. Bowling ball missing. Man on diving board in really bad mood. £30ono. Box FE8100

3" MARCONI TV. Buyer to collect. It's in my lounge somewhere. Find it, it's yours. Tel Framley 855 501

GROWN UPS

MAMAS & PAPAS pushchair. Cyan. With vomiting Michelle Phillips doll. Converts to pram. £15. 01999 855 411

6-BERTH FLOATING dollshouse. Elaborate gypsy pontoons, tiny kitchen, Edwardian-effect bannistering. £325ono. 01999 965 422

245,000 Tiger Tokens. Enough to get six wine glasses or 3/8 of a tiger. Offers. Whoft 8651

HUFTY

"HUFTY" SLIPPERS, from TV's "The Word". Unwanted gift. £5. 01999 894 765

EGBERT NOSH

SNOOKER TABLE / Diving board, with conversion clamps and switch. £80. Box FE8711

"SPIN ME" toilet seat. Rotate while you defecate. Really quite pleasant. £12. 01999 822 2021

OVER twelve hundred farts in screwtop jars. Some labelled 1978-81. Some vegetarian. £2 each, or offers for full collection. 01999 953 3001

BREVILLE Sandwich Chimney. Flue blocked with cheese, hence quick sale. £10. Box FE8016

TELEPHONE conversation with ex-wife. Includes row and phone number. £5. Box FE8083

The Framley Examiner

"I sold all my hair to the fourth caller. I hadn't even placed an advert. Thankyou, Framley Examiner!"

Mr Auntsally, Molford

CORBY Christmas Tree Press. Flattens and de-tinsels. Ruins Christmas. £45. Tel 01999 807 762

SOUP TOILET. Hot flush and simmer-tight lid. 14 Bloo crouton blocks. Some Mulligatawny staining under rim, hence £90. Framley 823 649

FOR SALE: Man's black dinner jacket. As new. Would suit me, hence no longer for sale. No offers. £115. Do not tel 01999 819 997

TREE BUNGALOW. High, and yet also low at the same time. "A building, a paradox, a delight" Solihull Evening Echo. 01999 877 742

GIRL'S WORLD "Man's World" adapter set. Moustache comb, lipstick, ball ribbons. £8. Framley 801 1818

TUPPERWARE SCABS. Airtight. Never heal, hence £2. 01999 821 209

BATMAN KETTLE. With remote control and Cesar Romero kneepads. Makes occasionally delicious boiling water. £4. Tel Wripple 9054

REMINGTON Babycase. Vinyl carrying case with brass clasps. Ages 2-4. Some scratching inside. £16. 01999 854 421

SOFA SHOES. Size 10. Seat six, or eight standing. £26 the pair. 01999 872 232

NEON "Alan Titchmarsh" sign. No longer required. £40. Tel Fram 986543

TWENTY-THREE minute video of my sister taking one off the thumb. £10. 01999 851 111

SODASTREAM. With several flavouring bottles: Brocolli™, Hollandaise, All-New Marmite, Hundreds & Thousands, Jalfrezi, Milk, Vaseline, and Plain. £15. Box FE8191

CHILD'S Cot Parrot. With "No-Nonsense™" peck. £9. Box FE8033

The Framley Examiner

76,000 passports are sold every day through Framley Examiner Classifieds.

GREENHOUSE CARAVAN. Ideal for holiday tomatoes. £1800. Tel 01999 888 942

MAGPIE extractor fan. Removes them cleanly. Never used. Never bought. £28. Tel 01999 890 913

CORNWALL, Duchy of. £28million. Mine to sell. 01999 853 310

SUNBED. Clouded over, hence £4. 01999 866 456

GROCER. Retired. 5'8". Ideal garden ornament. 01999 965 764 before 4am.

FOLDING bath and bathroom. £245ono. 01999 832 320

MATCHING bridesmaids' chickens. With lace-up wings and "Something Borrowed" beaks. £36 the pair. Will not split. 01999 894 462

12-PIECE Spain. Velour bulls. No Barcelona. £18. Tel Whoft 6543

COMPUTER SOFTWARE. Microsoft Trampoline 95. £20. Adobe Shoeshop 6.0, with "Laces" CD. £25. Tel 01999 810 007

FISHER PRICE Menstrual Mickey Play Set. £12. 01999 866 309

OVER 150 Hitler salutes. 4' / 6' / 2' / 1'6". Fire damaged, but moustache gesture intact. Offers. Box FE8042

TWO DOZEN loose hymns. Jumbled. Some all chorus, Some all verse. Chords hideous. £50. Previous applicants welcome. 01999 894 492

NEST of bunkbeds. Sleeps 18 progressively smaller people. £190. Box FE8795.

SHARI LEWIS and Lambchop Vietnam-era memorabilia sought to augment peacetime collection. Will trade for Watergate-hearings Charlie Horse toys. Good prices paid. Call 01999 894 475

DINING / snooker / fishing table. £110. Tel 01999 871 523

MAGIC PORRIDGE POT. Lovely mauve glow. And they pulled, and they pulled, and they pulled, and they pulled. £210. Molford 7854

BUDGERIGAR with Mike Reid's sideburns and attitude. Laughs like a tug. £35. 01999 842 825

INFLATABLE war memorial. Adaptable for Boer / Great / Cod. £170ono. Box FE8740

CHILD'S Formula One chassis. "You'll think she's a car!". £25. Tel 01999 895 501

FREEZER full of individually wrapped eyebrows. Mainly ginger. £180. Fram 976 641

BLACK & DECKER fire drill. With detachable muster points and head count. £28. Fram 988 818

200,000 housebricks with Roni Size's face embossed on side. Would suit really big Roni Size fan planning to build extension. £150 the lot. 01999 876 653

FIVE out of ten. Would half suit perfectionist. £50. Call 01999 854 754

ALREADY SOLD

GRANDFATHER clock, with real hands and human face. Optional second (third) hand. £200. Tel 01999 854 413

EARLY LEARNING CENTRE "Too Many Crayons" Set. Not too many crayons, hence quick sale. £6. Sockford 98541

INCREDIBLY BEAUTIFUL woman, £45. Only joking. Pig. £44. Box FE8976

WARMLITE humane gas blanket. With instruction video and scoresheets. £30. 01999 822 209

The Framley Examiner

Only **137** people died as a result of replying to Framley Examiner small ads last year!

This year, let's make it 136!

GIANT white teddy, holding heart-shaped cushion; "I'm dying". £5. Fram 809 943

INSENSITIVE carer. Racially intolerant. Poor listener. Methadone habit and some spitting. £16/hr. 01999 830 083

STAR WARS "Minnellium Falcon" skis, with "Saucy Yoda" design. £12. 01999 854 987 NC.

WICKER BODYSOCK. Very itchy. No longer a good idea. £11. Tel Whoft 9654

GLASS fish tank, with thirteen glass shebunkin and a perspex carp. £40. Fram 800 907

NINTENDO 16 games console with games. "Simon In The Land Of Chalk Drawings", "Naughty Triangle", "Maverick Milkman" and "SpyPuncher". £20. Tel 01999 895 950

The Framley Examiner

"I sold my aquarium to the second person who came to see it. I must have been drunk."

Mrs Strinoline, Creme

RED HOT Dutch Spirograph. Beautiful curves. Leaves nothing to the imagination. £14ono. Tel 01999 809986 after 6pm.

COW AND GATE. Cow kicks. Gate doesn't. Will separate. £15 each. 01999 803 336

PISSFLAPS. Set of five. £9. Box FE 8321

GINGERLILY PIGWEED

OTHER TOILET HERBS

McQuarrie's Natural Remedies

MAIL ORDER SERVICE

Also crofter's soap, bat droppings and hairdressing crystals

BOX 444 FREEPOST FR3 4UZ.

GIRAFFE PELLETS. Ideal for gardeners. Kill anything smaller than a giraffe. £16 per 10 gallon drum. 01999 850 613

PARKER KNOLL chair. £45. Lady Penelope Knoll sofa. £115. Fram 874 986

CHAD Valley "Skinheads On A Raft" beans-on-toast playset. 01999 947 657

TATTOO of Lady Olga Maitland. Unwanted gift. Slight scarring. £12. Tel 01999 852 212

TRIVIAL PURSUIT, Russian Roulette Edition. Kills one in six. £5. Tel 01999 899 437

WASTED youth. Hardly used. £22. Box FE8054

JEREMY Bowen's moustache alarm clock. £10. 01999 853 021

PRINTS of Whales. £3 each. 01999 873 322

MESS YOURSELF

UPTIGHT freezer / frigidaire. Will only open when drunk. Guilty meals inevitable. £145ono NC. Whoft 65297

LIMITED EDITION, framed Brian Jacks squat-thrust, from TV's "SuperStars". £150ono. Tel 01999 822 097

ALL MY BLOOD. Delivered in 1 pint instalments over a period of whens. Will swap for all your bone marrow, or Black & Decker DinnerMate. 01999 820 940

ACTUAL SIZE statue of elephant made of billiard balls. Ears red, rest yellow. A lifetime's work. £45. Box FE8654.

FRIMPTIMPTIMPIMP

FRANCIS MONKMAN doll. Plays Where Opposites Meet Pt.1, vgc, £12. Adapter for Tristan Fry doll, £6. Box FE8744.

BARBIE Hospice. All dolls dead or dying. £25ono. Fram 821 96

TALIBAN "Egg" game. Requires 146 AA batteries. £6. Fram 811 732

COCKNEY Lord Of The Rings action figures, with Pearly Frodo. £16 the set. Framley 873900

A PICTURE of you and your partner as conjoined twins. The Ultimate Gift of Love. Joined at head, heart or hair. Chang & Eng Industries, Unit 149a East Cossett Ind. Park.

THE BIG YELLOW Fawlty Towers. Slide slightly broken. £8. 01999 644 343

SOLO FROM SONG. Not sure which song. Fast. £10. Box FE8110.

A POUND. Get yourself something nice. Don't tell your mother. Phone Grandma 01999 977494 after 5am.

IF YOU DON'T USE A TALENT GIVEN TO YOU, God takes it away. Pay attention. Box FE8140.

PADDY MUSICAL

CAPITAL H. Fell off my name. Phone arry 01999 894091.

SLEEP WITH YOUR HAND DOWN YOUR TROUSERS. I can teach you how. Box FE8417.

EARN ££££s

using your loft to store immigrants

MITCHISON'S STORAGE

01999 952 952

FOR SALE Metallic blue 1992 Ford Mondeo ono. Box FE8696.

PHILLIPS BabyShave. £52, or £1 a week for a year. 01999 894 921

MICHAEL RODD

NEVER MIND. Perhaps next time you'll listen to me when I spend half my life screaming my head off. Goodbye Julie. Box FE8742.

BREED WITH ME. There are only a few of us left and we MUST multiply. Box FE8181.

1980s MIRROR covered in 1980s stickers. 'That's Patrick Bossert!' 'Chew A Chunk Of Cheese,' 'I Am 1982,' 'Say Yes To Chess,' 'Owl Club,' 'Angels On The Head Of Shitty Little Pin' and far too many more. £5. Box FE8693.

MADE OF SNOW? I am made of snow. Box FE8168.

GUITAR STRINGS £4.50 per pack. Guitar, £400. Guitar case, £15. Lawnmowing incident, regrettable sale. Also gloves. 01999 900542. No well-wishers.

M O B I L E HAIRDRESSING. I will cut your hair while you sit on my handlebars. Box FE8621.

HOLE, empty, used once, £15. Box FE8273.

PHONE US FIRST if you wish to speak to my wife and I before someone else. 01999 752970.

BAG HATRED

ANYTHING done (within reason) £1/hour. Box FE8888.

TELL ME SOMETHING I DON'T KNOW. I have run out of things to say. Box FE8294.

Just in!

Colindale BF800XL Back-To-Front Piano.

Runs high to low. Blew my mind. Grieg has never sounded so back-to-front.

Call Messerman's Piano Grotto

01999 875 575

MY FRIENDS ARE BORING ME. Phone me now. 01999 331 044.

SIMPLE TEETH. So simple a child could use them. £40 a set. Box FE8613.

1000 TAP DANCING 8 YEAR OLDS needed for private occasion. Apply Framley Police (Vehicles Division)

WELCOME!

MIDDLE OF NOWHERE for sale. Sought after location. Box 8297.

TRAVEL TWISTER. dangerous gift, unsuitable for driver, £30. Box FE8324.

OWL WIG, £5. Also vole hanky and robin glasses. 01999 704277.

CHASE THE BAD THOUGHTS FROM YOUR HEAD with new eyes. Modern, interesting surgery in louche surroundings. Free car parking. Box FE8302.

NO CALL OUT ON ALL WORK UNDERTAKEN

Washing Machines
Freezers
Fridges
Electric Cookers
Dishwashers
Tumble Driers

WE WILL NOT COME OUT

'Anytime' Tom Bluebridge

01999 949494.

ASSORTED LADIES, size 22-28 plus, nearly new ladies, mostly Evans. Box FE8946.

SPOT THE DOG! Prizes prizes prizes! Can you spot the dog? Can you? Box F8728.

I'M COMING. Call me. 01999

The Framley Examiner

Each copy of The Framley Examiner is read by **24,000** people

source: unknown

Beyond the Behind

The Book (2001–02)

News In Brief

CONSUMER STATISTIC

People are buying more calculators now than they did 100 years ago, a survey for *Thing* magazine has revealed. People are also using shorter short cuts than they did in the 1970s, and are eating 65% less horse meat than they would if three quarters of their diet were replaced by horse meat.

BALLOON REACHES MARS

A party balloon full of helium (with a funny face on it has) entered the record books, thanks to local entrepreneur Capston Cacton. He accidentally let the balloon go in his back garden on his 40th birthday barbecue and, he claims, it has now reached Mars. Its next scheduled stop is Finland.

SCHOOL FETE

Pupils at St Icklebrick's School, Whoft, have collected over a hundreddd dddd ddd dddd dd dd dddddddddd dddd dgotmyfin gercaught in thedd dd dddddd ddd ddddd ddddddddd.

MANUSCRIPT FOUND

The earliest surviving manuscript of the New Testament has been found at a laundrette in Slovenly. The 1,200-year old tome, entitled *The All New Adventures of St Thomas*, had been sitting by the kettle with the washing machine service manuals and the clocking-in sheets for "ages," say nervous scholars.

BIKE SAFETY INITIATIVE

Schoolchildren in Molford are being given "I'm A Safe Cycler" stickers to help reduce road accidents. The stickers which are the size of an 8-year old and made of 40mm tensile steel plate will protect them from "anything short of a howitzer", say road safely officers.

COURAGE OF CONKER BOY

by Challenger Putney

IF CONKERS ARE THE root of all evil, then Chutney schoolchild, Milton Prentock, is smashing his way to a brighter future.

After his success in the local and regional Conker Championships, Milton has set his sights on the International Conker Crown Derby. With his current form, the newly-crowned district 'Conker King' could well be on his way to the top of the horse chestnut tree!

COURAGE OF CONKER BOY

Milton looks like any other child with a difference, except for the fact that his bedroom walls are covered in conker posters and there's even a tiny horse chestnut tree growing in the corner of his room!

Mitlon is the newly-crowned district 'Conker King' and with the national championships on their way, this means he could well be on his way to the top of the horse chestnut tree!

His parents, however, are all too aware of the fame that celebrity can bring.

"If there's one thing I know," said

3-year old Milton plans to smash his way to the throne of the King of Conkers.

PHOTOGRAPH BY BAT HARPSICHORD

one. "He's conkers!", said the (>m?)other. "Ever since he won that local title, the phone hasn't stopped ringing. We can't believe in it. It's the best thing that's ever happened to anyone."

COURAGE OF CONKER BOY

Tragically, however, Milton suffers from a rare form of condition, which, ironically makes him allergic to conker contact.

"'We've tried everything said his mother'", said his father, reading from a previously prepared statement, "'but not participating in the national conker finals is not an option. He's going to win'".

Allergy specialist, Putter Smith, was said to have said, "He's allergic to conkers. No more conkers. Probably best sticking to stamps or collecting clocks. Not conkers, though."

Milton's future opponent in the national finals, the self-proclaimed 'Conker Pianist', Putter Smith, was yesterday unavailable for comment, saying "I've been up all night with my conkers in a warm vinegar bath. I feel invincible."

Quantifiably Balti

Traditional Fine Indian Cuisine

Butterfly Jalfrezi
A selection of seasonal butterflies in a thick, spiky sauce. £5.99
Creme Egg Vindaloo
Fresh Creme Eggs with tomato, onion and silver foil. £4.65
Infinite Guru Josh
An endless plate of delicious vinyl curry £4.99
Rogan Polanski
A traditional Polish dish for children £3.75
Chameleon Korma
Dish of indeterminate meat. Really wants to hurt you. £2.50
Heinz™ BakedBean Tikka Masala
A traditional dish from the Moghal region of Stourbridge. £6.99
Spotted Dick Phall
Made with very hot raisins and ferocious suet. £4.50
Curried Curry
Dish. £3.25
Chicken Thor
The curry of war. Previous medical required. £4.25

SIDE DISHES

Keema Naan £1.50
Peshwari Graandad £1.75
Lager Bhaji £1.65
Roald Dhal £2.20
Bombay Plates £3.25
Pilau Biter £1.99
Chick Pea Dull £1.00
Strawberry Bootlaces £4.95

In our restaurant, hot, or to your door.

FOR EVERY £1 you spend over £50, we'll double your order.

FREE portion of pilau rice with every dish, up to a maximum of 18 portions.

FREE delivery within the European Union.

28 Christopher Tracy's Parade, Whoft **01999 855 651**

Composer tries to apply for patient

By our Arts Correspondent URSULA CLOYBEAM

A COMPOSER from Whoft has applied to the Patent Office for the retrospective rights to the key of F major.

His groundbreaking application comes in the wake of applications by corn companies to patent corn.

"Music is as natural as corn," explained Italian-born Raviolo Presto. "And if a big user of corn can patent corn, why can't a big user of F major patent F major?"

Presto, best known for his *Lift Music #13* (which is still being performed in Framley Library, in spite of two court injunctions), says he chose the key with care.

"I chose F major carefully," explained Italian-born Raviolo Presto, "because of its universal popularity. I can now expect back-payments from sales of *Yesterday*, *My Way* and *No Surprises*."

But his scheme has come under fire from the music community. Peter Werrill, conductor of the Framley Concert Orchestra, says Presto is a "fool waiting to happen."

"He hasn't thought this one through," said Framley-born Peter Werrill. "He should have chosen C major. Think about it: *Old Man River*, *Let It Be*, *Three Blind Mice*..."

Mr Werrill also listed a further 47 songs.

GORING'S CARVERY
Traditional Family Butchers
01999 299 3999 (ext. 328)

**PORK LIONS
GIRAFFE NECKS
PIG-PIGS
INNARDS
FISHES
SCOTCH EGGS
HEN BEAKS
DROP SCONES**

BUS ROUTE MAY BE CHANGED

The 37 hangs out the front of a shop – one of several bus stops that councillors insist "seemed like a good idea at the time".
PHOTOGRAPH BY KATHRYN PERHAPS

Computer Fair
14th-16th May Molford Showground

Toffee Apple Macs
Blue Screen of Death Train
Waltzer 98
Linux Dodgems* (crash 60% less often than ordinary DOSgems)
Madame Zaza's Virus Scan
If-Then Loop-the-Loop
Swingboats ME (beta testing)

Admission £1.50
FREE 8K of RAM with every stick of candyfloss

BY JESUS CHIGLEY

FRAMLEY TRANSPORT PLANNERS have called for the new number 37 Shopper Hopper bus route to be changed, or scrapped altogether, after a series of unforseen problems revealed that the route was "maniacally wrong".

Previously, the 37 bus skirted the High Street as far as Denegate with stops outside Moseley's, Jensen's the Pederasts and Newby's Wool. With the closure of Jensen's in summer 2000, the time was right to move with the times, the council claimed at the time, and a revised timetable was drawn up in time for springtime.

The new route, introduced in March after extensive consultation with local businesses, zig-zags across the town in a series of drunken loops and includes six-hundred incremental fare stages, a stop on top of the war memorial, and a series of exciting stunt jumps and ramps.

STUPID BUS

Shopkeepers, who were initially enthusiastic about the changes, are now calling for the bus to return to its old route. The owner of rare record shop Lionel's Vinyl, Lionel Vinyl, expressed the views of many.

"At first I thought a new bus stop in the Soundtracks section was a marvellous idea. I hoped it would bring more customers in, but now I realise that a bus coming through the shop every eight minutes isn't a good idea at all. It just smashes things up. I don't know what I was thinking."

Although the 37 will go back to its old route next Friday, councillors still say changes need to be made. A subcommittee of the Transport office are investigating the feasibility of making the bus look like a rocket and plans are afoot to introduce two extra stops, possibly in the river.

Lifts full of man chod

BATLEY DISTRICT COuncil Hygiene Officers have come up with a novel solution for the persistent soiling of the lifts in Eugene Terreblanche House, a high rise block on the controversial Dungeon estate.

"By installing fully plumbed-in toilets in each of the three lifts, we feel we are responding to clear public demand," said Gordon Speedbeadle, the senior engineer in charge of the operation. "People seem to need to pooh in these lifts, so we are sending a plain message to them: Go ahead, pooh away, just don't forget to flush."

However, the first week of the

Mortimer Acorns
PHOTOGRAPH BY

pilot scheme has not gone entirely according to plan – with usage far outstripping expected levels. This is due to since because of the fact that the new lifts are attracting users from all over the Batley area, eager to try out the new facilities.

"The gents lift is constantly engaged," complained one desperate tenant. "People who live here just can't get a look in. I haven't been in days. And yesterday afternoon, my eight-year old son told me that the disabled lift is up to the third floor in man-chod."

The council have had to declare a state of toilet emergency in the block pending the delivery of shovels and fairy liquid.

Well damaged

THE PUBLIC ARE BEING warned to be on their guard after the Sockford Green wishing well was broken into last Friday evening, and once again drained of wishes.

Fearing that the theft may have been carried out by a gang of opportunist black-marketeers, police are now warning potential wishers not to purchase their secret fantasies from unlicensed granting sources.

Bootleg wishing has been a problem in Sockford for yonks. Last year, antisocial St Eyot's misfit Benny Ulffph, 48, hit headlines when, after dropping a tuppence at the notorious illegal wishing urinal at The Fluff Lion Public House, his keen desire for all his critics to try living with his mother and see how they liked it came

immediately to pass, filling his house with hostile strangers. "I can't get into my room," he complained at the time, "Get out."

Responding to Friday's theft, Sockford Parish Council have issued the same statement as last time. "If the wishes are not returned before the end of the financial year then there are going to be a lot of disappointed kiddies come Christmas the 25th."

Local businesses have generously offered gifts to wannabe wishers as compensation. Joboxers Butcher's & Son have donated three beef pigs, and Hi-fi & Audio Repairs de Sockford are promising a state-of-the-art Sony Memorystick Walking-stick to the first six pensioners who can prove that their lifelong dreams remain unfulfilled at 9am on February 12th.

LEARN TO SPEAK BARCODE

Cuánto es la trucha?

Colloquial Dewey Decimal also available

CONVERSATIONAL COURSES TO GCSE STANDARD
LINGUAPHRANCA 01999 865 654

PENSIVE MISTAKE!

...NITURE AND HOUSEHOLD

...OWROOM IN THE

...ramley area!

"The Stout"
"Enormous" The Lancet
ONLY £4995.99

"The Snowball"
with orthopoedic fringing
ONLY £475.99

NEW!

- nest of occasional front doors £154.99
- crinkle cut mirror £39.99

L-SHAPED BEDS
- ideal for clowns who don't like taking their shoes off at night
- interesting and unusual
- probably ideal for other people
- warehouse full of the bloody things

£32.99

...BY'S
...ality furnitures **01999 866 865**
...tsite on 01999 www.newbysfruniture.ac.uk

Going for the spin!

by Adam Wrent

FRAMLEY CONSUMER campaigner Baj Curtins is at it again! The customer watchdog is planning his most rigorous benchmark test yet – crossing the Atlantic in a washing machine.

I met him at his office, where he receives over four complaints a year from irate shoppers keen to get justice for their pounds. He told me the reason for his transatlantic trek.

"I was sold this machine in good faith. Now for the good of the people of Framley, I'm putting it to the test. By sailing it to Newfoundland."

"If I come a cropper, you can be sure I will be wording a very strong letter to the manufacturers."

Mr Curtins plans to make a clean getaway!
PHOTO BY PONDA WILLIAMS

Curtins says he's well prepared for the journey, and will be taking 6 weeks' supply of food and Persil.

The doctor will write a poem about you now!

By BEAKY COXSWAIN

FEELING A LITTLE BIT under the weather? Doctor Shapiro will make you feel better! Feeling a little bit worse for the wear? Doctor Shapiro is always be there!

Last time you went to the doctor's, you probably came away with tablets or cream. Unless you're a patient of St Eyot's GP Lupin Shapiro that is in which case you probably came away with a poem!

"Everybody hates doctors these days," says a beaming Shapiro when I meet him at his surgery in Pleasant Crescent, "so I thought it was time we started cheering our customers up a bit."

Shapiro, who sees 35 patients a day on a good day, has been giving out rhyming diagnosises since last summer.

"I usually just come up with them on the spot, but I have a few favourites. For instance: 'You've come to me to get an answer / Well, I'm afraid you've got bowel cancer,'

which I follow, where appropriate, with 'If I were you, I'd hedge my bets / Your lungs and kidneys have secondary mets' or 'I'm going to feed you Carmustine / Razoxane, Cytarabin / and Methotrexate by the glug – / Basically, a load of drugs.' I like that one," he said.

AM I BETTER NOW?

Dr Shapiro has even had a poem published in the *Medical Gazetteer*. Called 'I'll See You In Six Weeks,' it has been nominated for at least one award to date.

"I hope to release some of my poems in an anthology called *All Better Now*. And I'm taking my one man show, The Doc's Bollocks, on tour later this year," he added, reaching for a speculum. "People have even started to recognise me in the street. Several young people have asked me to sign their prescriptions."

Just to keep the good doctor on his poetic toes, I set him a challenge: make up a poem about a drug that you regularly use and like. There were two we couldn't print (sorry, Lupin!), but I'll leave you with my favourite.

Ventolin, Ventolin,
I can't get enough of Ventolin.
Its bitter perfume is just right for a doctor
And reminds me a bit of a very cheap vodka
I savour it tickling my bronchial tract
When I'm in the midst of an asthma attack

Raise your glasses as Dog's Head sells millionth pint

By KENATHON STOREY

THERE WERE WET EYES and mouths all round last Thursday when the Dog's Head pub served its one millionth pint of beer ever.

Landlord Fred Winstnalye put up a plaque on the wall to commemorate it and another one given to local drinker and old man Arthur Gavinson.

Not only had Mr Gavinson personally helped them well on the way on the grand total of one million (!) clocking up some 440,000 pints himself, but more importantly it was

him who had in fact counted every pint of bitter pulled at the bar since he first entered the pub, in 1917, at the grand old age of 3 years old. He hasn't left since.

Asked if the project of counting every pint pulled at the bar since he first entered the pub, in 1927, at the grand old age of 3 years old was part of a school project, or just a way of passing the time until his father finished drinking and started hitting him home, he smiled and said, "No". Mr Winstlanley paid tribute to Mr Gavinson and his great endeavour. He

said, "It was a treat to see old Arthur sat there, on the same stool, every day in, day out, no, not that one, that one, over there by the charity collection thing, from 11am until closing time. We helped, of course, by not serving pints while he was at the loo, which in recent years, I must add," he added, "has been upwards of an hour at a time."

The Dog's Head is the holder of the Framley Examiner 'Nearest Pub' Award 1978, 1979, 1980, 1981, 1982, 1983, 1984, 1985, 1986, 1987, 1988, 1989, 1995, 1998, 1999, 2001, 2002.

Council clampdown on mindblowers

by Bunco Booth

COUNCILLOR GEOFFREY Cauchaugh has called for a clampdown on mindblowers at Framley Borough Council.

The problem, which first surfaced in 1997 when then Treasury Deputer Clive Yitch had the entire finance department decorated with mirrors, is back on the rise. One woman is still having a nervous breakdown after becoming trapped in a toilet cubicle where she became convinced she was being attacked by a million cisterns.

SNOWBALLS

Since then, reports claim, literally everything has snowballed.

"Pranksters are sods," chewed Cllr Cauchaugh when I found him. "The Park & Ride scheme is close to collapse since some sillyrollock moved the car park to the centre of town and the drop-off point to a disused MoD site in Slovenly," he continued.

"Pensioners aren't big on hitch-hiking," he ate a sausage.

"And there's definitely a mindblower working at the recycling centre," he continued. "We have internal reports that suggest that dustcarts are being recycled into giant cutlery for a planned Millennium Meal, which is already years overdue."

He continued, "There are no

What the bloody hell is going on?
PHOTO BY ELLIS SOUPFATHER

dustcarts left in Framley now."

And then he continued, "And the funny thing is, the Mayor has apparently signed off all these projects without a second thought."

BASKET CASE

The Mayor, who cannot be reached (generally), denied he had anything to do with mindblowing. He also denied being Mayor and denied being on the phone.

"Mindblowers are costing Framley Borough Council mi££ions every year," Cllr Cauchaugh went on, "mi££ions we could be spending on..."

What he told me next was incredible.

[>flag: MY OFFICE ASAP. Ed.]

Vetivers consulted

LOCAL SECRET SOCIETY the Wripple Vetivers have been consulted on proposed changes to the new US dollar bill.

The famous banknote, 233, is being redesigned for the second time in twenty years in an attempt to foil forgery, and includes the Vetivers' insignia in its design.

"We didn't want to upset them," said Jefferson Downberries of the United States Federal Reserve.

"Not after last time."

New choice for drivers

FRAMLEY MOTORISTS who break the law are being given a choice – points on their licence and a hefty fine, or buy the magistrate a pint and we'll forget all about it.

This new compensation scheme, say magistrates, will save paperwork, and improve relations with the community.

Sunday school teacher sacked

A 45-YEAR-OLD Sunday school teacher from Effing Sodbury has been sacked for his unorthodox teaching methods.

Patrick Mexico had been running his under tens' Bible study classes for six years before church leaders discovered that he had been teaching his pupils stories that have been described as "apocryphal" and "odd."

There had been no complaints from parents or students, but when a group of children from Mexico's class were asked to paint a mural in the vestry of Framley cathedral, organisers were bemused by their 14 foot illustration of the story of Judas and The Jaffa Cakes.

The story, in which Judas Iscariot eats all the Jaffa Cakes of Our Lord while His back is turned in the garden of Gethsemane, is not in any recognised version of the Bible, and, just like the story of Jonah On The Wasp which the children staged for Harvest Festival this year, was probably just made up. Mexico is 45.

DON'T MAKE AN EX

VISIT THE No. 1 FUR

GOODS SH

LOOK Great deals on relaxing sofas

"The Egg Nog"
Unique left-handed sofa
ONLY £299.99

"The Hot Toddy"
3 seater, 0-60 in 9.4secs
ONLY £299.99

All our sofas are also available in

human leather™

BEESKIN CUSHIONS
- available in yellow or black or yellow and black
- sting zips
- pollen stuffing

£9.99

BATH TENTS NEW!
- with non-slip groundsheet
- make being in a bath indoors just like being in a tent outdoors!
- soap on a guyrope

£85.99

NEW
Framley's premier supplier of
Warehouses throughout the region. Visit our

NEW IN...
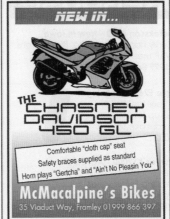
THE CHASNEY DAVIDSON 450 GL
Comfortable "cloth cap" seat
Safety braces supplied as standard
Horn plays "Gertcha" and "Ain't No Pleasin You"
McMacalpine's Bikes
35 Viaduct Way, Framley 01999 866 397

COME SUN OR CLOUD... WE'LL BE THERE
(excepting heavy cloud)

ALL TV AERIAL REPAIRS UNDERTAKEN
- wind damage
- balloonist trapped in spurs
- heavy cloud
- old programme caught in uprights
TELLYBOY AERIALS
61 Prairie Palace, St Eyot's 01999 766531

THANK CHRISTMAS
IT'S
XMAS

And it's Ursula Cloybeam

This week in our annual look at Christmas, we turn the focus to what's on in Framley this Xmas.

From the pantomime to late night shopping, there's bound to be something to keep you entertained on my page!

So crack open a nut and settle down in front of a roaring black and white fire, pour yourself a sherry and a mint pie, and get ready to go out shopping!

Lights up!

THE TURNING on of this year's Christmas lights on Framley High Street will take place on Monday night at 7.50 outside Clobbers.

Master of ceremony this year will be former TVam weatherman and local celebrity, Commander David Philpott, who will be switching the lights on using the traditional switch.

Five minutes beforehand, Cmdr Philpott will be switching off last year's lights from the same switch, and giving a vintage 1982 early morning weather forecast in his inimitably bluff style.

● *Fans of light will be pleased to hear that they can see more lights at the Framley Pagoda's production of Aladdin.*

In tribute to the late Norris Roman, who delighted us with his Widow Twankey year after year after year, there will be a two minute silence in the middle of the last song, during which strobe lighting will be used.

Sufferers of epilepsy should make themselves known to front-of-house staff by attracting attention to themselves during the light show.

'Kincheap
10 Downing Rd, Sockford, FM4 01999 865 656
WHERE CHRISTMAS COMES CHEAP

Treetop "Smiling Judas" baubles £2.50

Nativity crib with figures of Joseph, Mary, Donkey and arch-enemy Evil Doctor Octopus £8.99

Chocolate Tuna Santas for your cat's Christmas tree £3.50

Roxy Music's "Bryan Fairy" £2.99

Packet of 48 x 7ft Xmas trees £8.99

Frozen tinsel (6lb bags) £1.99

12 pack of 4-Megaton tactical thermonuclear crackers £2.50

Xmas fear grips Christmas

IT'S NEARLY CHRISTMAS, and that means it's nearly a year since twelve people were killed by an explosive device, possibly a sleighbomb, planted outside Screenbusters Videos on The Blobway.

The bomb, which had a bang "like a barn door with a bomb in it," according to one earwitness, is believed to have been the work of breakaway Christmas Separatists.

Members of this terrorist group want to assert Xmas's independence from the rest of the year by adding an extra 20-day month – called Remember – between the 24th and 25th of Christmas. Calendar experts, however, insist that this is impossible, and will make the year so long that by 2042, it will still only be 2006 in Framley.

A memorial to those who died at the hands of last year's explosion – a statue of Whoft victim Mr Alexander Nunt being blown apart in the blast – was unveiled at a quiet launch party this Wednesday.

Mr Nunt's family broke off from picketing the site of the statue to talk to a waiting journalist at the junket.

"We're glad he's being remembered," confessed Widow Nunt, "but I feel sick now. Does anyone have a barley sugar?"

The grieving woman was later cautioned for trying to take the statue of her bursting husband home on the bus.

A coded message from the Separatists, phoned through to Framley's top rating Zephyr AM, on Tuesday won the first prize in The Colonel's Noonday Quiz.

"We are delighted with this Zephyr AM 'Good

The festive High Street may be under the threat of a terrorism.

PHOTOGRAPH BY NOEL FURST III

Guy' sweatshirt, which I will wear with pride until our demands are met," said Separatist leader Chas Has.

With more bombs feared, Framley shops are refusing to open until February, leaving shoppers only 62 shopping days until Christmas restarts, or 82 if the Separatists get their way.

A special policeman has been sent in to look under things and generally improve the situation.

Newby's treats it's shopper's

THERE'S GOING TO BE a real Xmas treat for anyone going for a late night shop at Newby's famous stores!

The record-breaking store has an array of extra attractions planned to make this Christmas a special time for its customustomers.

In return for a small donation to Whoft Hospice, St Eyot's Salvation Army Band will follow lucky shoppers around, making up carols about their purchases.

"Whatever's in your trolley," said Admiral Prestatyn Ffyst, "we'll praise the Lord about it in brass. Hosannah in exceptional."

And one lucky 3-year old shopper will be nominated "Santa For A Late Night" and placed atop the Army's burning Nativity float. The so-called Sally Schooner will then patrol the tinned goods aisles, distributing flaming gifts to lucky girls and boys, and stealing presents from atheists.

Chairman and founder of Newby's of Molford, Roy Newby will be on hand too, to distribute samples from his Christmas dinner on Thursday 23rd, so be sure to be careful to be early.

Roy, who is a strict vegetarian, has made tomato drumsticks and cress chipolatas to give away, whether customers want them or not.

But if you want soup, you'll have to queue. This year's must have gift is Chunky Country Vegetable, thanks to the popularity of the hit film of the same name.

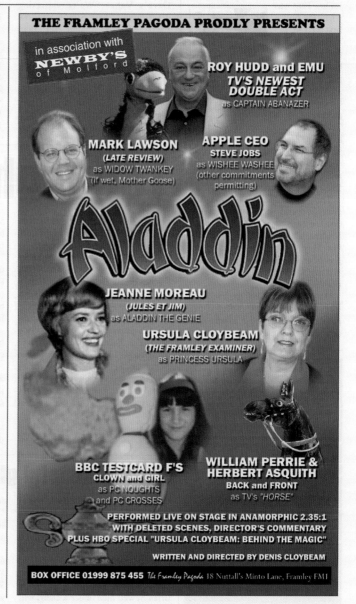

THE FRAMLEY PAGODA PRODLY PRESENTS

in association with
NEWBY'S
of Molford

ROY HUDD and EMU
TV'S NEWEST DOUBLE ACT
as CAPTAIN ABANAZER

MARK LAWSON
(LATE REVIEW)
as WIDOW TWANKEY
(if wet, Mother Goose)

APPLE CEO
STEVE JOBS
as WISHEE WASHEE
(other commitments permitting)

Aladdin

JEANNE MOREAU
(JULES ET JIM)
as ALADDIN THE GENIE

URSULA CLOYBEAM
(THE FRAMLEY EXAMINER)
as PRINCESS URSULA

BBC TESTCARD F'S
CLOWN and GIRL
as PC NOUGHTS
and PC CROSSES

WILLIAM PERRIE & HERBERT ASQUITH
BACK and FRONT
as TV's "HORSE"

PERFORMED LIVE ON STAGE IN ANAMORPHIC 2.35:1 WITH DELETED SCENES, DIRECTOR'S COMMENTARY PLUS HBO SPECIAL "URSULA CLOYBEAM: BEHIND THE MAGIC"

WRITTEN AND DIRECTED BY DENIS CLOYBEAM

BOX OFFICE 01999 875 455 *The Framley Pagoda* 18 Nuttall's Minto Lane, Framley FM1

A golden anniversary all round!

Screte & Sons, Framley's famous vegetarian butcher's shop, is 50 years old this week. Our reporter ADAM WRENT popped in for a joint.

IT'S 8.30am AND IT's all go at Screte & Sons, Framley's famous vegetarian butcher's shop.

The cabbages are being tagged and hung up in the fridge, the parsnips have been gutted, and the grapefruit chops have been dressed.

Len Screte, the oldest of the Screte family still behind the counter, is trimming a whole head of cheese when I arrive.

"I started here when I was twelve, working Saturdays. I was mostly the delivery boy for the first few years, but when I turned 15, I started out front, and that's where I learnt all the traditional skills – carving, shelling, peeling."

Screte & Sons, Framley's famous vegetarian butcher's shop, is known for its quality products like Boned Breast of Beetroot, Aberdeen Quorn Shapes and its Celebrated Leg of Flan, which the Queen has one of yearly.

BY 10.00AM

By 10.00am, Gil Screte, Len's oldest son, has finished the morning deliveries and there's just time for a sniff of tea as he prepares another handmade Wotsit Rissole.

"When dad retires, I'll take over," he told me as he tenderised a sprout.

Screte & Sons, Framley's famous vegetarian butcher's shop, sources all its produce from recognised organic sources. All their stuff is reared kindly and picked humanely, they reuse all their peelings – as pâté and vegan offal – and their sawdust is recycled.

IT'S 10.30AM

10.30am, and Len is complaining about the treatment of vegetables. "Squirrels hunt nuts for fun. They don't eat them. They're the only animal apart from man to hunt for pleasure. They should be shot."

10.32am, and Gil is arranging some choice cuts of plum. "There's an old joke in the veggie butcher's trade, about the assistant backing into the cucumber slicer and his boss saying, 'we're getting a little behind in our work.' It hasn't happened to me yet."

Screte & Sons, Framley's famous begetarian vutcher's shop, was opened 50 years ago by Len's father, Tricky. It is open from 9am to 5am daily.

Len prepares some prime cuts of grapefruit, ready for the morning rush.
PHOTOGRAPH BY KIERAN WENDIGO

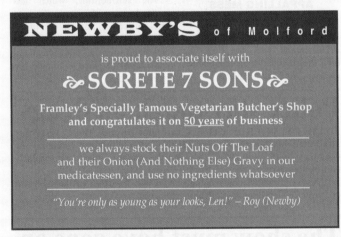

NEWBY'S of Molford

is proud to associate itself with

❧ **SCRETE 7 SONS** ❧

Framley's Specially Famous Vegetarian Butcher's Shop
and congratulates it on 50 years of business

we always stock their Nuts Off The Loaf
and their Onion (And Nothing Else) Gravy in our
medicatessen, and use no ingredients whatsoever

"You're only as young as your looks, Len!" – Roy (Newby)

TURN YOUR MEMORIES
"The 'Turn Your Memories Into' People"

congratulate Screte & Sons
on 50 years of busyness...

NEW! Write your will in a stick of rock for only £35!

Still Available! turn your passport into a cake!

...and thank them for all the potatoes that have helped turn so many satisfied customers' memories into crisps

The Perineum
gentlemen's club

tel. 01999 367785
fax. 01999 367785

The Perineum gentlemen's club accords Leonard and Gilliard Screte the warmest congratulations on 50 years in the trade

And cordially invites them to take drinks in the Marquis de Sade room at their earliest leisure

Dress Code:
Mondays – Smart, Clothes Optional
Wednesdays – Smart/Smelly
Fridays – Skeleton Costumes

**The Perineum Gentlemen's Club
12, Widow's Walk – FRAmley 550**

Lord Croissant

framley's biggest bakery

best wishes to Screte and Sons
on their 50 years producing
interesting vegetable by-products

Lord Croissant Big Bakers
35 Boiled Eggs Lane, FR1 5BE

PEACENIK 2000

says

NO

to battery apples

Nice one, Screte & Sons
from all at the live-in

SAVE ABSOLUTELY EVERYTHING™

VINCE'S WICKED WHEELS

'Two new cars and a refrigerated van does not equal £200, boys. I'm still waiting.'
from Vince (remember me?)
01999 429229 now

my Beautiful mother, the earth
organic bookshop

Congratulate 50 years of business on Len Screte & Sons

new this week

PRESTO ON PESTO *by Nigel Presto*
THE SUNFLOWER DIET *by Shower*
ORANGES ARE NOT THE ONLY ORANGE FRUIT *by J. Orange*
THE BROWN PAPER BAG (A HISTORY) *by Leaf Pinko*

bestsellers

MY HESSIAN LIFE *by Rosie Glow*
RECYCLING RECYCLED RECYCLABLES *by H. Pogle Hermann*
A HEDGEROW IN YOUR POCKET *by Summer Ovum*
GOLDEN DELICIOUSNESS *by Avril Greenapple*

The largest selection of organic books on our wonderful dying planet

MY BEAUTIFUL MOTHER, THE EARTH ORGANIC BOOKSHOP, 30 Wrong Way, off Clinton High St, Clinton FR12 3EE

we only stock books containing recycled words

The Framley Examiner

Framley's Traditional Favourite since 1978

FRIDAY, JULY 12th, 2002   PRICE 45p

PAT O'CAKE
BAKER MAN

Bakes you a taxi home
as fast as he can!
PAT O'CAKE BREAD TAXIS
01999 571 655
(accounts welcome)

STYLE
Fancy a punch up?

WIN!
One of two giraffes

PROPERTY
Unusual starter home

A big day for the area as pressure on Ordnance Survey finally prevails

LOCAL BUSINESSES PUT FIRMLY FRAMLEY ON THE MAP

Local businessman Gulliver Toast (inset and main photo) celebrates the new map.
PHOTO BY KIEFFER SLIPPERS

by Jesus Chigley

LOCAL BUSINESSMEN were yesterday celebrating the release of the new Ordnance Survey 1:120,000 Map OS8999. The publication, featuring the towns of Framley, Whoft, Sockford and Molford, marks the end of a decade -long campaign to have the Framley area included on maps.

At a special launch party held in the Rainforest Zone of Newby's Hardware and Ironmongery, retailers and community leaders toasted what they see as an exciting new development.

MAPPED OUT

"It'll bring plenty of business to the area," said Gulliver Toast of Gulliver's Electoral Supplies. "It's been unnaturally quiet since we were taken off the map, and I for one, am not alone in thinking the two events are connected."

Other businessmen agreed. Ron Staminabar, who runs the Bell Polish Superstore in Executive Way said he too had noticed a change in customer patterns since the map deletion decision in May 1991.

"People driving through who stop and come into our shops are often too confused to buy anything – they usually just ask where in God's name the town came from, then leave. They have that stare, like a soldier who's seen too much."

The cartographers responsible for removing Framley from maps over ten years ago have still not explained their actions, but many observers feel it was a deliberate final flourish in a tit-for-tat war between area residents and the mapmakers, begun in 1989 when cashiers from a Sockford bank stole a theodolite from a survey team and dressed it up as a clown.

ANCHORS AWAY!

FRAMLEY'S FIRST STOP FOR ANCHORS

With over **46,000** types of anchor in stock at our five branches

(all shops within walking distance of Framley Station)

Keep ahead of fashion with the NEWEST anchors, direct from the manufacturers

14 Unsworth Parade, Framley / 211 High Street, Framley
175 High Street, Framley / 46 Watterson Vault, Framley
Unit 34b, Level 2, The Bristow Centre, Framley

Records tumble as man, 122, strangled 58 times with world's longest red ribbon

By CHALLENGER PUTNEY

RECORD BREAKERS worldwide turned their collective head to Framley this week as two long-standing world achievements were simultaneously bettered.

Lifelong Framley resident Pop 'Sweet' Corn, who was a magnificent 122 years old and held the title of 'World's Longest Man', was killed on Monday as he attended the opening of the new Newby's All-Night Doughnutterium.

Local celebrity Corn was about to cut the 5,000 metre red ribbon stretched round the perimeter of the building and declare the Doughnutterium open, when he tripped and fell groundwards.

As he scrambled to regain his dignity, he caught his neck on the thin red band, turning as he rose.

The gathered crowd then watched silently as Pop unsuccessfully launched into a further 57 'escapes' from the scarlet noose, which appeared to be tightening slightly after each attempt.

After two hours an ambulance was called to cut loose the ribbon which, organisers noticed, was preventing entry to the eaterie.

Roy Newby, proprietor of Newby's, was quoted as saying "We'll all miss Pop. I'm sure it might have been one of the ways that someone might have thought that it was possible to die from"

On hearing the news, world record men were quick to declare the achievement "an achievement of human achievement on the grandest scale"

"We live for records such as this. It's much better than plate spinning or salad eating. The only problem is where to record it. Ribbons or strangulations?"

A: Ribbons.

DJ MAY BE GIVEN THE MARCHING ORDER

by Jesus Chigley

ONE OF FRAMLEY'S BEST known radio Shock Jockeys has, once again, been almost sacked after a string of inappropriate on-air stunts.

Zephyr AM ex-favourite, Robbie Nougat, has managed to lose the station 80% of its audience with his crazy show. According to Zephyr boss, Slim Beard, Nougat's antics provoke an "unprecedented level of unease and confusion within his listeners."

These incidents haven't gone unnoticed by the studio bosses either. Radio shows such as "Nougat's Watercolour Challenge" and more recently "Juggling Hour" were dismissed by Zephyr bighead, Slim Beard, as "dead air".

ARE ACTUALLY

"We've given him plenty of opportunities in the past, but his idea of entertainment doesn't seem to correllate with that of the average Zephyr listener," Mr Beard was reported last week as having said. "The fifty minute show we broadcast where Mr Nougat purported to be going over the town hall in a barrel is a case in point. None of these stunts are actually happening. He just uses them as an excuse to leave the studio."

Nougat, whose show.
PHOTO BY PINHEAD McMONARCHY

39 MINUTES

The final straw seems to have been when, during Nougat's recent "Boiling Thirteen Eggs In a Row" stunt, he was spotted by listeners enjoying a pint in The Warm Zippy with fellow Zephyr DJs Tenby and The Colonel.

Radio engineers rushed to the studio to discover a kettle with its switch taped in the ON position placed next to a microphone. Twenty minutes later, they watched in horror as the kettle boiled dry, melted and burnt the building, screaming, to its knees.

Fortunately, by the following morning, a new building had been erected in way of a replacement.

Pupils helped to improve their concentration

By Challenger Putney

PUPILS AT St Christ's School in Chutney are being encouraged to bring bottles of gin into class to improve their concentration.

The initiative follows research suggesting that dehydration can adversely affect children's health and learning.

Pupils are allowed to keep one 70cl bottle of gin at their desks, which also cuts down lunchtime queues at the school bar.

The project has proved popular with the pupils, aged 4 to 11. Twelve-year old Kylie Woyote, said: "Having your own bottle of gin stops you disturbing other people when you really really need a drink."

But headmaster Colin Thirtysmith has his reservations. "I'd rather they brought sherry," he moaned to listening reporters yesterday. "I've already had to confiscate 38 bottles of gin, and my wife and I don't drink the stuff."

St Christs's Jumble & Booze Sale will be held on Saturday in a hall.

THIS WEEK'S TIME SIGNATURES

Monday – Thursday: 4/4
Friday – 3/4 (7/8 from 6pm)
Saturday – mostly 3/4, moving to 6/8 in the early evening.
Sunday – 5/4, with bars of 4/4 towards midnight.

The outlook: scherzo.

News In Brief

POLICE PRANK

Two men dressed as a pantomime grand piano made off with £300 worth of conditioner from a branch of Llwylls the chemists. Framley Police, who were staging a 24-hour sponsored Come To Work As A Grand Piano day in aid of children with insects in their mouths, say they had nothing to do with it.

'HEALTH HAZARD' FOR SALE

Quattro Formaggi, the former home of eccentric bankrupt Miles Smile, is up for sale. Simon Cress, of estate agency Simon Cress, said he had "low hopes of a quick sale" for the cheesy property. "of a quick sale. It retains many original features, like Cambozola carpeting and Vintage Stilton wardrobes, there's no doubt it's a one-off, but you need to wear a mask." Mr Smile died earlier this year of colorado of the kidney.

NURSES UNIFORMS

Framley General Hospital's much vaunted Fetish Ward, opened three months ago by Melinda Messenger, looks to be heading for closure after complaints from nurses about the health and safety risks posed by giving a bedbath while wearing thigh-length pvc boots and studded collars. They also insist that disposable thermometers should no longer be attached to horsewhips. Aneasthetists' gimp masks will remain hospital policy, however.

CHANGE TO SINGING PLAN

Would event organisers please note that due to circumstances beyond human control, the Rotary Club of St Eyot's "Sing *Metal Machine Music*" evening has been postponed?

CLOTHES PERMISSION YES

Planning permission has been granted for a pile of unwashed clothes to begin to accumulate at the end of the bed of Carl Gennet, 22, of Lesney Road, Codge.

MY WIFE HAS LEFT ME

Abandoned typesetter Martin Leak was back at his desk again last night, after his wife walked out on him at the weekend. Mr Leak, 34, is said to be to have "had his life cut in four" by the thoughtless bitch. She also half-inched HIS copy of *Ruby Vroom* and HIS Travel Scrabble, which she can give back if she likes.

PAINLESS LASER REMOVAL
OF SPECTACLES OR GLASSES

CUSTOMER ANNOUNCEMENT

We would like to offer a pair of FREE SPECTACLES to any customer who had their glasses fitted by us between August 1997 and January 2002.

Acting on legal advice, we have recently had our machines recalibrated.

Your replacement spectacles should now be easy to remove from your head, with wider arms and an overall looser grip.

This FREE SPECTACLES offer shall count as "reasonable compensation" in a court of law, and invalidates any legal action currently being taken against us.

STEVLAND, JUDKINS & MORRIS OPTICIANS
160 E. HARBORSIDE BLVD, FRAMLEY 01999 877 921

EVER THOUGHT OF BECOMING AN OLYMPIC SILVER MEDALLIST?

Do you never settle for third place?
Do you dream of being the second fastest, the second strongest, the second best at swimming?
If your answer to some of the above is not no, then we have the course for you.

Course monitored by
Xavier "Sempre Segundo" Silarte
(Silver, Men's 400m Javelin, Oberammergau 1985)

Sorry, but we are unable to offer running and luge.

PHONE ESPERANZA ON 01999 855 755

Justice for giants

WRIPPLE HOUSEWIFE Linda Blinder is taking her Justice For Giants campaign to the steps of The Prime Minister.

Mrs Blinder, 14ft 9in, says that enormous people are still being unfairly discriminated against. She cites difficulties using lifts and public transport as among her highest priorities.

"You should try being me for a day," she laughed yesterday. Then she burst into tears. "It wouldn't be that difficult to make all buses and trains twice as high," she giggled. And started crying again.

Mrs Blinder is appealing to the Prime Minister [>FLAG: name please. Ed] to push through legislation banning heightism. She

by Jesus Chigley

points out that he is 6ft1in, which is above average for a man (although just below average for a socialist).

"I'm fed up with kneeling down when I use the stairs and falling off beds all the time," she smiled, as tears welled up in her big eyes.

Mrs Blinder is not a tall happy.
PHOTOGRAPH BY JOHNNY MYJINGO

Hospital gears up for winter

FRAMLEY GENERAL HOSPITAL has re-organised its medical beds and casualty wards to provide more care for victims of winter this winter.

Wards are being reduced to a temperature of -15°C and deliveries of carrots and coal are being upped to prepare for the annual influx of injured snowmen.

Hopefully this will avoid a repeat of last year, when lack of surgical beds led to many kidney transplant and radiotherapy patients being thrown into skips in the carpark to allow the overstretched wards to cope with emergency snowman admissions.

A spokesmen said the trust hoped the re-jumble would not lead to longer waiting lists. She said something about "this de-fragmentation of headcount" and "enable a partnership between consumer and provider" by which time I was nearly asleep. It

was one of the worst presconferences I have ever seen.

A patient looks out of one of the windows of the new cold ward.
PHOTO BY IPPY POG

The de-fragmentation (and so on and so on) will complement the Borough Council's new snow cameras, and the local Save-A-Snowman initiative.

Chief Exectuive Stan 'The Brain' Nickname said: "it is imperative that we keep up with the private sector, where some of our competitors have 24-hour snowman-only wards and television advertising. It's a tough market place in winter and we've got our league tables to think of."

Appeal for thief

A LOVELY GIRL had her mobile phone stolen last Wednesday evening at around 1.48pm by Malky Kingfishererer, 20, a self-employed mugger from the Batley area.

The crime occurred outside The 11-Elevenses Snackbar on Biscuite Street in full view of two deliverymen and their vans who described the incident as "precise and quite stylish".

She was white, stocky, about 5ft 7in and wore a clean frock and gingham baseball cap with one of those velvety bits at the back.

Please call 07999 837200 and ask for Malky.

In Court

TURTLEHEAD JOSPIN of no fixed address was jailed for 7 weeks for stealing 2 weeks' worth of whiskey and vodka and 5 weeks' worth of carrier bags from Newby's Stores, Molford on October 22nd.

MS PHEREMONE RUSH of Outside Avenue, Crème, was found quite guilty of a charge of unlawful marriage. She was banned from paying a fine of £800 and £65 additional costs for six months

JOLIFFE ARTEFACT, 42, was sentenced to Wickerman for setting fire to a bag of old rubbish on November 5th on November 26th.

EULILY UNDERCLOTHES was found Yes She Did on a charge of drink driving on October 28th, of Taito Crescent, Framley. She was jailed for three months and banned from drinking for two years.

ARNOLD GRASS, of Kedgeree Reach, Whoft, received a five minute discharge following gross indecency in the changing rooms at Dipsy Fashions in the Arnhem Centre on October 16th. He evades capture.

PETER DOIL of Sockford Magistrates Court was sentenced to 6 weeks imprisonment by Sockford Magistrates Court for beating a boy from Whoft in Sockford Magistrates Court.

LEE ORGANISN of Unit 17, DeLorean Industrial Estate, was fined £300 with £40 additional prosecution costs for trying to *TURN YOUR MEMORIES INTO CRISPS!* 01999 963 371 Call now!

ANTHONY WIMBLEDON of Gerter's Hat, Codge, was forced to pay £87 of bar tab after a charge of threatening behaviour at Framley Magistrates Court was withdrawn.

RABBI JOSEPH GORDAN, 68, was found guilty of eighteen counts of possession of material in contravention of the Protection of Children Act. He was sentenced to two years in a young offenders' institution, since it was his first offence.

MARIELLE HOUSESITTER of Yeldham's Crouch, Fracton, was fined £8 with £317 prosecution costs for not liking Captain Beefheart on October 18th.

Knyfe and Slaughter
MEDIAEVAL BUTCHERS

☞ Rotten Carrion ☞ Unboned Pyglets
☞ Fruites and Victuals ☞ Jackal Steaks
☞ Fermacies of Herbes ☞ Wolfes Lyver
☞ Choler of Boare ☞ Freshly Murdered Knaves

All our meets is thyck with blod and gristle

Diseases Certaine

Whoft Village bye the gibbet
Barter most wellcome

Success for Cancer Awareness Day

PROUD PUPILS at St Gregory's Girls' School in Whoft are basking in local glory yet again.

Last Friday the school held a Cancer Awareness Day, in which all 680 pupils were kept locked in the hall until they found a cure for cancer.

Headmistress Lullaby Crunch says she is "over the bleeding moon" with the result.

"It worked so well last year for the common cold, and we thought it was worth doing again," she explained to yawning reporters yesterday.

The girls spent Friday morning reviewing recent developments in genetic engineering, and a cure was found shortly before midday. The doors and fire exits were unlocked, and after lunch lessons resumed as normal.

Shortly before 5th period, The Men From The Ministry arrived and took the lucky child and her cure away.

TEACH YOUR DOG
DARTS!

Dogs love to play, and what better game to teach your dog than **DARTS**, the game of throwing darts?

The McLaughlin **DOG DARTS** course will teach your best friend everything he needs to know to play Britain's favourite indoor pastime, for fun or profit.

With an introduction by top darts player **BOBBY GEORGE** and a foreward by **A DOG**, the course guides your dog, step-by-step from **TAKING THE OCHE** to **GOING OUT ON A DOUBLE**, all lavishly illustrated with pictures of dalmatians trying to play darts.

Introduce your dog to a whole new world with the McLaughlin **DOG DARTS** course.*

PEAUX & SCHMIDT
SPORTING SUPPLIES (EST'D 874)
235 With The Beatles Rd, Hammertime, Sockford
Tel 01999 854 399 *after 6pm*

*Every book comes with a board, six darts and a bone.

Relax this summer...

BRITAIN AT WAR IN CRISPS £17.99
Accompanies the TV Series

2 FOR 1

DELIA SMINT'S BACK TO BASICS
Water *AND* How To Lay An Egg £30.00

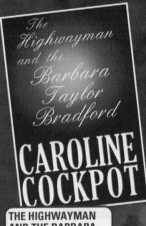

THE HIGHWAYMAN AND THE BARBARA TAYLOR BRADFORD
by Caroline Cockpot £16.99

THE COMPLETE JOY OF STAIRS
by Dr Butterfly Regular-Brandreth
For the first time in one volume:
UP and DOWN £19.99

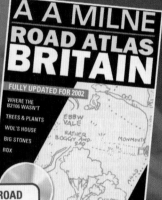

AA MILNE ROAD ATLAS OF BRITAIN
Updated for 2002
(Mr Shepard helpd)
Comes with CD-ROM of Willie Rushton reading this map £13.99

THE DIARY OF MY BUM AND SHOES
by Hellabella Wielding
"Indistinguishable"
The Observer £6.99

A BRIEF HISTORY OF TOAST
by Dr Stephen Hungry
"Stephen Jay Gould" Amazing £6.99

£8.99

THE IT
by Colin Schilling
"Sent a shiver down my lap"
Sunday Times

THE FUTILITY OF SEX
by Dr Gideon Ceefax FRDS
Not for children £17.99

NNNNNNNNNNN NNNNN
by Böri Øegg
Translated by Anthony Dull
"An exciting literary experiment using only the letter 'n' " London Review of Books £8.99

CAN'T YOU BREATHE LITTLE BEAR?
Martin Jezebel's charming cautionary tale for the under 5s £4.99

THE LITTLE BOOK OF SLIGHTLY BIGGER BOOKS
No 1 Bestseller 8p

HAIR
by Melestope Fassenhough
The true story of the 18th Century milliner whose researches led to the discovery of hair £9.99

a world of books from
NEWBY'S bookshops
15 High St, Molford

IT'S

The Examiner is once again Britain's second best-selling local weekly newspaper! *

YOUR TOP SELLING
Framley Examiner

Framley's Traditional Favourite since 1978

FIVE BIG REASONS WHY THIS NEWSPAPER SELLS THE SECOND BEST!

THANKS TO ALL OUR READERS

* 12.10pm – 12.13pm. Tuesday afternoon. Source: PMRB Statistics

Lottery boost for outdoors lovers

Mayor D'Ainty in ebullient mood.

PHOTOGRAPH BY IRONTEETH RUMSPIGGOT

by Adam Wrent

FRAMLEY'S EXCEPTIONAL Mayor, William D'Ainty says he's keen to bring back the heady days of free love.

In a new plan, announced on Wednesday from the steps of the town hall through a loudhailer, he offered dozens of free lottery tickets (worth up to £1 each) to anyone willing to "get it on in the bushes" outside the window of his office at Framley Town Hall.

Shouted D'Ainty, "I don't know about anyone else, but it would really cheer me up to see a lively young couple at it like knives and forks in the shrubbery."

Mayor D'Ainty explained that he had bought the lottery tickets from the all night Conch QuwikStop on the Molford turn off of the FR404, and was sure they looked "lucky".

"'Come one, come all!' that's my message," he bellowed. "Third window along, Tredegar Road side. I'm just doing some filing, so you can pretend I'm not there. Come on. Enjoy yourselves."

HOLY, HOLY, HOLY
religious relics

JUST IN!

ONLY £39.99

Turin Shoes
"leave the footprint of Our Lord!"

HOLY HOLY HOLY
15 Barrabus Way, St Eyot's   01999 777 670

Child progidy takes own life
By TAUNTON MISHAP

CHILDREN AT The Academy For The Precocious Child in Sockford were struggling yesterday to come to terms with the death of one of their least popular classmates.

11-year-old Macabee Massingbird, a concert-standard cellist who was flying commercial airliners at the age of 8, was found in the school's Geography Lab, hanging by the neck. Teachers say he had fashioned a noose from a diagram of an upper river course and tied it in a Moebius strip around a stalactite.

The tragic swot.
BY TRISHA GOB

Macabee, who was twice winner of the BBC's Young Introvert of The Year competition left a suicide note in Scrabble letters on a nearby board, blaming the pressures of relentless excellence.

Scrabble experts, called in by Massingberd's concerned parents, were delighted to inform the proud couple that the troubled junior boffin's last message to an uncaring world had earned a record 768 points, and was palindromic.

Beaver pack shown glittering world of opportunity at Poundmaster Stores

Stacey Poodes of Dungeon Beaver Pack watches the construction of a Persil display.
PHOTOGRAPH BY OPPENHEIMER BALLOON

DUNGEON BEAVER PACK were given the trip of a lifetime this Tuesday when they were taken round behind the scenes at Batley's Poundmaster Stores as part of a local initiative to lower their expectations.

Organiser Jonathan Sweets told the journalist writing this one column piece that the trip was part of a programme designed to break the young girls' spirits and teach them to accept their dismal lot in life.

"We've taken them to see the cells at Batley nick," said Sweets, "and tomorrow we've got a couple of hours at the Child Support Agency."

The grey-faced children jumped for joy when they saw our photographer, but only because they thought it was part of the trip and meant they might one day become photographers themselves.

"Don't get ideas," said Mr Sweets.

In Court

HUMPTY Waistcoat, 40, was arrested for being followed home from The Doig Nightclub by three policemen on May 5th. His hair was removed in error and will be replaced by a qualified arsehole.

PUSHALONG Jones, of no fixed age, Chutney, was found guilty of treason by Framley Civil Court. He will be replaced by an identical German counterpart for the rest of his natural life

JUSTIN Casey-Howls of Lollipop Stick Joke St, Whotten Plodney, was found guilty of receiving stolen moments and sentenced to 30 seconds' trolley dash through Newby's Audio Visual department.

PVT EMBARGO Escargot, of Whoft Barracks was fined a tenner for standing to attention without due care and attention.

FRAMLEY Magistrates Court was found guilty of everything by Sockford Magistrates Court on the 5th day of May. An apllication for demloition was refused by Framley Magistrates Court and a pre-frozen snowball was thrown.

CHARLES Barone of Quality Quality Quality Street, Chutney was found hiding in a cupboard at Framley Magistrates Court. He was ordered to pay a fine and get down.

Books of the sort Vice Dep. Chllr-I-W Pomodore wishes people could read.
PHOTO BY ILYA BEAUCOUPDEMONDE

Literacy plea

BY JESUS CHIGLEY

THE EDUCATION DEPARTMENT of Framley Borough Council has fired the opening salvo in its War on Illiteracy.

Acting vice deputy education chancellor-in-waiting Stronzo Pomodore led a crowd of well-wishers outside the Town Hall last week as a covey of pheasant was released from a third storey window and shot to the ground by twenty-six members of the Wripple hunt dressed as the alphabet.

"This is a great moment for Framley," beamed Pomodore as the last colourful bird was brought to the ground (by the letter R).

"We hope this will encourage people to do something about the naked crippling shame of not being able to read."

SPELING

But opposition councillor Geoffrey Cauchaugh is less than even moderately impressed.

"Last week in chamber, I sat through eight-and-a-half hours of debate about ways in which the word 'small' could be made smaller and the word 'big' bigger, ostensibly to help clear up a common point of error. In fact, no conclusions were reached and the sitting was abandoned at 9.45pm, by which time it was too late to put up the PA and the glitter strips, and the the weekly council karaoke had to be cancelled."

Cllr Cauchaugh is appealing for the money to be more wisely spent in future.

"My gut feeling," he explained, feeling his gut, "is that the kind of funds we're talking about here would be better directed at education, which is why we're proposing that everyone in the area who can't read is supplied with a book teaching them how to."

The debate continues.

Ornamental fountain kills twelve

by Taunton Mishap

WHOFT'S NEW ICE FOUNTAIN has been closed by council order after only three days due to fears for public safety

The fountain, which was opened last Tuesday by former TVam weatherman Cmmdr David Philpott, who cannot be named for legal reasons, cost over £300,000 to build and install, but now lays dormant awaiting demolition by controlled explosion.

Although questions had been asked about the suitability of the street decoration, pressure from groups such as The Real RIBA (the paramilitary wing of the Royal Institution of British Architects) had pushed the plans through.

ENORMOUS CANNON

The award-winning design – a fourteen foot cannon, shooting shards of sharpened ice directly at passersby – was the award-winning work of award-winning local architect Gethsemene Proops, and had won several awards.

Proops has said that he will not take the demolition order lying down, and is proposing to lash himself to the barrel of the cannon until his demands are met.

>> Twelve dead.

The fountain, awaiting smashing up.
PHOTO BY SIMEON SOMEONE

PIANIST FIGHTS FOR LITERACY

World-famous pianist Alexander al Sacha will be touring the region next month with his famous 'typewriter piano.' The unusual instrument, which al Sacha takes everywhere with him, types foolscap pages as it is being played.

Al Sacha's party piece is to play The Flight Of The Bumble Bee at breakneck speed while the piano simultaneously types The Declaration of Independence.

The brilliant pianist is back on the touring circuit after his six-month absence due to a tragic accident at Carnegie Hall in April. During a performance of Rachmaninov's Brief Encounter, he hit carriage return and the keyboard flew off the piano, sending all 88 keys into the audience. Three music lovers were killed.

News In Brief

SHOP FORCED TO CLOSE

Zebda, Framley's only ethnic shop, has been forced to move out of Denegate because it is becoming "too integrated," a local councillor has admitted. "What started off as a cheery little emporium selling lion's roar drums, rice flails and lucky fetishes has turned into this monstrous junkyard of bakewell mintcake, antemacassars and statues of fish and chips," explained Cllr Harris Parris then.

BIRD

Patsy Dole, a club singer from Molford, is to change her stage name to The Artist Formerly Known As Princess. However, she has abandoned plans to appear as a The Artist Formerly Known As Prince tribute person and only perform material from his rubbish years. She will, however, "do him a duet" with him at some point. Her relaunch is on 5th May at Vince's Car Spares.

DEAR ANNE

By the time you read this I will be dead. Marriage is a sham. If I knew now what I knew then, I'd have stayed being about to be a happy man in my own future. As it is, I'll never know what it would have been like to know, so I'll have to leave with the knowledge that I know I was a happier man in my past than I ever would have dreamed I'd be if I were transported into my own miserable future and made to look backwards. I'll always want you. Goodbye. Derek.

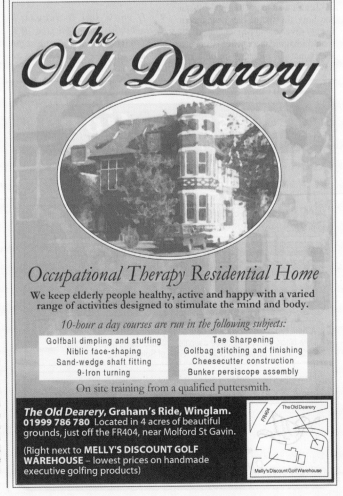

The Old Dearery

Occupational Therapy Residential Home

We keep elderly people healthy, active and happy with a varied range of activities designed to stimulate the mind and body.

10-hour a day courses are run in the following subjects:

Golfball dimpling and stuffing	Tee Sharpening
Niblic face-shaping	Golfbag stitching and finishing
Sand-wedge shaft fitting	Cheesecutter construction
9-Iron turning	Bunker persiscope assembly

On site training from a qualified puttersmith.

The Old Dearery, Graham's Ride, Winglam.
01999 786 780 Located in 4 acres of beautiful grounds, just off the FR404, near Molford St Gavin.

(Right next to **MELLY'S DISCOUNT GOLF WAREHOUSE** – lowest prices on handmade executive golfing products)

A touch of the Tinseltown hits Molford

by Katie Blirdsnest

IT'S A WELL KNOWN FACT, the fact that fact can be stranger than fiction. Being in the newspaper game all my life, I prefer facts, but some people prefer fiction and I'm sure that they're right!

And why not? Because the world of developing huge bags under your eyes at lonely preview screenings came to the Molford Conference Palace last weekend with the opening of the sixth annual *Film 88* convention. Fans of the late 80s film review show came from all five corners of the country and beyond, making it, according to the organisers, the third best yet. Fact is indeed as strange as fiction!

HUSBAND

But that illusion was smashed into 88 pieces when, on my arrival at Film88Con02, I was met by a woman who had just had her breasts autographed by star attraction, *Film 88* American film correspondent, Tom Brook. "He was very kind about them, and he certainly didn't make me cry like my husband usually does," she beamed.

Many fans made the extra effort to come and dress up as their hero, Oscar-winning *Film 88* star Barry

Fans queue up outside the hall to hear Tom Brook talk about talking about *Mystic Pizza*.
PHOTOGRAPH BY MATTEUS TRILOBITE

Norman, with elaborate, colourful costumes being the order of the weekend.

Something like 3,000 Normans and Normettes spent two days pressed up against each other in what most passing rubberneckers described as a "stifling and weird" atmosphere. They whiled away the while munching their way through 2,998 tubs of popcorn, 18 waxy pink hot dogs and a convention-tub of Haagen-Daz Chocolate & Revels.

WASPS

Film 88 first appeared on our screens around 15 years ago when a lot of today's parents were only knee-high

to a cinema-goer of that time. But there they were, swarming into the convention like a flock of wasps with the parents of yesterday on one side and the parents of tomorrow just to the side of them.

EXCUSE

"That's because the programme appeals to all ages," prouded Gunther Willinelzon, who came over via the Hamburg-to-Fracton catamaran the day before he said this: "It is a beautiful series, a great favourite in Germany along with *Allo 'Allo'* and *Der Hitmann Und Sie*. Excuse please, there is a re-enactment of the location report

from *Scrooged* on in the saloon bar in funf minuten."

CATAMARAN

As you can see, this is a programme that inspires a lot of love... and a lorra lorra hate as well! That hate was well and truly on display when a nasty incident turned into something that should have been quite easy to control but still wasn't.

Due to a horrible malbooking at the centre, the adjoining conference suite was hosting a *Film 85* convention at the same time! The lid of the bitter rivalry between the two factions couldn't be kept on top of the building for long.

Two *Film 88* fans, who had come dressed as Barry Norman interviewing Steve Guttenberg about *Cocoon: The Return*, got into a bloody fistfight with four Film 85 fans dressed as two Barry Normans interviewing two Steve Guttenbergs about *Cocoon* and *Police Academy 2*, but they still came out on top.

"I think that proves our point," crowed Guttenberg, 88, dusting the ceiling plaster from his curls. "And I'll definitely be coming back again next year. If they'll let me. And why not?"

And why not!

If you'd like to attend Film88Con03, visit www.gorillasinthemist.co.uk for an e-pplication form.

POTENTIAL PURCHASERS OF PUPPIES ARE STRONGLY RECOMMENDED TO PAY CASH ONLY AND CARRY NO ID

ODOURLESS DOGS NOW AVAILABLE

Home reared, KC reg (sort of), individually genetically modified dogs with **NO NASTY** afterlinger. **DOGS** you can show to your poshest friends **WITHOUT** fear of **NOSE CLUES**.

Also: Soil-Free Dogs, Pedigree Mongrels, Silent Dogs (with and without Subtitles), MiniDogs, MidiDogs and Oversize.

01999 926927

or visit our website at

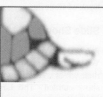

try our charming
PIES

tortoiseworld

all makes of tortoise repaired
written estimates
free valet and shell polish
parts and servicing

our award-winning redecorations include
half rugby ball, ashtray, farmhouse loaf, cardinal's hat,
soup bowl, hedgehog (some nails), cycling helmet,
spinning top and doorstop (dead models only)

www.t.o.r.t.o.i.s.e.w.o.r.l.d.com

ST EYOT'S & WHOFT HOME FOR
UNIDENTIFIED ANIMALS

01999 440962

donations welcome

CHAUFFEUR DRIVEN HORSE BOXES

Carpets, curtains, DVD, en suite paddock, full length mirror, champagne flavour hay

01999 420206

PET DISPOSAL SERVICES
"No fussing- No fighting – No fur"

All animals considered
Special Christmas rates
Deposit req'd for larger animals
Commemorative mugs and jigsaws
available at extra cost

Call Dennis, Barry, Wayne, Bomber or Oz
on 01999 677998 NOW for instant quote

Framley District Branch Cat Of The Week
C.A.T.Z.

SUTCLIFFE is a mainly white with a little bit of black around the mouth and a few flecks of ginger on his back and around the base of his tail cat who likes a bit of out and about. His brother, **NILSEN**, is a quieter sort, with a ravenous appetite and a habit of collecting bones. A little shy of strangers, these two toms need a good stable affectionate loving fussy home.

If you would like a cat, ring us.

01999 381460

(ask for Katherine, Cate or Kathy)

RECENTLY LOST A FOUR LEGGED LOVED ONE?

LET THEIR LIGHT SHINE ON FOREVER

We take charge of your deceased pet after the cremation, and turn all the remaining body fat into candles. You get about 18 from a typical family dog.

FOREVER PET CANDLES
24, The Groggings, Whoft

BIRDS AND FISH NO GOOD

CHUTNEY ANIMAL RESCUE

Have lots of spiders, frogs, moles and one tiger in urgent need of warm homes

PLEASE HELP THEM AND US

01999 329561

Police plans to introduce tagging

by Bunco Booth

Police in Framley and Molford are to adopt a novel new scheme for tagging prisoners, designed to stop the criminals reoffending once they leave custody.

Framley Chief Constable Rupert Bone, a regular churchgoer, explained the new plan to journalists and prison officers on Tuesday.

"The tagging starts in prison. One of my men, dressed as a police clown, will visit prisoners due for release, handing out balloons," Bone explained.

"Lags love a balloon. After years in the drab prison environment, they are fascinated by a balloon's round shape and gay colour.

"The hope is that, after returning home, the released prisoner will become attached to his balloon, taking it everywhere he goes."

The helium-filled balloon, tethered by an eighteen foot string, will bob above the rooftops, Bone explained, making the felon a great deal easier to keep tabs on, particular in a helicopter the Chief Constable hopes to get soon.

COLOURFUL TOO

To allay public fears, the balloons are to be colour coded so that more dangerous criminals attract police attention first.

White collar criminals, like credit card fraudsters and Russian spies will be given beige balloons, whilst murderers and serial rapists will be given bright orange or blue ones.

The public are being encouraged to help with the new system too.

"If victims would kindly try to remember what colour balloon their mugger or rapist was carrying, we'll be able to identify their attacker far more quickly, or, at the very least, establish what sort of crime has probably taken place," Bone said, swigging helium from the neck of a green polkadot balloon the shape of a crinkle cut chip.

"Balloons fight crime," he squeaked.

A multiple offender is released into the community yesterday.
PHOTOGRAPH BY FABULOUS BEE

mint?

mint!

(mint)

propelled by the mint marketing board

UNCOMMONLY ANIMALS
for all your animal needs

JUSTIN!

DEFENCE HENS

£1100 each
or eggs for £22.89 a dozen

BEWARE OF THE HEN

Cat-to-Dog lead with male and female fittings	£15.99
Takeaway kittens	£6.95
Vintage 1960s valve parrots	£POA
Tortoise chews	£1/doz
Snake knots (reefer, granny, half-shank)	£75

124 GODMOVESINAMYSTERIOUS WAY, FRAMLEY
01999 499 610 www.defence-hens@demon.co.uk

Library book finally returns

by Katy Blirdsnest

AFTER AN ABSENCE of nearly thirty years, Framley's Most Haunted Library Book has been returned to its rightful home.

The hardback edition of *American Shoes,* a pulp detective thriller by Kauffer Whitman, had been missing from Framley library's shelves since 1972, when it was rendered overdue by a mysterious nun, later found to have died in 1855.

The surprising find was made by senior librarian Twerrin Speck, who reported seeing a headless monk amongst the Book Amnesty boxes in the corner. Ghoulishly enough, Mr Speck investigated and stumbled across the spook-tacular volume.

The book's whereabout had been the subject of intense speculating since it's disappearal in the year of Ford Capris, Squlchie bars and The Bay City Roller!

Readers of the clumsy thriller had previously reported cold pages, the sound of footsteps coming from chapter eight and the sense of up to twelve 'presences' reading over their shoulders at any one time.

A team from Molford Polytechnic spent a night reading the book in the dark in 1968, under the gaze of infra red cameras, tap recorders

Framley library to where the book has been returned to.
PHOTOGRAPH BY PEACOCK STRUTMASTER

and temperature monitors. Nothing unusual was recorded, although two of the investigators claim to have heard snoring.

The book is now back in storage where Mr Speck can keep it from falling off the wrong pair of hands.

In Court

IAIN EUAN JAN, of Corrosion of Conformity Street, Molford was fined £10 for driving and drinking a car at Framley Magistrates Court on November 8th.

THE LATE ERIC DOUGALSUGAR of 14, Tey Road, Whoft, was fined £1000 with £520 prosecution costs for failing to obtain air traffic control clearance to fly a light aircraft into the roof of 14, Tey Road, Whoft.

HENRIK GABERDINE of Henrik's House, Wripple, was sentenced to the middle four years of an eight year sentence for trying to leave the court without permission.

KEREN LANCET of Humbert Avenue, Whoft, received a one year conditional discharge with £55 additional costs for possessing 5.4mgs of Framley Magistrate's Court on November 3rd.

JENIFFER VAN VAN, of Nimble Road, Framley was forced to undergo one day of manilow ® for theft of a Newby's napkin. Costs of £100 were impossible.

JUSTICE CONSTANT WAXY, of Berner's Leap, Whoft, was fined £100 for building his own special little court inside the big court.

KEVERETT ENNETH, of The Canal, Molford St Gavin, was awarded five 5.9s and a 6.0 for threatening behaviour.

MRS ISSY NOHO of Mothership Lounge, Molford was fined £4 at Framley Magistrates Court for breaking the unwritten law. The jury is still far out.

MRS JUSTICE CONSTANT WAXY of Berner's Leap, Whoft, was fined £1000 with £295 costs for not having the dinner ready when I got home.

LESLEY GRANDDAD of 14,Tiger Woods, Wripple was lowered into the Well Of Sundials for driving with defective lights on October 28th.

Exciting new proposals point to a brave new start for St Eyot's Castle

Brave new start for St Eyot's Castle

by Katy Blirdsnest

ST EYOT'S HISTORIC 14th Century castle is heading for one of the biggest shake ups in its four hundred year history!

Because the ancient building, built in 1462 to defend St Eyot's from dandy highwaymen, is to be bulldozed to the ground to make way for a new Medieval theme park – The St Eyot's Family Heritage Experience!

The new attraction is sure to have visitors flocking into the area from far and wide, because of due to the fact that it features rides, greeters dressed as the middle ages and a three-quarter scale replica of the original castle with Europe's loudest rollercoaster threaded along the battlements!

So what's it all about then? I sent myself as a roving reporter to find out exactly what it's all about then.

OUT WITH THE OLD

After a horrid journey through the traffic outside Codge, and a spot of bother turning right off the FR404 (sorry, whoever it was – I've got your wing mirror and driving gloves), I met project manager Ogilvy Grapes at the site office.

"This is a marvellous opportunity for the area to move out of the 14th Century once and for all," Grapes

Enjoying the castle grounds before they are smashed down.
PHOTOGRAPH BY MONTMORENCY BOAT

told me, indicating a model of the old castle.

"This sort of visitor attraction has a high foot-through and a proven unit satisfaction index," he explained, absentmindedly crushing the outer bailey of the model with the flat of his hand.

"Just you wait," he concluded, carelessly climbing onto the table and jumping repeatedly up and down on the tiny castle until it looked like wooden jam.

HOW THE NEW PLAN WILL GOING TO WORKS

Here's what the developers are planning to do to the old castle...

OUT	IN
The Great Hall	Animatronic Dipso The Dragon teaching kids about global warming & safe sex
The inner bailey & walls	Cap'n Chaucer's Velcro barfly trampolines & diner
Carp-filled moat	Go-Kart paintball track
The De Tournay Tower	Actors dressed as teddy bears re-enacting Heath Ledger's hit movie *A Knight's Tale*

What the new castle will mean for local people in the St Eyot's area

I ASKED Developmental Project Manager Gavinder McMountain what the new castle will mean for local people in the St Eyot's area.

"Though this new development isn't a castle in the traditional sense, people have to understand that our theme park does exactly the same job as St Eyot's Castle has always done. Just as the old stone building kept people safe from marauding vikings and pillaging Visigoths, The St Eyot's Family Heritage Experience will keep people safe from boredom.

"With our interactive themed rides, spectator-centred edutainment events and nourishment concession zones, we're lowering the portcullis on the prospect of stimulation-shortfall, and raising the drawbridge on sharp-end user-non-engagement. Now get out."

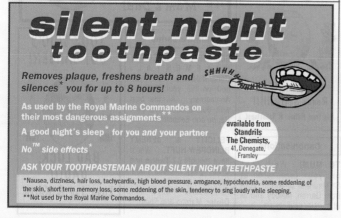

silent night toothpaste

SHHHH

Removes plaque, freshens breath and silences* you for up to 8 hours!

As used by the Royal Marine Commandos on their most dangerous assignments**

A good night's sleep* for you *and* your partner

No™ side effects*

available from
Standrils The Chemists,
41, Denegate, Framley

ASK YOUR TOOTHPASTEMAN ABOUT SILENT NIGHT TEETHPASTE

*Nausea, dizziness, hair loss, tachycardia, high blood pressure, arrogance, hypochondria, some reddening of the skin, short term memory loss, some reddening of the skin, tendency to sing loudly while sleeping.
**Not used by the Royal Marine Commandos.

Britain's first batman found in castle grounds

BY KATIE BLIRDSNEST

ARCHAEOLOGISTS, called in to have a look at St Eyot's Castle before developers bash it up, say they have found startling evidence of Britain's first batman.

Rathbone Twiddrington and Oswald Underclown say they were digging by the teashop when they unearthed an elaborate Renaissance courtier's hat and mask, sitting on the passenger seat of a horsedrawn batmobile.

Though the actual finds have been hidden under orange crates to stop magpies getting at them, the two men were more than willing to outline their theories.

Over tea and jam scones in the castle cafe, Twiddrington showed me conceptual drawings his partner had made of the so-called "ycaped crousadier".

"This batman worked under the patronage of the Wheelwright's Guild, solving crimes and foiling the wheel-hating plans of various 14th Century supervillains."

But the pair's investigations are under threat from the fact that the castle's tea shop area is due for demolition on Monday, to make way for a Third Place Coffee Lounge and Organic E-Point.

"This is a find of amazing historical significance. My partner and I must be allowed to continue our research. The site must not be disturbed."

Although the developers have insisted the archaeologists show them evidence of the finds, Twiddrington is

An artist's impression of the "Darke Knyghte". **BY OSWALD UNDERCLOWN**

The 14th Century batman's arch-enemies (L-R) Catlady, The Renaissance Joker and Mr Fruit. The Renaissance Joker's relentless jokes about mistaken identity and allusions to cuckoldry were a particular thorn in the batman's side.

adamant that he and his friend not be moved on.

"There is nowhere else in the country that shows better evidence of Renaissance costumed vigilante activity, or serves better tea," he insisted.

"We must stay, and dig, and have another eclair."

That'll be £6284.22, please!

by Taunton Mishap

FRAMLEY mother-of-one Judith had the fright of her life just recently when she opened her latest phone bill and read the total.

Judith, 39, who works in a shop, is used to receiving phone bills of about £40 per month. She thought the phone company had made a simple mistake, fainted and had to be revived by her husband's smells.

However, when she took a closer look, she discovered that her 14-year old son had spent some 660 hours on the phone to himself in the last month.

HOW MUCH?

"I was absolutely livid," she mumbled yesterday, "I had no idea he spent that long on the phone. And he was ringing his mobile. Why he couldn't have rung himself on the land line, I can't imagine. He knew

Judith's son, with (inset) the terrifying bill that he ran up using the telephone.
PHOTOGRAPH BY BALLISTA MEMORIAL

where to find himself."

Mrs Judith's son, whose name begins with a D, was last night recovering from stab wounds in hospital. His condition was described as "stable, but dead."

Police have arrested a 39-year-old woman on suspicion.

Tom Capstan's washing up column has been moved to page 1

Good times not so good

IT'S BEEN another disappointing year for Goode Stores, the oldest shop in Framley's Arnhem Centre.

In spite of rising profits in the retail sector over the last year, Goode's is still fighting low sales.

Goodman Goode, managing director of Goode Stores, complained, "People say these are the good times, but they're not that good at Goode's. Sales of Goode's luxury goods, for instance, have not been good at all. Even our brand-leader luxury good, Goodman Goode's Goodie-Goodies, isn't going particularly well."

Goodie-Goodies, Goode's famous hand-squeezed truffles with added vitamins, outsell every other Goode's luxury good. Last year's "It's a Good Time For Goodie-Goodies!" advertising campaign saw the sweets outsell Ferrari Rochers two-to-one. But the good times haven't lasted for Goodie-Goodies, or Goode's Stores or Goodman Goode.

Goode's fail to make good on good start.

"We've tried every aggressive marketing tack known to man with the Goodie-Goodies," continued Mr Goode, "and the most successful of those was our Blue Swastika week. We shifted a good 300 Goodie-Goodies that week. That was a good week, actually. But apart from maybe one good week, it's not been a good year at Goode's."

Mr Goodman is now considering a frivolous proposal to re-name Goodman Goode's Goodie-Goodies "Goodman Goode's 'Not So Good' Good Times Goodie-Goodies", and a rather less frivolous proposal to sack an unbelieveable number of staff.

FRAMLEY'S NEWEST BOILED EGG ATTRACTION

CONCH ™

COME ON IN... THE EGGS ARE BOILICIOUS!

Eggsby ™

BOILED EGG HILLS

THE WORLD'S GREATEST BOILED EGG THEME PARK

Come and meet Eggsby, the Boiled Egg Hills boiled egg !

Ride a saucepan round the Big Boiler, Britain's HOTTEST rollercoaster !

All rides last 3 minutes (or 10 minutes hard)

Son et Lumiere display every day at 5am (The Boiled Eggs Story)

£25 adults / £12 children FAMILY TICKET (£28) includes FREE stick of boiled egg floss and "I'm A Dippy Soldier" bumper sticker

JUST OFF THE FR404 BETWEEN FRACTON AND CLINTON open every weekday until 11am (except Easter Sunday)

"Eggsby" and the boiling of eggs are registered trademarks of Conch Oil Plc

WILLS! WILLS! WILLS!

Your name included on the will of your choice!

Join the Codicil Will Of The Month Club and earn £££££s

Simply choose one will every month that you want a stake in, otherwise, the Solicitor's Choice of money will be sent to you. If you don't want the money, simply send it back.

Members also get free entry into our Big Prize Tontine, with the option of an exciting duel to the death.

CODICIL sponsors of the anna-nicole smith gold-digger prize
www.codi.cil 01999 822 186

possible to remove without killing one of the twins? 01999 865 428, ASAP.

WRIST MAGNETS. Set of two. Prevent unwanted clapping/waving/movement of lower arms. Fram 01999 888 946

EASTEND FOREPLAY KIT. Includes Stepney Tickle, Mile End Feathering and Bow Road Finger Insertion. Batteries included. £12.50. Call Guy on 01999 865 456

50'S SINGLES COLLECTION. All divorced/widowed/cold and confused. Some later ones missing. To complete collection or for spares. Fram 01999 821444

BICYCLE WHISK

BOX OF DELIGHTS. Push button to the left to go small, push to the right to become Poet Laureate. £19.99. Phone Mrs Hawlings on 01999 801934.

LIFT FARTS, fake gangster, some giggles. Will exchange for These Bleeds™. 01999 866 466

LIPSTICKS, assorted. Salt and vinegar, smoky bacon, soup. 9 of each. £45 the bunch. 01999 393031.

QUICK SALE. Would suit speedy Manchester. Offers. 01999 871 109

HUMMINGBEARS

QUANTUM CLOCK. Tells the time and doesn't tell the time at the same time. £20 oqo. 01999 268834.

YOUR FRONT DOOR. Get it back on 01999 835 310.

MAGIC EYE Teach Your Child To Read. Alphabets, simple stories and helpful pictures represented as 3-D images only visible when eyes are defocused. Would suit advanced 3yo that doesn't cry as much as mine. Good luck. £5. Framley 849727.

THE BLING BLING. Giving it for all the St Eyots District Domino and Billiards League Massive. Keep it safe, yeh?. 01999 832 455

FRAMLEY area phone book, complete with handwritten alphabetical index. All my own work. £450. 01999 360361.

BUZZARDS, BUZZERS & BUZZ. 3' x 8' watercolour reinterpretation of 2nd man on the moon as bespace-suited quiz show host under attack. On the moon. £500 framed. 01999 875 522

BILL & BEN, the flowerpots. Plant receptacles, red clay. Too much personality for flowerpots. Hence slightly intimidating. £12 the set. Will not be separated. 01999 800 632

BLACK & DECKER Garden Devil. Left in neighbour's garden overnight will soak oil into flowerbeds, hide sheds and turn spades inside out. It really works! All of mine moved within three months. £48. 01999 819019.

BOX SET OF BOOKS by Douglas Adams. A five part trilogy in increasingly large type. £8. Tel 01999 855 981

1974 SLOW COOKER. Far too slow. Still waiting for boiled egg. £12orwhatever. 01999 231664.

JUNIOR GRAVITY SET. Let your child experience the joy of staying on the ground. Certificate of authenticity signed by Lord Howe. No responsibility accepted. £24 01999 865 456

MONEY CAN'T BUY YOU LOVE but £2.50 will get you a cuddle. Call Vernon on or around 01999 834440.

> The Framley Examiner
>
> Framley's Traditional Formulae Since 1839
>
> **"I have no idea who you are or where you came from. Pour that back in the bottle and get out of my lounge."**
>
> Mrs Limoges, Sockford

LIONS AND TIGERS and bears, all mine. Fake or real, it's up to you. POA. Framley 844 644

NUMBER ONE SINGLE, Top of the Pops appearances, fan club. Will exchange for less difficult second album. 01999 844 093

GRIEF CYCLE. Denial/anger vgc, some acceptance refusals. Can't believe that I have to let this go. £16ono. 01999 849 589

A PLAYGROUND RHYME ABOUT YOU by professional 8-year old poet. Please indicate whether you have nits or fancy Kelly Vinton. 01999 850006 after 3.45pm.

POSTMAN PRAM. Keeps your postie safe and warm, rain-hood, post-Consignia design, 300 of. £750ono. 01999 831 030

OFFICIAL "ALL YOUR MEMORIES" 1982 PANINI STICKER ALBUM. Complete except for penguin falling over at London Zoo (28), that thing with Paul McDowell in it (141) and Dan & Mandy's wedding foil badge (436). £100ono. 01999 875 055

PIGGY BANK for sale. Contains roughly £38. Call Mr Hollyhock on 01999 482762 (please hang up immediately if Josie answers). £41.50

CAT LITTER. Also hamster graffiti. £6. Box FE8511

CAN YOU WAKE ME UP? I've got a train to catch. Please call 01999 872359 between 5am and 6am.

FIDDLE-STICK™. Provides evidence of child abuse by gluing offender's appendages to your kiddie. Approved by European Court of Human Rights. Box FE8009

BANG & OLUFSEN Speakers of the House of Commons. Excellent treble, Boothroyd / Martin separation exceptional. £450. Framley 802 223

WANT A NUT? I've got plenty. Selling due to protein efficiency. Must be seen. POA. 01999 866 954

READY-TO-HANG Union Jack, printed upside down, perfect for TV productions, will provoke letters of complaint to Points of View. £40. 01999 94R880.

LAVA LAMPOST, £35. Box FE8249.

BUS QUEUE in twenty foot lengths. First and third sections may contain pensioners or pushchairs. £8 per foot. 01999 845902.

REGRETS, I've had a few, but then again, too few to not sell, so call, call Gary Vest, I'm in the phone book.

GREYHOUND STABILIZERS. Once used by Romford Champion Hurdler, Miss Princess Fififi d'Bigbitch. Michelin tyres, chrome finish. Will swap for weasel mittens. Box FE8274.

CRAP. This is all crap and none of it's for sale any more. You're all such slow-witted fools. I've already bought it all. Box FE8193

TELETEXT ONLY TELEVISION. 32" widescreen FST, Dolby 5.1 Surround Sound, but ONLY teletext. £1400. Tel. 01999 824487.

INDUSTRIAL LAMINATOR. Laminates anything. I've just done my face. Can I do yours? Or your hair? Or your house? Call me now! Framley 567833.

BORING RELATIVE. Goes on and on and on. Will swap for sultana or postage stamp. Box FE8815.

WHO WILL BUY?

BISSELL "Ceiling Master" Ceiling Shampooer. Three foam rollers, stepladder and sou'wester. £55. 01999 428166.

ANTIQUE LAPTOP, 1938 Imperial, hurts lap, needs new ribbon, £101. Box FE8001.

YEAR'S SUPPLY of tampons – regular, heavy and crikey. Hysterectomy, hence quick sale, £30. 01999 610978.

BOY FOR SALE

CELL SITE, currently in children's ward of local hospital. Carcinogenic, hence controversial sale, £160. No journalists/parents. Box FE8413.

TORTOISE CRUCIFIXION KIT. 2' cross, fits neatly inside shell. Some staining. Comes with hydraulic nail-gun and crown of lettuce. Offers. Call Mr Hollyhock on 01999 482762.

CHRISTIAN paraphernalia: 'Judas Was A Sodding Catholic' t-shirts, £10 each. 'Holy Shit My Lord' mugs £3.50 each. Turin teatowels, £1 the lot. Framley Christian fellowship, 01999 231664.

OOM PA PA

HARRY BELAFONTE and The Prisoner of Azkaban. Early J.K.Rowling draft manuscript, written on the back of 500 twenty pound notes. No longer legal tender. £8. Box FE8735

BEARD, £10. Moustache, £5. Soul chip (stylish lower lip beardlet), £2. HairWare, 01999 950950.

OFFAL BALLOONS. Already full, tricky to burst, but it is possible. Great for children's parties. £4 each, raw or cooked. Call Mr Jimmy on 01999 258187.

VAGUE TAPE MEASURE. Marked "Near" at one end and "Far" at the other. £2.50. 01999 822985.

CONSTABLE'S HAYWAIN and other police pictures incl. Desk Sergeant's "Whistler's Mother" and Copper's "Bod Snap". £98 the lot or £99 the lots. Fram 01999 801010

PLANET for hire. Small, cold, barren, insufficient oxygen. Call Vince on 01999 348792

FEATHERSTONEHAUGH'S Dyslexia Remedy. This is not a cure. Box FE8719

BURGLAR FLAP. fits any door, opens on detection of ankle tag. £35. 01999 352920.

TEFAL CHICKEN TOASTER. Pops up when the chicken is done. Ruined, hence £5. 01999 357553.

SPLENESMATIST

20GB C: DRIVE, full. Try to avoid My Pictures>Oh! Isn't that a really interesting thing in that folder over there?>Faeces. Offers. BoxFE8374.

100% COTTON TESTCARD, never transmitted, beautiful rarity. £250. 01999 360241.

TURN YOUR KEYPAD TONES OFF. All of you who have a mobile phone that beeps every time you touch a button, it's really fucking annoying. Sort it out, you wankers. Call 01999 871336 if you can do it without me having to punch your face off. I'll see you on the train, no doubt.

MOULINEX OrangeBigger™. Makes oranges bigger. Satsumas – 4ft, Seville – 8ft. Plus CheeseGreater™ £20. Box FE8234.

CONKER, championship-winner, Stuttgart 1983. Filled with glitter for spectacular ending. 29lb. £29. Call Friedrich on 01999 373119

BESTGLOW log effect 2kW scissors. Too hot to hold, honestly. £7. 01999 442700.

SCREAMING BLUE MURDER alarm clock. Screams really really really really loudly all the time. Stops when it's time to wake up. Everlasting batteries. £FOC. 01999 487555.

TWEED EFFECT pet igloo with two hotplates and grill. £25. 01999 258 476

GOBLIN TEASDRUNK Wake up every morning to a hot, empty cup. £15. 01999 841569.

FAST SHOW shampoo and conditioner. Rub those catchphrases into your hair and scalp for a longlasting, hilarious shine. Box of ten. £8. 01999 846466.

CARAVAN COSY. Six years of knitting. No longer required. Caravan now cosy. £8ono. 01999 895523.

TOOTH HOOVER, adult and milk. Sucks or blows. Variety of nozzles for high corners and narrow gaps. Slightly damaged root extractor (doesn't cope with wisdom very well). Divorce threatened hence £25. Box FE8363.

DOG PERISCOPE. Fits most breeds (except retrievers). Russian Navy surplus. £160. Box FE8747

MILK. Will separate. £100 Whoft 3554

KRAUT ROCK, 13 sticks. Has "A Present From Amon Duul II" written all the way through. £14. 01999 845519.

THE REAL PAULA YATES bread-bins. Inspired by the hit Channel 4 programme. Made by local carpenter, twelve designs, mostly tasteful. All £25 each, except 48 Litre "Geldof Jereboam" (£50). All proceeds to charity or CSA. 01999 899 765

ENORMOUS MINT IMPERIAL decorated with elaborate scrimshaw design of 1100 anatomically correct birds in flight. Signed by Rudolf Hess / Rolf Harris (?). £110. Framley 01999 822745.

INFLATABLE BREADBOARD. Used once. Very disappointing. £2. 01999 854488.

ZILDJIAN / PEARL 5 piece exercise kit. With cymbals, 22lb rack toms and drumbells. £200ono. Will separate, except hi-hat. Take the hi-hat. I said, "take it". Here, I'll put it in the boot of your car, just so you don't forget it. 01999 893995.

THE LIPSYL STORY

FRIGIDAIRE 'Refrigerator' – miraculous! A very cold cupboard! £4.11.6d, FRAmley 330 before 1949.

SCRABBLE CHEATING MACHINE. Over 50,000 imagined words. Accepts all new entries programmed in during games. Has some trouble with legitimate words. You will win. 01999 845354 OIRO £300.

A BONE OF YOUR OWN! I have your ribs, your ulna, your patella and part of your spine. Phone me to find out how. 01999 378858.

MIRROR THAT REFLECTS THE 1950s. See yourself as a Teddyboy or Teddybird, Daddy-O! Call Chip on 01999 849010.

MOUSE TIMPANI

HALF HOUR DELAY. Would suit busy person wishing to be late. £99 or £180 for an hour. Box FE8770.

IMITATION CHESHIRE CHEESE SOAP. I wouldn't use it, would you? OK, then, it's yours. £40 nqa 01999 841211

> The Framley Examiner
>
> Framley's Traditional Formulae Since 1839
>
> **Over 1300 tonnes of fried eggs are sold every day through Framley Examiner Classifieds.**

UNWANTED CHRISTMAS GIFT. Given by unwanted aunt. Will swap. £20 Fram 01999 867955

ASSORTED MEXICAN Jumping Men in low ceilinged container. Some concussion. A quid. Fram 01999 857743

BLUE PULLOVER full of kittens. Kids love it. Kittens don't. Don't do it. £30 Fram Evenings Only 01999 822256

BORSTAL BAILEY annuals 1942-78. Private sale, best not to shout about this one. £50 ono. Box FE8599.

BRIAN GLOVER GLOVES and Brian Jacks Jacket. I wore both and looked like neither, neither will you. Or will you? No you won't. £800. Fram 01999 865545

GIANT CHILDREN'S PLAY CRANE. Suitable for small home improvements. Vertiginous fun for the giant child in your house. Fram 01999 899566

COLLECTION OF Shredded Wheat pencil case stickers circa 1980. inc. "I saw Sir on Top of the Pops", "Sums are Gay", "Sir's crack pipe stinks", "My Smart Desk", "I'm A Two Tone Tyrant". Offers. Fram 01999 956666

MIKE NESMITH'S HAT

WHAT'S IT ALL ABOUT? This is what. I'm placing an advert for a lovely chair. It's yours if you can tell me why I'm selling it, but be quick, it's on fire! Fram 01999 844566

COCONUT MATT. Likeness of Matthew Perry made entirely from coconuts. Makes sound of galloping horses when operated. Chewing mechanism disabled for child safety. Fram 01999 856111

STETHOSCOPE TELESCOPE. See the stars and hear them thump at the same time. £15. Box FE8433.

CHILD'S CHARLIE CHAPLIN RUG. Teaches children how to tie and eat their shoelaces. Fram 01999 845221

BABY GROW. Results in minutes. As recommended on TV's Big Brother programme. Fram 822113

ALL-IN-ONE COOKER/ FREEZER. Hot on outside, cold on inside. Difficult to open due to heat. May still contain all my food. Buyer to collect. Whoft 5879

LUCKY PREGNANCY TEST KIT. Used once. Negative. Sealed bids to BoxFE8284.

VERRAY PARFIT Fyn Coverchiefs Golde, alle clene and faire and nat too olde. 10 quid the lotte. Fram 889 765 before 1365AD.

TUESDAY AFTERNOON AT WORK. Really boring. Would swap for Friday, 3pm with prospect of drink afterwards. £5. Whoft 8888

PAT COOMBS SEX doll. Polyvinyl, asexual, rat-voiced supporting cast-member fetish action. Will deliver and watch. £30 flat or £40 inflated. 01999 893 300

ADULT POPCORN MAKER. Popcorn's never sounded or looked so much like adults. Tastes of Rum Punch. Fram 856556

FLUFFY DICE, 18-sided, crate of. Would suit Advanced D&D fan with haulage firm? £200 01999 800007.

DREAMBOAT, 'The I Can Fly Can't I?', luxury, 60'. Toffee galley with infinite fridge, cloudy beds and priest wearing all the lifejackets at once. Nightmare dinghy, full of burning glass. £6,571. Call Dr Glacier on 01999 864177.

PLAYSTATION 6. Quick. They're after me. £offers. 01999 877 653

tea break

BIG PRIZE CROSSWORD COMPETITION
SOLUTION

Solution to Big Prize Crossword Number 1161

BRIDGE
the gathering
puzzle set by **Mongo**

ALL BIDS CLOCKWISE are parried. Held cards are frantic, except **spades** and **deuces**, which count double. **Baggage**, and paired **"wet" cards**, pass to dealer's left, unless declared by a player holding either *The Hanged Man* or *Secret Tunnel Discovered In Chapel.*

WE JOIN the game just after the first round of secondary bidding has left all the court cards **open.** Though this gave East a possible folded-trick advantage, West has opted to freeze the table at **twelve (12)**, and the face card on the discards (the **2 of balls**) is now the boundary suit, unless the bid is **raised.** You have won second prize in a beauty competition!

North to move first and win in four months, before food runs out.

BIG PRIZE CROSSWORD
Set by "Invictus"

Number 1161 Here's your chance to win one of hundreds of Framley Examiner t-shirts or a brand new Saab 9000 Turbo in the **Framley Examiner Coffeetime Big Prize Crossword.** (We regret this competition is no longer open to employees of The Framley Examiner or "Invictus")

FRAMLEY EXAMINER TEATIME CROSSWORD #1161

Name _____

Address _____

_____ Framley   Postcode FM _____

Preferred prize: T-Shirt ☐ S ☐ M ☐ L ☐ XL ☐ Saab 9000
(please tick)

Send to THE FRAMLEY EXAMINER Unit 149b, East Cosset Industrial Park Parkfields Bypass, Framley FR1 6LH

Quick Quiz

1. If the answer is half of two, what is the question?
2. Tiny Tim is finishing his Christmas Turkey with Scrooge. He is asked what he wants for dessert, but politely refuses. What is the name of his 1968 top ten hit single?
3. Complete the following sequence:
   NAME'S, BOND, JAMES, _____.
4. Solve the following picture conundrum:

LAST WEEK'S ANSWERS: 1. Body Odour 2. There was no known answer to this one 3. You're taking fucking liberties, son. 4. 87 similar-sized lozenges should block the hole

---

ACROSTIC
This week's alchemical acrostic is:

S	A	T	O	R
A	R	E	P	O
T	E	N	E	T
O	P	E	R	A
R	O	T	A	S

Answers to THE FRAMLEY EXAMINER Unit 149b, East Cosset Industrial Park Parkfields Bypass, Framley FR1 6LH

Last week's winner, who cracked the puzzle and revealed the Enochian language of the angels, was Mr Hugh Passiter from Molford St Malcolm, who can now turn base metals into gold and converse directly with God.

Well done, Hugh.

DOWN CLUES

1 TV weatherman (8,4)
3 Half of French & Saunders (2)
4 David _____, actor and inventor of hand cream (5)
5 "___ break every bone in your body." (3)
6 Eurovision winning Swedish group whose hits include *Waterloo Sunset* and *Come Dancing Queen* (4)
10D & 28A You've got to buy it to be in it to win it! (plural) (7,7)
11 TV weatherman (6,7)
12 Not Bloody Likely! (acron.) (3)
13 Now, where did I put that old box of shoes? (2,4)
14 First name of politician Mo Mowlam (2)
15 Cow / cat noise (2)
17 ___s against ___s, Brighton, 1963 (9)
19 Standard measure of Angel Delight (6)
21 A dozen (1,12,4)
22 TV superhero (3,3)
24 The first three letters of "assembly", perhaps? (3)
26 Bi (anag) (2)
27 James Bond's bosses (1,1)
29 "____, tyger, burning bright" (Kipling?) (5)
33 Swedish group who won Eurovision with *Dedicated Follower of Fa-Fa-Fashion* (4)
35 Ballbag (3)
38 Two (3.14159)
40 "Can you put the cat out?" "___" (2)

ACROSS CLUES

2 TV Weatherman (3,10)
3 lb (anag) (2)
8 English national dish; fish and ____ (3)
9 Eurovision winning Swedish car whose hits include *A Winner Takes It All* and 6 Down (5)
12 Geographical area of Britain containing Manchester (2)
13 "On your marks, get set, ____" (3)
15 "_____, a drop of golden rain" (Sound of Music) (2)
16 Cock (6)
18 Basic error leads to lost duel (2,3)
20 "And all because the lady loves ____" (4)
22 "I'll have a nice ____ ____, please, Mr baker" (5,4)
23 Gravy vessel (5,4)
24 "Able was ant, ____ ____ saw Elba" (3,1)
25 San Fran ____ (5)
28 see 10 Down
30 The company that makes pencils (2)
31 Regiment of Bennies, we hear? (11,6,3)
32 "Look at ____ _unt!" (2,1)
34 More than one 'I ' (2)
36 SH + DR UGS (5)
37 A long, snakelike fish (4)
38 "Look at me, ____! Top of the world!" (Cagney & Lacey) (2)
39 "Old MacDonald had a farm, ___ E-I-O!" (2)
41 TV weatherman (8,5)

SIMON CADELL'S WEEKEND IN DORSET WITH A LIME
#37754   By Rollo

Mayor's actions show he has finally lost all respect for town

STONES

by Challenger Putney

Have YOU got a story about a circle of ancient stones being demolished to make way for a public bypass or something? If so, we'd love to hear it!

Send all correspondence to
THE FRAMLEY EXAMINER
Unit 149b, East Cosset Ind. Pk
Parkfields Bypass, Framley FR1 6LH

THE FUTURE of the famous Framley Stones, Britain's oldest earthwork, has been plunged into uncertainty yet again.

The famous Stones, a 3rd century circle of 'standing stones' (or menhirs) – presumed a place of worship – and Britain's oldest earthwork, were under threat of construction from the borough's proposed Outer Ring Road Project (ORRP).

The Stones became the subject of a compulsory purchase order by the council, prompting local architectural historian Sir Cocoa Wufflemere to claim that Billiam D'Ainty, Framley's colourful mayor, has "lost all respect for the town."

Wufflemere, who has done three books about Framley, made his startling allegation after a ten-minute meeting with the mayor in his plush office last week.

"I asked him about the future of the Framley Stones, and he told me not to worry, they were being preserved," gasped Wufflemere.

HERE'S THE MAYOR

Mayor D'Ainty, long since the ORRP's noisiest approbator, had

A proposed map of the project.

ILLUSTRATION ARCHIE BUBBLES

already signed compulsory purchase orders for a 14th-century mansion house, the village of Whoft and the world's largest penny farthing. At an Extraordinary Meeting last week, D'Ainty told councillors that the future of the Stones was "under my review."

"I asked him where his review was at," warmed Cocoa, "and that's

when he told me that the Stones were going to be included as a feature on a roundabout on the road.

"Then he whispered that actually, the road scheme wouldn't be going ahead, but that he was going to build a roundabout around the stones anyway. And he blew a fart at me.

"I just lost it. I flew at him and punched him on the nose," went Sir.

POLICE TOLD ABOUT

Mayor D'Ainty has told policemen and people dressed as policemen that he plans to press charges of common assault against Wufflemere. He has also brushed off claims that the Stones are as old as everybody thinks, claiming the earliest photograph of it dates from the 1920s.

"I'm on the side of proof," spat the Mayor as he gripped his blood-drenched handkerchief to his gushing nostrils as he passed me as he left his office where I was on the spot.

ENTER THE HIPPIES

A pride of hippies has arrived at the site of the Framley Circle, claiming they will "make love to the stones right up til the bulldozers get it together," says a red-faced farmer from St Eyot's.

"They've arrived in their Volkswagen Caravans, covered in beads, and they're sicking up joints all over my farm," he boiled last night.

Edwin Nimby, 42, jokingly threatened to "go on a hippy-peppering spree with a couple of friends from the National Front."

The Framley Examiner
Framley's Traditional Favourite Since 1978

YOUR AD HERE

could be reaching

62mm x 74mm

Thinking of Decorating?
talk to the
EXPERTS

Blue
01999 780 001
Yellow
01999 780 002

GINDY & SONS

All In A FLap!

FRAMLEY BOROUGH COUNCIL today warned of further chaos as industrial action by the local owl community entered its fourth fortnight.

The dish-eyed birds, who are demanding their own parliament, have been working to rule for 8 weeks, doing only the bare miminum required by the terms of their contracts

The majority of Framley's owl population will now only move their heads 90 degrees in either direction when looking for mice, while one breakaway wolery is operating a "fly slow", moving through the air at less than 4cm an hour, crashing slowly into pedestrians' heads and obscuring lines of sight for drivers and lollipop people.

One teenager boy was last night being councilled by his family after

by Katy Blirdsnest

he froze with fear because of the fact that an owl flew at a constant 30cm from his face for two and half hours last week.

Tawny owls, who are refusing to follow the co-operative's hardline "one whit, one whoo" policy, have been crossing picket lines and manning a skeleton owl service, but this is proving nowhere near enough to cope with demand for owls in Framley, which was at an all-time high until this.

A spokesmen for the Department of the Environment, Traffic and the Regions (DEFRA) has invited the nocturnal birds to arbitration in Athens.

There is a species of owl called the New Zealand laughing owl.

An owl, refusing to budge
PHOTO BY BURGER BOY

MOTÖRHEAD

with Oliver Singultus-Hiccup

Sockford comes up trumps with new car

SOCKFORD MOTORWORKS hasn't produced a new model in over 150 years, so I was more than excited to be asked to road-test their latest prototype, the Sockford Narwhal R150.

On first impressions, I was impressed by the car's roomy, warm interior, with its impressive array of climate controls and 8" temperature gauge, situated unexpectedly in the centre of the windscreen. Right, Oliver, I said to myself, let's you and me see what this baby can do.

With a throaty roar, I pulled out into traffic, licking my lips and mopping my brow. With engine response like this, I thought, things might get too hot to handle!

At 60mph, the windows shut automatically, and my glasses began to really steam up. Quite a ride!

My fingers started to sizzle and pop on the steering wheel, and I thought it best to prick them with the dashboard fork provided. Just outside Whoft, I reached for the gearstick, and slammed the car into Gas Mark Six. Soon the skin began to blister and lift from the bridge of my nose. Excellent.

Partway up the F420 to St Eyots, there was a loud ping and I knew that I had been done to perfection. All that remained was to get home and find that cranberry sauce!

With this thrilling new model, Sockford should find themselves back at the top of a tree. But, if you, like us, can't wait to get your hands on one, you'll have to wait. Pending investigation of a few undisclosed teething problems, Narwhal production has been suspended indefinitely.

If you want details of this or any of Oliver's previous recipes, call us on 01999 877 7777 ext 467.

PERSON4LI5ED NUM8ERPLATE5
from LARRY PLATES

ME4T M4RK3T	B4YLE4F
MR CLUM5Y	BBC CHO1C3
CR15P5	OLD M41D
P4EDO	AM15H
7 DW4RF5	HA7 5HOP
83TTY 800	CL4MB4KE
TYN3 TEE5	TE4 PO7
833TROO7	ESSO OIL
WE7 BED	SHELL OIL
8LOW OFF	5ENIL3 COW
NUTM3G	E4RLY B4TH
RO4LD D4HL	WOOL
QU33R STR33T	70YS R US
5TE4L ME	7E7RI5 K1D
COCKY CUN7	W1NDMILL
R4VIOL1	AN7 5 D3C
NO7 YE7	DU5TC4RT

IDEAL GIFT   H4PPY CHR15TM4S
last few remaining!

CALL 01999 886 443
FOR A FULL COLOUR CATALOGUE

FRAMLEY SCHOOL OF CARMANSHIP

We offer a wide range of courses in popular road and fancy driving for the discerning 17 year old

JOYRIDING LESSONS   STUNTS
BROKEN BRIDGE   HOTWIRING
ENDOS & BUNNYHOPS
LOOP-DE-LOOPS
ROAD RAGE   HANDBRAKE TURNS
GETAWAY   SKYWRITING
also: DRIVING FOR GIRLS

01999 800 656
www.01999800656.co.uk

FSM

Molford St Malcolm Motors
Loretta Swit Stableyards, Molford St Malcolm, Molford FM7

01999 876 5300
www.molfordstmalcolmmotorslimited.demon.co.uk

the excperts in used cars !

AUSTIN MUSTARD

- 1972 L reg
- Brown tyres, mauve roof and yellow leather seatage.
- Overbearing smell of flock wallpaper and Wet Ones.
- Would suit student, I suppose.

£2995 ON THE ROAD

VOLKSWAGEN BEATLE

EXTREMELY RARE

- Original 1964 B reg vehicle
- Undulating wax John, Paul, and Ringo 'passengers' on back seat
- Slightly distracting when driving, (especially Paul)
- One Beatle owner (George)

£11995 NEAR THE ROAD

MORE OF OUR FAMOUS GREAT CARGAINS!

FORD SH-BOOM 1.3 ULTRA POPULAR
N-reg, fsh, one lady owner killed in car crash.
THIS WEEK ONLY £150.

FORD CLOWNMOBILE, 1998(S)
coupe, square wheels, bright yellow with flower motifs, doors that fall off, 23 horns, backfiring exhaust etc, vgc   **CRAZY PRICE £225,000**

VAUXHALL AVERAGE 1.8i
1996/P, with unique seat-mounted airbags to break passengers necks (presumably).
THIS WEEK'S DEAL £9,550

WOLSEY POLICE DRAGSTER
0-120 in 3/8s overshoots crime scenes by miles.   **UNBEATABLE OFFER £8,995**

FORD WEBMASTER
Internet-ready roadster with full DNS history. Available in any one of 256 colors, as long as it's Mac (compatible).   **UNMETERED ACCESS FROM £14.99 A MONTH**

DAIHATSU WESTMINSTER
Horsedrawn-effect with gilt coachwork, and woolsack, DVD-R player, Karaoke parliamentary debate machine and full Manga library (Hansard 1982-97). One Prime Ministerial owner.
PRICED AT £48,995 ono

PEUGEOT 830L
Cardboard box with felt-tip lights, cushion seats and saucepan lids for wheels. Ask a grown-up to cut you a door. Also fort, aeroplane or boxmonster.   **POCKET MONEY PRICE £26**

DOUBLE DECKER BUS.
Seats 65 on ground floor, with stairs leading down further, seating 190 below road level on mezzanine deck. Full HGV and structural engineer's licence required.
AVAILABLE BRIEFLY AT HALF PRICE £37,000

VOLKSWAGEN SPASMA 1.5GL 93
K-reg (shed shape), 5-speed gearbox, 3-speed sunroof, electrical doors, fsh
ESPECIALLY OFFERED AROUND £5,675

CITROËN MEASLE DIESEL 2.0Hdi.
Mostly red. 1 careful owner, fsh. Airtight sunroof, contaminated aircon, itchy windows. Comes with 18 pairs of driving gloves, 1 face mask.   **UNREBEATABLE OFFER £450**

CUSTOMISED AUSTIN MARTIN DB5.
Silver paint job. Oil-squirting seat and ejector wheels. Be just like James Bomb!
AND IT'S ONLY £10,595

SEAT GIEDROYC
650cc GTI, 1997(P) 1-door, automatically gears, marshmallow pink, powered by magnets.
IF ONLY £2,150

TOYOTA WEATHERMAN GX AUTO.
Snow-white, wind-screen, sun-roof, fog-lamps, mostly dry-seats and muggiest steering-wheel since records began so don't forget to wrap up well.
ONLY £1400 FAHRENHEIT

MAZDA EGGSHELL ESPRIT.
Inflatable bodywork, childproof Brittle™ seatbelts, shatterproof-proof front/rear windshields with 'Baby On Fire' sticker. 67 careful miles, 18 owners.
TODAY ONLY £1,595

VAUXHALL BLAND 1.4
1999, special edition Super Furry Animals Guerrilla model. Hidden track under spare wheel.   **SPECIAL OFFER SPECIAL PRICE £5,950.**

BENTLEY BEEFMOBILE
1984 B Reg. Limited 'Mince' edition with shortcrust pastry trims and sausage nozzle for exhaust. Complies with British safety standards, but requires constant freezing.
BENTLEY'S VALUE ONLY £5.99

FIAT CRISPS.
Plain with silver interior, full service history, driver/passenger bluebag, crunching gears. Only 12000 crisps on clock. Multipack – not to be sold separately.
BARGAIN OF THE WEEK £2.99 FOR SIX

BRISTOL POSTGATE
M-reg (1995), walnut dashboard, duck leather upholstery, chandelier, open fire, resident domestic staff of six.
AMAZING BARGAIN AT ONLY £3,255

MITSUBISHI PIRATE 1.6GLi.
Jolly Roger bonnet, headlight patch, 1 mahogany wheel, side-firing cannon / grappling hooks, streamlined crow's nest, mutinous abs, onboard parrot.
THIS WEEK ONLY 1000 PIECES OF EIGHT

ROVER PIXAR CGi 820.
Woody finish, hopping headlamps, glove compartment full of talking de-icing implements, Randy Newman soundtrack. Great merchandising possibilities.
YOU'D BE A FOOL TO MISS ONLY £2,590

FORD TURNIP 3.9 VOGUE
3-speed, met blue, includes 250 used tyres. Will not separate. £4,500. No timewasters or zookeepers.
ST MALCOLM'S SPECIAL DEAL £2199

ROLLS ROYCE 'FANCY FELLOW'.
Handsome vehicle with posh seats and numberplate moustache. Complete with original Niven Steering Balloons.
LUXURY EXECUTIVE PRICE £26,000

THE READERS OF THE LORD MAGAZINE VOTED MOLFORD ST MALCOLM MOTORS 12TH BEST USED CAR DEALERSHIP, 2001. THANKS FOR YOUR SUPPORT, YOUR LORDSHIPS!

It's never toi-late to go to the toilet!

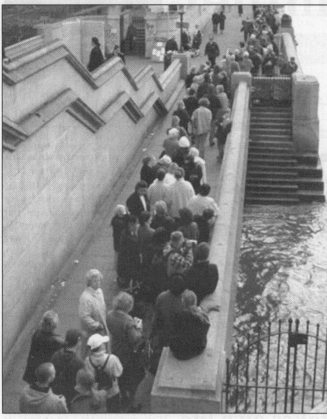

The queue for the award winning toilet that many are calling "the most exciting thing ever to happen in Framley"
PHOTOGRAPH BY MATTEUS TRILOBITE

by Damiun Clavalier

By Damium Clavalier

FLUFF STREET conveniences have been voted the best in Framley, only a year after they were voted the worst in Framley.

Gus Wetherlady, the conveniences' sole attendant was present at the presentation at Framley Hall. "I'm going to put the award on the wall under last years'", he announced to the gathered, "Clean toilets are more fun. And the extra cash helped."

And indeed he's right! More than £150,000 was ploughed into the project, most of which was targeted at two serious blockages that had troubled visitors for years.

These weren't the only improvements that were noted by the judges. All areas of the conveniences are now accessible to wheelchair users, including the famous pitched roof and store cupboard. There's even a coffee shop, lift and museum celebrating 100 years of effluent.

Q

If you'd like to use the facilities, however, you'd better cross your legs. On a good day last week, the queue for the cubicles stretched back past the war memorial a mile away, with many more people joining the line 'just in case'.

"I didn't need to use them when I first joined the queue," I quoted someone as saying, "but I'm grateful to be here now, I am telling you."

The regulars seem happy as well. After inspecting the facilities, one of the judges locked himself in a cubicle and refused to leave. Staff have since fitted a glass window in the door so you can see him smiling and enjoying his visit.

Archaeoaelogists find evidence of the past

THE NEWS is just in for golfists – if you want to score a golf-in-one, you'll have to steer clear of Molford Golf Course for the next few weeks. The greens have been cordoned off by a pair of local archaeologists who have declared the course a "site of ludicrous historical significance".

Rathbone Twiddrington and Oswald Underclown of the Framley Archaeological Survey have been digging in the bunkers of Molford Golf Course since the beginning of last month, and they have already unearthed a veritable corn-on-the-copia of treasure troves.

So far, they've uncovered a viking longball, a woad club dating back to the 3rd century and a fossilized dinosaur carrying a golf bag.

RIDICULOUS

"This is a site of ridiculous importance," Twiddrington said yesterday from the bottom of an eight foot trench in the fairway. "Every day we're learning more and more about the evolution of the game of golf. If these early finds are anything to go by, I wouldn't be surprised if, before long, we find evidence of the fabled 'Missing Links', a prehistoric

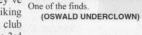
One of the finds.
(OSWALD UNDERCLOWN)

golf course built by sabre-toothed tigers."

Senior clubmembers at Molford Golf Club however are annoyed at this disruption to their game, and insist that the archaeologists are "making it all up".

PENFOLD HEARTS

"The course has only been in use since 1982," one told me. "So the discovery of these artefacts is extremely unlikely. What's more, neither of these so-called archaeologists has shown us any real evidence, just shapes under a tarpaulin most of the time."

Another clubmember was concerned that the few 'finds' he had seen were obviously shoddy fabrications. "That viking longball was just a Slazenger No7 with a beard drawn on it. If you ask me, they're just inventing stuff so they've got a reason to stay"

Twiddrington pooh-poohs the clubmembers' concerns.

"Of course we like it here, and I won't deny that the bar is excellent, but this is a sensitive and serious piece of scientific field research. Look at all the stuff we've found. Only this morning, I dug up a golf cart with the skeleton of Henry VIII in it. It's over there, under that blanket. Anyone fancy a snifter?"

GARDEN VACS LAWN TWEEZERS TREEDRYERS and other vain stupid rubbish

Talk to the experts! **RUPERT'S UNNECESSARIES** 855, A High Street, Framley.

Just had a baby? Stuck for a name? *Talk to the experts.* Just give us the sex, length and heaviness of your baby, and your's and you'r partner's names, and we'll match it with a beautiful name for your new arrival. Some of our most popular names at the moment: Ribena, Marmaduke-Sue, Bag O'Nails, The Operator, Doc Morrissey, Og. **babynames** 01999 300800 (Prices range from £80.00 to £2000.00)

BEING ATTACKED BY A DUCK? Talk to the experts. Whittington & Mead Special Services **01999 770 944**

Mayor Mash

by Challenger Putney

MAYOR D'AINTY faced a formidable sight when he arrived for his weekly Council briefing this Monday evening, at 6 for 6.30pm, on floor two of the Town Hall (please avoid using the lift.)

As he attempted to enter the conferencarium, the mayor's path was blocked by a dollop of dinner ladies from The Teapop School, Sockford, all throwing mash and calling him a bender.

From their colourful placards, it was clear that the disher-uppers were peeved at The mayor's plans to withdraw free school dinners from local school pupils.

Chairs were overturned and a glass statue of a clown was thrown, missing the mayor by only a few minutes.

RATED

The "D'Ainty Dinner Plan", that made them so very, very cross will phase out the school's traditional menu of free chips and cheese pizza in favour of an à la carte selection from Framley's Michelin rated Belgian restaurant, Alimentaria.

"Children love posh food," Mayor D'Ainty told reporters at the launch of the plan last March, "and the proposed winelist is first class."

Controversially, the children will be billed at the restaurant's usual rate, with Visa, Diners Club and Newbycard all accepted.

Alimentaria owner Jacques Shit, who bankrolled the Mayor's winning election campaign in 1974, was delighted with the plan.

"No discount for groups," he chuckled, rubbing all his hands together.

The old dinner scheme cost the council to the tune of £2.750,000m a year, the new one will cost nought.

"The children will finally pay for their own lunches at last, saving us money, and teaching them valuable restaurant skills that will help them in future lives," said D'Ainty, climbing into bed, "Goodnight, dear."

DEMI-BOUTEILLE

But the daily cost to pupils (starting from £20, based on three courses and a demi-bouteille of Chardonnay) has upset school meal staff. No, they are not happy one bit, turning up in mass on Monday to make their protesting felt.

"A lot of our pupils have learning difficulties. They're bound to have trouble calculating the 12.5% service charge," whinged a spokesdinnerperson. "And none of them like mussels anyway."

But the mayor dismissed their protests.

"Mussels are delicious and nutritious. I have them all the time. These people are talking rubbish," scoffed Mayor D'Ainty, speaking of the incident at a presconference. "If there's one thing I know, it's how much children like mussels. Popeye eats them."

Ianbeale Steeplecocque
MP!
Representing YOUR interests

MP Holds regular surgeries

Come and talk about:
Mon-Tue: Visitors from the future
Wed: Children ageing backwards
Thu: People stuck in old photographs
Fri: Wormholes in fabric of space and time
01999 800 987   www.com

YOUR AD HERE COULD BE REACHING OVER £14,000 READERS!

Phone Leia-Rizzo Price BA Hons (Durham) at the Framley Examiner on
01999 800 987

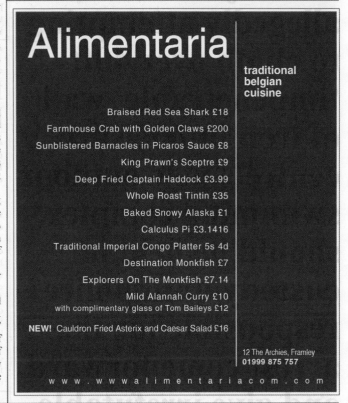

Alimentaria

traditional belgian cuisine

Braised Red Sea Shark £18

Farmhouse Crab with Golden Claws £200

Sunblistered Barnacles in Picaros Sauce £8

King Prawn's Sceptre £9

Deep Fried Captain Haddock £3.99

Whole Roast Tintin £35

Baked Snowy Alaska £1

Calculus Pi £3.1416

Traditional Imperial Congo Platter 5s 4d

Destination Monkfish £7

Explorers On The Monkfish £7.14

Mild Alannah Curry £10
with complimentary glass of Tom Baileys £12

NEW! Cauldron Fried Asterix and Caesar Salad £16

12 The Archies, Framley
01999 875 757

w w w . w w w a l i m e n t a r i a c o m . c o m

Mayor is so chuffed with new railwa7

by Challenger Putney

FRAMLEY'S CHARISMATIC Mayor, William D'Ainty announced a mayor new building project for the Framley district at a presconference on Tuesday.

"I have drawn up blueprints for a new underground railway system, which will drag Framley into the 20th century, once and for all. I am glad to announce that building work will start right away," he said.

The Mayor insisted that the creation of this vital rail network will bring hundreds of construction workers to the region from all over the country, and probably boost the economy or something.

LIKE

The tube system, which will have two stations and almost four hundred yards of tunnels, is sure to be the envy of neighbouring tubeless boroughs, like Bellaire and Prince's Freshborough.

The Mayor's desk, with the exciting new blueprint on it that he drew himself.
PHOTOGRAPH BY SUE PUTNEY

"I have designed a new municipal crest with a train on it too, and smoke coming out," the Mayor insisted. "Within a couple of years I'll be confident Framley will be known as the pivot of a brave new railway world."

Defending the cost of the enterprise, Mayor D'Ainty pointed to the £2.750,000m surplus that had

recently appeared in the Council budget. "That'll be plenty," he beamed.

Troublemakers have already started asking questions about the proposed route of the Framley tube, but it's "the usual bloody suspects and they're talking rubbish."

Trains will run every six minutes between the mayor's house and

Framley golf course. An express service will also run at 10.45am and 11.30pm, with a fully licensed buffet bar.

Mayor D'Ainty stressed what good news this was for the people of the area as he left for work.

PARTICULARLY

"These two stations are essential for the smooth running of daily life in the borough. Commuters will be able to make this journey in half the time it would take by car. This will reduce traffic congestion along the FR404 between my house and the golf course, and there's a slim chance it could attract tourists and discourage foxes."

"And, as an added bonus, the tube line will prove very useful for me. I have always said how important it is that the mayor keep in touch with the citizens of Framley, and this will enable me to forge a close personal bond with local people, particularly those who live in and around Golf Station. Or my house."

Framley

Final competition

FRAMLEY CAMERA CLUB. – The club's final competition had the theme of "Framley – or something else" and was judged by guest Little Willy Spanish, picture editor of Magazine! magazine. The following gained the highest awards. **Prints** – Beginners – Colour: Prize, Marlon Wild, *Foot*; Merit, Bernardo Wild, *Feet*. **Advanced Monochrome:** Prize, Cmdr David Philpott, *Hamster Enjoying 'Ground Force'*; Merit, Duncan Dunkerque, *Hoverjew*. **Advanced Colour** – Prize, Wendy Bendy, *Where Children Shouldn't Really Play*; Merit, St Dave Yates, *Peacock & Thumb*.

The club met every Tuesday at 8pm on a rotating basis. Guests were never welcome.

Crack morning

THOSE BLOODY METHODISTS AGAIN. – There will be a crack morning tomorrow (Saturday) from 10am to midnight in aid of Doug 'The Destroyer' Pettygrew, currently doing a 14-stretch in HMP Chutney. There will be refreshments, a cake stall, bring and buy, and chill-out room.

Tudor Life

AFTERNOON WI. – At their fortnightly meeting, members welcomed three new members, Mrs Robinson, Mrs Robinson and Mrs Robinson. They also welcomed three visitors to their afternoon meeting, Mrs Robinson, Mrs Robinson and Mrs Robinson. Mrs Robinson proposed a toast to Mrs Robinson, who was celebrating her 85th birthday and supplied cakes for fellow Mrs Robinsons to enjoy. The speaker was Mrs Robinson, who took on the guise of 'Mrs Robinson,' a tudor Mrs Robinson at Robinson Hall. Any members who accidentally returned to the wrong lives after the meeting are urged to call Mrs Robinson on 01999 418010.

Family film

ETHEL DUNNING CLUB. – On April 2nd, members of the club enjoyed a special BBC1 screening of popular film, *The Wizard of Oz*. In her vote of thanks Ethel Dunning said it had been a wonderful afternoon's entertainment and that it had reminded her of when she was a little girl. During tea, Ethel announced next week's visit to the supermarket to herself and that she also missed her late husband. With no more business, members had a soda biscuit and an early night.

Sockford

Organ recital

MOTHER'S UNION. – Sockford MU members were treated to a special organ recital from world-renowned organ reciter, Leo Hopkirk. Leo recited a list of all of the notes played by all of the keys on all of the three keyboards of the Sockford church organ. At last, he finally encored with a lengthy sequence of noises that each of the stops make when the organ is actually in use. Secretary Mrs Beryl Mothers noted the members' disappointment that Mr Hopkirk had failed to mention the third octave F# but that they all went home humming the sound of the 8' diapason.

A Busy Week

SOCKFORD WORKHOUSE. – A week in Sockford Workhouse was organised by Framley Conservatives. Members were made to scrub flagstone floors with lye, sleep in draughty cellars overridden with rodents, and were forced to subsist on a diet of gruel and heavy beatings. At the end of the week, several members asked for more, but were denied this by club beadle Gavin Bumble MP.

Guest Speaker

SOCKFORD WI. – The speaker at the monthly meeting was Oliver Benz. Under the title 'It Could Have Happened To You,' Oliver described growing up in a hessian potato sack, and how he had been taught to swim by a man dressed as a man doing a handstand, and of how unhappy he was working as a quality control officer in a jazz quintet. Oliver displayed a large selection of maracas, air fresheners, boxing gloves and loft insulation. The floor was opened to questions and members unanimously asked Oliver to explain any of what he had been saying in the previous two and a half hours.

Chutney

REFITTED UNARMED CHURCH. – At 10.45am on Sunday, the service was led by guest preacher Mr Clem Froust, with Mr Basil Bedouin in the organ. The subject of the sermon was "Why Are The Poor So Annoying?". Mr Froust took as his text a 160 character message from his mate Bob about that bloke who lies around on the ground near the cash machines in the Arnhem Centre. The service

NEW SIGNS MEAN SAFETY

NEW SIGNS have been erected outisde the village of Gartside Green in response to a series of near misses. In the three years since the first "Gartside Green: Please drive carefully" sign was erected, over four hundred vehicles have struck the sign, killing almost a thousand people. The new signs read "Please drive carefully" to warn drivers of the presence of the sign, then, twelve yards later "Thankyou for driving carefully" to signal that the emergency is over. The signs have been worded by a local poet and cost over a quarter of a million pounds.

PHOTO BY EDWARD IAN FURNITURE

concluded with a game of Bingo, using the new font balls. Attendees exchanged the peace and snogged. After the congregation had left, Mr Bedouin was teased out from the organ with a saucer of milk and humanely destroyed. Next service will probably be on Sunday too, led by the minister, the Rev Jonathan Bang. Tickets limited to three per caller. Book early to avoid disappointment.

Molford

Delicious apple

LADIES' GUILD. – The weekly meeting of the Molford District Ladies' Guild was held on Monday, 3rd at 3pm. A record attendance welcomed Mrs Sarah Convoy who brought a delicious apple for everyone to look at. This proved a popular theme for the meeting, which was a great success and adjourned at four in the morning. Those members who were unable to attend and so missed the delicious apple will be glad to hear that Mrs Convoy has promised to come back next week with either a pear or a glove. Crowds expected.

Magnificent Illness

MOLFORD CONSERVATIVE CLUB. –

The first meeting of the new bimester was held on Friday, 28th, in the Treasurer's Hall. Chairman Peter Unguent was absent, citing his recent acquisition of a majestic dose of clap. His place at the head of the meeting was taken by his five year old daughter Hannah, who led an entertaining round of "If You're Happy And You Know It Clap Your Hands" and drew a rabbit. The drawing was passed unanimously round the table. Meeting adjourned.

Molford St Gavin

Fascinating Talk

MOLFORD LITERARY CIRCLE. – The third anniversary meeting of the Molford Literary Circle was held on Thursday and a great success. Mrs Honeydew Melton, acting chair, welcomed newcomers and old members and others and introduced Mrs Aggeline Fant, who spoke about the world of Jane Austen. Aggie illustrated her talk with slides and was born in 1775, lived her early days as the youngest of seven children, Northanger Abbey. She illustrated her talk with slides of places Jane Austen had visited and was buried in Winchester Cathedral.

Meeting Cancelled

ANY OTHER BUSINESS. – The February meeting of the Molford St Gavin Any Other Business Club was cancelled due to the over-running of the January and December meetings.

Molford St Malcolm

Gentle exercises

ROYAL BRITISH LEGION WOMEN'S SECTION. – The chairman, Mrs Etta Pulse, welcomed those members who had turned out on such a frosty night. Apologies for absence were received from Mrs Luge, Mrs Front and Mrs LeTroux, all of whom had perished in the snow on the way there. Mrs Euridice, who had become stuck fast with cold to the latch of the church hall was chipped free by a vote of 8 to 6.

CORRESPONDENTS PLEASE NOTE:

WOULD village correspondents <u>wherever possible</u> please e-mail their copy to the following address:

damiunclavalier@framleyexaminer.com

Please title your e-mail "my tiny little life" and indicate which village it is that you're on about. Oh, and send your village news piece as plain text, not an 8MB Bitmap scan of your bloody minutes, and yes, I *am* talking to you, Robert.

The Wand Guide to

Framley

Edited by Ray Floor

Framley and district

Framley

Pop. 20,255 (1976). The first part of the name refers to the river Fram. The second means "shambles" or "upside-down horse".

The former Roman settlement of Frimulodonum, Framley was first mentioned in the Domesday Book, where the *"uglye hamlet, Franley"* is recorded as a *"ditche or ponde."*

Once famous as the centre of the fluff industry, Framley is known world-wide today as the home of Rawlinson's Awls, *"the finest way to make a hole there is.™ "* Framley is not a one-industry town, however, and a new industrial estate has opened on a brownsite site near Cossett Park.

Framley town centre is popular with shoppers.

The church of St Dog-in-the-Manger's contains many fine 15th century architectural features, including tweeves, archiblodes, mnesmenomes and flying fux.

Here Be Turnips was a 16th century coaching-house, in the yard of which was a mediaeval brew-shed from an earlier inn on the site, The Big George.

Framley has good shopping facilities, with the modern **Arnhem Centre** its centrepiece. There is a large car park at the rear of the 1960s' development in which many of the original graffiti survive. Early closing is frequent and unpredictable.

Famous men whose names have been heard in the same sentence as the word "Framley" are reformer Gosnert Evenmore, later Bishop of The British Empire, engineer Sir Bluff Furrow Gullimurph, and composer Alwyn Tittershear, who wrote **HM The Queen**'s only single, *"Coronation Serenade,"* released in 1953, which was number one in the hit parade for four and a half years.

Many M.P.'s from the town later became national figures, including Brian Furniture, Albit Mpeg and Dame Polly Wedgwood-Pott, who started as a humble secretary and went on to become Secretary to the Deputy Secretary of the Home Secretary's Private Secretary.

Although Framley has some of the best sports facilities in this part of the country, its first brush with notoriety was in 977, when **Bishop Dunroamin**, hanging from a rope tied to the town walls, asked everyone to walk beneath his feet as he kicked those he'd never liked in the hair. There are two swimming pools and a four acre crazy golf course with 837 holes.

>flag THIS IS THE WRONG WAY UP KEITH.

Wripple

Pop. 1,976 (1976). "Silly upland."

A charming village of TV fame, lying beneath the Gloveswold downs. Cunnymede, the model village which depicts the entire village which depicts the entire village which depicts the entire model village Cunnymede, lying beneath the Gloveswold downs.

A charming village of TV fame, lying beneath the Gloveswold downs. Cunnymede, the model village which depicts the entire village which at twice its actual size, was built by Sir Constant Tiger in the grounds of his estate, Tiger Woods.

Codge

Pop. 500 (1976). "Cough; pandemonium."

Five miles N.W. of Durbiton. Darling House is posh, Plonkney's Farm and Sterling Mansion very posh, and Flutherhuther Towers, with its 3,000 peacocks, is not only astonishingly posh, but perilously dangerous.

Chipney

Pop. 840 (1976). "Field of potato."

Once the world's most prolific grower of potato, the land around Chipney is now completely potato-free, thanks to the Forestry Commission, which has reafforested the fields and streets with English Teak. Thereby, Chipney has given our language not only the word "Chip" but also the phrase "ploughshares into sideboards."

Bellaire

Pop. 460 (1976). "Fresh air."

Home of the Bellaire Hillock, which has dominated the landscape since the nice age. The mighty rock, which climbs over 200ft into the sky, has never been conquered, despite attempts by Lord Bile in 1902 and a team of Blue Peter pets in 1977.

Princes Freshborough

Pop. 460 (1976). "Fresh breath."

Bellaire's next-door-neighbour, this village and surrounding farmland was purchased by Joseph Nitsy in 1828, and most of the houses date from the Nitsy occupation. Nitsy's insistence that the houses should have no roofs or ceilings, "because only the Almighty and his elements ought look down us," lasted almost a fortnight.

Batley

Pop. 3,280 (1976). "Batley."

One of Framley's most deprived suburbs, Batley is the most deprived suburb in England. The name derives from Batley in England.

One of Wripple's loveliest corners

The underground car park of St Kitten's, Glibley

Clown

Pop. 0 (1976). "Mr Cellophane"

The forgotten village of Clown used to lie between Sockford and Whotten Plodney, until it was swallowed by grass in the 1560s, following the levy of the disastrous Scythe Tax. By the turn of the 17th century, the village had completely disappeared under acres of overgrown lawn, an all too common occurrence at the time.

Glibley

Pop. 52 (1976). "That's easy for you to say."

Three miles north-east of the river Sock. Home of the famous Glibley point-to-point races, held every Easter Saturday, when young and old alike ride across the fields and hedgerows in pursuit of chickens dressed as seasonal bunnies. The winner pulls the bird from its rabbit costume and makes it lay a chocolate egg.

Dungeon

Pop. 1,310 (1976). "Hill of bad shit."

Built on a Native American burial ground, Dungeon has since been swallowed up by Framley's suburbs, and is now the most crime-ridden estate in the world. Its unwieldy population, cramped into stinking award-winning brutalist blocks of flats is mainly made up of aggressive ex-lags with quadruple buggies full of industrial-strength pilsner. It is also impossible to avoid crunched-up men resembling seriously injured wolves, who should be avoided.

Durbiton

Pop. 4,860 (1976). "Where ducks gather" or "Nice bingo lady's wobbly arms".

At Durbiton used to be found the headquarters of MMC, makers of Mixture Mate, the nation's favourite mixture. Their adverts famously boasted "a box and a half of mixture in every box of Mixture Mate." The town's principal employer for over 70 years, Mixture Mate finally closed its doors and sacked its loyal workforce in 1989. Since then, the town has slowly started recovering, although many people still have trouble making mixture without their loyal Mate.

So Mr. Mixtures, what's the good of making a meal without any Mixture Mate in it?

"*Well,* for a start you'd never get that flavour that your family expect from their food. You wouldn't get that authentic *freshly laid* smell. There'd be nothing to drink with your meal."

"And after you've eaten, how would you clean the plates? Or, for that matter, dry them again afterwards? You'd have nothing to eat the meal on, or to wipe yourself with after a *little accident.*"

Next time you're considering cooking a meal without Mixture Mate, just think about what you've just been told and what you'd be leaving out.

It's almost impossible to comprehend.

Shilillingbury Lillingbury Illingbury On Ingbury

Pop. 850 (1976). "Ing's estate on the river Ill, by the L-shaped turn in the river Ill".

England's prettiest village. Gloveswold-stone houses rising from a stream in a sylvan combe, where pretty girls in flower-pattern dresses wave and smile as they float past on hot buttered bicycles, and hot sweet tea is served with hot sweet cream horns covered in icing sugar and sauced in hot sweet honey. Not for the faint of tooth!

Thoxtoxeter

Pop. 260 (1976). "Thoxton's poisonous-smelling farm".

The five almshouses in the main village street are known locally as "The Fingers". The poet Owen Eyebrow wrote *"My Life As A Cauliflower"* at Index House, and both Little House and The Thumb are said to be haunted or sticky.

Effing Sodbury

Pop. 880 (1976). "Peat house, unsuitable for children."

Home of the famous Effing Sodbury carnival, held annually. Fire-eating pantomime horses race each other around a crazy-house shooting coconuts full of goldfish, while a parade of wicker cheerleaders tight-rope-walks across a giant teacup, and steam engines driven by tigers run amok through the crowds. A wondrous local spectacle *(not pictured).*

Ovenly

Pop. 355 (1976). "Certainement il fait chaud aujourd'hui".

Unlike its soundalike, Slovenly, Ovenly is heavenly. The church of St Sharpener has a beautiful futuristic chancel arch, and contains the 16th century tomb of Ludby Chantrey Chappell in a lovely chantry chapel.

St Eyot's and district

St Eyot's

Pop. 5,266 (1976). "Church of St Eyot".

St Eyot (pronounced "Eight") founded the monastery at Deyaughthcan's Chine (pronounced "Chine") in AD320 and gave his name to the town that now bears his name. The town formed part of the Glansby estate until the 1600s when it was given to a man in a pub by the then Earl of Glansby in exchange for a spectacular pair of shoes that the next morning turned out to be a design on the pub flooring. The famous 14th Century castle is one of the most complete examples of late Norman showing-off in the region.

St Eyot's Castle is one of the best preserved examples

Slovenly

Pop. 1,116 (1976) "G of Dorset, inheritance is hidden behind dressing table"

Birthplace of Framley's ebullient mayor, William D'Ainty. The beautiful 12th Century Priory at Ogden's Mount is mentioned in Thackeray and also in the middle eight of *The Magic Number* by De La Soul. Slovenly has a vibrant harbour district that attracts tourists and crabs. The elaborate medieval cobblestone high street was built by midgets captured in the crusades.

Urling

Pop. 408 (1976) "Garden full of old lawnmowers"

Nestling in the arm of the river Fram, Urling is home to the Urling Grandfathers, Britain's smallest football team. The seventeenth century pond was built on the site of a sixteenth century pond and was the first in the region to be treated with duck-resistant artex.

The church at Urling contains relics from the 1976 FA Cup final

Fracton

Pop. 1,893 (1976) "Settlement behind enormous ditch"

Genteel Fracton sits in stark contrast to its gaudy neighbour, Clinton. Its inhabitants resist change, and its Regency seafront is refreshingly untouched and closed to non-residents. Fracton was used as the location for the cult 1960s TV series *The Enigmatist* and fans gather every year in Clinton to squint wistfully up the FR411 in the vague direction of the exclusive resort town.

Clinton

Pop. 3,609 (1976) (origin obscure) "Clyn's ballbearings thankyou grape mountain" or "Clyn's settlement"

Originally a tithed smallholding to the Rumphall Estate, Clinton expanded dramatically in the 1800s with the coming of the railways and the vogue for gaiety bathing. The pier and pleasure gardens were completed in 1896, with characteristic pornographic ironwork by Sir Daniel Factfinder. The domed ceiling of the pier head ballroom is visible from space but not visible from the pier itself, a trick of the light that has led to the pier being adopted as the international calibration standard for orbital survey telescopes. There are four times as many fruit machines in Clinton as there are anywhere else.

Flapton Nogley

Pop. 315 (1976). "Nuaga's farmstead in a terrible bother".

Flapton Nogley old town is now almost entirely deserted, the erection of the GEV Telecom Mast on the village green in 1998 having driven out any residents with strong views on brain cancer. House prices in neighbouring Flapton Nogley Carnival Village however remain popular. The sports centre was opened in 1981 by Suggs and features Britain's only indoor waterskiing pool.

Stanglebridge

Pop. 85 (1976). "St Anne's disappointing holiday"

Once the home of St Anne's Dye Works. The dyemakers here popularised the colour orange in the early nineteenth century, eventually influencing plant breeders to develop the tie-in fruit. When the factory closed in 1936, the town was given back to the flood plain, after long negotiation between representatives of both the dye works and the river.

One of the least annoying parts of Stanglebridge.

Yopney St Oh!

Pop. 92 (1976). "Yapp's meadow by the river sacred to St... I've fallen in"

A picturesque hamlet on the main Roman road out of Framley, Yopney has always had great strategic value for anyone wishing to attack the town. In 1943, British Intelligence discovered that the village had been entirely populated by German spies in deep cover since August 1918. Yopney is also a favourite stop off point for birdwatchers keen to see the last breeding pair of Gold-Hooped Rabbit Buzzards in captivity, in the family room of the Bear and Cretin pub. Please keep children's hands inside the pushchair.

Queff

Pop. 284 (1976). "Dirty boy"

The village name derives from the Old English word *Cwéad* meaning mud or dirt and refers to the mud which fills the streets to calf height for most of the year while the river Fram is in high flow. George Mousehat wrote *Manderby Chase* while trapped in a barn here, transcribing the entire novel in longhand onto all the paper he could find in his pockets before realising the door opened inwards.

Gartside Green

Pop 147 (1976). "Smooth patch of grass (by the) smoother patch of grass".

Home of the Gartside Fusiliers who acquitted themselves so nobly at Rourke's Drift that they were preserved in bronze in Framley Regimental Museum, killing them. The remains of an early motte-and-bailey castle can be tasted in the shepherd's pie at the Gartside Lounge. The church of St Anne-Le-Knife is said to be haunted by the ghost of a pair of trousers left by a bridegroom in 1911.

Molford and district

The Kentucky Fried Chicken Drive Thru in Molford St Gavin

Molford

Pop. 8,401 (1976). "Shallow crossing point of river, filled with dead moles".

A modern suburb, 3 miles in any direction away from Framley. Molford was revitalised in the 20th Century by the arrival of Roy Newby, and his octopoid Rakes and Essentials shopping empire. After decades of heated negotiation, all retail outlets in the town are now owned by the Newby corporation, and the pound is no longer legal tender (having long since been replaced by Newbytokens each worth £1). Molford is also also the official birthplace of Mayor William D'Ainty al Molfordi. D'Ainty's actual birthplace, Slovenly, celebrates his birthday on a different day of the year, in accordance with royal precedent.

Molford St Gavin

Pop. 698 (1976). "St Gavin's drowning of the moles"

Simply dripping with cash but known locally as a particularly sensitive village, Molford St Gavin's main feature is St Gavin's Chapel. Built of flints, pudding stone and hamster teeth, the church has an unnaturally gaudy 15th-century tower carrying a peal of bells. None of the three bells are inscribed. All three are replacements made from parachute silk, installed after the original bells were taken away to be melted down to make bells for the war effort.

Molford St Malcolm

Pop. 1,264 (1976). "St Malcolm's artificial respiration of the moles"

By a curious geographic quirk, Molford St Malcolm is actually closer to the moon than it is anywhere else. In the 13th century permission was granted for an official weekly market in Molford St Malcolm and the ancestors of the original stallholders are still trying to sell exactly the same goods today.

Houseboats and Domestic Submarines crowd along the

Molford St Arahim Rhamal

Pop. 1,962 (1976). "Non-permanent member of the UN Security Council"

Weather managed to cause disruption in 1833 with gusts of up to 100 mph uprooting a windmill. The sails spun at such a rate that the mill tunnelled through the earth's crust and soon reached Brisbane, leaving Molford St Arahim Rhamal with a literal tourist trap, the Antipodean Chute. For a small fee, Victorian danger seekers could visit the other side of the planet on a fire-resistant bungee rope in less than 15 seconds. A bronze engraving of a man in a deerstalker emerging from the ground in front of confused kangaroo, feet first and at great speed, is on display in the Framley Museum.

Robot Oak

Pop. 39 (1976). "Deciduous aluminium; a boogie-boogie acorn"

An inorganic hamlet situated at the gateway to Iffing Forest, developed as an experiment in utopian living in the early and all of the 1970s. No natural materials whatsoever are used in Robot Oak. Polyester hedges divide nylon allotments where acrylic fruit and vegetables are grown to feed the steady population of thirty-nine cellulose automatons, who keep themselves largely to themselves. Home to the largest municipal dump in the Northern hemisphere, the sky above which contains an average of 75.1 seagulls to every square foot.

Ghastley St Matthew

Pop. 558 (1976). "Minnie Riperton once slept here"

Formerly known as Absolutely Grotesquely St Matthew, the village changed its name after the old church was bulldozed and replaced with a marginally more pleasant looking one. Home to The Old Barn which runs both sides of The Old Barn Street. The barn once housed the largest brood of gala pie-egg producing hens in the world until animal rights activists released them in 1987. The fowl were left free to roam the streets where they now lay terrifying quantities of free-range eggs measuring anything up to a furlong in length. A local industry manufacturing long spoons and stabilized eggcups flourished briefly in the late 1980s although it collapsed soon after, as the employees were too busy trying to finish their breakfasts.

Crème

Pop. 202 (1976). "Pleasure, but not necessarily for pleasure's sake".

The name is pre-English. Once a haven for peasant thrift, the wars with Little Godley and the influence of wealthy landowners have made Crème a place of commercial thrift. Pre-decimal currency – including groats and denarii – are still accepted in the delightful Post Office, where penny chews remain ten-a-penny. The mediaeval church of St Dragon's has an authentic Norman kitchen which still employs a Norman cook.

A homeowner receives her test results in Crème

peaceful riverside at Strawbury Magma

Tollephant

Pop. 397 (1976). "Many a muckle makes a mackleackleackle"

Almost entirely parkland, Tollephant is home of the wettest park bench in Britain, adorned with a plaque which reads, *"In loving memory of Arnold Flower, 1889-1967: he loved this place. It may have given him an arsehole like the Japanese flag but he still loved it anyway".*

Strawbury Magma

Pop. 149 (1976). "Hot purée within crust of village"

Once a major Saxon settlement, picturesque Strawbury Magma now regrets the parish council's 1932 decision to employ the renowned artichect Sir Brian Clough Ellis-Bextor, a self-made alcoholic and recovering millionaire to modernise the village. After his plans for a redesign of the main thoroughfare were approved and built to his exact specifications, Sir Brian stalked the streets with a bullwhip, grievously injuring anyone not standing in the exact pose and location of the tiny figures in his original scale model.

Diesel Park West

Pop. 4 (1987) "Dylla's farmland in the West"

The village of Diesel Park West released its first album in 1989, having signed to Food Records, home of Jesus Jones and Blur. Though the village encountered some commercial success through the support of parent label EMI, a breakthrough eluded it and the sleepy hamlet retreated from studio and live work, eventually resurfacing on a series of smaller labels in the mid 1990s.

Sockford and district

The only surviving Sockford Squab, a prototype wheel-less one-seater, takes pride of place as the centrepiece of the the Museum's car garden, which is deemed an area of special scientific interest, so we never mow it.

Sockford

Pop. 2,680 (1976). "Ford by the river Sock".

One of the fastest growing towns in the area, Sockford was originally a smallholding. By the late 1900s, it had become a bigholding, and was home to many light industries such as Tomskworth Gas Lights and Possibly Fittings.

The coming of the motor-car meant the motor-car arriving in Sockford, when, in 1922, the Associated Motor Works opened. The twelve-acre plant mass manufactured the Model One and the Bitmap MkVII.

By the time of the Second World War II, over 800 people worked at Associated. The plant was adapted to manufacture munitions and tin shoes during wartime, but returned to carp roduction in the early 1950s, turning out over 2 million of their best-selling model, the Operator.

Associated Motor Works grew with the success of the Operator, and by 1971 had over 8,600 employees. Despite rocky times during the 1980s, when they faced competition from the new Apollo Creed 4 Series, the plant is still productive today.

The last Operator rolled off the production line in 1976, and is buried in the churchyard at St Wednesday's.

Lessbury Moreborough

Pop. 511 (1976). "Large Village" or "Small Village".

Following the Poor Law of 1836, picturescue Lessbury was chosen as the site of the new Sockford District Workhouse. Overseen by social reformer Sir Malcolm Bunglebonce, the home cared for the tramps and "casuals" who passed through the town. After a hot meal and bed, the staff would send tramps off the next morning with clean ears and a purse containing £11,000 for the journey. The Workhouse closed in 1837.

Sockford attracts art lovers keen to visit the streets that inspired local artist Ibrahim Bethsheveth to move elsewhere.

Whoft and district

Whoft

Pop. 8,440 (1976). "Silent but violent".

Whoft lies in the centre of the region and was once the county town before Framley was discovered to be 1/16th more attractive and thus more likely to be featured on the *Antiques Roadshow*. The area's history can be traced back to before prehistoric times; a mammoth penis is proudly displayed in the foyer of the library on the first Tuesday of every month. Two Whoft men, Abel and Babel Luscombe sailed on the Mayflower to the New World in the 17th Century but got mashed by sharks whilst attempting to invent water-skiing. There is also a miniature railway running through woodlands which is great for families although not so great for wildlife.

Whoft is currently in the process of reconstruction, after a planning blunder in 2002 destroyed the whole town. Sights used to include the then-intact ancient seven-sided cross which was by what used to be the river, near the since-pulverised church where a heap of rubble now stands.

It also used to be possible to enjoy the 16th century tanning salon and nearby Happy House, with its famous bass line. The site is now given over to builders' portacabins, and looks a bloody mess.

Wotten Plodney

Pop. 710 (1976). "You are leaning against an open door, sonny". Variously recorded as "Rotten Rodney," "Whatter Plonkney" and "Wombling Wembley".

Home to the world-famous Puddles brewery, winner of the Whotten Plodney only employer of the month award for six years running. Other places to visit include the Georgian mansion, Bresslaw Halt. This dilapidated property was landscaped by Cacophony Taupe and has subsequently been disowned by English Heritage. A light skirmish on the outskirts of the town in 1639 finally escalated into the Boer War several hundred years later when the ancestors of the instigators were sent to Boerland.

Right Angle Cottage, Whotten Plodney

Queues Likely

Pop. 772 (1976). "Of, for, or relating to the nose".

The Black Death was launched in 14th Century Queues Likely and became so widespread that 127% of the villagers perished from the disease. The negative number of villagers had huge families over the following years in an attempt to repopulate and by 1398 the population numbered -571 until they were all turned inside out by order of the King and the problem solved. Lord Nelson is reputed to have frequently stayed at The Roach & Horse Inn with his lover, Mr Hardy, where the landlord was perfectly happy to turn a blind eye to that sort of thing so long as he could watch.

Little Godley

Pop. 828 (1976). "Crafted from the thighs of tiny giants".

The Foreign Office has advised all British nationals to avoid Little Godley due to the prospect of civil unrest in the area since Councillor Haris Paris's military coup in 1994. The Witchradar General, Nightnight Hopkins, once sat in judgement on women thought to be witches at the Crown Inn. His verdict would be announced at the end of an all day session, generally "Grfffthmp" as he slumped into a plate of cold meat and boiled potatoes. 512 suspected sorceresses were burned at the stake until Hopkins died in 1967.

Chutney

Pop. 2,639 (1976). "The Best of Roger Whittaker".

Until the 17th century, Chutney was home to a population of indigenous mermaids. The villagers lived in civilised harmony, combing their hair and seducing sailors. Then, in 1685, they were completely wiped out in the famous Chutney Clearances. A group of hunters and thrillseekers arrived in skiffs and culled the fish. Their oily bodies were made into soup, and their scales into gloves. Glovemaking thrived in the town until the 1920.

One of Chutney's biggest claims to fame is as the ancestral home of two former presidents of the USA – Richard Nixon and J. Danforth Quayle. The parish church contains a reredos displaying the Quayle family's coat of arms with their motto, *"Ich bin ein potatoe"*. The church greets you as you approach the town centre; local opinion is divided as to how and why the church does this.

King's Mustard

Pop. 68 (1976). "If this is Mustard then I'll be an uncle's monkey".

The vertical main street is a rarity in the county, and was recently awarded a lottery grant due to its 1:0 gradient. Abseiling equipment has been provided and a temporary lift installed, although the oxygen tanks needed to visit Shandy's Chemists of 68 Tall Street have recently run out.

The parish church of St Maplin's in Steeplecocque boasts an olympic-sized font

Without Sir John Battleship's revolutionary sewage system of 1881, this view down Chutney High treet would have been entirely obscured by dung.

Clifton James

Pop. 145 (1976). "(Some kind of) doomsday machine".

The fine, sweet Gloveswold turf was made by nature to be the home of sheep: champion sheep that yield rich Clifton James mutton. Champion sheep that compete with other champions at the country show, being carefully groomed, along with all the other champions. Where, in a holiday atmosphere, the country and the town get together: farmer and statesman meet over a pint of mildly drinkable.

Pity, then, that no sheep have ever been reared in Clifton James, and that no such country show exists here. Sometimes it is a lonely planet.

Steeplecocque

Pop. 109 (1976). "Chicken-like tower structure".

Once the seat of the Steeplecocques, influential landowners and fraudsters, the area is now very different kettle of people.

At Pancake Rectory, the Rev Albert Prickles was born, whose diaries record his father's weekly target practise on his benighted son. Prickles was made to stand in a shed, while his strict Presbyterian father fired boiling apples at him, inspiring his later memoir, *"On Being The Target Of A Madman With An Armful Of Hot Fruit"*.

Outlying districts

Carnaby Constable

Pop. 54 (1976). *"Green Dock".*

This tiny village is noteworthy for two reasons; its church's unusual altarpiece – a giant wooden bear eating Whoft church – and being the birthplace of the C16th architect Average Po. There are numerous examples of Po's work to be found on display, such as the *Raven House* in the middle of the village green and the post office's ornate *Fountain Go-Round*.

Cloxted

Pop. 5 (1976). *"Where the Oak Trees roam".*

Possibly the smallest village in the area, Cloxted isn't really much to talk about. There's a house, a farm and that's it. In fact, I'm not even sure the house is there anymore. It's got a nice sign.

Rockney

Pop. 157 (1976). *"Place of the pub and the rock".*

Just after leaving Purge on your way east out of Framley, you pass through Rockney. This village is home of the famous *Humpty Horse* public house and in turn the birthplace of *Eggstone's Batter Bitter* with its distinctive foaming bottom.

The famous pier at Hazeldean Inchmistress

Hazeldean Inchmistress

Pop. 975 (1976). *"Hazeldean Inchmistress".*

Coastal town. Hans Christian Andersen famously spent 5 nights at Hazeldean Inchmistress' fire station and it was here that he wrote *Charles Dickens*.

Billberry Buryborry

Pop. 4872 (1976). *"Berry and Bile Heap".*

At the centre of the high street in this quaint town still stands the original *Berry Spinner's Arch,* where market traders would hang their berries to ripen before spinning to market. The berries found in the locality are highly poisonous and would have been sold as a novelty.

The market square at Billberry Buryborry still looks similar to itself.

Nyth

Pop. 320 (1976). *"Too Near"*

There is evidence of early settlement at Nyth dating back to the Iron Age. Extensive Roman remains, including a beautifully preserved Roman archaeologist, were found during construction of the A999 in 1986, as well as a fine example of a medieval wristwatch.

WHEELBARROW EXERCISE FOR ALL.
"The Foe of Lethargy"

This is a pastime of the greatest utility to the busy gentleman, as it gives the same results as would otherwise only be obtainable with a whole week of swimming or polo mallet tossing. The gentleman reclines whilst pushed in a barrow of considerable comfort. Exercise of the mouth is also displayed by the commands 'Stop!', 'Go!' and 'Faster!'. The wonder of the modern age. Encourages respiration and checks the ossification of the blood.
Price three week course £1 8 0

LADIES' SANITORIES
"Discretion an Imperative"
Linen curse flannels.................................... 4/6
Lockable nightgown....................................12/5
Wooden swaddling jockeys
(For gentle exercise)....................................8/6
'UNCLEAN' placards.....................................2/6
Lengths of carefully poisoned bandage.........2/6

BUTCHERS' OFFCUTS
(For the Needy)
Blood, urine, freshest melancholy.
Offal..0/2
Goat's Tails...0/1
Pig-Eye Porridge 0/1
Dog Gut...0/2
Braces of uncured crow...............................0/4
Rat crackling...0/1

CRAVEN'S
"CAREFUL CADDY"

Faith restored! Now the happy golfer need never forgo his tea or tee again.
Can be set to brew the perfect pot of Indian tea at intervals of 1, 2 or 18 holes.
There is a broad strap running along the top of the caddy that can contain up to 3lb of snuff.
Comes with pack of fifty tees.

Best make (The Maharajah) .... each 49/9
Second quality (The Marylebone) ...... each 34/0
Cheapest quality (The Pardon-Me) ... each 0/3½

BERRYMAN'S PATENT DANCING SHILLING

Endless entertainment for ONE SHILLING.
Mechanism comprises ingenious combination of clockwork and the Dark Arts.
One Dancing Shilling........................ each 1/0
Two Dancing Shillings (Waltz)....................2/0

CHILD'S POPPING WEASEL

The perfect accompaniment to nursery story telling.
Send unquiet children to sleep effortlessly with a tear in the eye and hair full of weasel innards.
Popping Weasel...............................½lb. 0/2 rice

LADIES' HEAVY VESTS.
(White Silk and Cast Iron.)
(unshrinkable, so-called.)
Low necks, metal sleeves .... 5/6   5/9 – 6/3
White merino, rust-resistant .... 6/3   6/6 – 7/0
Silver trim, light flow .... 7/6   7/8 – 8/4

LUNCHEON HAMPERS.

Suitable for travellers, excursionists, policemen, escapologists &c. Each box contains 3 tins and will be found sufficient for a light luncheon when travelling. Suitable to be eaten with either a bread or Fenworthy's Patent Air Biscuits.
No. 1. Consisting of Pate, Opium and Crushed Plum Pudding .... per box   1/6
No. 2.   "   Grain, Maize and Corn .... per box   1/6
No. 3.   "   Cake, Tongue, Tonguecake .... per box   1/6

DIGNITY BUREAU

This handsome, burr walnut bureau with exquisite Mother-of-Pearl detail, comprises honesty drawer, Bible well, collar press, moustache mirror, and cane hook. Comes complete with upright chair.
Gentleman's Bureau as described.................2 19 5
As above with hair tonic dispenser...............2 20 6

ENGLISH CHIMING CLOCK
("Old Bastard")
Size about 15 in . high, 12 in. wide, chiming bells on seconds, gongs on minutes, "cuckoos" on hours and small explosions at midnight........ £26   8   0
Ditto. Larger size, 10ft. high, 5ft. wide, small wooden characters enact play set in belly of whale every hour. Some coarse language...... £50 16   0
Shotgun.. £6 10   0

SUNDRIES & COLLECTABLES
From the Lands of the East
Elephant's tusk croquet hoops.......................3/6
Tiger Hide Top Hats...................................13/6
Servants (each)..1/2

RESTLESS SPIRIT STOVES.

This stove is the p e r f e c t accompaniment for Camping, Races, Picnics, Seances, Regattas, &c.
Capacity 4 pints and one occupant of the spirit world.
Spirit likes: Egg, Cut Ham, Pigeon Pie, Mayonnaise.
Spirit dislikes: Condiments, Roast Fowls, Sweet Sherry.
Stove containing spirit..............................3/6
(not available without spirit. Spirit lives in stove)

YOUTHS' BATMAN CAPES
3 button, Tan, Black Reindeer mask..............3/9
4 button, Black, Slate Gazelle mask...............5/11

DUNKLEY'S PATENT PAPIER MACHE TEETH.

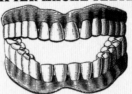

Unrivalled for the consumption of soft, dry foodstuffs, these teeth will give hours of merry mastication. On softening, they can be dried in the oven and reused - giving a pleasant toasted aroma.
3 sets...2/3

GUIDES TO DANCING.
How to Dance (Scott) 0/9
How not to Dance (Scott) 0/9
Crompton's Electric Boogaloo 0/9
Guide to dancing without music 1/6

NEW & POPULAR DANCES
Ball of the Belle...............1/4	Man on my Face................1/4
Bid me Good Riddance...1/6	My Horrid Hair 2/6
Dancing thru the Ceiling..1/6	Sinking Boating Song......1/6
Drunk's Promise................1/4	They Love Eating Soil ...1/6
Five Knuckle Shuffle........1/4	Two Lovely Broken Legs..1/6
Garden of Manure............1/4	When I was on Fire..........1/4
Jolly Arsonist (The)...........1/6	Whoft Tommy.................1/6

UNPOPULAR DANCES
(The) 1/4	24 Hour Waltz 9/0

Pianofortes by Archibald Ricicle & Sons.

Paris Exhibition 1900   GRAND PRIX   Highest Award.

PIANOFORTES, PARLOUR & GRAND.

No. I.
THE BECHSBERG "LITTLE ANGELS" KLAVIER.

A compact upright piano of the smallest possible size. The tone is pleasing and the touch responsive.
Overstrung.
Complete iron framing.
Patent repeating action.
Ivory key.
One key only (middle "C")
Rosewood case.
Length, 1ft.
Width, 1ft. 2in.
Height, 3ft. 0 in.

Price 40 Guineas.

No. II. THE LEVIATHON.

A full-toned grand piano of responsive touch and distinguished exterior. Twenty-one octaves of music, ten yards of astonishing length. A new system of construction renders the instrument indestructible.
Reinforced cast-iron framing.
Compass, 21 octs. A to A.
Patent hammer felts.
Under damper action.

Suitable for rooms of very large dimensions.

Length, 10yrds. 2ft. 2in.
Width, 4ft. 11in.
Height, 4ft. 2in.

Price 150 Guineas.

THIS PAGE, taken from *Bollingley's Summer Bazaar 1890*, shows the wide variety of goods available at Bollingley's, Framley's oldest department store. A permanent fixture on Framley High Street, Bollingley's reflects the changing spirit of every age and is always ready to delight customers with its high standards of traditional service. Bollingley's was demolished in 1991, rebuilt in early 2012 and then demolished again in late 2012, due to being knocked down.

A New Dusk on the Horizon
The Rest of the Book (2001–02)

The Framley Examiner

Framley's Traditional Favourite since 1978

FRIDAY, JUNE 7th, 2002

PRICE 45p

EarRing
NITECLUB
Tuesday night is...
POLKA INFERNO!
with DJ Mad "Max" Velour
15 Viaduct Way, Framley

STYLE

The latest beards

WIN!

Two months in bed

PROPERTY

It's a full house!

De'spite Queen's past snub's to town, its Golden Jubilee fever!

LEFT: Scenes of spontaneous celebration were arranged to mark Her Majesty The Queen's fifty years since wearing the crown. **ABOVE:** the local man who celebrated.

PHOTOGRAPHS BY NESQUIK RUBETTE

FRAMLEY CITIZEN CELEBRATES 50 GLORIOUS YEARS

by Taunton Mishap

TWO-HUNDRED THOUSAND half-grapefruit hedgehogs, bearing over a million portions of cheese and pineapple on sticks went uneaten as Framley celebrated HM the Queen's glorious 50th jubilee last weekend.

The event, which had been dubbed "the party of the century" by organiser Glasner Pommedeterre, marked the glorious 25th Anniversary of the Queen's glorious Silver Jubilee in 1977, with street parties, souvenir mugs and cake, just like in the historic summer of The Stranglers and *Kramer Vs Kramer*.

Though the Queen is still widely resented in the area for having taken away Framley's prized Seaside Status – following a disappointing holiday to the landlocked town in 1954 – the scars of the past were soon forgotten in a riot of iced gems and Onion Jacks.

Everywhere I went, people were in the party mood.

"I'm going to watch the football," said Graham Unch, 78, an unemployed candyfloss vendor from Framley's now derelict promenade district. "What party? Is there a free bar?"

And from behind the smoky doors of the Sailor's Wave pub in Harbour Way, I could hear the sound of a game of Jubilee snooker, and the occasional hearty cry of "you're barred" as a Jubilee dart hit the Jubilee board.

Back at the scene of the street party the next day, organisers were clearing away the pickle-smeared plate and cup. Mr Pommedeterre mopped a tear and congratulated the unnamed Framley man who had helped make the party go with such a bang.

"I'd like to thank you," he said yesterday, "whoever you are. Please contact me to collect your commemorative coin.

"Actually, you can have a couple if you like."

Rain forecast

By PHARAOH CLUTCHSTRAW

EXPERTS predict that a light shower, heading for the Framley area and due to arrive in the early hours of Wednesday morning, may last some years.

The shower, of the genus *fluctus in simpulo*, will be enough to ruin drying washing, says John Never of the St Eyot's Meteorological Society. However, he insists, it will not send people rushing for cover, and drivers will not need to use the fast setting on their windscreen wipers.

The last time it rained for several years in Framley was several years ago.

FIND OUT MORE ABOUT THE QUEEN'S HISTORIC 1954 SNUB TO FRAMLEY INSIDE p6

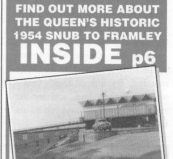

FRAMLEY'S grass pier, 1961, just prior to its tragic, unnecessary closure.

HARVEYHOUND
THE OLD FASHIONED FOOD STORE

NOTHING QUITE COLD ENOUGH

DRINKS MAINLY BROWN

THINGS GOING A BIT OFF

WHAT'S THAT SMELL?

SUGAR ROUND THE LID

NAN'S FAVOURITE™ FURRY CAKES

EXTRA VIRGIN LARD

"FRESH" MILK / CHEESE

20% DISCOUNT ON EVERYTHING AT THE BACK OF THE BOTTOM SHELVES

UNIT 46 ARNHEM CENTRE, FRAMLEY
* OLD 50P COINS STILL ACCEPTED *

MORE JUBILEE NEWS AND PICTURES IN OUR HALF PAGE PULLOUT – SEE PAGE 26, COLUMN 2

Judge rules that man, suffering from multiple fractures and self-inflicted chin injuries after allegedly attempting to climb over 40ft 'impenetrable' wall of iron into leisure centre's new outdoor swimming complex, should be held in custody until police responsible for the arrest come forward and give irrefutable evidence that it was him and not them who had broken into the building, slid up the the water flume backwards and caused more than £250,000 of damage to the new facilites

by Challenger Putney

The police are searching for a receipt which shows they were at the cinema on the evening in question.

Raisin' Arizona

A LUCKY FRACTON schoolboy is set to jet off to the Americas after drawing a dried fruit.

7-year-old Egbert Nosh beat off five other hopefuls to come first in a PlumpBoy Raisin™ competition to design a 'New Raisin For the Millennium'

As well as having the kind folks at PlumpBoy put his raisin into mass production, Egbert is also set to fly to Arizona as part of the prize, where he will get to wear the costume of Grapegomery, the PlumpBoy mascot.

PlumpBoy spokesperson Tina Intricate said, "This is a once in a lifetime opportunity for Egbert to spend 4 weeks in a sweltering factory in Tucson dressed as a grape. He'll get to see first hand how raisins are made."

"The transition is more effective without water", she said as his plane departed, "The sacrifice of the Shrivelled Child will appease the god of our vineyards."

Key to town found in large jacket

43 YEARS AFTER its mysterious disappearance, the key to the town of Framley has turned up... in the pocket of a huge jacket in the Town Hall!

The jacket was discovered hanging up in a disused wardrobe by cleaners, who were turning over the mayor's office looking for dust.

In the years since the town key's disappearance a huge cardboard key has been used as a replacement for special occasions and presentation ceremonies. This key was destroyed in 1972 after it was found to fit the vault door at the Framley Safe Deposit. Since then Framley has been officially keyless.

Council officials are currently discussing plans to fit a huge, flashing fob to the key to avoid the possibility of it going missing in future.

News In Brief

MAN JAILED FOR LIFE

Due to a judicial error, a man who had been found guilty of murdering four children, was jailed by Justice Headley for the "length of my natural life". Justice Headley who has terminal bowel cancer is not expected to see next spring. The man, who is still a danger to the public, will be released, almost certainly, within the next six months.

RUB-A-DUB SHUT

The Golden Ticket public house in Ocksted has been closed to the public while pest controllers deal with an infestation of Pearly Kings. Verminists found a twenty foot Pearly Queen's nest under the floorboards of the saloon bar where up to 1,200 drone Kings, would service the Queen, bringing her cockles and mussels. The nest was neutralised on Sunday by PC Officers who eventually managed to roll out the Queen in a barrel. The pub remains closed while experts check the site for loose shiny buttons that may attract the Kings back.

AND FINALLY...

Framley residents are reminded that they are strongly recommended to evacuate the town on Saturday 13th in order for essential crop spraying experiments to take place. Failure to do so will, in all cases, result in paralysis, mental vomiting, dry saliva, mix-ups, and may also cause some pleasant hallucinogenic effects.

MANURE SALE

BRING YOUR OWN
ROOM CLEARANCE
SIZZLING SPECIALS
HOT! HOT! HOT!

Wednesday 28th May
Meadowlands, Whoft

SIXTIES BAND NITE

GRAN'PA FLUTE AND THE WHISTLIN' POPS
with their 1967 top 10 hit 'Cough Drop'

the operators   THE ORIGINAL SWAYERS

THE NEW SWAYERS

BERNIE   1645 Peppercorn Slipper Factory
together on tour again for the first and final time

ALL OF THE SOUND! – ALL OF THE NIGHT!
Friday 30th May @ The Orange Vine, Clinton Rd FR1 11pm 'til late £1 door

TRIATHLON WINNERS CELEBRATE IN STYLE

Stan and Edie toast their victory shortly before Edie tried to put her tongue in my ear.
PHOTOGRAPH BY ALISON HANDSOMEBOYMODELLLINGSCHOOL

IT WAS ADVOCAAT snowballs all round as Molford's all-conquering triathletes celebrated their historic win last Thursday.

Stan Rimshot (76) and his wife Edie (71) walked away with the Framley District Athletic Association Special Achievement Cup after a stunning victory in the Modern Triathlon – a newly introduced event consisting of Bowls, Knitting and BMX Freestyle.

Though the pair won through with ease, Stan told me that the event hadn't been plain sailing.

"My wife and I have been keen bowls enthusiasts for years, and we both enjoy knitting, but I have to admit, the BMX was a surprise. We hadn't really trained for it. But once I was up on the halfpipe, I found it surprisingly easy.

"I suppose riding a bike is like riding a bike. You never forget," he chuckled.

Edie then made another round of snowballs for the assembled journalists while Stan visited the smallest room and was sick down his shirt.

Sockford fisherman wins a personal best

ANGLING
Framley Municipal Park Open

SOCKFORD HERO, ATLANTIS GREENE, beat the regional records tumbling when he landed a superb personal best of nearly catching a fish at the Ned's Atomic Dustbin-sponsored Framley Municipal Park Open.

Greeen was overcome with emotions after landing the severed torso of the late Robert Shaw, using alternate maggot and caster baits.

The paddling pond was teeming with salmon, perch and a bream flown in especially for the competition – which was donated by famous fish farm, Keith Moon.

Second place went to Boz 'Alfie' Scaggs who tempted a 27lb mirror carp with a lot of skill and a Milkybar all covered in Marmite, winning himself a holding net full of two damp £5 notes.

JUNIOR WINNER

The title of Junior Angler of a Year was claimed by Minogue Hoffman,

12, whose resounding victory was never in doubt after scoring an eighth for 16lb50 off of Big Mick at the poolside hot dog stand. Proud parents, Anastacia and Valerie Helpmann were said to be very pleased with Minogue's catch and immediately offered to double his stash.

The victorious Minogue
PHOTO BY STAN MOOD

The first annual third annual angling contest was deemed a huge success by spectators, organizers and fish alike and there is expected to be fierce bidding for the television coverage rights of next year's second annual third annual angling contest from rival channels Sky Fishing 12 and Sky Fishing 139.

SPORTS extra

The football action is never far from away

SOCCER
Framley Veterans Cup

By Pigshit Nelson

IT TOOK EXTRA TIME, penalties and a quarter-pound bag of aniseed balls to split **Whoft Moonies** and **Batley Spinner**. The match ended 0-0 with goals from Cyd Shariff (Whoft) and Basil Jet (Whoft) early in the second half. Batley finally edged the shoot-out 8-0. The replay will be next Wednesday.

•

FRAMLEY POLICE called on their excellent home form to claim a 124-6 victory over **Molford St Gavin** after nine of the visiting side were arrested under the Prevention of Terrorism Act (1973) shortly before kick-off. MSG keeper, Richmond Nettle, was stretchered off within two minutes after a nasty clash of head and truncheons, leaving brave centre-half Andy Vlap to put up a spirited 88-minute performance against the eleven burly coppers. Surely it won't be long before the County Intermediate League comes knocking as Vlap never looked out of his depth despite being forced to score 91 own goals.

•

IN AN EXCRUCIATING game at Wripple Celtic Park, the away side **Framley Caledonian** Thistle lost out by the odd goal in two to **Wripple Glasgow Celtic** whilst **Benjamin Disraeli Town** beat **Bad Seagull** absolutely bloody hollow.

NEWBY'S OF MOLFORD CITY ran riot at home with just over half of the team on the scoresheet and just over two-thirds of the team tipping the **Framley Pagoda** team bus over after having set fire to the visiting players.

•

FRAMLEY NORTH-EAST CONSERVATIVES new signing, Westcott Malaise, scored a dubious offside on his debut against **Wripple Old Nonagenarians**. FNEC ball/manager, Marcus Help!, was delighted with and by Malaise's contribution to the team's performance which was marred only by the necessity to substitute local MP and wing-back, Ianbeale Steeplecocque, five minutes before the end of the match and, again, five minutes before the beginning of the match.

•

THE SEMI-FINAL line-up was completed with a convincing display from **The Sockford Reverends** whose absent opponents **Tuesday Wednesday**'s chutzpah was rewarded with a bye into the final. Wednesday's coach, The Marty Marty, revealed at a local presconference that there was no point in them turning up for the game as they would definitely have tonked the in-form Vicars 5-0 anyway.

SPORTS ROUNDUP

BRITISH BULLDOG
After a series of grazed knee injuries, Leanne Pelvis has been forced to pull out of next Monday's British Bulldog Championships. According to her coach, Mrs Maureen Pelvis, she's had a bit too much blue pop and she's just tired and overexcited. Concerns that there would be tears before bedtime were also a factor in Pelvis' withdrawal from the competition.

NEW SIGNING
Molford Descriptive FC have signed a new bass player. Juice Oblong, 19, will make his debut next Saturday.

SEMI-FINAL CLASH
The semi-finals of the Sockford Intermediate League Basketboxing championships will take place on Tuesday. Leroy "Wildtrack" Ingle will face The Fracton Windmills. Winner to be decided by two slamdunks or a knockout.

SPORTTALKTEXT from **Zephyr** **1375** am

ZEPHYR AM's popular sports phone-in, every weeknight from 8-10pm.

A radio show converted nightly into a lengthy series of 160-character text messages.

50p per message

To subscribe send 'BORING/ANNOYING?' to 07999 702818 FR2 8PF

Our food critic visits Framley's newest restaurant and finds it lives up to his high expectations

Ladies first

EATING OUT
with Vernon Palliard

IT TAKES SOMEONE of particular vision to bring their own particular vision to the world of top-end dining, but if there's one thing you can depend on, it's that that someone is going to be local gourmet and restauranteur Cameron Stad.

Stad's unconventional sense of design first caught my eye when I visited *Chez Cap'n*, his fishfinger restaurant in old Framley harbour in 1996. With its distinctive cod-shaped dining area and cutlery anchors, this was a whole new experience for the jaded food critic, but I'm pleased to announce that the ever restless restauranteur's arresting new restaurant outstrips it.

Called simply *Ladies*, Stad's new eatery stands in the centre of Van Dyke Park, at the bottom of a flight of steps, its exclusivity guaranteed by an 8 foot railing, which my dining partner, Django, and I negotiated with some difficulty.

DINING STALLS

Access to the dining area is via a skylight and there's a lengthy drop onto broken glass for all guests. The Maitre d' seated us in adjacent "dining stalls", and pointed us towards the menu, which had been cleverly printed onto a long roll and mounted on the cubicle wall.

Most of the dishes on offer were cold. Gazpacho, green salad, or nice 'n' spicy Nik Naks for starters; biscuits and cheese for main course. As Cameron explained to me from his facing stall, the kitchens at *Ladies* are not equipped with anything as vulgar as an oven – a kitchen utensil which Stad regards as "a distraction from the real business of washing and arranging food on the plate".

And I had to agree that my food was clean as a whistle. My Nik Naks had been washed thoroughly, removing all the gaudy flavouring, and bringing out a pale, pure, beige colour I had never anticipated. In a

Cameron shows us round the facilities at *Ladies*, his new premium dining experience. **CLOCKWISE FROM TOP:** the welcoming sign; the kitchens; one of the dining stalls; entering the restaurant. **PHOTOGRAPHY BY ARRIFLEX WELLING**

similarly imaginative touch, Django's simple glass of tap water was frosted with a pink, soapy substance that acted as a marvellous palate cleaner. As bubbles floated above his stall divider, my appetite was truly whetted. I couldn't wait for my main course to arrive.

BISCUIT

And what a main course! A fan of spotlessly clean Sports Biscuits, topped with a single Emmenthal Baby Bel.

My partner opted for a pyramid of Krackawheat, washed in their own juice. I was delighted to note that the chef had decorated each cracker with

a smiley of Primula cheese spread, a straight-from-the-tube flourish that is typical of Stad's diligent approach to *la cuisine moderne*.

Fully sated, we skipped dessert and went straight to the delicious bill and mints. Still reeling from the heady flavours, we congratulated the *patron* and clambered back out into the night air by shinning up the cistern by the skylight. I was in love.

VERDICT: This is a truly exceptional restaurant, and well worth a visit.
★★★★

LADIES, Van Dyke Park, Framley. 01999 644 379. Typical cost £45 per head with bottle of house water. No dogs. No toilets.

RESTAURANT ROUNDUP

PULCINELLA'S ★★★ Just opened on Carpet Street, this new Italian restaurant is intimate, with distinctive red and white decor. Book well in advance – there's only room for one diner at a time – but it's worth the effort. The menu offers a choice of sausages, or crocodile stuffed with sausages, all cooked by the owner's long-suffering wife, Judy. Children are welcome to watch, but must stay outside, laughing and clapping and indicating when things are behind you. Average meal £17. Service charge not included, but a hat is passed round for tips after each sitting.

MIKE'S UPSTAIRS ROOM ★★★★
Framley's long-running Only Fools And Horses theme restaurant just goes from strength to strength, with special guests queueing to turn up. This week, there's live dinner jazz with Sue Holderness (Boycie's wife Marlene in the hit TV show). Sue will be singing and playing her famous saxophone solo from the *Theme From Blockbusters*. Book too early and ensure disappointment. £2.

THE CROWN OF MARMITE ★★★★ ★★ Inspired gastro-pub recently refurbished by the people behind Bar Humbug, this is a dining experience guaranteed to make you drunk. The choice of dishes ranges from deep fried bitter to lager carbonara, all served in pint-glass shaped glass plates. The selection of beermat appetisers is excellent and the staff are always cheerful, helpful and shit-faced. £2.45

it's child's play to read

The Framley Examiner
Framley's Traditional Favourite Since 1978

NEW KIDS' EDITION

- stories rewritten with happy endings
- illustrated by Quentin Blake
- 20% more princesses and lions
- big bath-time pages
- strawberry flavour

free crayons with issue 3371

Every week! Order yours today!

01999 974 977 £4.50 rrp

way too much Restaurant

every meal too big to eat! GUARANTEED

JUST LOOK AT WHAT'S ON OFFER! YOU WON'T BELIEVE OUR PORTIONS!

NEW! all you can't eat buffet **£5.99**

WOW! 3-course a la carte menu **£7.99**

NEW! meal for 6 for 2 **£9.99**

Doctor's certificate required for all diners

way too much restaurant
76 Grandebouffe Drive, St Eyot's Tel 01999 744 371

A La Carte Menu*

A YARD OF ANCHOVIES
&
A JULIENNE OF 32 BAKED POTATOES
&
FROGS LEGS DE TRIOMPHE

ENTIRE HORSE ON A KINGSIZE BED OF SPAGHETTI
(GARNISHED WITH EXTRA HOOVES)
&
A DALE OF YORKSHIRE PUDDING, FILLED WITH A PUB OF BEER
&
STATELY HOME OF CORNED BEEF
(SERVED IN FIFTY ACRES OF ROLLING, WINDSWEPT ROSEMARY)

BREAD PUDDING (£1.50 PER SQ FT)
&
AN ICEBERG OF KENDAL MINT CAKE
&
MELON ZEPPELINS

WINE HYDRANT

Clean plates compulsory before bill will be brought

Local National

have vacancies for bus passengers. Full training for suitable applicants, life insurance, paid holidays, free uniform, free travel, employee share scheme.

If the idea of combining being a passenger with meeting bus drivers appeals, call **01999 877 677**

Local National

Hamster monitor

£65K p/a.

Suit ambitious 8-year old, good team player, with interest in pets and summer holiday free.

St Icklebrick's Primary School
"Excellence in Education"

01999 985 005

£50,000 P.A. OTE

Yes! I have been here 12 months and have made £12,000 already! Halfway there! You could be halfway there too! - 01999 688 754 -

BEE REQUIRED

by trainee beekeeper
Call Simon Eminem on
01999 963 023

FRAMLEY DOG RESCUE

Framley Dog Rescue have vacancies for butchers, sous-chefs and experienced waiting staff.

Framley Dog Rescue also require unwanted pets for use in promotional film. We're sorry, we can't return any of your pets, but there is a prize for all those shown.

Call Isadorabella on 01999 600 610

VEGETARIAN BINGO CALLER

Must have own complete set of 1-100 cherry bingo tomatoes. £5 per hour p/h

PODIUM BINGO
01999 677 865

St Gahan's School for Boys

are looking for a
BAD LANGUAGE ASSISTANT

3 years min experience as sailor, dockworker or squaddie preferred.

Salary negotiable depending on salary.

01999 470 872

MILKMEN AND WOMEN

The Onion Milk Company Ltd require milk men and women to turn around sales figures on our new range of Onion Milks. Previous deserters need not reapply.

01999 744 743

THE ONION MILK COMPANY
So misunderstood...

PART-TIME EVENING CLEANER

required to partially clean office.

£4.50 / hr. 7pm-9pm. Don't touch that drawer.

01999 939 018

RAIN MAN WANTED

to act as human spreadsheet for Framley technophobe.

Must not be taller than Tom Cruz, and preferably able to sing theme from "Goodnight Cowboy".

OIRO £1200 pcm.
01999 851 711

TEMPORARY BAR STAFF / ASTRONAUTS

needed for Sockford wine bar. Previous bar experience preferred.

5 days p/wk
(4 days bar work / 1 day suborbital satellite maintenance)

Some on-the-job training given.

Mandy 01999 850 080

DESIGNER
required

to design this advertisement

successful applicants will already have this job

WHOFT HOSPICE
STAFF WANTED

Do you think hospices are places of doom and gloom? Not all of our patients come here to die. But they all do. In the end.

We're looking for a sensitive, caring individual with their own spade and a strong back, who understands that life can be short as well as long, and wants to join us in this fast-moving, high-turnover business.

For job details, call Amylase or Saliva on 01999 842 842

BUILDER'S MATES

Builder's mates required.

I've just woken up in a skip. Where is everybody?

Mike? Dave? Jimbo? Come on, a joke's a joke.

07999 908 651

CAN YOU COOK?*

The Horse and Further Horse pub / restaurant needs you tomorrow*!

Are you prepared to work hard*, be part of a team*, deliver top quality service*?

Morning, lunchtime and evening work available*. Good pay*. Excellent scope for promotion*.

*Tuesday 16th April only.

Applications by 3pm today at the latest.

The Horse & Further Horse, Adrian Mill, Wripple, Nr Framley FM5 6RE

SOCKFORD HAPPINESS CAMP

has vacancies for a delighter, a pleasurer and a laughterist. Apply to the chief conjuror on
01999 620 105

MOLFORD EMPLOYER

seeks
FULL TIME PERSON

Must be a person ALL THE TIME. Must not sometimes be a pot plant or an octopus or a cloud.

Previous applicants may reapply if they are now a full-time person.

01999 855 902

WEB DESIGNER

wanted for crap spider

01999 833 901

WINE DEMONSTRATOR

We have a vacancy for a wine demonstrator at our busy Molford Retail Park outlet.

You will be between 40 and 60 years of age and covered in dribble.

Slumping, sleeping, swearing, stealing packets of jelly and sicking up wine will be just part of your job, which will also include some urinating against the back wall.

Good interpersonal skills a must. £48K starting salary. Uniform provided.

Call Cathy or Spagger on 01999 932 022 or send CV and beard sample to

CORKER'S WINE

Unit 48b, Molford Retail Park, FM7 6TT

We have 20 vacancies for
SALESPEOPLE

to sell double glazing in Whoft to Mr Jack Bicknacre of Basement Flat, 38a, Woollen Grove. You will join a committed existing team, working long hours on this project. £38K pa. 58h p/wk (+OT)

Call Stevhen, Marhie or Colhin at
THE JACK BICKNACRE WINDOW DEVELOPMENT SALES FORCE
Units 12-19, Cormorant Industrial Estate, Whoft FM3
01999 854 711 / 712 / 713 / 714 / 715 / 716

FRAMLEY POLICE

WE HAVE A VACANCIES FOR A

BENT COPPER

Must be disliked. We're looking for someone who doesn't do things by the book. You will preferably be motivated by greed, power and money and be an excellent team traitor.
Apply Det Ch Insp Barry Judas, Vice (Ref 7754)

BURGLAR

Traditional burglar required. Striped jersey, bag marked "Swag" and Fred Flintstone Five O'Clock shadow. Easily spotted melodramatic tiptoeing motion if possible. For training new officers. Previous inexperience inconsequential.
Apply Supt. I. Triangle, Training Dept (Ref 7710)

MURDERER OF JOANNE PEST

You'll be a socially awkward loner, 5'8" – 5'10" with a loping walk, goatee beard and distinctive blue shoes. This is a permanent position and the successful applicant must be prepared to do long hours (30 years minimum).
Apply Det Sgt Ulan-Bator, Framley CID (Ref 7710)

For full details of all these vacancies, call Framley Police on 999

DESPATCH CLERK

required by retired Sockford businessman to send A3 envelopes full of hot gravel to everyone who's ever annoyed me.

Des on 01999 710 940

We have a
POSSIBLE VACANCY

for an invisible receptionist. This post may already have been filled. We're not sure.

Phone the front desk on
01999 622 192
and see if anyone answers.

Calls cost £8.75 per minute.

Framley Community College
FINE ART DEPARTMENT

Require a

TRANSFORMER

to teach sculpture and ceramics.

You will be over 8 feet tall and able to turn into a lorry.

16K, 36h p/wk 01999 954 968

Time running out for tiny farm

THE FOUR WEEK SIEGE at Wripple's Rappapoort Farm has entered its third week. The owner of the smallholding, Mr David Futumsch, has barricaded himself in and is refusing to leave the farm, which has been in his family since the age of Robin Hood. The authorities, who have surrounded the farm with little tanks, insist it is still too tiny. PHOTOGRAPH BY RANDALL OMEN

Vandals attack statue

"SHITKICKING THUGS" are being blamed for damage valued at £4,000 caused to a statue in Van Dyke Park at the weekend.

The statue, Venus Tumescing by Dame Olga Cello, depicts womankind as a orgasm-shaped baby holding a frying pan full of ironing, and has been a favourite with locals since its unveiling in 1969.

"It's a pornographic disgrace that this slur on the mysteries of womanhood is brazenly and publicly on display," said one enthusiast recently, "and I love it."

Even Sid, the notoriously poker-faced park-eeper, loves it!

"What, the climbing frame?" he told me as we went through the dog bins for change.

The vandals wrote "PIF PIF PIF" all over the frying pan and drew treble clefs on the baby.

Ne'er-do-wells from the nearby Dungeon estate are being blamed, largely because they're easy targets but also because most of them can't read.

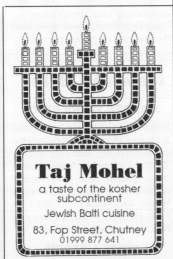

Van Dyke Park
PHOTO: DOMINO RUIN

Taj Mohel
a taste of the kosher subcontinent
Jewish Balti cuisine
83, Fop Street, Chutney
01999 877 641

CONTUTER REPAIRS

we sell and repair all makes of contuter

we are experts in the field

cd-run, nodem and contuter tv's all fixed while you wait

PANGOLIN CONTUTERS
32, Dragon St, Framley
01999 581 582

PENDULUM III NOW IN

Record shop raided

by Adam Wrent

THE OWNER of Bob's Records, Sockford's only independent record shop, has been imprisoned for fraud.

Bob Eliteonemodellingagency, who has run the shop for over twenty years, was found guilty of conspiracy to deceive the record-buying public, and sentenced to four years sitting in a prison cell.

The court heard how the 47-year old shopkeeper, finding it hard to afford new stock, had taken to recording the albums himself and passing them off as the work of the original artists – pop stars like Celine Dion, The Crazy World of Arthur Brown and Autechre.

EDS OF SCREAMING F

Although Bob's actions were apparently against some law or other, the vast majority of his customers were horrified by his arrest, with hundreds of screaming fans turning up outside the court to stand behind him.

"Bob's version of the Zero 7 album pisses on the original," said one. "The artwork was better as well."

Similarly, Bob's version of Sir Georg Solti conducting the Berlin Sinfonietta doing Mahler's Third had critics raving ("The best music ever made" – *Boston Globe*). The record, which came with a bonus CD of rarities and a signed poster, is now changing hands amongst collectors for over £200.

BONUS TRACKS

Though they were aware of Eliteonemodellingagency's deception, police didn't act until the 47-year old shopkeeper began to get carried away, inserting his own extra tracks

Bob's record shop, Bob''s Records, with (inset) the fraudulent owner.
PHOTOGRAPH BY IMMAC NOSTRIL

into the middle of well known records.

Det Insp Jerutha Damaja of Sockford CID told reporters, "*Sgt Pepper* never had a track called *Uncle Albert's Handlebar Moustache* on it. That was the giveaway. We had to move in. It may be one of my favourite songs on the album, but I'm afraid it's still fraud."

SIM TIMENON

A benefit concert in aid of the 47-year old shopkeeper is being organised by Bomb The Bass singer Tim Simenon and Peter Gabriel (from that video with all the fruit). Stars such as Celine Dion and The Crazy World of Autechre will be performing their versions of some of Bob's greatest hits.

Bob's daughter Stephanie says she will be running the shop in his absence. She is described as having a pleasing descant quality to her voice and a good ear for countermelody.

Man waits two weeks to be served in restaurant

By JESUS CHIGLEY

WHEN JEAKE PERKIN ordered a plate of grilled cod with asparagus and lime jus at Squaffables Restaurant, he didn't expect to be quite so hungry by the time it arrived at his table.

"I only came in for a light lunch after a business meeting in the area," he told a reporter yesterday. "I ordered the cod and a glass of Pinot Grigio, and waited. I was still waiting when the restaurant closed that night, but I thought there might have been a mistake."

HIS LIFE IS RUINED

Three days later, Mr Perkin told the waitress he was still waiting. A day later, he asked again. But, despite his two protestations, it would be a further ten days before the hot fish sat between his cutlery.

The restaurant, which was not asked for its opinion, refused to comment.

"It's ruined my life," sobbed a blubbing Perkin, 41, "I've lost my job, my wife thinks I'm Martin Guerre and, to be honest, I'm still hungry.

"How could they treat me like this? I mean, what were they doing in there? Growing the sea?"

the FRAMLEY Examiner

Thursday March 16th 1978 7½p if sold

Framley's traditional favourite since March

BOFFINS SAY "THE COMPUTER IS HERE!"

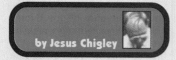

by Jesus Chigley

FRAMLEY POLYTECHNIC has brought the pride of the computer age to town!

After two years of fundraising, the college has finally been able to pay a record £7,350 for a brand-new Quickticus Wolf III, one of the most powerful computers in the world. Roger Lemon, head of engineering at the poly, is beyond delight.

"This is a marvellous acquisition," he explained through his beard. "The Wolf is a giant of technology: it has six screens, five banks of valves and a breathtaking 400-bite magnetic storage and retrieval system."

The state-of-the-art machine has left the engineering department stunned.

"We'd never even seen a computer this big before The Wolf arrived. We're actually at a loss to make full use of it, so infinite is its power," continued Prof Lemon.

COMPUTER CHIPS

But one bright spark has found a cheeky use for the futuristic beast. Physics student Daniel Tidd is writing a programme that will produce dozens of computerised school dinners.

"I've tested it," admitted Mr Tidd, "and so far it can do 22lbs of potatoes in two hours. With that kind of power, it should be able to manage a staggered system of complete lunches for up to eleven hours at a time. Look out, dinner ladies!"

Meanwhile, back on the serious side of the story, Prof Lemon has high hopes for the future.

INTO THE FUTURE

"If this kind of technology continues to be developed at this pace and on this scale," I think he said, "we could see computers the size of entire office blocks by the mid-1980s. And imagine what a machine that crikey big could do."

"I feel invincible," he added.

The polytechnic professors plan to spend the next 18 months writing a programme that can add two numbers together without overheating.

This new mechanical brain challenging the way we live.

PHOTOGRAPH BY TARTAN CARBLANKET

New newspaper

FRAMLEY woke up to a bright new day on its doormat this morning with the arrival of the area's first COLOUR newspaper!

It's called the Framley Exanimer, and it's packed full of all your favourite local news, but told in a new COLOURful way!

The newspaper will mark a new era for local news. The Franley Examiner will be the first to inform you of all the breaking stories, from bus timetable changes to new BBC radio frequencies *as they happen.*

In these fast-changing times, you can be sure of one thing – The Framley examiner will be he

Foreign Secretary coming

The Foreign Secretary, Dr David Oven, is visiting Little Godley next week, to try to repair relations with the genteel village after it declared itself a hostile state by resident renegade Haris Paris.

Councillor Paris, 41, orchestrated the coup de village in December, after somebody threw a snowball at his wife's legs.

Chamber of Commerce welcomes drop in inflation

FRAMLEY's Chamber of Commerce has welcomed the drop in inflation, and predicted that it will start to reverse the decline of manufacturing in the town.

The monthly rate has dropped to 99% – the first time it has been below 100% since 1973.

STYROFOAM ROOFING

A 1980s ROOF AT 1978 PRICES

If you're thinking of replacing all the tiles in your roof with something else, don't forget **STYROFOAM** – roofing material of champions.

No wonder "Central Heating Engineer" magazine said "Styrofoam is STYLE-O-FOAM"

PHONE CRANHAM'S HOUSETOPS ON FRAMLEY 776 or TELEPROMPT 460CNM

NEWBYS OF MOLFORD

Just in! The MOUTARDE 9800 LX SYNTHESIZER KEYBOARD

2 EXCITING NEW SOUNDS! "Electrical hum" & "Bees"

As heard on the TOP 40 hit "Level Best" by TEXTURE

He's got the whole world in his photograph!

by Adam Wrent

FRAMLEY EXAMINER PHOTOGRAPHER Matteus Trilobite is going for the big one! On July 18th, the snapper, who specialises in group shots, is going to try and get over 3 billion people into a single photograph.

Trilobite is one of the newspaper's trustiest snapsmen, and reprints of his photos are amongst the best-selling pictures in the Framley Examiner's archive.

His wide angle view of seventeen local rotary clubs all fighting to give big cheques to a man from Unicef was very popular amongst members of local rotary clubs, and his pin-sharp sports pictures regular sell to every single spectator in the ground.

8 x 10 PRINT

"People love to have a picture of themselves making the news, and at £9.99 for an 8x10 print, these group shots are very lucrative for myself and the paper," he told co-workers who wrote down what he said and put it in this story.

"I used to specialise in portrait shots, but that barely pays for

Smile! What the earth might look like from space..
PHOTOGRAPH BY NATHANIEL AERONAUTICSANDSPACEADMINISTRATION

chemicals," he explained yesterday. "For every couple of yards I step back, I get four more people in the shot. Big money."

For his next photo, accompanying an under-tens' chess report, Trilobite is planning his most populated picture yet.

"This job is a dream come true," he told us. "I am going to cover the story from space."

CHESSBOARD

Using a special handmade rocket, Trilobite will travel outside the earth's atmosphere. He then proposes to take the picture from geostationary orbit, 600km above the chessboard, hopefully getting every man, woman and child in the Northern Hemisphere into the frame.

Local inventor Babbage Wilson-Wilson, who is building Matteus' rocket, is convinced the mission will be a success.

"I'll certainly be buying a copy. I'm not much interested in junior chess, but I will be waving from my garden, and the photo will make a lovely present for my grandchildren."

If you're going to be in the Northern Hemisphere on July 18th, and would like to pre-order a copy of Matteus' photograph, send £9.99 to the usual Framley Examiner address.

KEGS!
the family pub

Everything for a great family day out, set in 8 acres of rolling car park, with space for up to 2000 children

FOR THE KIDS!

Crèche bar
with fully trained nursery assistant (not Thu)
Soft darts
Bar bikes
Children's pints
The Game Of Scissors

FOR THE BIG KIDS!

Adults' playground
Sky BloodSports 1, 2 & 3
Dad's Club
(breast-feeding strippers Mon am only)
Uncle Room
4 types of beer
400 types of crisps

SPECIAL OFFER
CHILD'S FAMILY SIZE MEAL (OR ADULT SIZE MEAL) ONLY £3.95

NEW BOILED EGG CRISPS
"LOOK FOR THE LITTLE BLUE DIPPY SOLDIER BAG"

PLUS
A free pint for every half hour the kids KEEP QUIET

Junior last orders 10.30pm

KEGS FAMILY PUB, YOPPING OLLEY, WHOFT
(Just turn right by Grandma's Warehouse)

EARN £££s
FROM HOME

AS A POST BOX
HOURS NEGOTIABLE
CALL NOW 01999 655 645

40% of drivers would fail test says top copper

40% OF DRIVERS would fail a new blood test, according to PC Damascus Bitesize of St Eyot's Police.

The new test, introduced last week by the same policeman, tests for purity and flavour and is reportedly the hardest yet.

"I'm the only one who's passed so far," said PC Bitesize, picking a clot from between his teeth.

Drivers' groups are not yet impressed.

News In Brief

BUBBLE TROUBLE

Rapscallions and guttersnipes who spit their bubble gum onto the pavement will in future be publicly named and shamed, Framley Borough Council has decided. From next January, anyone caught expectorating masticatable rubber paste products onto a public foot surface will be forced to spend an entire day walking around the town centre blindfold wearing a suit made of tomatoes.

MORE TROUBLE

Fighter pilots at nearby RAF Harmonium are threatening a work-to-rule if conditions aboard aircraft carrier HMS Who Wants To Be A Millionaire are not improved. Talk of industrial action follows complaints from serving officers in The Sea's Own 32nd Regiment Mounted Marines about the treatment of horses. "They keep slipping over when they gallop around the walkways. We lost 14 in the steeplechase," said one anonymous floating soldier.

CCTV TROUBLE

CCTV closed circuit television cameras are to be installed in the control room of the town's CCTV monitoring system after a series of thefts which led to the hi-tech office's 22 staff being stolen and all 58,000 hours of videotape being replaced with copies of *The World's Craziest CCTV Footage.* Police will investigate when they can work out where to start.

(NO) TROUBLE AT T'MILL

Plans to convert the decrepit Framley Fluff Works into a museum and crafts centre are to go before the council next month. The famous Fluff Works were the area's biggest industrial resource for nearly a century, milling and bundling fluff, and later, supplying power to an area of 50 square miles from its unique fluff-powered turbines. The building was decommissioned in 1963 when I was two.

Sadly Missed

Albert "Chalky" Snowdon

Gored in Spain, 20th February, aged 91.

Dearly loved father of Jesus and Concepcion and the finest matador Framley ever produced.

In Loving Memory

Gordon Clive Sinclair

"The boy stood on the burning deck,
His legs were all a-quiver,
He gave a cough,
His leg fell off
And floated down the river."

Thanks to the Framley River Police and the staff of Ward 3J for all their efforts.

"United again in heaven"

Mum and Dad xxx

Your advert here could be reaching over

14,000 readers!

The Framley Examiner

Acknowledgement

Dandy Hummingbyrd

Humbert wishes to THANK all relatives and friends for their kindness and support following his recent loss, but it's not going to bring her back. It was a great comfort to see so many other funerals taking place at the crematorium. Please accept this as my most sincere acknowledgement, and if you've got any lonely female friends, why not give me a bell?

Michael Bettenden

accidentally during mining disaster at Bee Gees concert, Framley Pagoda, 11th March

In our thoughts.

Carol, Stephanie, Robin, Maurice and Andy

Jim Cleuworth

"Dad, we miss you in our lives,
In our hearts you live forever.
But where did you put the car keys?"

Miriam, Lance & Hansel

In Memoriam

Toby Bostrum

1972 - 2005. Lost in space while orbiting the wrong planet. Sorry Toby, we still can't find your head.

Experiment unsuccessful

In Memoriam

Maureen Sprent

Mother to Alan, Grandmother to David and Great Grandfather to Diane.

February 19th. Peacefully, in our sleep.

Fucking Hell & Sons

Funeral Directors

"When you see our logo on the hearse, you know it's a Fucking Hell funeral..."

01999 875 908

Bertie "Fred" Bassett

of 35, Leslie Rise, St Eyots, died, as he had lived, noisily in his sleep.

"The snoring may have stopped, but you will be with us whenever we are awoken by a dustcart or a man with a jackhammer."

all at number 33 xxx

Eirich Chapnelle

suddenly in hospital, March 2nd.

Confused as to why he was suddenly in hospital, he passed away, immediately, of surprise.

We missed you. J & F.

Carol Bettenden

accidentally during mining disaster at Bee Gees concert, Molford Odelisk, 12th March

Your spirit lives on.

Stephanie, Robin, Maurice and Andy

Missing you...

Ian David D'Avid

"I'd swap everything I have for one more day with you. Or a speedboat."

Leanne xxx

Stephanie Bettenden

during mining disaster at Bee Gees concert, Sockford Plantaganet Centre, 16th March

Stayin' Alive in our hearts,

Robin, Maurice and Andy

Irene "Lispy" Scissorssenhurst

Thanks to all the staff of Ward B6 who kept Irene on a gurney in a corridor with a sheet thrown over her whilst we finished our cruise.

Cheers!
Jeremy and Charlotte

New Arrivals

WILLIAMS

DeForest and Rococo (née Roxanne). Congratulations on the birth of your beautiful chinchilla Doughnutz, born on 1st February, a welcome daughter for Loopie and a fellow pet for Fleas, Fangs, Sgt Mincemeat and The Comptroller. With love from Rain.

IT'S ANOTHER BLOODY GIRL

James and Tessa Herringhamham announce the birth of Emma, on Feb 22nd. A sister for Chloe, Hermione, Cassandara, Siobhan, Jane, Emma, Emma and Emma.

HAPPENSTANCE

Janet and Mark Happenstance are delighted to announce the arrival of their new son, Daryl, born 7.20pm, Feb 17th, and would like to thank all those who may have taken part in his conception.

IT'S A ABORTION!

Karen and Robert Misterman are delighted to announce that their daughter Sharelle will no longer be having the baby of Gary Skag.

FEATHERSTONEHAUGH

Nigel and Robyn Featherstone would like to announce the birth of a beautiful baby person, D. An excellent additional challenge to the nanny's job managing A, B and C. She's from Gstaad, you know. Very pretty girl.

IT'S A GIRL

Martin and Lesley Wiltham are delighted to announce the birth of a beautiful, 32-year-old daughter, Miss Regina Divine (né Tony Wiltham)

IT'S A GIRLFRIEND!

The parents of Richard Jeremy Paynting, 39, are pleased to announce the arrival of Donna, a 5'6", 37-year-old County Records Office filing assistant with sufficiently low standards.

Property, page 86, Richard!

BLIMEY!

Ciaran and Daine **Meltis-Fruit** are surprised to announce the birth of a beautiful Aunt Sally, "Aunt Sally", 175lbs. Feb 27th, 5am.

SIXTIES

Terry and Julie Sixties are proud to announce the arrival of a daughter, Ringo. A beautiful sister for John, Paul and Georgeharrison.

IT'S STILL A GIRL

Leah and Andrew Slippers are pleased to announce the continuing birth of their daughter, Alice, 11lb 4oz, 14' 6" and still apparently plenty more to come.

NEW ARRIVAL!

Arreta Trains are delighted to announce the late arrival of the 8.32 from Winchhandle Junction. This was due to driver action.

NEW BABY

To Jennie Dowell-Bishop and Ian Walden-Sutherland, a strapping son, Jack. Congratulations my darling girl, Jen. For God's sake don't give him all your surnames. Love Mum.

Occasions

Happy 18th birthday

CHUNDERTHWAITE Kelly. To Smelly Kelly with the big ears and the national health glasses and the bad breath and these days, frankly, raging thrush. Dad. xxx

NOT LONG NOW, ELSIE!

J & L xxx

LOOK who's on holiday for a fortnight!!

My parents. Everyone round to my place. Bring rocks. Steve.

CONGRATULATIONS on your ENGAGEMENT

Nana Belmarsh and Uncle Mike

Love from all the family

LOOK WHO'S 35

KEITH JARRY, YOU **WANKER**

LOOK who's not getting a penny!

Right, Jody, that'll teach you to try and put me in a home.

Look who's a baby again !

Professor Arthur Bostrom FRSRC

Experiment successful!

Your ad here could be reaching almost

14,000

Happy 80th Birthday, Rosemary !

Love from Paul, Michelle, Ma, Pa and Nana Dad-dad

LOOK WHO'S STARTED DRINKING AGAIN

KEITH WENSLEY come anywhere near me or the kid and I'm calling the police.

UNCO-OPERATIVE FUNERAL DIRECTORS

INDIFFERENT, INDISCREET SERVICE
UNMARKED GRAVES A SPECIALITY
HEADSTONES FROM £8.99
(WITH A THREE WORD MESSAGE OF OUR OWN CHOOSING)
STROBE LIGHTING / MULTIGYM
DORMITORIES OF REST
BRING YOUR OWN FLOWERS
ALL CEREMONIES GUARANTEED DOUBLE-BOOKED
(MAKE YOUR DECEASED LOOK MORE POPULAR)

Ask about our great **2-for-the-price-of-one** deals !

self-drive rental hearses ...by the hour!

un co op

YOUR CHOICE!
LOVED ONE PRESENTED TO YOU AS ASHES IN ORNAMENTAL URN, OR CHUTNEY IN JAR

un co op packing them up and sending them off

*PLEASE ADVISE US IF TAXIDERMY NOT REQUIRED
OPEN 9AM-1PM MON-TUE
01999 824 242   WWW.BYEBYEGRAN.CO.UK

.............FRAMLEY EXAMINER SPECIAL REPORT.............

Why don't you eat it all up now, won't you?

By Beaky Coxwain

THE YOUTH OF FRAMLEY ARE ALL going to die if they carry on like this.

Children as young as yours are eating all the wrong things like we never used to and they're running the risk of planting a cancer or heart disease time bomb in their arteries because they should eat up their vegetables.

A recent poll into the eating practices of kids throughout the county rang warning shots when it produced alarming evidence that no child in Framley has eaten any fruit or vegetables since November 1978.

It also revealed that whilst families living in the Framley area eat more fast food than almost anywhere else in the country, it was still only a quarter of the Government's recommended amount.

So with this at the back of my mind I invited myself to lunch at St Icklebrick's Primary School to see what teachers really eat these days.

AND A MINT VISCOUNT

Headmister Dr St John St Peter held his gut in and put his arms around my shoulder as he showed me what a well-oiled army of primary schoolchildren really eat these days.

School dinners have certainly come a long way since my last one was finished! No longer the mountains of rotting brown cabbage, stale plastic mash and pork substitute of my miserable schooldays – the choice on offer was simply more than my poor stomach could understand so I made my excuses and left. But it looked lovely.

NEW BALLS, PLEASE

Out in the playground it was a different story. Boys and girls alike showed that packed lunches and huzzing tennis balls at each other can mix. Looking inside their boxes I found that sandwiches were made with maybe a yoghurt or even cheese and meat as well as the traditionally compulsory bag of crisps.

Wendell Theefff, spokesresearch scientist for The Healthy Eating Disorder Researching Campaign, told me on their website that the risks are high.

"We all know how difficult it is to encourage people to eat more green. But what we don't know yet is whether this will lead on to problems later in life. There may be all sorts of stuff that they won't be able to be encouraged to do when they get older. It's very scientific."

Although bread is good for children, this boy's diet could cause rickets or scurvy.
PICTURE BY ARAPAHO CENTRIFUGE

WEB PAGE DESIGN AND G R A PHIC DESIGN

WORK UNDERTAKEN

TALK TO THE EXPRETS
01999 477 90
NEW WORLD GRAPHICS

European Weather View

35   26

>> Christ alone knows what this is all about. Give it to Wendy, she's usually got sod all to do on a Tuesday. xxxxxxxxxxxxxxxxxxxxxxxxxxxxxxxxxxxxxxxxxxxxxxxxxxxxx

2-Dimensional Bookbinding

The perfect gift for a loved one – a favourite volume rebound in sumptuous two dimensions.

The newly bound book will bring pleasure and elegance to any table or lap*

EDWIN A. ABBOTT
THEORETICAL BOOKBINDERS
01999 820 976

* LEGAL DISCLAIMER

Rebound books are impossible to open without breaking the laws of 2-Dimensional physics. Only the cover will be visible, and the book will vanish if placed spine-out on a shelf.

DOES YOUR BATH BITE YOUR BOTTOM?

If not, call us!

Our baths sever your spinal column with their taps and drive hot nails into your thighs and shins while you soak.

Call now for a free, no-obligation obligation. Your plumbing remains untouched and your statutory rights affected. No fuss, no mess, no smart answers

BARRINGTON'S 01999 876 611

GARDEN AND HOUSEHOLD RUBBISH TO CLEAR?

Don't hire a skip!
I'm hungry, and so's my wife.

Call Dennis on 01999 692 750

WHAT YOUR CHILD SHOULD BE EATING?

Source: Healthy Eating Disorder Research Campaign.

Breakfast

Semi-skimmed Coco Pops with wholegrain milk
or
porridge made with half-fat Sunny Delight
or
chips on toast

Lunch

Trebor Sugar-Free Extra Strong Mint and cucumber sandwich on wholebread
and
cheese, beer and veal pie
and
a plum in an eggcup
and
pizza with extra mussels and pinenapple
and
another cheese, beer and veal pie
and
something to drink, I should think

Dinner

To start
a light lasagne salad with tinned cherry tomatoes and a sprinkling of Scotch eggs
followed by
a whole roast chicken stuffed with a whole roast beef
and then
a spotted custard
to finish
coffee and After Eights
or
whatever's left in the fridge

Statue honours Framley mayor

by Challenger Putney

THE PEOPLE OF FRAMLEY received a special surprise this week from its friends across the Atlantic – a statue of its elegant mayor!

The statue, which arrived by skip together with forty-eight lengths of broken plywood and a binbag full of grass clippings, was sent as a gift by the citizens of Framley's twin town, Baden Schleissgarten.

CEMENT

Cllr. Geoffrey Cauchaugh greeted the statue with open arms, saying, "That we should be blessed with this beautiful statue shows the unique relationship we have forged with our German neighbours."

Framley was twinned with Baden Schleissgarten in September 1943, a controversial move now recognised by the Guinness Book Of Records as Britain's last attempt at appeasement with the then Third Reich.

The statue, which is nearly four feet tall and made of cement, with a removable plastic bucket inside, has been erected at the southern edge of the swan pond in Philpott Park.

Although the opening ceremony attracted many local dignitaries and some swans, the statue has, so far, elicited only a guarded reaction from its subject, Mayor William D'Ainty.

"Go away, Challenger, I'm trying to watch *Never Mind The Buzzcocks*," he told journalists at a presconference yesterday. "When's dinner ready?"

A handwritten message taped to the skip read simply "Dein Stadt nicht richtig geschmeckt. Claus xxx", a sentiment which the Framley Community College German department has so far been unable to translate.

CAPTAIN

Local primary school pupils, excited by the gift, are currently designing a statue to send to Germany in return. Initial leaked blueprints indicate a 28' tall animatronic gold-plated octopus, called Captain Fishfingers, that shoots rays from its beak and solves underwater crime. It will bear the face of Baden Schleissgarten's Mayor, Claus Freneddt and cost over £280,000, plus postage.

The cement statue will be a symbol of the close relationship between Mayor D'Ainty (inset) and Mayor Frennedt (not pictured).
PHOTOGRAPH BY RANKIN, STYLING BY MIRABELLE

Headline here

A MAN WHO WAS REFUSED PERMISSION for a an extension to his bathroom has taken his protest to the roads.

Gilliam Sensible, 42, of High Hopes, Whoft, has been having a "whopping Crippen of a row" with Framly Borough Council since they refused him permission for an extension to his bathroom in 1990.

"I've started this fight, and I don't intend to continue it without finishing it," he explained to passing reporters yesterday.

"The council have treated me like fluff," he went further.

UNCOVERED

Mr Sensible's latest protest was UNCOVERED by policemen who pulled him over on the FR404 for travelling at 4mph. However, when they knocked on the window of his Ford Turnip, he was in the shower.

On further investigation, they discovered that the glovebox had been converted into a soapdish and that one of the rear seats was a toilet. Mr Sensible was banned from driving for 18 months.

"I've got to wash somewhere," explained a soapy Gilliam from his passenger seat yesterday.

ROAD REPORT

with Oliver Singultus-Hiccup

A MAJOR ROAD REDESIGNATION is planned for this weekend in Codge. Little Passage, between Killiard's Pet Shop and The Bride and Best Man pub is being reclassified from a one-way street to a three-way street. Motorists are advised to negotiate the three-way system using a new virtual roundabout that has been erected at www.littlepassageroadworks.gov. uk. Double click your mouse when you wish to leave the roundabout and leave plenty of time for your journey.

TEMPORARY TRAFFIC LIGHTS are in operation every four feet along the FR303 to slow speeding traffic during the Vetiver's Bachanaal at Molford County Showground. So, that's a road to avoid this week, unless you really like traffic lights.

MAJOR STRUCTURAL ENGINEERING WORK is taking place on the pedestrian bridge by Sockford Fire Station. The work, to raise the footbridge over 40 feet, will allow the passage of the fire engine's ladder at full perpendicular stretch, and seemed a good idea at the time.

Boy robbed

A TERRIFIED 8-YEAR OLD was attacked at rulerpoint and locked in a horrid toilet during a partly armed robbery in Chutney.

School Counsellor Tricky Dixon of Chutney Junior School told reporters how it happened.

"It was the last day of term," he said, "and, like her classmates, the little girl had brought a toy into school. Everything was fine until a robber, tempted by the look of the girl's toy, jumped on her in the bogs.

The suspect smacked his victim in the chops, calling her a 'stink' and a 'frutter,' before making off with her favourite toy – a million pounds.

He then came back, tied her hands to her face with rubber bands, stuffed stuff up her nose and locked her in a toilet that had not been flushed for several days.

The girl, Sarah Pepperkite, who cannot be named for the usual reasons, cried for "ages and ages and ages and ages," said a spokesfriend

Police are baffled by the attack. "Why would anyone want to steal a million pounds?" asked Sgt Stig Bluff of Chutney Constambulary.

Her attacker is described as white, 4ft tall and about eight. He wore grey and blue trainers and school uniform, and smelled of cheese and onion crisps.

Anyone with information should contact Molford Police on or Crimestoppers on 0800 555111.

DEBT PROBLEMS?

Bills unpaid? Being chased by creditors?

DON'T PANIC!

Call Piltdown Debt Management and let us take the strain.

We can take all your household bills, loan demands and bank letters, and hide them tidily and neatly, unopened behind the microwave.

If it comes through the door in a brown windowed envelope, we can hide it.

PILTDOWN
DEBT MANAGEMENT
01999 860 861

PARSLEY

The great new taste for today's dishes...

Now in 4KG bags!

BRITISH PARSLEY BOARD
*serving suggestion

'Tis the season to be missing!

by Katy Blirdsnest

A POPULAR MP screamed non-stop for seventeen hours this week when he realised what kind of a world he was living in!

For it was he – Ianbeale Steeplecocque, a popular MP for Framley NE – who first noticed that Codge, where he lives, hasn't had an Autumn since 1998!

According to the time-watching MP, the blame for the missing season lies with calendar manufacturers. Since 1997, a persistent printing error has caused the W.I. charity calendar (used by most of Codge's residents) to be printed with the Autumn months missing. Knowing no better, for four years, the village has gone straight from Summer to Winter overnight. It is only now, Steeplecocque told me, that the cost of three years' worth of missing September's, October's and December's are starting to count their own cost.

DEAD HEDGEHOGS

Steeplecocque first noticed that something wasn't quite alright when he found "a load of dead field-mice,

Mr Thubnall's aeroplane lies in the wreckage it caused with its crash.
PHOTOGRAPH BY JEMMA SVENGALLIGAN

tortoises and hedgehogs" literally around his back garden. The sudden change in climate from very hot to not hot at all must of happened far too quickly for them to be able to collect any nuts or warmth, I'd expect, and he agrees.

"After I'd cleared up their sweet little corpses with my favourite Newby's rake I realised that this was the first time that I'd used it for several", whimpered Steeplecocque, "years.

BAD FRUIT

"Then, staring at my fruit trees, I realised that not a single leaf had fallen from them since the birth of my son, Peterbeale, in 1999."

Steeplecocque

"The trunks had buckled, branches were creaking at me and there were thousands upon thousands of grotesquely impacted apples and strawberries still hanging from their swollen stalks."

And it's not just MPs! Local scientists had until recently been baffled as to why darkness tended to fall just as they took their elevenses. Apparently it's just something to do with clocks.

"I only hope we've caught this problem in time," fretted Steeplecocque.

SHAVEN

It may not be that easy, though. The ladies of Codge Women's Institute have warned calendar users that they have already prepared themselves for next year's *Shaven W.I.* and it will now be too much bother for them to find three more volunteers who are willing to participate in any way at allsoever.

So it looks like Spring, Summer, Winter for the village of Codge for a while to come!

AIR CRASH HORROR

Squirrels find themselves frozen before they have time to buy nuts for the winter.
PHOTOGRAPH BY SIMON ROAST

RESIDENTS of St Eyot's have been restaging the terrifying moment when a light aircraft hit overhead power cables and crashed into their homes.

The pilot of the Cessna single-engine aircraft, Terry Thubnall, was trapped in the cockpit for ten minutes after it hit the 440,000 volt power line and plummeted pilot-first into innocent villagers' lives a month ago.

Mr Thubnall, 46, of Copcobmanbury, was shown to Framley General hospital, but later pronounced dodo.

HUGE

Sindy Doyle, of Kidney Lane, St Eyot's, said she was outside cleaning the lawn when she saw a "huge" flash and heard a "huge" bang. She later called the emergency services with a phone.

Ms Doyle was among 250 villagers involved in the restaging of the incident last Thursday, which included a perfect replica of the Cessna and a Mr Thubnall lookalike.

"I did my bit – I went out and cleaned the lawn again and waited for the huge bang," wizened Ms Doyle yesterday, "but I didn't really enjoy it. Especially the huge flash and the huge bang. They were a bit too huge – not really in keeping with the spirit of the original crash."

However, one villager who wasn't taking part is Tim and Sally Shoppington, whose daughter Flax was being born during the explosion.

"We couldn't really commit to it, what with the baby," explained busty stunner Sally yesterday, "but we might join in next month."

"Queen 'will never die' say voices" says man

A DOCTOR from Whoft claims to have heard voices telling him that Her Majesty The Queen will never die.

Overweight GP Colyn Graveyard, 62, said yesterday, "I regularly receives testimony concerning the monarch's immortality.

Her Majesty will probably live forever. I believe everything they say. Would you like a gypsy cream?"

One neighbour described Graveyard as a "old queen with a whopping barbiturate habit" who asked to remain anonymous.

Police say they do not understand.

Framley Pagoda
prodly presents

Beauty and the Beast
ON FIRE!   ON ICE!

a fairytale love story told in a whole new way

JUN 17 – MAY 11   01999 873 103
BOX OFFICE OPEN NOW!

WILSON, KEPPEL & BETTY
FUNERAL DIRECTORS
We put the FUN in FUNERAL

Complete funeral arrangements carried out with some dignity.

Full procession through local area in comedy ricketty hearse.

Whoopee coffins

Antics with a ladder, mishaps with buckets of glitter.

Corpses embalmed in full clown make up
(Choose fromCaroli / Grock / Ronald McDonald)

74 JUNTA CRESCENT, SOCKFORD 01999 765721

We offer 3 levels of slapstick:
- *The Wisdom*
- *The Chaplin*
- *The Mayall*

mobile citadel

for all your mobile phone need*

DEREKSSON 3L

Great all-rounder. Denim case. With 35 different vibrates, including Back of The Bus, Walking Machine and San Francisco Earthquake. 300 free buttons a month.
If you don't use all your buttons, they roll over to the next month, and are incorporated into a new, larger, monthly handset.
(Zzz-Mobile ButtonPlan 100 tariff only)

NOW WITH UNPREDICTABLE TEXT MESSAGING

£39.99

MELANOMA 4500

The perfect One-Call™ disposable handset. For that important just-can't-wait call. Just throw it away after your first three-minute conversation. Perfect for students and people on benefit.

£19.99

ACCEPTS LUNCHEON VOUCHERS.

PONY 350e

THE classic mobile. THE *classic* mobile.

£49.99

Crashes, cuts out for no reason, says INSERT SIM CARD every twenty minutes, rings too loud, fills up with text adverts, loses your numbers, hides behind things when you're in a hurry.

OPTIONS: LOOSE-FITTING HANDSET, RANDOM BATTERY, NOBODYTHERE FUNCTION

WANKIA iCARCINOMA

Unique traditional-style phone. Strapped on your back in a handy three-quarter size telephone kiosk (available in K3, K6 and K7 designs). An impressive 49.7kgs, and a great talking point.

You don't pay a penny until you make your first call. From that moment on, you're charged for every minute you own the iCarcinoma.

£299.99

Non-WAP compatible

PAY-AS-YOU-TALK-AS-YOU-GO VOUCHERS
Available in 1p and 6p denominations. Min call charge 25p.

EXTRA! EXTRA! EXTRA!

CELEBRITY TEXT MESSAGES

0129	Hi! It's Lisa from Steps!
0130	YO YO YO - DJ Alexndr Th Gr8
0147	Congratulations! from Alan Ruck
0155	GET WEKL SOON LUV TUCKER
0155	Happy Birthday To You / I Just Bought Some Glue / And When You're Not Looking / I'll Stick Me To You - Sir John Harvey-Jones MBE
0161	Hi, itsk Popeye. Well, whaddayaknow?
0167	HRH Princess Eugenie says FLOWERS!!!!
0183	Your Gonna Live Forever from Erika Gimpel (Coco Hernandez from Fame)

EASY PAYMENT OPTIONS!

LIGHT USER PAYMENT PLAN
We charge you for the calls you make. Min call charge 25p.

OR

HEAVY USER PAYMENT PLAN
We charge you for the calls you DON'T make. 25p for every minute the service is not being used. Every second counts!

NEW! NEW! NEW! BBC RINGTONES!

4409 Greenwich time signal
4410 Curtains closing
4411 Door opens and slams
4412 Troupe of horses passing
4413 Milk float start, tick-over, depart
4414 Playground atmosphere
4415 State Funeral of Winston Churchill
4416 Martin Jarvis reads Just William
4417 The Shipping Forecast
4418 Blenheim Bomber, Deal, 1942
4419 Lulu the Blue Peter elephant
4420 TARDIS approaching
4421 Seal of Rassillon Atmosphere
4422 Brian Perkins saying "Radio 4. It's bedtime."
4423 2.4 Children (first series)
4424 The News

and remember...
If you can find a better deal anywhere
— *we'll cut you off!*

mobile citadel

*subjunctive

23-25 COSSETT PARK INDUSTRIAL ESTATE (opp Just Blankets) 01999 920992

CAN DO!

by Taunton Mishap

A WRIPPLE SCHOOLBOY who raised £4200 for a TV charity, has received the highest award ever given by long-running children's programme *Flagship*.

14-year-old Kerin Fitzperrin collected over 16,000 empty aluminium cans to send to *Flagship*'s annual charity appeal – more than any other viewer – entitling him to a Gold Flagship Badge with real fur and moving eyes.

The producer of the show, Baxterby Parnell, recognised Kerin's achievement at a special ceremony, held in Fitzperrin's absence at the Marbleborough Hotel, Sockford.

"Thanks to Kerin's amazing effort, we have enough aluminium to buy a whole herd of caribou for Eritrean blind children. We'd like to wish Kerin a speedy recovery. His was truly an amazing effort," Parnell told.

Kerin, most of whose cans had previously contained lager, India Pale Ale and stout, took a month

Kerin toasts our photographer shortly before his hospitalisation.
PHOTOGRAPH BY EMELINE AWARDWINNER

off school to prepare and recover from his charity project. Doctors at Framley Intensive Care Ward estimate that this is the most beer a human being has ever put in their body.

The award was given in Kerin's absence to *Flagship*'s second-best fundraiser, an 11-year-old girl, who had sent the programme 7 catfood tins and a box of spoons.

"I am not an emergency," screams Framley man, 42

THE ROLE of the emergency services in Framley is to be re-examined after a string of embarrassing incidents.

Martin Sister, an unemployed venerealogist from Whoft, claims he has become the victim of victimisation by police officers, firefighters and ambulances.

Three months ago, Mr Sister snagged a fingernail while opening a carton of milk in his kitchen. Within ten minutes, three separate crews of paramedics had arrived at his home and were fighting each other to perform cardiopulminary resuscitation (CRP) and inject Mr Sister with naloxone and adrenalin.

A few days later, Mr Sister was hosed with water cannon from six fire engines when he lit a cigarette in a pub. And, he claims, two lifeboats arrived when his bath was too hot.

A spokesman for Framley Fire

An emergency vehicle of the sort that won't leave Mr Sister alone.
PHOTOGRAPH BY PINNY SOUSE

Service apologised to Mr Sister, but claimed "we genuinely thought it was a genuine emergency."

Mr Sister, however, has yet to receive either an apology or compensation from the police, who arrested and charged him with GBH for clapping at a football match.

An unrepentant Chief Constable Rupert Bone yesterday woofed, "It seemed very clear to my officers that his right hand was trying to maim, or at least kill, his left hand – and they acted accordingly."

Ch Con Bone later went to bed.

THE REVOLUTIONARY NEW MATHIESSEN 800-X TOILET-WARDROBE

GENEROUS STORAGE SPACE

ROOM FOR TWO DOZEN BLAZERS

LUXURY STRING PULL FLUSH

CAPACIOUS BOWL (8 gal)

REAL DOORS

ONLY £179.99*

Stylish new home furnishing idea from Sweden
* Deodorising model also available (£229.99)

FROM FURNITURE IGLOO
UNIT 166, DELOREAN INDUSTRIAL ESTATE, SOCKFORD

Nit suitable for the children !

PARENTS are being warned not to let their children buy copies of a new hit film over the internet – because it has nits.

Skip Butane, Mall Jockey was the biggest grossing movie amongst US filmgoers aged 4-18 last summer, and youngsters on this side of the American Ocean are quite literally bursting with anticipation at the thought of seeing it before its official UK release date of 2012.

Many keen teens are resorting to ordering copies of the film over the net direct from the US, but doctors are warning that the American edition of the film may pose a health risk.

"We feel we must warn parents," said a representative of the World Health Organisation, "that the vast majority of copies of this film have nits."

But internet traders and film fans have tried to calm fears.

"It's not a problem," one told me. "These are Region 1 nits. They won't work on British children, who are coded for Region 2."

"There's nothing to worry about unless your child has been chipped."

SCOFFING & FEY

AUCTIONEERS AND VALUERS
29, Yafflegate, Wripple
01999 428663

FUTURE SALES

Friday 22nd February at 10.30am
WATER PAINTINGS, OILCOLOURS, PHOTOS OF PEOPLE

Tuesday 26th February at 11.00am
ENID BLYTON'S COLLECTION OF FALSE TEETH

Wed 28th February at 10.30am
GENERAL TAT

Thursd 28th Februray at 10.00am
STUFF THAT WON'T MAKE IT HOME IN ONE PIECE

Friday 1st March at 11.00am
SOMEONE'S GUITAR

Further information and advice available from our boys.

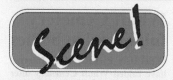

Twenty-one piece rap collective return as duo

Something familiar, something amusing, something for everyone, there's some comedy this week

Frankie, a well known Framley face, is hoping to tickle your funny bone "good and hard."
PHOTOSHOP BY RYAN STUBBLEFIELD

by Ursula Cloybeam

THE LAUGHING BULLET, Whoft's only comedy club will finally be reopened this Friday night after a protracted legal battle with Framley Borough Council Trading Standards ended in the horrific death of the main complainant.

And Frankie "Oh dear, are we crying now?" Hayes, the club's owner and compère, persuaded me in no uncertain terms that there's seven shades of fun to be kicked out of an evening at his new *Go On, Make Me A Laughter I Can't Refuse* show every Saturday night, and I'm certainly agreeing to write about it every week.

THREATENING NUTTER

"We're very excited about our opening night, aren't we, Ursula? Are you writing all of this down?" pointed out Frankie. "We've got a true star, Barrie Lyle, appearing on the main stage with what he's promised on his young son's life will be the best performance of his entire career."

Lyle opened for Jackie Mason during his Broadway run last year and whilst he received several Hollywood movie offers apparently he still needed to be reminded that he owed Frankie more than a few favours!

"Without me, Ursula, he'd be absolutely funning nowhere and if he ever treats me with that sort of disrespect again he'll certainly know which side his coffin is buttered on," he continued to scare me.

EIGHTEEN STITCHES

But don't be put off just because Lyle may be visibly shaking on the night. Frankie says that the *Puppetry of the Groin* section of Barrie's act will always go down a storm. From what Frankie told me, when Barrie asks for a couple of helpers from the audience, you should be prepared for some eye opening tricks with two safety pins and an elastic band.

And don't forget, if you're thinking of coming along on Friday that, by Frankie's popular demand, the Heckler's Gibbet will be operational from the moment the doors open.

And the moment that the doors open at the Gammon Way venue is 8pm. Tickets are priced at £10 or £8 for your dear old mum and can be booked in advance although woe betide you if you then fail to turn up.

cc this to Frankie for approval, would you, Stephanie?

by Adam Wrent

UP AND COMING local 21-piece rap collective The Christian Cross have relaunched themselves as a duo.

Leading lights of the self-promclaimed Soolin Liquid Beatz Bruthahood, The Christian Cross are Whoft's most popular crew, drawing crowds to their old-skool barn-parties and, in their words of one of their own songs, "keepin' it real from Whoft to the boundaries of St Eyot's churchyard."

The group's distinctive look, with clothes worn back-to-front and two days running, has sparked a craze amongst their fans, and forced several local launderettes to the brink of bankruptcy.

"It's all about unity and pulling together," said K-Rabbit, one of only two members to survive the brutal infighting that has decimated the group in the two weeks since their formation.

His partner, Mixmaster Timothy Bennett agreed. "Though many of our brothers have died in the course

The two remaining members of the group.
PHOTOSHOP BY STEPHANIE SCHLATER

of recording our demo, the message of our music is still 'Peace'."

The factional divisions within the group led to a clear "Eastside" and "Westside" split that had always threatened to erupt into murder. A series of tit-for-tat driveby poisonings in the past week was only the cherry on the cake of the violence that has driven the group to become smaller.

"Two members / is the way it's gonna be / goin' back to our roots / like Peters and Lee," rapped K-Rabbit to me, before looking suitably embarrassed.

The Christian Cross' first demo *Help Tha Police (With Their Enquiries)* is available by sending a cheque or postal order for £1.99 (made out to Mrs Bennett) to The SLBB, 27a Browning Crescent, Whoft, FM4 6PP.

THE DOIG
it's 80s week
at Framley's DOIG

MON	**BOBBY G'S DAVID VAN DAY'S BUCK'S FIZZ** Contains original member
TUE	**BAKER'S FIZZ** Contains original member
WED	**THE MIKE NOLAN SISTERS** They're in the mood for making their mind up
THU	**BUCH'S FFYZZ** Welsh tribute band
FRI	**DUCK'$ FI$$** Featuring Therese Bazaar
SAT	**BILL BERRY'S FIZZ** Ex - R.E.M.

Tickets £8 (Thursday £1.50) Full week ticket £25
167 The Bizzares, Framley. 01999 965543

Lorem ipsum dolor sit amet

LOREM IPSUM dolor sit amet, consetetur sadipscing elitr, sed diam nonumy eirmod tempor invidunt ut labore et dolore magna aliquyam erat, sed diam voluptua.

At vero eos et accusam et justo duo dolores et ea rebum. Stet clita kasd gubergren, no sea takimata sanctus est Lorem ipsum dolor sit amet.

Lorem ipsum dolor sit amet, consetetur sadipscing elitr, sed diam nonumy eirmod tempor invidunt ut labore et dolore magna aliquyam erat, sed diam voluptua. At vero eos et accusam et justo duo dolores et ea rebum.

Every Wednesday at
Budwigs
The
Exeter Textsetter --- -Sextet-------------
modern jazz tea dance fusion trio
12 noon – 11pm £2 entry
Basement of Saucy Pertwee's, Ipp Wharf

FRAMLEY PLAYERS
proudly present
"Waiting for Champion the Wonder Horse"
(en attendant champion le cheval merveilleux)
NEW PRODUCTION
Framley Pagoda
FROM FRIDAY
Box office 01999 873103
Circle £10, Stalls £15 Restricted view £25

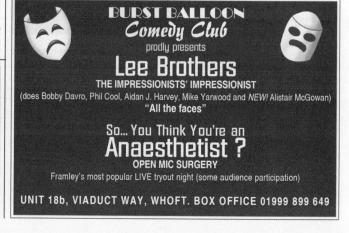

BURST BALLOON
Comedy Club
prodly presents
Lee Brothers
THE IMPRESSIONISTS' IMPRESSIONIST
(does Bobby Davro, Phil Cool, Aidan J. Harvey, Mike Yarwood and NEW! Alistair McGowan)
"All the faces"

So... You Think You're an
Anaesthetist ?
OPEN MIC SURGERY
Framley's most popular LIVE tryout night (some audience participation)

UNIT 18b, VIADUCT WAY, WHOFT. BOX OFFICE 01999 899 649

dredged the lake for four solid hours but only one of the trolley wheels and a bobble hat was recovered. A vote was unanimously passed that safety measures be reviewed before the next race.

Smashing

Interesting guest

GARDENING CLUB. – The speaker for the February meeting was the gardening correspondent of the *Whoft Sentinel*, The Amazing Dantini. The Amazing Dantini talked at length about the history of conjuring, showed overhead projector drawings of master magicians like Harry Houdini and David Nixon, and pulled a tulip bulb from behind the chairman's ear. Questions from the floor about gardening were dismissed, but some rings were made to link and unlink at will. As the appreciative members passed a unanimous vote of thanks, The Amazing Dantini had a bit of a cry.

Fracton

Just desserts

WOMEN'S INSTITUTE. -The meeting opened at 11.20am, and attendance records were taken. All were welcomed and a birthday kicking was administered to Mrs Jowett, Mrs Franklyn and Mrs Overboard. A plea of "mercy" was passed by 3 to 1. Next meeting on the 19th.

Litter discussed

FRACTON AND AREA LITTER WARDENS ASSOCIATION. – A meeting was held on Tuesday 4th at Lismond House under the chairman Leonard Flintlock. The following is a brief resume of what took place, although a full account of the minutes would blow your mind. Increased litter levels in Oscarwinninganimatornick Park were noted by the committee. The new bags were given out, with all members expressing their delight at the new logo. A vote was taken regarding the choice of refreshment for the next meeting, with Bacardi Breezers and Nik Naks being passed by 183 votes to 171. The secretary, Mrs Josephine LaPatapap, in her report, outlined the activities of the society during the year, highlighting those of special interest, such as the informative weekend spent trapped behind the curtains in August. The issue of hiring bands of alien mercenaries to help with the wardens' work was again brought up by committee member Mr Voules, but gained little support.

St Eyot's

The waste of a time

ST EYOT'S FRIENDS OF A GREEN. – Invited speaker, Frank Boseunit, gave an insightful presentation by explaining, in particularly graphic detail, how he recycled all of his own waste. After several members made their excuses and fainted, he went on to produce even more of his award-winning mucus. In retaliation, the committee

voted unanimously to present the speaker with an ice cream cone stuffed with handfuls of members' loose pubic hair. Mr Boseunit was finally forced to play his trump card – setting fire to his toenails. The evening was adjudged a huge success as Boseunit ran screaming towards the boating lake with great purpose.

Semi-skimmed

THE BROTHERHOOD OF CHRISTIAN MILKMEN. -The St Eyot's Dairy BOCM met at their monthly meeting in the monthly meeting hall of St Eyot's Dairy. The meeting was opened by chairmilkman Br Nicholas "Creamy" Simpson, and the minutes of the previous meeting were read. The power of the Lord was felt moving the table to discuss gold top orders in Welling Street, and prayers were taken for an increased natural yoghurt uptake in the northern districts. Br Galadriel Float witnessed to the love of Christ through his gift of the Dairylea Cheese Triangle, and showed slides. Truly, the assembled members were told, the Lord moves in a mysterious way, gently, at about six miles an hour under electric power, with a slight rattling sound, quite early in the morning, his wonders to perform. Prayers and milkshakes.

Codge

Well Adjusted

WELL GREEN RENOVATION GROUP. – The Well Green renovation has been attractively completed, but within a matter of days, despite the raising of the perimeter wall to 11 inches,

the new benching had been struck by a pigeon lime and the inverted cross was back. A motion proposing the addition of a twelfth inch was passed by 13 to 1, and it was suggested that a protective copper dome be constructed just under the sky, where pigeons live. A vote of 13 to 1 passed the motion that the inverted cross be removed by the Green Warden.

Bellaire

Appalling Acts

UNITED FELLOWHOOD CHURCH. – Members welcomed the Rev Timothy Lipschitz, from Christ's Church UFC in Framley, to lead their service. Timothy opened with the words, "The Lord is all I have, so I put my hope in him" and the hymn *And Did Those Feet In Ancient Times Walk Upon England's Mountains Green And Was The Holy Lamb Of God*. In his talk, Timothy said that he needed a ladder to see over such things as the World Trade Center, and was promptly arrested by police under the Prevention of Terrorism Act. As he struggled with armed officers and was bundled into the back of a car, he was shouting about the ladder in the dream of Jacob as described in the book of Genesis.

Slide Show

RENDEZVOUS. – On Wednesday, members and their wives were given a slide show entitled 'The Land of Chalk Drawings' presented by Rendezvous member David Frigg. He explained how he remembered visiting the land in the 1970s quite clearly, although he admitted it might just have been on the television.

Sponsored Bollocks

BELLAIRE PENSIONERS. – Bellaire's elderly residents took part in a Sponsored Bollocks this month. Entrants' speccialist subjects ranged from 'Why We'll Never Join The Common Market' and 'Here, Don't Tell Your Dad' to 'Even Doing Nothing Costs Too Bloody Much' and 'This New-fangled Running Water.' The event raised £380 towards new DJ decks at the Retired Persons Tea Dance.

Prince's Freshborough

A party

GRANDPARENTS, PARENTS AND TODDLERS FEDERATION. – The Grandparents, Parents and Toddlers Federation recognises that up to 100% of grandparents, parents and toddlers spend time with each other. Many grandparents care for their grandchildren while parents care for their parents (the grandparents) and their children (the grandchildren). The Grandparents, Parents and Toddlers Federation has funding to set up Grandparents, Parents and Toddlers Federations throughout the district, and is linking with the Toddlers, Tinkers, Tots and Pre-Tots Group that meets every year in the home of the Grandparents, Parents and Toddlers Federation, Grandparents, Parents and Toddlers Federation House in Molford. A party will be held on September 5th to try to decide the joint federations' purpose and a new name, as it is now unanimously agreed that The Grandparents, Parents, Toddlers, Tinkers, Tots and Pre-Tots Group Federation was too expensive to put on stationery. The party will also give everyone a chance to offer help to absolutely everyone else.

Slovenly

Namesake

ROTARY CLUB. – The Slovenly Rotarians were treated to an evening's entertaining anecdotes by guest speaker Stanley Lebor. In his delightful and lively address, 'Not THE Stanley Lebor!' he described some of the hilarious pitfalls of having the same name as a famous celebrity, the actor Stanley Lebor, who played Howard Hughes in the BBC TV Series *Ever Decreasing Circles*.

The big one

SLOVENLY SURVIVALISTS. – Mr Norris led an interesting discussion on tinned food and showed members his Armalite

What's on

MONDAY

The South Molford Players present 'An Evening in Wripple' by Adrain Showler, The Social Club, Molford St. Darren, 7.45pm. Tickets £5, concessions £3.50. Residents of Wripple are advised that they will find some scenes distasteful and consequently are asked not to attend.

TUESDAY

Barn Dance with Grand Funk Railroad, The Dressingham Memorial Hall, 7.30pm to 11pm. Tickets £7 including ploughman's breakfast and raffle entry (top prize - white label copy of the Rollo remix of GFR's *Time Machine*).

Keep-Fit for Good-Looking Frustrated Mature Ladies, The Hightower Rooms, Sockford, 3.30pm to 4.30pm. For further details contact Vince on 01999 480 086

WEDNESDAY

Lunchtime Recital with Malcolm Breach, violin, and Martin Ridgewell, Playstation2. Selections from Bruch, Fifa 2002 and Rodgers & Hammerstein 2002. St. Darren's Church, Molford, 1pm to 2.30pm, admission free but there is a savings-linked exit charge.

Story & Song Time, Adult Literature section, Framley County Library, 10am to 12pm. Hosted by Suzi DD, an occasion for all the family men, strictly no audience participation.

THURSDAY

Quiz Night, teams of up to 2-82 people. Entry fee £3 per person, answers available beforehand at £5 each, £2 the day after. The Naked Landlord, Big Godley, tel 01999 722693.

FRIDAY

'From Explosive Anger to Inner Peace for a short time and then right back to Full-Blown Rage', Troy Griffiths shares 20 years of intermittently successful research into controlling his temper around the wife & kids. Sockford Mill, Sockford Green, 7.30pm, wear loose clothing.

Charity coffee morning in aid of Robert Mugabe's election fund, the grounds of Wensleydate Manor, 11am to 1pm. Bring your own damn coffee.

SATURDAY

Fundraising sale, Framley Wildlife Reserve Visitor Centre, 10am-4pm, Thu. Many rare birds eggs, otter teeth, commemorative stuffed and mounted endangered species from our own wetlands.

FOCUS ON... BATLEY

with Katie Blirdsnest

This week in our weekly A-X of Framley District Councils, we reach B, and that's for Batley!

Batley is one of Framley's most deprived neighbourhoods, and home to the notorious Dungeon sink estate, but that doesn't seem to get the locals down!

We sent our roving reporters to bring us the skinny on the Framley district with the fastest growing population in the Northern Hemisphere! And that must be something to SHOUT about, probably!

FOCUS ON FACTS
Dungeon

In Dungeon, you're never more than 30 feet from a social worker.

The number of pupils shot in the head by staff at Dungeon Infant School has fallen for 2 out of the previous 3 years.

Due to repeated incidents, local pub The Drink & Drive has had all glass removed "by police request". Window panes have been put into storage and beer is poured straight into customers' cupped hands.

Dungeon was built on an ancient Indian burial ground.

The estate was opened by Enoch Powell in 1964 and made the headlines in 1987 when Princess Diana visited the new Community Centre and was not attacked.

Every single home in Dungeon is broken into every single night, often, police believe, by the same man; a burglar dressed as a different burglar.

Dungeon has more single fathers than there are grains of sand in the mighty desert.

Residents of neighbouring estates have complained about the level of noise on the Dungeon Estate caused by Dungeon residents complaining about the level of noise on the estate.

A CRY FOR THE HELP

THE TREE, which Batley Council installed two weeks ago in an attempt to brighten up the Dungeon Estate, committed suicide on Tuesday by felling itself. Stump psychologists believe the felling to have been a cry for help. The Council is next proposing to erect a CoffeeStop on the site, where residents will be able to enjoy a wide range of executive business breakfast options and a shiatsu sausage.

PHOTOGRAPH BY JEREMY OW

Whores' plumbing "all messed up"

THERE WERE FRESH calls

One of the popular calling cards, swapped with a child by our reporter.

yesterday for the authorities to act to introduce legislation to attempt to begin to encourage moves to start to curb the activities of prostitutes operating on the Dungeon Estate, writes one of our writers.

The Framley District Plumbers guild, who are the main movers behind the new demands, are up in arms, citing the level and number of services being offered by enterprising streetmadams.

"No-one minds the ladies of the night earning an honest crust, but there are some things they are simply not qualified to do, like bleed radiators or service a boiler," said Grand Plumber Christopher Testquardc. "We want to stress to the public that, should you find a build up of waste matter in your outflow pipe, please call a certified plumber, not a tart."

But local residents think the prostitutes are merely plugging a gap in the markets.

"I waited four months for a registered plumbist to fix my storage tank," said one smiling local homeowner, "but a quick call to a number I found in a phone box got me a whore with an adjustable spanner, who not only did an excellent job in under an hour, but took it in the gob. And swallowed too."

And it's not just plumbing! According to delirious residents, the women of easy virtue are doing everything from babysitting to satellite television installation, all alongside their usual excellent work up trap two. Plumbers are furious.

"We could try and claw back some of the ground we've lost, but there are some things my members just won't do," shrugged Mr Testquardc, and hung up. Click!

If you require a prostitute, call our 24 hr helpdesk on 01999 854 766.

NEXT WEEK
we turn our focus to
CHUTNEY
(beginning with C)

Joyrider bother

YOUNG HOOLIGANS from the Dungeon estate, some as old as fourteen, have been crying havoc and letting slip the dogs of joyriding!

Car theft has always been a problem on the estate, but gangs of teenages have now begun welding the stolen vehicles together to make one big car, which they then race around the streets, keeping residents awake at all hours of the day and all of the night.

Annoyed residents have told police of a car the size of a cross-channel ferry looming out of the fog at them, shattering windows with a single blast on its massive horn, then vanishing into the night as quickly as it appeared. The car, which is crewed by up to eighty joyriders, rips up pavements and eats postboxes as if they were Shredded Wheat Bitesize. Although officers have searched several lockup garages for the enormous car, they have only found a skateboard and some old paint with a stick in it.

"They'll soon get bored of it, they always do," said community liaison officer PC Mary Pleistocene. "Last year all we had were complaints about the kids stealing lampposts to play 'Street Snooker', now there's this big car. Until a third person is killed, it won't be high on our list of priorities."

Playground vandaled

A PENSIONERS' playground on the Dungeon estate has been vandalised by rioting children, who sprayed the word "bum" on the side of the slide then set it all on fire with their tiny children's torches.

The children had rioted after their last remaining play area was eaten by Wolves.

Former midfield dynamo and England international the late Billy Wright was unavailable for comment yesterday, though chairman Sir Jack Hayward has issued a formal apology.

PARKINSON'S
TATTOOING AND BODY ART
of Dungeon
ANIMATED TATTOOS
HAIR PIERCING
BODY EXTENSIONS
YOUR FACE TATTOOED 1/4" TO THE RIGHT OF YOUR ACTUAL FACE

TUESDAY NIGHTS SPECIAL :
PIERCINGS & TATTOOS
BY JEFF, OUR TRAINEE AT
SPECIAL DISCOUNT RATES
Ears £1, Genitals £1.50p,
Tattoos £4, or £30 for ten.

14, Tennyson Dungeon, Dungeon, FM16
01999 874 444 No more firemen.

Zoo arrival nerves

by Pharaoh Clutchstraw

STAFF AT FRAMLEY ZOO are keeping their fingers crossed for a historic new arrival this spring. For the fifth year in succession, veterinary experts are trying to persuade two zookeepers to breed successfully in captivity.

Zookeepers *(bestiarius vulgaris)* are an endangered species, their numbers in the wild having dwingled to around 1000 globally, with perhaps another approximate 110 in possible captivity maybe.

"They're notoriously shy creatures," explained Breeding Committee chief Danny Vemble in his broad Australian brogue, "and although they're not without charisma, they do prefer to sit around eating for twelve hours a day, which isn't very horny."

Zookeepers mate between March and May, and predicting the female's fertile period remains a frustratingly elusive challenge.

"We test for raised levels of oestrus in the female zookeeper," explained Vemble, "but the mating period only lasts three days, so we have to be as accurate as someone trying to land a cut-glass jumbo jet on a grain of rice.

IT GETS WORSE

"And the real danger is if we

Look at the penguin.

PHOTOGRAPH BY INSERAT BONT

introduce the female to the male too early, because they end up fighting over the bamboo buffet or kicking the daylights out of the staff toilets."

The pair, Xiao Lin and Bun Hat, were first introduced to each other six years ago. Xiao Lin is on long term loan from Ueno Zoo in Szechuan, and Bun Hat was one of three cubs born to a pair of zookeepers from San Diego Zoo in 1972.

There were concerns at the time that, because the father of Bun Hat was The Man From The Elephant House, their birth-line may have been weakened, but he has since sired three other offspring, one in the wild, so the team from Framley have little doubt about the fertility of their prize specimen.

THEN

Mr Vemble showed me pictures of Bun Hat's visible arousal, which were fascinating, if uncomfortable, and explained how zookeepers communicate by scent released from glands under their peaked caps. He then showed me further pictures of genitalia, and commented on the similarities between the "undercarriage" of a male Red Zookeeper and the "Sunday lunch" of a Giant Zookeeper.

"We'll know if we've been successful by July," concluded Mr Vemble. "Look at the Xmas stocking on that one!"

Woman shrugs and drives off after being killed

A woman shrugged her shoulders and drove off after being killed as she attempted to reverse her car into her kitchen, a court was told.

Pamomile Kilter, 41, of Kidney Bean Passage, Whoft, posthumously admitted driving without much care and attention and failing to submit to a breath test after the crash at a car park in Wripple. Kilter was fined £200 with £55 costs and had her licence endorsed with points.

Hunt for right bugger

Police are looking for a man who broke into Stapney's Nudist Supplies in Codge on Tuesday. The man, described as a "right bugger", stole a marble statue of a bear and four copies of *Exchange and Mart*.

The public are being warned not to approach the man, who is also wanted in connection with the theft of a matelot's costume from Pegg's The Chemist and the removal of the colour violet from the Sockford Reservoir rainbow.

Murder amnesty

Feb 14th has a special significance this year – it's being declared a controversial Murder Amnesty day, when murderers can freely declare themselves to anyone who likes being murdered. What have I got to do to get sacked? Love, Damiun.

DAFFODILS CAN KILL

FIT AN ALARM *TODAY*

If you already have a daffodil alarm
CHECK THE BATTERIES

Issued by Framley Borough Council Department of Health & Safety

---

Man, 78, sees own reflection for first time

ALBERTON BEASTMASTER, a retired monogamist from St Eyot's, had the shock of his life last Wednesday when he caught sight of his reflection for the very first time in his life.

"I'd just left the chemists, having bought a lollipop and some Bonjela. There was a noise behind me – I later discovered it was a moth – so I turned round, and, bless my soul, there was another me, still inside the shop."

Mr Beastmaster attempted to leave

Rev Beastmaster

the shop again, but "it turned out to be impossible. I couldn't work out what was going on."

"It was like I had an identical twin, mocking my every move – but an identical twin who looked nothing like me."

Alberton, whose only previous encounter with his appearance was through a photograph of himself taken in 1951, is having a great deal of trouble coming to terms with the collapse of his face over the last fifty years.

"I didn't know it was me at first. I mean, I never had this stupid haircut before, and loads more teeth, and I was on a donkey. What in God's name is going on?"

Vernon Tutbury, senior lecturer in Physics at Framley Community College said Mr Beastmaster's reflection wasn't likely to be a one off.

"Everyone has a reflection, it just depends what you're standing in front of. You will see your reflection quite clearly in the highly polished surface of my silver shoes, for example, while your reflection in a brick wall is very dim indeed."

Mr Beastmaster says he will be staying indoors from now on, near some cloth.

VANDAL ATTACK ON 'OLD PERCY'

By BUNCO BOOTH

MINDLESS vandal no-do-wells have added a saucy 30-metre tall figure around Chutney Hill's famous ancient chalk phallus.

The original Anglo Saxon cock, the only one of its kind in the whole wide world, is generally thought to have been discovered in 1952 by a passing lawnmower.

The addition to the turf penis, or 'Old Percy' as locals have been known to call it, was executed in white paint late on Saturday evening.

Local archeologists believe that the jubilatory gentleman may have been added by beer lags as part of an ancient booze ritual.

Robert Hilfiger of Whoft Archaeological Society, who's an expert on these things, appeared horrified by the addition.

"The sick individuals responsible for this are the scum of the earth. They're not fit to lick the shoes off my feet"

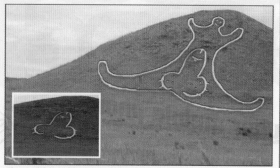

The vandals' work and the original figure (inset)

PHOTOGRAPH BY WILMINGTON LONGMAN

A local parent is also worried. Worried about the effect that the hill figure could have on her children.

"Everyone loved 'Old Percy', but this is pure filth.", said she. "It leaves nothing to the imagination. Imagine if one of my own saw it and tried to copy it?"

Not everyone is annoyed at the recent appearance of the paint man, however. Trevor St Saint, an upstanding member of Chutney parish seemed pleased by its presence.

"It's fantastic", he said gesturing at me using fingers thick with white paint, "It was only a matter of time before someone revealed the joyous owner of this god-like nob"

Mr St. Saint went on to suggest that in a matter of weeks, hundreds of chalk offspring could appear on surrounding hills, bowling greens and perhaps even on the walls of municipal buildings.

"Now that Old Percy has been given arms, legs and the wherewithal to walk, it's entirely possible that he may attempt to make congress with the prehistoric chalk vagina on the other side of the hill."

Drugs star in rock charge

by CHALLENGER PUTNEY

Local celebrity Leon Orbit, former rock guitarist with the former rock group Deaf Horse, is spending some time in the company of the police after a raid at his home in Wripple.

Following an anonymous tip-off from a local magistrate, a search warrant was issued and fourteen uniform officers arrived at Shangri-La-De-Da, Orbit's luxury 9-bedroom bungalow, in the early hours of Saturday afternoon.

They seized an extremely large quantity of illegal substances including canasta, purple parliaments, methamphethamphethameths, hundreds and thousands, and several bottles of barbarbarans.

They also took away scales, mirrors, rolling pins, bungs, exhaust pipes, children's socks, birthday cards, needles, thread, two boxes of non-safety matches, a Ladyshave and a copy of the Reader's Digest Book of Herbs. Oh, and they rolled up his lawn and took it away for analysis.

Mr Orbit denies absolutely anything.

Looking for books about smell?

THIS WEEK'S BESTSELLING TITLES

1. THE SOUND OF PEPPER by Martin Rash £7.99
2. YOU'VE BEEN WITH ANOTHER WOMAN by Lesley Shite £6.99
3. THE PENGUIN BOOK OF AFTERSHAVES by Zanzibar Orlando £12.99
4. ORANGE IS NOT THE ONLY SMELL by Janet Lesbrian £5.99
5. I'D LEAVE IT FIVE MINUTES BEFORE GOING IN IF I WERE YOU by Greg Yoffy £7.99
6. THE MEAT AT THE BACK OF THE FREEZER COOKBOOK by Easel Quilliot £17.99
7. A FAREWELL TO ARMPITS by Pugil Macho £4.99
8. TIGER FEET (sheet music) by Mud £3.75

The complete scratch n sniff Encyclopedia Britannica £300 – OUT NOVEMBER 8 – TAKING ORDERS NOW

LEONARD FRAGRANT & SONS, BOOKSELLERS
34, Iolanthe Street, Effing Sodbury 01999 711 973

Codge vicar suspended

A VICAR from Codge has been suspended after an investigation into his activities revealed he ought to be suspended, a conclusion reached after an investigation proved this to be the case.

The Reverend Easy-Peasy Carlton, 61, has been stripped of his dog collar and ordered to "become an ironmonger or something" by the General Synod of the Church of England, the standard punishment for clerical misdemeanour.

Although details of the activities that led to his suspension are hazy, parishioners suspect his practice of "riding" the bells during Sunday services may have been a factor.

"He'd clamber onto the 12-3-21 Tenor bell, over the bearing, and across the gudgeon, onto the headstock, wrap his legs around the sound bow, and read his sermon from there, swinging back and forth," said one churchgoer confusing me completely with too much information about bells.

The Right Reverend Gussard Prime, Bishop of Framley, was "horrified" by tales of Rev Carlton's activities.

"This is the sort of behaviour that would have God turning in his grave," the Bishop said.

SECONDARY SCHOOL ADMISSIONS **SEPTEMBER 2003**

MAKE SURE THEY'RE HOME BY SIX
Educational year 2003/4

Framley Borough Council

Will your child be starting secondary school this September?

If the answer is yes then you should have received a brochure entitled *'Make Sure That They're Home By Six'*. This contains important information about not letting your child hang around outside McDonalds intimidating bearded single men and tells you how to dissuade them from drinking too many Bacardi Breezers in Bay 9 at Framley Bus Station.

If you have not received this brochure then ask your child's primary school and telephone the police. They're probably out raping a war veteran as you read this.

Framley Borough Council 01999 988119

WHOFT ANTIQUE PEANUT FAYRE

CHEWY HALL

DRY LANE

SUNDAY 31st JUNE
Adults £1.00
Children £3.00
Cats and Dogs £5.00

Keep On Munchin!

Adults £1.00!

The Original and Best Peanut Auction Company
01999-544628

Arts Scene

THE DOIG

MONDAY

Battle of the Dance Troupes!
INTERPRETING THE HITS OF 1983...
TO THE DEATH!

BETTY BOOTHROYD'S
HOT CUSTARD
From TV's Kenny Everett Show
- VS -
PAM FERRIS'S DARLIN' BUDS
Contains original member

TUESDAY
CAPTAIN BEAKY & HIS MAGIC BAND
Avant-jazz blues poetry

WEDNESDAY
JOEY DEACON, BEAKER, Mr MEAKER & LITTLE TICH
Unorthodox 1960s chart-toppers

THURSDAY
LLYVYL 42
Welsh tribute band

FRIDAY
THE AUSTRALIAN DUDLEY MOORE TRIO
Just like the real thing

SATURDAY 'N' SUNDAY
STEPPES
Ukrainian Steps tribute act

Tickets £6 or £9.50 with free sandwich
167 The Bizzares, Framley. 01999 965543

I come to bury school production not to praise it

Julius Caesar
St Gahan's School, Framley

by Ursula Cloybeam

NO WORDS OF MINE can adequately describe the shambles masquerading as a production of *Julius Caesar*, that was presented to an audience of about a hundred snoring people at St Gahan's School last Saturday evening. But I'm going to try to try to convey it as best as I can.

This was supposed to be the swansong of retiring Head of Drama, Colin Frilly, and certainly bore comparison with what he apparently considers the fine work that he has been produced at the school over the years.

UNMITIGATED BALLS

As in so many school productions, cast members were practically inaudible and mumbled their speeches – in sharp contrast to this reviewer, whose excellently projected criticisms were shouted at the stage with considerable vigour and clarity.

The cast and scenery included Martin Ffooulkess in the lead role, whom was considered a controversial choice by this reviewer as he was significantly too young and too short and too ginger to play someone less like a schoolboy than Julius Caesar than could be imagined by this reviewer.

I understand that Mr Ffooulkkess harbours some desire to become a professional actor one day. On this showing, I would advise him to pay a swift visit to his careers Advisor for extra car park attendant lessons, and believe me if there's anything I know about, I know about acting! And music was composed and performed by (mosaic teacher?) David Daddy.

HOPELESS CRETINS

Also appearing were Barry de Lemon as an immature Brutus, Denny Bin as an underage Cassius, Martin Ffooulkess doubling up as an underdeveloped ginger man in a dress called Calphurnia, and Mark Anthony in an unimpressive debut as Nathan Haircut.

The audience were little help at all and refused to join in either my rousing chants of "Ceasar, he's behind you!" or "the director's a wanker", both of which are usually considieried a highlight of any Frilly show.

BRILLIANT AEROPLANE

However, things improved after I made a paper aeroplane from my programme to repeatedly throw at the actors. The little dance I did every time I went up to retrieve it certainly livened things up onstage, and I was beset by parents during the interval eager to speak to me about it. (Does anyone know how to get orange squash and biscuit stains out of a cream polyester blouse?)

Then the second bit of the play got underway and I had to start humming again to keep from falling asleep.

STUPID COLIN

There were tears aplenty after the final curtain as Mr Frilly was called upon to give a farewell speech to the strangely upset cast. As they consoled each other, it fell to the many former pupils, who had foolishly attended the

Barry de Lemon as Brutus confronts Elizabeth Nounce as Fagin in this unengaging production.
PHOTOGRAPH BY JEREMY FONZ

final night of Colin's godawful final production, to escort me from the hall into the waiting police van.

After what has to be described as a wasted evening for all concerned, I can only repeat what I said to the arresting officer, and hope that new head of drama, Burton Touche, has considerably more joy than stupid Colin did with the empty pool of talent that St Gahan's School has to offer! Stupid Colin!

URSULA'S VERDICT: Shit

POP JACK'S

NEW RELEASE

BETH ORVILLE   £12.99

Stop Going On And On About School Fees And Trust Funds And Noisily Pushing Your Langustine Around The Plate, It Took Me Ages To Record This Album And You're Not Even Listening To It, You Bastards

COLIN PHILLIPS
No Album Requested
£13.99

McALMONT & BUTTHEAD
The Sound of
£10.99

NIRVANANANA
Na Na Hey Hey Bang Goodbye
£12.99

PINK KEITH
A Distant Scraping Of Barrels
£17.99

CLEARLY MINGE
Can't Get Your Lycra Pants Out Of My Head
£2.99

CHLAMYDIA 69
I Have Control Issues With My Parents
£12.99

POP JACK'S RECORDS & TAPES 01999 858 856
487, Monopoly Parade, Arnhem Centre, Framley

I just hit paydirt

By our Blues Correspondent, GEECHIE WRYLY

DADDY BEAT me as a kiddy. Daddy used to beat me. Got myself a brand new rifle. Gonna draw a bead on him.

Oh Lord won't you help me save my Daddy's farm? Oh Lord won't you send me one last kind word? My sister got sick and I'm stinging from the weals. Got a tin of a tobacco and a blade to hawk.

My bones is dry. Them horses is whinnying.

I'm going up to the red barn with a ax. I just hit paydirt.

Next week: Where's my Jesus now?

ST EYOT'S RAILWAY CENTRE

MAY DAY WEEKEND

GRAND STEAM FAIR

♦ Many visiting engines
♦ Fairground organ
♦ Rowenta iron display
♦ Kettle rides
♦ Children's pressure cooker
♦ Special attraction "A Good Hot Bath"

Open 10.30am-11.00am. Last entry 4.30pm.
Adults £8. Children from £5. Senior citizens banned.

Recorded information service 01999 655355
Chff-chff-chff! 07999 400626
Binnington Road, Binnington, St Eyot's.

Reader annoyed about something

MISS, -- Regarding the alleged 'Wishing Well' on Sockford Green.

I have been using this 'well' regularly for over eleven years, and yet I still haven't sprouted wings, or had an everlasting dinner with Lorraine Kelly.

How much is that to ask?.

MRS RENARDIE GRALEFRIT
Wishing Well Cottage
Sockford Green
Sockford

Sponsored event raises £470

MISS, -- On behalf of Batley Safehouse, I'd like to thank the clear majority who supported our Sponsored Spend last month.

After twelve long hours in The Arnhem Centre, we had raised well over £469, and managed to spend a magnificent total of £33,000. Although this was sadly short of our intended target of £50,000, we feel the whole event was still a roaring success nonethenevertheless.

Well done, everyone!

Our next event will be the auctioning of the 26,000 loaves of bread and 1052 shirts we now have blocking our hall.

TANSAD PARIAH
Batley Safehouse,
255 cummings Dungeon
Dungeon Estate, Batley FM6

Everyone's rubbish

MISS, -- People say things always come in threes, but I'd be hard pushed to agree. What on earth can they be talking about?

Since Framley Council contracted out refuse collection to Pegasus Disposal at the end of November, my front lounge has been full of bins.

Apparently my home was reclassified from a 'collection point' to a 'delivery point' in the administrative changeover.

I have written to Mayor D'Ainty on several occasions, but he insists that nothing can be done until I provide over 15,000 photos of the dustmen responsible.

So can I have a Framley Examiner mug (Botham)?

RON OSCALATOR
Duncannorvellin', St Eyot's

What about my children?

MISS, -- I was distressed to hear that they intend to close the Gypsy House at Framley Zoo, apparently because of "human rights concerns".

I have to ask, if the Gypsy House closes, where will my children ever see Gypsies in their natural habitat, dancing and playing their caravans? Through the television?

It's political correctness gone mad!

TIMOTHY RUHR
Monk's Hoover,
Whoft

Gives her side of the story

MISS, -- I wish to complain about the tone of your coverage of my visit to the chemist's last Wednesday ("How Many Plasters Does She Need?" FE1709).

Usually your standards of journalism are of the highest. Your story about my reversing into a parking space on Denegate was a model of clarity and restraint, and the supplement on my new trousers was not only well-designed but informative and fun.

But in the case of the chemist visit story, you let yourselves down badly. I did not put my hands on my hips by the War Memorial, and the Zovirax was not £2.99, but £3.45.

JOAN TWEED
Lissop Cottage, Creme

For the latest on Joan Tweed, see main feature page 7, and 'Comment' on page 42.

Sad news isn't it about hog

MISS, -- Your readers may be sad to hear of the death of Lazenby, Framley's Biggest Hedgehog.

He had been ill for some time with prickleworm, but was making a recovery, until the unfortunate incident at St Eyot's Steam Fair on Sunday.

His tireless work for charity will not be forgotten, and a special children's ward will bear his name in memory of the many ill children he made happy and itch.

He is survived by a wife, Eleanor, and 76 hoglets.

MARGARET HELFPUL
Millbury Mollymandeigh

This is madness

MISS, -- I am absolutely furious.

In 1959, after happily using my address for many years, I was informed that it needed to be extended, by the addition of a 'postcode' (FM4 6TY) at the bottom, just below where I live.

Naturally, I protested, setting fire to the Post Office counter at the Spar on forty-six separate occasions, until the police intervened and I was finally forced to accept this ludicrous situation.

Little did I imagine that, shortly after moving house in 1999, and having had new stationery printed at great expense, I would be told that we were back at square one – my postcode had been *changed* – to FM9 1RE, of all things.

What the hell is going on? There was nothing wrong with the old one, and it had served me well for 40 years. Apparently, the powers that be had given *my* postcode to someone else!

How much red tape have I got to eat in this day and age?

I'm sure many of your listeners will feel the same way, and would love to join my campaign to bring back my postcode.

COLONEL JACK "HAPPY" ISTAMBUL, DFSC (Ret)
The FM4 6TY Campaign
96, Chocolate Spiral
Fracton
FM9 1RE (née FM4 6TY)

She must of known

MISS, -- It's been said before, but I of to agree with your front page last week.

She must of known.

DR ALCOCK BROWN
Roy Newby Villas
Molford

Help me find my old pals!

MISS, -- I wonder if you can help me track down some old chums?

I was in the Whoft Blackshirts from 1935-7, and wish to get in contact with any old boys.

If enough people get in touch, I'd love to organise a traditional cockney open-air barbecue, so we could celebrate my release after 65 years of internment. It'd be great to meet up with the lads, and, who knows, maybe re-enact some old memories.

SPODELEY ARTHRITICLE
196 Tazo Collection Terrace
Massingborough Boxjunction
Whoft
FM3 6TT

Quotes of the Week

"Young people love very old people and we're giving them all a chance to see how it's done."

"We have no recollection of Mr Nugent's letter and won't be doing anything about the sky."

"This is a fantastic opportunity for the people of Framley to see my new bike."

"I know it sounds unbelievable but every single dinner lady is outside."

"That's not my bike."

"A single feather from this bird can take your arm clean off, so we're closing the park."

"Have you done the Quotes of the Week yet, Trish?"

"The boy's definitely got a future at this club, if he can just stop scoring so many goals."

"We are interested in talking to anyone else who may have been inside the barrel at the time."

Letters should be kept as brief as possible, and preferably be about something. Please include a name, an age, an address, your daytime phone number, and preferred size of Framley Examiner mug (regular, medium, standard or Botham). No correspondence will be entered into, and the judge's decision is final. In the event of a tie, the winner will need two clear legs advantage. Letters should be sent as quickly as possible. No cash. Why not send us letters to THE FRAMLEY EXAMINER, Unit 149b, East Cosset Industrial Park, Parkfields Bypass, Framley FR1 6LH ?

EMERGENCY SERVICES

CHEMISTS
The following chemists are opened on Sundays and in the middles of nights.

BILL'S PILLS 14, The Runs, Molford
WRIPPLE VETIVERS herbal apothecary (elixirs and balms to soothe and succour) The Old Lodge, Gibbet Lane, Wripple
SQUIRE PUFF'S OPIUM DEN Gentleman's club. Finest snuff in Christendom, D--- you! By invitation.
MIKE (07999 965544) outside The Warm Zippy. Crack, speed and speed II.
JACK TAR'S SAILOR'S REMEDY ground cuttlefish, soluble seahorse, wifestoppers and everlasting gumplops. Shed 8, Fracton docks.
WHOFT HOSPICE RADIO AMBULANCE Call Tenby or The Colonel on 01999 866566
BARON SAMEDI'S HAITIIAN CHEMIST for love, for money. Wripple churchyard.
LIBRARIAN WITH HEADACHE CHEMIST librarians with headaches ONLY. Unit 18a, Sockford Smelting Works, Sockford.
DUNGEON PHARMACY only armed chemists in Framley, twin 18mm tills in cupola, barbed wire Lemsip display. Passports must be shown and customers MUST be accompanied by a policeman. 6 Tennyson Dungeon, Batley.
FAT TRISTRAM'S The Best Deal In Town. This joint's always jumpin'. Lock-in Fridays. Upstairs nightly at the County Records Office.

DENTIST
In event of dental emergency after 9pm, an emergency drill and mouthwash are kept behind the saloon bar of The Coach & Woody Boyd public house, Wripple.

FIREMEN
The Framley Fire Service is available on 01999 827 1947 (during office hours, except religious holidays).

POLICE
The relief police force covering this Wednesday and Thursday evening will be The Sockford Aeromodelling Society.

OFF-LICENCES
The following off-licences are open illegally in the tiny hours to serve the extremely thirsty.
ST TRUDE-IN-THE-FIELDS CHURCH Chest NCP CARPARK KIOSK 8 Meaker St, Molford
THRESHER'S Arnhem Centre, Framley

M*A*S*H UNITS
The following M*A*S*H units are operating all night: **4077th** and **853rd**. That is all.

RECORDER LESSONS
ADRIENNE WOODGATE Please, genuine emergencies only. 07999 977754.

PUPPETS
Late night puppets on duty between 11pm and 6am are Alan Tracy and Edd The Duck

RELIGIOUS SERVICES

Kick off at 3 o'clock unless otherwise stated.

PENGUIN CAFE BAPTISTS Worshipping Simon Jeffes through parping and beeping since 1997. Whoft.

MOLFORD FREE CHURCH rejecting the papist conspiracy and regular jumble sales. Whoft.

ST MOSSAD'S REFORMED CHURCH counter espionage, light weapon training, carols. Whoft.

NEWBY'S PENTECOSTAL (State) Be baptised and enjoy attractive discounts on sausages, ornamental swans and Vim. Molford.

POPEYE ECUMENICAL CHURCH Setsk sail every weeksk at four pm Sunday. Well, waddya know? Whoft.

CHAPEL OF OUR LADY OLIVE OYL Closed for refurbishment. Reopening October as *Swee'Pea's Late Nite Chemises*. Whoft.

FOURTH BROTHERHOOD OF SLACKERS Meeting probably Thursdays. Whoft.

THE BOWLER HATS Vesperal brotherhood. Matins 10am. Postmortems 2pm. Matinees Saturdays onlies. Whoft.

FELAFEL FELLOWSHIP now incorporating Kebabs For Christ and Bibleburgers. Whoft.

ST JUDAS IN THE MANGER Unconventional bible study. Whoft.

DOVETAIL PENTECOSTAL CHURCH symmetrical worship, shampoo and set. Whoft.

MAGIC CHRISTIAN FELLOWSHIP cutting a choirboy in half, linking Ringos etc. Whoft.

SECOND AND SEVENTH DAY ADVENTISTS Wednesdays and Thursdays good for anyone? Whoft.

ST PETER & THE WOLF Pastor D. Bowie on bassoon (as the narrator). Whoft.

SCHINDLER'S MOSQUE Whose idea was this? Whoft.

ST WHIPPY'S ICE CREAM VAN AND CHURCH Mind That Jesus! Whoft & environs.

PETER WEIR'S WITNESSES HALL Whoft.

THE WORSHIPFUL COMPANY OF ENTHUSIASTS YOUTH CLUB squash and snogs. Biscuit mornings Tuesday. Whoft.

ST MAUREEN OF AVILA NEW! Whoft.

AUSTRALIAN ORTHODOX CHURCH Fancy dress Thursdays. Whoft.

●*A.A. Gill is on holiday.*

TAKING YET ANOTHER TRIP DOWN MEMORY DRIVE

Class of 1932

with Arcady Belvedere
Framley's premiere historian

I WAS BORN IN 1909 – but I'm only as young as I feel! So, of course, I can remember the 1930s as if they were the 1970s.

Although I should rather say that I can remember some of it, not all. And I bet that you weren't even born at the time! I didn't live in Framley either.

But I do know what I like, and what I like is reading about the ancient people from history from the Framley district from the books in Framley District Library.

Just before the library closed last Thursday evening I stumbled across a very interesting piece of fact concerning the first Framley resident ever to appear on a television, which, in those days, we still called "the variety box".

NINETEEN THIRTY-2

I can't know if you remember a success-full quiz show of the time, called *The Early-Evening Frolic,* or any of the panellists that used to feature on it? Well, it ran from 1932 to 1932 and one of the regular guests was Sir Edward Elgar, then still one of this country's most respected and popular knights of the realm.

Sir Elgar was well-known for his irascible composing and grand old English temper and they combined to add a certain frisson to his numerous appearances which, of course, was why we all loved the old goat, bless him.

On the show, a panel of celebrities would have to guess the social class of a sequence of people from all over Britain, the answers to which were only revealed after much offence had been taken.

One of the contestants – Mrs Ethel Notton, a former debutante – was a Wripple resident of many years standing and that's why I'm writing this. On the night in questions, after Mrs Notton had completed round one by reciting the show's famous tongue-twister with a whelk in her mouth, Edward Elgar turned to Wallis Simpson, seated directly to his left, and, in that endearingly blunt way of his, described Mrs Notton as a "fat cow".

SYMPHONY

How the audience laughed but Sir Edward, realising that he had metaphorically stepped over an invisible line, offered Mrs Notton an immediate apology – by composing his second symphony on the spot and dedicating it to her.

Mrs Notton, 1932

It was a memorable night for Framley folk, and even though poor Ethel failed to beat the panel and win the submarine, she received the usual consolation prize: a "Plastic Bertram" – the show's smiling mascot. Her evening later ended in tragedy when lightning struck her eight times on the way home, the tin hat on the booby prize attracting lightning after lightning to the dashboard of her brand new open-topped car. She finally succumbed to her own death during the penultimate strike.

What a year!

HAD A TIGER OF A DAY?

...have you really??

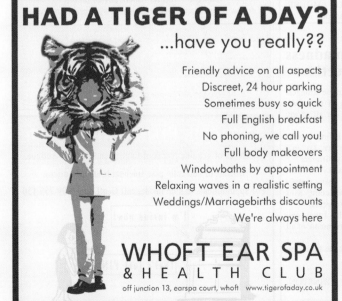

Friendly advice on all aspects
Discreet, 24 hour parking
Sometimes busy so quick
Full English breakfast
No phoning, we call you!
Full body makeovers
Windowbaths by appointment
Relaxing waves in a realistic setting
Weddings/Marriagebirths discounts
We're always here

WHOFT EAR SPA
& HEALTH CLUB

off junction 13, earspa court, whoft   www.tigerofaday.co.uk

50 years ago today
From the St Eyot's Flugel, 14th March 1952

ON THE ROUTE OF THE MARCH OF THE PROGRESS!

The denizens of St Eyot's and Whoft looked on agape as the Electric Age finally arrived this week.

Not that there was much to see, mind. A simple brick construction, technically termed a 'sub-station', was commissioned on Tuesday by local councillors.

"Looks like nothing so much as a windowless shed," observed one spectator, Mr Juff.

"Bully beef," quipped another.

How electricity works

The 'sub-station' contains a series of 'transformers' which channel electricity into the village from the its internal generator, a 2000 mega-ton atomic bomb. A single light-bulb on the roof of the sub-station indicates that Watts, Volts and Ampères are in rich supply!

However, representatives from Standard Telephones & Power say that demand for the new, clean energy source has so far been sluggish.

"It's early days yet," said Mr Greenhalgh for ST&P, "in fact, so far, this marvellous device is only powering the light-bulb atop the building. But we expect more interest once the hairdryer has been invented."

Traditionally, St Eyot's and Whoft have been lighted and heated by dung, although some local gentry employ hot, shiny peasants.

100 years from today

ITALY CAVES IN AT LAST

Italy has finally made assisted suicide finally legal.

The so-called AS law was first adopted by Britain in 2035, the same year that Sir Steve Coogan was assassinated, the Liberal Government made hanging illegal for the second time and Wimbledon was finally abandoned due to the country's heavy summer snow.

Italy has only agreed to pass the law, though, after decades of obstinance. Only last August street riots wrecked what was left of Venice before it all fell into the sea. In addition, the Italian Congress insists the AS law is "on a renewable short-term contract" and that only people who are already dead will have the right to be helped to a peaceful end.

Italy is the last Catholic stronghold in Europe. Latin is still a compulsory second language there, although the European Federation plans to challenge this, along with other accused "atrocities" (like Clapping Prayers – *Scicciccicicini* – and the continuing ban on marshmallows).

Elsewhere: where now for snooker?

FIRST BANANA

St Eyot's has finally seen its first real banana since before the war. The banana, which arrived in the village with great flourish on a velveted dray, is the purchase of local fruiterer Giles Molquhoun.

Molquhoun paid the princessly sum of £3 4s 6d for the yellow wonder from a contact at the Brazilian Embassy in London, which was later eaten.

Mr Molquhoun pronounced the banana "ba-na-na".

Tried everything? Then try

Bum Massage

in the comfort of your own home!

Relax as our expert, Vince, kneads and rubs your bum.

You'll feel like a new woman!

01999 480086

(sessions typically last 4 hours)

The Healing Power Of
SHOUTING

with Kathy Fraud

"Belief rather than technique"

Relax, de-stress, unwind and discover more about yourself through SHOUTING. Kathy Fraud will lead you gently through a sustained programme of shouting about your past and and help you open new wounds and unheal old ones.

Kathy Fraud MZCF
01999 728370

*Author of the bestselling
SOMETHING TO SHOUT ABOUT*

DO YOU REMEMBER...

HORSE JELLY AND CURTAIN PUDDING?

"TURN THAT LIGHT ON!" ?

HIDING FROM THE "COUGH POLICE"?

PAYING THE BUS DRIVER IN ACORNS & HAY?

WHEN MILK BOTTLES WERE MADE OF WOOD?

THE BEATLES WINNING THE WORLD CUP?

Then it's time to preserve those precious moments in a way that your grandchildren will be able to enjoy again and again and again...

FREE CLOCKS FOR THE OVER 70s

TURN YOUR LAST REMAINING MEMORIES INTO CRISPS

01999 963 371

FOCUS on
Robbie Nougat

Robbie stands prodly in front of the new £2.75m Blend AM transmitter.

PHOTOGRAPH BY CRAZYHORSE REDGRAVE

He's king of the air!

by Beaky Coxwain

YOU'D HAVE TO GET UP pretty early in the morning not to have heard of Framley's very own radio superstar Robbie Nougat.

The controversial DJ, who was sacked from local station Zephyr AM after a series of zany stunts and record-breaking absences certainly does things his own way, and his new dream project is no exception!

Because Robbie's started his very own station – Blend AM – and it's taking the airwaves by storm.

CARCINOGENIC MAST

Broadcasting from a 400 foot tall supertransmitter that cost Robbie every penny of his life's savings, Blend AM beams pure Nougat all over the Framley area, blocking out the Zephyr AM signal for a 60 mile radius and interfering with some emergency services too!

The transmitter – which is recognised by the United Nations as an offensive weapon – is sited in the playground of a local school and has been vital to the Blend AM success story – a story that has seen the new station become Framley's third most listened to sound (next to traffic and the boiler filling up).

50s, 70s, 80s, 90 & 92

Blend AM plays all your favourite tunes, promising its listeners "the very best of the 50s, 70s, 80s, 90 and 92". Robbie himself presents the top-rated "Breakfast Drivetime" programme every day from 4am-11am. The show is broadcast in the inimitable Nougat style from the driver's seat of Robbie's Mercedes SL55 on the hands-free set.

What's more, Robbie chooses the playlist himself, with most of the songs coming from his own personal collection of tapes in the boot.

So what better way to celebrate Framley's newest radio sensation than to take a look behind the scenes at the man who made it all probable, Robbie Nougat!

All about Robbie

ROBBIE NOUGAT'S career has always been dogged with cuntroversy. Although often in conflict with his bosses, his crazy stunts and no-nonsense style have made him one of the area's best-loved radio faces.

Robbie's shows are always shows with a difference. Whether it's boiling 13 eggs in a row, or sorting through his wallet live on air, you never know what he's going to do next.

This year, he famously took 7 months off after the death of John Thaw "out of respect" for the smooth-haired, silver-tongued actor-turned-hardman – a period which he now claims to have spent in Thailand taping the Bangkok Open Snooker Championships over his mother's collection of *Inspector Morse* videos.

But Robbie doesn't come cheap. His astronomical wage demands have made him the highest paid DJ in the country, and the fourth richest man in Europe.

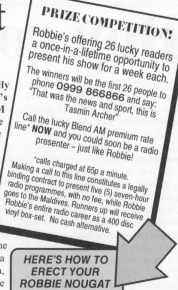

Robbie relaxes at home.
PHOTO BY CAPULET HOOB

Where it began...

ROBBIE got his first start initially as the breakfast DJ on Framley's previously top-rated Zephyr AM – home of the legendary "Teatime Twosome", Tenby and The Colonel, and Britain's forty-sixth most popular medium wave station.

Zephyr AM has existed in one form or another since the late 14th Century, and the breakfast presenter's job is a hereditary title. Usually it is passed to the first born son on the death of the father, however in a break with tradition, Robbie inherited the role while his father, Richard Coeur de Nougat was away fighting in the crusades.

His abdication from the position caused a constitutional crisis at the station, only resolved when Tenby and The Colonel stepped in to the breach, adopting the titles of breakfast presenter and breakfast presenter consort.

PRIZE COMPETITION!

Robbie's offering 26 lucky readers a once-in-a-lifetime opportunity to present his show for a week each.

The winners will be the first 26 people to phone **0999 866866** and say: "That was the news and sport, this is Tasmin Archer"

Call the lucky Blend AM premium rate line* **NOW** and you could soon be a radio presenter – just like Robbie!

*calls charged at 65p a minute.

Making a call to this line constitutes a legally binding contract to present five (5) seven-hour radio programmes, with no fee, while Robbie goes to the Maldives. Runners up will receive Robbie's entire radio career as a 400 disc vinyl box-set. No cash alternative.

HERE'S HOW TO ERECT YOUR ROBBIE NOUGAT FACT PYRAMID!

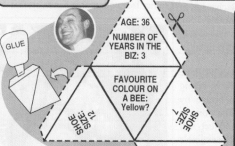

GLUE

AGE: 36

NUMBER OF YEARS IN THE BIZ: 3

FAVOURITE COLOUR ON A BEE: Yellow?

SHOE SIZE: 11½

SHOE SIZE: 7

blend a.m.
4AM – 11AM

HOT TOP TWENTY

here's robbie's top playlist this week

1. Tasmin Archer – Sleeping Satellite
2. Richard Marx – Hazard
3. Ugly Kid Joe – Everything About You
4. The bottom 14 of the 28/5/92 Top 40
5. A £2.99 Supertramp Greatest Hits tape
6. Teach Yourself Colloquial Spanish
7. Ce Ce Peniston – Keep On Walking
8. En Vogue – My Lovin'
9. Dictaphone 14 – Bank Letters
10. Dave Lee Travis Show 11/6/86 (20mins)
11. Some Fleetwood Mac-ish thing (?)
12. Shakespear's Sister – I Don't Care
13. Unlabelled tape
14. Jet Set Willy (Commodore 64 vsn)
15. Ron and Maggie's Xmas tape from Australia
16. Singles Going Steady (end chewed up)
17. Driving Tunes 6
18. Old Kevin Bloody Wilson tape from school
19. Robbie Nougat Zephyr Breakfast 2/9/01
20. Wilson Phillips – You Won't See Me Cry

blend a.m.

broadcasts a left and right signal on two parallel AM frequencies, bringing stereo to Medium Wave for the first time. Blend AM is best listened to on a pair of ROBERTS RADIOS radios from **ROBERTS RADIOS (01999 755 655)**

In Court

NATWEST Ovenglove, 28, of Magulliger Bottom, Framley, was bound over for ever and received a Chinese burn for punching a motorbike in the face outside The Warm Zippy public house on May 13.

JIGSAW Giant, 18, of Hitlerdale, Chutney, received a suspended burning at the stake for drinking while under the influence of alcohol on February 29.

MR JUSTICE Bitmap Johnson, QC, was fined a million gazillion pounds by a jury of eight year olds who didn't appear to understand the legal process at all, at St Cardigan's CofE Primary School last Wednesday last Thursday.

SEBASTIAN Finger, 35, of Beauty Parade, Molford, was jailed for seven weekends and denied access to his television remote control for driving with undue care and attention on April 3.

RATTIGAN Disney, 39, of Original Glade, Whoft, received 120 seconds community service for murdering his wife and three children. Magistrates said there were special reasons not to impose a custodial sentence, saying it would be excessive in view of Disney's duties and employment as a Home Secretary.

SUNRISE Smith, 31, of Chlamydiagate, Whoft, was fined £100 with £1 costs, but received £350,000 compensation due to a clerical error at Framley Magistrates Court on Wednesday.

PRINCE Schoolboy, 22, of The Alarm, Sockford, was fined six years' interest for inflating himself to the size of an ambulance and releasing radioactive gases outside Here Be Turnips on May 21.

AMANDA Childsniffer, 12, of Golliwog Prom, Whoft, was fined £5 with £3 costs for possessing enough pickled onions in her loft to make a 4.5kg vomit bomb.

Less than the warm welcome

by Adam Wrent

POLICE had to be called to a a a street in Chutney at the weekend after a fighting threatened to become a rioting.

Residents of Waxworm Reach took to the streets en masse at the weekend in protest at the arrival of a further dozen foreign asylum-seekers. Bricks were thrown and locals demanded the removal of the newcomers, the third immigrant family to move into the area in the last six months.

Ever since their country was torn apart by wars between rival fractions, immigrants seeking to escape the *trouble and strife* have been flooding into Britain at the rate of check this figure.

The displaced families, many of whom cannot speak English, are finding it difficult to integrate into their chosen communities. Chutney Social Services director, Concept Nicolas, pointed me that, because Waxworm Reach is predominately white, "the new red, yellow, mauve and green faces are easy targets" for a well-deserved punch in the head.

Amid cries of "send them back" and the throwing of pots, the twelve migrants were escorted from their flat. They were then taken to Chutney Police Station for their own safety, where they were given toast and custard.

"They're trouble," said one bigot [>flag: LEGAL. Ed.].

"This used to be a niceneighbourhood."

And, you know what? The violence isn't just coming from people who belong here, either. In Batley, where most of the immigrants have washed up, the refugee community is dangerously split along tribal lines.

A household of twenty-eight green refugees was deported home last week after they pleaded sorry for burning a maisonette full of yellow ones to the ground.

A spokesfax from Framley's immigration department yesterday read, "we make every effort to welcome new arrivals to the area, and see that they settle and integrate comfortably into Chutney. We are

Look at the little bleeder, waving like an Englishman.
PHOTO BY BALLIOL SASQUATCH

horrified by the events of the weekend, but shit happens."

The Framley Examiner is pleased to announce it will again be sponsoring next Wednesday's anti-immigrant riots. Come along and bring a bottle.

Man attacked by nerds

BRAVE Stanley Poubelle was last night recovering in Framley General Hospital after being attacked in Shirtshrift Street on Saturday night by a gang of nerds.

Umemployed builder Stan, 56, said he felt lucky to be "alive, and" appealed to Framley Examiner readers to help apprehend his culprits.

"I was a-strolling home from the pub," he went, "and all of a sudden I sees these six nerds on the other side of the street, whereupon they laid into me, like. It was with words at first, you see."

After berating their terrified victim for not knowing that the atomic number of Iridium was 77, the nerds ran across the road. One of them was heard to shout, "it's the most corrosion-resistant metal known to man, you bag of old farts."

All six of the social misterfits then took off their spectacles and started hitting Mr Poubelle with them.

The violent intellectuals attacked Stan with eancylopaediaes, inserted chess pieces, and kicked him to within a sixpence of his life under a torrent of machine code abuse. "One of them called me a FF1G 5H178AG3FF00," said Mr P, shaking and sobbing.

Police are appealing to anybody with information to come as far forward as possible, since some policemen are short-sighted and are professionally obliged to wear glasses.

A spokesman for The Encyclopaedia Brittanica last night pointed out that the corrosion index of Iridium is only slighter lower than that of Osmium.

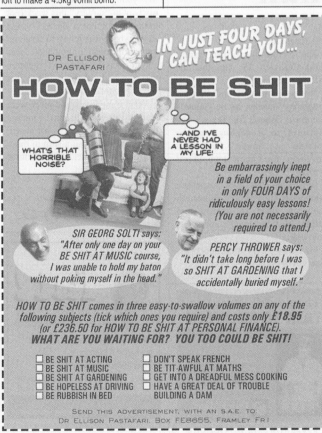

DR ELLISON PASTAFARI

IN JUST FOUR DAYS, I CAN TEACH YOU...

HOW TO BE SHIT

WHAT'S THAT HORRIBLE NOISE?

...AND I'VE NEVER HAD A LESSON IN MY LIFE!

Be embarrassingly inept in a field of your choice in only FOUR DAYS of ridiculously easy lessons! (You are not necessarily required to attend.)

SIR GEORG SOLTI says: "After only one day on your BE SHIT AT MUSIC course, I was unable to hold my baton without poking myself in the head."

PERCY THROWER says: "It didn't take long before I was so SHIT AT GARDENING that I accidentally buried myself."

HOW TO BE SHIT comes in three easy-to-swallow volumes on any of the following subjects (tick which ones you require) and costs only £18.95 (or £236.50 for HOW TO BE SHIT AT PERSONAL FINANCE). WHAT ARE YOU WAITING FOR? YOU TOO COULD BE SHIT!

☐ BE SHIT AT ACTING
☐ BE SHIT AT MUSIC
☐ BE SHIT AT GARDENING
☐ BE HOPELESS AT DRIVING
☐ BE RUBBISH IN BED
☐ DON'T SPEAK FRENCH
☐ BE TIT-AWFUL AT MATHS
☐ GET INTO A DREADFUL MESS COOKING
☐ HAVE A GREAT DEAL OF TROUBLE BUILDING A DAM

SEND THIS ADVERTISEMENT, WITH AN S.A.E. TO: DR ELLISON PASTAFARI. BOX FE8655, FRAMLEY FR1

Plan refused

PLANS for a new fire station in Wripple have been rejected by the borough's planners.

Staggerback Rollerby Properties had submitted plans for a 109-storey development including a vibrating restaurant at the top, and a load of shops at the bottom, with 28-storey wings extending from either side as far as the church and the WI hall, in case the building ever needed to fly.

A representative of Framley Borough Council told local paper The Framley Examiner reporter me that Wripple village green was "not even slightly the right place for this enormous thing. The firepole alone was over 1100 feet long."

The developers are planning an appeal which the council plans to reject.

WOW! A KETTLE THAT COUGHS!

that's unnatural

KOF! KOF!

BELPIT LF1400 EXPECTORANT KETTLE

only £49.99 from NEWBY'S OF MOLFORD

also now it's also available in POT and CUP

WARNING! MAY CONTAIN THE DEVIL

WEEKEND TV
SATURDAY

PICK OF THE WEEK

With Ursula Cloybeam

READERS WILL be excited to discover that this week I am choosing a programme originally shown several weeks ago! Yes, you're not dreaming, my pick of the week is episode 6 of *Hospital Corners* (with Michael Flipflops) which, on Wednesday evening, after fish fingers, tinned carrots and angel delight, I will be watching for the seventh time! And I encourage you to do the same! Of course, to join in, you'll need to have one of these new VCRs or Video Channel Recorders like me and Denis, but Roberts Radios sell them at reasonable prices and they're not too heavy! You won't want to get left behind when everybody's talking about episode 6 of *Hospital Corners* at work the next day! VCRs are the future and stuffy old televisions are the past. I've already thrown my set away, and I know you will too, when you see episode 6 of *Hospital Corners*. **That's my pick.**

TV SWAPS BOARD

If you have something you want to swap via the Framley Examiner Swaps Board, just call Janet or Gary on

0999 4545

GOT	WANT
01 BATMAN vs COLUMBO BOARD GAME	PROFESSIONALS WEEBLE SET
02 BEST OF BRIAN REDHEAD LP	KHMER ROUGE FATIGUES (AGE 8-10)
03 "EVIL" EVEL KNIEVEL	EVEL KNIEVEL
04 ADVENTURES OF HAROLD WILSON ANNUAL	BETAMAX "DRILLER KILLER"
05 ACTION MAN KITCHEN	REAL, CRYING "TINY KIDNEYS" DOLL
06 THE BIG YELLOW SLIPPER PLAYSET	4' x 3' BOX OF DUTCH PORNOGRAPHY

ROBERTS RADIOS

only **£895.99**

The Findus Repeat Archive Televiewer 8000LX (basic)

- records up to 12 minutes of TV
- with 2 x 6 min Benelux cassettes
- clear 11" channel display panel
- on *and* off
- big orange switch (volume?)
- plug and wires

65 UHF House, Promenade Way, Framley

BBC

8.30 Pages From Gagfax

8.35 Scrappy Doo, Why Are You?

9.00 The Saturday Speedboat Sarah Smith & Keith Philbin steer randomly at Newton-le-Willows and the Prime Minister interviews Roman Holliday.

12.12 Weathercock Bill Giles

12.15 Olympic Sportsnest including (approx. times)

12.20 Miniature Swimming

1.05 Equus

3.25 Men's Sanderson (Final)

3.50 Women's 100x4m Relay (Semi-Finals)

4.10 The Adventure Game

4.50 Table Dancing

5.5 News (8,589/53,112) A bomb goes off in Ulster and Jan announces a royal engagement.

5.20 'Ello 'Ello Jack Warner and Gorden Kaye pound the beat.

5.45 Jim'll Unnerve You

The weekend starts here! There's plenty of fun for younger viewers when Sarah Smith and cheeky puppet friend Mr Cabbages meet the secretary of the Transport & General Workers Union and Emu

SATURDAY SPEEDBOAT 9.00am BBC

6.20 The Two Ronnies of Hazzard Unpopular spin-off with Barbara Dickson as the Balladeer.

7.10 The Late Late Breakfast Time Selina Scott and Debbie Greenwood attempt to jump over eighteen double-decker buses in a double-decker bus.

8.05 Summertime Nuisance Laughter with Keith Harris and his new puppet, Wasp's Nest.

9.05 Carrott's Shtick Jasper beats his donkey of an audience.

9.35 News (as 5.05) (rpt)

9.50 Match of the Unexpected Highlights of Brighton & Hove Albion.

10.25 The Big Saturday Big Night Movie: *Carry On Freaking Out* (1968) Television premier of Nixon-era rock opera

Bongo Star ... Jim Dale
Sid Dylan ... Sid James
The Acid Queen ... Kenneth Williams
Pearl Necklace ... Barbara Windsor
Swami Yogi Bear ... Charles Hawtrey
Kyoko Ego ... Joan Sims
Dr Robert ... Kenneth Connor
Keith Animal ... Peter Butterworth
Cynthia Plastercaster ... herself
Paul McCarthorse ... Terry Scott
Screenplay: Talbot Rothwell & Terry Southern
Dir.: Jack Nicholson

12.00 Penisbobs Yukkie uses his scampi fingers to help him get wood.

12.15 Last Orders

12.25 Closedown (rpt)

BBC "2"

6.25 Open Polytechnic

6.25 The Politics of the Penis

6.50 Nuclear Holocaust: Newton-le-Willows **7.15** Two Plus Two Is Maths

7.40 How Green Is My Yellow?

8.05 Italian Pour Les Anglais

8.30 Shakespeare's Many Lesbians

8.55 Biscuits in Edwardian Britain

9.20 I Fancy You, Joyce

9.45 Management Is The Eighties

10.10 How to Photograph Your Insides **10.35** Does Tennis Work?

11.0 The Miracle of Fluff

11.25 Games Sans Waring

11.50 Important in September

12.15 The Duvet of Christ **12.40** How We Used To Think We Lived

1.05 Dividing a Horse

1.30 Saturday Cinema:
The Brevet Bunch (1943) War drama. Disgruntled, underpaid tommies wish that for them the war was nearly over.

Brevet Major Rufus ... Jack Hawkins (dubbed by Marni Nixon)
Brevet Sergeant Grimshaw ... William Hartnell
Brevet Private Lavender ... and introducing James Perry
Dir.: William Joyce

3.20 Playing Away Brian Cant & Toni Arthur spend the weekend in Brighton.

3.45 One Man And His Mary Poppins More competitive kite-flying, bird-feeding and making an anagram out of Dick Van Dyke's name at the end, with Phil Drabble.

4.35 Labour Party Conference 1982 Day 6 of the continued live coverage, including the retrospective Denis Healey 'Silly-Billy' montage. Presented by Robin Day.

6.05 The Old Grey Whispering Test Bob Harris struggling to make himself heard above the music of Cabaret Voltaire.

6.45 Weather and Sport A look back at the week's forecasts with Bill Giles.

7.05 Live From The Albert Proms The London Sinfonietta plays John Adams' *Fast Ride In A Short Machine* and a specially commissioned work for parrot and orchestra by Alwyn Tittershear.

8.40 One Foot In The Future Young Scottish researcher, Kirsty Wark, investigates how British architecture will be represented on television in the 1990s.

9.10 So You Think You Want To Be... Made Into A Ball

10.00 Pissed-Up Nannies Quarter-final action introduced by David Vine.

11.05 Newsnight At The Zoo

11.10 Third Degree Burns Gordon Burns meets Sheila Ferguson.

11.50 Alfred Hitchcock Presents Agatha Christie's Michael Cimino's "Sir Arthur Conan Doyle's The Chinese Detective Investigates Barbara Taylor Bradford's Strange Case of Columbo vs Gerry Anderson's The Mysterons" Double Bill

12.45 Last Orders

12.55 Closedown (first shown on BBC1)

ITV

6.25 Open Sesame

6.25 Counting 1-2-3 Cookies ah-ah-ah

6.55 Spanish For Junior: *Agua*

7.25 The Mike Morris Breakfast Hour Celebrities refuse to wake up for their interviews.

8.25 The Amazing Underwater World of Captain Nimmo Animation.

8.30 The Grizzly Life and Times Of Douglas Adams Lazy author Adams worries that Denver Pyle will sell the last remaining Siberian-toothed bear as a pelt.

9.30 Today Is Saturday, Where's Our Speedboat? More or less fun with TV doctors Graeme Garden and Magnus Pike. Phone in to offer your organ swaps or to swear at Buck's Fizz on 01 999 8055.

12.25 Moustache of Sport including live coverage of the Winter Olympics

12.30 Snowballing

1.10 Bob The Slayer

1.55 Speed Snorting

2.45 Ice Hockney

3.45 Skier Jumping

4.00 Kent's Big Granny Haystacks

4.45 Score Drawer Dickie can't quite hear Brian's match report from Upton Park.

5.05 Weekend News Leonard Parkin washes his car and takes his mother shopping.

5.15 Metal Machine Mickey Locked groove feedback.

5.45 The InCredible CHiPs Jon & Mr Punch get angry and turn into a big green motorbike.

6.40 Russ Meyer's Pussycathouse With special guest Bella Emberg.

7.15 That's My Typecasting Mollie Sugden acts all posh.

7.45 3-2-0-2-7 The quiz that makes no sense with Dusty Springfield.

8.45 Weekend News (as 5.05) (rpt) Followed by a nice cup of tea and a sit down

9.00 It Was Actually Alright On The Night 3 Denis Norden introduces more of the final, transmitted versions of the outtakes we know and love. Peter Sellers delivers a line in a lift and a man says "Not one thing" without moving his head from side to side.

10.00 An Audience With Harold Macmillan (B&W) (rpt)

10.45 Over The TISWOS Carolgees gets into a drunken fistfight with Gorman over James. *Not Whoft.*

11.15 Last Night Movie: *No Sex Please, I'm Not Robin Askwith!* (1972) Television premiere of Heath-era simulated comedy-sex comedy.

Robin Askwith's boss ... Tony Booth
Mary Pentagon ... June Whitfield
Arthur Lowe ... Robin Askwith
The Wife of Bath ... Valerie Leon
Dir.: Allan Smithee (Alan Smithy)

12.45 God, Why Hast Thou Foresaken Insomniacs?

12.55 Closedown (first shown on BBC1)

TEDDYBOY MARTIN

01999 865465
www.tedbozmaz.com

175 YEARS OF EXCELLENCE

GOOD OPPORTUNITY TO OWN THIS HOUSE

MOLFORD ST MALCOLM
£450,000 Teddyboy Martin are pleased to offer this rarely sought after property for sale.
A magnificent Tudor, four-storey Georgian style house set in 8 acres of unspoilt, rolling lounge, belonging to another, larger house.
On market unexpectedly due to owners currently being on holiday in Magaluf. Quick sale preferred.

GRAEHAEME GARDENS, FM12

SASQUATCH HEIGHTS
£82,950 Mind-expanding semi-detached rotating Edwardian residential swimming pool, retaining many period features.
This pool is offered fully furnished, with wall to wall carpets and functioning fire place.
Pool floor hatch leads to thatched cellar with wine storage, parking and mains electrical points. Also wave machine and flume to loft.

NIGHTMARE COTTAGE

BATLEY **£225,000oro**
Grossly underrated House In A Mood. Doors always slamming, water always too hot (except in shower), windows mysteriously wide open when you get home. Draughty when jealous. Doesn't like you having your friends round.

NICE ONE, CYRIL

£64,395 GASCOIGNE, PLINTH
One way house with "In" door and "Out" door ("Out" door switchable to second "In" door via exterior switch). Please arrange viewing well in advance, allowing plenty of time to get out.

LOFT CONVERSION

£46,550 THE POPS, BELLAIRE
We are disappointed to offer this former house, converted into seventeen lofts. A baffling property which would be ideal for, I don't know, an ambitious loft-lover with seventeen lofts' worth of stuff.

£155,000 OREO

THE BUTTOCKS, SOCKFORD
Superbly converted flat. No windows, no lights, radios all over the place. Ideal for extreme antisocial type. Or blind person.

£78,000

TRIREME CIRCUS, WHOFT
Beautiful 5-bedroom detached house on unfortunate electrical ley line. Taps occasionally live, carpets occasionally standing on end. Some chance of strobe lighting and hard disk erasal. But at the moment, worth a look, to be honest.

HIGHLY TALKED AFTER PROPERTY

THE TRUMPTONS, WHOFT
£113,500 Badly thought out 14th century maisonette situated conveniently on the fold of the map. 4ft ceilings, no doors on ground floor, fluffmill-powered windows, greenhouse cellar, that sort of thing. This is your last and own only chance to own yourself your own highly talk-provoking home. NB Susie it's ALSO on the flight path!!! Me and Paul PISSED ourselfs.

GOING, GOING, GOING

£170,950 MOLFORD ST GAVIN
Traditional French bungalow with circumflex glass roof and fully fitted neighbours. Gas fired spiral escalators and easily movable windows. Fashionably situated on the underneath of the town, with commanding upskirt views.

£36,000

Teddyboy Martin are pleased to offer this modern, 2 bed house, with a door, windows one, two, three, four. Full GCH, garage, garden, cavity wall insulation. One window contains film about two dogs visiting a biscuit factory.

SOLD

SHILILLINGBURY LILLINGBURY ILLINGBURY ON INGBURY, FM12

£1.1M Gobstoppingly, filling-looseningly vulgar mansion. Everything bright pink, including giant glass pissing flamingo waterfall feature in living room. Several bathrooms wallpapered in royalty cheques. Home of former newsreader.

Altogether & Hopscotch

LETTING AGENTS
01999 966 862 www.....co.uk

KITCHENETTE WAY, FRAMLEY FR2 £323 weekly (£1400pcm) A well-presented first floor flat ideal for professional couple willing to share with other professional couple unwilling to move out. Bring a sword.

THE BLUETONES, SOCKFORD FR3 £1200pcm Aerial flat, loosely tethered above this desirable warehouse development. Ribbed steel structure, hydrogen / helium mix. Excellent views, but unsuitable for vertigo sufferers, the elderly or smokers.

FALTERMEYER'S WHARF, FRAMLEY (£1 million pounds pcm) Light, spacious whorehouse conversion, built over the middle of the Wharf's historic 15th century bascule bridge. All fittings bolted to floor. Living area splits and tips to allow passage of tall ships. Some warning given.

Le POP-POP, WHOFT (£1,500pcm) Architect designed, thermometer-shaped house. 1st floor bedroom leading to 10th storey bathroom in hot weather.

BATTLECAT, MOLFORD. (£1100 pcm) Unconventional 2 dimensional apartment (depth and height, no width) situated right up against left hand wall of 3-dimensional victorian townhouse. Security guard and counsellor. Must be seen (by standing at angle).

GRAND COLONNADE, WHOFT (£15,000pcm) Over-bright last floor roof in this ever populated crescent. Commanding views of the moon and the elements. GCH, loft, pets.

ALTOGETHER & HOPSCOTCH "WE LET IT ALL OUT... "

Ron's new poems are sheer poetry !

by Ursula Cloybeam

Ron gets his inspiration from the natural world around him, and likes gravy.

PHOTOGRAPH BY FRANK CHICKENS

THOXTOXETER resident and amateur poet Ron Plural has his eyes set on the biggest prize in poetry, the Poet Laureate Prize.

I met Ron, who has been writing since he retired from professional wrestling in 1998, on a park bench in Thoxtoxeter, where he was having a Forest Fruits drink and inventing a ballad. Ron told me he thinks his newest poems are exactly the sort of thing that Poet Laureates ought to be writing.

"These two new poems are the best things I've done, far better than either of my previous poems. Acquiring all the skills of poetry was hard, I'll admit, but I've got it now, and I'd like to be Poet Laureate please."

POETRY IN MOTION

Ron has written both his new poems out and sent them to the Queen, accompanied by a short couplet (written in January) explaining in ten words or less why he wants to be Poet Laureate.

"I done them in a binder," he explained as he rolled me a menthol cigarette on his poet's notebook. "Her Majesty can't fail to notice that."

Ron's poems are personal, he says, but he sees no reason why he couldn't turn his hand to grander, national themes, like Coronations or the state of the railways.

"How hard can it be? I've done four poems, that's true, but I've got loads of words left."

The current Poet Laureate, Andrew somebody, was not in the phone book.

HERE ARE RON'S TWO NEW POEMS

The Old Man With A Drawer
There was an old man with a drawer
Who decided to open the drawer
So he opened the drawer
And inside the drawer
There was an old man with a drawer

The Old Man Who Was Old
There was an old man who was old
Who was asked by an old man "How old?"
"How old am I old?"
said that old man so old,
"I'm as old as those old men of old."

© Ron Plural 2002

Chinmey Sweeps

Chinmey sweeps for all occasions

Sale, hire and personal use

All sweeps guaranteed for 2 hours

Safe for machine washing

"Where're my sweeps?" They're here!

"You boys look as if you could do with a sweep!"

NACKVID KEYD ENTERPRISES, 17 Cherry Tree Lane, WHOFT
tel. 01999 664793
fax. chinmey@sweep.org.chinmey.co.uk

What's on...

Arts Scene

OIL PAINTINGS OF BOATS KICK ARSE

Oliver Mouth, Oils
KEYSEL GALLERY

Review by Amy Llarona

THIS NEW EXHIBITION of oils by Fracton artist Oliver Mouth is just the sort of thing to take your kids to this half term. And if they complain that they'd rather be playing

"More Bloody Boats" oil on canvas, Mouth 2001.

Battlebat on their PlayCylinders, explain, as patiently as you can, that these oil paintings of boats KICK ARSE.

Let them know who is PAINTING BOSS. Let them know that Oliver Mouth is KING OF BRUSHES, and that every time he picks up this BRUSH, of which he is KING, and every time he chooses a subject, as long as that subject is boats, you can rest assured that the painting which he makes is going to KICK ARSE.

Write it large, across the clouds of the sky, that Oliver Mouth is THE MAN WHO PAINTS BOATS. Let no child wake, crying in the night, saying, "Mummy! Who will paint boats for me?", for the answer will be known. Whenever boats need painting, one man will always be there, and that man is OLIVER MOUTH and his boat paintings, in oils at the Keysel Gallery until the 5th, KICK ARSE.

(our regular art columnist, Delawarr Louche, is on holiday.)

Theatre audience "extremely patient"

BY BUNCO BOOTH

THE OWNER OF CLINTON'S Promenade Theatre paid tribute to the patience of his audience this week.

Bob Catapult showed me round the auditorium, where a full house has been waiting for a matinee performance by genteel TV drag act Hinge and Bracket since October 1998.

"I come out onstage every few months to explain that the performance was cancelled long ago due to ill health, but the ladies and gentlemen always tell me they don't mind waiting a bit longer. You know. Just in case."

The happy theatregoers have been surviving on a diet of Neapolitan ice cream and interval drinks for four years now, and although several audience members have died from scurvy and liver failure, Bob says the crowd's enthusiasm shows no sign of flagging.

"People round here love a good show, and, although most of them are now aware that Patrick Fyffe (who played Hilda Brackett and not the piano) died earlier this year, they're convinced this will still be a fine entertainment, if and when it ever happens."

There was excitement last week when news reached the rear stalls that the late Mr Fyffe had been replaced by 1980s Rubik's Cube expert Patrick Bossert. Hopes are now high that a new "Hinge & Bossert" show may be underway by spring.

A poster advertising the show.
PHOTO BY LESLEY OGRE

TRANSFORM YOUR WINDOWBOX

- crazy paving
- tarmac
- concrete
- climbing frames
- patios
- decking
- swings
- watchtowers, fences and searchlights

JOHNSON'S WINDOW BOXES
01999 548 778
www.johnsonswindowboxes_themovie.com

I may not know much about about about art but I know what I'm like!

GREAT RINGTONES

FREE DOWNLOADS

www.ringtones.gov.uk
09999 9999XX

01 OSCAR WILDE	49 A DAY IN THE LIFE (LAST CHORD)
02 C4 NEWS THEME	50 A DAY IN THE LIFE (ORCHESTRAL CLIMAX)
03 ROUND OF APPLAUSE	51 A DAY IN THE LIFE (ALARM CLOCK)
04 WELSH KITTEN	52 MARIELLA FROSTRUP
05 TREE FALLING DOWN	53 TAXI BRAKES
06 400dB WHITE NOISE	54 NUTCRACKER
07 FENELLA FIELDING THROWING UP A KIDNEY	55 GIANT HAILSTONE GOING THROUGH ROOF
08 LATVIAN WEDDING	56 SWEETEX (TASTE ONLY)
09 "YOU TERRIBLE C**T!" (WITHNAIL AND MARWOOD)	57 DRIPPING TAP
10 WB CARTOON GUITAR SLIDE	58 THE FIRST HALF AN HOUR OF "SAVING PRIVATE RYAN"
11 CHARLOTTE CHURCH SINGING THE WORD "CUM"	59 BINGO CALLER (CALLS THE INCOMING NUMBER IN BINGO PAIRS)
12 FALSE TEETH	60 "HAPPY BIRTHDAY, MR PRESIDENT"
13 "THERE IS NO SUCH THING AS SOCIETY!"	61 POLICE MEGAPHONE ("YOU'RE SURROUNDED")
14 MILKBOTTLES	62 DRUM ROLL
15 OUTLOOK EXPRESS SPLASH	63 SIMON SINGH'S ENIGMA (TXT ONLY)
16 TUMBLEWEED	64 TRAIN CRASH (XXX)
17 SPAGHETTI WESTERN RICOCHET	65 FINGERNAILS ON BLACKBOARD (4 INCREDIBLE VOLUMES)
18 "YOU'RE DRUNK"	66 ROARING FIRE
19 BIG BEN	67 JULIA CARLING (FAKE)
20 BABY MONITORINTERCOM	69 STOMACH RUMBLING
21 ZIPPY SWEARING!! (XXX)	71 £1,000,000
22 APPROACHING FOOTSTEPS	72 HARP GLISSANDO (DENOTES TIME PASSING)
23 BONFIRE	73 LION BEHIND YOU
24 FOUR-MINUTE WARNING	74 "TIME AT THE BAR"
25 BUILDER'S BUM	75 GHOSTLY WAIL
26 ECHO	76 THE CENTRAL HEATING COMING ON
27 MELTING CHOCOLATE (SMELL ONLY)	77 BORING PENSIONER
28 THE KINGS SINGERS SING "FITTER, HAPPIER"	78 BAGPUSS YAWNING
29 IRRITATING PENTIUM JINGLE	79 BEE
30 SNORING	80 CHILDREN IN PLAYGROUND
31 REASSURING WORDS FROM NICK HORNBY	81 SPIN CYCLE (WITH UNIQUE VIBRATE)
32 WEDDING MARCH	82 "I DON'T BELIEVE IT!" (VICTOR)
33 1300 MOBILE PHONES RINGING IN AN EMPTY WAREHOUSE	83 THERE'S SOMETHING IN THE LOFT
34 WHISTLER'S MOTHER	84 MOOOOOOOOOOOOOOO!
35 FLUSHING TOILET	85 DENTIST'S DRILL (WITH GHOULISH LAUGHTER)
36 IAN DURY SHOUTING "WHERE'S JIMMY HILL? BURN HIS CARAVAN!"	86 DOG PANTING AND WHINING
37 PLOPTROTS AND NOSECLUES	87 CHAINSAW (BACK BY POPULAR DEMAND)
38 ¡BONK!	88 DELBOY FALLING THROUGH THE BAR
39 OPTICAL ILLUSION	89 BOMB-LIKE TICKING
40 FATHER CLANGER SWEARING	90 JAPANESE NATIONAL ANTHEM (DJ F1NG3RT1P REMIX)
41 SOMEONE MUGGING YOU FOR YOUR PHONE	91 NORMAN MAILER TELLING EVERYONE TO FUCK OFF
42 LORRY REVERSING	92 X-RAY (VISION ONLY)
43 DOG WHISTLE	93 HERD OF RHINO
44 CAR ALARM (20mins)	94 SPITTING SKINHEAD
45 VERY LOUD SNEEZE (VERY VERY LOUD)	95 CHAMPAGNE CORK POPPING
46 SEAGULLS	96 RECORDBREAKING BELCH
47 1978 F.A. CUP FINAL	97 ALEX FERGUSON (SINISTER BACKWARDS MESSAGES)
48 SUNDAY TIMES RICH LIST	98 TOM & JERRY ANVIL
	99 THE BAD THINGS IN YOUR HEAD

all calls charged at £5 a minute*

THE MINISTRY OF RINGTONES

* peak rates also apply, up to a possible £95 per minute. Most ringtones take upwards of two hours to download. Please consult a doctor before downloading any of these ringtones.

by Adam Wrent

(From left to right) Fabien Giraffe.
PHOTOGRAPH BY HOTPANTS COLORADO

LOCAL ARTIST Fabien Giraffe was last week sensationally fired by the subject of his latest portrait.

Giraffe, 35, of Television Spinney, Whoft, has described his dismissal as "a thundering blow to the balls of what was to be my finest work."

Cpt Giraffe started his self-portrait last Autumn, but only two weeks ago called work to a halt when he announced, in a shock to the art world, that he was the wrong man for the job.

"I've been a bit hard on myself, but I just wasn't cutting the mustard," he metaphored yesterday. "I'd been working from a photo, since I wouldn't be able to be present at all the sittings, and unfortunately the process didn't afford me a decent level of detail.

"So, after much thought and some more thought, I fired myself. It's the first time I've been sacked, and I have to admit, it's the worst thing that's ever happened to me."

APPALLING MESS

However, his subject, local artist Fabien Giraffe, remains unrepentant.

"It doesn't look anything like me," the artist and subject explained clearly. "And I'm not paying £3000 for a load of square-jawed rubbish that I wouldn't even hang in my dog's bathroom."

But Giraffe was quick to retort. "The fee isn't important, although I will miss paying myself. The picture is rubbish, I'm right," he argued, "but I quite like it. It's got a certain smirk. If I had any sense, I'd be proud of it, rightly and wrongly."

The self-portrait, which has a "certain smirk" (according to one source) is now likely to be completed by another artist, who may paint some of his own features onto Giraffe's face. Should be interesting.

Police stay tough on drugs

FRAMLEY POLICE Chief Constable Rupert Bone yesterday attributed his team's tireless hardline stance against crime to the excellent quality of the amphetamine sulphate they had recently confiscated.

"This is some of the most binging gear my boys have ever got their germans on," said Ch Con Bone through bloodshot eyes.

"I feel invincible."

The show must have gone on

The Framley Pagoda is shutting its theatrical doors for the first ever time tonight in order for essential renovations to take place.

The theatre has famously kept a twenty-four hour open-door policy throughout its colourful history. This was intended by its original owners to provide a constant cultural focus for the local community.

After much deliberation over when the renovations would begin, it has been decided to close the doors, somewhat surprisingly, midway during the first performance of the *The Cocktail Sailor*, Framley's Newest Show in Town. The cast and crew are delighted.

"What better way of celebrating this historical theatre than to be playing while it's closed for stage repairs?", said one sailor.

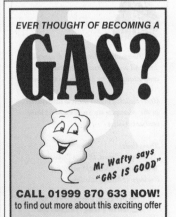

EVER THOUGHT OF BECOMING A

GAS?

Mr Wafty says "GAS IS GOOD"

CALL 01999 870 633 NOW!
to find out more about this exciting offer

Our roving reporter meets Framley's refuse men, and learns how sanitation is a dirty job but somebody's...

A dirty job but got to do it

The daunting piles of rubbish I had to face in my job. I couldn't believe my eyes!
PHOTOGRAPH BY HESELTINE GRENADE

by Katie Blirdsnest

THE BLIRDSNEST REPORT

WHEN THEY TOLD me what my report was going to be about this week, I couldn't believe my eyes! Me? Join the dustbin men and pick up rubbish, like a dustman? I couldn't believe my eyes.

But when I turned up for work with the Sockford Refuse Disposal Crew (1 Team), I just had to "muck in" with the rest of the boys, even though I was a girl, which makes things quite different, in a man's world!

I met team manager Mike Roulade for my first shift, and asked him what the job was like. For instance how were the binmen treated by the people they served?

"We're like Marmite, us," he told me.

I asked him if he meant that people either loved dustmen or hated them.

"No," he replied patiently but sternly. "We're *exactly* like Marmite."

FIRST SHIFT

We pulled up for our first stop in our dustcart, and I began loading rubbish out of the alley behind Watterson Avenue. I couldn't believe my eyes!

"People throw away the oddest things," said Mike, laughing at my reaction.

He wasn't joking. There was what looked like a tar-baby in one bin, and the bottom half of a statue of Ronnie Barker poking out of the top of another. I asked Mike what was the worst thing he'd ever found in a bin. He paused to think.

"A dead leprechaun," he said eventually. "They're always trouble. It's the paperwork."

CONTROVERSY

Conversation was heated on the way to the next pick up. Everyone had their own views on the controversial MaxiBin scheme that has made the headlines recently. These new king-sized bins are emptied every six months and have found few friends among the public, but are surprisingly popular with the dustmen.

"I'm off to Cyprus with the lads from 2 Team, for the next eight weeks," Mike said. "It's a straight choice. My lads are coming round twice a year, no more, no less. Now do you want one big skip full of rubbish blocking your driveway or forty-five wheeliebins? The choice is yours."

The binmen themselves seem unconcerned about public disapproval of the scheme.

"It's just like it was with the alphabetical rubbish idea," said Keith Mumbles of 3 Team. "At first people resisted it, and made our lives difficult, throwing away potato peelings into the bin for P for potato, rather than P for peeling, but they soon got used to it."

He lit me a fag, and we laughed.

THE WASTE LAND

At the end of a hard day's graft, I rode with the bin lorry back to the landfill site where all Framleys' rubbish is dumped.

It was an amazing site. I walked round, trying to take it in.. As I climbed to the highest point of the pile, it felt like I was literally wading through a pile of rubbish. Crows were ranged along the perimeter fence like birds, and the stench was overwhelming, rich, and creamy, like salt.

My journey was at an end, and I knew with every roly-poly I did down the pile, I knew it would take longer to wash the smell from my clothes.

I had joined the binmen.

FRAMLEY FACES RUBBISH PROBLEMS

WHILE FRAMLEY itself is planning to adopt the controversial Maxi Bin scheme, most other collection zones in the borough have rejected the idea. Here's how the rubbish is dealt with elsewhere...

FRACTON	turned into feed for cattle and old people
SOCKFORD	shot from a gun towards France
CHUTNEY	denial
WHOFT	hidden under a big bed in an enormous room just over the district border
WRIPPLE	fed to a giant iron beast that lives in a hill
MOLFORD	ski-bins pushed downhill towards less prosperous districts, where residents use the contents as currency

Crime awareness week

By Katie Blirdsnest

FRAMLEY POLICE have announced a Crime Awareness Week as part of their Community Outreach programme, to take place between the 5th and June. Plain-clothes officer, Jemmy Guvnor, popped into The Framley Examiner offices to give us the low-down on protecting your property.

The week will include a "Bogus Callers Blitz", with Jemmy's team knocking persistently on the doors of many of the community's elderly residents.

They will prove how ineffective door chains can be and will be offering to open a high interest savings account for bewildered pensioners if they'd like to bring that wad of notes out from the tea caddy. No hiding place is safe from Jemmy, it's like taking caddy from a baby!

FANCY PARKING

There will also be a chance for young drivers to undertake an intensive course in road skills, to be run by Guvnor's right-hand, Driver Maurice. Young men with no other way out will be able to learn ancient handling methods in the 2-day "Drive! Drive!! Drive!!!" course, which Maurice himself learned off his old man.

Modules include 0-70 In 8 Seconds, Cornering Under Pressure and Dumping The Wheels In A Bit Of A Hurry. And Jemmy tells me that a one-off job may be on offer for any sprog what proves their bottle.

BURGLARY WORRY

And if you're worried about house-breaking, Framley Police are happy for concerned residents to pop into Jemmy Guvnor's local nick, which is somewhere in the north of Scotland apparently.

"Just give my boys a bell on 07999 762237 when you get there, and don't forget to give them your address with a rough estimate of value of contents," rubbing his hands together.

BAD DREAMS AT NIGHT? NO DREAMS AT ALL? YOU NEED...

The **no nightmares** *Pillow*

from **NEWBY'S** of Molford

™

The pillow that gently and naturally releases pleasant and relaxing dreams while you sleep.

+ VAT

£139.99
refills £9.99 each

- Be a shepherdess in a French orchard
- Be an Xmas present covered in tickly tinsel
- Be an Edwardian fireman on a steam railway in the Chilterns
- Fly high above your old school while your teachers dance happily with your homework
- Eat a neverending candy-floss while floating in a sea of warm olive oil (plus eye massage)

The No-Nightmares™ Pillow's unique Herbal Essences will lull you gently into a beautiful dream world every night. Now, for the first time, you can finally eventually sleep super soundly at long last.*

*Subject to offer. Subject to availability. While stocks last. Products may vary. Sizes may vary. Dreams may vary. Availability may vary. Offer may vary. Credit checks may be necessary. Things may then become subject to acceptance. Acceptance may vary. Written details available upon request. Details may vary. Details may be subject to varying. While details last. Details correct at time of going to press. Subject to changes, availability, size, acceptance and necessary variation. Variation correct at time of going to press. Press may vary. Press may be necessary. While press lasts. Offer only applies at time of going to press (subject to offer). Not to be used in conjunction with any other offer. Any other offer may be subject to all the above and more. This offer includes, but is not limited to, any of the above. Subject to all of the above. And availability.

Your first stop for value

TO CELEBRATE the opening of the newly refurbished Conch Quwik Stop store and services at Sockford Orient Parkway, The Framley Examiner Group have joined forces with Conch Oil And Poultry Products Plc, to give away three chance-of-a-once-upon-a-lifetime chances to spend a dream holiday.

The Framley Examiner
Framley's Traditional Favourite Since 1978

〜 CONCH QUWIK STOP are the ultimate one-stop shop stop, offering everything you will ever need under one roof.

〜 You can use the instore internet kiosks to check the weather, through our window cams – trained 24-hours-a-day on the forecourt – or surf the web with access to six selected websites (£5 per hour or £10 for adult premium sites)

〜 Quwik Stop changes the way you live your world today. Now you can surf your e-mail while you check your tyre pressure, or read the whole of the web while munching on scotch egg.

〜 And if you're feeling peckish, why not take time out to give your taste buds a treat with a freshly prepared selection of gourmet scotch eggs and a glass of dry, white coleslaw?

〜 The 24-hour Quwik Stop should be your destination for any of life's last minute essentials: from newspapers to magazines, from periodicals to scotch eggs.

COMING SOON!
Picnic eggs

To mark the opening of the new Sockford Orient Parkway Conch Quwik Stop Stores, Conch are offering readers the chance to win a 3-day break at their refinery on Tayside*

The prize can be for a family of FOUR or FOUR families (please tick)

☐ YES   ☐ FOUR

Prize includes travel to the offshore refinery by Chinook helicopter and first class death slide or rappel cable. You'll have a chance to taste the new oil and meet the refinery manager. This is a great opportunity to see a refinery in its natural habitat.

For your chance to win an oil-fuelled Conch weekend break, simply the answer to a simple question is below.

A: Scotch eggs

Call our premium rate line **0999 882 882** after 6pm.
If Charlotte answers, ask for Jenny.

competition not open to employees of Conch Oil Tayside Refinery

---

Framley prepares to try and remember war dead

By TAUNTON MISHAP

Framley's War Memorial is gathering crowds again.
PHOTOGRAPH BY JACKPOT CONNOISEUR

AFTER YEARS of neglect, Framley's War Memorial is expected to attract large crowds again this Sunday.

The suddenly-popular obelisk was until recently scheduled for demolition, but a sudden resurgence in interest has gained it a stay of execution.

The monument commemorates the men of the Framley Rifle Regiment – the local batallion who were completely wiped out on the night before the historic battle of Limoges, in 1917. According to British Army records, the entire regiment was shot in the back while attempting to desert, a statistic unique in the history of warfare.

The regiment, most of whom, the memorial reveals, had German names, was disbanded immediately afterwards, when Framley declared itself neutral. The mayor of the time said he was not prepared to send any further men "to certain death at the hands of the merciless guns of the British Military Police".

Attempting to explain the appeal of the monument, Sockford entrepreneur Capston Cacton told me that many people feel it is time to acknowledge the sacrifices of the war years.

"If we do not learn from the past, we are doomed to repeat the future," he explained. "This memorial is important to Framley, which is why I have bought up the land surrounding it and, every Sunday lunchtime, will be screening popular films onto the marble sides of the needle."

This week memorialgoers will have a chance to see the middle third of Wayne's World 2, and next Sunday there will be a showing of the left hand side of Carry On Spying.

Redaing week a success

A READING WEEK at Newby's cannery supervised by Molford Library was judged a "great success" according to event organiser Lumpy Jungle.

"This is part of our community outreach programme," she said. "We chose books, which would have relevance to local people, and made them available in a way that would exist in harmony with their lives."

The books – *Under The Greenwood Tree* and *Firefox* – were printed in two paragraph installments onto the labels of tins of skipjack tuna, allowing employees to read while they worked.

A similar scheme has been proposed for Oriel Fruit Farms in Sockford but experts have warned that growing the text on to the sides of grapes will take considerably longer.

Take up your egg and leg and walk

by Pharaoh Clutchstraw

THERE WAS GOOD news for local drug addict Mowbray Melton when doctors at Framley General Hospital gave him the good news: "You will walk again."

Surgeons had amputated the Sockford thrillseeker's left leg two weeks ago, due to complications arising from long term intra-venus herion use. Pre-operative X-Rays showed that one of Melton's leg veins had become blocked by an object – later revealed to be a scotch egg.

"I was starving, so I nicked it from a garage. I couldn't wait to eat, so I just jacked up and spiked myself with egg," he explained at length at a presconference at the hospital at the time.

LIMB SALVAGE

But now, thanks to a revolutionary new procedure, the junkie may be able to kiss his old leg hello again.

"We still have Mr Melton's leg on ice," said Chief Speculative Surgeon Dr Torben Bumhammer, "and have successfully removed the scotch egg. Though reattaching the severed limb is impossible, we are proposing to liquify the leg, and simply inject it back into Mr Melton's body."

Doctors say they are pretty certain that injecting the bad leg into Mowbray's one remaining good leg will enable him, within days, to walk faster than ever before.

"Four hundred miles an hour," Dr Bumhammer insisted, revving his blender.

Mr Melton, in happier times.
PHOTOGRAPH BY RICTUS LIPS

Charity fat

THE CHAIRMAN of Chutney Parish Council has set himself a "countdown conundrum" of a sticky wicket. Stuart McO'Shea, 1947, is asking his parishioners to guess how much weight he willl lose during the month of Lent.

After the challenge is over, Stewart will put the weight back on before having the exact same amount removed again via the liposuction process. The extracted human fat will then be presented in a commemorative soup-bowl to the lucky guesser of the closest guess.

Mr McO'Shea, 54, has said he's determined to beat last year's total, when his poor dieting skills led to a weight gain of 17lb. As promised, he was then forced to undergo the standard fundraising failure forfeit of drinking a pint of cat bile through a straw full of dead skin.

ROBOTS! ROBOTS! ROBOTS!

your slippers, m'lud

We've ALL SORTS of ROBOTS!

THEY SERVE TEA!
THEY DANCE!
RIP YOU A NEW ARSEHOLE!

CAPEK'S ROBOT WAREHOUSE
Unit 18, DeLorean Ind Estate

Permission OK'yed

PLANNING PERMISSION has been granted by Framley Council for a new commemorative statue to be built in Van Dyke Park.

The proposed monument has been described by its artist as a "religious work", and depicts a scout pack eating their packed lunch on a rollercoaster, from the opening titles of *Jim'll Fix It*.

The statue, which was designed by bedbound Sockford sculptor Ibrahim Bethsheveth, will be built and opened by TV funnymen Bill Oddie and Mica Paris in the the spring.

A Man Is Being Questioned By Police (right, inside the police station) yesterday.
PHOTOGRAPH BY POMPIDOU CENTAUR

Man questioned

BY PIGSHIT NELSON

A MAN IS BEING questioned by police in Wripple after changing his name to A Man Is Being Questioned By Police, it was revealed yesterday.

The man in question, whose name is too complicated to use again in this article, claims he is being constantly questioned by police, in a series of spurious arrests designed to wind him up.

"Last week, they had me in for seventy-two hours while we went through the spellings of 3000 famous men. I got about half of them wrong.

Saint-Saëns took me nearly three quarters of an hour. It's a disgrace."

Chief Constable Ruuuuuuuuuuuuuuuuuuuupert Bone, himself a champion shotputter, said that "the spelling incident" had been hugely exaggerated, and that "we just needed to check the name Ayman Al Zawahiri for a charge sheet."

He also insisted that his conviction that there was "something not right" about the man in question, which had led him to set up 14 separate lines of heavily policed enquiry, would eventually bare fruit.

KILLS BOTH KNOWN GERMS

YOUR FAMILY ARE AT RISK FROM ATTACK FROM INFECTION FROM GERMS EVERY DAY

PROTECT THEM WITH NEWBY'S GALAPOGAS BLEACH

GALAPAGAS KILLS BOTH KNOWN GERMS... DEAD*

*May not totally kill one or either of the stated germs. This statement is not legally binding, and will be interpreted as reasonable lassity of fact for advertising purposes in a court of law.

Galapagos
RASPBERRY FLAVOUR
KILLS BOTH KNOWN GERMS

NEWBY'S
OF MOLFORD

Molford St Malcolm

A Humorous View

MOLFORD ST MALCOLM TWINNING ASSOCIATION. – An exciting talk got this month's meetings off to a cracking start. The association welcomed guest speaker Jean Pierre Richelieu and tea was served. An attendance of more than 8 members came along to hear Jean Pierre who had travelled all the way from St Eyots. He gave a humorous view of the typical French year starting with the clearing of the hedgerows and the barrow decorating and the eating of grouse at Whitsuntide, the winner being the one whose grouse contains the coin and becomes king for a day. Members then had a short interval, with refreshments, during which they calmed down. Next week's meeting will be cancelled due to unforseen circumstances.

Beard With Sauce

MOLFORD LUNCH CLUB. – A delightful luncheon of smoked salmon with lemon sauce was enjoyed by all at last week's meeting. Treasurer Trevor Treasureton kept everyone royally entertained by growing a full beard in 20 minutes which, for the third year in a row, was long enough to reach his lunch. He then astonished members by picking up his piece of salmon with his beard and tossing it in the air. A motion was passed to applaud Mr Treasureton, and clapping and coffee followed. Apologies were received from Sgt Lowther and Mrs Appleby, who are having an affair.

Whoft

Anniversary celebrated

WOMEN'S INSTITUTE
To mark the 75th anniversary of the Whoft Women's Institute, president elect Mrs Prudence Juris re-enacted the full minutes of the very first meeting, culminating with the act of institution of the WI. As a result, there are now two Women's Institutes in Whoft. Anyone wishing to help draw up new rotas for use of the hall, or to join either WI, or move from one WI to the other, should contact Mrs Juris or the Department of The Environment and ask for a leaflet.

Enjoyable Trip

DARBY & JOAN. – Mrs Swain presided at the meeting held in The Running Mayor and everyone agreed that the trip to Wovlingham had been enjoyable with agreeable weather. A considerate driver took members on a countryside tour of all the pubs between Wripple and the coast, ending with a delightful meal at The Squirrel's Problems. The driver was sentenced to a lifetime ban and 8 years' imprisonment.

Triangle Cheered Up

PARISH FELLOWSHIP. -Tertiary meeting. Twelve members of the inner council were in attendance. Minutes were read, and a triangle of grass just outside the church was cheered up by taking it to the zoo.

Creme

Harvest Supper

A CHURCH. – A harvest supper with games and competitions arranged by members of the congregation was held on Friday in St Saint's Hall. The service was a harvest festival and nine courses, led by Mary Josephs. Harvest For The Hungry boxes destined for Bulgaria and Macedonia and a collection for the Framley night shelter were blessed by the Rev Phantom Brown, and everything was eaten. Three recently baptised children were welcomed into the church, but ran screaming when they saw a horse struggling on a spit.

1970s Housewife Day

UNITED FELLOWHOOD CHURCH. – Morning worship last Sunday was '1970s Housewife Day.' All members of the church who had been housewives in the 1970s took parts of the service, and Maureen Barber gave the address. Readings were taken from Fanny Cradock's *Puff*

NOT SO N-"ICE CREAM"!.

LOCAL CONSUMER RIGHTS campaigner Baj Curtins is at it again! He's taking Clinton seafront ice cream vendor Roger DeBear to court for false advertising. Apparently, although the ice cream cones pictured on the side of Roger's van appear to be over a yard tall, and filled with up to a gallon of ice cream, the actual cones Roger is selling turn out to be much smaller. "And another thing. His 99s cost a quid." Mr Curtins has contacted his Euro MP and hopes to force Mr DeBear to attend a war crimes tribunal in the Hague to account for his blatant deception.

PHOTO BY SCOTT CHEGG

Pastry Bible and *The Reader's Digest Book of Hoovering.* The guest was the bearded man from *The Joy Of Sex*, who was very very very popular.

Window on the world

PHOTOGRAPHIC SOCIETY The new season's programme of meetings got of to an eye-opening start with a display and talk by local photographer Galleon Prompt. Mr Prompt showed photographs of faraway places with exotic names like "America" and "Hart-le-Pool", all of which made members feel dizzy with possibility. The talk was followed by a sit down and glasses of water. Next week's talk will be by associate member Jumbo Rheims, who will show his world-famous photographs of grass.

Wripple

Silent tribute

WRIPPLE WOMEN'S INSTITUTE. – The meeting opened with a minute's silence in memory of the still late Jim Henson. This was followed by Noah Cudihogs who offered us 'Something Different' in the form of a cookery demonstration. The theme was one of speed of preparation, simplicity of flavours and overall tastelessness of the finished product. He certainly managed to achieve this as he produced dishes ranging from a potato sandwich to strawberry mouse. During social time there was an opportunity to sample the dishes but members remained unimpressed. Elizabeth Benteene won the evening's competition with her 'Easy Pie & Pea' and a fierce left hook. In-form challengers are invited to the group's next meeting at the Wripple Arena where Mrs Benteene will be defending her title.

Lively meeting

DARBY & JOAN & MANDY. – The September meeting of the over 55s wing of the Wripple Bigamists was held on Tuesday, with the admission of new member Mr Tony Biscuits and his wives almost doubling the attendance. A motion to move to a bigger hall was passed. Coffee and houmous.

Flower Arranging

WRIPPLE VILLAGE HALL. – Enrolments are being taken for two new courses starting soon at the Village Hall. These are very friendly, informal sessions, this summer focussing on 'Transforming A Front Garden' and 'Transforming A Back Garden.' The course will be led by Julia Poveney, whose front and back gardens will be converted by students into 'a glowing and brilliant riot of colour' while Ms Poveney makes tea and looks on from her recently restored oak kitchen. Classes may last all day.

A rare treat

WRIPPLE ARSONISTS. – The new chairman of the Wripple Arsonists was sworn in using the traditional brazier and sirens, while petrol was

Framley Town Plans

119 Kimberley Row, construction of single-storey sex annex at the rear. **48 Cox Street**, display of free-standing boards, flags and swastikas. **20 Urban Myth**, Molford, resiting of public payphone facility to second bedroom. **Orchard Cottages, Cigarettes Lane**, conversion of four existing cottages to provide accommodation for six elephants in a line. **108 Mill Road, Whoft**, replace existing bungalow with identical bungalow. **Bakers Arms, Sockford**, raising a section of the northern boundary wall from a height of 1ft to a height of 170ft to stop the people on the 13th and 14th floors of the neighbouring tower block from seeing any of the property. **43 Pestle Close, Little Godley**, to retain existing satellite dish, rocket silos and perimeter fencing. **High Street, Molford St Malcolm**, conversion of police station to art gallery. **22 King**

Creole Terrace, Chutney, lifting of concrete slabs from rear patio, burial of two unpleasant adults, hyperactive 4-year old child and noisy dog all belonging to 20 King Creole Terrace, relaying of patio. **Wallaby Kirk, Molford St Gavin**, redevelopment of existing single-storey lean-to to provide forecourt (including canopies, pumps, underground tanks, car wash and parking for 2500 cars). **St Margaret's Church, Whoft**, installation of two-storey half-pipe in graveyard. **77 Cotton Fields, Sockford**, construction of a PROPER toilet to replace the existing overflowing monstrosity. **St Merton's Church**, Thoxtoxeter, conversion of existing church building to forty-five foot sealed concrete cube containing two of each kind from the congregation. **18 Welwyn Garden Gardens, Framley & 19 Welwyn Garden Gardens**, linking monorail.

6 Eugene Terreblanche House, Batley, addition of 14th Century church tower housing 23cwt tenor bell to front door. **236 Pencil Street, Sockford**, single storey extension to first storey, suspended by cables from geostationary dirigible in low orbit. **Junction of Millichope Ridge and Pethig Arch**, conversion of unexploded WWII rocket propelled bomb to two 1-bed flats with garden access. **Urchin Road, Clinton**, replacement of existing flat roof with party susan containing 48,000 picnic eggs and ¾ metric tonne of dry roasted peanuts. **207 Animal Crescent**, erection of a 22ft statue of Moby on roof gable **St Greavesie's Christian Community Centre, Awkward Lane, Codge**, painting of go-faster stripes along east and west walls. **139, Cunard Heights, Molford St Gavin**, re-siting of chicken goujons from freezer to fridge.

Zephyr 1375 am

TENBY
Midday Madness

THE COLONEL
Coffee Time Request Show

ROBBIE NOUGAT
Breakfast with Nougat

GREGORY ROBERTS
An Evening with 'The King'

TRINA OXGLOVE
Weather Hour

TOM BELT
'Don't Ask Me!'

DAVID VALVE
Housewife's Choice

RON BOVRIL
4am Breakfast with Bovril

CLAIRE KINVIG
The Best Recent Playlists

CHRIS BIDDEFORD
News Argument

ADRIAN MATCHBOX
The Matchstick Report

ROSIE CHAMPION
The Sound of the Eighties

The great sound of Framley

Fracton

Clinton

Wotten
Plodney

Slovenly

odley

St Eyot's

Whoft

Urling

ple

Chutney

Sockford

Framley

Molford

Molford
St Gavin

Lessbury
Moreborough

Molford
St Malcolm

Codge

Molford
St Arahim
Ramal

Effing Sodbury

History on your doorknob

with Arbroath Smokie

EVER SINCE THE DAYS of William the Conqueror, when "Franley" was first recorded in the Doomsday Book, and registered for tax purposes as a "ditche or ponde", history has been being made every day right here under our doorsteps.

Though many of the buildings and people of the past are now sadly no longer with us, their remains still remain.

So let's take a closer look back in time round the area in which we live in, today in this day and age, and peep behind the curtain, to discover the history that lies under everyone, right here in Franley, at the end of the day, at this point in time, when all's said and done.

It's like history on your doorknob!

EFFING SODBURY WALRUS MILL

THIS FAMOUS MILL, colonised by families of walruses (not walrii, I checked) delighted and mystified visitors and tourists to Effing Sodbury during the latter half of the 19th century.

With its remote hilltop setting and no visible entrance, the old corn mill was generally assumed to be empty. This was to be the case until 1852 when legend takes a turn for the fuller mill.

In spring of that year, a passing traveller spotted a lone walrus barking from a single window situated in the roof. A cloud of blue smoke was then said to have emerged from the mill's flues and chased the petrified fellow down the hill.

Over the next 30 years sightings of window walruses became commonplace, and the alternate clouds of blue and orange smoke emerging from the chimney could be seen from as far away as Whotten Plodney and Durbiton.

In 1899, however, the building was demolished to make way for a new corn mill and walrus sanctuary. Within the walls, Victorian construction workers were delighted to discover two children playing. They were never discovered.

FRAMLEY SEAFRONT

IT'S A SOURCE of great local displeasure that Framley's historic seafront now lies in ruins.

Until 1958, Framley had much-sought-after Seaside Status. The designation had been granted to the town by King George III who loved holidaying here, but only because he was a mentalist. (According to the diary entry covering his 1774 visit to the town, he thought he was in a balloon).

However, an in-depth study into Framley's suitability for the role of Seaside Town was commissioned in 1957 after HM Queen Elizabeth II spent a "disappointing" two weeks on Framley seafront. The study revealed that Framley was landlocked, and Seaside Status was rescinded by royal decree. This was a huge blow to the then mayor, who had, in a spirit of coastalness, brought in four buses of gulls for the royal visit, beached a dolphin outside the Queen's hotel, and manned the reception desk with crabs.

In recent years there have been moves to pressure the Royal Family to reverse their judgement. Councillors and representatives of the Framley tourist industry have said they are willing to do whatever it takes to comply with the terms of the original ruling, even as far as moving every single resident, street and building 20 miles up the FR404 to the coast.

Although the glory days of Framley-on-Sea are long gone, you can still get a flavour of how the town used to be. Many reminders of Framley's glorious maritime heritage do still remain – Adam Faith the donkey still gives rides up and down the high street, and the last candyfluff stall only closed in 1998. Sadly, Framley's beautiful grass pier (pictured) now has an estate under it, and is usually on fire.

CHUTNEY VIADUCT

ASK ANYONE who was at the Great Exhibition of 1851 what their favourite bit of British engineering is and, chances are, they'll still say the same thing – The Viaduct between Chutney and Lessbury Moreborough.

The construction of the huge viaduct took place on the 16th of February 1850. The speed of the building process was largely due to the utilisation of Victorian 'Steam Mules' to propel the engineers up and down the side of the viaduct to work.

However it was the groundbreaking 'Suspension Engine' that marked this as a triumph of early Victorian engineering. This hydraulic pump raised the viaduct essential inches in clement weather to allow passage underneath to top-hatted gentlefolk. The toll? A penny.

An interesting side-effect of the suspension engine was that it allowed water to travel uphill across the viaduct. It was so efficient that flooding occurred twice daily at Lessbury Moreborough, creating an inland tidal system and successful summer tourist attraction.

Unfortunately, the viaduct fell ill in 1921 and had to be put to no further use. It can only be seen now in memory.

FRAMLEY MONUMENT

THIS QUIET memorial at the corner of Belling Street and Wharf Parade is the only reminder today of the catastrophic 1994 fire which destroyed much of Old Framley.

At the time, historians say, most of Framley's buildings were wooden framed, meaning that the whole town "must have gone up like a tramp". Contemporary accounts describe a "conflagracioun of greate ferocitee and fearsome vigorous as if the mouthe of helle itself were agape upon the streetes" *(Smash Hits)*.

Although the fire flattened much of Framley, it did clear the plague that had been raging through the town, and, parish records also note, cleared a backlog of suspected witches awaiting processing in the district pens.

Studies show that the blaze started in a monastery kitchen in Cake Walk, and spread quickly down Butter Lane, as far as Hat Street, destroying 90% of the town over four days, before firemen were called not a moment too soon. A statue of some water was erected in Cake Street to mark the aversion of disaster but it burnt down almost immediately and was replaced by the current monument depicting a monk reading the safety instructions for a Breville Sandwich toaster.

Tired? Sleepy? Thirsty?

All these three could cause an ACCIDENT

So, pull over, and we'll pull you a long, cool pint... or a Guinness with some car keys drawn in the foam!

4-pint pitchers of lager £6.50

Happy hours 7-10am 4-7pm

Darts! Pool! Bobsleigh!

Had "one too many"? Our valet parkers will bring your car right to the door of the pub, so you don't have to worry about negotiating the car park. You'll be back on the road in minutes!

PINTSTOP　The Roadside Travel Pub

Just off the FR404 near Crabbing – PINTSTOP – a refreshing break!

Time to run!

By Pigshit Nelson

RECORDS FELL like clumsy rain last Thursday, at the annual Framley and District Athletics Club "Race Against Time".

As usual, the challenging road race attracted both experienced athletes and strange plush-covered man-beasts, all competing to see who could reach the 6.00pm finish line first.

This year's winner, with an impressive time of 5.57pm, was Strimony Bimmelmann, a prizewinning temporal steeplechaser from Crème. Spectators watched as a faint ghost of the runner streaked past the six o'clock mark a full three minutes early, eyes bleeding with the strain.

The popular race started from outside the Bruce Dickinson Memorial Fencing Lounge in Denegate, and ended, as is traditional, at six. Crowds lined the route, waving clocks and appropriate pictures, many of former Six O'Clock Show hosts Michael Aspel and Kenny Baker.

There was, however, a worrying moment of controversy towards the middle of the race, when bad signposting along the route led to seven competitors finishing at 3.38am the previous day. Fortunately, having been forewarned,

Runster Bimmelmann smashes a record.
PHOTOGRAPH BY BENETTON PRELLT

WINNING TIMES	
1st: Bimmelmann, S	5.57:00
2nd: Wendigo, B	5.59:26
3rd: Big plush wolf	5.59:28

course officials were able to rectify the problem so it had never happened.

Bimmelmann's new record smashes the 5.58 six o'clock barrier set by Sir Roger Bannister in the Molford Hundreds in 1962. The record had stood for so long that many were beginning to think it unbreakable. In 1976, sports physicist Richards Richard declared, "If man had been meant to arrive at 6.00 at 5.57, God would have created him three minutes earlier."

Local MP, Ianbeale Steeplecocque, who picketed the event with a sign, has promised race fans that next year's event will be cancelled.

A match with something for everything

WHOFT BERBERS.........................1
MOLFORD BUTTERFLIES..............1
(Electric Entertainment League)

By BARBOUR ZADAGIO

SATURDAY saw Whoft come within a tantalising 1 points of their first ever victory.

Actually winning a game is still nothing more than a sweet little nightmare for the Berbers, but this, their first game of the season, was also their best so far.

Conditions were messy underfoot after two weeks of torrential fluff, making handling difficult and sneezing inevitable.

A row before the kick-off failed to resolve the matter of whether this was a league or union game, and Molford insisted on playing 15 league men against Whoft's 13-strong union side. As a compromise, each team was allowed to bring its own referee.

Molford kicked off and immediately started winning – a strong position on which they disappointingly failed to build on for the rest of the match. The players all started running around shouting numbers at each other, which I found rather distracting above the noise of the 8-strong crowd.

The Butterflies, fresh from their astonishing 2-1 win against the Sockford Clownes, stormed into the match, their referee awarding them no fewer than 28 penalties in the first five minutes alone.

After further struggling and a fist fight between the two refs, Whoft goalie Adrian Rugby (what an amusing name for a rugby player, isn't it!) made a valiant save from the crossbar onto which he'd climbed, although in doing so, he clumsily avoided not falling off and rupturing two of his famous kidneys.

Butterflies centre winger God Johnson then sent the ball on to skipper Sir Frostie Canuderbitch who passed to left hook Ravenal Showboat on the blind side who powered his way to a showstopping try, landing the ball right in middle of the face of spreadeagled Adrian Rugby, who was by now being attended to by beleaguered ambulancemen.

Rugby was declared dead minutes later, just as four of the flagging Berbers found themselves locked in a scrum. They continued to play as an indivisible sixteen-legged mess for the rest of the game.

The second half whizzed by in a flapping of arms and more shouting of numbers (which I found less distracting because I left at half time) and apparently it was a drawer.

![SPORTS extra]

Sports day means sport

St BARRABAS' Infants' School sports day went with its usual bang, this Saturday, writes one of our staff. Parents and children cheered as pupils lurched about the lower field, confused by the rules of the Knife & Fork race, until teachers intervened.

The 110 Metre Hurtles also hospitalised several young competitors. Eventually, after hurtling through a nose-breaking eight sheets of plywood, a victorious and bloody Gawain Bethlem, 8, was helped to the podium by his mother.

At the Optical Course, designed for the school in 1946 by Mauritz Escher, hot favourite Oliver Hans fell at the "Neverending Staircase". With the field wide open, year 3's Maysie Ballon stormed to victory after a stunning "Which Line Is Longer?".

The Three-Legged Pole Vault was won with the bar at 47'6" by the unseeded Sorcha Cockrill and Evan Elevan, after their chief rivals were disqualified for going "one under – one over", a foul in the rules, I'm led to understand.

The great-grandparents' race went to Mr Wisty Memorial, 84, after great-grandmother Mrs Eileen Thoth came over all faint and sicked up in the last few yards.

- Spanish darts
- Swimming weights
- Extra balls
- Reversible cricket bats
- World Series "Walk The Plank" planks
- Sweat bags
- Double hockey sticks
- Judo belts: 2nd Dan Brown ONLY
- Dungeons & Dragons ladders
- Konami Hypersports moustaches and headscratching kits

PEAUX & SCHMIDT
ESTD 874
235 With The Beatles Rd,
Hammertime, Sockford
Tel 01999 854 399 after 6pm

Molford District Darts League Results

The Drink & Drive	11-4	The Fluff Lion
The Broken Arms	9-6	The Famous BBC2
The Chandelier & Grandad	6-9	The Naked Landlord
The Prince of Peas	2-13	The Goldilocks & Bear & Two Bears
The Drummer Out Of Def Leppard Who's Only Got One Arm's Arm	7-8	The Knitting Noodle
The Eighteen Bees	1-14	The People On Fire
The Frank Finlay & Firkin	6-9	Here Be Turnips
The Carry On Abroad	9-6	A Anchor
The Crush & Grape	4-11	The Warm Zippy
The My Family And Other & Groom	0-15	
The Chitty Chitty Bang	10-5	

FRAMLEY'S SPORTING PAST

NEW!

200 Years of Tradition

Wripple Anthemic AFC, Framley District League Champions 1960-1961.
This photograph, from before the introduction of home & away strips in 1975, shows the home team in traditional "whiteface". Please allow extra time for your order since the original cover, showing the away team, has been pulped.

TWO CENTURIES OF SPORTING MEMORIES BROUGHT TOGETHER FOR THE FIRST TIME

A NOSTALGIC GIFT FOR SPORTS FANS
£18.99 FROM ALL GOOD BOOKSHOPS

PUBLISHED BY MESTHETE AND WAND, 149b VIMY TERRACE, FRAMLEY

Television treasures are found in treasure trove

by Taunton Mishap

TV BOSSES WHO PUT out a call for lost episodes of classic television shows from the golden age of television were shocked and stunned by what has turned up in a loft in Whoft – a treasure trove of television previously thought lost forever.

Mahabarat Robinson, 52, found the unlabelled film cans amongst the effects of his late dead father, a former Comedy Classic wiper for the BBC.

"We'd presumed these rare historical artefacts had been wiped. But, goddamn it," said a BBC spokesphilistine yesterday, "we were wrong."

THE GOOD LIFE

The hoard, which contains the forgotten pilot episode of popular seventies survivalist documentary *The Good Lives* has shocked media historians, particularly in the many subtle ways this early draft differs from the hit show as we now know it.

In the newly rediscovered pilot, the title role of Tom Life is taken

Mr Robinson is delighted that his finds have been found.
PHOTOGRAPH BY ANDREW DEFINITELY

by much-missed adulterer Leonard Rossiter.

,

In the show, Rossiter, together with his wife Barbarah (Diane Keen), decides to build a farm in his lounge, much to the annoyance of stuck-up neighbours Jerry (*Rising Damp*-star Don Warrington) and Hanna (Minnie Riperton). Soul legend Riperton also performs a medley of her smash hits *Les Fleurs* and *Inside My Love* in the middle of the programme, backed by The Mike Sammes Quantity,

while Rossiter delivers a pig.

Warrington, who claims to not remember recording the show, was delighted that it had turned up. "What do I do in it? Oh, good."

Also in Mr Robinson's nostalgia haul were the missing Christmas episode of *Fawlty Towers*, where the cast go to Barcelona to stay in Manuel's brother's guest house; the final episode of *The Sweeney*, in which Denis Waterman gets eaten by a seal; and Arnold Ridley – Private Godfrey out of *Dad's Army*.

All the forgotten gems will be returned to the BBC archives, where they will be taped over with weather reports and closed circuit footage of the car park. Mr Ridley will be humanely destroyed on the June 13th edition of *Rolf's Animal Hospice*.

News In Brief

PENSIONERS RAIDED

A retirement home in Fracton was raided by police from Framley Drugs Squad in the early hours of Saturday morning.

Drugs worth a pavement price of £58,000 were seized, mainly aspirin, paracetamol and mogadon. 35 frail and infirm people were arrested and further 113 harassed. Unconfirmed reports say there are no survivors.

HOUSE HAUNTED HOUSE

Whoft resident Grammaticus Throttle has called in experts following claims that his house is haunted.

Throttle, 59, is convinced that his house is being haunted not by ghosts, but by living people. Exorcist Fulton Wonderful, however, says the so-called ghosts are Mr Throttle's upstairs neighbours, whom Grammaticus has been trying to evict since they installed glass floors and a 76-trombone doorbell.

JEFF'S WEDDING STORY

A woman whose husband fell asleep during their wedding vows has filed for annulment. "It was so embarrassing," says 23-year old stunner Lorraine Plums. "He was supposed to be saying 'I do', but all we could hear was him snoring." Her new soon to be ex-husband, Victor, later explained he was "bored".

AIRPLANET FLAPS

FLIGHTS FROM SOCKFORD INTERNATIONAL AERODROME

Destination up!

THIS MONTH'S SPECIAL OFFERS...

NEW Wrexham from £109 return

The Centre of The Earth £11

The Land of Chalk Drawings £38 retn

"The Buddy Holly Experience" £250 all in

Sandown, IOW £78 one way   **BARGAIN FLIGHT!**

The End of Your Road £12

BARGAIN FLIGHT! Sockford Aerodrome Arrivals Lounge £5

The Pub from £69

OrkneyDisney £575

Full English Breakfast £3.50

Ham, Egg & Chips £1.80

"See-Gulls" Cruise 4 whole weeks at a steady 27,000 feet in a glass-bottomed plane (no stopovers) from £109 return

EXCLUSIVE OFFER

24-HOUR BOOKING LINE
01999 940 940
www.aeroplame.com

Time for a wash

FRAMLEY TOWN hall's famous 20th century astronomical clock is to have its face washed for the first time since its construction almost as many years ago.

The huge clock, which is rumoured to only be fully visible from space, has been a favourite amongst old residents since it was built into the shopping precinct roof in 1968.

The passing hours are marked with a chime from one of the twelve bell towers scattered around the town. Every quarter hour, a wooden joust takes place above the clock face between the mediaeval characters of 'Jack o' the Hours' and 'Molly o' the Minutes', the result of which determines the length of the following hour.

By request of local MP Ianbeale Steeplecocque the essential

The clock figures who will have a special bath.
PHOTOGRAPH BY KEVVIN CHIPS

renovation works are to be undertaken while the clock mechanism is still running. This procedure will involve careful hand holding and numeral lifting during cleaning to avoid "time standing still".

to leave the hotel for three weeks now, because of the snipers. This is the only phone number I can remember, so I hope this gets through. Jenny, I love you and miss you terribly. Look after the kids. Donald.

COLANDER that lets the lumps out but leaves the liquid in. £15. Box FE8741. And no, I don't know how it works.

ETCHASKETCH "Curves" edition. Only draws curves. A giant leap sideways. 01999 722444.

LP for sale, 50p. 01999 240971.

FORD TURNIP 3.0 Touring, R-reg, very clean, fsh but no reverse gear or brakes. £3,000 asap because I've been driving round the block for 2 months and I want to get out. Tel 0906 480991.

HOSTESS TROLLEY. Fits two hostesses or one hostess and one client. £120 after 6pm.

TRAMPOLINE REQUIRED Any condition accepted. Mine's been stolen. Please hurry, I'll be coming down in a minute. 01999 733 008

STANNAH stairlift, lifts your stairs so you can't get onto them, vgc, £3500. Box FE8440.

INVISIBLE MAN, good nicker, £500. First to see will buy. 01999 673382.

CAN YOU TELL by the way you use your walk that you're a woman's man? No time to talk? We've helped six people like you. Call 01999 450981.

JOE & PETUNIA

THE FACT THAT I SMOKE IS YOUR FAULT forehead-mounted 3ft placard. £10 ten pound a tenner. 01999 460171.

HAYNES MANUALS for sale: Vauxhall Ciao 1985-89, Zanussi Z101 pocket fridge, Robin CurlyGirly hairdryer 1990-92, IKEA cutlery (new shape) and wallpaper. 01999 871298.

BLACK & WHITE MICROWAVE oven. £75. 01999 238664.

KEITH HARRIS ventriloquist's dummy. Comes with Orville ventriloquist's dummy ventriloquist's dummy. Call 01999 648 877 any time before the item is sold.

ROOFING CONTRACTORS, guttering and points. Will frot. Discreet service. Box FE8300.

BABY, Winnie The Pooh design, vgc, £10. 01999 313453.

INCOMPLETE KITCHEN. Bits of wood, bits of tiles, plughole, some other things, rest somewhere (might get round to finding bits). 01999 688140.

WICKER RADIO, geuine twiggy sound, AM only. £15. 01999 429420 am only.

250 x 2 piece jigsaw puzzles, each showing scenes of bits of harbour/sky. £1 each. Will separate. Box FE 01999 454120.

WHEELCHAIR, lightweight, folding for a car, little used. Good fun while it lasts. £45. 01999 866426.

PINK FLOYD'S Dark Side Of The Moon. Royalty cheques not quite as large these days, hence quick sale. Other satellite properties also available. Phone Roger on 01999 878 930

HOLY CRAB

GLASS GARAGES, self-assemble, show off your stuff to burglars, 8ft x 6in x ft, £8000. Freephone 09999 100600 (calls charged at £35 per min at all other times).

CAN'T SLEEP at night? Get up. £35. 01999 238117.

DANNY BAKER VIDEO "Football's Craziest Linesmen Vol 3". Still in box. £1. 01999 896 033

01999 845763. Offers 01999 863741.

INEXPENSIVE CHILD-MINDER required to look after sensitive 6 year old (Josie) while rest of family go on 3-week holiday to Disneyworld. References / experience not essential. Call Mr Hollyhock on 01999 482762

PINSTRIPE chimney pots, 32" waist, £20 each or £20 the pair.

RAWSORE Breast Pump & 50 litre feeding churn with Nipple Replacers. Box FE8280 after 6pm.

SLEEP-EASY INFLATABLE QUILT. Fully inflated forms 4' patchwork sphere floating eight inches above mattress. £15. 01999 560125.

FRAMLEY EXAMINERS for sale. Complete set 1978-2012. £offers Call Prof. Arthur Bostrom on 01999 429006. Experiment successful.

The Framley Examiner

"I sold my bicycle to the firth person who bought it. Thanks, Framley Examiner."

Mr Ing, Molford St Gavin

DANCING TABLECLOTH. Ashtray Polka / Cutlery 2-Step / Flower Arrangement Cha-Cha-Cha-Cha-Cha. £20. Box FE8631

"MRS COD" Ladies' Fish-n-Chips Umbrella. Take your mind off the weather by letting it rain delicious fish and chips straight onto your head! Wrapped, or open. £12, pickled onions 50p. 01999 852 872

IRON-ON GENTLEMAN'S PENILE TATTOO for urethra wall. Reads "Get In Lane". No longer required. £8. Whoft 855 341.

LOFT LADDERS, £135. Use your loft! We have thousands of ladders and nowhere to put them. We'll pay you £135 to store a few dozen in your loft. 01999 866 400

VOLKSWAGEN QUAGWAT 2.0E, not right from day one, handles like a rowing boat full of drugged children, £6,790 if necessary. Tel David (not "Dave") 01999 520998.

CHOCOLATE LOG effect electric fire. Just turn it on and it melts all over carpet. Already melted so £2. 01999 705590.

SIDEBOARDS. Italian. Job lot, 2 doors blown off, you're only supposed to bloody phone 01999 290000.

The Framley Examiner

"My spiral travel scissors sold within 24 hours!"

Mrs Eth, Wripple
sold for £50*
(* spiral travel scissors sold for £75)

1930s dinner service. Complete: 74 spoons, 3 forks, half a knife, tureen, gravy boat and soup yacht, £120. 01999 420425 after £120pm.

MY EX-WIFE'S NEW MAN'S MOBILE PHONE NUMBER IS 0999 766 533. Call it anytime between 1am and 4.20am and ask for Mr Cunt. That's 0999 766 533 and "Mr Cunt".

PAIR OF 18th Century "Bad Kitty" cat handcuffs. £200 or what? 01999 871289.

PUSH / WHEEL CHAIR, £45. No phone so write.

RYVITA? / RIBENA?

3-BEAN BAG. Tiny. £1. 01999 811111.

EVER WONDERED how a magicia n saws a lady in half? I think I can show you how. Box FE8311.

COFFEE TABLE, tea towel, Bovril slippers. The kettle's just boiling, pop round any time! 01999 552170.

NOVELTY CHESS SET Pieces representing Burger King (Dovercourt branch) relief staff. Board and Jessica Leonard (white bishop) missing, hence £35. 01999 885490.

CHILD'S three-quarter length grown-up, never used, £350ono. Box FE8230.

DOG BISCUITS, 3 flavours, Poodle, Labrador and Custard St Bernard. £5 a box or £5 a box. 01999 219335.

CLASSICAL GAS

INTENSIVE CARE BEARS Full set of upsettingly realistic children's toys, including Sunshine Coma Bear and Love-a-Lot Serious But Stable Bear. IV capoc drips on furry stands, and Wolf Nurse. Offers. Box FE8166

400 CONDOMS. All pink. Inappropriate gift. Obviosuly for girls. Will swap for blue ones for boys. Box FE8982.

DODGIMIX food processor with blender, 4 blades & 28 recipes. Requires some emptying, hence £no idea. 01999 885166.

VAUXHALL SPASMA 1.3L F-reg, vgc, no paperwork except MOT valid until 2047. £3,000 and no questions. Tel 01999 859120.

DOWNRIGHT PIANO. So piano. Really piano. £450 after 01999 381150pm.

SET OF SIX novelty cycling helmets. Sombrero, deerstalker, topper, fez, porkpie and scotch egg. Owner to collect. £8 each except £12. 01999 631408.

GIRLS mountain penny farthing. Used once. Also chest of girls clothes and effects. £yes. Box FE8137.

TIRED OF GOING UNNOTICED? Try one of our 'Stare At Me And Win £1000' t-shirts. M, XM, XXM. Call Vince 01999 450887 after today.

LAURA ASHLEY wetsuit, size 14. Black velvet bodice, long sleeves, with crepe de chine skirt. Bargain, £2000. Box FE8086.

HORIZONTAL baby bouncer, fits most halls, £45. 01999 882531.

MORPHY RICHARDS BeardMaker. Watch your beards grow and rise! £35. 01999 838440.

TABLE TENNIS table, half size, no receiving end, £65. 01999 352920.

ALL SCOTLAND'S BUTTERFLIES. You wondered where they'd gone. I've got them in my garage. £150 the lot. 01999 842 098

ELVIS COSTELLO This Year's Model train set, £15. 01999 487101.

"FUZZY PUMPER PUBERTY SHOP" TOY. Supplied with "Brunette", "Mousey" and "Ginger" Play-Doh tubs. Box FE8922.

NAN VARNISH, 5 litres, £30. 01999 328600.

GENUINE Victorian television cabinet. Mahogany with ormolu brass handles and ivory aerial attachment. £350. Will sell to the first person who calls, whether they like it or not. 01999 461023.

UNCONVENTIONAL DINNER SERVICE. Jack knives, tuning forks, satellite dishes, crown green bowls, that sort of thing £60. 01999 713382.

BABYGAP maternity dress. Ages 4-5. £70. 01999 681290.

THE CORN LAWS

LADIES' EROTIC ACCESSORY. Battery-operated vaginal swingball. Stimulates and bruises. Comes (every time) with two fanny racquets. £25. 01999 844 812

SINGLE "Z" BED, will fold out into double "N" bed or a pile of I's. £12. Box FE8533

Last year,
The Framley Examiner
readers sold more than 22,000 rare birds' eggs through our classified pages.

OAK EFFECT pine-style dining table with elm-plated mahogany finish, £200. 01999 862380.

TOTTENHAM HOTSPUR bedroom accessories, including bedlinen, pitch, turnstiles & bunkbed shaped like Pat Jennings tipping one over the bar. £offers. Box FE8385.

SALT & VIAGRA CRISPS, for nibbles that keep you up ALL NIGHT LONG! Also Dry Rohypnol Peanuts. 01999 Box FE 230886.

MATSUI digital nappies, with action replay and 10x macro, £300 each. 01999 300500 (T).

1967, lovingly restored in glass pack. Fiancée beginning to embrace free love, hence quick sale. £43 quickly – now nearly December. Box FE8109.

SLIPSHOD

SNOOKER BOARD, complete set of six balls, Jocky Reardon signature flights, Jim Bowen's "Bull Pocket" quiz book, £45. 01999 841971.

ALUMINIUM LADDER, 13ft long, 3 rungs, up only, £15. 01999 837414.

COLLECTION OF EARLY prototype vinyl CDs (1979-83). "Lexicon of Luxury", "Drat!", "Legionnaire – Just The Hits", "Nik Snood Live At The Blackheath Oregano", "Infrastructure IV", "Ickenham Dartboard – Sharp Pants and Piano Ties", "Walnut Whip" and "More Shillingbury Tales". Also half jar of jam and one six-inch nail. Acquired through work. £20 the lot. Call 01999 866 732 and ask for Michael Rodd or Judith Hann.

WEBSITE SOILED CLOTHING? Crusty with bollock marmalade? You're not coming in. Framley 895 544

PORT DECANTER and set of six solid Stilton glasses. Ripe. 01999 827454.

DICK VAN DICK

NISSAN THROATGRIPPER 4x2, terrifying 7.0L 3-gearbox, 6-wheel chrome and reinforced leather nightmare covered in roo bars and spotlights. The worst investment I ever made. I only needed it for the school run. £12,000 or anything. Tel Linda (not her real name) 01999 492217.

BARBIE ROLLERSKATES, will fit Barbie aged 6-9. £13.29ono. 01999 830987.

FRONT DOOR. Single panelled 77" x 35" glazed white uPVC door leading to my house and all my possessions, £35 the lot. 01999 901999.

GOODMANS Slightly Too Personal CD Player, plays songs relating to your life and details those areas in which you have failed miserably to live up to your own expectations or the expectations of those around you. Unwanted gift. Box FE8377.

SINGLE BED with mattress, storage drawers and me in it. £30, or £10 with annual hand-job. 01999 842151.

SCENES FROM HOLY BOOKS CRISPS, available in Bible, Koran, Bhagavad Gita and Chokey Bacon. Also, turn your visions of the blessed virgin into crisps. 01999 963 371.

TOILET DUCK. Turns water blue but pecked my arse. Removes crust under rim. £4. 01999 863 373

SPEAKING CLOCK RADIO, tells the time every 10 seconds. 2 (very insistent) voice settings: Naughtie / Wogan. £0. 01999 352133. Need not collect.

CLIPART CD "Saluting Fried Eggs". Over 240,000 images of fried eggs in a variety of saluting poses, including cub, National Socialist, senior officer, RAC, twelve gun and high-five. 01999 822 920

The Framley Examiner

"I got excellent results from The Framley Examiner. I sold everything I own except what I advertised."

Mrs Roophie, St Eyot's

COCKER SPANIEL KITTENS, superb temperament, quizzical look. 01999 480161.

PINE CD STORAGE towers, 14ft tall, store 4 CDs in luxurious splendour. En suite bathroom. £4500 each. 01999 381666.

PAIR OF galvanised haystacks, £15 each the lot each per pair. 01999 492294.

INCOMPETENTLY DRAWN hand-made Father's Day card depicting some sort of blue square holding hands with larger green shape (possibly car?). Message inside reads "Please Love Me Daddy from Josie", but spelt wrong. £offers. Unwanted gift. Call Mr Hollyhock on 01999 482762.

ARMITAGE SHANKS handbasin on pedestal. Ivory, with skid marks, £85. Box FE8626.

CAMCORDER WANTED, must be in good working order. Needed ASAP – baby about to fall out of high chair. 01999 829737.

Last year.
The Framley Examiner
readers sold more than 13,000 feet of purloined rushes from Star Wars Episode 3

CROWD SUBBUTEO. 48,000 pieces. Extremely slow play. Kenneth Wolstenholme's "Some People Are On The Pitch" Edition (1966). £12 in original box. 01999 872 421

BILLS. Gas. Water. Council Tax. £387 the lot. 01999 8

CHILDSPLAY™ carrier bag. Safe for putting over head. Fully breathable. £6 Also Wendy Abandoned Freezer. £45. Tel 01999 848 221

CUB SCOUT uniform, size 16 with 38" bust, £30. 01999 761443onn.

MELTED CHEDDAR bubble bath foam. 50cl. Produces one huge bubble. Do NOT pop. £3 01999 855 188

PRINGLES JUMPER. Full of crisps, very itchy and I just can't stop wearing it. Will swap for Pickled Onion Monster Munch jockey shorts. 01999 844 902

A final slice of the pie

by Bowery Tarpaulin

Britain's oldest pie is about to serve its last slice. Clinton Pie, baked in 1951 as an exhibihit for the Festival of Britain and relocated to Clinton seafront in 1952 is now down to its last portion.

For the last 50 years the pie has provided, in total, hour after hour of enjoyment to visitors and local residents and visitors alike.

The first slice, served on Saturday 5th June to King George VI by Winston Churchill, became a symbol of hope, prosperity and nourishment for the nation.

After this, slice after slice was served, until the following year,

The pavillion housing the pie.
PHOTO BY HARRISON COMPARISON

when the pie was relocated to the jetty on Clinton seafront to act as a "Pastry Beacon of Peace".

Since then until now, hundreds of visitors have visited the 25m diameter savoury tart, including some celebrities and some politicals.

That is until next Saturday, when the last few morsels of the pie will be auctioned off to local charities with the intention of funding a "Save The Pie Trust".

The Trust will endeavour to protect the last few crumbs of the famous pie, and return the jetty to the ocean as a memorial.

"It'll be a great and tragic day for all of us who come to Clinton, year after year for the Pie", says Pie enthusier, Canard Leghorn

"I've been coming here since I was 30, and that's twenty-three times. My daughter's still missing and where will the pie be when it's gone?".

Donations and concerned relatives can contact Mr. Leghorn on his Pie Helpline during low tide.

Train man dies

A DEPRESSED train driver who was on the verge of bankruptcy has committed suicide by throwing himself under a passenger.

Rufus Boing, 31, was said to be at "both ends of his tether," according to his doctor, when he deliberately dived under the front wheels of Carolyn Morphene's Vauxhall Average as she drove through the town centre.

Ms Morphene, who is suffering from post traumatic stock, was a regular passenger on Mr Boing's 0732 from Framley station, and had even accidentally slept with him on "one or two" occasions.

A spokesmen from MidCentral Journeys offered Mr Boing's family his deepest sympathy, and presented Ms Morphene with new wheels. There was a strike that day which explains why he wasn't working and she wasn't on a train.

In Court

BALLYHOO Bullknuckle, 46, of Manic Street Preacher Street, Molford, was hanged and banned from driving after he admitted parking all over 65-year old Denise Poverty in the Arnhem Centre one day.

MY MOTHER, 54, of My Family Home, Framley, heaped shame upon the family by being found guilty of parking a vomit bomb outside Framley General Hospital on All Saints' Night.

REG Edit, 43, The Address, Crème, was fined £50 for paying a previous £50 fine without due care and attention.

ANNIE Pandy, 27, of Slag Heap, Molford, was fined £35 with FF68,00 costs and A$200 compensation for possessing 8.1g of marshmallow at his address on October.

KERRY Perry, 23, of Boysenberry Spiral, St Eyot's, received a 35-year conditional discharge for damaging the corner of an envelope belonging to Glans Cliffcakes on July 14. He was ordered to cough up £400 compensation and his first born child (as yet unborn) in costs.

PAUL Discovery, 29, of Hexagon Rhomboid, Thoxtoxeter, was raised two metres and blown through an open window for 'becoming lighter than air' on two separate occasions during the Summer of '69. He was asked to pay a heavy fine.

EVEREST Blessed, 19, of Manilow Retreat, Effing Sodbury, had his head separated from his shoulders for assaulting a grizzly bear at Framley District Zoo on the sixth Friday of May last year. An additional fine of £80 remains unpaid.

VIOLET Complexity, 76, of Cake St, Whimsy, was returned by second-class mail after being inadvertently posted to an illegal address. Her statuatory rights remain, as ever, unaffected.

BESTHEMANE Fisticuff, 31, of Steam Crescent, Fracton, was released into the wilderness last Friday as part of an experiment to determine the shelf life of lime cordial. She may never return.

ELEPHANT McCartney, 24, of The Dodecahedron, St Eyot's, received a damning 3 minute summation of his shitty life after being lowered on top of Justice Constant Waxy during Big Court. His sentence is being punctuated.

School concert "far too loud"

By not Our Arts Correspondent, TAUNTON MISHAP

THIRTY-TWO children from Molford Children's School are recovering in hospital after a school concert went disastrously wrong last week.

The end of term jamboree had been organised by head of music Nigel Merry, who was due to conduct the senior orchestra through a medley of light popular hits from the 1960s, using his favourite 5-inch-long conductor's baton.

However, a sudden outbreak of flu caught Mr Merry off the hop, and his place was taken on the night of the concert by his deputy, Sally Quaskling. Parents are blaming the tragedy on this decision.

ENORMOUS VOLUME

"It was terrible," said the mother of one of the trumpeters, "Miss Quaskling had a huge baton, nearly a yard long, much bigger than Mr Merry ever used. When she started conducting, the children just followed, but her baton... Her baton was far too big..." She broke down.

Another parent told emergency services that the piece was so loud that "people started to run screaming from the hall in fear of their lives."

"The children were only following orders," said another mother's brother. "But... too... too loud..."

Within moments of the band striking up Petula Clark's *Downtown*, windows in neighbouring streets started to shatter and the earth was momentarily tipped off its axis.

The concert was called to a premature halt when a have-a-go hero attacked Miss Quaskling with a fire extinguisher, killing her.

The horn section's eardrums burst painfully.
PHOTO BY MORDRED FRONT

Children were reportedly led away with burst bloodvessels and bleeding mouths. A CD of the concert will not be available ever.

DOES HE TAKE **SUGAR?**

LIKE YOU GIVE A SHIT

Framley Social Services

Tel. Framley 01999 900 900

NOW IS THE WINDOW OF OUR DISCONTENT!

MADE GLORIOUS SUMMER BY NEWBY'S WINDOWS

SMASHING JULY SALE

ONLY £1000 FOR **7** WINDOWS

1 Square window
2 Round window
3 Three-way window
4 Window of opportunity
5 Revolutionary single-glazed window
6 Window envelope
7 Quarterlight from Ford Psycho SRi

"THAT'S NOT A LOT OF MONEY FOR QUITE A LOT OF WINDOW" says WINDY, Newby's Windows's mascot!

FIND A WINDOW TO FIND A WINDOW!

COME WINDOW SHOPPING AT NEWBY'S WINDOWS!

VINCE PREVIOUS IS INNOCENT

THE WORLD HAS NEVER LOOKED NICER THAN THROUGH A NEWBY'S WINDOW?

YOU'RE NEVER MORE THAN INCHES FROM A NEWBY'S WINDOW!

100s OF ACCESSORIES! including locks, polarizing filters and shabby leathers.

*Fitting and glass not included though.

NEWBY'S OF MOLFORD WINDOWS OF MOLFORD
56 HELVETICA BLACK CONDENSED STREET, MOLFORD 01999 877 577

Developments announced in missing charabanc case

The coach party in the road outside The Running Mayor public house, shortly before they set off for Fracton and vanished.

PHOTOGRAPH BY MOGADON SPOOK

Difney FIGURES

celebrating
**70 years of not
being able to sell
these Difney figures**

*Set of 6 hand-crafted bakelite
figurines of popular Difney
characters.*

DS1 Steamboat Mickey
DS2 Steamboat Mowgli
DS3 Steamboat Chip
DS4 Steamboat Herbie Goes Bananas
DS5 Princess Steamboat

and one more

celebration
price
£1 each

Adrian Butterfly Collectables

56, Jammy Dodger Terrace, Molford St Malcolm
01999 584 657 www.loftclearance.co.uk

by Jesus Chigley

POLICE WHO HAVE BEEN INVESTIGATING the mysterious disappearance in 1953 of a charabanc full of holidaymakers have announced that the bus and its passengers can now be officially declared "presumed missing".

In a neatly typed press release, released to the press last Thursday, chef investigating officer Det Sgt Ronald Sodastream said that his team were now almost 99% certain that the coach was no longer on its way to Fracton, and that there was no reason not to assume that it was probably missing.

"In police work, it's important not to jump to any hasty conclusions," the sergeant's statement read. "We couldn't rule out the possibility that the charabanc was just taking the long way round. I assure the public that my officers have been watching the main Fracton arterial road for the last fifty years like hawks, just in case."

WHERE IS THE BUS?

Having redesignated the errant pantechnicon's status from "late" to "presumed missing", the police are confident that enquiries into its whereabouts can now begin in earnest.

"I'm glad that, after all these years of uncertainty, the anguish is over for the families and friends of the unaccounted for holidaymakers,"

Sodastream told me yesterday.

"To those patient people, I say take comfort from the knowledge that your loved ones are undoubtedly missing."

And things are already moving fast. A special group of detectives are looking into the possibility that the coach and passengers may have simply gone invisible, while other experts are searching all the drawers in the police station to see if someone just filed the bus away somewhere and forgot where they put it.

New paving stone

A new paving stone is to be laid to replace a damaged one. The stone, made by Dabney & Dabney Brick Works, will occupy 45cm of the pavement at the corner of Slops Steps and Prefab Way in Sockford. The stone will be laid by a top pavementer rushed in by contractors Wonham Foreign de Foreigner. Saturday is expected.

This month's
**LOTTERY
PREDICTION**
from Megalithic Meg

6

"I predict 6"

DAMIUN'S RECIPES

WEEK 6: CURRY DISHES

No 23: CORNFLAKE CURRY

Ingredients
1 curry
1 family size box of cornflakes

Method
Take the cornflakes and add them to the curry. Eat.

No 25: RICE KRISPIE ROGAN JOSH

Ingredients
1 curry
1 x 500g box of Rice Krispies

Method
Take the Rice Krispies and add them to the curry. Eat.

No 24: BOUNTY BIRYANI

Ingredients
1 curry
1 milk chocolate Bounty

Method
Take the Bounty and add *both* bars to the curry. Eat.

No 26: CORNFLAKE & RICE KRISPIE MADRAS

Ingredients
1 curry
1 x 500g box of Rice Krispies
1 x family size box of cornflakes

Method
Take the cornflakes and the Rice Krispies and add them to the curry. Eat.

Variations: try Honey Nut Loops or Newby's Morning Glory™.

**All recipes on this page
serve one (eleven times)**

Damiun's recipes are available online at www.damiunishungry.com or by sending a SAE and £50 cash to Damiun Clavalier, c/o The Framley Examiner, Unit 149b, East Cosset Industrial Park, Parkfields Bypass, Framley FR1 6LH

Voter apathy to blame

BY BUNCO BOOTH

THE LOWEST EVER turnout in Framley at last week's local election is being blamed on voter apathy.

The council elections, held on Thursday, broke all records for turnout, percentages and majorities, in a surprise that psephologists (who are people who study voting trends)* weren't expecting.

One of Framley's most famous political faces, Cllr Geoffrey Cauchaugh, managed to poll the most votes in his ward, with the returning officer declaring him elected with a majority and total of 1 vote. All the other candidates polled none.

"I only put in my vote for a photo opportunity, and naturally, I voted for myself," shouted Cllr Cauchaugh from his fifth-floor office as I interviewed him from the car park.

ROCK THE VOTE

When asked why they did not even vote for themselves, Cauchaugh's rivals remained unapologetic.

"Politics doesn't really interest me," said one. "It doesn't have any effect on my life. And anyway, you can't really change anything, so what's the point?"

Exit pollsters at a polling station in Whoft find it easy to cope with an influx of no voters.
PHOTOGRAPH BY FORGETMENOT EVANS

Perhaps more surprisingly, others did not even know the election was taking place.

"That's perhaps even more of a surprise – I didn't even know the election was taking place," said others.

ANARCHY FOR THE UK

None of Cllr Cauchaugh's 15 opponents lost their deposit, luckily, thanks to the D'Ainty Poll Act Bye-Law 1997, which states that "a candidate need only poll no (0) votes to be deemed legitimate."

The act, which the High Court and House of Lords have declared "illegal, unethical, undemocratic, overtly and unfairly partisan and entirely empirically contradictory" has been declared "awesome" by Mayor D'Ainty.

* Source: British Airways in-flight dictionary.

In Court

ELEANOR VIRTWHISTLE of Lom Street, Molford, was fined £12 with £8 costs by Sockford Magistrates Court on October 23rd for failing a driving test. A charge of genocide was withdrawn.

GRAHAM HANDSOME of Suez Canal, Wetting, was sentenced to A Journey Into Sound, for Letting The Beat Drop, with £200 additional costs at Framley Magistrates Court on November 9th.

THOMAS MALALLEY of no fixed address was fined £250 with £80 costs for going against God by building an owl.

M'LEARNED COLLEAGUE MR CHRISTIAN DENNNIS was fined £300 with £45 costs for boring me stiff on November 3rd at Framley Magistrates Court.

JENSEN INTERCEPTOR of Coffeepot Park, Fracton was banned from driving for six months for driving for six months.

MICHAEL SPIDERMAN of Ditko Avenue, Sockford, was jailed for 5 months for driving a Batmobile while under the influence of Superman.

GORDON TUMBLEDOWN of One Street, St Eyots, received 100 minutes of Simplification for stealing a bread.

Conman made pensioner get him a glass of water

A MAN DESCRIBED AS "a dangerous conman by police", tricked his way into the home of Wripple pensioner Jerome Leading, 72, last Thursday and persuaded the unsuspecting old man to get him a glass of water.

The conman then sat down in Mr Leading's lounge, drank the water, and left.

Police say this is one of the oldest scams in the book, and have warned all pensioners to be particularly vigilant, remembering to check the identification of all callers.

The glass of water, filled from the cold tap in Mr Leading's kitchen, was yesterday being ground into a fine powder by forensics experts in case it turns out to be full of clues.

Mayor stoned

BY BUNCO BOOTH

QUESTIONS are being asked about the future of the mayor, Mr William de D'Ainty, after claims that he was stoned last week in his office.

Mr Mayor, 44, was found slumped over his desk in hysterics by his secretary, Herod Williams, on Friday lunchtime.

Miss Williams, who famously won the boat race in 1960, also claims that she had to cancel the mayor's appointments for the rest of the day because she thought his fingers were ten little milkmen. Mayor D'Ainty spent the rest of the afternoon happily practising his signature on a blotting pad.

"He was blapped," she illuminated.

When questioned about the events by interested reporters, Mr Mayor admitted that his memories of Friday afternoon were "hazy, at best," but insisted that he had no recollection of anybody throwing stones at him.

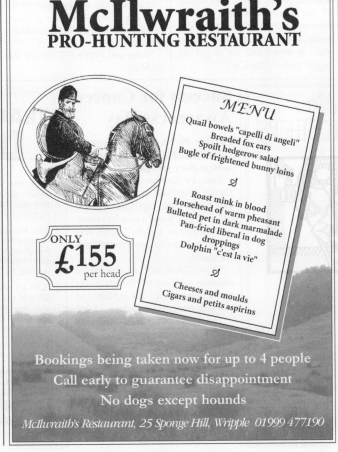

McIlwraith's
PRO-HUNTING RESTAURANT

ONLY
£155
per head

MENU

Quail bowels "capelli di angeli"
Breaded fox ears
Spoilt hedgerow salad
Bugle of frightened bunny loins

Roast mink in blood
Horsehead of warm pheasant
Bulleted pet in dark marmalade
Pan-fried liberal in dog droppings
Dolphin "c'est la vie"

Cheeses and moulds
Cigars and petits aspirins

Bookings being taken now for up to 4 people
Call early to guarantee disappointment
No dogs except hounds

McIlwraith's Restaurant, 25 Sponge Hill, Wripple 01999 477190

PARANOIA LESSONS

EVERYONE ELSE IS HAVING THEM

WHY AREN'T YOU?

01999 800 756

Scott is certainly a top of the class!

by Jesus Chigley

SCOTT JOPPPLIN, a Year 12 pupil from St Gahan's School For Boys in Framley, is definitely top of the class! His record-breaking haul of SIXTY-FIVE! A-Levels has made him become the most successful pupil in the school's three hundred year history.

Normal pupils at the school usually take no more than three A-Levels, with an optional fourth for swots. Scott made special arrangements with the examination board in order to achieve his achievement, often sitting two exams at once and, in one case, entering the same set of answers for three papers in different subjects.

It was unconventional examing by anyone's standard, but the results speak for themselves.

"I was nervous before the results envelope arrived," he told our reporter when I phoned him, "but when I saw I'd passed nearly all of them, it was a huge relief and I got drunk."

The only subject that proved too tricky for the exam mastermind was Geography, in which he did worse than me. "I'd been up for eight days' straight by that point, and could only draw circles," he said in his defence.

Scott, whose father is married to local TV weatherman Gareth Smee, is to be immortalised by a tapestry draped over the west wing of the school like a blanket over a parrot's cage.

Here are the exam results that made Scott the cleverest boy in the world:

English (D)	Spirograph (A)	The Farm (A)
Maths (D)	Pub Quiz (B)	Showing Off (A*)
French (D)	Woodwork Oral (C)	Crumb (Robert) (A)
Geography (U)	StickleBricks (A)	Crumb (Charles) (A*)
History of Soup (A)	Jugs (A*)	Marijuana Cuisine (B)
Tommy Cooper (A)	Rugs (C)	The Unbelievable (A)
Whisk (B)	Burning It (C)	Alphaboni Rigatoni (C)
Mouse Hunt (C)	Homebrew (C)	Write Anything You Like (A*)
Stopping (A)	Somebody On A Beach (A)	If... Then... (B)
Kettle Maintenance (A)	Umbrella (Opening) (A)	Lucky Dip (A)
Hiding a Bus (B)	Umbrella (Closing) (C)	Fire Exits (B)
Manchester (C)	Cannonball Run 2 (B)	Walking In A Straight Line (C)
Playtime (A)	Big Coins (C)	GCSE (A)
Applied Carpets (B)	Surprise (A)	Pure Maths (Best In Show)
Captain Sensible (B)	The Blustery Day (B)	Worm Husbandry (B)
French Smiling (A)	French Kissing (A)	Sandwich Spread (B)
Mud Wrestling (B)	Pin The Tail On The Answer (B)	Showboat (A)
Body Popping (A*)	Roundie or Squarie (A*)	Bullshitting (A)
Hula Hoop (A)	Dominoes (B)	I Spy Roadsigns (A*)
Measles (A)	Guinea Pigs (B)	When I Grow Up (B)
Shoegazing (B)	Fancy (A)	Battleships (B)
Practical Kitten (A)	Highland Fling (B)	Lists (B)

So, think you could do better? Try our sample questions from some of Scott's papers and see if you could beat Framley's own Stephen Hawkings!*

1. In one word describe how long it takes for the sun to travel the sky.

2. Two men start walking towards each other at the same speed on different days. When will they learn?

3. "Discuss the significance of 'Trial By Eating Sweetcorn Niblets With A Cocktail Stick' in *Gawain and The Green Giant*." Discuss.

4. Now close the box.

5. What is the essential difference between a web spun by a cat and that spun by a mouse?

6. A triangle has four sides. The sum of the internal angles is 270°. Using this information, rearrange the sides to spell the word "Hut", without breaking any of the matchsticks.

7. "There is light at the end of the tunnel." How do you know this?

8. Make an ox-bow lake.

9. Use both sides of the paper if necessary.

*These questions are for fun only, and are not exchangeable for A-Levels.

Ernhold Swiss (Left), the headmaster of Teapop Prep School, expressed concern at the hygeine of the Sewerside Leisure Centre (Above)

PICTURES BY TESCO DICKBARTON

Big bug

by Pharaoh Clutchstraw

FRAMLEY ENVIRONMENTAL HEALTH OFFICERS closed a local leisure centre and took samples of school canteen food after a mystery bug hit pupils at Teapop Preparatory School on Monday.

The children, aged between 11, complained of "feeling all sick" after attending a schools' fishing gala at Framley's Sewerside Leisuredrome on Friday evening.

The leisure centre, which attracts more than 14 visitors a day, was sealed off with gaily coloured sellotape. Urine samples were taken from all three mezzanine pools and one was put in the outdoor pool as a control.

Teapop School head Ernholt Swiss said: "I knew that something was terribly up when every one of my 90 children failed to be at my school on Monday. All but 86 of them were back in my classroom the next day so that's alright then."

The source of the contamination is not yet known. Teachers first thought that the Sewerside pool was to blame because pupils had attended the Friday gala and fished there the day before Friday. Leisure centre staff, on the other hand, insisted the infection had started from improperly cooked school dinners, such as Sloppy Semolina and Spotted Dick With Dead Flies In.

Council Health officials say they are keeping an open mind until all the samples have been looked at, with results expected to be available at the end.

A Framley Borough Council press officer said, "If samples from both the pool and the canteen turn out negative, we may have to conclude that the bug was brought into the school by an infected pupil, perhaps one carried into the playground on a gust of wind."

Day raises £250

PUPILS AT Gregory's Girl's School in Molford St Malcolm have raised £250 towards the cost of new textbooks during a sponsored fancy dress day.

"This year we chose a special theme," said Headmistress Wendy Redrobin. "Everyone, staff and pupils, came dressed as Stephanie Webster from Year Nine."

"We wish Stephanie a speedy recovery. In retrospect, maybe we should have warned her."

Stephanie, who is currently lying in a trauma-induced coma in Framley General Hospital, was the only pupil not to dress up specially for the day.

Stephanie's music teacher, Miss Brie, has prepared a special tape, which doctors say may help bring her out of her catatonic state.

"It's a recording of her favourite song, sung by the whole school, doing an impression of exactly the way Stephanie used to sing it."

Good levels

A Year 12 pupil from St Tuscadero's County High School For Girls has passed 94 A-Levels. Yasmin Strost, is, according to the pictures editor of a local newspaper, an unphotogenic bespectacled goink.

THINKING OF TURNING YOUR CAR INTO A PIANO?

It's harder than you think, so talk to the experts.

Whether it's fitting a candelabra, or installing lid mirrors, our trained mechanics and piano tuners are here to help.

aldente PIANO CARS

01999 855 430

READER'S OFFERS

COLASANTO COACH TOURS

Established 1985

Get away from most things inside of a deluxury coach by COLASANTO

01999 844 444
for free brochure

BANANA GARDEN ABBOT

2 trips for the price of 1

Come and visit one of Britain's most unique holiday destinations, on this 3-week coach cruise round Banana Garden Abbot.

Bananana Garden Abbot was designed in 1921 by compulsive serial architect Sir Brian Clough Ellis-Bextor, his final masterstroke being the installation of a 3 hectare mirror suspended over the village.

You can see what's going on anywhere in Banana Garden Abbot by simply looking at where the sky used to be! Watch yourself pedalling a Penny Submarine or fighting a bear. Look at what's on the roof of the Orrery! And at the end of every day, why not stop in at the hospital for a neck massage?

QUOTE REFERENCE BGA11
(both trips must be taken by the same customer within a two month period)

foghorn hoy
"just imagine..."

Foghorn Hoy on the South Coast of Scotland advertises itself as The Darkest Place On Earth, so why not go and try and see for yourself?

There's plenty of spectacular scenery to hear and you can visit the famous Black Beach and have a go at making out the famous stranded dolphins.

"See" the famous Auld Woman o' Hoy

This trip includes full board for one week (14 nights) in the Penumbra Majestic Hotel, a free torch (not to be used during hours of darkness), and a rope to keep the whole family together.

QUOTE REFERENCE FHY23
With every voucher you give us, one of your kids goes free.
No funny business.

Lessbury Moreborough Model Village

Come to Lessbury Moreborough's beautiful model village, where there's never been a better time to take in a small show, win big money in the miniature penny arcade, or visit the tiny IKEA.

It's your last chance to enjoy this listed Heritage Attraction, before it gets bulldozed next month to make way for a model motorway linking two neighbouring model towns and relieving model traffic on the model bypass. So roll up roll up.

We're offering our Framley Examiner readers
2 last chances for the price of one!
when they present this coupon at the tiny turnstile

W. Seafields, Lessbury Moreborough (off junction 17 of the FR12)

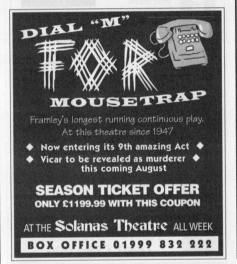

DIAL "M" FOR MOUSETRAP

Framley's longest running continuous play.
At this theatre since 1947

◆ Now entering its 9th amazing Act ◆
◆ Vicar to be revealed as murderer this coming August ◆

SEASON TICKET OFFER
ONLY £1199.99 WITH THIS COUPON

AT THE **Solanas Theatre** ALL WEEK
BOX OFFICE 01999 832 222

BILLY TURPS
THE BOOKMAKERS

We'd like to take this opportunity to give readers of the Framley Examiner the following special offer odds on a selection of popular bets.

	WAS	NOW
MAN UTD TO WIN PREMIERSHIP	7 – 2	20 – 1
TIGER WOODS TO PLAY US OPEN	EVENS	35 – 1
CYCLIST TO WIN TOUR DE FRANCE	EVENS	50 – 1
BY-ELECTION TO RETURN MP	2 – 1	75 – 1
QUEEN ALREADY DEAD	3 – 1	80 – 1
PORTUGAL TO BORDER SPAIN	NO BET	100 – 1
DECEMBER CHRISTMAS	3 – 1	150 – 1

11, Rayndon Parade, Whoft 01999 854 633 www.bt.com

SWEEP UNSQUEAKED

The smash hit, fresh from its sell-out run at the Theatre Royal Drury Lane.

For the first time, Sweep performs, uncensored, in his own voice. Over forty years of pent-up aggression released at last.

Featuring the DISAPPEARING BONE trick that got Sweep and Charlotte Church thrown off The Royal Variety Performance, this is a show that is strictly NOT for children.

**SPECIAL FAMILY TICKET OFFER
TWO ADULTS AND UP TO NINE
CHILDREN AND ANOTHER ADULT
ONLY £45**
QUOTE REF. FE8776

AT THE *Framley Pagoda* FROM FRIDAY
BOX OFFICE 01999 875 455

NcNewby's

Roy NcNewby

Everyone's favourite clown, Roy NcNewby has some mmm-mindwatering mmmm-meal offers for mmm-NcNewby's diners. Readers just have to cut out these NcCoupons and hand them in at the Molford Station drive-thru restaurant as the train passes the service window. Not available in standard class.

25p Off

Egg NcMilkshake™

Regular, Chocolate or Omelette*
*may contain traces of bacon

It's NcBack!

The Sage NcBun™
A whole quarter pound of prime, chopped sage, all wrapped up in a freshly pickled bun!

ONLY £1.99 while stocks last

Kidz Deal

With ev'ry Kidz Heavy Meal™, get a FREE Medium Tar Kingsize NcFag™

20 different NcFags™ to collect. Collect all 20 and get a free NcPack™ to put them in!

Only £6.99

Roy's NcSpecial Breakfast Menu™

NcBoiled Egg™ and a cup of tea
OR
NcDippy Soldiers™ and a nice cup of tea
Available between 11am.

Still HUNGRY?

NEW NcDouble Meals™
2 x Brisket NcBiscuit™
2 x 3lb Cow Bar
2 Frapuccino NcFries™
2 Sausage NcFluffy™
Cumberland Ripple, Pepperamipolitan™
2 tins Mushy Pears

Only sold on presentation of still warm clean plate from previous NcNewby's meal. £4.75 EACH.

Get On With Your Dinner

Give this voucher to any member of staff and we'll tell your kids to Get On With Their Dinner.

BBC

9.00 Joliffe The cloth crab descends from his cloud and tells the story of a hand grenade that falls in love with a bunch of keys. Narrated by Oliver Postgate.

9.15 Hey You! Yes, You God! It's Sunday! Leviticus 11:2 sung for under-10s.

9.40 Worship On One The playful choirboys of Winchester Cathedral. Narrated by David Attenborough.

10.10 Aslan Magazine A look back at this week's events in Narnia.

10.40 Does He Take Sugar? (6/10)

10.55 Hear Say! Programme for the tone-deaf.

11.20 We Are Experiencing Technical Difficulties (18/26) (rpt)

12.35 The Computer Programme Fred Harris investigates the government's pledge to get a BBC Microcomputer into every home by the year 2000.

1.00 Farm The kids from The New York School Of The Farming Arts get upset when heifer Doris is sent to the abbatoir. *followed by* **Farming for Weathermen** with Jonathan Bell

1.25 Thousand Island Discs Roy Plomley methodically dips all Barry Cryer's favourite records in salad dressing.

1.50 News Headlines A look ahead at next week's storylines.

1.55 Film Après-Midiée: *Whistling at Hayley Wind* (1959) When children discover a rapist on the run hidden in a barn, circumstances cause 12-year-old Hayley to believe that the stranger means her no harm.
Mills ... John Wind
Hayley ... Hayley Wind
Man ... Oliver Casterbridge
Billy ... Frank Sorry
Dir.: Bryan Numan

3.30 The All-New Adventures of Foghorn Rabbit

3.40 Alias Stephenson & Atkinson (rpt) Comedy western adventure series with Bob Goody and Chris Langham

4.25 Julian Balloon The storyteller (Michael Gambon) weaves another yarn using his fridge magnets.

4.35 Go With Groom Simon Groom returns to his family's Dethwick farm for the eighth time this series.

5.05 Charlie's Gordon Army Gordon Honeycombe, Hannah Gordon and Buster Crabbe are pressed into service by Captain Drake.

5.55 News (8,590/53,112) Jan grows suspicious when she has to cover Kenneth's shift for the third time in eight weeks.

6.05 The Edwin Drood Mysteries By Andrew Davies, dramatised in six parts by somebody Dickens.

6.35 Stanley Lebor appeals on behalf of the Neighbourhood Watch.

6.40 Screams of Praise Human sacrifice.

7.15 Sweet Jesus Sitcom. Audrey (Penelope Keith) falls for the teenage Christ.

7.45 Polpot Drama. Ross goes into hiding in the tin mine when Angharad finds the ditch full of bespectacled skulls.

8.35 It Ain't 'Alf Cramped, Mum Wartime sitcom with Melvyn Hayes as Anne Frank and Windsor Davies as Obergruppenführer Stertzlitz.

9.05 That's Enough Sausage-shaped vegetables, dogs allegedly saying 'sausage-shaped vegetables' and Cyril Smith reading us one of his Odd Odes in which he apologizes for breaking Cyril Fletcher's armchair.

9.50 Magnusmind Specialist subjects include Specialist Subject Questions I Asked During the Last Series of Mastermind and Little Known Facts About Iceland.

10.20 News (as 5.55) (rpt)

10.30 The Heart of the Thinking-Man's Crumpet Nude studio discussion. David Jessel disappointingly stands in for Joan Bakewell.

11.05 What Tastes Salty And Slithers Across The Dancefloor? David Jacobs and Terry Wogan cha-cha-cha to find out who will be Host of The Next Series.

11.45 The Sky Tonight Patrick Moore accidentally swallows the sky and Chicken-Licken can't remember if he or she is in the wrong story or not.

12.10 Phil Silvers as Steve Biko

12.35 Weathercock Michael Fish's

12.40 Last Orders

12.50 Closedown (first shown on BBC2)

BBC "2"

8.05 The Pope Pope Karol Wojtyla I returns to his birthplace where he will be facing penalty kicks from General Jaruzelski and Lech Walesa.

10.10 Open Polytechnic
10.10 This Lime's Bleedin' Diabolical **10.35** Squat Betty **11.00** The Rock n Roll Years: *1927* **11.25** I Cried When Charlie Got Blown Away **11.50** Collecting Crabs **12.15** The Brittlest Hobo.

12.40 Sviatenski Plays Ravel *Quarter-final.*

1.05 That's a Queer Sort of Ball, Mother Opinioned England v Twickenham. Highlights from yesterday's international in New Zealand with commentary by Alan Bennett.

1.55 Indoors Indoors Annie Farmhouse cooks lunch for James Burke.

2.20 Vertical. Science. James Burke eats his Sunday lunch.

Post- closedown music show. Late night tunes from Kawasaki Wetbike, The Collective, and Organ Dispute, plus an exclusive play of the new Hudsons' single. Presented by Ellen McArthur

THE OLD FLANNEL FUNNEL
BBC2 4.45am

3.10 Rather Be Lord Olivier says he'd rather be Osvaldo Ardiles, Peter Purves or Justin Fashanu. (B/W) (rpt)

3.40 The Second World War In Crisps (rpt) (6/26) Wotsits over Berlin.

4.30 The Great Crisp Race Three more teams of engineers attempt to drive a Ringo across the ocean floor. With Professor Heinz Siebenundfunfzig.

5.05 Whicker's Lounge This week Alan talks us through his magazine rack.

5.40 Around With Alice Another of Czech animator Jan Svankmajer's subversive anti-state golfing films. Jan's guest this week is Dennis Waterman.

6.10 News Review Ludovic Kennedy and his panel look back at this week's events in White City.

6.30 The Monkey Programme Tripitaka gets it on with Valerie Singleton.

7.15 The Natural World About Us The life cycle of *homo sapiens* filmed over the course of seventy-four years by a dedicated team of Brazilian rain forest ants. Narrated by Roy Skelton.

8.05 Bent Coppers In 1974 producer Paul Watson produced an extraordinary fly on the wall documentary series about two of Britain's top policemen. Tonight he revisits the pair to discover if their dishonesty has been exposed eight years after his documentary that no one watched first exposed their dishonesty.

9.00 Jack High The world's best flat-green bowlers compete to score the world's worst poker hand. Semi-final: David Bryant v Bill Moseley.

9.30 35 Minutes: *The Harlem Bogtrotters* Film following a dismal Irish basketball team trying to get a cartoon series made about their non-existent exploits.

10.10 Samuel Beckett Season: *Not Yet* A close up of a woman's mouth as she cycles up the steep slopes of the Alpe d'Huez, chasing the peloton. Billie Whitelaw gives a tour de france performance.

10.45 Betjeman in Birmingham (rpt) Buying a spade in the Bullring.

11.30 Your Socks Are Giving Me The Horn

11.40 Kirk Douglas Season: *Falling Down* (1961) Psychopathic sympatheth I-SPRCS, goes on the rampage in ancient Rome after his wife abandons him on the cross. May be badly edited for bad language.
Ian Spartacus ... Kirk Douglas
Maggie Spartacus ... Lee Remick
Det Sgt St Matthew ... Shelley Duvall
Persian shopkeeper ... Karl Malden
Dir.: Stickley Brick

1.10 Last Orders

1.20 Closedown (first shown on BBC1)

ITV

6.00 I Am-TV David Frost.

9.25 Bob The Biscuit (rpt)

9.30 Minipopska 8-year old Marek Strzelecki dresses up as the Pope and makes a pronouncement on chocolate biscuits.

10.00 Sport Dickie

10.30 Good Morning Faith from St Nedwell's Chapel, Shillingbury Illingbury with readings from Percy Filth.

11.30 Pant Along With Nancy Lamaze class.

12.00 Weekend Waldheim Former UN Secretary-General Kurt Waldheim denies direct knowledge of any of this week's alleged events in "Europe".

1.00 Out Of African Township Meryl Streep and Jack Hargreaves fall in love with a carthorse.

1.30 Les Schtroumpfs Hergé's Aventures de Tintin Schtroumpf et Hercule Schtroumpf test Papa Schtroumpfette's little grey beards. Translated by Eric Thompson.

2.00 Mork & Dawber Documentary. Robin and Pam take a break from filming but, even though the cameras aren't rolling, Robin can't stop performing.

2.30 The Big Moth Highlights of Brian Moore eating a jumper.

3.30 Major Charles Winchester & The Bear

4.30 Just Catworzel Geoffrey Bayldon scratches his head as the eleventh-century scarecrow gets into more trouble with his dog, Jumble.

5.00 Sunday Flipping Sunday hosted by Gloria Beaumont.

6.00 Brasseye Top darts players are made to look foolish by Jim Bowen in the seemingly innocuous quiz.

6.30 Weekend News And finally, Martyn Lewis reads a newspaper and potters about his flowerbeds in a sunhat.

6.40 Steve Heighway Harry Secombe sings *You'll Never Walk Alone* and recreates his classic goal from the 1971 FA Cup final.

Hard-hitting current affairs. Britain's clown community faces its toughest crisis yet with the closure of Billings' Circus, laying off over 14,000 full-time and 6,500 part-time clowns. Tonight Berys Jervis talks to every single one of them.

WORLDABOUT
BBC1 10.30pm

7.15 Me & Me & My Girl Sitcom. Simon (Richard O'Sullivan) is unable to finish his new libretto after Samantha (Stephen Fry) steals his credit card.

7.45 You're 'Aving A Laugh Practical jokes backfire on presenters Rusty Lee and Martin Say "Yes, Father" Daniels as they visit the East End.

8.45 Fingers Crossed At Her Majesty's Veteran entertainers in more death-defying performances.

9.45 Weekend News (as 6.30) (rpt) Followed by a nice pot of tea and a really long sit down. Lovely.

10.00 Clive James On IV Drip-feeding endurance show with the least hungry man on television.

10.30 The South-East Show Melvyn Bragg proposes that culture should only be available in London.

11.30 It's Not Like The Old Days An invited panel laments the unfestive feel of today's Christmas Day schedule.

12.00 Christmas Meditation Lord Rabbi Lionel Bluebird of Happiness offers some of his own thought.

12.10 The Queen Repeat of her message to the nation after one and a half bottles of Gordon's.

12.20 Oh No! It's The Moomins Nightmare-inducing animation. Narrated very, very quietly by Nick Ross.

12.30 Closedown (first shown on BBC1)

B/W indicates Black & White
Rpt indicates a repeat
Times indicate times

WEEKEND TV
SUNDAY

Great Deals At WAND Stores

Family pack 6 bags of Sir Spuddingham crisps:
2 x steak & kidney pudding
2 x bread & butter
2 x soup

45p

Jammy Jigs jigsaw shaped jammy biscuits (20 packets required to make full jigsaw of Cotswold cottage)

18p

Chippy's "Gravy Magic" pour Gravy Magic over your dinner and watch as it forms a crispy sage and onion shell... delicious!

27p

Sailor Suds bubble bath 300ml available singly or "Sailor Suds and Mr Sailor Suds" twin pack

64p

Frye's Maestro bar

10p

Wand... your local stores

12, Main Street, Sockford
68, Goose Green Road, Chutney
8, Lemonade Parade, Wripple

Fireman rescued from big tree by cats

By Odgar Cushion

A WHOFT FIREMAN had a lucky escape on Wednesday when a routine cat rescue operation turned out to be a lot more!

The cat's owner, Mrs R. Webster, had called Whoft Fire Services after hearing plaintive miaowing from a tree high in her garden.

"At first I thought it was the wind, miaowing through the leaves, but then I realised that my cat, Lucky Webster was up in the tree," she said.

I ran to the kitchen, where she continued, "I ran to the kitchen and phoned the Fire Brigade. A neighbour had told me they'd be the men for the job. Firemen can climb trees, just like cats, you know."

HOORAY FOR FIREMEN

On receiving the call, the Whoft Fireman bundled into their engine. Within minutes they were at the scene, laughing and joking and doing skids.

Mr Sautée takes up the story.

"The lads offered me a ladder, but I turned it down. I was pretty sure I'd heard somewhere that when cats in trees see ladders they expand to fill

The cat and (inset) the fire engine responsible.
PHOTO BY MARY MARTHA O'GOD

the branches. That sort of thing would just make our job twice as hard.

"So I put on my new climbing boots and got stuck in!"

The plucky fireman then began his careful ascent, breaking branch after branch in a clumsy, inconsiderate fashion.

"I thought it'd never end,", Trevor recalled, "by the time I'd reached the top of the tree I decided that I'd had enough and stopped climbing."

Unfortunately his final resting location had put him tantalisingly 'just-

out-of-reach' of the kitten, who was busy pawing honey out of a bee pot.

BUTTERFLY LUCK

The other firemen, realising that their ladddders simply weren't long enough to reach man or cat, quickly admitted defeat and ate a slice of cake and mackerel sandwich.

"I can't move."

"Come down!"

"Miaowwww!"

And so it would have gone on, had not a group of local cats started gathering around the base of the tree.

"It was quite beautiful to watch," said the pets' owners. "Our cats were getting excited. They must have been attracted by the matching butterfly designs on the bottom of the trapped fireman's shoes."

The cats, who had been following the fluttering shoe motion, suddenly pounced, bringing the broken fireman down to earth with a terrified ankle.

Said Fire Chief Keith Cimbalom, "Cats love butterflies and it was fortunate that the soles of my fireman's shoes depicted two such wonderful specimens, The Red Admiral and The Cabbage White'

Lucky Webster floated down from the tree some time later on a breeze.

Fig Friday is a figging success!!!!

A Framley mother and daughter have been drawn closer together after a school 'role-swap' charity event left them unable to fig-ure out who was who.

Shannon Cannon and her daughter Duke swapped places last Friday – Shannon attending classes at St Icklebrick's Primary, while Duke stayed home doing the household chores and reading *Bella* – in order to raise money for awareness.

Both of them adjusted to their new duties so quickly and effortlessly that they're considering changing for good.

"School's a piece of piss", Shannon declared, "much easier than it was first time around, when I was at school."

"I never realised how much work my mother did, it's great! More! More!" Duke let on later.

Shannon's husband, Thomas agrees. "I wasn't convinced at first, but the swap has left me feeling like a new man too. This is too wonderful for words."

The school is considering cancelling 'Fig Friday' in future, since the success of the event has raised the average school leaving age in the area to thirty-three.

School prize day congratulates pupils

By THE CREDITS

KING TUBBY VI Grammar School, Framley held its annual prizegiving this week, honouring the achievements of boys and girls from all years of the school.

The prizes were presented by local celebrity, ex-TV AM weatherman Cmmdr David Philpott. Philpott stood in at the last minute for absent guest of honour, Mayor William D'Ainty, who was unable to attend due to an urgent breakdancing appointment.

Special prizewinners, who all got copies of The Framley Examiner book are listed on the right. There were also loads of A-Levels and

excellence in sport and lemon squash.

Thanks were offered to all those who had helped make the event such a success, particularly those who had generously given photographs, or agreed to be photographs themselves.

Framley Examiner Prize for completing their book project	Robin Halstead, Jason Hazeley, Alex Morris, Joel Morris
Year 7 Divinity Prize	Rowland White
Year 8 Good Conduct	John Hamilton
Baden Schleissgarten Friendship Medal	Cat Ledger
Class of '68	Jonathan Gibbs, Philip Morris, Jason Whyte, Ben Parker, Mark Whitehead, Jonathan Parkyn, Simon Ansell, Andy Waterworth, Wendy Albiston, Nick Sommerlad, John Sparkes, Bob Lock, Bo Bloke, Bobby Locque, B O'Block, Robert Lock, Robin of Loxley, Lucky Bob, Bobert Blockington, Robbie L'Oc, Bob Block, B. Oblong, Rock Bollock

your comments here

News In Brief

HANGED

Laurence Edward Hanged, an estate agent from Molford St Malcolm, returned to Framley Crown Court on Monday. 48-year-old Hanged caused a sharp intake of breath to be heard all round the court just before his punishment was read out. He received a suspended sentence from Justice Sir Splendid Sentence.

WHAT A STORY

1000 local children have raised £1 million for the Mayor's charity, which has something to do with hospitals and the by-pass. At the day-long event, which may become an annual fixture if successful, 100 huge cheques were presented by policemen dressed as clowns, who then gave everybody a balloon and a complimentary puppy. Then there were fireworks. Journalists and photorophers who omitted to attend the event were said to have been "sacked".

CAR STOLEN

A car stolen from the Asda car park in Whoft was found three minutes later in the Asda carpark in Molford, full of shopping. The car continues.

THERE'S LEARNING TO KILL... ...AND THERE'S LEARNING TO BE KILLED !

Do you enjoy a real challenge?

Do you like the idea of SERIOUS injury?

Want to get more out of the rest of your life?

AND get paid AND get killed for it?

Why not spend the weekend lying in a puddle of your own guts with the PROFFESIONALS?

To find out what makes the THE ARMY such a great alternative to the rest of your life, come and be pressganged by our roustabouts on Clinton Docks, every night from 10.30pm.

THE ARMY

Framley Imaginaire
JSC
JUNIOR SUPPORTER'S CLUB

Meet Zebedee!

Say hello to Zebedee, the zebra! He's our new mascot, and he's recently been transferred from local premiership side Framley Zabadak, following an incident.

You'll see him at every Framley Imaginaire match from now on, cheering from the touchline, or maybe in the wall if there's a free kick on the edge of the eighteen yard box and we're down to ten men. Zebedee will always give 110% over the full ninety minutes!

artist's impression

FRAMLEY IMAGINAIRE FOCUS ON FACT FILE

HOWARD ANTHITLER

Date of Born: April 13th, 2002
Place of Birth: The Mirror End Stand, The Imaginaire Stadium o'Flight
Height: 4'12"
Previous Clubs: Tufty, Chip
Position: TBA
Squad Number: 83
Joined Imaginaire: October 1996.
Debut: TBA
International Debut: NA
Played: 0
Goals: 0

Howard has suffered badly from injury ever since the idea of playing football for a living was first suggested to him. With his 28st frame, chronic asthma and prosthetic legs, eyebrows were raised at the time of his £2.4m transfer from Whoft Hospice reserves in 1997.

However, he soon proved his critics right with an unbroken run of seasons brilliantly spent at home with his feet up. Though playing in this position naturally made him more of a backroom boy than a star of the field, cometh the time, cometh the man, and many fans fondly remember his stunning display of sitting quietly on the bench against Molford Incredible during the historic 1-0 victory that prevented Framley Imaginaire's expulsion from the World of Football.

Sadly, a combination of injury and related loss of form has denied Imaginaire fans the chance to see their hero's inaction, confining Howard to the saloon bar of The Warm Zippy for the past season, from where he relays the other football results to the stadium via the pub payphone (authenticity subject to random teletext reception).

Membership

Imaginaire Junior Supporter's Club members get lots of benefits and free gifts! Look what membership could get you...

0 – 5yrs
- *Standing tickets to all home matches.*
- *Complimentary, personalized packet of 20 Bensons signed by Mr Shaq Tehrani, reserve team physio and proprietor of Tehrani's News.*
(no more than 2 schoolchildren at one time)

5 – 16yrs
- *Complimentary set of 11 Framley Imaginaire first team butt-plugs, courtesy of Blackjack's Shagshack, sponsors of Imaginaire since 1932.*
- *Eligibility for half-price knuckle-duster & nunchakas gift set*
- *Discounts on Junior Away-Days*
- *Priority waiting list for membership of the Imaginaire Hardcru (includes The Cute Hooligan badge with real fur and moving eyes).*

IMAGINAIRE BIRTHDAY CLUB

Zebedee says HAPPY BIRTHDAY to this week's Junior Imaginer: *Subraminiya Raj* **who will be 3 on Wednesday**

Happy Birthday!

NEW FACES!

Good news for fans of The Imaginaries, Framley Imaginaire have just signed a new spectator!

Diego Malvinas, who cost £8m, is an exciting signing for the club because he also supports Argentina. He caught the selectors' eye after a fantastic couple of seasons at the home end at Boca Juniors.

Imaginaire's new hot property is much in demand, and there is talk of him supporting England next year, if he impresses at his new home.

Competition Corner

Last week's competition was won by Johnny Ann Miller, 6, of Molford St Gavin, who correctly guessed that Framley Imaginaire had scored seven away goals between 1995 and 2001.

Johnny's prize was to get to sit on the lap of Imaginaire's goalkeeper during the penalty shoot-out at the end of Thursday's vital qualifying match for the FA Cup.

If you want to join the Framley Imaginaire Junior Supporter's Club, just send a banker's draft for £175.99 to JSC, Framley Imaginaire, Administrative Office, Stadium O'Flight, Embankment Way, Framley FR1 6LS. Remember to write your name, age and address clearly on the back of the banker's draft. Please allow up to 6 months to receive your badge.

F**O**CUS *on* Roy Newby

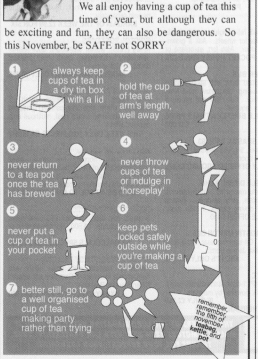

A promotional cut-out of Roy stands outside the very first of his shops, now Newby's Bulbs and Screws.
PHOTOGRAPH BY HARRIET FILLIGREE

He's king of shops

by Beaky Coxwain

ROY NEWBY is one of the area's best known figures. Over 90% of the shops in Molford bear the Newby's logo, and his name appears above street signs, on bin bags and within the curlicues of every £20 note spent in the town.

The debonair philanthropist vegetarian entrepreneur millionaire is a long way from the humble immigrant refugee who first arrived in Molford in the late 1950s, but Roy has never forgotten his roots as a humble immigrant refugee who first arrived in Molford in the late 1950s, but Roy.

So, this week, we take a look at the career of Framley's very own Roy Newby, Roy Newby.

Roy's autobiography "From Rakes To Riches" is published by Newby's Books and is available from all Newby's bookshops, and in the bedside drawer of every hotel room in the Framley area, priced £12.99.

Roy Newby TIMELINE

1949	Roy born, Prestatyn, aged 0.
1958	9-year old Roy becomes a refugee, leaving Wales after being chased out by a dog. He settles in Molford, claiming political asylum.
1959	Young Roy starts his own business, doing chalk drawings of himself cutting out silhouettes of people in the park.
1960	Roy secures a lucrative government contract to supply his drawings to the Middle East.
1967	Having made his fortune, Roy invests in commercial property in the Molford area, buying a vacant retail space on the corner of Hooky Street and Youave Avenue.
1968	Roy's shop "Just Rakes" fails to entice the public, and closes.
1970	Undeterred, Roy opens a new shop on the site, "Simply Rakes".
1971	After the failure of his second shop, Roy takes stock and raises investment capital for a new project.
1972	"Roy's Rakes" opens.
1973	Roy has reason to celebrate. His shop is a roaring success. The store's Unique Selling Point – that every rake has Roy's face carved into the handle – really pulls in the punters. It's a practice that he continues to this day – Roy's face can still be found on every Newby's product, on the side of every dinghy, in the heart of every cabbage.
1973-4	Roy opens twelve more "Roy's Rakes" shops, all in Molford High Street. They are a huge success.
1975	Roy's luck runs out. His prestige 13th branch of "Roy's Rakes" in Molford High Street fails to attract customers, and remains derelict to this day.
1976-7	Sensing that the time has come to try something different, Roy labours day and night to open a revolutionary new shop.
1978	"Newby's Rakes" opens.
1979	Success! Roy's new "Newby's" brand takes the area by storm. The money rolls in.
1980	Newby's Airport opens.
1981	First branch of Newby's Grocery and Newsagents opens, cashing in on the public appetite for grapes and magazines, popularised by glamorous movies such as the James Bond series and *Glitterball*.
1983	Newby's Toys opens
1985	Newby's Hats starts business
1986	First branch of Newby's Cushions
1987	Newby's Cushion Hats opens
1989	Newby's Walk-In-Hospital opens
1990	First branch of NcNewby's
1991	Newby's Swank Fashions
1994	Newby's 24-7-51

SAFETY FIRST

With Chief Fire Officer Kenneth Blan

This week:
The Cup Of Tea Code

We all enjoy having a cup of tea this time of year, but although they can be exciting and fun, they can also be dangerous. So this November, be SAFE not SORRY

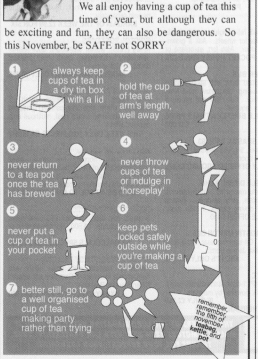

1. always keep cups of tea in a dry tin box with a lid
2. hold the cup of tea at arm's length, well away
3. never return to a tea pot once the tea has brewed
4. never throw cups of tea or indulge in 'horseplay'
5. never put a cup of tea in your pocket
6. keep pets locked safely outside while you're making a cup of tea
7. better still, go to a well organised cup of tea making party rather than trying

remember, remember, the fifth of november teabag, kettle, and pot

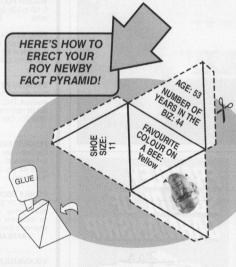

HERE'S HOW TO ERECT YOUR ROY NEWBY FACT PYRAMID!

AGE: 53
NUMBER OF YEARS IN THE BIZ: 44
SHOE SIZE: 11
FAVOURITE COLOUR ON A BEE: Yellow

GLUE

Suffering?

Injuries in relaxed conditions

Full consultations

Dr Friedrich Punschmensch
(B.C.M.A., A.B.H.)

I will only hurt you as much as you want to be hurt

Back conditions, kidney damage, bowel conditions, greenstick fractures, sinus, dental and many other problems

Safe word? What safe word?

Confidentiality must be assured

56a The High Street,
(above Mr Hammer)
Framley FM1 3HH
Tel 01999 481092
And ask for Punchy

The Framley Examiner

Framley's Traditional Favourite since 1978

FRIDAY, MARCH 11th, 2003   PRICE 45p

KILTS KILTS KILTS
many new designs
● mondrian
● testcard
● tube map
● scrabble
KILTS KILTS KILTS
01999 588 977

KIDS

Meet your sporting heroes

PROPERTY

Plans for town centre

STYLE

Make the most of your shadow

Framley MP is caught with his hand in the packet

"CRISPS FOR QUESTIONS" ROW HITS FRAMLEY MP

by Taunton Mishap

DYNAMIC local MP Ianbeale Steeplecocque was last night in hiding in his expensive Wripple home, after the Parliamentary Behaviour Committee (in London) put the controversial member under official scrutiny.

The knucklebattering follows a string of revelations about his business dealings with Framley millionaire entrepreneur and former bankrupt Lee Organisn.

SLEAZE

Steeplecocque, 23, has found himself at the centre of the so-called "Crisps For Questions" scandal. Documents leaked to The Framley Examiner (Framley's Traditional Favourite since 1978) suggest that the MP has been accepting "bungs" in return for asking questions in the House of Commons.

The portfolio of smoking guns shows that Mr Steeplecocque was paid a total of £19,000 over six months by local crisp magnate Lee Organisn.

LIES

Mr Organisn, owner of Turn Your Memories Into Crisps (The 'Turn Your Memories' Into People), denies any wrongdoing, and denies handing over crisps in little blue envelopes to the beleaguered MP.

But, since Steeplecocque spent most of the same six months asking questions in parliament about the crisp industry, Organisn's denials have so far fallen on thin ears.

BULLSHIT

"This looks smelly," said Mayor William D'Ainty in a press release, "and sleaze should confine itself to the kitchen. But, until the parliamentary committee has published its report, Ianbeale Steeplecocque should be presumed innocent, no matter how badly I treat him in private."

Mr Steeplecocque MP flees the scene of a crime.
PICTURE BY GERALDINE SKINHEAD

The soon-to-be-disgraced MP has not made himself available for comment, and refused to speak to unexpected reporters early this morning as he trouserlessly fled a prostitute's flat.

The case continues to continue.

Taxi driver attacked

TAXI DRIVERS in Framley have been warned to be on their guard after a minicab was boarded by pirates.

Stanley Bogwig, 42, had just dropped off a foul-mouthed customer at Here Be Turnips, a pub known as a popular pirate haunt, at 8.30pm on Saturday when the attack took place.

Three men armed with cutlasses boarded the dark blue Vauxhall Average and ordered Mr Bogwig to drive to a quiet car park on Stuffing Lane.

They threatened to make him walk the plank if he didn't do what he was told. One of the men blindfolded Mr Bogwig with two eye patches while the other two seized maps, tissues, beaded seat covers and boxes of traffic-light-style air fresheners.

The three bearded corsairs then tied up Mr Bogwig with towing rope and made off in the direction of Madagascar.

INTERROGATION

Police have applied to magistrates for a extra 24 hours to question the parrot they took into custody two days ago.

Detective Constable Inspector Gregan McHough yesterday told waiting reporters that although the brightly-feathered suspect had been helpful at first, it was now refusing to say anything other than "hello, Sarge" and "for the benefit of the tape."

MERRIWETHER'S CLOUD PROJECTIONS

Ever dreamt of having your face projected onto the surface of a cloud? With Merriwether's, the reality is just a phone call away. Simply choose a cloud, send a recent picture of yourself (in vapour form, if possible) and leave the rest to us
- - - - -
Impress your boss!
Make new friends!
Leave mental scars on your kids!

visit: www.my-face-is-on-a-cloud.net.uk
or phone 01999 252243 and ask for Windy

LENTILS P19 & 20   PARK RANGER FASHION P61   NOSE CLUES P11   SPORT P69 – 79   BRAS P51-112

Sockford .W.I take step into a future

THE LADIES OF Sockford Women's Institute are sending a message into the future, by using a time capsule to preserve a snapshot of how local life is at the moment, in this day and age.

The historic capsule will be buried on the waste ground behind Tibb's Angling Supplies, with instructions not to open it for twenty-five years, by which time the future will have arrived. Sealed inside the 6 foot by 4 foot box will be all the members of the Sockford W.I., except Mrs Arglesocks who has offered to stay behind and nail the lid shut.

Mrs Beryl Cormorance, who came up with the idea for the project, described to me how the buried ladies will be the perfect way for the moon men of the 21st Century to understand our current world as it is today in this day and age.

"Inside the capsule, we will adopt a variety of poses, representing all the richness and diversity of life on earth. For example, Mrs Ardennes will be dressed as a rainforest, and Mrs Please is going to be playing the bassoon."

TWENTY-FIVE YEARS

Although the chief purpose of the capsule is to allow the people of the future to see how we used to live, Mrs Cormorance explained there was another eriment to the expelement.

"I can't wait to get dug up, so I can see how the world has changed in twenty-five years," she enthused. "I would imagine there will be rockets. Everyone will probably be blue and have wrinkly foreheads, and,

by Adam Wrent

hopefully, they might be able to do something about my hip."

BUCK ROGERS

Learning from the disastrous experiences of other time capsule makers has been important for the W.I. time-travellers, Beryl told me.

"There's always the chance that, by the time the people of the far future unearth our capsule, the container may have become waterlogged, destroying the contents. Just in case, we are going to make a video of us getting into the box, which the astro citizens of 2027 will be able to watch, should they crack open the capsule and find it's just full of sludge.

"We've also asked the TV people to show the video of us climbing into the tin once a year, on *Focus On Framley*, so our great, great grandchildren will be able to see that too. We think we've thought of everything."

● *If you'd like to suggest a representative pose for the W.I. ladies to adopt in their plastic coffin of doom, call Mrs B.Cormorance on 01999 843 877.*

Mrs Cormorance stands next to the capsule that will take her into the future.
PHOTOGRAPH BY ABRAM TUMULT

Minstrel arrested

BY BUNCO BOOTH

FRAMLEY POLICE were glad to move quickly on Tuesday, reacting to reports of a public disturbance outside Clots Estate Agents in Denegate Parade.

Fourteen officers piled out of a lovely big van and arrested the troublemaker, a Mr Conerry Seuss, 38, from Neu Funfundseibzigstrasse, St Eyots. Seuss, who had been singing *Greensleeves* to passersby, was then put in the lovely big van and driven to Framley Police Station, brrrm brrrm where he was charged with minstrelcy.

At a press conference, held in the snug of The Warm Zippy, DCI Gregan McHough indicated the feathered hat, lute, rebec, shawm and stuffed rats on a string that Mr Seuss had used in his act.

"With only these simple tools and a pair of excessively pointed shoes, Mr Seuss was not only able to perform random acts of senseless minstrelcy, but also indulge in fol-de-rol and public displays of olde-worlde merriment.

"Some witnesses insisted they had even seen evidence of wassailing, but this cannot be confirmed at this time."

Conerry Seuss
PHOTO BY BO OWLS

This is not the first time Mr Seuss has come to the constabular attentions of Framley police. In 1996, after reports of a jesting incident, police raided his flat and seized several belled hats and a pig's bladder on a stick.

"We don't need this sort of thing in Framley," summed up DCI McHough, wiping beer froth from his moustache. "For goodness sake, this isn't the medieval ages, this is the twentieth century."

Mayor visits new ward

FRAMLEY'S INDOMITABLE Mayor, William D'Ainty visited Framley General Hospital's new Intensive Care ward this Tuesday.

The ward provides beds for 97 critically ill patients, all of whom were stacked in the corner while Mayor D'Ainty tried all their beds to see which one was his favourite.

While 27 of the beds were "too soft" and 69 of them were "too hard", the final bed, belonging to the late Harald Whipsnow, 71, was "just right".

The Mayor will be staying in the bed until he's sucked all the butterscotch Angel Delight out of a specially erected intravenous drip.

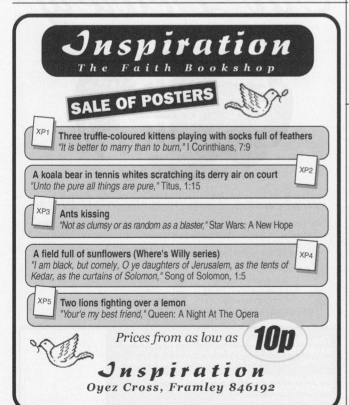

Inspiration
The Faith Bookshop

SALE OF POSTERS

XP1 Three truffle-coloured kittens playing with socks full of feathers
"It is better to marry than to burn," I Corinthians, 7:9

XP2 A koala bear in tennis whites scratching its derry air on court
"Unto the pure all things are pure," Titus, 1:15

XP3 Ants kissing
"Not as clumsy or as random as a blaster," Star Wars: A New Hope

XP4 A field full of sunflowers (Where's Willy series)
"I am black, but comely, O ye daughters of Jerusalem, as the tents of Kedar, as the curtains of Solomon," Song of Solomon, 1:5

XP5 Two lions fighting over a lemon
"Your'e my best friend," Queen: A Night At The Opera

Prices from as low as **10p**

Inspiration
Oyez Cross, Framley 846192

Legs... Bums... Frontbottoms
Excellence in exercise

Lose pounds from your legs, bums and frontbottom using our isotonic programme of rubbing.

We specialise in frontbottoms.

"Anything else you want rubbing?"

Call Vince on 01999 899 759

Funday Examiner!

HELLO GANG! Well! What a week it's been at the Funday Examiner for your Uncle Damiun!

I've been asked to write some really big stories for the grown-ups, and, phew! If it hasn't worn me out! And it hasn't left me much time to come up with new things for you to do, I'm afraid.

So, if some of this week's puzzles seem to be the same as last week's, don't worry. I'm sure you'll have just as much fun working out the brainteasers and finishing the puzzles again as you did last time.

I've had some letters from your mums and dads too! To all of you who sent their pocket money for the Funday Examiner badges and codebooks, thanks!

I give you my word that this week, I will send them. And if it's not this week, it might be next week! If you really need yours, you might want to try sending the money again.

Happy waiting!

Damiun

COLOURING-IN PICTURE PUZZLE

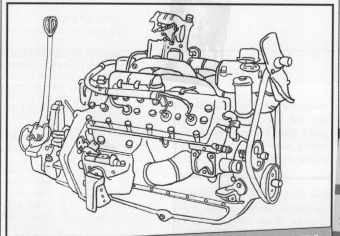

Colour in the COLLETS red and the SUMP FEED blue. Make the OIL PUMP BAFFLE a nice, clear yellow. Now, what do you think is wrong with Uncle Damiun's car? Send your completed pictures to me at the Funday Examiner, and try and get it right this time.

GAME ZONE

Here's some more hot new tips and cheats for the Nintendo PlayCylinder II...

PLANET OF DACHSHUNDS
From options screen press L, R1, R2, D, R, □, O, ⊠, L, L, L, R, R and game will change to "Submarine of Dachshunds".

PRINGLE MOUSTACHEMAN AND THE WOTSITS OF DISAPPOINTMENT
The fewer crumbs you get in your moustache, the higher your garlic bonus.

SUPERMARIOWARD
To avoid a malpractice suit, make sure you're hiding under the ambulance whilst the princess miscarries. The security guards can't see you there.

SONIC THE ROADKILL
On level 1, to avoid getting crushed the moment you leave your burrow, press L2, R1, power off.

METAL MICKEY SOLID
To make Irene Handl "Boogie Boogie", use the Fruitbat from the tank bunker.

FUN FOR THE HOLIDAYS

WHY NOT come along to Framley Town Hall (floor 6, avoid using the lift) and have some more fun on one of the council's Kids' Kourses this holidays?"

ARSE PAINTING
Back by popular demand. £150 + meals. (Tue-Sat, residential, 9am prompt check out.)

TXT MESSAGING
Includes oral tuition and day trip to Portugal. One day course, last few places. £3. (Mondays, Wednesdays)

ACCOUNTANCY
Ages 5-11. To BACA standard. Guaranteed placement at local firm. (Mon-Fri. 10am)

only two schoolchildren at any one time.

HERGÉ'S ADVENTURES OF CANCAN

Tintin is on holiday.

HERGÉ'S AVENTURES DE PÔP-POP

Tintin est toujours en vacances.

DAMIUN'S SEARCH WORD

```
I A M S I C K O F T H I S J O B I M
T R E A T E D L I K E A N A P E I F
I H A D A P O U N D F O R E V E R Y
C O L L E A G U E I V E D R E A M E
D O F D R O W N I N G I N S T A R V
I N G P I R A N H A I D B E A M I L
L I O N A I R E G O D K N O W S I D
R A T H E R B E S T U C K O N A S P
I K E T H A N S P E N D A N O T H E
R H O U R S T A R I N G A T A S T U
P I D B L O O D Y G R I D O R D R A
W I N G A N O T H E R M I C R O S C
O P I C M A P O F H O W T O F I N D
A F U R N I T U R E S A L E I M I G
H T F E E D T H E E D I T O R T O H
I M S E L F A N D A F I V E R S A Y
S I M T H E O N L Y H A C K H E R E
W H O C A N S P E L L P I R A N H A
```

LORD
OVAL
SOON
CAT
FOREVER
DUNN
FINE
SPRY
OFF
VET
THERM
RIPE
IF
BRA
WISE
GIN
IKEA
HERB
GOSH
BAA
PWOAH
EUK
IAN
SARI
DOGWAR
TAO
FERG
LADA
HRH
HERO
MEAL
OAT
OATS
GOT
NONE
TUB
NEST
COGNEAT
BONT
HARWUNK

ROGER THE HORRID BEAR

10455 "Roger The Babysitter"

Roger is watching Under Siege. Which triplet has the worst colic?

Last week's solution: The cut-and-shut was made from cars 1 and 5.

Just what they wanted

DOCTOR COBWEB'S COBWEB FACTORY £18.99

Spin miles and miles of real cobwebs... Make a cobweb picture! Build a cobweb bike! Fill your bedroom!
But don't make Doctor Cobweb angry or it's no more cobwebs!

"BILLY BRAGG" HANDHELD WATCH-A-GAME GAME £14.99

LCD game based on the popular singer songwriter.

WALLET & GRIMACE TALKING ALAMRM CLOCK £11.99

Wakes you up with a choice of four phrases. "You owe me big time" / "Time's up" / "In your dreams, pal" / "About fucking time". Distressingly persistent.

BATTENBERG THE GAME OF CAKE £31.99

With over 5,000 questions, battenberg-shaped question box and 36 pieces of cake.

BLUNT INSTRUMENTS' SPICK & SPAN £27.99

Talking educational toy.
"Do it again"
"Those aren't hospital corners"
"You could eat your dinner off that"
"Spell 'Clean'"

GUESS WHEN £17.99

The mystery time game
"Are you nearly dinnertime?"
"Am I up yet? Why am I here?"
Guess your opponent's time before they guess yours.
Oh yes, it's never too late to play Guess When, the family fun game that'll have you in clocks!

DAVID BRYANT SUBBOWLEO £21.99

Reproducing all the thrills of real tournament bowls by fingertip control. With 00 scale self-balancing teams, bowls, jacks, pipes, slacks etc.

BUGGEROO £16.99

The game of anal stuffing.
"Take an object
Try and stick
It up the arse...
...But watch it kick!"
Not suitable for anyone.

WHO WANTS TO ANSWER THE SAME QUESTION A MILLION TIMES? £24.99

Try the challenge of a lifetime! Based on the long-running TV show. "Are those all your final answers?" "Do you want to phone a hospital?" "And I understand your wife's a welder." "Hurry up, I haven't got all day..."

with christmas toys from

NEWBY'S bookshops
15 High St, Molford

into gold, cures all known diseases, makes possible unaided human flight. No trade enquiries, no police, no customs & excise. £15 a bottle. Box FE8741

LARGER THAN LIFE pottery dog collection. Dog collection beautifully rendered in pottery. Owner to collect. £200 01999 266698

'HOW TO STOP TALKING HUNGARIAN', book and tape set. Ideal gift for anyone not planning on visiting Hungary. £12. Tel 01999 865 433

HUGE GONGS

KID'S Hungry Onions game complete with sack of onions and time-locked isolation chamber. Who will eat the most onions over a month? 30 days' silent pleasure £150. Tel 01999 577889

PAIR of DJ turntable mats for twin mixing deck. Logos: "Mrs Mills" and "Rock-a-doodle-dandy!" Strangely timeless. Call Maxy on 01999 752 129

LOST: Cream coloured shoulder bag. Answers to the name of Sooty. 01999 731 403

BOOKS REQUIRED to complete collection. I require paperback copies of "Bridget Jones' Diary" and "Ainsley's Barbecue Bible" to complete my collection of all the books ever written. Good prices paid. 01999 499 313

BABY HARNESS and adult chariot. £22. Tel 01999 844 621.

MEAT, MEAT, MEAT! Pantomime Horse Steaks. £22 a kilo. Tastes a bit like pork, but wrapped in polkadot fabric. Delicious with golden eggs. Contact Milham's Pantomime Farm Produce Plc 01999 835 200

LONELY BOFFIN Great Night Out kit. Includes inflatable club, drunk tablets, taxi bedspread, 20 Bensons and a dressing gown with "All Back To Mine" embroidered on the breast pocket. Still in box. £65. 01999 701 904

HANDLEBAR moustache. Fits most bikes. £14. 01999 855 596

BED WETTING KIT with three refill packs. Two liquids, one solids. Ultra realistic and completely random. Offers? 01999 131124

SNOW TREES. In bloom and covered in blizzards. Deciduous and evergreen. £32 each. 01999 800 345

NOVELTY PUBIC LICE. Real lice, novelty gift idea. £10. Wripple 875

THE COMPLETE Underwater Chef. Volumes 1-5 bound in waterproof coating (Asparagus to Barbequing). £15. Fram 446523

HOME BREWERY Kit. Planning permission required. £3000 Freehold. BOX FR52234

GIANT BATH TAPS. Half the length of your bath, eight foot tall, two foot diameter. Fill your bath in seconds. £80 a pair. 01999 730 811

SIR SPINALOT™ TOP HAT. The original and still the best. Powerful clockwork brim. With No-Grip shoes for full spinning action. £40. Tel 01999 865532

BLACK & Decker 0.33" hammer drill with 500W amplifier and two 12" speakers. Council injunction pending, hence quick sale. £90. Mike on 01999 722 932

WATERTIGHT alibi. Used hundreds of times. £50 BOX FR57883

STAR TREK Collectibles, including trading cards, videos, books, action figures and Nichelle Nicholls' (Uhura) right hand. Pre-imprisonment sale of effects. Offers. 01999 501 765

JACK-IN-THE-MOUTH jack-in-the-box. A real surprise for the victim. "A laugh riot" The Catholic Herald. £45. 01999 612 633

PAIR OF fat ladies £88 Whoft 81490

ALMOST infinite number of manuscripts full of monkey typing. Left over from recent project. Experiment successful. Contact Prof Arthur Bostrom via BOX FE8664

SET OF 3 ornamental garden gases. Oxygen, Helium and Radon, all beautifully rendered in Helium. £40 ono Framley 357753

DRIED ORGASMS, available in handy tablets. Take effect immediately. The only swallowing you need ever do. MANDY'S PERSONALS, 01999 362118.

AUTHENTIC 1940s Republic Serials' "King Of The Rocket Men" gimp mask and straps. £200 Dave 01999 433 820

ROGER SLOMAN

GOOD Cop / Bad Cop Slippers. Break your right ankle, while massaging your left instep. £15. 01999 711 838

RARE BLUEPRINT of abandoned MoD sand castle project (1953). Great tablecloth. 01999 920 165.

FOUR SUITS for ventriloquist's doll. Doll now outgrown them, so no longer required. £130 Tel 01999 754 120

BLANKETY BLANK chequebook and bank account. Contains millions of pounds of undeclared, untraceable BBC money from the late 1970s. 01999 355 429

X-RAY PHOTOGRAPHS. Ladies' Day at Ascot, Roedean Prizegiving and What's Really Inside Your Travelcard. £40 each. 01999 410 933

IT'S PROBABLY MINE

EDIBLE chess pieces, with Yorkie knights, carrot pawns and a Weetabix king. Great game. Disgusting meal. Eaten (but thrown up again almost whole), hence only £5. 01999 621 199

ELECTRIC COT FENCE. £300. "Now Junior ain't going nowhere!". Unique American design. Slightly frightening at European voltage, but they only need find out once to learn. Contact Jeavons and Fitch Kid Control Ltd Box FE8021

"QUINCY, The Batman Years". Video collection. £32. 01999 622 095

FOUR HUNDRED AND NINETY-NINE "I'm Leaving You, Geoffrey" T-shirts. Minimum print run, but slightly excess to requirements. Call 01999 876 431, but hang up if Geoffrey answers.

SUNGLASSES, many designs. Also Moonmugs, Jupiterjugs and Plutothimbles. Also from £10. Also 01999 438660 and also ask for Patrick.

FALSE EYELASHES made from black shuttlecocks. Property of the late Dame Barbara Cartland. £65. 01999 707 844

ENORMOUS back-mounted hourglass that ticks away the passing seconds of your life with grains of inexorably falling sand. Would suit someone born on 4th April 1972, in reasonably good shape, light smoker, with family history of heart disease. Freaking me out, hence quick sale. £offers. 01999 831 911

10 LITTLE PILCHARDS™ children's lunchbox and flask. £5. 01999 398 766

HAND-KNITTED brown, purple and orange jumper, with slogan "I KNITED MY JUMPER". £25. Tel 01999 864 812

FIELD OF DREAMS for sale. ¾ acre. Some nasty back-at-school bits in the lower corner. £offers. 01999 622 988

POCKET Billiards table. Slight tear in baize. Balls need attention. £290 Chutney 689

14FT CARDBOARD CUT-OUT of Alice Beer. Used once (ie covered in sick), hence £3. 01999 327555.

The Framley Examiner

"I sold my bike within 24 hours, and, barring nausea and some hearing loss, thoroughly enjoyed the experience of advertising with The Framley Examiner. Thanks!"

Imogen Liss, Codge

INCOMPLETE set of bound partwork magazines. "Sew Today With Bruce Springsteen" Vols 1-4 (Cross stitch) and 14-16 (Denim). £10 the lot. 01999 633 097

10 Pilot's Licences. Genuine. Make your stag night go with a bang. 01999 755 490

FLASH-ME bathroom lighthouse. Guides you safely out of the bath and back into the bathroom. £200. Fr 833 112

TEAPOT, T-shirt and T-Bird for sale. Also T-bone, Teepee and black and white TV. Call Mr T on 01999 755 301

SELECTED ANAGRAMS £50, A Grandma's Celeste £05, A Gent's Crème Salad 5£0. Grade Salesmen Etc. FR. 01999 90199

ALONE? Join Date-A-Gibbon and meet the moron of your dreams! Partners you can manipulate, partners who never say a thing, partners who make you look like a casual professional brilliant hilarious billionaire sexual athlete compared to them. Call today! 01999 657657.

T-SHIRTS T-SHIRTS T-SHIRTS £150 the lot. Also F-Shirts (for one-armed people with colostomy bags) £35 each. Grey, yellow, foil. Box FE8473.

DANCING on The Ceiling, Turn Back Time, Live Forever and other well-kept secrets revealed in this fascinating set of instruction manuals. £20 each. 01999 800 735. Also available "Help!".

MOBILE PHONE, £30. Hairbrush, £5, driving licence, £150 nice wallet, £10. 07999 930919.

E.T. SCARF. Head at one end, body at the other. Very long neck. Simply grotesque. I had nightmares, now it's your turn. £12. 01999 624 320

EVERYTHING you've ever dreamed of. In underbed storage boxes. £45. 01999 300 976

FOUR BARS OF INTRO (drums, trumpet, Nelson Riddle). Unsuitable. Will swap for half a middle eight (steel guitar, congas, duelling banjos). Box FE8211

FOR THE love of God, get out of my way. 01999 855 176

TEBL Teacher required (Teaching English as A Belgian Language) to help confuse and bewilder home-schooled child. Call Mr Hollyhock on 01999 482762.

OX-BOW LAKES

'THE THREE LITTLE PIGS and the Big Bad Three Little Pigs'. Subtle moral tale for advanced toddlers. £5 Framley 01999 822324

TRADITIONAL rustic bongs made from wellington boots and gunbarrels. Horseshoof handles. Haystack lids. £80 each. Box FE8755

IDEAL GIFT for him! Treat your boyfriend or husband to five laps of Silverstone on the back of a goose! Prices from £250. 01999 844 099

REAL FRUIT in imitation wax bowl. £15. 01999 755 400

SECOND HAND HOLIDAY. 4 days in Ibiza with a blonde girl called Liz. August 1998. It was alright, I suppose. Used once. Call Dan on Fr 743 822

SIMPLY RED airbrush kit. "Disguise Your Full Potential". Doesn't work, hence £1 / Works hence £100. 01999 735 404

HANGING BASKET. 1955 collectable Ruth Ellis souvenir wicker basket. £25. Fram975458

BABY BOUNCER. 18 months old. 8 weeks' experience handling Friday night crowds. Comes with double breasted babygrow and clip-on bib. £30 p/hr 01999 802 133

POLTERGEIST chef. Makes unwanted dinners at quarter to three in the morning. £400. 01999 661 892

23 BOXES of Pickled Onion All Bran. Didn't take that much to get everyone vomiting and shitting themselves. Plenty left over. £offers. Box FE8640 (>FLAG: Who ARE these people, Julie? This bloke's rung up before)

'PERRY COMO Live and On Fire, Again'. The album that started it all. %offers BOX FR73343

JUST BECAUSE I'm having dinner with you, it doesn't mean you're in my pants. Cut this out and stick it to the menu. Failing that, try shutting his dick in a drawer. 01999 377 651

AEROPLANE GLUE

KEVIN ROWLAND's mind, encoded in COBOL. Now your home computer can think, dance and sing just like the Dexy's Midnight Runners frontman. Extraordinary. £20. 01999 599 320

BOOGIE WOOGIE

BABIES' ELECTRIC CHAIR, with rattles and Petra The Pig skullcap, £100. Non-lethal but persuasive. Box FE8673.

4' diameter child's swimming pool shaped like an open mouth. Forms centrepiece of 18' diameter "Screaming Face" garden feature. £75. Melinda on 01999 761 433

FOR SALE. Classified advert advertising set of six saucepans, vgc, £25. £15. 01999 650 388

SWORD of light. Shield of truth. Bag of crisps. Will not separate. £30. Box FE8720

INSTRUCTION CASSETTES. 6 vols: "How To Eat Spiders". 3 vols: "How To Eat Everything Except Spiders". £20. 01999 776 800

ELECTRIC SOCKS. Deliciously warm when you climb into them. £9. Whoft 8431

PIRATE FLAG, cannon and grappling irons. Redundancy sale. £30. Also assorted plunder. £15. Call Mr Tillotson on 01999 601 511

COFFIN DODGERS. No job too big or small. Other containers avoided. Call us for complete pricelist BOX FR5498

COLLECTOR'S SETS of certified bone china artistic wall plates. "Reach For The Pot – NAAFI Canteens of The Battle of Britain", "100 Years of Carsickness", "Scenes From The Life of The Infant Bresslaw", "The Milli Vanilli Files" £150 each, or £600 the lot. Call Elsie on 01999 411 902

HUMPTY FROG designer cardigan. Web-spinning cuffs, wooden underflaps the lot. Worn once (while writing this advert). Fucking uncomfortable. 01999 788828

MAN & VAN. A man with a van. Anything. 07999 923441.

ALARM CLOCK that wakes you up with the sound of people burning to death. Lacks charm but I was never late for work once in the three months preceding my nervous breakdown. £18. Tel 01999 655 451 after 5am.

VINTAGE FLIGHTS to 1960's New York. Two discount tickets to visit the States during this exciting and liberating period. Couple must be over 50 and accompanied by a piano. £10 Whoft 594

BOY'S NAVY BLUE. Dad's Army Green. When I am king, dilly dilly, you shall be £50 ono. 01999 844 754

WET-LOOK bowler hat. Extra saucy. Adults only. £16. 01999 344 811

HAVE YOU got a novel in you? Most people have. We remove them using the latest techniques. General anaesthetic and no scarring. Private consultations, $65. 01999 299951.

ACTUAL SIZE Morris Minor made out of cigars. All my own work. What on earth was I thinking! £45. Tel 01999 633 209

WEDDING DRESS, black and yellow, fuzzy velvet, with four huge crepe wings, calico pollen sac and 'compound eye' style veil fitted with delightful 3ft antennae, £400oao. Box FE8630.

SOFA shaped like Salvador Dali's moustache. Formerly the property of Mae West. £offers. 01999 740 843

JOSS STICKS. Various exotic scents: Teacher's Breath, Auntie's Duvet, Pub and When Did You Buy This Chicken? Packs of 12, £4 each. Call Rainchild on 01999 855 491

LEISUREKING Abdonimal Teaser, £35. Comes with tummyrubber and timing pants. Box FE8182.

"PAIR" of ladies' shoes (one orthopedic boot, one stilt). £12. Tel 01999 508 729

MICROSOFT WARDROBE 3.0. Sorts your clothes into type, colour or alphabetically. Except trousers. £25. Framley 850 046

CAPTAIN FLIPTABULOUS

DECK OF CARDS. Spades slightly aggressive (some biting). Also Queen of 9s missing. Otherwise vgc. £2 01999 722 960

DOORBELL, 12 string acoustic. bass, kit. You pay, we play. Covers or original material., Will travel. 01999 654 377

"MR SAFARI" self-adhesive windscreen lion. Fits Vauxhall Nova, obscuring most of your view with lion. £30. 01999 744 300

SOAP ZEPPELIN. Flies and cleans. £400. Box FE8562.

BLACKCURRANT CORDIAL Moustaches – I will model three different styles for you. All at once or separately. I await your call. 01999 909099

BAKING POWDER, tons and tons of it. Went through a phase of thinking I was a baker. Realise now I was a judge. £offers/medicine, 01999 347796.

Last year,

The Framley Examiner

readers sold more than 25,000 minutes of dog pornography through Examiner classifiueds

MIKE OLDFIELD'S old suit. 32" inside leg. 3" sleeves. Not what you'd expect. Can be played as Bodhran. £185. Box FE8976

TWENTY-THREE PIECE SUITE in velour with duckdown cushions and seat belts, vgc, £350. 01999 227865.

MOTHERS HELP. 01999 354792. I'll help your mum.

ECHO & THE BINMEN

ALL CENTRAL HEATING, boilers, radiators, tanks etc removed discretely while your ex is on holiday. Call Gavin 07999 419872.

FRANK ZAPPA sex doll. With Moon Unit / Dweezil costumes. £30. 01999 851 934

BAKED ALASKA – the greatest cover-up of the last century? Cold and hot? I think not. What aren't they telling us? www.thebiggestconspiracyintheknownworld.ac.fr

THERE IS NO GOD and I've got the proof: wasps. £12 per 100. 01999 582239.

PACK OF THREE tournament quality ping pong balls. Ideal for enthusiastic player, or that trick I saw in that Thai nightclub. 01999 733 218

GINGER BABY with black and white scan photo. £35. Will not separate. 01999 766 511

AMAZING saucy party trick. "Chipolata" which expands to size of bratwurst and sprouts two meatballs when bitten. Embarrasses and delights. £11 ono. 01999 855 210

SET OF FRAMED PHOTOS of Brian Blessed building a kite. £30 ono. 01999 733 701

AROUND & AROUND

taking a closer glance at rural Framley with Arbroath Smokey

Country Walks

WALK 132

Thoxtoxeter to Glibley

APPROXIMATE DURATION OF WALK 4 HOURS
DISTANCE COVERED 20-30 MILES

Butcher's Old Field at Ovenly   **PHOTO: MALCOLM HOUDINI**

THIS IS a mildly diverting stroll of between twenty to thirty miles, mainly in woods but with some farmland, from Thoxtoxeter to Ovenly and Boxing-Glove Mt Bellround, returning by Cloxted Farm and the edge of North-South Heath to Glibley.

Starting the walk from the top-floor of the multi-storey car park in Thoxtoxeter's main street, an easy jump takes you to the flat roof of The Cauliflowery Public House. Turn 90 degrees to your right and slide down the building's historic 15th century hexagonal drainpiping.

About four hundred yards to your in front, you should see a tall field. Turn right on marked path over stile into field, keeping fence on right.

Go under the pond and then up and over the top of the trees beyond (use a compass if you wish). This should take you to an opening and a leisurely amble across the FR404.

Turn right for an hour (it is safe to err on the side of caution here), then finally turn left into Ovenly Billiards Course and, keeping off the astrobaize, follow the signpost into the top left hole.

The next part of the trip takes in some hard walking, including an overwater sprint of approx. 500m, in the approach to Boxing-Glove Mt Bellround.

Walk vertically upwards, then right and finally down again, landing to the left of where you were originally. This tricky manoeuvre requires practice but looks great and should be no trouble to the seasoned country walker.

You should now be in the kitchen of Cloxted Farm. Make your apologies and leave by the nearest exit (usually the stove). Turn left uphill, and, when the path divides in two after six or so steps, take the righteous fork.

The pure of heart will emerge on North-South Heath. Follow the track North or South (it doesn't matter) and after a couple of days you should emerge outside the Pig and Valve public house at Glibley. Reward yourself with an evening in the company of one of their many celebrated whores. *You've earned it!*

A trip into your memory lanes

DO YOU REMEMBER when Whotten Plodney was bordered by Whoft on one side and Spain on the other?

If so, you're probably old enough to remember the first *Around and Around* feature I did on the dangers of crop migration.

Crop migration, for those of you unfamiliar with traditional country practices, is where a field of produce is herded to a new location nearer its target market.

In the days before steam, this significantly reduced transportation costs. Good farmers could direct whole orchards to new locations, while more mature crops could be left to relocate themselves.

Unfortunately, as is often the case with unfortunately, the increase in crop migration often led to whole areas relocating and huge gaps opening up around the countryside.

The Association of Wheat Walkers was set up in the late 18th century to oversee the practice of crop migration and ensure that any gaps left in the land were refilled as soon as possible.

It was Dr. Brian Bolland, however, who was to come up with the true solution to this conundrum.

By discovering that seeds are far lighter and more obedient than sprawling fields of produce, he found where certain crops were required and planted them there.

Crop migration is still practised in certain areas, but these days it's done under controlled conditions and for enjoyment rather than profit.

So next time you eat a wheat, *think where it may have come from!*

Storing nuts for winter

WITH AUTUMN still ringing in one's ears and the excitement of Christmas children spinning smashingly into focus, it's all too easy to forget about preparations for the festive season.

I've been collecting a few wise country tips on how to plan for and survive the Christmas season. All from the country, *of course!*

When hens start burying their eggs, it's time for you to stock up on plenty of hot soup and warming cocoa because it's more than likely to be a cold month ahead.

Look out for broken twigs and bruised leaves. We can always learn from our arboreal cousins. This usually means *red sky at night, shepherd's delight.*

Domestic animals' behaviour can also guide you during this period. Dancing cats and whistling dogs indicate a white Christmas, while stinging hamsters often spell rain.

Look in your garden. If you find wroms, then dig them out of the soil and measure them. Generally, the longer the wrom, the better.

In short, don't get caught out this winter. The clues are in the countryside around you, *just listen.*

FRESH FARM PRODUCE

----- all-year round freshness fresh from the farm -----

**FREE-RANGE KESTREL, FRESHWATER BRINE, ACORNS
PICKLE CHUTNEYS, PUDDLE PUDDINGS, CLOTTED CHEESE
HOME-MADE MARLAMADE, FRESH FRUIT & VAG, HAYWAINS
WILD SALT & PEPPER, PLOP-TROTS, CLING PEACHES
BUTTERBALLS, OAK DROPPINGS, HORSE EGGS**

Farmer Geoffrey's Farm Produce, Field, Chutney – 01999 805667 email: geoff.farmer@farmergeoff.co.uk

Sheep Marathon cancelleda gain

THE ANNUAL St Eyots to Glibley Sheep Marathon has been cancelled for the 50th year running due to growing pressure from angry Cloxted residents.

The route, which follows an almost perfect straight line between start and finish, traditionally meanders in the middle.

"The sheep have usually lost interest in the race by the time they reach Cloxted and graze.", one organiser said. "That's why we have trouble with this event time after time. Maybe next year."

Tumblehedgehog Farm

A holiday but mainly a farm

There's nothing like a day out in the country. Apart from a month in the country, that is! At Tumblehedgehog Farm we believe that every day in the country should be a month in the country. That's why we're offering free month-long holidays over the harvest period. All we ask in return is that you sleep in the barn, eat woodshavings and let us film you while you defecate. There's no catch. It really is as simple as that!

FOR FURTHER INFORMATION PLEASE CONTACT MRS TIGGYDINKLE ON 01999 557788

tv guide saturday july 6th 2002

bbc one	bbc two	itv one	four	chanel no 5

bbc one

7.45 The News at Ten Babies (rpt) Sandy Gall and the Blustery Day

8.10 Dr Who (rpt) Animated series

8.35 Rolf's Cartoon Hospital (rpt) Rolf helps a kitten squashed flat by an anvil.

9.00 SMBBC with PY & Duncan Avec Pierre-Yves Gerbeau et Duncan Goodhew.

12.15 Sportsnest including (approx. times)

12.20 Football Mucus

1.05 Pillow Fighting from Lingfield

1.25 First Bollard Back

1.40 Second Bollard Back

2.35 Half-Time

2.45 Ice Eisteddfod

3.40 Who Ate All The Pies?

4.00 The Adventure Game with Sue Barker, Steve Rider and Lesley Judd.

5.05 News (16,061 / 53,112) Huw refuses to wear a tie at Peter's funeral.

5.25 Cartoon 80:20 it's a mouse of some sort.

5.35 Hi-De-Hi-De-Hi-De-Ho (rpt) With Simon Cadell as Cab Calloway and Ruth Madoc as Minnie The Moocher.

6.05 Jim Davidson's Generation X Slacker fun with guests Ethan Hawke and Daniel Clowes.

7.05 Better On The Radio Inappropriate TV transfer of previously endearing comedy

7.35 Only Thing That David Jason Does That Isn't On ITV And Horses (rpt)

8.10 BorehamwoodEnders Local residents complain about the nearby late-night filming of a popular soap opera.

9.00 No. THIS Is Your Life Aggressive reappraisal of the life of wind-up merchant Trevor Bayliss.

9.30 News (as 5.05) (rpt)

9.50 Parkinson Classic interview with "The Greatest", Ali Bongo

10.40 FILM: Don't Tell Mom The Baby's Dead (1990) Harrowing screwball comedy

12.05 Top Of The Pops 1 with Manuel's Pyjamas, Twoozer, The Outstandings, Vulnerable and Kid Shit (rpt)

12.35 Are You Being Repeated? John Humphries sitcom (rpt)

1.50 Panoramic Last week's Panorama resized in 16:9 for widescreen TVs.

2.50 Last Orders

3.00 Closedown

REGIONAL VARIATIONS

ITV 4.00pm – 5.00pm **FRAMLEY NORTH EAST** Farming Week **WHOFT** Building an Igloo **FRAMLEY SOUTH** Roger The Horrid Bear **ST EYOT'S** Factory Club **FRAMLEY NORTH WEST** Interviewabout: The Framley Barrier **WRIPPLE** The Mrs Susan Wiltham Show **CODGE** Biscuit Time **CHUTNEY** The World Cup Final (LIVE) **SOCKFORD** Agaton Sax And The Sockford Computer Plot **MOLFORD ST MALCOLM** The Story of Cork **MOLFORD ST GAVIN** FILM: Ai No Corrida **FRACTON** Summerside Special **CLINTON** Tides (LIVE) **SLOVENLY** Closedown

bbc two

7.00 News 24/7 Rolling news service piped directly from MTV Europe.

8.00 Open Polytechnic

8.00 How To Get Out of a Loft

8.30 Valves (unit 4)

9.00 Gestetner Maintenance

9.20 Tidying Your Telephone

9.40 Gasthaus Glockenspiel

10.00 Saturday Cuisine. Cookery. Monty Rissole rustles up something involving bacon and tea to kill the pounding behind his eyes.

10.35 The Sexist Gourmet (6/8) Where in blue blazes is my bleeding dinner, woman?

11.10 Ant Kitchen A colony from Peru make a finger buffet.

11.40 You Only Live Once Incest and country dancing.

12.15 Wildlife On Toast David Attenborough pops some tree frogs under the grill

1.05 FILM: A Black & White Film (1930s-40s) Series of 11-minute scenes of women crying on railway stations and men in flying helmets. (B/W)

2.45 The Middlebrow Mysteries Det Insp Jack Middlebrow investigates the mysterious appearance of a line manager. (rpt from Sunday)

3.05 Labour Party Conference 1982 Day 7478 of the continued live coverage including Barbara Castle being interviewed by Sir Robin Day.

4.30 TOTP7 Gary Davies introduces the very best of his links from 1985.

5.10 Last Of The Summer Olympics Britain's gold medal hopes rest with Bill Owen in the Bathsleigh.

5.40 Robert Wars X-treme Robinson vs Hardy. Presented by Lord Charles.

6.10 They Think It's All News For You Public School vs State School.

6.40 Good Weather Isobel Lang

6.45 Bad Weather Christopher Walken

7.00 Yes, Paul Eddington Sitcom. Paul (Don Warrington) agrees to appear in a new political sitcom (rpt)

7.30 CrimeWave UK Nick Ross wraps a stolen GTi round a phonebox.

8.05 England Inch-By-Inch Bill Oddie's painstaking odyssey reaches 100657'N, 001765'E.

8.35 World's Strongest Young Musician of the Year Semi-final: Emma Johnson v Adrian Spillett.

9.05 I Don't ♥ Staying In On Saturday Nights Celebrity sofa reminiscences

10.35 Reputations A look behind the public façade of Changing Rooms' Mr Fixit, Handrew Andrew. Narrated by God.

11.05 I'm Andy Partridge The regional entertainer's abrasive style gets him into conflict with his producer again.

11.35 When Louis Met... Louis Louis Theroux spends three days with Louis Theroux impersonator Louis Laroux. (Edited for language and violence)

12.25 Last Orders

12.35 Closedown

itv one

4.35 GM-AM Environmentalists protest at the enormous, unnatural size of Lorraine Kelly's breakfast.

9.25 Tiswos 2000 Bob Carolgees and Spank the Monkey get the kids all sticky. Also starring Den Hegarty in a leather skirt as Sally James.

11.30 CD on Saturday... OK? Cat Deeley asks more pop stars if they can tell what it is yet.

12.30 World Really Championships

2.00 Framley Fortunes Local quiz

2.30 Fen Practice PC Muffin finds an owl. (rpt).

3.30 You've Been Patronised

4.00 Magpie P.I. Tom Selleck shows children how to make a coconut bird feeder. (rpt)

5.00 Weekend News John Suchet trolls round IKEA looking for 60W pearl bayonet-fitting bulbs

5.20 Lily Savage's Blank Attack

6.00 The Death Of... Another chance to see Jeremy Spake drive a tube train into the sea.

6.30 Data Entry Idol After eighteen weeks Ant & Dec are down to the last 12 contestants. Will Darius finally make it big?

7.30 Cilla's Surprise Date Cilla's in for a real surprise surprise when her blind date is with former manager Brian Epstein.

Stoner Zone BBC1, 3.10am

8.30 Pyramid Game 2000 Archive footage of Steve Jones poses the same questions he asked in 1983 to new contestants who can win the chance to repossess the prizes from their original winners.

9.00 Who Wants To Earn c11Kpa? Chris Tarrant introduces three more lucky contestants who want a job in a petrol station.

10.40 I Know Absolutely Everything About Footballs Two comedians in a sofa

11.10 PICK OF THE DAY FILM: The Real Morph: Through The Table (1991) Biopic depicting the amazing adventures of the stop-motion plasticene homunculus. Morph's career is in the ascendant until he and Chas fall out over a racist comment. *Morphine Lord* – Richard Pryor *Charles Sproxton* – Gene Wilder *Mr Bennett* – Wallace & Gromitt *Anthony Hart* – Robert Lindsay *Grandmorph* – Peter Cook
    Dir: Brian Cosgrove & Mark Hall

2.40 Movieline This week's releases reviewed by their own press departments.

3.10 Stoner Zone Unedited close up footage of a plate of spaghetti bolognese. (rpt)

four

3.50 Witch Hunts Live US sport

8.00 Transglobal Underground Baseball with Natacha Atlas

9.00 Tnage4 Cross-stitch.

11.00 Political Behaviour Last year's General Election re-staged as an eviction-based phone vote talent contest in order to interest all the 18-21 year olds who otherwise can't see the point in voting for anything. John Prescott performs *Mack The Knife* and Oliver Letwin has trouble with the chickens.

11.55 Enough Graham Norton! Graham meets J.D. Salinger, Joel & Ethan Coen, Chris Morris, Captain Beefheart and Lord Lucan. With music from The Beatles.

12.00 Littlejohn On The Prairie Uncompromising views on frontier grassland from the outspoken journalist (rpt)

1.00 Returning New series in which celebrities revisit their old haunts. This week Courtney Love returns to Liverpool to get off with the two people she missed last time. With Pete Burns and Cilla Black

2.00 I Love Lucy Speed Vintage comedy with Desi Arnez and Sean Williamson Jr (B/W) (rpt)

2.30 Aintree from Newmarket

4.00 The Bronze Age Kitchen (6/8) Bones

4.30 Clockword Baffling quiz presented by HRH Prince Edward. Magdalen College vs Blur.

5.05 Merseyside *Omnibus*. Sandra is concerned that Maggie is turning into a bear again until Reg flies by with his new friends from the galaxy of Andromeda to help open the leisure centre. Phil expects an audience-friendly explosion soon.

6.30 Big Baby Highlights from week four. The poor side refuse to share the nappy (rpt).

7.00 Trading Places Spagger, an HIV+ heroin dealer from Hastings swaps jobs with dental nurse Godiva Shuffle

7.30 Holding It In The series visits three more people whose jobs prevent them from regularly going to the lavatory. Narrated by Michael Kitchen.

8.00 The Upside-Down House The Gibson family continue their attempt to spend six months living upside-down. This week, Colin falls out of bed again and Marianne's bath floods the attic.

9.00 David Blane: Making The Sky Disappear Spectacularly special US TV special.

9.50 Heroes Of Comedy André Preview.

10.00 The 1000 Greatest 'Had An Accident Lately?' Adverts Of All Time

11.35 Boxcar The Bastard Cripple Cat Animation from the makers of South Park.

12.05 Ally McCoist Single, Scottish and falling apart. (rpt)

1.00 Late Night Sculpture Semi Final. "Cowgirl" Hepworth vs Jac Ometti.

1.50 Sparrows (rpt) Hard-hitting drama by Jimmy Truthwright set in 1978, about the IRA's breakaway birdwatching ring.

chanel no 5

7.50 Little Mr Men and The Mr Men Mr Small Uppity and Mr Uppity.

8.05 The All New Adventures of The Same Old Popeye

9.00 Rear Of The Year 1933 Vintage repeat featuring Somerset Maugham's winning swimsuit round.

10.00 FILM: That Darn Walrus! (1969) Disney comedy including (approx. times)

10.10 Rollerskate chase

10.22 Mechanical breakfast maker

11.16 Parent struck with cream pie

11.29 Villains dunked in harbour

11.35 Ratdog Unappealing cartoon

11.50 The World's Worst... Television series

Clockword C4, 4.30pm

12.45 Lord Peter Wimsey The Vampire Slayer (B/W) (rpt)

1.40 David Dickinson's Manhunt Newton-Le-Willows (rpt)

2.10 Xerox Warrior Princess Unoriginal fantasy series.

3.00 News at Ten A classic episode from the much loved third series. (First shown on ITV)

3.30 FILM: Tupelo Ass Station Gizz Guzzler (1987) Pammy Cum and Rocky Neville star in this family matinee. (Edited for bad language)

4.55 Bollocks To Bathtime Up-to-the-minute current affairs show for the under fours.

5.10 Lovejoy: The Next Generation *Into The Ormolu Quadrant*. Captain Tinker flies the USS Chippendale into danger.

6.05 Knight Fever Suggs and his singing car.

7.00 Millionaires Want To Be The Who *I Can See For Miles* and *Boris the Spider* rehearsed and performed by Stelios Haji-Ioannou and Michael Winner.

7.30 Harry Enfield And Less Sketch comedy without Kathy Burke or Paul Whitehouse.

8.00 The UK's Worst... Breath

9.00 FILM: 3 Men & Syd Little & A Lady (1991) Malone, Magnum and Mahoney look after the straight-man when his wife goes away on business.

10.45 FILM: Night Mail (1993) Hollywood remake of W.H.Auden's 1930s GPO promotional film. Sylvester Stallone attempts to thwart Lance Henriksen's plans to plough a hijacked mail train through Grand Central Station on Christmas Eve. *Score by Benjamin Britpop.*

12.35 FILM: Dark Side (1974) Pink Floyd's memorable live performance from the surface of the moon, with guest vocals from Michael Collins.

Big, bigger, and bigger!

Judy's sunflower towers above the corner of Alphabet Street and Maxink Way.
PHOTOGRAPH BY HERBIE FOWLERS

BY TAUNTON MISHAP

A sunflower growing race at The Teapop School has proved to be a blooming marvellous success as one of the plants entered has grown really large!

The flower, named 'Sonny' by its owner Judy Sausages, has grown at least tenty times higher and wider than its friends and the growth shows no signs of stopping there.

"At first I thought it would stop as soon as it reached the top of my garden fence," Ms Sausages told me,

"but now it looks like it has only one destination in mind. The moon."

Horticultural experts have been called in to try and curb the plant's relentless self-enlargement using kitchen scissors, but to no avail. If anything the plant seems more determined than ever to grow.

"You cut one stem and two grow in its place. Our only hope is that this thing's not intelligent," said one 'expert' as layer after layer of hot pollen ate through his jacket.

The winner will be announced on Thursday.

ROADWORKS NIGHTMARE

by Challenger Putney

FRAMLEY motorists have voiced their extreme concern over the 'nightmare' state of roadworks at junction 12 of the FR403 motorway.

Over a period of three days, over 2000 individual complaints were registered with Framley Borough Council concerning the 'essential' repairs.

"It was a nightmare," said one happy motorist, "I was driving along and then all of a sudden the road surface was replaced by what seemed to be nothing. It felt like I was falling through the earth's crust, but unpleasant."

Other car users reported seeing Cornish road cones, strobe warning lights and crazy tarmac.

"It was quite literally just a nightmare. I was driving my father home from the all-night garage when all of a sudden we were being chased over a waterfall by a swarm of bats", said ten-year-old Elverton Crest.

However, when council officials were called to investigate the situation, they claimed that no roadworks were present, or had ever

A road, like the one in the story
PHOTOGRAPH BY SUE PUTNEY

been present, at the stated location.

"We're currently investigating the situation, but these roadworks never existed", one of them said yesterday.

The motorists seem to agree. "Yes," said one later today, "My journey to work took me 2 hours longer than normal, thanks to these nightmare roadworks, but then I woke up and it was all a dream".

All charges against the roadworks have now been dropped and an out of court settlement now seems likely.

GENERAL MEETING

(A review of any of the events of the past few months that seem significant for discussion)

MID NEXT WEEK ABOUT NOON

VENUE T.B.C.

NB: A meeting involving the same people may well be taking place in the next room at the same time

For further information, please contact one of our representatives or send a letter to one of our addresses.

crabley's music

Framley's largest stockist of musical notes, staves and key signatures.

Why not ask for a short tour of our new pizzicato department?

Remember, you just cun't make music without Crabley's!

15 Dotonthe Lane, off Framley High Street
01999 123 4123

Police discover the same body again and again

POLICE investigating the discovery of a body on wasteground near Cossett Park Industrial Estate have identified it as 38-year old Samantha de Tricycle of Honeyman Circus, Whoft.

However, they have also opened an immediate investigation into the investigation, since DNA tests had already positively identified Ms de Tricycle when she was found dead on a bench in Cossett Park three years ago.

"I just don't understand it," said police forensics expert Foster Nice when I started asking him things, "people can't die twice, they just can't. It simply isn't possible."

Events took a further extraordinary turn on Friday when a third de Tricycle corpse was discovered during a sponsored police treasure hunt by a field near some trees in a ditch.

by Taunton Mishap

At the post mortem, Mr Nice broke down in tears, falling to his knees and challenging the Almighty for proof or denial of resurrection.

"His faith has been sorely tested by this," admitted Chief Constable Rupert Bone. "But we remain resolute. Ms de Tricycle died thrice. Our tests show this beyond any doubt."

Fourteen similar incidents are under further investigation. Mr Nice will be buried voluntarily next Tuesday.

Carnival Queen has best arse yet

Annelise Gullivard, the recently chosen St Eyot's Carnival Queen has "the best arse yet", according to the judging panel.

She will hold the coveted position for the next twelve months, during which time the panel will enjoy looking at her arse as she goes about her duties.

Sockford Auction Rooms

Auction of British Television Memorabilia

LOTS INCLUDE

Third grapefruit from Morecambe & Wise breakfast "Stripper" routine. Split slightly off-centre

Defective branch of Record Breakers domino topple attempt, Tokyo 1981. Floral spray. Still standing. McWhirter certificate of disappointment.

Unconvincing rat puppet in biscuit tin, formerly property of Andrew Sachs.

Very hot judge's outfit. As seen on Nationwide. Clearance of effects.

August 14th, 2pm. Bring a bottle.

Sockford Auction Rooms
21 Chapparal Lane, Sockford 01999 622 848

Stiffs

Nichola Logan

aged 30 years
of Onmy Parade, Whoft.
Peaceful until the end,
then kicking and
screaming.

Sadly Missed

Patient

slipped away at Whoft
Hospice on July 2nd after
a lengthy illness.

Not too sure what his
name was actually. Lovely
guy, shame about that
huge purple lump on his
neck, wonder what it was.
He always made us laugh
with that huge purple lump
on his neck.

Fond memories – all the
staff at Whoft Hospice.
Something like that. How
much would that be?
£14.50?!! You're having a
laugh! Oh, go on then,
stick one of those crosses
at the top too

DEREK RIFLEMAN, sneezed
himself out of a window in his sleep,
July 3rd, aged 86. A loving,
wheezing parent and grandparents
to Michael. Love Billy, Madge & the
kids xxx Funeral to take place at St
Humbert's Chapel, Wripple on 27th
September. **NO FLOWERS**.
Donations to the Hayfever and
Asthma Research Foundation.

Acknowledgement

Florence May Sexton

The family of the late
Florence May Sexton wish
to apologise to relatives and
friends for the last few years
of her bitter life, during which
time she made things
extremely difficult for those
around her.

Particular thanks to the
more than tolerant Mr
Baker next door, who
received a daily letter from
Bitchnanna detailing the
many and varied ways in
which his budgie could be
made into a glove.

PET FUNERALS

Family pet dead?
Don't want to lie to the kids?
We help soften the blow.

We'll take the
corpse of your
late pet and place
it with a loving
farm family.

We have hundreds
of accommodating,
caring, rural
families on our
books, none of
whom mind
having the odd
dead dog on the
hearth rug.

*Rover's gone to
live on a farm*

*THINKS:
Must get rid of the
body somehow...*

*Now you don't
have to lie...
Rover and you can
BOTH go to heaven!*

**DOOLITTLE'S PET
PLACEMENTS
01999 388 680**

DANIEL ROTISSERIE quickly, at
the hand of an aggrieved dealer, on
Framley High Street, June 27th, just
outside Boots. "They broke the
mould when they murdered you."
Funeral has already taken place.
Donations if desired to the "He owed
me 15 grand, Mrs Rotisserie. Now
that debt belongs to you" Fund.

Taken From Us

Why did you do it?
Alan Ant
1987 – 2002
*"Ridicule was nothing
to be scared of"*
Mum & Dad

HOW IS MY TYPESETTING?
01999 974 976

Peter Ointment

Died December 8th

He was a kind, loving man
with an infectious smile and
disease that affected all who
were close to him. He will
be missed, sorely by
everyone whom he touched.
From the patients, nurses
and staff of Ward 20
Framley General Hospital.
We must find a cure.

New Arrivals

It's NOT a boy!

CONGRATULATIONS
Tom and Linda Squirts
on giving birth to
what you claim
is a bonny,
bouncing boy,
even though it clearly has
a sixpence where it ought
to have a winkle. Call it
David and dress it in
trousers if you have to,
but we've taken a vote,
and it's definitely going to
grow into a lady.

*Love from the staff of
St Germain's Hospital,
Molford.*

IT'S A BOY!
GRUNDY
Alexander Yusuf,
born 26.05.02.
Announcing your
wedding to
Barbara on
03.08.31 and
your untimely passing on
16.11.48. You will be
sorely missed by Barbara,
Michael and Daphne.

Grandad xxx

LOOK! GREAT VALUE!

if you'd like to take advantage
of our great 3-in-1 offer, call
Denise on 01999 974 974

BAZALGETTE A wonderful baby
boy, Changing Rooms, a big brother
for Food and Drink and a third child
for Peter and Sir John.

IT'S A BOAR!

It's A Boar! Toctoc Erwin
Born June 30th 2002,
weighing 300lb
to proud
parents Asterix
and Obelix.

*Scrunch! These
announcements are crazy.*

GOUNOD-RELEASE 06.06.02,
Reginald. A beautiful second
grandfather for Adam and Jasmine.

MIKE DENNISON would like to
announce the birth of baby Ella,
18lbs 6oz on 03.06.02. Martine
Dennison, would like to announce
that this is never ever ever
happening again and is looking
forward to being able to sit down at
some time in the future.

It's a family announcement!

£35 boxed
£15 plain
£40 pop-up

01999 94 76 94

JANE & DANIEL IGLOO are
delighted to announce the
appearance of a smaller version of
themselves, but amazingly
combined into one tiny person.
How on earth did that happen?
Enlighten us. 01999 655 543

ELLIOT

Louise & Patrick are
delighted to announce
the safe arrival
of Delboy
Jason, born 30
June, weighing
8lb2oz.

A beautiful baby boy for
either Louise & Patrick
or Louise & Keith
MacGowan (blood test
result pending).

*Thanks to all the staff at
St Grandad's.*

OPAL & SOFT FRUIT wish
to announce the birth of Penny
Chew, a beautiful sister for Bazooka
Joe, Black Jack and Bubblicious.

WANT TO APPEAR on the
Announcements Page? I can kill
you, marry you or get you pregnant!
All services performed discreetly in
the privacy of your own home.
Competitive rates. Call Vince on
0999 754 544

It's a phantom pregnancy!

Karen Delling, you
attention seeking muppet,
you can throw up all you
like, you're
never going to
throw up a baby.
Now do a nice big
fart, and get out
of that bed, someone with
a real foetus needs it.

*Love from the staff of
St Germain's Hospital,
Molford.*

Adversaries

50th Anniversary

50 years ago you
stood me up outside
the Paragon Cinema,
Mildred Witting.

*"Though night draws in cold
My heart remains true
Love never grows old
I wait here for you"*

Never forgotten

Oliver Dixon xxx

DIXON Happy 49th Wedding
Anniversary Susan. From Oliver.

ANNIVERSARY
Congratulations, Mum and Dad
on the forty-sixth anniversary of
the invention of the hovercraft

*"Together forever, hearts
entwined on this special day"*

All our love, Carl and Mandy

CRAZY-GOLF, MICHAEL &
JEANETTE. Eleven marvellous
years. Happy velcro anniversary.
Thank goodness she never found
out that you don't really work on an
oil rig. From all the girls at Maxine's
24-hour Bowling Whorehouse.

Annoncements

LOOK WHAT OUR SURVEY SAID!

**You've always been like
a Les Dennis to us.**

From William & Ffion

HAPPY BIRTHDAY TO YOU!

Happy birthday to you
Happy birthday dear
Mildred and Patty Hill
Happy birthday to you
Lawsuit pending.

GOOD LUCK DAD!

Wishing you
all the best
on this, your
special day!

05.06.02
6am EST

"See you in hell, asshole"

LOOK who's under your bed!

**Sweet dreams, Josie.
Love Mr Hollyhock and
"Old King Pipe"**

Look who's 3 and a half!

Scott! Who are you
on the phone to?
Oh, for goodness sake...
Give me that. Who is this?
Oh, dear. Sorry, don't
listen to him. No we don't
want to take an advert out.
Yes. Sorry to have
bothered you.

LOOK WHO'S STILL WETTING THE BED !

**Is this what I have to do
to make you stop, Roger?**

*No-one drinks 12 cups of
tea before bedtime – I know
you're doing it on purpose.*

Eleanor xxx

CONGRATULATIONS
Josie, on finally finishing
your dinner. You know you
can't afford to miss that
much school and dinner is
good for you.

*Pease pudding hot
Pease pudding cold
Pease pudding on the plate
Three weeks old !*

Mr Hollyhock

**LOOK WHO COULDN'T AFFORD
A BOX AD WITH A PICTURE OF
YOU IN IT!** (Imagine that photo of
you in the bath as a baby with ice
cream all over your chin printed in
an oval here). Happy Birthday,
Simon! All our love, Mum and Dad.

**ABSOLUTE-BLEEDING
DISGRACE** The wedding of Julie
Absolute-Bleeding and David
Disgrace will unfortunately take
place on Tuesday the 5th despite all
our well-intentioned advice.

LOOK WHO'S RUNNING OUT OF OXYGEN !

**Keep shouting, Dennis!
Love Chris and Lynsey.**

Announcement

**Mr & Mrs
Ivor Engine**
Would like to
announce the
forthcoming
marriage of their
son Peter to Olivia De Steam
on 12th June at Llaniog Golf
Club, but we can't because
he's just slept with her dad

LOOK WHO'S 208

Happy birthday, Cecil.

From Auntie Mirabelle.

Look who's 3 and a half!

**I nearly four.
And rockets up the side.
Please. VISA 9432 6543
764 9999 16
Fankyou.**

TO ORDER a Father's Day
Massage call Trixie or Vince on
01999 322 191

LOOK who's fucking my wife!

Peter, you first class turd. I
thought you had more taste.
And you can forget
about getting your
lawnmower back – *Ray*

Adoptions

ADOPTION LETTER to
ADOFRM548. Dear Birth Mother.
Mother Helga and devoted father
Frank would be honoured to help
adobt your baby. We love being
parents to our adorable, adopted 2
yr. old son who's looking forward to
becoming a father. We're helping
him to help you. Thanks. BOX
FR6988

OUR PROMISE TO ADOPT YOUR BABY

(ADOFRM085)

We promise to raise you in a
home with laughter and
tears. We promise birthdays
with fake trees and Christmas
with real eggs. We promise
to create a home for you that
is full of heat. We promise to
remind you that without us,
you'd be
somewhere else.

*Please help us fulfil our
promises.*

01999 587776

(calls charged at 50p minute,
min call length 5min)

Life'style

with style guru Eugenie Solids

Bodystockings are in, in and still in this year, so show off your lovely shapes with a skintight orange number. You'll certainly be a hit with some of the ladies!

Don't be shy to show a little more on the beach this été. Cover up unwanted hair with a hat. Can't stretch to beach-flops? Seashells make an adequate alternative.

Always be aware of your proportions. Short waisted? Wear a smile and a neat bowler hat. Petite torso? Not my problem. Fat arsed? Try dieting, Porky.

Furs are very definitely in! My Italian spies tell me that otter is in the ascendent this week. Forget those moaning namby-pamby animal rights, fur is pretty.

Wear a **Newby's Fart Enhancer** from Newby's Health Saloon of Molford to distract from that embarassing moustache problem. People will be falling over themselves to get out of your way before it happens again!

With winter over for another year I've been turning my eyes to summer. I've been leafing through some magazines so that you know what to wear without breaking a bank.

Sprinkle talcum powder on used socks and twice-used underwear to mask your unpleasant odours. Prevents chaffing I'm told, but I wouldn't know about that, I'm told.

Eyeliner. Fairy Liquid. Persil. K-Y jelly. Condoms. Preparation H. Fish fingers. Bread. Clover. Econ cheddar. Frascati. 10 x Ben & Jerry's Dbl Choc. Light bulb (40w). Lunch with Darren. Pick up Jessica from school.

Hollywood stars always look their best but you can achieve this year's Gene Hackman look with nothing more than a coat-hanger and some glitter.

Low shoulders are raging on the Supermodel catwalks of Paris and Framley. If you can't afford the neck extensions, try **Newby's Neck and Chin Tincture (£13)** from Newby's Health Saloon of Molford.

Tired eyes? Try **Newby's Cucumber Pirate Eye-patches (£5.99 a pair** from Newby's Health Saloon of Molford) to flatten those unwanted retina wrinkles and widen irises.

Don't be afraid to show a little less on the beach this summer. Cover up unwanted hats with hair.

Finding hats and hair a beach-time nuisance? Cover yourself from head-to-toe in toothpaste and, as a bonus, you'll save a fortune in sunscreen. Stripes are *most definitely in!*

In belly-buttons are out this season – if you have difficulty converting yours to an 'outie' then I usually find that a partially-sucked malteser fits nicely in my hole.

Team fuchsia lipbalm with a *The Damned* album sleeve on each knee to achieve that elusive punk look. And then try gobbing in your own face as you speak to your boss like that.

Newby's Health Saloon is open Mon-Fri 9am-5.30pm (Sat 5.30am – 9pm) for all your health and beauty needs and ladies. 10% discount available on wrong treatments.

HIGH STREET OFFERS: Newby's Pharmaceuticals are offering a *2-for-1* deal on eye-concealer make-up, for that smooth-faced look that's so popular this year. **Mellard & Esst** have slashed the price of organic leggings. **Flammings** have a promotion on eyelash perms – remember afro lashes are *to die for*. **Ms Outside** are celebrating the opening of their new beautarium by offering a free arse-wax for you and your dog.

NEW SMELLS FOR THE MEN THIS SUMMER

SPIRIT OF EDEN
£2 a bottle from Newby's Pharmaceuticals

Splash it all over with this wonderfully delicate fragrance. Used sparingly it suggests innocence, copious amounts reek of betrayal. This jolly little scent comes in 4 litre, easy to carry bottles, so you'd never need not smell of *The Spirit Of Eden*.

BODYSOCK for men
£10 a bottle from shops

There's no excuse for not "pulling the ladies" with this effort from the laboratories of Conq. The smell reminded this journalist of Edwin Starr, but I could have been mistaken. It's equally effective used as an all-over body lotion or mouthwash. Killer.

BEANS ON TOAST SHAVING BALM
£2.75 a gallon from 6am, weekdays

There's a whiff of the hardy outdoorsman about this ingenious combination of robust aftershave balm and hardwearing varnish. The finish is smooth and tough, bringing out chin grain in bold tones, and with the alluring fragrance of a freshly cooked midday snack, you'll be beating them off with a splintery plank, Dandy Dan!

LOSE A STONE A DAY -the sugar and water way!

Advertising promotion

We all know that crash diets can be a good weigh of losing those extra stones quickly. Much better than Sit-Ups or DanceDiets or Aerobic.

This is why a company has produced a set of simple-to-follow diet books designed to allow you to lose weight faster than you can put it on.

The Sugar and Water Diet can be used throughout the day in place of your three regular meals. Sugar for energy. Water for rehydratration.

Here are a few sample recipies to make your appetite go all whet and hungry.

* * * * *

BREAKFAST
Ice Cold Sugar with Water

Fill a cereal bowl with

250ml of cold tap water. Add sugar and stir violently for a couple of minutes or until all the sugar has been absorbed. Stir again and eat immediately

LUNCH
Sugar Glacier Lollies

Add some sugar to some water, stir, and freeze in plastic lolly molds. Using the above amounts should make enough lollies for some people. I have found that these tasty treats can keep for up to forever.

DINNER
Sugar Lumps in thick and dreamy 'gravy'

Arrange 4 sugar lumps vertically on a plate. Warm some water in a saucepan and simmer for 5 minutes or so until thickened. Pour carefully over the sugar tower. Add sugar and

water to taste.

SNACKS
Bite-sized Treats

Diets shouldn't be boring affairs with long gaps between prescribed meals. If you get hungry, munch on some sugar lumps. Thirsty? Try water.

* * * * *

By following your 3-Stop Diet Plan you should soon feel the pounds falling off and you won't miss a meal.

TIP If you haven't got a sweet tooth, swap sugar with salt.

Squatters evicted from bouncy castle

Mrs Scholes in jubilant mood after her legal win.

PHOTOGRAPH BY POGLESWOOD ADAMS

A THREE-YEAR battle to evict a group of rowdy alternate lifestylists from a bouncy castle in Molford has finally come to an end.

Residents and campaigners looked on as bailiffs arrived in the back garden of 42 Leonard Rossiter Way and served legal notices on the five badly dressed squatters.

"This is a personal victory for me," said Marion Scholes, in whose garden the bouncy castle was inflated for her daughter's sixth birthday party. "The last three years have been a living hell of loud music, marijuana and constant bouncing."

CARNABY GROOVERS

Mrs Scholes' long fight to rid her garden of scruffy hipsters has been the subject of a huge publicity campaign, and has even featured in an hour long documentary in the television.

"This must never happen again," said Mrs Scholes, "and if it does, the council should deal with it much more quicklier. I handed in a petition at the Town Hall a year and a half ago, signed by everyone in Leonard Rossiter Way and Bruce Bould Close, and no-one even rang to thank me. I'm not a complete tit, you know, but I know when I'm being treated like one."

Mrs Scholes, whose daughter has had to hold her last two birthday parties in the loft, now plans to deflate the castle and return it to the hire company she now owes £42,500.

New roadmarkings "erratic and wrong"

MOTORISTS have given a lukewarm welcome to a new series of roadmarkings in Sockford town centre. The controversial road-mounted instructions are the work of a guerilla team of town planners and civil engineers known only as "The Black Wing". This elite cadre of urban signage contractors strike by night, then melt into the darkness like gossamer upon the winds of eternity. The signs will be replaced with proper ones next Friday.

PHOTOGRAPH BY SEXTON DELICIOUS

CORRECTIOSN & CLARIFICATIONS

In last week's feature 'The A-may-z-ing World Of The Nature Of Our World!', we reported that people who live on the equator can sneeze rainbows. We have since discovered this to be uncertain.

There have been consonants in the alphabet since language first evolved, not since 1842 as we suggested ('200 Years Ago, You Would Have Been Reading The Ae Eaie,' Framley Examiner last week) last week.

Some of our birdwatchers have been wrong ('It's Not Just A Hot Ball Of Feathers,' last week's Framley Examiner) to suggest that crows and sparrows fly by building tunnels in the air. Furthermores, ostriches do not spin webs and Rod Hull is not mentioned in the Old Testament.

Charlie Drake ('A Celebrity In Your Letterbox', last week's Framley Examiner) was the not the bass player in the Plastic Ono Band. He played the spoon.

The earth is not 13cm from the sun ('No Wonder It's So Hot!' Framley Examiner last week) but much, much further. We should also like to point out that bees do not collect pollen to make banana yoghurt, and that the tomato is not really an insect: it is a fruit / vegetable.

George VI ('Queen For A Day', last week's Framley Examiner) did not have a wooden heart, he had a real one. In addition, he was not killed by his wallpaper: this was King Napoleon.

Alfred Hitchcock's first film was not *Grease* (Film Review, Framley Examiner last week) it was something else.

Doctor Proctor ('Doctor Proctor', last week's Framley Examiner) was wrong to suggest that you can catch cancer by walking under a ladder. Nor was he correct to suggest that 96% of men are women or that sex is an aphrodisiac. However, in a correction to a previous correction, Doctor Proctor has reassured us that farting can make you blind.

Church minibus vadnalised

A NEW CHURCH MINIBUS has been vandalised only two weeks after it was bought with money raised by parishioners in a series of demeaning sponsored activities.

Hooligans seriously damaged the vehicle, – belonging to St Damonoutofblur's church, Molford – scratching the paintwork with cufflinks and smashing the stained glass windscreen.

The Revd Julius Pantomime, vicar of St Damonoutofblur's, told churchgoers in his sermon on Sunday that, although the windscreen was beyond repair, there was a bright side to every silver lining.

"It is a terrible shame that we've had to tape polythene over our once beautiful parish windscreen. But I have to admit that we seem to be having far fewer accidents now the driver's view of oncoming traffic is not blocked by colourful scenes of The Ascension."

We then sang hymn number 149 and ate magic Jesus biscuits.

Cruelty to dog - help wanted

The RSPCA is appealing for help after a 10-month-old bulldog was left in a sack in a hot car with concrete wheels with all the windows shut in the middle of a motorway for three weeks before being hanged by the throat from the "St Eyot's 3 miles" sign by irate motorists.

Anyone with any information about why the animal had been forced to wear orange lederhosen and a prescription monocle throughout the incident should contact the RSPCBD on 01800 PORDOG.

FROM FRAMLEY WITH LOVE

Need a holiday?
Need a new car?
Need to pay off that debt?

Need to raise that extra bit of cash?

Got a Framley boy going spare?

FROM FRAMLEY WITH LOVE is Framley's number one introductions agency. We supply affluent Filipino housewives of all ages with Framley boys. All our clients are extensively vetted and cleansed.
(Catholic brotherhood certificate of approval)

"We Filipino housewives like Framley boys - they're compliant and have very small feet."

FROM FRAMLEY WITH LOVE
27, Purple Passage, Framley FR1 3AD 01999 92074F

BUBBLE BURSTS ON CRISP MAN

TURN YOUR MEMORIES INTO CRISPS, the Framley firm that promised to TURN customer's MEMORIES INTO CRISPS, has gone into bankruptcy after only 6 months' trading.

Unlike successful businesses, 22-year-old Lee Organisn's Internet-based family-run firm has hit the financial ocean floor.

A hastily organised presconference yesterday saw Lee announcing his intention to fold the firm like a "foolscap envelope" and "post it to the receivers".

As news reached the marketplace investment men rushed to buy any stocks and shares that weren't connected to the the crisp enterprise, and to sell all of the ones that were. Something crashed.

"If there's one thing I've learnt from this business adventure", Lee told us, "is that not enough", he continued, "people wanted their memories turned into crisps"

"At first we sold some, and then we sold lots, so we thought we'd try and sell lots and lots," he explained quite clearly. "Unfortunately not as many people wanted lots and lots as wanted some, and so we found ourselves with lots left over."

The Framley Examiner's own business expert, Jennifer Oat, says that this phenomenon is quite commonemon and the news is unlikely to have a significant effect on the worldwide crisp memories market.

What's he doing?
PHOTO BY CHICK BEAK

"There will always be a small global contingent who would like to see a treasured memory captured on the face of a potato chip,"she gasped.

But as they say, you can't bury a good man for long. Towards the end of his speech, Lee announced that he wasn't planning an early retirement bath.

"We've got to move with the times. The World Web has opened up whole new boulevards of opportunity for us. Now is the time for us to consign the crisp memento to the dustman of history and seek out brave new horizons for business expansion."

Mr Organisn pulled down a curtain revealing a freshly painted logo: "Turn Your Memories Into Shoes!" Then, with the aid of an overhead projector diagram and a pair of shoes, he outlined the possibilities.

"You can do a lot with laces," he said. "Platform soles are a happy memory, brogues more melancholy."

Trading was brisk.

Business to Business
with our businessman, Nigel Drivel

The future starts tomorrow!

ARE YOU PAYING TOO MUCH IN MANAGEMENT CONSULTANT FEES?

IT'S A SCENARIO not unfamiliar to many businesses. It's been a good few years, the company is growing, and the management consultants have started to shape your future.

And then it all seems to go so wrong. Overheads are rising, the consultants have to re-think, capital gets sold off and even headcount can suffer. Short- and short-to-medium-medium-term debt can be crippling, especially with interest rates being so low: there's always the prediction that your future debts will cost more because inflation is bound to rise.

It can be utterly dreadful being in business some times, isn't it, businesspeople?

But just when you think you're walking around in circles, you find the answer around the corner marked 'management consultants.'

Consultancy costs can be astronomical, and often chisel away at budgets that will suffer after they've borne the cost of those costs. The inside track from The City is that it's time to ditch those consultancy costs. But how?

Well, here's where you turn the corner marked 'next generation of management consultants.'

In the competitive consultancy environment, more and more companies are competing to offer more and more more cost-effective services at more and more and more affordable prices. Fortunately for those of us in the business-to-business business, the new wave of consultants are leaner, fitter and faster.

Based in a converted 20th century barn on the outskirts of Wripple, The Company Company is one such "2G" team of consultants.

Managing director (or "team stag" in 2G-speak) Steve Glibbs is roundly optimistic (and a millionaire).

"We're taking on major projects at the moment, by accumulating a huge portfolio of consultancies and consulting on all their consulting. They consult us for decisions that help them cut the costs to make their decision making more profitable."

"It's absolutely astonishing. I can't believe what these companies will pay. I'm minted. You saw the Jags on the drive?" he continued. "One of our 'team leverets' took home £13,000 last month. We're all laughing."

It certainly looks as if the future will belong to companies like The Company Company. If your consultants are costing you too much, perhaps they need consultants? The future starts today.

OPPORTUNNITIES

HAVE YOU GOT WHAT WE TAKE?

These varied and demanding posts require desperate, pro-inactive depressives who have prior experience of the real world. You will need worn-out organisational skills, highly developed manipulative techniques and piss all charisma

We have permanent vacancies available in the following sectors of the finance industry:

- Fiscal Nancies · Self Financiers · Derivative People·
- Money Management Managers · Bond Agents · Senior Liars ·
- Field Saleswideboys · Risk Ignorers · Ordinaries ·
- Statistically Analysts · Insurance Badgers · Superhighwaymen ·
- Televaluers · Poundstretchers · Moneylickers · Underestimaters ·
- Team Brigadiers · Cocaine Addicts Who Can Shout · Tiny Chancellors ·
- People Who Are Prepared To Sack People · Team Brigadiers ·
- Account Manglers · Floor Dandies · Blank Managers ·
- Gamblers · Further Accountants To Do Other Accountants' Accounts ·
- Deal Stealers · Hollow Traders · Assistant Shysters · Sheep ·
- Needle-Eye Camel Troublers · Arguethe Tossers · Trained Apes ·
- Dicemanshipsters · Shit-Stirrers · Rumour Mongerers ·
- Welsh Marketeers · Chestbursters · Executive Belittlers · Thieves ·
- Human Ladder Climbers · Legitimated Bank Robbers · Flash Harrys ·
- Artful Dodgers · Chief Money Launderers · Yobs ·
- Team Player Managers · Penny Distillers · Michael Douglases ·
- Wall St. Shufflers · Manhattan Transferers · many more available

FOR BIG MONEY PLACINGS CALL JEFF OR CINDY ON 01999 800 810 NOW!

UNDERMONEY TELEPHILANDERERS Milk bottle shaped position. Upwardly conceived for hungry televaluers Opportunities aplentiful £300 funeral expenses

BLINKBROKER Full-time Scale 4 £16,000 – £17,999 plus PRP Fixed term post until final breath

COIN CONSULTANT All-the-time. Scale 6. £10 – £100 inc. Inclusive of Weighting

MONEY MANAGEMENT MANAGER Secret Scale tbc Variably honest contract

OVERANALYSTS/INSURANCE BADGERS Jobshare (2dpw on, 2 dpw on, 2dpw on, 1dpw on/off). Bad position.

SUICIDAL RECRUITMENT
JOBS FOR YOUR LIFE

WJC&S
Wee Jimmie Crankie & Salterton
SALES & LETTINGS

THOXTOXETER

We are proud to announce the sale of this genuine 1960s shrinkwrap maisonette in much sought after area. The property shrinks to fit, snugly smothering the occupants every summer. Previous owner only recently escaped during unseasonal cold spell. Quick sale preferred before weather changes. **£110,395**

FIELDINGFIELD

Well-mannered Gemini property. North facing and south facing. Gregarious. Gets on well with Libran neighbours. Lucky colour: Magnolia bathroom. You will meet a handsome stranger in the cupboard under the stairs. **£210,000**

CHUTNEY LE BASIL

Compact one-bedroom magical fungal feature, convenient for all local amenities, Economy 7 storage heaters. Fully fitted kitchen. Off road parking. But still, essentially, let's not beat around the bush, a big mushroom. **£40,595**

WANTED

Due to unprecedented demand and an abundance of customers seeking a property in your area, we urgently require **YOUR PROPERTY** and no other properties in your area.

Face it, it's too big for you now the kids are at University, with you rattling around it like a pea in a skip, and frankly what you're doing with the garden is knocking a couple of grand off the asking price every time that cowboy squeaks up the drive with his wheelbarrow, so give us **YOUR PROPERTY.** Mrs Eleanor Jessop

CALL MIKE OR CAROLINE IN PRESSURE SALES
WJC&S 01999 864 722

RUBMY

Delightful 3-bed family house. Large garden. Open plan lounge. Kitchen / breakfast room. Squatters. Excellent location, near to shops & transport. Period features. Screaming headless ghost of a 9-foot nun. Off street parking for 2 cars. **£11,985**

TOLLEPHANT

Spacious church conversion. Owner must put up with loads of people turning up unnanounced once a week to sing *Immortal Invisible*, drink your wine and eat your crisps.  **£495,950**

WRIPPLE*

*ON THE MOVE! One-of-a-kind 5-bed house, currently situated in Wripple. Soon to be situated in Molford. Two long metal legs extending from bottom of property, walking at 10mph up the inside lane of the FR404, heading east. Conveniently located (phone to find out for what at the moment). **OIRO £160,000**

YOPNEY ST OH!

Surrounded by walls and ditches, this charming 6-bedroom 17th Century property has been unoccupied since the 17th Century. Advances in Mole Machine technology mean this fine family home is finally uncovered. **£585,995**

WRIPPLE

Desirable bargain 2-bed property. Photograph recently airbrushed to remove toppling chimney and damp outside wall. **£85,795**

SOCKFORD

Flat-roofed house, 25' x 25' x 25'. Number of windows on opposite faces adds up to seven. Currently facing in highly sought after lucky direction, hence **£114,390**

COMMERCIAL

FOR SALE: Chocolate factory. 2 previous owners. Glass elevator (fucked). Chocolate river choked with dead midgets. E-mail Mandy at Bucket's Golden Ticket Enterprises. mandy@buckettents.com **£POA**

PETER BOLLOCKS
LETTING AGENTS AND GREENGROCERS
HIGH ROAD, WHOFT 01999 499 299

PERIOD COTTAGE

- Contrary facing
- Sudden swings (back garden)
- May need painters in
- On the B108
- Rent payable once every 28
- days, date to synchronise eventually with all other rents in the neighbourhood.

£600pcm*   (* non negotiable)

ST EYOT'S, 3 bed house, airy, sunny, rainy (no roof). £355pcm (not including roof) or £400pcm (including roof) (but there is no roof)

FRAMLEY town centre, flatshare with 1 other much larger person, fitted kitchen with 3 gas cookers. Tenant must know how to cook many different meals and be able to order and afford up to 8 pizzas per evening. £300pcm (service discount not included)

WHOFT ENVIRONS, room available in purpose-built flat, convenient location, new carpet in toilet, deep pile, no need to flush. £70pcw

WRIPPLE, large small room, clean, quiet, discreet, fully fitted professional female. £30ph, no kissing on mouth, actual photo.

CHUTNEY, delightfully situated 4 bed flat (4 beds, 1 bedroom), would suit sharing couple that like to share, previous snorers need not apply. £41pw or offers.

SOCKFORD HEIGHTS, 2 bed house, desirable location in middle of busy road, easy access to transport, some through traffic, also traffic lights in lounge. £380pcm incl 6 months road tax.

MOLFORD VALLEY, well decorated 2 bed house, exclusive location, suit professional sharers, no DSS staff. £82pw.

FRAMLEY FR2, 1 bed flat, would suit professional w/machine, available immediate. A quid all in.

CRESSLEY BRIDGE, Art studio. Garret location, North light, en suite ballroom. Previously property of Garfunkel out of Simon and Garfunkel. £115pw.

WHOFT, Pleasant enough house offering unpleasant accommodation. Gas "cold air" heating. Patio-style bedroom. Kitchen with wasps' nest 'feature' in corner. Hideously overpriced £1000 pcm (per calendar minute)

FRAMLEY, Noisy end-of-terraces house situated at the end of Framley Imaginare's prestigious new stadium. Commanding views of the corner flag. Hot and cold running commentary. £2,000 pcm.

QUEFF, Idyllic "off the beaten track" location yet offering easy access to unbeaten tracks. Fitted walls, double kitchen, lounge feat. ceiling frescoes depicting stages in the building of next door's conservatory. £690 pcm

WHOTTEN PLODNEY, Large, former Rectory in the middle of this unpopular village. Off-road parking for tiny vehicle (poss. skateboard?). 20 reception rooms, leading to master bedroom. Would suit light sleeper. £1,600 pcm

SOCKFORD PEVEREL, Victorian 2-bed detached house with garden, close to town. Actual house, unfortunately, not close to town. To be honest, not sure garden belongs to house at all. May be wishful thinking on our part. Try organising a barbecue in it and find out if anyone gets upset. £1100pcm.

Excited shoppers wait along the sliproad by the DeLorean Industrial Estate, Sockford.
PHOTOGRAPH BY ST EMILLION POPDANCER

SALE MUST START SATURDAY

POLICE HAVE ORDERED that a sale at a shop in Sockford "must start Saturday".

Officers say they were forced to act after receiving a number of complaints from local members of the public.

Sockford residents had expressed concerns that traffic and emergency vehicles might have trouble negotiating the three miles of queues that have built up outside the shop since the first "Sale Starts Soon" signs went up in March.

Local schools have reported that truancy levels are at an all time high, and no firemen have reported for duty since June.

The owners of the shop, Anna-Barbara Production, and her common-law business partner Phil Mation have both been cautioned, and the sale, at Key Cutting City on the DeLorean Industrial Estate, will start, by court order, this Saturday.

CLEARLY A NEAR MISS

by Odgar Cushion

A MAN I MET YESTERDAY told me that a cyclist was involved in a bizarre near miss in the town centre last Thursday.

At around 2.30 in the afternoon, glaziers were delivering new windows to Gossip's Florist's in Purple Passage. But as they crossed the busy four-lane Cockson Road, carrying a 3m x 5m pane of glass, a cycle courier, rounding the corner at some speed, came within inches of losing his life.

"It was shocking," said a bystander (my man), "the cyclist didn't spot the pane of glass until the last minute. He didn't have time to brake, and I saw one of the workmen carrying the glass gasping with shock."

STROKE OF LUCK

But what happened next was an astonishing piece of luck.

"The cyclist just passed seamlessly and perfectly through the glass. It was like something out of Narnia. It was so peaceful and sublime that I almost barked my yop."

A representative for the glazier's, F.H. DeSmith, declined to comment, but Colin Yaffle, a professor of physics, logic and brilliance at Framley Community College, thinks there might be an explanation.

"They may have been carrying a pane of air," he said yesterday. "No, hang on, let me think about this. Some panes of glass have huge bubbles in them. No, that's not it, either. Just a minute. They may have achieved a perfect molecular velocity and just existed within each other for a moment without any of the usual interference, like the cyclist having his face smashed to bits.

"Yes, that'll do," he said.

The glaziers were reportedly so shocked that they dropped the pane of glass and it shattered into millions of annoying pieces.

Child dies of garden

A SMALL CHILD which had a severe allergic reaction to pollen was last night lying dead in hospital, say sources.

The little child, which has no name for legal reasons, was playing happily in its mother's friend's garden when it suffered anaphylactic shock (very bad for you) after coming into contact with a flower.

The owner of the deadly 24-foot back garden, 38-year-old Gwynyrd Skynyrd, offered her sympathies, but said the garden was a good garden that had never killed anyone before. Despite her protests, magistrates have ordered that the garden be put down.

The mother of the tiny little child, known only as Mrs ?, last night called for dangerous gardens to be muzzled.

"The Home Office," said Mrs ?, "must."

Bulldozers are already on their way.

Children missing since Saturday

By TAUNTON MISHAP

FOUR SCHOOLCHILDREN who went missing while on a hiking holiday to abroad have now not been seen since Saturday, say calendar experts.

Jolyon Hurrah, the co-owner of Higginson's Adventure Holidays – who was supervising the kids on the outward-bound course, told reporters that the children's disappearance had got everyone stumped.

"We don't have a clue what happened," he explained yesterday. "The group was playing an innocent game of blindfold hide and seek on the brink of a precipice in the middle of bear country when it happened.

"I had been chosen to be 'seeker', so I turned round for half an hour to count to ten thousand before going to find them.

"And when I did, I was horrified to discover they'd simply vanished into thin air."

Hurrah says he searched the area for nearly twenty minutes before giving up and walking to the nearest town to alert the police.

The four children, the only survivors of the rollercoaster accident that last week claimed twenty of their party, had been due to come home this Sunday, but their parents are now being encouraged to forget about them and have some more kids as soon as possible.

The last photo of the missing children.
PHOTOGRAPH BY JOLYON HURRAH

HIGGINSON'S ADVENTURE HOLIDAYS

WHETHER IT'S EATING POISONOUS REDBACK SPIDERS FRESH FROM THE TREE, OR ABSEILING DOWN THE SIDE OF A TIGER, NOTHING BEATS THE CHALLENGE OF A HIGGINSON'S ADVENTURE HOLIDAY. WITH DOZENS OF FLIGHTS TO HUNDREDS OF EXOTIC DESTINATIONS, YOU'RE NEVER FAR AWAY FROM ADVENTURE WITH HIGGINSON'S.

19 Blue Montague Terrace, Framley 01999 677 540
or visit our sponsors at www.dangeroussportsclub.co.uk

MILHAMHOUSE RADIATOR COSIES

A Milhamhouse cosy keeps even the coldest heating appliance toasty and warm, the natural way.

Call Milhamhouse on 01999 765 821 for a free conversation about heat and wool.

St Eyot's DONKEY MUSEUM

Hundreds of donkeys on display

See Europe's largest diorama on the evolution of the donkey

Just off the FR404 (Previously St Eyot's Airfield)

01999 811 542

Railway designer killed by new Framley loop-the-loop rail link

by Jesus Chigley

INVESTIGATORS were yesterday looking into the future of Framley's new £200m corkscrew railway after a disastrous test run killed the track's designer.

Maverick engineer Christopher P. "Rice Crispy" Rice was tragically flung from the buffet car of an experimental test train as it negotiated the second of a series of loop-the-loops that were intended, in Rice's own words, to serve as the "crown jewels in the crown" of the new rail route, linking Molford and Framley stations. After falling 180 feet, bouncing from strut to strut of the superstructure of the loop and landing on a grass siding, Rice died instantly, doctors say, of lung cancer.

EYEWITNESSES

Eyewitnesses described the scene.

"It was brilliant. I don't know how he did it," said Petra Wilkommen, who watched the accident from her bedroom window. "It's definitely the most death defying stunt I've ever seen. Except for the bit where he died."

Rice's deputy engineer, Helen Belljar, said that, though the tragedy was tragic, the construction of the rail link had to go on – and studying what went so horribly wrong this time would avoid further deaths in future.

Framley Station is closed by some police tape. (Inset) The unfortunate designer.
PHOTOGRAPHS BY BESERKELEY GRENADIER (INSET POSED BY DEAD MODEL)

"Though this is a difficult time for all of us, we can learn from what has just happened," she told me and I wrote it down.

"For instance, the first loop, above Chutney Junction, worked brilliantly. People on the platform heard Christopher and the test-monkeys all going 'Wooooh' as the train went round, and there was a lot of waving. It's a blinding loop, that."

PLUNGE OF DOOM

"It's the second loop that's the problem. We need to examine it carefully to see what might have gone wrong."

This second loop was Rice's pride and joy. Using a new design never before seen in railway engineering. it formed a revolutionary "figure of six" in the track. Experts are now keen to discover what tiny flaw in the construction of the loop might have led Rice's test carriage to be flung hundreds of feet into the air at over 90 mph.

"We're going to try everything, but the rail link will be built," said Ms Belljar, "and it will have Chrsitopher's beloved loops."

Plans for a revised "figure of four" shape are already on the drawing board, and the railway should be.

Whoft Cemetery full of stolen bodies

FOREIGN POLICEMEN Interpol have raided Whoft Cemetery after sustained allegations of grave robbing.

Cemetery manager, Emily Locque, we can exclusively reveal, has definitely been pinching the graves and headstones of celebrity corpses from other cemeteries around the world, with a view to reburying them in her own graveyard and attracting tourists to the area.

Police found famous communist landmark, Karl Marx, who was stolen from his Highgrove resting place in 1994, propped up against a still warm furnace in the crematorium.

The bodies of Dustin Gee, resident comedian on TV's *The Laughter Show*, and tree/car accident victim/singer, Mark Bolam were traced by police kiff-dogs to the staff quarters, while the ashes of Lizard King Van Morrison were found in a biscuit barrel labelled "BURY THIS – URGENT."

Mrs Locque has previous.

Cannibal woman innocent, apparently

THE FRAMLEY Examiner would like to offer its most sincere and humble apologies to Mrs Emily Locque and her family. In last week's top-selling Examiner we stated that Mrs Locque, manager of Whoft Cemetery, ate partially-cremated bodies for her tea. This is not the case and The Framley Examiner is happy to correct any misleading impression that they may inadvertently have created. Sorry.

Appeal lodged to speed up treatment for mentally ill

By ADAM WRENT

THE COMPANY RESPONSIBLE for a new home for mentally ill patients next to a Sockford housing estate has lodged an appeal in an attempt to up the speed at which patients recover.

"These people aren't helping themselves," said Graham Grahamsson, CEO of WellbeingProfit plc. "We urgently need to spearhead a more efficient turnthrough in our patient-to-bed ratios. Basically our clients are going to have to get better quicker."

The company, valued at over £13bn, is hoping to see people with depression being allowed home the same day as they are admitted.

"It's not impossible," said Mr Grahamsson, "I'm no scientist, but if you inject someone with enough Prozac or electricity, say, they must get better almost immediately. I would have thought that was obvious."

The entrance to the nut unit.
PHOTOGRAPH BY DEANNA OH

The home, which is one of the company's flagship franchises, is planning to offer special one-off bargain treatments for autism, OCD and [not being able to get a hard-on] (>FLAG: whats it calld?), with same-day cures for shyness, fecklessness and jumping to conclusions.

The centre was at the centre of a controversy last year, when a former patient was found trapped in his own microwave ten minutes after being discharged.

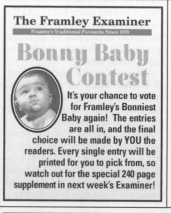

The Framley Examiner
Framley's Traditional Favourite Since 1978

Bonny Baby Contest

It's your chance to vote for Framley's Bonniest Baby again! The entries are all in, and the final choice will be made by YOU the readers. Every single entry will be printed for you to pick from, so watch out for the special 240 page supplement in next week's Examiner!

Beauty **for you!**

MON TUE WED Tanning
THU FRI SAT Mermaid conversions

Get that healthy glow, or turn yourself into a mermaid at

LUCY NEREID SALON
01999 875 988
Tanning not suitable for mermaids

PEST REMOVALS

THINKING OF INFESTING A NEW PROPERTY?
WE LOOK AFTER EVERY ASPECT OF MOVING,
FROM BOXING UP DUNG TO NAILING TINY CRATES SHUT
- - - NO JOB TOO SMALL - - -
COCKROACHES, MICE, ANTS, MIDGETS WITH JACKHAMMERS
ALL PESTS CATERED FOR, ALL CRAP MOVED
BUGSHIFT PEST REMOVALS **01999 865 665** 24 HRS

Framley's in a safe pair of hands, as long as its safe pair of hands is on duty

A safe pair of hands

by Katie Blirdsnest

THERE'S AN OLD SAYING that says "If a job needs doing, it needs doing well". Well, that could equally apply to Ron Aerosmith!

Ron has worked the lockside at Urling for over forty years, acting as Framley Barrier – a traditional craft dating back, I suppose, more than forty years. On Wednesday, after getting my hair done and buying some binbags and toothpaste, I went to see him to find out just what it is that it is that he does.

THE TIDE

I met Ron in his cottage by the lock and asked him actually what the Barrier's role involved in fact.

"The whole of Framley is built on a flood plain," he told me as he poured some tea. "Twice a day, the tide sweeps in up the river Fram all the way from Fracton.

"By the time it reaches Urling, it's a tidal wave almost forty foot high, that frightens cattle and ruins the washing. A fearsome sight, to be sure."

"My job, as it was my father's job before me, is to stand in the deepest part of the river and drink the incoming tide before it reaches the town."

I'd never heard of this before, but Ron assured me it was all true, and showed me a framed swimming certificate which had been changed to read "swallowing certificate".

£4000

It didn't take long for me to become convinced that Ron's work is clearly a job and a half! Although he recently negotiated a nominal wage of £4,000 a year from Framley Borough Council, he sees his work as more of a calling than a career.

"If I don't do it, who will?" he

Ron stands guard by the upper course of the Framley and Tedlingford canal.

PHOTOGRAPH BY PEASON GRATEFRIEND

asks. "Show me someone else who can swallow nearly a million gallons of floodwater a day, and I'll gladly pass the job on to them."

ARMY OF ROBOT PIKE

Ron never married and has no children of his own to teach the Barrier's craft, so he fears for the town's future.

"One day I'll have to retire, when my lungs can't take the pounding any more. The day after that, you'll be pulling seaweed out of your upstairs windows, mark my words."

His job is made harder, he told me, by the actions of a woman he calls 'Kan'Thor the Evil One', who lives only to thwart Ron's good work.

"Last week I had to fight off an army of robot pike, controlled by her mind waves," said Ron. "Next week it'll be a yacht manned by skeletons." Check this.

DISTRIBUTORS REQUIRED

The Framley Examiner Group Plc require paperboys and papergirls, aged 3 – 65, to deliver newspapers in the following areas:

- ◆ Whoft
- ◆ St Eyots
- ◆ Molford St Malcolm
- ◆ Molford St Gavin
- ◆ Molford St Arahim Rhamal
- ◆ Rockney
- ◆ Jism
- ◆ Nyth
- ◆ Billberry Buryborry
- ◆ Weekend-On-Speed
- ◆ Lower Stabbing
- ◆ Frontal Stabbing
- ◆ Square Inch
- ◆ Hazeldene Inchmistress
- ◆ Clipping St Newspaper
- ◆ High Egg
- ◆ East West
- ◆ West West
- ◆ Mizzenmast
- ◆ Twatford
- ◆ Truffaud-On-Hitchcock
- ◆ Corpsebury
- ◆ Toxic St Syndrome
- ◆ Bad Seagull
- ◆ Bean-On-Toasts
- ◆ Gaza Strip *(Palestinian Edition Only)*

Would you like to earn extra money to spend on alcopops and shoes?

You'll need to be keen, reliable and sign a standard minimum wage waiver form, but you won't have to collect any money* and very few of our employees are eaten by dogs**.

* wages, payable at 45p/ hour paid directly into insurance fund
** figures available on request from Framley Examiner Group Plc

Brownies reunion

HAVE YOU EVER been a member of the 2nd Molford Charlie Brownies Pack?

Current pack leaders are trying to organise a reunion of anyonewho has ever worn the distinctive yellow and black, zig-zag uniform. It'll be a chance to relive memories and there'll be root beer and chocolate chip cookies.

The Crest of the 2nd Molford Charlie Brownies'

The Second Molford Charlie Brownies, the last active group in Britain, meet on the pitched roof of the Village Hall every Tuesday evening, as they have done since the pack was formed in October 1950.

Former packmembers who wish to attend the get-together are invited to contact newly appointed Woodstock, Mrs Patrick Peppermint. The pack are particularly keen to contact that little red-headed girl, or the one with naturally curly hair.

Obituaries

Born bad

Dame Margaret Le Fontleroy Duq-de-Granmercy (née Bad)

Shockwaves echoed round the Framley social scene with the death last week of evergreen debutante Dame Margaret LeFontleroy Duq-de-Granmercy, one of the area's most respected rich old ladies.

Born in Whoft in 1909 to a wealthy family of landowners, Margaret Bad was elevated to the high life by her marriage in 1931 to Reg Le Fontleroy Duq-de-Granmercy, the man who came to fix the boiler. Leaving her stuffy life behind, and much to the disapproval of her family, she joined the bright young set, and ran with it.

Fortune smiled again when, in 1934, while holidaying in Marakesh, she invented the device that makes the sound of a door slamming when you slam a door, a gadget that is fitted to every door in the world to this day.

Already rich beyond dreams, Margaret put the proceeds from her invention towards finding a cure for being hit by a bus, the illness that had dogged her estranged mother years before (throughout the war, Margaret drove an ambulance, picking up people who had been hit by buses during the blackout.)

Sadly, after her husband died in 1971, when he coughed up his own mind, Margaret became a recluse, only venturing off her country estate four times a week to organise parties and charity dinners and go and watch snooker.

Tragically hit by a bus, at 92, she leaves twin sons, Quentin and Um.

Local journalist and "character"

Odgar Cushion

It is with great sadness that we announce the death of one of Framley's best-loved journalists, Odgar Cushion, self-appointed chronicler of the bizarre.

Always cautious about revealing his age, Odgar was born at sometime between 1932 and 1994. He attended St Shoebingon's Grammar, Chutney, where he excelled and left before taking any exams.

Keen to make a name for himself, he began working for The St Eyot's Flugel at the tender age of either 15 or -47, and soon had his own column, *"We'll Fancy That"*, that bears his name in The Framley Examiner to this day.

Dedicating his life to the pursuit of the unusual and peculiar, Odgar made the news himself as often as he reported it. In 1961, he became the first man to ride a bear across the English Channel, and was well known locally as the owner of Framley's biggest ice cube.

He died suddenly on April 11th, after falling eight stories from the pavement to the roof of Denegate carpark. Relatives say life has returned to relative normality since his death, but were delighted to notice that on the following Sunday, all the flowers on Odgar's favourite roundabout had burst into bloom, spelling out the date, time and manner of his remarkable death.

He is survived by two daughters, Whoopi and Pin, and Framley's biggest ice cube.

an honest woman of her, Ricky! So it just remains for me to lead this toast to the happy couple. Please charge your glasses. Richard and Julie! Buyer to collect. After 6pm. 01999 387 664

BEETLE WIGS. June, Potato, Ground and Rove Beetle hairpieces. One size fit head. Also bag of Monkee Nuts. £100 the set. FR 01999 662334

OCTAGONS

GET A JOB, you bone idle waster. Excellent working order. £6. 01999 729 690

DOLL'S HOUSE. Burnt out husk. Complete with two sets of charred furniture and dolly smoke detector with flat dolly batteries. £25 01999 887265

BOY. Boy for sale. Going cheap. Only joking. Girl for sale. £2,500,000 ono. Call Mr. Hollyhock 01999 654722

BOX of early 90s memorabilia. "Vanilla Ice is Vanearly Nice" T-shirt; Picture of Mike Edwards from Jesus Jones beating Lady Miss Kier at Super Nintendo; 4000 cans of Cucumber Classic Coke®; a 22p stamp. £offers. Box FE8911

BOOK "How To Make Pencils" £5, or will swap for copy of "How To Stop Making Pencils". Help me. Please. 01999 733 291

MINDGAME GAME

STANNAH Stairlift to Heaven. "The last gift Grandma will ever need". Fits most stairs. £250. Fram 944 321

YODASTREAM. Star Wars tie in drinks dispenser. "May the fizz be with you!" £16. 01999 734 299

WISHING MACHINE. Ever wanted really expensive clothes but never been able to afford them? The new Sinussi 4500 turns rags into ballgowns, pumpkins into carriages and glasses into slippers. Comes with three refillable wishes and four mice. £599.99 from Ranfurly Electrical. 01999 646 900

RARE "RAINBOW" merchandise. Bungle bag. Geoffrey Hayes backpack. Rod and Jane pencil cases. £10 the lot. 01999 765 409

LIGHT LIFTING. I'll take all your lamps and bulbs and raise them up to six inches higher. £12 p/hr. 01999 644 802

Last year only 6 complaints regarding The Framley Examiner classsified ads were upheld by the Advertising Standards Authority, resulting in a fine of only £375,000

24-HOUR DOG WALKING. I can outlast your pet. Drive hounds into the ground. Look on my walkies ye mighty and despair. 01999 403 651

SHIP'S BELL, £2. Also ship, £42m. 01999 444 864

MOUNTAIN BIKE with 400W amp and 2 Peugeot bass bins. £350. "Cycling has never been so audible" *The Grocer*. 01999 611 310

THE SKY AT NIGHT. £350. It's alright. Nobody uses it at night. Call Vince on 01999 911 055

FREE HARDCORE from damaged brick wall. Approx 5 – 6 cubic yards. Some girl-on-girl. Must collect. 01999 398 878

BREAST MILK. Vintage. Marked "HRH Queen Mother 9/6/98" with crest and certificate of authenticity. On its own, £250. With 3 Union Jack straws, £274. Call Box FE8202

SHOWER. Vgc. £30. Five minutes only. Put the mat down and remember to turn the boiler off. 01999 629 299

FRIDGE FREEZER with 3 drawers and tie rack. £100. 01999 744 347

WHIZZ-KIDS

GLASS DARTBOARD. Used once. £3, with some bits loose in Newby's bag. 01999 511 951

"ONE SMALL Step For Jazz, One Giant Leap For Satchmo" by Louis Armstrong. Autobiography of first trumpeter on moon. Rare marked up galley. £offers. Box FE8432

MICROWAVE Radiator. £60. 01999 400 958

PINE BREAKFAST BAR with pine stools, pine bacon, pine egg and eight slices of pine toast. Inedible but hardwearing. £350. Call after work on 01999 533 280

The Framley Examiner

Make your ad stand out high light it with a box

DOES HE TAKE SUGAR? diabetic testing kit. £6. Box FE8511

400 TONS of well-rotted horse manure. 3 years old. £1 a bag (a bag holds 400 tons). 01999 971 703

CAN OF STELLA. 3cl left in bottom. Would suit smoker sitting some distance from ashtray. £350 pcm. 01999 622 924

KENWOOD CHEF. £35p/h. 4 years experience working in one of London's top stately homes. 01999 709 996

CHIP-ITES

DRUG HABIT. Also bongwimple and tonsure with an acid house smiley shaved into it. £20. Call Brother Francis on 01999 877 601

TOPSOIL. Free to collect from gardens up and down my road. Bring own spade. 01999 248 860

RAT, 50p 01999 698 787

BRIAN ENO'S Oblique Strategies coaster set. 6 designs including "Maybe this isn't your drink", "Imagine you're still thirsty". £15. 01999 710 252

MOTORISED WHEELCHAIR. 5 gears. Top speed 180mph. 0-60 in 4.8secs. Sun roof. Alloys. 3 times London Marathon winner. £18995. 01999 252 977

MY CHEQUEBOOK. 6 cheques left. All signed but otherwise left blank. OIRO £20. Danny on 01999 499 032

SPICE RACK. 1 jar each of Oregano, Lemon Grass, brown powder, something that looks like leaf litter, and a load of little sticks that taste like Blackjacks. £4. Call 01999 533 912 before I finish all the little sticks.

We now offer a FREE 24 hour voice-ad phone line.

If you want to hear any ad on this page read by the person who originally placed it, simply call 0999 974 978 and, when prompted, clearly say the first word of the ad you require.

Or, if you'd rather hear the ad read by Martin Jarvis, say "MARTIN SAYS" then the first word of the ad you require.

The Framley Examiner

CARAVAN. £2,500. 6 berth Crusader Convivial. Isobella Ambassador awning. Top of the range. In beautiful mahogany frame for wall mounting. 01999 399 629

OLYMPIC BID. Unsuccessful hence £28m. Call 0121 999 4638.

BATTERED WIFE, £3.50. Saveloy, £1.00. Mushy peas 85p. Call Cap'n Fist on 01999 486 688

HOLE IN THE GROUND. £16. Ideal for looking like you only exist from the waist up (in my garden). Buyer to collect. 01999 676 273

BOILING ice skates. Ruin the rink! Hard to put on though. But then isn't everything these days? Call Elsie on 01999 641 318 to talk about anything. I'm waiting for your call. Don't get cross if I don't have any ice skates.

SAMPLING KEYBOARD. £160. Tests your blood and urine while you type. National Food and Drugs Administration approved. 01999 749 841

UNSATISFYING SEXUAL ENCOUNTER with Michael from Data Inputting. Over in seconds, with some awkwardness at work for 3 months afterwards. Will swap for going home with Darren instead like he offered earlier in the evening and not getting shitfaced. Call Emma on 01999 616 563

YORKSHIRE TERRIERS, £65. Yorkshire puddings, £1.50. 01999 529 300

INVESTMENT OPPORTUNITY. Bring in a fiver and we'll turn it into ££££££s instantly. Call Dean at the Photocopy Shop on 01999 655 855

MISERABLE ROGER™ PIRATE TRUCK. Unsatisfying toy for dislikeable children. Makes a loud whistling noise when unattended. Unbreakable. No batteries required. 01999 558888

BURTON'S TEACAKES

MARBLE ASHTRAY, £3. Doubles as spare marble ashtray for person with marble ashtray. 01999 233 954

THE FEAR OF GOD. £30. Box FE8028

UNIVERSITY CHALLENGE "Dusty Bamber" booby prize circa 1984. £offers. 01999 732 888

WAITROSE culture range / twenty tins of haiku shapes / in tomato sauce. £22

LEATHER briefcase, £10. Open-crotch PVC pantcase £12. 01999 646 119

REDNECKS

THERE GOES a nice pair of legs, pair of legs, pair of legs and other Crack-a-joke-book punchlines, in presentation box. £18. 01999 212 624

UNDERAGE deodorant. £5. Box FE8771

GIRL'S WORLD CUP. £12. Dress up the Jules Rimet trophy in a range of ribbons. Make its hair grow. Great gift. 01999 423 331

LE CREUSET pans. £45. Set of 5. Suitable for hob, oven or evening wear. 01999 498 788

RISING unemployment figures, £15. Would suit Leader of the Opposition. Also appalling record on public spending, £20. Many more available. 01999 644 842

LOTTERY TICKET. £4.3m winner. Used once. £1. 01999 659 590

COLLECTION of 1960s boardgames. Including "Backstreet Operation!" (plastic coathanger missing), "Carnabopoly", "Hungry Hippies", "Turn On Tune In Connect Four", "Ringo Bingo", "Profumo Downfall" and "Ken Kesey's Drop Out". Offers. Will split. 01999 644 372

YOU'RE BOTH WRONG

CASE OF 36 bottles of red wind. 1996 vintage. Strong, fruity bouquet. £90 ono. 01999 800 750

PIG HUTCH. 4' x 2'. Freestanding. Feeding bottle and bowl. £12. Call 01999 646 630. **GUINEA**

1500 COMMEMORATIVE Royal Wedding of Princess Charles and Prince Diana souvenir mugs. Slight factory printing error, hence £25 the lot.

Last year over 1,924 classified ads for his burst spacehopper were placed by Mr J. Ottingham in the pages of The Framley Examiner Well done.

FAT BLOKE. Up for just about anything. Call Tony on 01999 510 655

WASHING MACHINE REPAIRS. It's never been easier. I get in your machine. Put me through a cycle and I'll see if I can tell you what's wrong (no boiling). Also spindryers, hoovers and ironing boards. 01999 268 430

EARN £3000 A MONTH! Get a really good job, apparently. Call 01999 629 801 if you know more.

LEGO. 650,000 pieces. Makes bungalow or 3rd floor flat. £450pcm. All bills except water. 01999 733 221

3-PIECE FRIDGE £120 ono. 01999 449 374

SPIRAL HEIDI

A MAN AND A VAN needs another man to drive the other van. Call a man on 01999 302 088

SINGING LESSONS. For children and adults. No callout charge. 6 months parts and labour. Free estimates. Everything I Do (Adams) £18. Automatic (Pointer Sisters) £25. Call 01999 500 232

FANTASY FOOTBALL World Cup Video 1966. England 9, Germany 2. Geoff Hurst 8-trick. Beckenbauer killed by final penalty. People on pitch throughout. £7. 01999 543 286

1 DOZEN Gala Pie eggs in 6-foot long box. £4. 01999 522 940

POCKETLESS billiard table. No end of fun. £175. 01999 319 050

COMMEMORATIVE Mel and Kim Silver Jubilee souvenir plates, with Appleby Mint certificate of authenticity. £65. 01999 744 380

SICK 8 times this morning. Had to take day off. Pissed in a carrier bag. Lizzie bloody furious. 01999 765 488

GARDEN SERVICE. Pissing. Slumping. Shitting. Home-made compost. Call Bill on 01999 643 939

HALL FOR HIRE. Nice telephone on sidetable. Hatstand. Stairs on left leading to parents' bedroom. Call Stacey on 01999 300 843

FISH and chips tank. 4' x 1' with cabinet, filter and light. £20. Pickled egg 50p.

KIDS' POOL TABLE. 1" x 2". One ball (brown). No pockets. Possibly just a bit of baize and a Malteser. £offers. 01999 299 721

WEDDING DRESS. Size 24. Ivory jockstrap and depilator. Call Sweaty Malcolm on 01999 833 065

PARENT COSTUME. "Any time is bedtime when you look like your Dad". £15. 01999 400 211

JIM ROYLE humour destroyer. 6" plastic replica, will repeat previously amusing one-liners until rendered unpalatable Tomlinsonisms. Belches Mambo #5. Also GenuineManOfThePeople Top Trumps. £16.99. No time wasters. Call Jenny or don't call Jenny. The choice is yours. 01999 653 766

MOBILE BATHROOM. Comes to your door on time, whenever your girlfriend is spending hours and hours and hours and hours doing Christ knows what in yours. £1300. 01999 865 400

FIAT STILETTO SPACEWAGON 2.0i, one lady owner, middle-aged, divorced, WLTM mechanic with heart full of lust, £6,800. Tel Simone 01999 671444.

AND THE YEAR...? Call Noel on 01999 811 8055

ECSTASY TABLETS, Penguin logo on reverse, 10 thou., street value of up to £22,000. Doubled up order for staff party by mistake. Contact Rowland on 07999 871920

BAIL, £20,000. All donations will be delightfully received. Hopefully I won't be burning the fire station down for a third time! Box FE8510

FRAMLEY EXAMINER FLATSHARE

MAN BROKEN into millions of pieces offers room to homeloving woman who will sweep me neatly into a corner. £80p/w. 01999 754 654

ONE BED FLAT, WHOFT. Would suit one bed flat keen to convert to 2-bed maisonette. £65 p/w. 01999 844 311

ROOM TO LET in 3-story house. "Jeff's trip to Australia", "Annabel meeting Elton John", "How we got the landlord to knock £4 off the rent". Bring your own. £320pcm. 01999 622 812

CODGE – Room to let in small house in large room. Removable period facade. All original 1/12 scale fittings. Share with 5 other females of differing sizes and age. Ideally suit contortionist or professional doll. £doll

PRINCES FRESHBOROUGH – Entire second floor to let in quiet, first-floor house. No kitchen but sitting room has 'kitchen design' and smells of cookery. No time wastrels. £1200pcm

WELL-BEHAVED GHOST seeks room to haunt. No chains. 01999 399 804

FRAMLEY – Busy drawer to let in quiet Mayor's office. Stripped pine floor, high ceiling and washing machine. All bills inc. ex council tax. £85 pw.

The Framley Examiner

"So, Denise from the telesales desk of The Framley Examiner classifieds department, we meet again. You appear with the inevitability of an unloved season. Well, it would appear you've stumbled upon my little plan. But no matter. Soon it will be too late..."

Mr H. Drax, Codge

DURBITON – Flat to rent in smart 1960's terrace. Dble bedroom and 1/4 "skinny" bedroom. Kitchen/Cafe. Purple heart-shaped bed and shared back alley inc. fitted Lesley Ash. All mod cons. Would suit Shepherds Bush geezer. 12/6 pw.

SMALL SPACE available to rent in child's wardrobe. Would suit professional, light-sleeping smoker. No rent, but tenant must lurk at bottom of wardrobe in dark, rhythmically chanting "Old King Pipe, Old King Pipe! Coming to eat your hair!" for eight hours a night. Call Mr Hollyhock on 01999 482762

Terry HOLLYWOOD LETTING AGENTS AND VIDEO RENTALS

Flats, houses and latest blockbusters to rent.
£2.50 a night.
Some I.D. required (gas bill or addressed junk mail)
Weekend special – 2 for 1
Please rewind before returning.
If we're shut, just post the keys or tape through our letterbox.

01999 266 084

trapped under the chassis of the tank for over half an hour until the emergency services pulled the couple free with the help of Stromboli, the World's Strongest Man. Black coffee was served and sandwiches.

Fireman's Helmet

Musical Treat

ARTHRITIS CARE. – It was music, music, music for members who had a visit from three buskers. They sang *Kum Ba Yah*, *I Will Always Love You* and *It's The End Of The World As We Know It* at the same time and later treated their captive audience to some duets and, eventually, some solos. Everybody had a most enjoyable afternoon and members were sad to learn of the death of two of the buskers during the performance. Arthritis xmas cards were on sale and Rubik's cubes were left outside.

Silent Tribute

PARISH COUNCIL. – A meeting was held on Thursday at Whoft Memorial Village Hall. The meeting started with a fortnight's silence to remember the sixteen guest speakers who have died on the platform in the past month. As usual, the ceiling fell in on the person in the middle chair at the table, guest speaker Lollyrod Perkins (inventor of the long-forgotten Erg) on this occasion. Mr MacKenzie was again called to mend the ceiling, and arrived escorted by two parole officers.

Creme

Exciting film show

CREME FILM CLUB. – The society has arranged a film show on the village of Creme to take place in Creme Village Hall. The show will be open to local people. Viewers will be taken on a journey around this lovely village and have a chance to meet the many interesting people who live there, including themselves and each other.

Little Godley

Back To nature

RETIREMENT HOME. – Residents at Malgrave Hall were treated to a demonstration of sexual intercourse by Pammy Cum and Rocky Neville, two of America's most celebrated pornographic actors. The delighted audience were invited to go off in pairs and practise some of the exercises, including the popular double-lapper. After tea and soggy biscuit, residents were then shown Ms Cum's most famous film, *Tupelo Ass-Station Gizz Guzzler.*

Quiz Afternoon

FLORAL CLUB. – Just for a change, members of the Little Godley Floral Club were

Framley Town Plans

21 & 23 Walliams Hurrah, Friern Benedict, erection of illuminated sign "Fuck off, Dennis" along dividing fence. **Gents conveniences**, corner of Hopalong Row and Hartnell's Farm boundary, St Eyot's, construction of adjoining regional sales office, ancillary departmental offices and mezzanine reception for lavatory facility. **49 Bulgaria Tassel**, Sockford, installation of 24-hour oompah band on first storey flat roof. **11 Winton Terrace** Removal of house to make way for statue of same house being demolished. **29 Buccaneer Place**, Creme, addition of 2nd storey to garden, with upstairs pond. **38 Jalapeno Crescent**, Molford, removal of front of house to allow neighbours to see what John's done with the kids' bedroom. **112 Gotobed Vale,** lowering of entire street to make house look bigger. **102 Gavin**

Corners, Whoft, modification of front of house to let it smile again. **6 Ciconne Avenue**, Thoxtoxeter, erection of huge bow on roof to make house look like a big present. **94 Yowling Bench,** Urling, extension of back garden by five minutes. **3 Gabbitas Rd**, St Eyot's, removal of 6-foot blinking eye from cellar **19 Kevin Toms St**, Codge, transposition of house into key of B♭. **52 Glove Rd,** Wripple, removal of tennis match from television and replacement with episode of Quincy. **14 Peyote Villas,** Fracton, election of 2-storey MP. **81 Devoto Ramble,** Chutney, 2-blanket extension of existing den using pegs, beach towel and auntie's duvet, to allow extra comic storage. **32, Windsor Gardens**, removal of annoying bear. **41 Candida Rd,** Whoft, silencing of Yankee Doodle doorbell at number 43.

CELEBRATING A LONG LIFE

CANDLES APLENTY there were at the birthday party of Wripple's oldest resident, Nichola Logan, who reached the grand old age of 30 last week.

Nichola was born in Wripple during the reign of Elizabeth II and has lived there for the whole of her lifetime. At the time of her birth man setting foot on the moon was over a week away, the Titanic was just a dead boat, not a film at all, and public houses closed at 11pm to allow the armaments industry to make shells for the Great War.

Her 9-month old son, Max, described Nichola as "still on the ball and enjoying life to the full". Nichola also received the traditional congratulatory text message from Prince William and was later led away for a ride on The Carousel. **PHOTO BY FURCOAT AGGUTER**

locked into the garden centre and questioned by American intelligence experts. All members were released after 36 hours, with the exception of Mrs Buckley, and the CIA described the siege as "productive."

Coppernob

Grape Apes

A BUS STOP, COPPERNOB.- A disorganised shambles of a walking human pyramid was arranged to 'freak-out' certain elderly members of the parish. The motion was put forward by a young gentleman at the front of the busqueue who thought it a necessary step to prevent complacency during the autumn years.

Thoxtoxeter

Sweet Jesus

THOXTOXETER CHRISTIAN COVE.- A delivery was taken of 500 marzipan Jesuses as a token of friendship between Thoxtoxter Christian Cove and Thoxtoxeter Christian Club. The confectionery Christs, depicting scenes of His life and what He may have got up to afterwards, are all over 7ft tall and of variable stickiness. A return gift of 10,000 Our Lady Marmalades is planned for early this afternoon.

Chutney

School Success

RUBMY INFANT SCHOOL OPEN DAY.- Another school open day was planned for early next year after the success of last Thursday when all 400 pupils managed to enter the school and participate in a full-day's education. The school remains closed in the interim period until the headmaster's annual 360 day adventure holiday comes to an end.

Inspirational speaker

CHUTNEY MOUNTAINEERING SOCIETY. – This Thursday, in a change to our previous plan, inspirational speaker Mohammed Al'Mutah will come to visit the Mountaineers. This is due to the continued, inexplicable failure of the Mountaineers to make the trip in the other direction, despite all our best efforts.

Sockford

Mobile Church

ST. CHURCH OF THE GREEN, QUEFF.- Repairs to the historic bell tower were once again suspended after recent structural inconsistencies caused the building to topple heavenwards. A tarpaulin, set-

up to prevent such happenings, came loose and created a 'brick balloon', which is now heading towards Sockford. The congregation are praying for clement weather and a favourable wind.

Bum's the Word

1st SOCKFORD BROWNIES.- This year's sponsored swear raised over two hundred pounds and eyebrows as the Sockford Brownie pack swore their way into the history book. The event, which coined three hundred new swear words and two inaudible to the human ear, was interrupted by an impromptu display of the effects of gravity on brick church towers.

Successful Event

PEOPLE'S GUILD – Meeting at their new venue in the car park, members enjoyed a splendid talk by Jim Twin, who entertained the assembled crowd with repeated questions about where the A999 was. He left after five minutes in a red Vauxhall Average, complaining that he wasn't their bloody guest speaker and that he didn't seem to be able to get a straight answer to a straight question from anyone in the village. Members voted by 28-3 to invite Mr Twin to return to the guild. Anyone with information about his whereabouts should join.

First stone

INTERNET CLUB – The recently-formed Internet Club, going from strength to strength, invited Mr Bill Gates, the inventor of the computer, to lay the first stone of their new website, being built on brownfield land on the site of the former air factory. Mr Gates politely declined, but did send a message of goodwill, 'GR8! b xxx ;-)' which members voted unanimously to use as their mission statement. The first stone was eventually laid by robots.

Well Done!

WINNERS' CUP – The Sockford Enthusiasts were represented in this year's community riots by six suitably violent residents. Although not among the winners, all six gave creditable preformances in the bricking, the clubbing and the looting, some beating their own personal records. A special exploding prize for excellence in petrol-bombing was presented to Doug Bunnit by guest speaker Ch Con Rupert Bone.

Local hospitals and bystanders thrown into shock as
Ambulance crash happens

by Taunton Mishap

AN EMERGENCY AMBULANCE rushing to the aid of two ambulances that had crashed into each other dramatically crashed into the Accident & Emergency department of Framley General Hospital in the early hours of Thursday morning.

The ambulance, believed to have been driven by driver Gregor GitzFerald, smashed through plate glass, steel, concrete and patients at what Britain's speed chiefs have described as 45mph. Twelve doctors, seventeen nurses and 28 people in a serious condition are now either dead, dying or in a serious condition.

The patient being carried by the patently out-of-control vehicle, Julian Chaucer, who was pregnant with a child, was yesterday said to be in a stable condition. His baby is just as likely unharmed.

Emergency doctors were called several metres to attend to things like internal bleeding, as a state of emergency was declared by

What Thursday's carnage might have looked like, had our photographer not been at a fete.
ARTIST'S IMPRESSION BY TAUNTON MISHAP

Framley's emergency services.

SUSPICIOUS MINDS

Framley General Hospital's A&E department hit the headlines earlier this month when it was closed off and surrounded by police for 28 hours after a man walked in claiming to be Elvis. By the time he was released and arrested, a crowd of 20,000 had gathered to look at The King.

Three further ambulances were called to the scene on Thursday morning, but they crashed into the other two ambulances and the crashed ambulance.

There was no survivor.

If you are concerned that a friend or relative may have been injured please call the emergency helpdesk on 01999 542 542 and ask for Maxine. Hang up if Chris answers.

I have decided to resign

By DAMIUN CLAVALIER

AFTER SOME six months here, I have decided to resign. Try as I may to get sacked or find a reason to stay, nothing seems to work. (I set fire to the editor's laptop yesterday morning and he failed to notice.)

I, 19, deny being too good for this job. "I am no egotist," I said yesterday.

"But things have got to change," I continued. "It's been an enormously enjoyable and educating experience

and I shall miss it."

And, as I also pointed out, I thought long and hard about taking this decision. Mind you, I thought long and hard about taking the job in the first place, and yes, I was wrong.

I also denied describing my job as "like being locked in a shed full of cretins" and pointed out, accurately, that my resignation would not be noticed even when I shoved it under their noses in 32pt headline, and looked forward to many more blissful and tortuous months filling time here.

Fish auctioned for over two trouthand quid

The mounted trout that is selling for
PHOTOGRAPH BY KICKASS VAN HALEN

A TROUT caught at Framley Municipal Baths in 1911 is being auctioned for £2500 at Sockford Auction Rooms next week.

The stuffed fish on a bed of stuffed wild rice in a glass case weighed 18lb when caught by S. M. Norris just before a war, and is now thought to be the most valuable fish ever caught in the pool – worth the equivalent of more than a lifetime's pay.

The auction catalogue also mentions that another trout caught in the same year by an S. M. J. Norris is valued at £300. It is not clear if this was the same angler or a father and son or even if it's the same fish.

Anyone with any information about this sort of thing should call our Vague History desk on 01999 603282.

The CARPHONE WHOREHOUSE

Dereksson 8450 – New in town
Curvy handset and big, firm buttons.
WAP me! WAP me hard!
01999 866 001

Mottorhoople E26 – Barely legal
Let me be your fantasy
Fascia dress-up fun
Wipe-clean bukake screen
01999 866 002

Purves KS2000 – Adventurous
18 year old's phone
Waiting for your call
Pay as you go. Filthy ringtone.
01999 866 003

16 Peanust Street
Framley
Open 8am – 5am daily

News In Brief

POP'S POWERFUL FUTURE

A report published this week has revealed that by the year 2029, every third song will be called *The Power Of Love*. In addition, says the report in Thing magazine, every fifth song will be called *Ship Of Fools* and people will be able to download millions of mp3s in seconds from credit cards made of recycled fingernails.

NEW HOSPITAL MACHINE

Framley General Hospital continued its long-term investment in more up-to-the-minute technology this week, when it became the proud recipient of a new Flymo lawnmower. The machine, valued at £79.99, hovers above the ground while cutting the grass. Skeptics say the two may not be logically possible at the same time.

VICAR ARRESTED

A Church of England vicar who was found having sexual intercourse with part of a tortoise at Framley Museum has been released from police custody on bail. Rev Nester Thrilling, 58, yesterday said "alas, there is a beast in all of us." He now plans to wrestle with the idea of taking his own life.

CEMETERY TO MOVE

Framley's famous Victorian cemetery is, after many years, set to rotate again. A National Lottery grant has allowed the gigantic complex of subterranean machinery to be spruced up and restored to working order, and from next month, the cemetary will rotate five times daily just as it did in 1843. "It's nice," said one resident, "we get some fresh air."

AIRPORT SABOTEURS

The saboteurs of the proposed Molford St Gavin airport will meet this Sunday at the corner of Skullion Farm and Porterhouse fields. When the diggers roll up, questions will be asked but answers will be scarce. Placards.

FACT OF THE WEEK
Every human being spends 68% more time thinking about sneezing than they do actually sneezing!

SALE
AT GERRISON'S NEWSAGENTS
EVERYTHING MUST GO!
LAST FEW ½p CHEWS!
3 FOR A PENNY!
ONLY 100 REMAINING!
A CHEW MAKES A GREAT PRESENT
43 Hermitage Lasso, Whoft

Plans for church anger just about everyone

MISS – I feel I must respond to your article ("Church moves with the times" Examiner Aug 17th) and state the case of Wripple residents more strongly.

The plan to move St Mauve's church six inches to the right to allow the passage of an approaching snail is, quite frankly, a slap in the face to tradition. Protestors' feelings run high on this matter, as your excellent full-colour photograph of the burning verger showed most clearly.

Regardless of what so called animal rightsists may say, a church is a church. I'm sure Jesus would have turned in his empty tomb had he known what was being proposed.

TETBURY GRANDMORPH
Mittelnachtstrasse
Wripple

St Mauve's church, Wripple – threatened with a six-inch movement.
PHOTOGRAPH BY PERSEPHONE MAGIC

MISS – The scenes of violence that marred last week's protest at St Mauve's will have lodged in everyone's minds like a marble in a fallopian tube, but we should not let that distract us from the real issues.

The snail – currently on the verge by the lych gate – has clearly indicated the path it wishes to follow. It would be against nature for man to place a church in its way.

The church must be moved. It is as simple as that. Remember, if we don't inherit the earth from our parents, we steal it from their children.

MISTRAL STARLIGHT
The Wickery
Molford St Gavin

MISS – Moving St Mauve's historic 15th Century church six inches to the right for the benefit of a snail is madness.

What about the worm coming up the side of the vestry? Surely the church needs to be moved six inches to the left.

HOXTON WINNEBAGO
Non-Alignment Pact Way
Chutney

MISS – I wonder if you might help me trace the attractive woman I met at the St Mauve's church-moving riot last week? Around 5'8", slim built, pro-snail, with strawberry blonde hair and a sharpened chairleg. I was the pro-church bearded man with the under-over assault rifle. Do get in touch.

DAVID EOHIPPUS
The Gondolas
Wripple, FM6 9QT

Hear, here!

MISS – Well said! (Editorial, Examiner Aug 17th). If God had meant man to be descended from monkeys, he would have given us a tea party.

Prof. YOSEMITE VEGEMITE,
Creme

The importance of being him

MISS – I recently received a letter from Framley Borough Council asking for my comments on a proposed mobile phone transmitter mast to be erected only a few feet from my next-door neighbour's house.

I strongly object to this proposition. My neighbour, Mr Frank Holder, is a decent man who simply does not deserve to have this scabrous monstrosity located within eye distance of his immaculate patio.

However, those wankers, the Dennisons at number 67 should be subjected to any form of cancer-giving totem there is going.

For too long we have suffered their annual anniversary party and constant car washing, not to mention their three young children who, I fear, will only ever be taught not to say their bedtime prayers at 8pm every evening by a healthy dose of radiational mindwipe.

My good lady wife and I would be further delighted to witness the demolition of their house in order to build some kind of imminent motorway.

Please pass my comments onto the relevant council.

DEVON PLANXTY,
65 Sapphireandsteel Walk,
Sockford

You're all c*unts

MISS – You know who you are. Yes, you. Parking in my church reserved space. What part of "reserved space" don't you understand? C*unts, every man jack of you.

And what's so hard about not pissing in my flowerbeds? You lot. Yes, I'm talking to you c*unts. C*unts to a man. C*unts,. c*unts, cunts. The lord may forgive you, but I never will. Bunch of c*unts.

Rev OILY WINDSCAPE,
Molford St Malcolm

Police to write letter to paper about article

MISS – I wish to clarify your story "Police To Ignore Intruder Alarms" (Examiner, Aug 17th).

Your story stated incorrectly that under our new policy, Framley police would only respond to intruder alarms if there was nothing good on the telly.

As Framley Police Station is located at the base of an extremely steep hill we can actually only receive BBC2 and ITV. So we will respond if there is something good on BBC1 or Channels 4 or 5 so long as there is nothing worth watching on BBC2 or ITV.

For a copy of our pamphlet "What Your Constabulary Watches" please phone us on 01999 999899 (having first checked to make sure that Emmerdale and Ready Steady Cook aren't on).

DESK SGT JOE MOUSE,
Framley Police Station,
Framley.

Political madness gone correct!

MISS – I object in the strongest possible meaning of the word. I've been correct for all of my life until now.

Not only do I find myself having to refer to my " " " "intellectually different" " " " son as Thicky Thicky Malcolm Johnston rather than simply Thicky Thicky Malcolm, as I have called him for years.

Now I'm told that I must call a policeman a 'personman' of all things.

And this is just the tip of my iceberg.

MRS RONETTE JOHNSTON,
The Pinny,
Whoft

Ask Captain Mitchell

The Framley Examiner's very own agony aunt answers your questions

Lawn trouble

DEAR CAPTAIN MITCHELL,
I have been happily married to my husband of ten years for ten years now, and until recently I couldn't have been happier.

My husband has always been interested in gardening, and we used to enjoy discussing his hobby, but recently his focus has narrowed to a point that I feel I no longer know him.

In the old days, we would visit garden centres together to buy plants and furniture, and I would help by maintaining the pots, trellises and ornamental features in the garden. Now he simply locks me in the kitchen every morning before going out to buy lawnmowers.

Since the weather turned in April, he has purchased over 350 lawnmowers, all of which are currently parked in the back garden, obscuring the landscaping and dripping oil on the lawn.

Sometimes my husband rides one of his favourites up and down the patio for hours, staring at me in silence as I gaze mournfully out at him through the kitchen window. When it rains, he puts a grassbox on his head, and shifts into reverse.

I have tried to show an interest in his new hobby, but every time I try and crawl out through the catflap, he just comes at me on his Qualcast, crying.

Please help me – RW

Captain Mitchell says:
Try soaking the clothes in a vinegar-water solution overnight. That should bring back the chip-shop freshness you miss so much.

Sex problem

DEAR CAPTAIN MITCHELL,
I live in a flat, and when my neighbours make love, I can see them through the wall. I don't want to sound like a fuddy-duddy, but it's a bit much, even in this day and age – PT

Captain Mitchell says:
Try applying bicarbonate of soda to the affected area until the stain lifts and becomes wearable again.

Gun worry

DEAR CAPTAIN MITCHELL,
Following a row about driving gloves, my fiancee has just fired a gun at me. The bullets are heading towards my face as I write. What should I do? – JY

Captain Mitchell says:
I'm sending you my leaflet "Duck: What To Do When Someone Fires A Gun At You". I hope its advice comes in helpful.

Whoaaaaah!

DEAR CAPTAIN MITCHELL,
I am becoming worried that my husband thinks I'm Tom Jones.

For the last four months, he has refused to go to sleep until I've sung him The Green Green Grass Of Home.

Now I find I've been booked in at Rockfield to record a comeback album of collaborations with contemporary indie artists, such as Starsailor and the Sugababe who looks like Nicholas Lyndhurst. I'm at my wits end. Please help me. This is destroying my marriage – Mrs G

Captain Mitchell says:
What's new, pussycat?

Captain Mitchell offers advice on the following problems on her exclusive 0999 premium line:

Itching	0999 980 980
Tins	0999 980 981
The Ottoman Empire	0999 980 982
Glassblowing	0999 980 983
Hairy lady	0999 980 984
Fridgefright	0999 980 985

calls charged at 75p per minute, except TINS (£3.50)

ANTIQUE PINE WAREHOUSE

Hundreds of genuine pieces of English and Cornish Antique.

Dozens of authentic pine sideboards at trade prices.

For appointments to hide inside, call Geoff on 01999 755 150

I'm inside now!

That's just PINE!

www.hidingincupboards.co.uk

SPORTS extra

Cricketing idiot found

GROUNDSMEN AT SOCKFORD GREEN cricket ground, working at clearing the rough scrub from the perimeter of the pitch, say they have found a player believed missing since the beginning of World War II.

The lost batsman, a Mr Bob Jaundice from Lissom-by-Trench near St Eyot's, hadn't been seen since the summer of 1940, when he went in to bat for Sockford Second XI.

Sockford needed 48 to win against local favourites Wripple Cosmologists, who had declared for 216, but the game was never completed. Conscription was unexpectedly announced after tea, and both teams were immediately flown to the Egyptian Front, leaving the scoreline tantalisingly inconclusive.

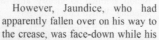

By Stan Rubbish

However, Jaundice, who had apparently fallen over on his way to the crease, was face-down while his team mates were being loaded into the Hercules transport plane, and missed the whole thing. Not realising the game was over, the lone batsman stood his ground.

Since this time, Jaundice has been fighting a guerilla cricket match from the bushes near Silly Mid Off, making use of low ground cover and an improvised bat.

THE SUMMER GAME

Sixty years later, the grounds crew stumbled upon the batsman's nest. They ordered Mr Jaundice to leave the bushes, but he became agitated, flailing at the undergrowth with his rudimentary cricketing stick and screaming, "Not Out! Not Out!"

Experts believe the only way to remove the entrenched sportsman is to bowl him out legitimately using a vintage 1940s ball. Groundsmen are searching the shrubs where he was last spotted, to see if they can find evidence of a primitive wicket which they think he may be guarding.

"It does seem," said chief groundsman Arnold Laramie, "that until we prove to the gentleman that his marathon innings is at an end, he is going to refuse to return to the pavillion. It's like Geoff Boycott all over again."

Jaundice is currently 5004 not out.

Mr Jaundice, hiding from the undergrowth.
PHOTOGRAPH BY MICHELOB PAOLOZZI

SALE!

The Framley Examiner
Framley's Traditional Favourite Since 1978

AD SALES DEPT

every inch must go!

CLOSING DOWN SALE

big, big savings on box-outs and WOBs

CALL DANNY OR KAREN ON
019 94 76 94

Number 01866
The ball has been carefully removed from this picture of Wripple Anthemic vs Bayern Sockford. Use your skill and judgement to guess where it is, and mark it with a clear 'X'.

SPOT THE BALL COMPETITION

Oily   Soft / Hard
Send your entries to THE FRAMLEY EXAMINER Unit 149b, East Cosset Industrial ParkParkfields Bypass, Framley FR1 6LH

NAME:_____ ADDRESS_____, Framley

POSTCODE: _____

MARITAL STATUS: ____ DAYTIME TEL. _____ SHIRT SIZE: S / XL / XM

(01865) with the location of the ball indicated. There were a record number of correct entries. All winners listed here get a crate of champagne, a night in the Miami Motel, Sockford and a Mini Cooper.

Mrs Elsie Remindme, Whoft; Jeremy Liphippo, Codge; R. Tumbril, Wripple; Wendy Redknapp, Framley; Stephen Missat, Framley; Wayland Smithy, St Eyot's; Youngman Grand, Framley; Montgomery Waste, Whoft; Richard Lionfoot, Whoft; Ursula Cloybeam, Molford; Dennis Cloybeam, Molford; Witchy Poo, Creme; Haris Paris, Little Godley; Hopeful Jefferson, Bad Sandal; Trebus Announce, Fracton; Paul Ryman, The Close; Whistledown Jones, Wripple; Hootle Bellend, Clinton; Ippy Pog, Framley; Messerschmitt Ouch, Sockford; Yolanda Nameagain, Creme; Outside Nugent, Lessbury Moreborough; Riley O'Riley, Frant; Mrs L. Mouse, Framley; Mr Grovenly, Slovenly; Hatbitch Crowdnoise, Whoft; Flakey-Foont, Crumb, Mr Natural, Crumb; Sgt Neil Howie, Framley; Helpme Warrington, Framley; Windmill McMasterman, Wripple; Mr O. Churchflower, Molford; Aggie Legs, Codge; Pinhead McMonarchy, Framley; Ms J. Wheelarch, Fracton; Hopalong Osmond, Framley; Longman Wilmington, Molford; Cerne-Abbas Giant, St Eyot's; Michael Pikle, Whoft; Beverly Everly, Wripple;

Jazz meet their match at Framley

BASKETBALL

Newby's Amateur Shield

THE COUNTY'S PREMIER basketball team, Sockford Jazz, suffered a severe mauling at Framley Tigers last Monday.

The friendly invitation match, held in the tigers' basketball enclosure at Framley Zoo was finally halted by giggling keepers after six Sockford players and a basketball were swallowed in seventeen minutes by Sheba, a Bengali mother of three.

This week's game will be preceded by eight bars of syncopated silence for the late Sockford stars after a special request from their coach, Chick Corea. Local bookies have closed the books on a victory for the visiting Spaniards, Newcastle Basketball Players.

FOOTBALL GOALS

LONG DIVISION

	P	W	F	A	Pts
Bungalow	1	0	0	11	0
Battery Flatford	1	0	0	59	0
Wripple Wetsuits	1	0	0	33	0
Mrs J. Hargreaves	1	0	0	24	0
Chutney Gloves	1	0	0	18	0
Framley Area Referees	5	5	145	0	15

NEWBY'S PREMIER

	P	W	F	A	Pts
Tallboy Valves	999	999	999	999	999
St. Eyot's Folders	999	999	999	999	999
Fracton Crackers	999	999	999	999	999
Batley Berettas	999	999	999	999	999
Effing Ball	999	999	999	999	999
Slovenly Emcellent	999	999	999	999	999

NONE-LEAGUE

	P	W	F	A	Pts
Busy Wednesday	999	999	999	999	999
Werther's Originals	999	999	999	999	999
Delighted United	999	999	999	999	999
Bisto Impossible	999	999	999	999	999
Durbiton Unreasonable	999	999	999	999	999
Round The Block FC	999	999	999	999	999
Whoft City Slickers II (The Legend of Curly's Gold)	999	999	999	999	999

>>MIKE GET THESE STATS FRM WENDY – IVE DUMMIED THEM IN BUT NEED DOING B4 TUESDAY DDLN – CHRIS

to remake in the image of my dead wife. No timewasters. Box FE8433

TEACHER, 27, petite, loves teaching Sociology and PE seeks male, 25-35, with gaps in his education. 01999 281930

CAPRICORN, genuine, honest girl (Pisces) WLTM man able to believe me. I am sisters. Box FE8938.

GREEN-EYED Sockford girl, 13, seeks beautiful, strapping chestnut mare for long bouncy ride, hymen-popping and nosebag if compatible. Box FE8361.

LIKEMINDED man would like to meet likeminded woman who likes Minder and doesn't mind that I like her for her mind. Box FE8140

WHOFT FEMALE, 36, medium build, eyes, magnetic, enjoys going to gym & picking up iron filings WLTM similarly charged male for evenings of nearly kissing. Box FE8366

DESIRABLE LADY, 38, WLTMarry man called Lee in August 1985 that won't end up shagging my best friend in our own bed, you utter shit. I'll be at my mother's, the solicitor will be in touch. Box FE8048.

CONNECT PRIVATELY TO THE HOTTEST WOMEN IN FRAMLEY!
JUST CALL 0906 800 8-- FOLLOWED BY NUMBER BELOW
01 OVERWEIGHT WOMAN COOKING SPAGHETTI IN WINDOWLESS FLAT
02 SPORTY LADY IN CABLEKNIT JUMPER LATE FOR BUS
03 NATURE-LOVING DIVORCEE, 57, TRAPPED IN GREENHOUSE. IN A PLASTIC MAC.
03 SHOPGIRL DRESSING SHOP WINDOW ON SUMMER'S DAY IN PVC BODYSTOCKING.

WRIPPLE MAN, 24, likes loud music, dancing, drugs, bottled lager and night-buses, hates clubbing, seeks accommodating female with own flat/bungalow where we could probably do all that sort of thing. Box FE8482.

STUNNING BLONDE
NEW TO AREA
offers sensual massage followed by beans on toast

0906 877 651

BUBBLY LADY, very very soft skin, lemon-scented, clean to the squeak, fell into cauldron of Fairy Liquid as a baby seeks short male with leather gourd and own helmet for mistranslated French-language fun. Box FE87ix.

SINGLE FEMALE, 35, seeks male (any) for marriage, three kids, growing old together, maybe more. 01999 714592.

POLICEMAN, 40, seeks man, 20-22, approx 5'8", shaved head, tattoos of Johnny Mathis on both forearms to eliminate him from our enquiries. Phone 01999 999899 in complete confidence.

ELDERLY GENT, 78, seeks vivacious redhead, late 20s, for one last night of messy passion. Never done it ginger before. One remaining ambition. Boxes FE8574 – 89.

I'M NOT WEARING MANY BRAS
CALL ME UP & EXPLAIN YOURSELF!

0906 854 852

I'VE GOT a cock with a 10-second trigger but I can still make you come before I do. Box FE8595.

GAY MAN, 33, professional non-smoker WLTM gay woman for sex (by gay I mean happy). Box FE8517

KIDS GROW UP so fast these days, don't they? 07999 744 355

TOUCH ME IN THE MORNING Blue eyed Chutney female. Varied interests. Only tangible before 12pm. Box FE8137

COULD I BE YOU? 43yo widower, into submarines, cross-stitch and mango chutney seeks 43yo male into cross-stitch / mango chutney and submarines. Box FE8667

DAVID BOWY LOOKALIKE circa 1973, now looks like Shane MacGowan WLTM person. No longer fussy. Box FE8933

MAN DRESSED AS SCATTER CUSHION WLTM man able to stop man dressing as scatter cushion before wife discovers man dressed as scatter cushion. Box FE8332

EXPLICIT ADULT BINGO

JUST DIAL. 0906 765 7.. (followed by)
88 FAT LADY ON FAT LADY
22 DUCK ON DUCK ACTION
11 LEG FETISH
69 UNLUCKY FOR SOME
82 BESTIALITY
all calls charged at 60p/min

BABY-FACED MAN, 48, into Art Nouveau, oil, windmills and the music of The Spheres seeks unintelligible, lanky female(?) for spoon-bending and quiet evenings in with a bottle of gripewater. Box FE8112

SHY PROFESSIONAL MALE, 29, seeks someone that might laugh at one of my jokes. M or F, I don't mind. Not that you'll be reading this anyway. I'll be over there if you want me. Box FE8709.

ARE YOU FED UP WITH friends letting you down? Look no further – I hate you & I'll let you down. Box FE8380

WELL-SPOKEN MALE, 52, GSOH, seeks like-minded person interested in current affairs who enjoys talking to literally millions of people at the same time. Must be able to pronounce Matabeleland. And now it's over to Michael Fish for a look at tomorrow's weather. Box FE8941.

LONELY POSTMAN, 19, 7'2", interests include tombolas, bisto sniffing and The Fonz WLTM broad-minded female to test the edges of possibility. Box FE8996

TELL ME WHAT TIME YOU'LL BE HOME FROM THE PUB

AND I'LL BELIEVE YOU
NO HOLDS BARRED!
0906 855 599

HANDSOME CHUNK, good-looking male, 32, enjoys going to the gym / coming back from the gym / being at the gym seeks women to impress with chunkiness. Box FE8111

INCREDIBLY BUSY MAN, 34, seeks attractive woman for 30-second relationship, possibly marriage. Box FE8127

FLAT STANLEY seeks welcoming family with spare wall to lean against. I won't be any trouble. Box FE8433

LOOKING FOR MR WRIGHT? So am I. He was my geography teacher & he still hasn't marked my essay on terminal moraine. Box FE8006

INSENSITIVE BASTARD, unreliable, bad in bed apparently, unable to commit, some baggage from previous relationship, seeks woman 24-30 for new start. Box FE8001

PLUG SEEKS SOCKET for electric relationship. I'm not actually a plug but I do have a thumb on each hip and would welcome a chance to meet someone with appropriate holes. Box FE8722

WHEN WILL YOU MARRY ME? Anybody? Tel 01999 238764

FILM-LOVING Framley male, interested in prisons / schools / oil rigs and public places seeks Simon Bates lookalike to inform him about pirates. Box FE8778

DIVORCED FEMALE, 38, likes TV, cooking, decorating, hamsters seeks rugged male with similar outdoor interests. Box FE8129.

OCTAGONAL MALES, seek smaller square females for tesselation and problem-solving. Box FE8237

SINGLE MOTHER, 23, five kids, gets drunk easily seeks genuinely caring man that won't take advantage. Box FE8873.

CONTINENTAL CLIMAX
Reaching unusual German heights
- Das Lied von der Erde
- Bulletproof bra
- Exploding necklace
- 26 Wristwatches
- "Berlin Hot-Toddy"

0906 510 514

AFFLUENT MALE, 34, diagnosed iron deficiency WLTM meat. Last three girlfriends vegetarians, can't fucking handle it any more. Need chops. Box FE8390.

MAN WITH MOUSTACHE seeks woman with beard. You'll understand when you see me. No kissing. Box FE8119

FIREMAN seeks non-smoker for lasting relationship. Box FE8300

WRIPPLE CHILD, 5, WLTM Father Christmas. Tel 01999 200572

I CAN BE what you want me to be. I have coloured contact lenses, wigs, a prosthetic cock and interchangeable limbs. Must be able to love me for being myself. Phone Sally on 01999 835472.

CHANNEL HOPPING guy seeks ferry for safer journeys. Box FE8499

MYSELF & MY G/F are looking for compatible friends to go out on day trips to hairdressers, Tescos, work & meeting the kids from school, possibly more. Box FE8089

I CAN GET INTO A FIGURE 8

IF YOU CAN WORK OUT WHERE TO PUT IT
0906 488 488

I'M YOUR KNIFE. Are you my fork? Let's plate! Tel 01999 000100

HEAR ME REPEAT EVERYTHING YOU SAY...

...IN A HIGH-PITCHED VOICE!
Really really annoying!
0906 788688

BREEDING PAIR of endangered people WLTM zookeeper with dirty mags, test tube, spatula and lots of patience for unconventional 3-way. Tel 01999 707278

ARE YOU A SLIM, attractive, successful blonde? Are you looking for love through the Framley Examiner personals? Didn't think so. Box FE8766

SEMI-ATTRACTIVE FEMALE, raspberry-blonde, WLTM divorced male, 55, 5'5", into the music of 1955 and the Waffen SS. Box FE8433

YOUNG-LOOKING MALE, 81, seeks slim-looking woman, 18 stone. Tel 01999 970911

SUCCESSFUL SOCKFORD BUSINESSMAN, 46, GSOS wltm very clean female with extremely diligent standards of hygiene. Box FE8646

FRAMLEY MALE, likes cinema, hates films, WLTM huge, noisy woman with tall hat and bags of crunchy popcorn to sit behind during visits to the Odeon. Box FE8993

28-YEAR OLD MALE enjoys eating, people and eating people. Seeks gregarious, hungry, delicious woman for short term relationship. Box FE8622

BOND GIRL LOOKALIKE (Klebb) WLTM a man who thinks he can do a Sean Connery impression. There must be someone out there! Box FE8992

BEN, 23. Handsome, black Escort for women. Clapped out blue Nova for men. 07999 656504

YOU CAN'T ALWAYS GET what you want, and I'm what you always wanted. Bye! Box FE8261

ELEGANT LADY, mid-30s, seeks irrationally dependent male who will fall in love on the first date, propose to me even though we've never slept together and will step in front of the 44b bus when I reveal that I'm just toying with him. And that I'm a bloke. Box FE01999.

SOLUBLE MAN seeks woman with dry skin condition, saliva deficiency and vaginismus. Box FE8087

OLD-LOOKING MALE, 21, WLTM young-smelling woman. Tel 01999 287874

I SAW

FIRST CLASS LADY, I licked the back of your head. You tasted of glue & looked like the queen. You weren't a stamp, I've already asked that once. Box FE8736

MOLFORD DENTIST. You touched my teeth. I was 36. Now I'm 38. Box FE8949

I WAS THE ENORMOUS woman on table 14. You were a roast potato on table 2. Where are you loved one? I'm stilll hungry. Box FE8207

HELP! I SAW YOU standing there, Lady Madonna. With a little help from my friends at the Framley Examiner Personal Desk we could all come together. Everybody's got something to hide except me & my silver hammer. Why don't we do it in the road? Call Frank Ifield fan on 01999 873410

I ROAST POTATO (table 2). You nice, handsome man eating with fat, ugly lady. Where you? Box FE8422

I WAS FEEDING GRAPES to Marianne Faithfull and writing the words to Jumping Jack Flash. You were writing the bassline. Who were you? Box FE8126

FANCY DRESS PARTY, March 2001. I was dressed as a bonfire. You were dressed as an invitation to another fancy dress party. Is it still on? Box FE8926

WHERE DOES MY ROSEMARY GROW ?
FULL-ON GARDENING CHAT!
0906 454 plus code below
010 PRUNE MY BUDS
011 I'LL TAME YOUR CLIMBER
012 WATER MY GNOMES
013 TOPIARY
014 SHIT IN MY BED
015 TRIM MY BUSH
016 DRAIN MY WATER FEATURE
017 PLANT YOUR BULB

YOU TOOK THE PISS. I cried. You laughed and laughed and laughed. Want to meet for good times? Box FE8739

ARE WE HAVING SEX YET?

YOU WON'T KNOW UNLESS YOU PHONE
0906 555 545
* You must be under 18 years of age to get off on this service

I WAS SEDATED. You were supposed to be doing root canal. Did you steal my bra? Box FE8541

PHANTOM LIMB SEX
I HAVE NOTHING

COMPLETELY SAFE
0906 357767

YOU WERE SHAPELY, STYLISH BRUNETTE eating alone. Michaelantoni's Brasserie. I was Italian-looking 20-something waiter. What did you order again? Box FE8961

BLACKPOOL PIER, 1961. You swallowed the rollercoaster. Why did you do it? How did you do it? When will this ride end? Tel FRA308

THERE'S FRUIT IN THE BOWL OR YOGHURT IN THE FRIDGE
I'LL BANG YOUR HEADS TOGETHER IN A MINUTE
KISS YOUR NAN
MUM LINE

0906 551 541

YOU WERE LOOKING FOR a 3-bed semi in Whoft, I was working the night shift on the Framley Examiner telesales desk. I'm pregnant. It's yours. Tel 01999 939234

I WAS 6-YEAR OLD with overactive imagination, you were 19ft blue piggybank called Mr Waggy. Please call. We could really make it work this time. Box FE8165

HOT HOT HOT
TRIED OUR HOTS?
HORNY BANANA FIGHT 0906 458601
HAMPSTEAD FLAVOURING 0906 458602
SHOP FOR AN ASHTRAY 0906 458603
HEN 0906 458604
POSH CARTOON 0906 458605
ADAM F SOUNDALIKE 0906 458606
RUSSIAN SALAD PARTY 0906 458607
I WILL MAKE YOU GO 0906 458608
HUMPING LIKE MAD FURNITURE 0906 458609
YOUR LITTLE SISTER'S DOLLS 0906 458610
FRUG ME FROM THE SIDE 0906 458611
I AM HIDING IN YOUR MOUTH ALREADY 0906 458612
LISTEN TO MY PHOTO (UNCENSORED) 0906 458613
FOUR HOUR SILENCE 0906 458614
STICK IT IN MY HANDBAG 0906 458615
RATZENBERGER DELUGE 0906 458616
* All calls charged at £2.99 per minute from the moment you first think about calling until the moment we receive an official death certificate from a recognised authority.

CINDERELLA – We met on the slopes at Montgenèvre. I still have one of your glass skis. Box FE 8419

1964 – you were screaming 16-year old girl with horn-rimmed glasses. I was Billy Crimson & The Corsairs, Whoft Hippodrome. Box FE8195

SWAP MESSAGES WITH UP TO 60 OTHERS
POST-IT NOTE XXX NOW!
01 REMEMBER! TOM SAUCE
02 DON'T TOUCH KEYBOARD
03 JENNY'S – KEEP OFF
04 IT'D BE NICE IF SOMEONE ELSE BOUGHT SOME BUTTER FOR A CHANGE
0906 4954 + code

The Framley Examiner

Framley's Traditional Favourite since 1978

FRIDAY, DECEMBER 13th 2002

PRICE 45p

Santa's Grotto is **FULLY LICENSED** open nightly till 11
no stag parties
NEWBY'S OF MOLFORD

FOOD

Hot hot pies

STYLE

Even numbers

WIN

A lifetime's supply of spiders

Local area flattened due to planning irregularity

OUTRAGE AS DEVELOPERS DEMOLISH WHOFT

Cutting a swathe through some Edwardian cottages.
PHOTO BY REEPERBAHN GRAPE

by Adam "Peppercorn" Wrent

THE PEOPLE OF WHOFT were this week coming to terms with what might be the biggest shock of their lives. Furious residents are claiming "an act of unparalleled and shocking vandalism" after the entire suburb was accidentally razed to the ground by property developers.

The alarm was raised at 3pm on Tuesday by computer cleaner George Fazakiel, when he returned home from work early to find his house gone.

"I turned into Psittiter Circus, and round the bend by the community centre, and realised that my house wasn't there," he recounted, 38.

"Then I noticed that the community centre was also missing, and that the road I thought I was on wasn't really there either, except for a load of rubble," he recounted.

Whoft was home to 15,800 people until this week. Much of the area, which included two primary schools and five pubs, was built in the 1880s by Victorian speculator Excelsior Melon, but that doesn't matter any more.

Present-day developers Wonham Foreign de Foreigner put in a planning application to build two one-bedroom houses with car parking in January. They say that residents were given until February 30th to write to Framley Borough Council with any comments.

THIS IS OUTRAGEOUS

"This is outrageous," said elderly Noreen Twaith at a specially-convened meeting of former Whoft residents at Framley Town Hall on Thursday evening.

"The council sent us a letter asking for our opinion and emphasising that our comments counted, but then the bulldozers and the wrecking-balls go right over our heads and do whatever they want."

Developers do not need planning permission to demolish a building unless it is listed. However, they do need to agree a means of demolition,

which WFdF claim they applied for.

Unfortunately the council now admit that a "simply frightening" amount of paperwork – possibly including the demolition form – was used in Mayor D'Ainty's highly successful Grand Framley Paper Aeroplane Race at the beginning of February. Normally, if the council does not respond to a bashing-up request within a certain period of time, the demolition can go ahead. It is thought that this technicality led to Tuesday's disaster.

NOW

Now-homeless residents are now taking their fight to court, and have formed an action group to take their fight to the courts.

"Our lawyers think we have a very good case," says campaigner Curly McWurly. "And if our initial hearing goes well on Monday, we may have our houses back by the end of the week."

A spokesman for Wonham Foreign de Foreigner made no comment except to confirm that the time for the council to reply to the demolition application had elapsed several weeks ago and that "it said 'Whoft' on all the forms – what have we done wrong this time?"

Charity jailbreak goes with a bang

THE ANNUAL RAG WEEK at Framley Community College ended on Friday with a sponsored Jailbreak that raised over £900 for drunk children.

The police, who had co-operated with students of the college to help organise the jailbreak, told reporters they were delighted with the results.

"It was great to be involved with the college," said a police spokesman. "This forges ties with the community and raises money for a good cause into the bargain. The whole event was a great success, with over 38 criminals sprung from chokey. Well done.

"We advise the public not to approach these men as they are probably armed."

SATUR-DAY IS FUN-DAY ON ZEPHYR AM

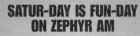

The Hot Hot Pie Show
with Mario Paradiso

Fun Fun Fun! Fun Fun!
Saturday   4.30am-11.00am
Sunday   3.30am-4.00am

Zephyr **1375**AM

LETTERS P18 & 19 LETTERS P11 & 23 LETTERS P37 LETTUCE P79 – 79 THIS BANNER P1

134

The Gathering Storm

Internet Updates (2002–04)

New CCTV system fails to entertain

A scene from the disappointing film with (inset) the camera responsible with (inset) the scene from the disappointing film again.
PHOTOGRAPH BY SUSAN PILLOWTALK

By JESUS CHIGLEY

A NEW £150,000 CLOSED CIRCUIT TV system at the corner of Denegate and Rittenden Row that cost almost £151,000 to install has come under fierce criticism from the residents for whose whom it was set up for.

The cameras were installed after Framley police decided that a 24 hour watch needed to be kept on the notorious crime spot, but when members of the community were invited in to view the footage, they weren't slow to voice their disapproval.

"It's shit," said Luxuria Ottoman, a hermit's assistant from Whoft who stormed out of the control room after only an hour and a half. "Really boring. We were told this would be some sort of crime film, but it's just a montage of shots of bins and bus lanes. There's not a single symapthetic character."

TERRIBLE LET DOWN

Others were similarly disappointed.

"£150,000 for that?" scoffed roundabout warden Dennis Memory. "We could have got three eighths of an episode of *The Onedin Line* for half the price of all this rubbish about the Fisheries Street carpark."

Some residents tried to look on the bright side. "It's not what I'd call laugh out loud funny, but I managed a couple of giggles," verdicted Trisha Wrindow, landlady of The Mouse And Mouse's Friend pub in Denegate, while Gordon Bonnet from the chip shop said he'd enjoyed the bit where his wife came out of the post office, and so had his wife.

BLAZING BUILDING

After two and a quarter hours though tempers were beginning to fray and so Mrs Arglesocks from the W.I and local rotarian Kenneth Grabs offered to go out and set fire to Debenhams to liven the film up a bit.

"That's when things really picked up," smiled Chief Constable Rupert Bone yesterday at the inquest. "Everyone joined in. It was spectacular."

It certainly was! The sequence with the blazing shop went down so well with residents that from Friday this part of the footage will be released for a limited run at the Sockford Polyhedron. The film has been edited slightly for nudity and violence and is not suitable.

Box Office: Tel 01949 800 600

More paella

People in the Framley area are eating more paella than one might expect, according to a new report from the Framley District Paella Board. The promising figures are put down to paella's delicious taste and ease of preparation, but have been pooh-poohed as "spin" by representatives of the Sockford and Area Hotpot Club.

Mayor mugged

By ADAM WRENT

IT'S been a bad week for Framley mayor William D'Ainty who has been mugged.

The mayor had been attending a meeting at a pub in the town centre on Tuesday morning. At 11.30am, he left The Clown & Pudding in High Street Road and made his way to a planning meeting at The Accident Blackspot public house on Sewer Steps.

As he approached the pub, he was approached by two youths who asked him the time. According to police, D'Ainty reached into his handbag to find his watch, asking the youths to hold his wallet, mobile phone, pager and car keys.

The thugs then ran off in the direction of north, relieving the mayor of his pager and mobile phone, as well as the keys to his car and his wallet, containing credits cards, three driving licences and £700 in travellers' cheques.

HOPSITALISED

Police have described the mayor's condition as "he's in hospital," and say that he is badly shaken, but not that badly. He is not thought to be injured, and is thought to be annoying hospital staff.

Speaking to reporters from his bed in the maternity ward, Mayor D'Ainty issued a statement saying "they should be hanged up and throw away the rope. The only language they understand is too good for them."

The mayor, in impassioned form, added that "someone ought to be doing something about this town."

DARKER ONE

The two youths are described as both wearing hooded jackets, although one was lighter than the other, with the one in the darker one being about an inch higher and with lighter hair than the one in the lighter one, who had darker hair than the one in the darker one and was fatter and wore blue trainers and jeans like the one in the darker one except his trainers were slightly different and probably lighter than the darker ones of the one in the lighter one.

Anyone with any information about the muggery should find themselves a policeman.

NEW! from NcNewby's

Newby's **PORK McSLURRY**

SENDS YOUR STOMACH AND BOWELS FROM 0-80 IN LESS THAN 3 HOURS... GUARANTEED!

... OR WE STOP MAKING THEM!

OILY **£1.49**

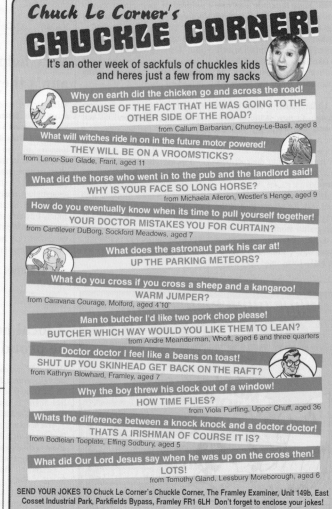

Chuck Le Corner's CHUCKLE CORNER!

It's an other week of sackfuls of chuckles kids and heres just a few from my sacks

Why on earth did the chicken go and across the road!
BECAUSE OF THE FACT THAT HE WAS GOING TO THE OTHER SIDE OF THE ROAD?
from Callum Barbarian, Chutney-Le-Basil, aged 8

What will witches ride in on in the future motor powered!
THEY WILL BE ON A VROOMSTICKS?
from Lenor-Sue Glade, Frant, aged 11

What did the horse who went in to the pub and the landlord said!
WHY IS YOUR FACE SO LONG HORSE?
from Michaela Aileron, Westler's Henge, aged 9

How do you eventually know when its time to pull yourself together!
YOUR DOCTOR MISTAKES YOU FOR CURTAIN?
from Cantilever DuBorg, Sockford Meadows, aged 7

What does the astronaut park his car at!
UP THE PARKING METEORS?

What do you cross if you cross a sheep and a kangaroo!
WARM JUMPER?
from Caravana Courage, Molford, aged 4'10"

Man to butcher I'd like two pork chop please!
BUTCHER WHICH WAY WOULD YOU LIKE THEM TO LEAN?
from Andre Meanderman, Whoft, aged 6 and three quarters

Doctor doctor I feel like a beans on toast!
SHUT UP YOU SKINHEAD GET BACK ON THE RAFT?
from Kathryn Blowhard, Framley, aged 7

Why the boy threw his clock out of a window!
HOW TIME FLIES?
from Viola Purfling, Upper Chuff, aged 36

Whats the difference between a knock knock and a doctor doctor!
THATS A IRISHMAN OF COURSE IT IS?
from Bodleian Toeplate, Effing Sodbury, aged 5

What did Our Lord Jesus say when he was up on the cross then!
LOTS!
from Tomothy Gland, Lessbury Moreborough, aged 6

SEND YOUR JOKES TO Chuck Le Corner's Chuckle Corner, The Framley Examiner, Unit 149b, East Cosset Industrial Park, Parkfields Bypass, Framley FR1 6LH Don't forget to enclose your jokes!

Contributors must be aware that some editing or rephrasing of jokes may be undertaken by the editor of this column. The Framley Examiner Group will no longer enter into heated correspondence with children or parents regarding this practice. We can't return any of your jokes, but there is a prize for all those shown.

READER'S OFFERS

ONE WEEK ONLY!

MR ADRIAN TEASDALL'S CIRCUS

meet **CORDUROY THE ELEPHANT**

ROLL UP! ROLL UP! DROP OUT!

With this advert, one adult will be admitted dressed as a child

SOCKFORD COUNTY SHOWGROUND
JUNE 5th – JUNE 11th (except Mon, Wed, Thu, Sun)

Bear Baiting!

Britain's palest clowns!

Dance with Humphrey the Blue Peter tiger!

Live Bee Swallowers!

Wooden Seals!

Go two rounds with Mercury Rev and win a goldfish!

See The Amazing Nesmith swim in shark-infested Tippex!

This voucher entitles you to TWO recurring nightmares about pale clowns for the price of ONE

COLASANTO COACH TOURS

Established 1985

Wouldn't you like to go away inside of a deluxury coach by COLASANTO?

01999 844 444
for free brochure

AROUND THE WORLD IN FIVE DAYS!

Half price offer!

You'll be amazed at what you will see in just *FIVE DAYS*, as our tour whisks you past sites in lively Whoft, Fracton (where you'll be shown a photograph of a pint of local) all the way to Bellaire and Portugal in the first hour and a half, then on, on, on... near the temples of Bangkok (day four), even leaping spectacularly over the spectacular Grand Canyons of the USA of America (lunchtime).

Dinner will be included each hour, with entertainment ranging from a traditional twentieth century banquet to a ride on a balloon, all from the comfort of your seat. All of this in such a short time will give you a tantalizing taste of what a longer stay on the world can offer you – and whet your appetite for a return visit!

ROUND THE WORLD TICKET – NORMALLY £1999, now £999

QUOTE REFERENCE BGA11

(due to the excessive speeds involved in this tour, passengers are warned that they must NOT ATTEMPT TO LEAVE the coach at any time)

Meet your Waterloo at one of our...

ABBA MURDER MYSTERY WEEKENDS!

ALL THE HITS!
ALL THE MURDER!
ALL THE MYSTERY!
ALL IN SWEDISH!

Spend a luxury weekend in full weekend luxury at Ygdrasil Hall, Chutney Le Basil and join in the fun, as you try and work out which Swedish member of ABBA has murdered an actor playing a member of the public.

You'll be dancing like a queen and singing "gimme gimme gimme a piece of substantive evidence after midnight" as the murder unfolds to the great sound of ABBA in an authentic Edwardian mystery setting!

Did Bjork the butler do it? What is the dark secret of Anfred or was it Benny the ballroom dancer? What does Abbanetha's mother know?

Perfect for office parties or the easily pleased, it's singalong investigative fun all the way!

*Murder and crime are real. Investigation overseen by Framley CID, other commitments permitting.

SPECIAL OFFER PRICE THIS WEEKEND ONLY £69.99 or £879.99 with FREE immunity from prosecution should it turn out that you are the murderer. Bring a gun and an alibi.

BOOK NOW ON 01999 766 656

Why not come and visit...

Little St Buttery

"The most English place in the known universe"

Down the lane, past the pond and into Little St Buttery – an English delight.

Take a stroll around the Cream Tea Museum, have a refreshing flagon of Diet Mead (only 70cal/pint) in the snug of The Highwayman & Hooligan, enjoy the local Morris Beefeaters performing songs from EastEnders at the Harvest Festival Experience, or just relax on the green and watch the neverending cricket match from a jam sandwich deckchair.

At £900 per person per day, Little St Buttery is a one-in-an-English-lifetime opportunity.

- HomeMade™ cakes in the post office
- Wenchwolding competitions
- It's sunny every day (controlled environment)
- Bakelite furniture in most rooms
- XTC gift shop

DISCOUNTS FOR MIDWIVES ON BICYCLES
No swearing
Parking for 3,000,000 cars

(Just off the A, near the B)

don't drink and drive!

special offer call **subman** *it's easy*

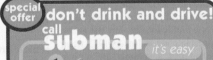

1
2
3

you go out and drink!

call us on **0999 433432**

a trained operative in a miniature submarine will surface behind the bar. The sub then packs flat into a tiny backpack which you wear while walking home

this voucher entitles you to one free call out, or can be exchanged for a complimentary beret at any branch of Newby's Tamoshanter Express

HELOTRON

thursdays at the doig

Themed Fetish Nights

Feel free to come dressed as any of the following:

Pound Note + Nude Man + School Dinner + Stephanie Webster
The Guv'nor + Billiard Ball + Smelly Old Fat Man + Mayor D'Ainty
Jeeves + Duvet Boy + Darts Trophy + Woodcut + Goalkeeper
Disguise + A Funny Robot + Sterling Void + Yourself (But Bigger)

No streetwear or regular clubwear allowed

The DOIG – 167 The Bizarres, Framley. 01999 965 543

Here today! Hair tomorrow!

A SNIP ABOVE

A special offer from Craig Blloon, Framley Hairier Area Champion International Pro-Celebrity Scissors Championships 1993

HAIR MILES
IF YOU HAVE 5 HAIRCUTS WITH US THIS MONTH *IN DIFFERENT STYLES* YOU'LL GET THE CHANCE TO CUT MY HAIR IN RETURN!

OAPs SHAMPOO & SEX £15
BLOW DRY £10

15 Hair Cuttings, Framley Tel: 875 439

Have you seen this woman?

THE FAMILY and friends of 96-year old Fracton resident Dotty Muffins are appealing for information on her whereabouts.

Miss Muffins went missing in January 1990. At the time, she was wearing a pink and white floral nightdress, having decided to get out of the family car halfway along the A999 near Slovenly and walk the rest of the way home.

"She was most insistent at the time," said her daughter, Bronco yesterday, "so we let her get out into the snow and get on with it."

A photofit picture of the missing woman has been assembled by police canteen staff.

Detectives and caterers say Miss Muffins is now believed to be 107 and living in the Wripple area.

Framley Police Department Photofit   CASE GT6664
The police photopicturefit, yesterday.
PHOTOFIT BY CRISPIN BOWL

No to model villillage

TIME HAS FINALLY RUN run out for Cunnymede, Wripple's famous model village.

The once popular tourist attraction, which was built by local eccentric Constant Tiger in 1918, depicts the village as it was then, at twice its actual size. Its popularity has waned since the 1970s, when the gigantic three-times-actual-size MegaWripple model village and theme park opened nearby.

Owner Viven Tiger says that the closure was inevitable, but is considering a partnership with a local chipped potato supplier to market a Turn Your Village Into Crisps website.

For dinner, for worse!

A RETIRED COUPLE from Molford have celebrated their ruby wedding in unique style – by eating each other.

Titus and Molly Blank wanted to commemorate their fortieth year of marriage by "doing something everyone would remember," said their son Groovy yesterday.

"It was a beautiful occasion," he expanded. "The three of us sat down for a meal, and after a light starter of orange and pecorino bibouillette, my parents exchanged a few words, kissed, and tucked into each other."

Solicitors for the happy couple's estate confirmed that Mr and Mrs Blank left their teeth, hands and digestive system until last.

There was a finger buffet afterwards.

Business is baby-booming for small bank manager

by Katie Blirdsnest

IT'S OFTEN BEEN SAID that a child and his money are soon parted, but that's certainly not a word you'd apply to 8-year-old Gideon Poco!

Because according to the latest end-of-year figures, Gideon's set to become the most successful bank manager in Molford!

Gideon, who is in top set for maths and owns his own calculator, has been managing a bank in his free time for two years now and things show no sign of slowing up for the mini financial whizzzard.

His business, "This Bank Belongs To Gideon Plc" named after the sticker on the door, has attracted customers from all over the Framley area, including former TV-am weatherman Commander David Philpott and Mayor William D'Ainty himself. The week that saw the announcement of the encouraging figures also saw Gideon opening the Molford branch's 100th piggy bank in a short ceremony with pop and pass the parcel. I was impressed.

BAP CASTLE

I met Gideon at a working lunch at NcNewby's Bap Castle a few doors down from his bank and after a short competition to see who could blow the biggest bubbles in their omelette shake, he explained how he'd managed to succeed against stiff competition.

"My overheads are very low," he told me. "Apart from certain unavoidable expenses such as stationery and strawberry bootlaces, the bank costs very little to run, and I can pass these savings on to my customers. Or spend them on Frazzles."

Gideon's innovations – such as join the dots chequebooks – have made

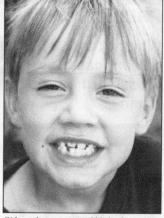
Gideon shows me round his bank.
PHOTOGRAPH BY WHATALOT MISTERMAN

his bank a big hit with the business community. His latest plan is for Magic Painting Statements which reveal your balance and interest when you paint them with water. He is confident this will attract young families and first time housebuyers.

CUSTARD PROTEST

However, not everyone is pleased with the youngster's banking decisions. As we tried to return to the branch so he could show me his new mortgage interview room filled with balls, we were stopped by a crowd of protestors picketing the building.

The angry crowd, including Bono from U2 and Tom York from The Radioheads, were cross about Gideon's investments in the Third World, particularly his efforts to encourage African mothers to feed their babies pink custard instead of Nestlé powdered milk, but police soon dispersed the mob and we were able to get inside and have a play.

MUM AN DAD

As we sank happily into the balls, I asked him what his parents thought of his success.

"I would hope they are proud of me," he said, "but we're not speaking at the moment. You see, they tried to send me to bed early last week, so I turned down their application for a second mortgage."

I laughed and threw a ball.

Calling all our readers born on a Friday between 1978 and last Friday!

A COPY OF THE FRAMLEY EXAMINER FROM THE DAY YOU WERE BORN!

CHILD BORN "He'll look like this," says mother

There's no argument that the most precious gift is the gift of love (and money can't buy you that!)

But studies conducted by the marketing department of the Framley Examiner Group Plc have proved that the next most precious gift is the gift of a copy of the Framley Examiner from the day you were born, which money can buy you for just £11.99!

So why not buy the gift of love for someone in the form of a copy of the Framley Examiner from the day they were born by taking this special opportunity to obtain a copy of just that?

Name: _____
Address: _____
_____ Post code _____
Date of Birth: Friday, __ / __ / __

I enclose a cheque for £11.99 and acknowledge that this newspaper is not a reasonable substitute for my love.

All Juice

the refreshing juice-flavoured drink

in 3 great natural flavours
* bright blue
* startling mauve
* jet black

79p

- contains minimum 1% juice -

WANDMART '7-11' STORES
7-11 Guevara Crescent, Whoft. Open 10am – 5pm

CANVASSERS REQUIRED!

We require door-to-door people.

NO SELLING!

Just knock and run away!

call Richard on 01999 643499
or e-mail www.knockdownginger.co.uk

Planning blunder leads to yet another ugly local eyesore

Storm brewing over new council offices

by Taunton Mishap

FRAMLEY TOWN PLANNERS were asking themselves some tough questions to themselfs this week when the scaffolding came down from the new District Council offices. Dignitaries and local scaffolding enthusiasts looked on in horror as it was revealed that although the new town centre development was ugly, squat and uninspiring – as requested – an unwelcome eighty-six foot structure had been added to the roofline in contravention of planning regulations and the wishes of the architects.

The structure, a solid concrete spire with a rubber on the end and the words "WH Smiths 2H" written up the side, has got council representatives and structural engineers completely foxed!

"There was certainly no spire on our plans for this building," said Gordon Clairedelune of architecture firm Westinghouse and Monkey. "That would be a church. This isn't a church. It's a Framley Council offices. It said so at the top of the blueprints. Take the spire off. TAKE IT OFF!"

WILD SPECULATION

Theories as to how the unusual appendage came to be on the council's shiny new roof have

The unwelcome obelix pokes from the roof of the new council building yesterday.
PHOTOGRAPH BY LUCIFER GLUESNIFFER

arrived thick and fast, like milkfloats in a big race.

"It's a message from God," screamed one wild-eyed lunatic from the back of the presconference before being escorted out by police, but others are not so sure.

"I'm sure these things just happen sometimes," said Mayor D'Ainty at the unveiling. "Architecture isn't an exact science. Buildings sometimes just come out a different shape than you expect.

"Maybe this spike is like the sticky-up bit I get at the back of my hair when I've slept badly," he mused dreamily. "I rather like it."

Whatever the explanation, it looks like the spire is here to stay, at least until the fingers of blame can be pointed at someone prepared to pay to

correct the blunder.

"It wasn't us," said everyone.

CLEARLY THEIR FAULT

In response to a new line of enquiry set up in desperation by the Forensic Architecture department of Framley Community College, Construction contractors Boothroyd Rubberbaby have denied allegations that one of their staff simply left a pencil on top of the blueprints and got confused where the plans ended and the pencil began.

"It's a message from God," their chief supervisor of works, Jonathan Wheels screamed at me yesterday from the back of the presconference before being escorted out by police. "Didn't you hear me the first time?"

[> hold this story for next week]

The Framley Examiner
Framley's Traditional Favourite Since 1978

HAVE YOU GOT A STORY FOR US?

call Katie Blirdsnest on 01999 94 76 94 ☎

---

the perfect birthday gift!
TURN YOUR CHILD *into a* **PUPPET**

standard service! **£39.99**
MARIONETTE
☐ "Muffin"   *JUST ADD STRINGS!*
☐ Mr Spoon
☐ The Voice of the Mysterons

deluxe service **£119.99**
GLOVE PUPPET *
☐ Erroll The Hamster   Certified member of the British Association of People Who Turn Children Into Puppets
☐ Basil The Brush
☐ The Great Gonzo ☠

* *WARNING Turning your child into a glove puppet is a non-reversible procedure.*

Teeth and Sweetums Ltd
Call Today! 01999 4875877

The Framley Examiner
Framley's Traditional Favourite Since 1978

HAVE YOU GOT WRITTEN COPY FOR US, KATIE?

call Matt on extension 3226 ☎

THE MITCHELLSON SCHOOL

110 Bolton Wanderers Terrace, Framley, FR1
Tel: 01999 733 987   Fax: 01999 733 987
email the Mitchellson School via studentcouncillor47@
emailthemitchellsonschool.framley.sch.uk

We're looking for new pupils to join us at The Mitchellson School.

We have over twelve acres of grounds, a science park, technology block, arts and music centre, swimming pool, ice rink, eighty-seven academic staff, a helipad, gymnasium and five students (left).

If your children could be friends with any of our pupils, particulary Susanne, don't hesitate to call.

OPEN SESSIONS
Tuesday 19th Sept 2002 -Wednesday 17th Sept 2003
Drop in any time, day or night, it's no trouble.

Church backlog bak clog black og

FRAMLEY CLERGYMEN were this week calling for the withdrawal of thousands of recently reprinted Order of Service booklets after a typographical error replaced every occurence of the word "*Amen*" with the words "*The National Anthem*".

"This mistake is slowing my job up no end," expelled The Rev Joliet Filename of St Prendeville's Drop-In Church in Chutney. "The flow of the service is interrupted terribly if every time I read a short prayer, I have to spend four or five minutes listening to the whole congregation singing the National Anthem in response."

Weddings are now taking up to an hour longer than usual and the backlog of christenings has become

so severe that members of the Territorial Clergy are being called upon to step into the breach, conducting skeleton services from the backs of Green Goddess trucks in church carparks throughout the region.

Many local churchmen have expressed concerns that unless the service sheets are changed, their pews will be full of patriotic parishioners twenty-four hours a day until the end of time when Christ returns in glory to judge the living and the dead, the sky splits to admit the passage of a seven-winged ocelot and the seas foam thick with vinegar.

The printers responsible for the error have said that this is unlikely and offered free post-its as a sorry.

One small step for not only the Mayor but mankind

MAYOR LANDS ON MOON

by Taunton Mishap

MAYOR WILLIAM D'AINTy stunned protesters and press alike last week when he revealed that he has been to the moon.

D'Ainty, fiftysomething, made the shock announcement at a heated presconference to announce the new parking charges announced for the town centre.

A beleaguered Director of Controlled Parking Zones, Joe Vafanculo, was crumbling under the weight of noisy opposition to the proposed increases when the mayor stepped in. Aksed to justify why the cost of one hour's parking in Denegate had gone from £1.20 to £370, Vafanculo hardly had time to draw breath when the Mayor took to his feet.

"I've been to the moon, you know," he told the room.

NO HE HASN'T

Shortly after he had been pelted from the platform by angry traders and members of the Save Our Town Centre Yet Again pressure group throwing tins of beans and their shoes, I caught up with the Mayor in his newly-refurbished office, The Thinking Zone.

"Going to the moon is a unique experience," he told me, "and I'd like to do it again. In fact, I'd go there every day if I could."

The Mayor, who had to urinate in his own clothes during his unique experience, describes the moon as "a beautiful place. Miles of golden beaches full of hundreds of little moon people. I was only there for a few hours."

NO HE WASN'T

The moon, 4,000,000,000, is our planet's only planet (apart from the sun, which is a fire) and can be seen from everywhere. It has long been the subject of scientifical research and is the property of the USA.

D'Ainty made the 384,000km journey last year, courtesy of NASA and a controversial council grant of £17m. He is the first person to have landed on the moon since Dr H. Schmidt in 1972 and, as he points out, the first mayor EVER to land on the moon.

"I brought back some chocolate," he added.

Fifteen year old, 15, laughs himself to death

PUPILS AND STAFF from Our Lady Remarkable school in St Eyot's were among mourners at the funeral last week of Jake Scrower, a fifteen-year old who died tragically on 23 February.

Witnesses told how Jake, a lively and popular boy, had laughed himself to death after a friend broke wind. Last night the friend, Digger Adams, was said to be "deeply upset" about what he described as a "tragic thing to happen after such a really funny fart."

The teenager was playing *Hepatitis Rush* on his computer with two pals when the tragedy occurred.

"He was laughing so much, it was like h'ed never heard the sound before," said a distraught Philip Philips, the second friend, who had also laughed at the noise but nowhere

near as hard.

Jake's parents were too upset to react, but the Rev Lionel Loveboy, leading the funeral service at St Tiny's church, said that God had taken their only son because he scoffed at the sins of the vegetarian, and that at least he died smiling.

The head of Our Lady Remarkable, Karen Pritchard, described Jake as a "a lively" and "popular boy" and added that the whole school had been crying all week, she could just tell, it's one of those things you get to know when you work with kids.

Sadly-missed-from-now-on Jake is only the second person to die since King Nandabayin of Burma. The first was the bloke who had a heart attack at the 'Ecce Thump' episode of TV's *The Good Life*.

Hair raising!

KAREN CRESTA, 17, of Wotten Plodney High School for Girls, had plenty to comb her hair about on Friday, and it was all for charity! Karen, pictured centre, threw caution to the wind in aid of Action For Hiccups and dyed her hair brown. The crazy stunt netted over £200 towards her school's fundraising efforts, and though teachers have insisted she dye her hair back before returning to lessons on Monday, she and her classmates were determined to enjoy the wackiest weekend of the year! **PHOTOGRAPH BY SCATTERGUN BUNCH**

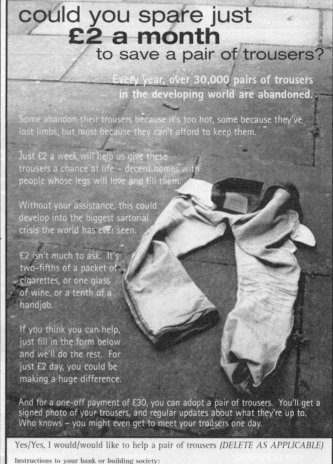

could you spare just £2 a month
to save a pair of trousers?

Every year, over 30,000 pairs of trousers in the developing world are abandoned.

Some abandon their trousers because it's too hot, some because they've lost limbs, but most because they can't afford to keep them.

Just £2 a week will help us give these trousers a chance at life – decent homes with people whose legs will love and fill them.

Without your assistance, this could develop into the biggest sartorial crisis the world has ever seen.

£2 isn't much to ask. It's two-fifths of a packet of cigarettes, or one glass of wine, or a tenth of a handjob.

If you think you can help, just fill in the form below and we'll do the rest. For just £2 day, you could be making a huge difference.

And for a one-off payment of £30, you can adopt a pair of trousers. You'll get a signed photo of your trousers, and regular updates about what they're up to. Who knows – you might even get to meet your trousers one day.

Yes/Yes, I would/would like to help a pair of trousers (*DELETE AS APPLICABLE*)

Instructions to your bank or building society:

To the manager, _____ Bank/Building Society,
Address: _____

Please debit my account by £2 a day/hour/moment (*LET US DELETE THIS BIT*) and send the money to FairTrouser, a registered for-profit charity.

Account number: _____ Sort Code: ___-___-___

I understand that I do not completely understand the smallprint (which is available on request but is commercially confidential and may not be read by anyone) and that by undertaking to confess to an incomplete understanding of something I haven't read, I am entering into a legally binding misunderstanding of a profoundly complicated contractual arrangement that I appear to have already agreed to.

Print name: _____ Signature: _____

SEND TO: FairTrouser, FREEPOST 19519, Wollesley TH3 1RA.

PROPERTY

Mister Movement

Estate Agents and Lettings and Wheelwrights   32, Condiment Row, Framley FR1 9LG

01999 565657 www.nicholasmovement.co.uk

ROCKNUTTERS, ST EYOTS

4-bed bungalow with lift conversion. 24ft kitchen with AGA-style sink, master bedroom with en-route bathroom, 3 mister bedrooms, glide-through bathroom, entertainy room and sitty down room. Interior doors have buttons instead of hinges, fridge fitted with entryphone, secret garden where garden should be.

£265,850

CHUTNEY

300ft x 140ft warehouse full of unsold caravans. Would suit group of 1800 agoraphobics wishing to recreate a traditional English holiday without the bother of daylight or fresh air, or wealthy caravan enthusiast wishing to add 447 Nelson Bombardiers Mk XXIX to his collection.

£OIRO POA ONO

SOCKFORD AWARD-WINNING GARDEN

Charming 3-bed terraced house with award-winning 10ft showgarden, divided into 64 themed areas: Mini Meadow, Titchy Town, Little Hill, Silly Valley, Ittybitty City, etc. Also water feature, Teeny Weeny Mississippi Steamer, with kitten paddles. All offers considered, including psychiatric help.

KNACKERHILL ESTATE

We are pleased to announce taking instruction of this one-off goldfish-bowl-style property. A house with walls, ceilings, stairs, roof, doors, kitchen appliances, furniture and fittings made from glass isn't to everybody's taste, but then neither is anal sex ha ha. The not-very-shy will pirouette in their graves at the chance to own this revealing property. No stone-throwers or Marty Feldman fans.

£89,000

WOTTEN PLODNEY

Unique Shakespearean cottage in breathtaking hamlet. This other Eden, demi-paradise, like a fair house built upon another man's ground, has commanding views o'er the dew of yon high eastern hill. 120ft unweeded garden that grows to seed, and there is a willow grows aslant a brook. Old Adam's likeness set to dress this best garden of the world, which has a fully functioning 'All's Well That Ends' well.
Our bodies are our gardens, to the which our wills are gardeners, but it is Rome indeed and room enough, when there is in it but one only man. Would suit he that outlives this day and comes safe home. Balcony. Grade IIb/Not IIb listed.

£545,000 or nicest offer

fax us on our fax machine! 01999 565657 and say you'd like to send a fax

BENNINGHAM & STUPID

01999 258258

Flapton Nogley Carnival Village

Unique heritage property on grade I listed roundabout. Architect-designed house with milkman-designed garden and stairs. Some bedrooms. Mint bathroom suite (flavour not colour).

£485,650

Bernie's Place, Thoxtoxteter

Spacious, bright school to let in this splendid period Victorian school conversion conversion. High ceilings, higher newly fitted kitchen and highest stripped wooden flooring guarantee that this is a house to be not to be missed, Miss.

£193,550

The Pingwingerie, Ibb

Furnished to an exceptional level throughout, this prestige apartment literally looks like a mi££ion dollars. Good investment opportunity for those easily fooled by brick things looking like cash. Easy money

£0, no pence

Delvedere Bo, Whoft

Curly-wurly property, benefitting from a prime location in front of me as I try and sell it with my words. Secluded garden with underground patio and Big Dipper leading to Spare Bedroom 4' x = 40'. Also available in Space.

£193,550

make your dream home a fantasy!
with BENNINGHAM & STUPID

55, Marble Helter Skelter, Whoft

Oscar Dribble
L E T T I N G S

FRAMLEY

£85pw
Bright, bland flat in university accommodation. Lounge/bed/diner/kitchen/front door, bathroom with pesto-coloured walls and Marmite-coloured fittings. Applicant to provide own central heating and ceilings.

FRACTON

A 'ROOM' WITH A VIEW
Delightful, self-contained cross-member underneath the pier with commanding view of the underneath of the pier and the sea. £60pw, payable in advance at least 2 years before moving in. 100% risk of drowning, but only at certain times. Would suit very warm person in diving equipment.

DURBITON

IT COULD BE YOU!
Miss H of Durbiton is looking for a flatmate who only appears as a reflection in mirrors and whose voice cannot be heard. If this is you, call us NOW or AT LEAST VERY SOON on 01999 424710.

FRAMLEY TOWN CENTRE

F/F FLAT
1-bed flat conversion very close to railway. Bright, sunny room with splendid collection of big levers. Easy access to Framley Station and the nearby railway arches. Some knowledge of signalling necessary.

FLATSHARE

L*SBIANS ONLY
Room to let in furnished house with 37 lesbians. We're an ambitious commune, and soon hope regain our place in the Guinness Book of Records for being the most lesbians ever to fit in one house. Please come and live like a real lesbian with us, and help take our record back from the Boston Bullhorns.

01999 424 710

Flat(s) for sale sold

By ADAM WRENT

RECLUSIVE SOCKFORD postman Tchud Burrows has found a novel way of selling his one-bedroom flat.

"I'm a very private person," he wrote to journalists, "and I can't bear having people look round my home, so I bought an identical flat on the estate, furnished it the same as mine and showed prospective buyers round that instead."

PROBLEM ONE

The shy postie says his biggest problem was explaining to confused househunters that although the flat they were seeing was exactly what they would be getting, it wasn't the flat they were seeing.

"I had to tell them that they'd be buying an identical property a few hundred yards up the road," revealed the bashful messenger. "But eventually, just after Chrismas, I exchanged contracts with an instant tan saleswoman from Long Rodneys."

PROBLEM TWO

The cloistered deliveryman then ran into a new difficulty. He was by now such a private person that he couldn't bring himself to look for a new home himself, so he decided to move into his show-flat temporarily.

Timid legate Burrows managed the huge task of swapping the furniture in his flat with the identical furniture in the identical flat entirely on his own, with the help of five removals men.

And now the introverted emissary says he's staying!

"I'm very happy with my new home," explained the ascetic facteur. "I was fed up with the old place, but I don't really like change, so moving to an identical flat was the perfect solution to my problem."

St Eyot's boundary property has an appeal all of its own and ample parking

With its charming mock Tudor frontage and mandolin-shaped reception room, this 5-bedroom house on the outskirts of St Eyot's is believed by some to have been designed and built by Jamie Theakston. The property sits in an attractive location convenient for Dullingham reservoir and within easy walking distance of the garden. This is a much sought-for district. The new FR999 takes cars well away from these leafy lanes and plunges them into the Victorian era. Ample parking is provided as are full details from Teddyboy Martin Residential who are selling the property at £375,995. No socialists

New name for Bardon Homes

Local housebuilders Bardon Homes will have a new name and image from this week. Signs bearing the new company logo will soon be seen over their current development of starter homes near Molford St Gavin, and on envelopes.

Owner Tony Bardon said the new name reflected a fresh start, not only for his construction company, but also for him personally, following his recent divorce.

"I hope that people will come to regard Michelle Bardon Is An Unfaithful Gold-Digging Trollop Homes as a byword for trust, reliability and excellent value," he told the board.

"He that toucheth pitch shall be defiled therewith" as -
Town cursed by forces of evil

by Jesus Chigley

THE TERRIFIED TOWN OF FRAMLEY was last night bracing itself for further sinister and painful deaths as frightened residents felt the grip of the seize of the jaws of a terrible curse.

The Curse takes the form of a bizarre satanic sign. Anyone who sees the dreadful Sign has only seven days to live as they die a horribly painful death. So far it has been 100% deadly.

Hopsitals and florists are "on the crest of a tidalwave," says local predictor Piers Llewellyn. "They have already confirmed 47 deaths because of The Sign, and are expecting as many as a further 285,000."

TERROR

The town's darkest hour is thought to be the work of local satanist and self-professed 'warlock,' Alexei Clawlust, aka The Beest.

The Beest, who has links with the witches whose bodies were found locked in a spooky dungeon after the great fire of Framley in 1994, keeps a low profile locally. His last public appearance was in January 1972, when he opened a school fate with a sandstorm, out of which rode a flaming red knight on a two-headed horse.

Police are warning people to stay calm, but also to keep their eyes shut as much as possible until scientists can invent SIGN-proof goggles.

An excited police source confirmed yesterday that highly-trained officers will wear these space-age goggles by night, when they go hunting THE SIGN on turbo hoverbikes armed with stun phasers that go peeoww.

HORROR

But while the police were looking forward to enjoying themselves, others were staring into a bottomless pit of peril.

A retired pensioner from Molford, Obi Bosling, who saw THE SIGN appear before him in the fog of a dark wood, died on Saturday after a shatteringly painful illness. He described the experience as "like being eaten alive by boiling snakes."

The Mayor was last night rushed to Framley General Hospital after mistaking a British Kite Mark on a fire extinguisher for tHE sIGN. He was attending a dinner at the time, and is said to have "shat on his shoeshine".

Anyone who sees

THE SIGN

should call 999 and, when prompted, ask for an exorcist.

The Catholic Church – to our members we're the fifth emergency service

The SIGN, the very sight of which spells doom for anyone who sees it.
ILLUSTRATION BY THE LATE COOKIEMONSTER HARRIS

News In Brief

MULTIPLE SHOOTING

A 38-year old unemployed man from Sockford shot and killed his wife and three children last week before turning the gun on himself. Police have described it as "a satisfactory end to the case, which didn't cost us a penny and was a good example of the efficiency of modern policing."

VILLAGE BOOK PUBLISHED

A man who moved from Wripple to Ghastley St Matthew in 1996 is to publish a book detailing the similarities between the two villages. "Both villages have two schools and three newsagents and grass," says Tony Kite. "It's mad." Mr Kite has also counted the number of bus stops and worms.

THE VIEW FROM HERE

When Joanne is sitting at her terminal, I can see down the back of her trousers. She usually wears black or grey pants, but my favourites are her white Victoria's Secret pants, which go better with her blue eyes. She also keeps a spare pair of pants in the outer compartment of her handbag, something I found out when I spent a day under her desk.

Owls about that then?

By TAUNTON MISHAP

A GROUP of delinquent owls have been causing misery for a family of five from the Wripple area.

The family of five, Mr & Mrs Keith & Penelope Hotscotch, daughters Jaclyn & Impedimenta & son Scott (41, 38, 15, 11, 5½) told me yesterday (Monday) that they were all at their wits.

Mrs Hotscotch explained more to gathered reporter.

THIS IS WHAT SHE SAID

"It all started just before Christmas," explained Penelope more. "Our eldest daughter, Jaclyn, 15, had been babysitting Scott one evening whilst my husband and I had attended a just before Christmas concert at Impedimenta's school.

"On our return we were horrified to discover that our bedroom had been ransacked and that all of Scott's Christmas presents had been opened. He was playing with his new toys and making train noises, surrounded by a huge pile of torn wrapping paper. The moment he saw us standing there he started to cry and told us after a pause that owls did it."

OWLS DID IT

Eldest daughter Jaclyn had been downstairs all evening watching Inpector More and spinning out on Sunny Delight but remained unaware of the incident.

And it didn't stop there. The usually law-abiding birds of prey(?)

struck repeatedly at the same address over the following days. Owls have since stolen a lipstick stick, hidden a portion of peas under a tablecloth and defaced a bathroom wall with bright red messages stating that "Scott can bonc lik Tiggr" and "owls diddit".

Scott Hotscotch
LIBRARY PICTURE

POLICE INVETSIGATE

"We're not too sure how they're getting into the property. They must have a key," suggested WPC Davina Bacharachach (Framley Carnival Queen Constable 1997), "although no featherprints have been left at the scenes of the crimes.

"Our forensic team is flummoxed. They've not seen owl crime like this since training college. We're very grateful to Scott as without his eye-witness statements we would have no leads to go on at all.

"Fortunately for him he doesn't seem at all traumatised by the events and he's always got a lovely chocolate-covered smile for us when we're doing all our investigating."

Anyone with any information on this crime is requested to phone Owlstoppers on 0999 555 655 in strictest confidence.

framley borough council
call our 24-our helplines

HEALTH AND SAFETY	01999 940940
INVISIBLE PEOPLE	01999 640640
FURTHER EDCUATION	01999 SKOOLS
IF PEOPLE ARE SHOUTING	01999 245865
DANIELLE IN PAVEMENTS	01999 426819
DRY OR WET? HMM...	01999 365484 HMM!
BICYCLES ETC	01999 808080
NEW! 18-YEAR OLD SUCKS COCK	07999 696969
CAN'T REMEMBER	01999 68?ETC

framley borough council
working with you for a better Framley!
all calls are FREE and charged at the usual
national free rate of 0.00p per minute

Vicar freaked out by harvest

by Bunco Booth

A POPULAR VICAR from Tollephant has gone into hiding after finally admitting defeat at the hands of the harvest festival service.

A shivering Rev. Eldon Puff told Church authorities from his makeshift bivouac on the beach at Fracton that he wasn't coming out until the congregation had "gone home" and "stopped it".

The harvest festival is traditionally celebrated once an annual at St Ungun's Exceptional Church in Tollephant. Parishioners are encouraged to bring gifts of food that are later distributed to the local poors after there have been hymns.

Rev. Puff, who has been vicar at St Ungun's since 1992 has regularly expressed his displeasure at the unimaginative nature of his congregation's Harvest donations.

"Every year, everyone brings the same thing", he told reporters from *Dog Collar* in 2002. "In 1993 it was all Campbell's cream of mushroom soup. Three hundred cans of it."

Successive years have seen the aisles heaving with Worcestershire sauce, baskets of strawberry opal fruits, and in 1998 it was fennel.

"This year was the final straw," grieved the Rev Puff last year. "Every man jack of them brought in a four-litre tub of Wall's vanilla ice cream. I put the heating on for morning prayers and flooded the chancel. Look. I'm still sticking to the floor. Where's my shoe?"

To avoid a repeat of the same thing, on the Sunday before this year's festival, Puff instructed his congregation to be more individual, suggesting they all bring something home-made. "Surprise me," he told them.

TOO MANY MEN

And what a surprise!

At the 9.30 communion service, Rev. Puff was faced with an altar stacked with an eighteen foot pyramid of gingerbread men.

The tower of confectionery men, each one dressed in an identical liccurice tailcoat and sporting a lazy currant eye, drove the vicar to tender his resignation and run screaming to the seaside with his cassock over his head.

Church officials, who have so far failed to tempt him out of his hiding place, are having no more luck removing the unimaginative congregation from the church.

"They're all just sitting there, staring straight ahead," one paramilitary verger told me. "They don't speak, and they each have a single tear running down their cheek.

"I think they're upset. They only wanted to make Eldon happy. We've tried playing tapes of his sermons in the graveyard to lure them out, but they're just too sad to move.

"I only hope we don't have to blast them out with ordnance like that congregation in Whoft," he laughed

holiday reminder

There will be no Framley Examiner for the next two weeks due to the festival of St Merriman.

Remember that, while all shops and services in the Framley region are closed for the duration of the festival, Yolland's Grocers, Farmfield Lane, Wripple will be open for emergency food supplies.

A police / fireman is on call during office hours on 01999 664 721 (ask for Geoff).

Have a good festival!

bathroom herons

quality bathroom herons at competitive prices

from **£350** plus VAT fully fitted

for toilets and baths

decorative and practical

howdy doody!

JUST IN! shower bitterns

HM GOVERNMENT HERON WARNING
UNDER NO CIRCUMSTANCES LEAVE A HERON UNATTENDED IN YOUR BATHROOM

NICHOLSON'S TOILET HERONS

Weddings

BENETTON CRAMPAGNE (right) of Cracknell Wiggstanley, was the Best Man at the wedding of his ex-fiancee **Trudy Grenades** (left) and some other bloke. The newlyweds will honeymoon on the Iberian peninsula, whilst Benetton will be sitting at home, crying into old photograph albums and caning it on White Lightning.

MERTON STINT of Guesswich Road, Molford St Gavin was not supposed to forget that he was marrying **Lucy Ketchup** of No Little Patience at Our Mrs Lady Immaculate's Church in Molford St Arahim Ramal. Live bait, standard 9' pole, 8lbs 7oz.

Photograph by Owen Piss Studios

GOOD OLD CHARLIE BROWN of St Paul, Minnesota was finally married to **a cute little red haired girl**, from Melendez Crescent, Wripple, at St Ulchz's Emergency Chapel and Donuts, offramp 8, I-652, Root Canyon, OH.

Photograph by Rerun Franklin

REV. CHEVY LEVY of St Cheese-on-the-Stick's Church, Fracton, married **sixteen couples** at St Cheese-on-the-Stick's Church, Fracton. He will be honeymooning in the Maldives.

Photograph (c) Church Times

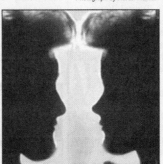

JEREMY TWO MEXICANSONABICYCLE of Longer Line, Framley and **Helen Giraffegoingpastawindow** of Shorter Line, Whoft, or possibly a vase, were married in silhouette at The Usborne Picture Methodists Hall, Chutney-Le-Basil.

Photograph by Odnald Cushion

BOB BANG and **Valerie Bang** both formerly of Stern Street, Framley, were divorced at Framley Civil Court after three years of increasingly strained breakfasts and a stand up row about the putting the hoover away properly.

Photograph by Don Logan Studios YES

ESTELLE DONNE of Topknot Villas, Whoft, and **Purves Scaramanga** of Culkin Walk, Framley, were married at Elim Penteteuchal Golf Club, Strawbury Magma.

Congratulations to Estelle who, by marrying her fifth husband this month becomes one of The Framley Examiner Weddings Page Frequent Flyers, entitling her to exciting discounts on honeymoons, cakes and foghorns from Newby's Marital and Maritime Supplies of Molford.

STAN LAMPS RD14557 of RAF Slovenly, Slovenly and **Dolly Mixamatixtures** of Stafford Cripps Villas, St Eyots, were married at the Royal Burma Club, Flapton Nogley.

Photograph by Clarence Jam Photographics

(Due to space constraints, this announcement has been carried over from the Aug 14th 1932 edition of the St Eyot's Flugel. Apologies to the family of the late Mr and Mrs Lamps for any distress caused.)

Whoft scientist to invent new speed of light

by acting sience editor
THINLY SPREAD

LOCAL SCIENTIST Professor Arthur Bostrum is again at the centre of controversy in the world of science, thanks to his latest experiment to see how fast light travels inside a toaster.

Bostrom, who is rapidly becoming something of a local *cause célèbre*, recently announced his attempt to re-evaluate the speed of light. And while the sience world has branded him "a waste of idiot" for his efforts, the professor remains convinced that he has uncovered a fundamental inconsistency.

"People always talk about the speed of light in a vacuum," explained Bostrom from his laboratory in his shed in his garden in Whoft, "but no-one ever measures the speed of light in any other appliance."

TIME FOR TOAST

The professor plans to build the world's largest toaster for his experiment, which he will fill with asbestos-insulated lightbulbs. He's even built a special customised egg-timer for the event.

"A typical egg timer has anything up to three minutes of sand in it, which is way beyond my needs," Bostrom Bostrom Bostrom. "My speed-of-light egg timer contains only one grain of sand, which is more than enough ."

The world of sience, however, has poo-pooed the professor's premise, pronouncing it "positively preposterous, profoundly provincial and punitively proofless peppercorn piffling."

A spokesmen for Framley Technical College pointed out that even a single grain of sand would be far too big to measure the time taken for a light to move through a toaster. Nerves have been particularly expressed that Prof Bostrom might be planning to cut his grain up with scissors to achieve his ends, releasing a beachload of bother.

"If Bostrom starts splitting atoms of sand, he could accidentally go as blind as a watchmaker and cause a massive sand explosion. It doesn't bear thinking about," commented Senior Physics Tutor Daniel Manual as he thought about it.

"God does not play Twister," he added, cryptically.

SIMON CRESS
ESTATE AGENTS

Experts in luxury bathrooms

Idiots in open fields

Hopelessly ill informed in a locked cupboard

01999 827 7611

JUNCTION SCRAPPED

FIVE YEARS of campaigning came to an end on Tuesday as Framley council final wom its battle to scrap junction 13 of the Molford ring road because it has an unlucky number.

Protestors from Lloydbridge, which the junction serves, were pushed back from the junction by police as construction workers severed the sliproad from the FR404 with grass, sealing the village off completely. Eventually, roadplanners say, the villagers will die off as supplies run out, and the ringroad will be lucky again.

Renumbering the junctions will begin next week with Junction 14 being redesignated Junction 13, and so on round clockwise.

PHOTOGRAPH BY HELENELLEN IMP

House prices still too complicated

ESTATE AGENTS in framley remain unable to show any sign of understanding the local property market with house prices still ranging from variable to intangible.

A study of recent sales in the three months to October compared favourably with a survey carried out at the same time concerning the relevant period last year, revealed Ben Partridge-Martin of Teddyboy Martin Residentials shortly before adopting a thousand yard stare at a council meeting last week.

Natthew Partridge-Martin – Mr Partridge-Martin's 12-year old son on a school-sponsored "Accompany Your Own Father To Work This Time" Day – took over and carried on reading from Ben's prepared statement, despite the intermittent speedboat impressions coming from his father's direction.

After advising the panel that prices currently fell somewhere between 24% and 4? – ?.17 Natthew was challenged to prove that this was the case. On production of his clear workings the matter was agreed with no dissenters.

SAME AGAIN ?

Chairman of the Beigefield Sites Planning Committee, Colin Bomdinghy, summarized the key

Mr Partridge-Martin at the start of his presentation, before he lost all hope.
PHOTOGRAPH BY BUSY KITTENS

points of the sunny afternoon for reporters who might have had a liquid lunch and had fallen asleep during the most pertinent moments of the meeting.

"Framley house prices have stabilized over the years. Gone now are the days of loft trading and brick-to-brick combat, and local property companies tend to meet UE regulations most of the time. It," he brought on migraines, "might be expensive to most of the people most of the time but it's Framley's expensive and nobody else's. Are you alright, Mr Chigley? Perhaps a glass of water…?"

In Court

BARRINGTON Paddington of Filmfair Meadows, Wripple, was fined £60 with £4 costs on November 2nd for driving while under the influence of alcohol. The court noted that he had a "terrible hangover" and exercised leniency accordingly.

CRESTA Froth of Haliborange Court, Creme, had a charge of threatening behaviour withdrawn at Framley Magistrate's Court after going through with his threat. He will appear charged with murder next month. Bring sandwiches.

BERNADETTE Hazzard was strapped to the back of a bear and ridden round the town by monkeys dressed as little pirates for no real reason after yet another misguidedly heavy drinking session at Sockford Civil Court.

EVAN Peterlee of Batey Oval, St Eyots, was fined £35 at Framley Magistrates Court on November 6th for becoming an endangered species.

JEBLOY Quadrant of Steps Street, Cough, received a twelve-year conditional discharge for stealing a £48,000 meat pie from Wandmart stores on Shebop Terrace. A charge of fraudulent pricing against the proprietor of the stores was withdrawn after the pie had been tasted.

MAXELLE Soundbarrier was fined £80 and ordered to keep her three dogs and two legs under control after all five were reported to be behaving in an erratic, excitable and dangerous manner earlier last month.

MICHAEL Sprint was fined £100 for causing £300 of damage to £200 of damage done by Stephen Pinchkiff on October 30th. Mr Sprint was also forced to repair the £300 of damage, reducing the £500 of damage to the original £200 of damage.

PEDALO Hovercraft of Emery Impression, Codge was thrown out of Framley Magistrates Court by Justice Constant Waxy (see page 5) for not being made out of enough seashells during 'Shell Court'.

danger of suffocation. Used once. No flowers. 01999 754 338.

ORIENTAL dRUGS, 15% OFF. 07999 320996.

THE PROPERTY MARKET, every Saturday 7am-3pm, Lion Square, Framley. Food, vegetables, handicraft, houses, offices, monuments.

MY TINY ATLAS novelty. A 1cm x 1cm atlas of the world? Surely that's not possible? Oh yes it is! It just isn't very helpful, hence £1. 01999 325390

IS IT GRAIN?

COMPOST BIN, black, sectional, full, still warm, £15. 01999 475099.

SCHOOL PHOTOGRAPHS, reports, piano certificates (Grades 1-5) etc. Shredded. Make ideal hamster bedding. Call Mr Hollyhock on 01999 482762. Hang up if Josie answers.

MICHAEL JACKSON meringue mould. Makes desserts in the lumpy likeness of the gloved dancer. £3 or 01999 714396.

BABYWEATHER. £10. 01999 611 961

TELEPHONE KIOSK style fridge. Phone rings when you open the door. £offers 01999 680559.

SOME OF our Some of Our Dinosaurs Are Missing are missing. Molford Mobile Video Library are offering a cash reward for any information leading to their recovery. 01999 622 630

LAMPSHADES LAMPSHADES LAMPSHADES lampshades lampshades lampshades. Call LAMPSHADES LAMPSHADES LAMPSHADES on 01999 370954 for all your lampshades lampshades lampshades needs.

32" WIDESCREEN TV remote control. The biggest handset you'll ever need to own. 07999 369404.

YEZYEZ

YAMAHA electric organ, 50cc, tax + MOT, one lady owner. £350ono, 01999 593017 after 5.52pm.

SILVER COINS, to sell and exchange. Princess Diana and Wayne Sleep commemorative 2p, Freddie And The Pacemakers half crown (rare mistake), Ratification of the Maastricht Treaty £99.99 note etc. Smithwick's 01999 340797. (T)

PLASTICENE Poptarts. Realistic plasticene pop tarts. Poison your children and burn their house down. £3 a pack. 01999 803 854

BLACK LEATHER arm chair. A chair just the right size to fit an adult arm. Take the weight off your arm! £299 each. For catalogue, write Box FE8933.

LION CUBS, all "rescued," need good homes. Kids love them! Box FE8523.

ABSOLUTELY ALL CARS AND VANS WANTED and so far I've only got 113. You will give me you car/van eventually – everybody will – and sooner would be better than later. 01999 400400 call now.

FINGERLESS WASHING-UP GLOVES £3 a pair, or send me your pair and I will return them with the fingers missing £2.50 a pair. Allow £28 for delivery. Box FE8491.

LOOKING for a mobile disco? Mobile disco detector. With straps and sensor hose. £165. 01999 748 211

PENCIL SHARPENER in the shape of a cement mixer. Size of cement mixer, hence £115. Box FE8241.

WATERFALL, unused, 3-part multi-tier, limestone, approx 60ft high, with elephant graveyard in secret cave beyond, £4500. 01999 239947.

BRIDESMAIDS' dresses. One size 16 in ivory. £100. Two children's in pink satin. £60. Very few bloodstains. Hardly used. Fram 941 411

NEVER BEEN ABROAD? Postcards of foreign places and things. £3 each or £25 the pair. Box FE8585.

"CANOE In My Pocket Snap!" card game. All new photos. Handmade. £5. 01999 722 065

Last year over 4,500 yards of strawberry bootlaces were sold through the pages of
The Framley Examiner
Yum yum.

CALLAGHAN GOVERNMENT ShrinkyDinks (Nabisco Shreddies 1978). Still in original boxes with original cereal. £25. Call Bryan on 01999 234 255

CROSS-CHANNEL FERRY in enormous replica bottle of HP Sauce. £47,000. 01999 439 555

SONY Playstation with Thomas The Tank Engine game and two fat controllers. £70. 01999 770 819

TWO-WAY MIRROR greenhouse. Now your neighbours can't see your tomatoes. Or your tomatoes can't see anything but themselves (depending on which way round you do the glass), £offers. 01999 238590

LADIES cricket boxes, £12 the pair. Doubles as sweaty plastic bra. Miriam 01999 238101.

A ROOM WITH A VIEW! A room without a view! These curtains could be yours! 01999 743 871. Offers.

LASERJET PRINTER. HP4. Fast and efficient. With cable. Slightly erratic. Has tattooed the minutes of the Sockford Amateur Dramatic Society AGM all over my face. £34. 01999 449 003

ADULT PRAM, 13' x 6' metallic blue. Air con, alarm, immobiliser, automatic rattle, many extras, £4540. 01999 358667.

ANG LEE'S The Incredible Fridge. "Don't make me ice cubes, you wouldn't like me when I'm ice cubes". £65. Wripple 11849.

POODLE-PROOF bike. Suit 6-8yrs. Enormous. Fairly good condition. £30. Tel 497 775

TWINKLE TWINKLE LITTLE SITAR, child's half-size Ravi Shankar signature model, £60. Palitoy TinyTabla £15. 01999 295861.

2kW ELECTRIC MIRROR, expensive to run and switching it on does nothing, although I think it's still working, hence I'm selling it. 01999 205172.

NO JOB TOO SMALL. I will tap the ash from your cigarette, brush the dandruff from your collar or move that salt cellar nearer that wine glass. No job too small! Call Mike on 01999 630 630

ZANUSSI fridge/freezer £50, fridge/hoover £30, fridge/hairdryer £15. 01999 574737.

STYLISH Yoko Ono – shaped bookcase, in white melamine with long dark hair, vgc, £70. 01999 327459.

HARP COSY, vgc, unfolds to disguise your harp as a 5ft tall butterfly with a 7ft wingspan. Not recommended for the easily startled, £350. 01999 238404.

SPIRAL STAIRCASE for sale. Stairs, handrails and balusters missing. Might just be metal pole. £10 oh all right 01999 209452.

JELLY & MASHED POTATO

PORCELAIN FIGURES, shepherdess, windmill, blacksmith shoeing horse, Dale Winton's face on a slice of toast, many others, £12 each. Framley Figurines, 01999 240995. (T)

THEIR DOG FREEWAY and you're Max. You look after both of them now. 01999 349 722

CASH MACHINE, holds up to £60,000. An unusual feature for your garden. £500 or £60,500 with cash. 01999 687444.

BLACK & DECKER Hover Barbeque, £140. Tel. 650651.

DENNIS HEALEY spacehopper with original "Silly Billy" eyebrow horns. £12. Bryan on 01999 234 255.

DID YOU SPILL my pint? What are you looking at, you four-eyed ponce? Sorry I'm late I've been hanging out the back of your mum. These and other sure-fire chat up lines available from 01999 467 933

SQUIRREL'S TAIL style penis socks. Grey £15, red £18. 01999 929469.

PATIOS LAID free of charge as long as you agree not to look at what I bury under them. 07999 961003

WANTED. Ladies' leotards. Best prices offered. Call Vince Previous on 01999 733 931

ROCKING HORSE. Handmade. Traditional. Wooden. Very rare. Needs some house training. £275. 01999 629 990

ARTHOUSE dining table with subtitles. £85. Tel 729 299

BABY MONITOR. Reptile licence req'd. £70. 01999 781 055

A DEAD penguin rotting behind the wallpaper? This could be yours, if you buy my flat. Call Chrissy on 01999 376 866

QUALCAST Technics Mix 'n' Mow sit down DJ's lawnmower with twin turntables, mixer and 200W grass bins. £175. Call Dan on 01999 844 901

FOR SALE: career. Will exchange for life. 01999 644 872

RUBBISH RUBBISH

BRASS TELESCOPE with commanding views of the Dave Brubeck Quartet. Must see. Oiro £75. 01999 390 005

THE TAO OF NORMAN WISDOM. Self-help audio tapes. Used once. Fell out of window. £15. 01999 755 544

CHILD'S HALF-SIZE jumbo jet plus runway and carrying case, £25ono. 01999 714383.

DUPLO DULUX DUREX LTD. We will fill your condoms full of paint and plastic bricks for a once-in-a-lifetime lovemaking feast. 01999 843 444

T-SHIRTS "Choose lifts," "Frankie says Radox," "You're with this idiot," "I started work in a t-shirt factory and all I could think of was this bloody slogan" and any others. Box FE8702.

TWO-WHEELED TRICYCLE, £55. 01999 235094.

HOUSE FOR SALE, 3 beds, living room/diner, fit kit, bath/WC, garden, single garage. Buyer to collect, hence £800. 01999 248694.

PINE AND GLASS fronted men's three piece suit. Buyer to wear. 01999 554 751

"SIMON SAYS" boardgame. £5 ono. Simon says "£24.99". Call 01999 380 365. Simon says call 01999 380 341

The Framley Examiner
"I sold my time machine to myself returning from the future where I'd invented it. Experiment successful!"
Prof Arthur Bostrom, Whoft

PADDLING POOL. Very large. Includes slip mat, coastguard and shark-repellent. £45. Framley 433 987

BREVILLE Sunbed. For best results eat lots of cheese before using. £65. Julie on 01999 722 900

TRAMPOLINE. 3" diameter. For the keep-fit enthusiast with pinpoint accuracy. £25. 01999 300 988

LITTLE TYKES "My First Last Will and Testament". £15. 01999 490 833

GREEDY LAMB toy. Eats mint sauce until it's sick. £12. Fram 861 606

WRIGHT Brothers Game. Frank Lloyd and Billy. Decide whether you're an architect or a footballer at the throw of a dice. £12. 01999 777 061

ELLEN MACARTHUR in a bottle. £40. 01999 529 859

BOY. Leather buckle shoes. Used once. Pristine condition. Navy blue. Size 4' 2". Framley 831 399. £25,

COMPLETE set of stamps. £478,000,000. Call Donald on 532 877

MISSING. "Patsy". Affectionate, gentle and loving, with white diamond shaped smudge on bridge of nose. Taken accidentally in skip to Meadowside Road Municipal Refuse Site on 15th of May. Patsy is extremely timid and may have wandered to any of the surrounding areas in an attempt to find her way home. Microchipped for identification. Any information gratefully received by her daughter, Linda or son-in-law Martin. 01999 599 723.

SEGA MEGADRIVE. Many games. Too many to list. Very good condition. Broken. £75. 01999 664 800

COWBELL for drumkit. VGC. Hardly used. £7. Also drumkit for cow. Used too often. Call 01999 337 520, ask for Farmer Geoffrey and speak loudly.

MAN WITH someone else's van. General removals and odd jobs. No job too large. Call before they find me and make me give the van back. Quick. That looks them in the rear view mirror now. 0999 465 778

CHINESE galleon ornament made of knotted balloons. Simply no idea what this is doing in my lounge. £offers. Whoft 434 365

YAMAHA Electone LE450 orchestral organ with stool. I'm sorry. I don't know how it happened. I can normally hold it in. £80. Sockford 533 876.

GEORGE THOMAS "Mr Speaker" Bubble Bath. £5. Call Bryan on 01999 234 255.

LITTLE ONES, YES

FOUR FLUTES. Boxed. Hardly used. Unwanted Christmas gifts. Apparently my stupid family don't want to learn to play the flute. £150. 01999 227 610

THE OFFICE chair. As seen on TV's hit show. £40. 01999 633322

FLOATER fishing set. With fragrant rules and easy-wipe hooks. £8. 01999 623 344

GRAECO-ROMAN pushchair with "Little Ben Hur" wheel blades. £37. 01999 533 932

HUNDREDS of expensive, ugly Royal Doulton mail order figurines. In boxes. And my late wife. Also in a box. Offers. Albert on 01999 822 982.

1970s dining table. Tubular steel frame. Bauhaus design. Four portions of prawn cocktail, set of well-done steaks and Black Forest Gateau. Served once. £230. Fram 955421

LARGE PINE chest of drawers. Internet ready. £180. 01999 228 943

SUFFICIENT BALROGS

COUNTERFEIT CURRENCY for sale: Russian Lire, Australian Levs, Welsh dollars. Best deals in town. Vince 07999 929927.

CD REWRITER. Put the chorus where YOU want it! £75. 01999 668 018

LOST; Three dozen fried eggs sellotaped to a photo of a fried egg. The only thing I've ever won. Reward offered for return. Box FE8942.

RSPCA What To Feed Your Kitten guide. Hardly used. Plus book "The Quick n' Easy Spicy Tex-Mex Roadkill Bible". Plus cat basket, bowl, blanket and collar. No longer required. £20. 01999 651 511

PETROL Lawnmover, vgc, moves up to 5 sq ft of lawn per hour. £01999 361877 tel 85.

A MAN AND A VAN Morrisson CD. Anything. Anytime. 01999 300 742

LOSE UP TO 4 STONE in a week by allowing me to hollow you out and use you as a canoe. 01999 462 477

THIS IS NOT the Bee Gees. How many more times? This is 01999 622 988.

XHRISTMAS tree with Xhristmas decorations. Plus tinned Eczema Pudding. £20. 01999 388 909

The Framley Examiner
"I sold my soul to the first devil who called in return for eight and twenty years of absolute power over the dominions of the earth. Thanks, Framley Examiner!"
Dr Basil Faustus, Codge

IT TAKES two people to be in a violent and abusive relationship. Come on! What are you waiting for? Tel 01999 476 620

NOT WITH A SPOON

2 UNWANTED TICKETS to St Icklebrick's School under tens piano recital. Might be interesting. Doubt it. Call Mr Hollyhock on 01999 482762.

PROFESSIONAL DOG GROOMER in your home. Call us if you find one – they're usually near the dog – and we will humanely remove him/her. 07999 140191

LARVAE LAMP in green, full of larvae and ova. Frightened it may hatch one day, hence 01999 327585. £20.

DONKEY JACKET. £10. Also Sancho Pancardigan. £5. 01999 831 322

TITLE DEEDS to Euston Square. £160. Northumberland Avenue. £140. Park Lane. £350. Call Vince on 07999 633276. No funny money.

SCRBBL. The exciting game of consonants. £6. 01999 509 366

LAURA ASHLEY jockstrap with tiebacks. 4" wide. 50" drop. Single quilt cover and pillow case to match. £45 the lot. 01999 665 801

JOHN CRAVEN'S new screwdriver. £10. 01999 733 944

DEPT OF AGRICULTURE Fisheries and Food magic painting book. £4. Call Bryan on 01999 234 255.

Name and Shame

Local celebrity Madeleine Up prepares for next week's Whoft fete.
PHOTOGRAPH BY QUEUES LIKELY

MISS – On Saturday 17th March, Whoft Hall hold their annual fete. If you know of anybody who isn't already involved with the fete, please call Petra in complete confidence on 01999 766 439.

There is a small cash reward for every name you give, with a free ride in the tombola for the person who gives the most, so speak up.

MORAG GRAGHOPPER,
Clap Street
Whoft

Radio Bias

MISS – If, to quote the Mayor (FE last week), Framley must shed off its "dusty image" and show itself to the world "grooving with the calypso beat" of our new times, perhaps the first place we should look is to listen to the local news reports on Zephyr AM – a station which seems to have no time at all for local area it supposedly serves.

I have conducted an independent survey of my own of over 28,000 news broadcasts from our local radio station, and, as anyone who wishes to inspect the files, charts and graphs in my new extension will soon see, my researches show that only a tiny proportion of airtime is being given to Framley,

To take a typical example from August 19th, 1998, we find that only 11 seconds of the four minute broadcast are taken up by the word "Framley", while the programme makers seem to dedicate yawning tracts of time to words like "France", "Prime Minister", "Thanks very much, Michael" and "Supertramp".

If I want to hear about exotic foreign lands and the habits of the whirling dervish, I can listen to the World Service. It's no wonder folks think Framley is behind the times.

I wonder if this bias against Framley has anything to do with the fact that Zephyr AM's new offices are based in faraway Fracton-on-Sea. What might this imply were regional government relocated to the nearest seaside area? We'd all be speaking candyfloss before we knew it, I'm sure!

S. W. CHUTLESS
8-10 Sunpat Avenue
Bodger-on-Badger

Wripple's legs above the rest

MISS – Although I never read The Framley Examiner, I would like to point out that last week's coverage of the "Wripple's Most Eligible Legs" contest left me seething.

Firstly, there was no mention of the excellent refreshments and sand served by Edna O'Clock at half time. These, as ever, were extraordinary.

Secondly, and it doesn't take a mathematician like Einstein to figure this out, was your inaccurate description of the event as 'A Blast'. This was inappropriate in this day and age

A more suitable description would have been 'Mexican', surely?

EVERARD PEPTALK
Framley Hospital Burns Unit
80 Krackerwheat Crescent
Framley, FM3 :-P

14 The Everlys Bellaire, FM8 9oP

MISS – I would like to express my displeasure in your decision to print my letter last week regarding the Bellaire Valves Sports and Social ex-employees evening.

The evening would have been a resounding success!, had the intimate event not attracted 5,000 attendees, of which 4994 present must have seen the letter in your paper.

Any notions of a 'good time being had by all' were soon quashed by the delivery into the hot, cramped hall of 10,000 inflatable pigeons, courtesy of your recent "Balloons for Bellaire" campaign.

Next time you print a letter by me, could you at least have the

DECENCY TO
Withhold the address.
Bellaire, FM8 9OP

Running the Marathon

MISS – I am intending to run the London Marathon this April and wondered if any of your readers would be willing and able to give me support in the form of sponsorship.

This is a worthy cause, and any money will be put towards helping this great race go ahead this year.

Donations, no matter how small, will be welcomed gladly and can be sent to:

Sir Michael Beresford
Managing Director
Flora Spreads and Marge
C/o London Marathon
Organising Committee
Shoes House
Charlotte Street
London WC2

They should of listened.

MISS – I of to agree with the title of your piece last week. They should of listened.

Ofd they listened, I'm sure they would of been here today.

DR ALCOCK BROWN
Roy Newby Villas
Molford

Grateful Thanks

MISS – May I take this opportunity, through your paper, to thank everyone who so generously gave raffle prizes for the Durbiton Choral Society's 40th Anniversary slap-up Iced Gem Supper and Fistfight.

However some of the gifts remain unclaimed, and we are keen to contact the holders of the following tickets:

478 Red (festive nut-free bubble bath selection), 479 Red (£479 Newby's Rakes Voucher) 139 Green (seven scented months in Barbados), 480 Red (permission to speak), 571 Blue (hand-crafted barbed wire dolly) and 000 green (chicken pox). Cheers, mate

GAVIM THORNALLEY
Durbiton Choral Society
St Eyot's

Goodbye

MISS – May I use the Framley Examiner to say goodbye to everyone in Sockford? I have now moved on to pastures new and although there are a lot of people I miss, none of them come from Sockford. Awful people. Simply awful. Ghastly, pissy, smallminded, deformed-looking people limping about the streets with their mouths open. Stupid peasents. I look forward to many years happily not ever coming back to Sockford.

FRANCINE MONOLITH
Sockford

YOUR STARS

with Captain Mitchell

The Framley Examiner's very own astrologer tells what the stars foresay

AERIES Mar 21-Apr 20
A pleasant wave from a stranger may indicate someone you already know acknowledging your presence on the street. Wave back. You will get a payrise and a hard-on.

SHENANIGANS Apr 21-May 20
With the ascent of balloons into the sky, this is a good week for domestic arguments. Beating up a spouse may or may not bring you into contact with a wealthy Hungarian. Recipes.

GIRAFFE May 21-Jun 20
You will be far too busy this week to finish crosswords or enjoy full-length orgasms. A plate of beans on toast means leopardskin is just around the corner. Touch me there.

BASTARD Jun 21-Jul 1938
Your child accepts a lift from a stranger and has to tolerate a plethora of celestial puppies. You will have stomach cramps, diarrhoea and a kite caught in your hair from 3pm Wednesday. Nothing new then.

CHLAMYDIA Jul 21-Aug 21
1978 Mini for sale, leather interior, wooden panelling, drinks cabinet, real fire, bakelite windscreen, desperate owner to pay loan shark what wants to kick the face off his otherwise head. £650.

LIKE A VIRGIN Aug 21-Aug 21
A chance meeting with the coastguard will have you staring at the top of a beautiful woman's knickers above the waistband of her jeans as she leans forward in a seat. You will never recover.

SH-BOOM Sep 21-Oct 20
You are not obliged to say anything, but anything you do say may be given in evidence against you.

PARAPLUIE Oct 21-Sep 20
You will suffer a myocardial infarction on Thursday and will spend two weeks recovering at a spa in Gstaad. You long-term prognosis involves a high protein diet and no strenuous exercise. Resign.

CHIGLEY Nov 21+Dec 20
Xmas is rubbish and will treat you like a baby treats its nappy. Buy your family perishable presents long in advance of the festive season – it's the only way they'll ever learn.

BUTTER Dec 21-Jan 200
A man in a raincoat augurs bad weather. Two and two is still four, but three and two throws up not five but a mysterious imaginary number expressed using the colour orange. Go figure.

TURINBRAKES Jan 21-Feb 31
If you want the spotlight, steal it. The local theatre will never miss it, and besides, they're subsidised by the council, so it's morally yours and you'll end up paying for it one way or another anyway.

HALFORDS Feb 20-Mar 21
Try not to be influenced by the opinions of horoscopers, since their powers of perception are overshadowed by their capacity to lie shamelessly about your coming week. I get paid today.

Next week: Captain Mitchell's Gardening Corner returns.

Captain Mitchell's columns are syndicated worldwide by United Independent Media Inc. www.advice_gardening_horoscopes_diy.tr.net

CHAMPAGNE RELAXED MASSAGE

DIFFERENT GIRLS DAILY
(SAME CHAMPAGNE)
£30-£60
Discreet entrance please
08999 654 657

GIRL NEXT DOOR
08999 740 5 - -
01 His fence is too high
02 Does he have to play his music all night?
03 That man keeps looking at me...

EXPLICIT REGIONAL ACTION
Call 08999 222 7 plus

CALL REAL NUMBERS NOW!
01 YORKSHIRE SHUTUP
02 CORNISH STARE
03 ESSEX TWANG
04 LONDON EYE
05 HIGHLAND CLEARANCES

Family enter her exam

Mica Robinson who done an exam.
PHOTOGRAPH BY ALAN FERRETY-HEXMIME

by K. T. Blirdsnest

AN EIGHTEEN-EAR OLD student from Molford has come up with a controversial way of sitting her AS-levels this coming summer.

18-year old Mica Robinson, a year [what?] student from Robot Oak Secondary School, has sub-contracted her three English AS-levels to her mother, father and brother, much to the heated foreheads of the school governors. "Not bloody on," is all one could say after an extraordinary meeting at the school last Thursday (which was odd, becaue I know him and he's normally more articulate than that.)

EXTRA MEN HERE, FAMILY!

IThe school has put Mica on a written warning, warning her that she is in breach of exam board and school regulations if her exams are done by proxy.

But Mica says she is standing firm. "The school is behaving like a closed shop," she said, "and it's about time they opened up the exam-sitting market to competition. Why shouldn't I have more choice in how I do my AS-levels?"

Mica's father, Derek Robinson, CEO or International Robinson, a company that specialises in sitting exams, said that he won the contract square on the basis of a very competitive tender.

"Mica raisedn the money for this herself, by selling shares in her revision notes to her friends. I'm very proud of my daughter, and, just as I thought, there is a market for this stuff. I might float her on the stock market next year, " he.

FETE "A REAL HYMN MIXER"

A ROW BETWEEN two factions of the St Cottager's Church Choir threatened to ruin their summer fete last weekend.

The choir split into three groups, all singing different hymns and competing for volume. The tombola was taken over by paramilitaries, and several breakaway Win A Goldfish stalls sprung up in the graveyard. A state of emergency was declared, and there was a 4pm curfew.

On Other Pages

set by 'Invictus'

News in Brief

"MY AXE FELT NEARER HIM"

A doctor's receptionist from Whoft is to be tried for murder for trying to murder her husband with an axe. Jenny Blamph, 35, is said to have attacked husband Kenneth whilst he was on business in Spain but she was at home.

Framley police say that, despite her massive error of judgement about the distance between herself and her victim, and even though he survived the assualt, Mrs Blamph is pleading guilty to the fatal attack.

THEY RELAX, MAN, I'M FREE

A dangerous and violent armed robber on the run from Chutney Prison has escaped police custody for the third time. Stigg Unt, 48, slipped unnoticed from Molford Police Station on Friday night after relaxing the two officers who were interviewing him,

"He offered us tea and Dundee cake, and read us a bedtime story," said an anonymous policeman, "and when the room cleared of pipe smoke, he was gone." Police are warning the public.

FIREMAN EXTREMELY "AH!"

Grown firefighters were said to be cooing and ooing at a Sockford gallery at the weekend. Framley Fire & Rescue laid on an exhibition of all the cats freed from trees in the last year.

Cries of "ah!" and the sight of hardened firemen moved to tears could be heard all weekend, say organisers. The animals were humanely destroyed afterwards and made into a pie.

Year menhir met a flex

LOCAL HISTORIAN Sir Cocoa Wufflemere is all of a tizz about the famous Framley Stones, Britain's oldest earthwork.

One of the circle of standing stones, he says, has been "plugged in." Mayor D'Ainty was challenged by Sir Cocoa at a general meeting this week in chamber.

"It's a lava lamp," said the mayor, "It's been plugged in since 1966, but no-one knows where the switch is."

Taxi female "hen merry"

35-YEAR OLD MARIA de Rea of Top Row Framley, is suing her best friend's hen party for getting her drunk. Ms de Rea was arrested for being drunk and disorderly last Saturday when she vomited up a grand night out all over the back of a minicab.

"The party should have come with a big health warning on the outside," she told reporters recently. The hen party, fourteen of Ms de Rea's best friends, are contesting the action.

EDUCATION! EDUCATION! EDUCATION!

FREE! **THE MARILYN EXAM**

Do you know who Norma Jean Baker became?

Do you know who married Joe Miller and Arthur DiMaggio?

Do you know who died of an overdose of Nembutal and chloral hydrate in 1962?

If you know the answer to any of these is 'Marilyn Monroe', then it's time you sat the MARILYN EXAM.

You answer 150 questions similar to thsoe above ABSOLUTELY FREE and, if you're successful, will be presented with a FREE certificate qualifying you as a MARILYN expert. All you have to pay is £450 to pass the exam.

WHY DELAY? WHY TODAY?

International and Global Learning Institue Centeal Faculty University School plc
PO BOX 07734, Framley, FR99 8HT

SEND NO MONEY NOW!*
*please enclose deposit of £300 make cheques payable to Vince Previous Ltd

**Arrested?
Injured?
Gone on holiday by mistake?**
Don't panic! Call...
**BEASTLEIGH,
MUDD & OOMSKAH**
Solicitors & Commissioners
for Oaths　01999 789899

25th ANNIVERSARY COLLECTOR'S HISTORIC COVER!

THE FRAMLEY EXAMINER

FRAMLEY'S TRADITIONAL FAVOURITE SINCE 1978

FRIDAY, JUNE 11th, 1981　　　　　　　　PRICE 12p

Investigations into mayor's wrongdoings become more and more and more and more

DAINTYGATE DRAGS ON

' And then I woke up and it was all a dream , CLAIMS MAYOR

by CHALLENGER PUTNEY

YET MORE ALLEGATIONS of gross misconduct came to light yesterday as a Council select committee continued grilling a yawning His Worship the Mayor of Framley, Cllr. William D'Ainty on day six of what has been dubbed 'Daintygate' by the headline up there.

At the close of play, Mayor D'Ainty took questions from the witness stand where he is living while suspended from mayoral duties. He explained to a reporters that he couldn't understand any of the charges made against him as he can only speak Portuguese and look! what's that over there? When the confused journalist turned back round two seconds later, it was discovered that D'Ainty had exited the courtroom and he is now believed to be on holiday.

MAYOR NOT GUILTY

The twelve new accusations – which I see in my notes that I have decided to call *The Dainty Dozen* – date back to the time that the popular leader first took office in 1973 and. include:

● the running of an unlicensed toffee apple stall at various civic occasions

● forcing work experience trainees to babysit his Froggy-went-a-wooing paperweight

● renting the gaps between the white lines in the middle of the road as premium advertising space

and many, many more!

INNOCENT MAYOR

D'Ainty's stubborn defence against the allegations – that "and then I woke up and it was all a dream" – has gone down well with the carefully assembled jury of his peers and relatives, though the court remains adamant that he will not be able to call his dog as a witness.

Only the day before yesterday, evidence given by a human pyramid of council staff requested by Mayor D'Ainty had to be discounted under legal "ringer" rules when it was discovered that several of the supporting witnesses at the bottom of the pile were trained acrobats and not council staff at all.

Concerns were expressed at the time that the case might collapse as quickly as the witness stand had done, but the prosecution appears to be rallying and local bookmakers Billy Turps are offering good odds that D'Ainty will be found "guilty of everything" and beheaded before the week is out.

Mayor D'Ainty photographed outside Newby's Independent Court in Molford on the first day of the investigation.
PHOTOGRAPH BY CHIRAC TOWNHOUSE

Celebrate the wedding of the year with the gift they'll remember...

There's no better way to celebrate the wedding of the year than with a Benton No.9 cigarette...

Professor Erno Rubik has personally designed this linking pair of mind bending puzzle fags in honour of the wedding of our future King. Will you be able to solve them and break the union apart?

SOUVENIR CHARLES & DIANA COMMEMORATIVE RUBIK'S FAGS
From BENTON'S TOBACCO Ltd

...lung cancer!

THE FRAMLEY PAGODA PRODLY PRESENTS

An evening's entertainment
to commemorate the marriage of
The Prince of Charles to a lady (Diana)
includes an impression of Frank Spencer and sandwiches.

JULY 30th 1981　Tickets £2　Box Office 675 731

**WHAT'S BLACK AND WHITE AND BLUE AND BLUE AND RE(A)D ALL OVER THE FRAMLEY AREA SINCE 1978?
WHY, IT'S THE FRAMLEY EXAMINER, FRAMLEY'S TRADITIONAL FAVOURITE SINCE 1978, OF COURSE!**
To mark the occasion, why not choose any of four historic best-selling replica front pages from The Framley Examiner's 25 glorious years of real front pages!
Collect all FOUR souvenir covers and be in with a chance of winning a bag of kittens – full details on page 46...

Parish life threatened

A SHARP RISE in the price of Gestetner fluid, ordered by the committee of OGEC (The Organisation of Gestetner Fluid Exporting Countries) is threatening parish life in St Eyots.

Since the cost of pale purple printer's ink went up to $45 (forty-five dollars) a barrel (a barrel), publicising local events has become prohibitively expensive, leading to several coffee mornings going unannounced, and many rotas for supervision of the Under 12s cricket team staying firmly on Stephen's desk.

Representatives of community groups have warned that while the crisis continues, newsletters will contunue to be expressed in tapestry form or inscribed by hand onto grains of rice.

ANNOUNCEMENT

THE HORSE AND FURTHER HORSE
Public House

would like to announce that its piano is now LOCKED on police advice

The Horse & Further Horse, Leonard Maltings, Wripple

Psssssst! Ladies!

NEVER HAD AN ORGASM?

...DON'T DESPAIR!

We will bring our specially adapted Land Rover round to your house and you will soon be in the throes of your first climax. *You'll be the talk of the neighbourhood!*

Discretion guaranteed and photos available.

Call Nigel at Functioning Women for a quote. 01999 820838 10am-5pm.

CAR / BOOT SALE

EVERY SATURDAY
AT MULLARD'S MOUND
(WHOTTEN PLODNEY)

The biggest selection of footwear and second-hand cars anywhere in the world probably

Undercover available
(includes fake moustache)

Public Entry £2 per car til 8am. £1 thereafter. 50p round the back.
EVERYONE WILCOME

01999 327230

Delight for winner of prize for design of sign on road

by JESUS CHIGLEY

IT WAS ALL SMILES this week for an award-winning nice little girl from St Eyot's.

Five-year old Jemima Flutterby won the Borough Council's 'Sign Of The Times' competition to design a new Get In Lane sign for the mini-roundabout on Beast Street.

The council organised the schools competition after the success of last year's 'SLW DWN 4 KIDZ' signs for the 20mph zone in Sockford. The signs, featuring a tortoise called Ant & Dec, have recently appeared in a national literacy campaign on the television set.

"This is a great way to make kids aware of road safety," said Highways Committee Vice Chairman Dan Flutterby, "we all agreed to that."

"When designing a sign that people will have to take in while driving past at speed, simplicity and clarity is key. We wanted something a child could understand, so who better to get in to do the job than my daughter Jemima, who won this competition fair and square."

PROBABLY AN IMPROVEMENT

Delighted Jemima told me how she'd come up with the judges' favourite idea. "That's a blue car and that's Daddy and it's sunny," she explained.

Drivers had complained that the previous sign, filtering traffic into eight separate lanes, was too confusing. The bright colours and lively design of the new version were felt by roadusers yesterday to be "probably an improvement, actually if you're already going this way, would you mind swapping cars?"

Last year's winner, nine-year old Derryn Leighey, has gone out to play.

Jemima Flutterby in front and slightly to the right of her prizewinning sign.   **PHOTOGRAPH BY ASTON VILLENEUVE**

Bellaire Hillock to be conquered

CLIMBERS from Chutney Mountaineering Club are set to become the first people ever to reach the summit of the Bellaire Hillock, just outside Princes Freshborough.

The hillock, which has dominated the landscape since the ice age, is estimated to be over 200 feet in height and may take as long as twenty minutes to climb, the team say.

VINYL BART
RECORDS CASSETTES & TAPES

SUMMER/AUTUMN/WINTER/CHRISTMAS/NEWYEAR/SPRING SALE NOW ON

Coldfeet
A Plank Of Wood To The Legs

as heard on *Children In Need* and *BBC South East News*

ONLY £10.99

Eno & Ono & Bono & the LSO
Music For Sealion Enclosures

Triple disc & frame

ONLY £15.99

The Sames
This Is Shit

* Bring this essential must-have album back within one week and weill swap it for the next one!

ONLY £11.99

The Fenn Street Preachers
If You Tolerate This Album, There Will Be Another One

ONLY £9.99

Jason Orange
Let Me Entertain You Instead

Reduced to clear

ONLY £5.99

Sixpac
Hang On, I Didní Cut Dis

* Includes new duet with Freddie Mercury

ONLY £14.99

David Beige
Beige Ladder

includes the hit *Beige Hello, Beige Goodbye*

ONLY £10.99

The Animatronic Brian Wilson
Sounds Like Pet Sounds

Recorded live at the Branston Pickle Hall

ONLY £12.99

SPECIAL OFFER!

Peter, Paul, John, George, Mary, Ringo, Mungo, Midge, Beaky, Tich, Nash, Young, Palmer & Dave
Onstage Fire Hazard

Collecting either of their hits together for the first, last and only time.

BOX SET! NOW £1.09

VINYL BART

38 Abbey Endings, Sockford, FM8 8LP
01999 0L1V3R Open all day except late and Wednesday

Cricketers play with themselves

by STAN RUBBISH

St Eyot's first team were the victims of a fixture foul-up on Saturday and ended up playing themselves, much to their own confusion.

The youthful side appeared perplexed as opening batsman and wicket-keeper, Carl Laurie, strode out to take his place behind the stumps. Out for no runs (b. Collins, st. Laurie) Laurie was replaced by second-choice wicket keeper, Tom Medocherty, who elected to concentrate more on his batting duties.

With the bat safely tucked under his arm, Medocherty caught each delivery in his clumsy gloves and notched up an impressive average of 78.4 runs per over, only eventually returning the ball to the bowlers after tearful pleas from the umpire.

St Eyot's struggle to work out who's doing what.
PHOTOGRAPH BY BINATONE STICKMAN

SAMWIDGES

A fine tea of ham sandwiches, egg sandwiches, ham & egg sandwiches, swan & cucumber sandwiches, cake sandwiches and a nice cup of tea sandwiches and a nice cup of tea was enjoyed by the St Eyot's players followed by a second similar tea which was rather less welcome.

Resuming at 15-45, spin bowler Ryan Lush vomited beaks all over the crease and Club Captain Jeremy Bluebeard's was forced to declare: "Judas H. Corbett! That's more than plenty. What the hell happens next?"

HAPPENS NEXT?

League officials called in yesterday to clear the pitch in time for next week's fixture told the increasingly desperate team that they still couldn't go home until either they beat themselves or were themselves beaten by themselves.

Anyone with any suggestions on resolving this situation is requested to telephone Jeremy on 07999 941077. Please do call, in absolute confidence.

(If you're the sort of person who'd normally tear out this headline and pin it to your cricket team noticeboard, you may be interested to learn that a 3' x 4' deluxe clipping is available from the Framley Examiner. Simply send a cheque for £15 to Damiun Clavalier, c/o the usual address, and remember to mark your envelope "Loathsome Tedious Cricketing Wag".)

NEXT WEEK IN YOUR GREAT VALUE
The Framley Examiner

BIG PRIZE COMPETITION

WIN CRAB PASTE SANDWICHES FOR YOUR SCHOOL

FREE COMPUTER GAME FOR EVERY READER!

YOU ARE IN ROY NEWBY'S MANSION. EXITS ARE NORTH AND EAST. YOU CAN SEE A BILLIARD TABLE.

> TAKE BILLIARD TABLE

SORRY, I DO NOT UNDERSTAND TAKE

ROY SITS DOWN AND STARTS SINGING ABOUT RAKES.

SHOELACES
BUY ONE... GET ONE FREE!

IN NOMINE DOMINO

Wripple dominoes player, Jim "Knock-Knock" Davison, is pictured here preparing to return his sponsored Bentley to Eggs & Co, the car showroom whom he claims had leant him the car as a promotional gimmick for the past domino season.

"As far as we're concerned, Mr Davison stole the vehicle. A test drive does not last six months," complained Alfred Eggs, spokesSales Manager for the family-run dealership. "We also understand that there may be some damage to the paintwork and the matter is now in the hands of our legal department."

New stadium improvements approved

Little Godley Wanderers AFC have received planning permission to build a network of "cheap hotel-style chambers" underneath their Ordinary Road stadium

but Chairman of the Unihomme League side and military leader of the village, Cllr Haris Paris, is yet to disclose the primary function of the 62 starkly-designed 10'x8' cells.

Rumours that the entire Little Godley squad will be invited to a correctional training camp if they fail to achieve seven consecutive promotions to the FA Premier League remain unconfirmed by former Wanderers Player of the Season, Ian Stanford, who defected to Whoft during a pre-season tour this summer.

In their final friendly match before the start of the season, Little Godley won 1-0 against Wripple Anthemic. The goal came from Ned Blungalow in the thirteenth minute and Anthemic's mascot, Billy Goat Gruff, who has been found guilty of adultery by a quorom of Little Godley scholars, was led to the centre-circle at half time and shot through the head of his costume.

Sockford Lad Wins Shop Prize

A trainee shoplifter from Sockford has taken first place in a regional competition.

Durwayne Punch, 19, won the award in the Junior Shelf Clearer category of the event, organised by the Guild of Shoplifters, with a record time of three minutes thirty two seconds. Durwayne goes on to compete in the national final at Harvey Nichols in Leeds.

A DAY IN THE SPORTING LIFE

This week, we spend a day with the life of Whoft's round-the-world cyclist Susan Milliniller.

PHOTOGRAPH BY GENOME ACGTCGGCG

"**I wake up at 6.45 every morning, and wash my tent, before preparing breakfast. It's vitally important to start the day with a good, filling meal to give me energy for the long bicycling ahead.**

I begin by cutting up some shallots and apples and frying them in a little oil – sunflower or 3M usually. I add raisins and cardomom seeds and a couple of plums, before mixing in 600g of oats, a box of bran flakes and a quart of semi-skimmed custard.

Bringing the mixture to the boil, I stir in twelve rashers of bacon and a family pack of Pepperami mini cheddars, leaving the whole lot to simmer while I chop some eggs and white pudding. The pan is usually quite full by now, so I reduce it down for half an hour or so before throwing in half a packet of Sugar Puffs and a cowboy hat full of duck stock.

After an hour or two, the meal is ready. I serve it in a tureen and garnish with mushrooms, beans and a fried slice, then I go to bed."

Susan Milliliner's Round The World cycle tour began at Whoft Cycle Club in June 1994. She reached Sockford last Tuesday.

TOO GOOD FOR FRAMLEY COMMUNITY AWARDS

by BEAKY COXWAIN

THE INFLATABLE-HEARTED stars of the local community were honoured last Wednesday at the annual *Kiss Framley Better Awards*, making anyone who might possibly have stolen three Cadbury's Crème Eggs from the Spar then denied it and whose mother might have taken legal action against the shop owner for false accusation of theft when they were 8 feel very ashamed.

Local heroes, brave heroes and plain ordinary heroes alike mingled with themselves on an evening of movement and tears. The annual guilt-inducing ceremony was this year held at the Sockford Hall of Mirror Halls where non-award winners were invited to contemplate the worthy lives that they previously thought that they had lived.

TATTY

Mrs Marmoset Baylon, chairman of the judging panel, who hosted the evening, was apparently moved to phlegm by every prize-winning sob story. "This makes all of my problems seem hopeless," she choked into a rapidly disintegrating tatty pink tissue.

CARE IN THE COMMUNITY: Roy Newby presents the awards.
PHOTOGRAPH BY POWDERKEG EVANS

The panel comprised Mrs Baylon, Ianbeale Steeplecocque, MP for Framley North East, local TV celebrity Wincey Willlis, and rake magnate Roy Newby. The regular place of Framley Examiner columnist Odgar Cushion was taken by his nephew Odnald, giving psychic-channelled voice to the voting preference of his late uncle. The awards were sponsored by Molfords of Newby again sponsored the awards of Molford.wby's.

BRAVE HERO WINNER

ADROCK PULPIT, who is 13 and lives in Little Godley, diagnosed himself with an ME-related sleeping disorder two years ago and has remained in and around his bedroom ever since.

Supportive parents, Mr & Beverly, are intensely proud of their only child's advanced diagnostic skills and hope that he might one day train to become a fully-qualified doctor retired early on grounds of ill health.

Adrock was unable to attend the ceremony himself, as he has to play on his X-box for at least 15 hours per day to stay awake. The prize money would go towards the cost of fish fingers and the green Sunny Delight that a specialist at Adrock's local bedroom has told his mum and dad he'd definitely die without.

LOCAL HERO WINNER

UKULELE BENNETT has devoted most of her spare time to working with local graffiti artists on the Dungeon estate in Batley since taking voluntary redundancy in 1976.

Ms Bennett, 39, has helped troubled youngsters to produce eye-catching spray paint tags and "urban landscapes" on many walls throughout Batley. A significant proportion of Ukulele's protégés have cunningly evaded court appearances under her tutelage.

The collective's latest work – which depicts Roy Newby reading the *Radio Times* whilst sitting on the toilet like Whistler's mother – can be seen sprayed onto Newby's formerly silver Rolls Royce which was left in an unlit parking area during last Wednesday's ceremony.

Autumn is her,e

By KATY BLIRDSNEST

It was a letter sent to the letters page of the Framley Examiner that got me sent on this mission by our editor after he'd started thinking about it!

Every year a Mr Stiltskin of Wripple traditionally writes to the paper informing us that he has spotted the first snowman of autumn! And every year the editor has traditionally decided to ignore his letters until now, possibly because August is traditionally a particularly slow time for news around here!

OSTLER'S WIPES

So with a notepad and a cameraman under the other arm, I arrived at Wripple Green and I couldn't literally believe my eyes when they saw what Mr Stiltskin was showing them! There, standing nonchalantly waiting for the snow to fall, was a fully-grown snowman, not twenty feet away from his nest.

Says Mr Stiltskin, "This happens every year! After six months of hibernation, the Early Snowman always returns to his nesting site on the Green! And if you can guess my name then you shall win your freedom!"

Before disconsolately sloping off, Robert told me that in olden times we'd know Autumn was on its way when we saw Old Mother Nature removing all of the leaves from the trees but it seems that she's a little bit too worried about global warming to sort the seasons out these days so now it's down to our old friend the Snowman to stir things up a bit!

I certainly learned a lot about snowmen and what they get up to that

A near-naked snowman stands by the nest what he built.
PHOTOGRAPH BY JARVIS ORRISS

KATIE'S SNOW FACTS

● **In olden times**, the first snowman of the season would be spotted by the Mayor on a beach near Fracton seafront, although it is not known whether it is the same snowman that we see first today!

● **Snowmen** became endangered after many of their eggs were stolen and sold at private auctions in the early 1970s, although today they are listed as an endangered species!

● **In 1912**, Frederick Deliusmith wrote a piece of classic classical music called *On Seeing the First Snowman of Autumn*, which would have gone straight in at number one on the pop charts if they'd had them then! Charts, not snowmen of course!

● **If you find a** snowman on your property then please call Framley Council on 01999 830761 who will send a Snowmanman round to look into the matter.

ORDINARY HERO WINNER

CHRIZ MUZ runs Duncan's Newsagent's in Rubmy and has done so for more than 35 years.

People of all ages are able to buy cigarettes, magazines and 40W pearl bayonet light bulbs at all hours of the opening hours and, along with his two staff, he has provided a never-changing standard of very basic newsagenting to the local community.

Chriz'z work pretty much meets the call of duty and includes early closing Thursdays. He also organizes the delivery of daily newspapers to the severely busy of the neighbourhood thus keeping young girls and boys on the streets on dark mornings.

Introducing

Experienced International Stylist

He says his name is Bert

Joining our team after seven weeks slumped in the corner by the magazines and eating all of our coffee beans

TRIAL OFFER: 95% off all *Cuts de Bert*

davide lounge
H A I R   D E S I G N S

The Baked Beanery, 26 Duchess of Duke Street, Framley 01999 755 870

Weekend will be full of music for budding musicians

by URSULA CLOYBEAM

FRACTON Festival of Music and Sound takes place from Friday, 19th This Month and St Darren's Hall and St Cheese-on-the-Stick's School, Fracton.

Described as "dedicated to music and sound or either," the organisers stress that no-one is too tone-deaf to attend.

On Friday evening, choir master Nick Food will lead a workshop dedicated to humming, which will end with an everyone-can-join-in rendition of *Mmm Mmm Mmm* by the Crash Text Dummies.

LONG LUNCH

Saturday sees more audience bullying, when pickled local soak Guy Folderol and an assembled scratch orchestra will play through his Concerto for Amateurs and Conductor, although his assistant will probably take the afternoon session, as banned driver Guy likes a long lunch.

The highlight of the weekend will be the appearance of the Framley Concert Orchestra on Sunday night at St Darren's. Their guest,

Christian folk duo Peter's Rock – Molford sisters Melissa and Crabtree Gland – will be performing floppily argued inspirational songs involving a close harmony (pictured).
PHOTOGRAPH BY TIVOLI GARDENS

composer Alwyn Tittershear, will conduct a programme of varied and no doubt barely listenable modern classics.

CLEVER

Opening with Iain Clever's *Farewell Overture*, the evening also includes Josephine Parallel's *The Music That Washed My Face Has Left Me Blind But Incredible No.4*, Tim Thinging's *Mellow Cello* and the premiere of Radiohead's *Go Away And Never Come Back*.

Internationally acclaimed Tittershear, who once told my sister that she played the harp like someone trying to pull a swan out of a cobweb, won an Emmy award last year for his score from the smash box-office comedy *Vice President Fuckwit*.

Entry is free, but participation is compulsory. Full details are available from Maureen, who lives in that foul bungalow with the fake well on the lawn.

The Sockford Amateur Operatic & Amateur Dramatic Society
PRODLY PRESENTS

HMS My Fair Lady

the rags-to-riches story of a professor of linguistics who takes a humble flower girl and turns her into a boat

FEATURES THE SONGS:

Why Can't A Woman Be More Like a Barge?

Get Me To The Docks On Time

I Could Have Sailed All Night

I've Grown Accustomed To Her Keel

On The Strait Where You Live

Limited Season **APRIL 4th – MAY 22nd**

 SOADS *Framley Pagoda*

Thanks to our sponsors... NEWBY'S of Molford The C.I.A. *A branch of the US Govt.* Benningford's STOOLS & TRESTLES

What's all this then?

The fourth annual Police Art show takes place at Framley Civic Centre next week.

Amongst the many exhibits submitted by the constables of today and the budding Constables of tomorrow will be PC Srichan Chaudhuri's inflatable chair made of breathalyser bags.

"The seat is over the limit," he explained, "but the rest of the chair tests negative."

Also being shown is Framley Desk Sergeant Joe Mouse's oil painting *Chummy Descending A Staircase* and DI Carrigan McRunch's *Bent Copper*, a 38ft copper statue of a policeman bending over to pick up a tramp.

What's On!

BROWNFRIARS COMMUNITY HALL, CHUTNEY PERCY

Graham Wantage's Bloody Tree. Musical by local playwright Jeremy Halt. The tuneful tale of how Graham Wantage's bloody tree overhangs Mr Halt's property by at least a foot and a half and keeps dropping its sodding apples through his cucumber frame. The cast features performers from the Chutney Mummers and a professional singer. Journalists and Framley Council Planning Department members are admitted free providing they promise to listen to all the words.

CLOXTED RIVERSIDE

Local artist Franklin Grout celebrates his 80th birthday with an exhibition of tapestries showing the heritage of the working river and a collection of watercolours of Biggie Smalls

TOLLEPHANT FOREST

Activity Day: "Living In The Woods". Build a wigwam; learn camoflage; hunt, dress, cook and eat a park ranger; Grade 4 Clarinet. Some gymnastics and double-entry, so not suitable for under 18s.

DURBITON BALLOON CENTRE

An exhibiton of shoes with margarine faces, and stuffed mice on bicycles by local balloon centre owner Harriet MacMillion. Admission free, children half price.

LESSBURY CORK EXCHANGE

Local band. The Davey Mattress Group. Presenting the opinions of Brian Sewell set to the music of The Eagles. Tues.

ST EYOT'S BILLIARD HALL

Posh film. With subtitles. Tuesday.

SOCKFORD MALTINGS

A Badly Double-Booked Evening Of Cajun Music and Dance and Swan Lake. Something for everyone in the main hall courtesy of the Sockford Zydeco Club and Ballet de Molford and Frances on the bookings desk who's new. Thursday.

GLIBLEY BOVRIL MUSEUM

"A Hearty Breakfast". 16mm film and exhibition, with actors in costume and original king-sized Bovril jar from 1948 Olympic opening ceremony. Final week. Queues expected. Book early and bring a sleeping bag or enormous, cosy glove.

WELSBY PARK, URLING

Dog walk. 6 miles. No dogs allowed.

ROCKNEY CARAVAN PARK

Open air film. *Plums of Dunkirk*, *The Morty Kitchen Story*. Unusual and boring bio-pic of the controversial tapdancer. Mon – Thursday.

THE PATTI BOULAYE ARTS CENTRE, WHOTTEN PLODNEY

A display of local crafts. Glass hats & crows, oak drulling, Spindle Nancy, mounted smells, Bollingley upside-downcraft, and an exhibition of traditional Fracton Valley handmade legs.

HOLLYWOODS
NIGHTCLUB
require a
CAPITAL L
for the sign above their front door

You will be a bright, flashing capital L with previous experience of working outdoors, available from 6pm until 2am every day (except Sundays). You will be working alongside an O and another L, and will enjoy being part of a team.

Salary is negotiable, based upon the manager's whim.

Although HOLLYWOODS NIGHTCLUB is an equal opportunities employer, we do need a capital L for this job: applications from lower case letters will be priority-downgraded, because of the costs involved in changing the name to HOILYWOODS.

Apply by letter (ie in person) to Max Hollywood, Hollywoods Nightclub, The Other Parade, Framley.

NO MONEY? NOT GOING OUT?

You're just what we've been looking for. If this sounds like it could be you then **call Janine** on 07999 746299 for a job that would suit you down to the ground.

JOE'S GARAGE is looking for a

MICHELIN MAN

You will be 9ft tall and made of concentric rings of inflatable white rubber. Your duties will include standing on the roof of the building and flapping slightly in the wind.

01999 285840

Framley Zoo

...where animals come to live!

IT ASSISTANT

Based in Framley Zoo
Salary: £12,815-12,820 per annum
(excludes life insurance)

This is an ideal opportunity to join the team at Framley Zoo. We require a young, enthusiastic assistant to look after the zoo's It. The It, a striking 13ft tall, seven-eyed hairy creature oozing a foamy substance and moaning, has eaten the past three assistants and is looking for a new friend.

The It is regularly fed dead lions and skiploads of turkey bowels, but occasionally eats staff, visitors, and the 3ft thick concrete walls of its secure compound. But on the whole, the It is a loving and friendly animal, who likes being tickled and chasing the giraffes.

Previous experience of Its is not necessary, but preferred. Any specialist knowledge of these terrifying creatures would be particularly welcome, since the zoo is having trouble controlling the It, which does not respond to tranquilliser darts or being set on fire.

For an informal discussion and compulsory application pack, please please please contact Alan Lawrence, Crisis Manager, Framley Zoo on 01999 696700 (on a telephone) or 3W673H (on an upside down calculator).

Would you like to earn extra pocket money to spend on the things you like?

We need 300 young boys and girls (aged 5 to 12) to play the parts of well-behaved pupils when Ofsted inspects our school in November. The children will 'work' every day for two weeks, during normal school hours. School dinners will be provided, and no learning will be expected.

If you would like to help restore our place in the league tables, contact Jessica Flynn, Headmistress, Robert Mapplethorpe School, Church Lane, Sockford in absolute secrecy. Our Ref: FE0628.

SAMARITAN INSURANCE requires two sympathetic listeners to counsel distressed and sometimes suicidal callers, before selling them costly life insurance.

Our revolutionary sales technique combines techniques from psychotherapy, family counselling, pressure sales and basic blackmail.

Every call will be a new challenge... The recently bereaved mother whose precious son died while playing the drums... The middle-aged man who's lost his wife, his job, his house and one of his socks... The depressed teenage vegetarian who wants to kill herself because she accidentally trod on a sausage...

Could you listen to their problems? Could you talk them down from the ledge of a high building? Could you sell them a competitive package of life insurance guaranteed to make you £££s in commission?

If you're ambitious, target-led and have a persuasive telephone manner, we'd like to hear from you.

Kelly Vinton, HR Personnel Person,
Samaritan Insurance,
138d Thumpton Parade (above Lovely Boy Kebab)

The Framley Examiner
Framley's Traditional Favourite Since 1978

SEN OR REPORTER

The Framley Examiner Framleys' Traditional FavouRite since 1978 is lookinf for a Senior Reportre. You willbe a traind news journalist with a apettite for workand desire to be part f a team where quality wrting matters.

You will you'll have a sharp new ssense and a fresh ideas. and the ability to focus on issue that hold the interets of the Framley Examine'rs 4,800 – 115,200,000* readers hip.

L'Examinateur Frambois, le favori traditionel de Frambois depuis 1978, cherche un reporter aîné. Vous serez un journaliste formé, avec le goût pour travailler dur, et le pom-pom-pom d'être un co-équipier.

Rien ne vous échapperez commes nouvelles, et vous serez plein des idées. Aussi, vous pouverez se concentrer sur les choses plus interessants pour le nombre de lecteurs d'Examinateur Frambois (de 4,800 à 115,200,000, on ne saura jamais – c'est la vie.)

The Editor,
The Framley Examiner,
Unit 149b East Cossett Industrial Estate,
Parkfields Bypass,
Framley,
FM1 6LH.

* Every copy of The Framley Examiner is read by 24,000 people

---

SDA OPERATOR

An SDA op, familiar with ISO/681 and PROCOL to 414 (F) standard, is required to work EBS with two BRI-LON techs on a PDK-667 system (10.3.4 – 10.4.0). A good working knowledge of P-Tex systems architecture and T9 series winforms is essential, and 881-Xbase2 basics are preferred.

GCHQ is currently recruting cryptographers. Encoded in this advertisement are all the details you need to contact us.

ROBERTSON MONTEVIDEO SOLICITORS

Temporary full-time receptionist.

6-month appointment to cover long-term illness. Anyone that feels the need to entertain staff by swallowing 100 staples at once need not apply.

Get well soon, Beryl, from all at the office.

Robertson Montevideo
29, Ladies Leap
Whoft
01999 375982

£6.50/hour + holiday pay.

No experience, transport useful but not essential as money can be earned from home. If you can pay me this (cash in hand) then I will be happy to accept. Strictly no job offers.

Ring Dudley NOW on 01999 489235.

"So proud" are bereaved parents of local drug hero

by PIGSHIT NELSON

One of Sockford's most popular tourist attractions breathed its last last week when the lights finally went out on resident drug addict Mowbray Melton.

The county coroner, Dr Timothy Bateson, revealed that by the time that Mr Melton's body, 43, was discovered slumped in his (Melton's) bedsit, he (Melton?) had already succumbed to a fatal heroin overdose.

FOIL-LINED BAG

Mr Melton was a well-known figure in the local community and was often to be seen lurching from shop to shop on Sockford High Street, carrying a foil-lined Newby's carrier bag filled to bursting with the stolen items that he claimed helped to fund his messy drug habit.

As a mark of respect, Mowbray's dozens of screaming fans were allowed to attend a special ceremony hosted by former Zephyr AM legend Robbie Nougat, where the contents

The late Mr Mowbray in happier times.
PHOTO BY LEVIATHAN THE UNCONQUERED

of Melton's famous carrier bag were revealed. The 48 AAA batteries will be donated to Framley Museum, the ear-piercing voucher from Claire's Accessories and the toffee Revels will be auctioned.

TEASPOON MILLIONS

Mr Melton's funeral was held at the same church in which he had married Lady Rosanna Hosannason, the millionaire teaspoon factory heiress, just six weeks earlier. His

new wife and many of his close acquaintances took part in a 22-syringe salute, lining the route as the coffin was carried to its final resting place.

TEASPOON MILLIONS

The parents of the deceased, Ross and Sian, spoke to reporters rubbernecking at the lych-gate. "It's what he would have wanted," explained his father. "We'd always encouraged him to follow his heart, live his dream."

"We're so proud," added Sian, a local magistrate, "although perhaps if he hadn't gone through all that rehab last year then his system might have been better able to cope with the shedload of Class A smack he managed to inject in the weeks since his lucrative marriage. Mowbray described himself as a "reformed reformed junkie" and that's the most dangerous thing in the world. Apart from helium canisters on a bonfire."

Mowbray Melton leaves a wife, two children that he didn't know about and a pet Cairn terrier, H from Steps.

On other pages

Whoft man finds face of Turin Shroud in picture of Christ (p9)

PENSIONERS GO SURFING THE NET

Firemen battle to save Old Cake Court shortly after Thursday's lesson. *Inset.* Vector Balrog.
PHOTO BY RAINSFORD FISTFIGHT

By TAUNTON MISHAP

THE TENANTS at Old Cake Court in Molford have been taking their first no-holds-barred rides on the exciting internet with the assistance of adult learning tutor Vector Balrog.

Balrog is running the NewToTheNet scheme in which six computers are installed in a sheltered housing complex for a morning so residents can get to grips with the world wide neb.

Once the lightning session has been completed, the residents will be left a broken Commodore 64 so they can get familiarise themselves with an unplugged computer.

Balrog says the scheme so far has been a rawing success. "You're never too old to flash your BIOS or shebang your perlscript," I think he said.

3-times BEST IN SHOW CHAMPION!
CHAMPION BILLINGSGATE PASTRAMI JACKPOT

says...

"It's Amazing!!"

It's HER!E"

it's

FAIRHAM'S PETS

*Advertisement designed by Champion Billingsgate Pastrami Jackpot

SOCKFORD PARISH COUNCIL
COUNCIL MEETINGS FOR JULY 2003

at the Lodge House, Butterbean Manor Gardens at 8.00pm
TOPICS UNDER DISCUSSION:

July 2   ENVIRON HEALTH: Litter in Greme Way / Mr E. Ranley's drain outflow
July 9   PLANNING COMMITTEE: Mr E. Ranley's new gazebo and herring farm
July 16   ENVIRON. HEALTH: Mrs D. Ranley's loud aerobics, Mr E. Ranley's bassoon
July 22   PLANNING COMMITTEE: Ms T. Ranley's lawn sculpture (heavy balls)
July 23   LEISURE COMMITTEE: Mr E. Ranley's anti-aircraft gun / Drugs in sport
July 26   ENVIRON. HEALTH: Mrs D. Ranley's loud opinions on Michael Barrymore
July 28   PUBLIC DECENCY FORUM: Mr E. Ranley's jogging shorts
July 30   POSSE DEVELOPMENT COMMITTEE: Running the Ranleys out on a rail

ALL MEETINGS OF THE COUNCIL AND ITS COMMITTEES ARE OPEN TO THE PUBLIC AND AVAILABLE ON VIDEO AND DIFNEY DVD

Roundabout becoming more difficult to exit

MISS – I am writing to agree with the comments made in your letters page two months back (Examiner, somewhere) about the need for new traffic signals at the Squatter's Road roundabout.

I have been waiting in the right hand feeder lane for three and a half weeks now in the vain expectation of a filter light, and am beginning to lose hope. Supplies are short. Judging by my radiator gauge, I'm running perilously low on drinking water. I ate my last Malteser on Thursday, and finished the Express crossword weeks ago.

I am now going to place this letter in an empty jar of Wet Ones and toss it into the road. With luck and favourable traffic currents, it will reach you.

TERRY ZANZIBAR
Squatter's Road, Framley

The Squatter's Road roundabout (in the distance) is a popular.
PHOTOGRAPH BY MARILLION SLEEVE-DESIGN

That bus letter

MISS – On behalf of Degville Highwayman Buses Ltd, I would like to respond to your editorial column last week (Examiner, last week) which claimed that passengers were confused about the fare structure of our new Park And Ride scheme in Framley.

The structure is simple. An off-peak single fare from Whoft to Framley Bus Station costs £2.20, and the day return fare is only £4. At peak times the single ticket rises to £3, and the return fare to £147,000.

For more regular travellers in Outer Zones 2 to 6, (Inner Zone 9), it may prove cheaper over a long period of time (such as a pregnancy or term of community service) to purchase a Highwayman Stroller Pass for £17, and make up the difference with your credit card every time you travel (using the slot in the automatic driver's mouth) or by working some shifts in the bus depot kitchens.

Children under 5 travel free, except ugly ones, who must sit in the luggage racks at their own risk, covered by a denim sheet.

SUSAN SHUTTLECOX
Degville Highwayman Buses
King's Mustard

Raffle prizes

MISS – May I, through your pages, thank all those who donated raffle prizes for our annual Charity Fun Run?

I personally carried the tombola and prizes the whole length of the 18-mile race, and sold over eleven tickets to competitors of all ages and levels of fitness.

Would anyone (everyone) who has not collected their prize please contact me and take some of this stuff off my hands? I will be running past Tipton's at 4.

MAUREEN TALLYACHT
Urling Harriers

Taking a leaf(let) out of their book

MISS – I have just received a yellow leaflet from Framley Council through my letterbox reminding me to put my wheelie bin round the front of my house the night before the so-called "collection day".

Last week, I received four further leaflets: one reminding me that the sixteenth letter of the alphabet was "P", two explaining how the traction engine was invented, and one covered in crude drawings of men's parts that seemed to come direct from the Mayor's Office and have been done by hand.

On none of these so-called "leaflets" was there any indication that they had been printed on recycled paper. What is going through their minds at the Town Hall?

I imagine they will have a different attitude to conservation when every giant panda has been turned into soup, if that's what they want, and I wouldn't be surprised!

JOSHUA PUDSEY-BEAR,
E-mail address withheld this time.

Syndicated heretic

MISS – As a regular churchgoer, I find it disgusting that you give space to the modernist, guitar-stroking prattle of the Rev. Marcus Boyband ("Thought For The Week: My, What A Lot Of Traffic!", Examiner July 3).

That a supposed man of the cloth could speak of owning a caravenette, when the Bible clearly tell us "in the days of Jael, the highways were unoccupied, and the travellers walked through byways" (Judges 5:6) is little short of sickening.

You pay lipservice to the needs of Framley's religious community, but show little concern or understanding for them. I wonder what Our Lord Chris himself would have made of this article!

Dr M.C. ULTRAMAGNETIC
Wripple

Horrid display "not horrid"

MISS – In response to Mr Harbison's letter ("My Eyes! My Eyes!" Examiner, 3 July), may I point out that the Denegate Traders' Association had no say in the choice of theme for the window displays over carnival weekend – this was a decision left up to the traders themselves.

While accepting that Mr Harbison was upset by Millings' window, it is also worth remembering that there were at least two conventional Summer-themed displays for every more challenging diorama, and that the right to the free expression of individual opinions, however unfashionable, is a cornerstone of our civilised society.

The staff at Millings had put a great deal of effort into their window decorations and we have had several letters of congratulation regarding the display from not only Burma Railway veterans associations, but also several doo-wop groups and two highly respected representatives of the pornography industry, so nobody depicted seems to have been offended.

Perhaps it is time Mr Harbison took off his blinkers and opened his eyes again! Wishing him a speedy recovery.

ALISON O'BREZHNEV
Chairman, DTA,
Denegate, Framley

Teaching concern

MISS – I read with astonishment that Framley is to axe more teachers Haven't schools in the area suffered enough from these cost-cutting measures?

At the school where I teach, I am the only member of staff remaining. If any more staff cuts were to be ordered, it would mean my being sawn in half.

And I know which half they'd continue to employ! The unskilled (and cheaper) top half.

PETER HARDLY
P.E. Department
Bellford School, Chutney

Quotes of the Week

"Our record in one-day cricket this year speaks for itself, but unfortunately I realise this is of little comfort to the families of those who died, and I hope they will find it in their hearts to forgive us."

"I have no idea who authorised this barn dance"

"There is no such thing as 'a hospital'. Hence there can have been no closure. Thankyou, gentlemen, now get off the fairway."

"Hit me there. In the stomach. WIth that tree."

"We would warn anyone thinking of copying this stunt that it wasn't just against the law of the land, but also against the law of gravity."

"Grass houses cost less and are attractive to buy and cows"

"It is unfortunately impossible to get your shoes out of the shredder. I put them there for a reason."

"All in good time. First, let us boogie-woogie."

"This has been a great week to be British. Or a sealion."

Pied piper reaches the end of line

FRAMLEY'S LAST remaining Pied Piper will pipe his last next Thursday.

"Things won't be the same," I asked Harry Christmas Truman at his Sockford home today.

"There's not the enthusiasm for it these days," he wandered lonely, "and there are more effective forms of infant crowd control available, my dear."

Truman, 54, was stung by an attempt to upend him in 1999 when south London wigger DJ Mashed Fr4it, aka The Pied Rapper, started piping without a licence only yards from his marketplace piping spot.

Fr4it was later drowned by a committee of senior warlocks from the mysterious Wripple Vetivers cult in what some commentators still believe to

Mr Truman considers a future.
PHOTO BY TINA BAVEL

have been a crass record company publicity stunk.

The Honourable Companie of Criers and Pipers, the fading profession's union, issued a statement, faxing "Mr Truman's sterling efforts to gather children about him with a tune" had not gone unnoticed.

Three men are under arrest.

We're back!
Re-opened following legal action!

THE FRACTON TEA ROOMS

Home of the famous "irritable waitress"

YOU BOOK...
... WE COOK!

YOU DON'T TIP...
... WE THROW YOU INTO THE HARBOUR LASHED TO AN ANCHOR!

MARINE VIEWS!

OPEN 7 DAYS
01999 492008

THE WRIPPLE PLAYERS
Present
LADY...

LAST FEW DAYS! BOOK NOW!
636091

**FLAT HAIR?
DROPPED SOME TORN-UP PAPER?
BALLOON-FREE CEILING?**

Call
POLLARDS

Framley's leading suppliers of static electricity

01999 850 850

NEW £100,000 SIGNS EXPECTED TO BE BROKEN BY WEDNESDAY

Councillor Euan Stripes shares a joke with the new signs that will greet visitors to the region.
PHOTO BY RAINSFORD FISTFIGHT

By BUNCO BOOTH

FRAMLEY's new digital village signs were unveiled on Monday at a brief ceremony on the verge of the B108 near Sockford, at the turning for CHECK WHICH VILLAGE<.

Councillor Euan Stripes, who declared the flagship sign open by cutting a pair of scissors, told villagers that these state-of-the-art village name boards would take the Framley region into the 2000s.

The new signs contain a highly sophisticated computer, which digitally recognises passing traffic, and a loudspeaker which doesn't. The sign will greet each visitor to the village personally, with a prerecorded message; "Welcome to..." (sung by the Keith Smarm Singers) and the name of the village, read by Councillor Stripes.

The signs also have internet access, DVD recorders and dozens of delicate china ornaments along the top and are expected to be broken by Wednesday,

Retail heir kidnapped

by ADAM WRENT

ROY NEWBY JR, the heir to Roy Newby's Newby's Of Molford retail empire, has been kidnapped and is being held to ransom, The Framley Examiner (hello) can exclusively reveal.

Newby Jr, 31, was snatched from his Molford mansion on Thursday night. His disappearance lay unnoticed until the following morning, when it was light enough to see that the Roy-shaped lump in his bed was not a Roy at all, but a load of duvet.

At a hastily arranged presconference and salad buffet, Chief Constable Rupert Bone gave few details of the ransom demands but confirmed that they were not seeking anybody else in connection with the crime.

"We are in dialogue with Mr Newby Jr," said the high-ranking policeman, "and he has confirmed that he has kidnapped himself. He is only prepared to guarantee his safe return in return for a large sum of money, to be paid by his father."

Roy Newby Sr, and (inset) his son in his work clothes as "Roy", the much-loved clown mascot of NcNewby's burgers.
PHOTO BY RUSTY TAMBOURINE

Amidst rumours that the millionaire's son may be trying to embezzle huge amounts of his future fortune, I had two tuna and cucumber sandwiches and a slice of melon.

But a source close to the family said yesterday that Roy Jr was hoping his eponymous father would "cough up about £10m."

"He didn't want to have to go this far," the source went, "he'll be furious with himself about this. He's a vegetarian, and won't be able to face cutting off one of his own ears and sending it to his father in a jiffy box."

Bus Lane confused with bus lane

by JESUS CHIGLEY

A QUIET ROAD IN WRIPPLE is at the centre of a massive traffic controversy this week after it was turned into a bus lane by mistake.

Bus Lane, named in the 1750s after its popularity as a short cut for carriages and prostitutional hot spot, these days connects the Mildworth estate to the village green.

However, due to a planning blunder at the borough Highways Department, the vital route was recently covered in red tarmacadamf and bus lane markings, and cameras were installed.

174

In the first week of operation, 174 penalty notices for driving in the lane were automatically issued to Wripple drivers, causing rivers of blood to flow at the Town Hall.

"We are investigating the matter as fully as human beings possibly can," said Highways spokesman Mike Joyce. "And we hope to clarify the matter in the next eight months."

But this simply isn't good enough for some people.

"Twat," said resident Caitlin Beckman. "There's no other way in or out of the estate. Twat. I'm not paying £80 every time I use it. The big twat."

OTHERS

Others are not alone in being livid too. Two of the five cameras were assassinated over the weekend. One was found burnt out in a field near Chutney and the other was tarred and cornflaked and hanged from a lamp-post on the village green.

But the mayor stands by Mr Joyce and the Highways Department. Speaking on the phone from a bar in Tenerife, he told The Framley Examiner, "I know, I know. Isn't it terrible? I know. It's so expensive being a motorist these days, isn't it?"

Whoft dinner ladies ignored repeated safety warnings

(continued from page one)

stopped and questioned.

Ooh, Betty?

- Discreet service
- 24 Hour call-out
- BAFS accredited
- Free estimates
- No hourly rate
- Free bottle of coke or vegetable dish if delayed by more than 30min

01999 454 541

* your home may be at risk if you do not keep up repayments.

HOPELESS & SONS

Call us if you need things doing and stuff

01999 366561
37-43 Ginger Biscuit Street,
Yopping Olley, Nr Bellaire.

Are you thinking of starting a fight?

The Framley Mixers' and Troublemakers' Association is pleased to announce that it is holding a one day seminar

■ **Wednesday, March 17th at the Stapleton Centre in Codge**

The seminar will cover all aspects of how to start a fight, with an emphasis on time management and efficiency.

Discover how pigheadedness, surliness and plain not listening can save valuable seconds in turning a difference of opinion into a full blown pub car-park barney.

The seminar will commence at 10.00am and degenerate rapidly. Lunch and broken bits of wood will be provided.

To book a place call Sam or Aysha on 01999 754545 and state clearly your name and exactly what you're fucking looking at.

FMTA
you and whose army?

SOCKFORD POLICE

"Getting to know everyone"

DRUG DEALERS

Drug dealers are invited to contact Sockford Police for an informal chat. *Don't worry, you're not in any trouble!*

We are planning a sting operation in which we need to find substantial quantities of cocaine and a small quantity of marijuana in the boot of a well-known Mercedes. We're all right for weed at the moment (thanks to our south-facing window box), but we need to get our hands on £20k or so of finest quality charlie.

Interested parties should ring Det Roger Rabbit on 118 999.

Framley General Hopsital

STAFF NURSE
Full/part-time
We are hunting a enthusiastic person to join our overworked staff casualties department. Previous experience in bandaging up doctors would be a advantage.

CARE ASSISTANT
Flexible hours
No qualification or reference necessary, just a willingness to apply for this job.

THEATRE STAFF
Full-time
Assistant anaesthetists, scrub nurses, follow-spot operators, make-up artists and rehearsal pianists wanted.

X-RAY ASSISTANT
Part-time
We are looking for a see-through person whose skeleton is distinctly visible to all, to assist in experiments, demonstrations and fund-raising events.

JANET STREET PORTER
15hrs p/w
A night porter is required on a short-term contract to cover the hospital's genealogy wing on the corner of Janet Street.

DISTRICT NURSES
Part/part-time
Nurses from East Anglia, The West Country and The Dales wanted for their affectionate, lilting accents and old-fashioned cooking, and because they're probably cheaper and more grateful.

RESEARCHERS, ADULT SERVICES
Full-time
We are seeking two dedicated researchers to join the team working on the hospital's lottery-funded Facts Of Life project. You will be investigating the theory that sexual intercourse is important, and will be an open-minded couple.

SEND YOUR APPLICATION TO THE RIGHT BLOODY DEPARTMENT

DORIS & FREDS ORIGINAL CAFE

is looking for a

PIE AND CHIPS

to join our saveloys and fishcakes in the hot cabinet.

You will be a pie and chips, including an individual pie and a (small) portion of chips. You will have a swimming in gravy certificate (50m) and a sachet of brown source.

SHORTCRUSTS ONLY NO PUFFS

DORIS & FREDS ORIGINAL CAFE, 118 Meadowview, The Arnhem Centre, Framley 670929

LIVE-IN COUPLE
required for maintenance, cleaning and general upkeep. Wripple area. Impeccable references required. Must have minimum 2 years experience of living inside a 38-year old man and own wetsuit. No more timewasters. Contact Mrs Milburn on 01999 739237.

SINGER REQUIRED

Blonde, adequate voice, preferably with photogenic terminal disease. I will manage you to success (after you're dead).

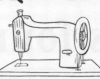

Send tape, passport photograph and lab sample marked with expected life expectancy to The Danny Bolero Talent Arena, Unit 7, Viaduct Way, Whoft.

AL QAEDA
(Whoft Cell)

is seeking an enthusiastic and experienced
SUICIDE BOMBER
for a post abroad (location tbc)
Salary: £26,000 rising to Martyrdom

You will, inshallah, be responsible for liaising with colleagues in a variety of continents, and will be thought of by your neighbours as the sort who keeps himself to himself. You will be neatly-presented and quietly spoken, with a respectable alibi, such as further education.

Previous martyrs need not apply.

FIRST CLASS JOB OPPORTUNITY

Travel the world as a stamp*.
27p OTE.

Self-adhesive for preference, must have silhouette of Queen tattooed on right ankle and perforated hair. Opportunities for promotion to £2.50 postal order. Applicants should not have been previously steamed off an old envelope.

*Mainland only.

RecruitMe Recruitment

SENIOR RECRUITMENT OFFICER

RecruitMe Recruitment is one of Framley's 35 busiest recruitment agencies.

As part of a recruitment drive, we are looking to recruit a Senior Recruitment Officer to manage a future recruitment drive to recruit four Junior Recruitment Officers, who will be in charge of day-to-day recruitment.

If you want to recruit the recruits that recruit the new recruits, we want to recruit you.

Apply: Rick Root, RecruitMe Recruitment, Recruitment House, 35-43 Labour Exchange, Framley FM3 4AZ.

FINTON WALDEMAR'S CIRCUS
is looking for NEW TALENT

Finton Waldemar's Circus is one of the biggest touring circuses in the country. As part of a hugely ambitious expansion plan, we are looking for the following acts:

- A one-legged tap dancer able to vomit fire
- A Dutch-speaking kangaroo with handler
- A giant clown with own shoes
- Anyone who can fly without the aid of wires or nets
- A three-headed woman who can sing all the parts of 'God Only Knows'
- Two superdwarfs, small enough to fit into a coconut
- A troupe of youngsters who look exactly like chess pieces
- A princess who has been asleep for 100 years

Call Roberto di Calamares di Scettivo de Caprio Waldemar on 07999 782944 for an application. Enclose a passport-sized photograph with your call (a photograph the size of a passport, not a photograph the size of a passport photograph – that would be a passport-photographed-sized photograph.)

EXPERIENCED BODYSHOP PERSONNEL.

We are looking for panel beaters, fitters, sprayers and preppers to help provide environmentally friendly cosmetic advice to some of our more ravaged clientele.

Contact Melgaret in first instance on 01999 399401.

GARDENER REQUIRED
Must be ever so sweaty

Apply: Janice Desire, Secret Cottage, Kiss Chase, Wripple.

Top Framley venue The Doig celebrates 10 glorious years
The Doig to close

by BOWERY TARPAULIN

TOP FRAMLEY music venue The Doig is to celebrate 10 years of great music by closing forever and never opening ever again.

The 10-year old nightspot, which has been the centre of Framley's music scene for almost a decade will stage one final concert on Friday to mark the historic milestone, with tickets going on sale £6.50 or £3.50 concessions providing proof of age or benefit claim is produced on request no readmission no casual shoes doors seven thirty for eight shots two for one until half nine.

FRY UP

Martyn Clwyns, Entertainment booker at The Doig, has high hopes for the grand closing party, and has arranged for local boyband "Fry Up" to perform as well as sandwiches.

"Fans can expect an unforgettable night to remember. The boys will be playing plenty of new material – *Three Hearts, Movin' On In, Dr Moon* – as well as old stuff like *Branston Pickle Polka* and *The Quasimodo Song.*"

The group, fresh from recent hit single *The Very Best of Alison Moyet* have made headlines all over the region. It's strange to think that only a year ago no-one had heard of Eggs, Toast, Howard, and Howie, and that they all have wooden legs – the source of the name "Fry Up".

Manager Simon Cress, owner of local property management firm Simon Cress Landholdings, kindly arranged for me to meet Toast from the band over a cream tea in the snug

Top regional boy band Fry Up have been booked to play the historic last night at the Doig.
PHOTOGRAPH BY JOHNNY H. JAZZ

of The Warm Zippy between rehearsals for the big night.

TOAST

Toast – real name Bacon Richards – is the self-styled leader of the band, and introduced me to the landlord of the Warm Zippy, Anthony Cloppurgh-Castle.

"There has been a pub on this site for over 400 years," he told me. "though the name The Warm Zippy only dates back as far as Charles II and derives, as you might have guessed, from the original landlord's wooden leg."

"We have an unfair reputation for being raided, and changes are being made," he explained as a team of policemen with dogs dragged two

half-naked men in bagpipe costumes from the upstairs room and into a waiting Black Maria.

And that's not all! Ashtrays are now emptied at least once a month to avoid obstructed views of the sport screens, there are plans to turn the saloon bar into an ice rink and, following the intervention of the council last month, Anthony assured me that the white wine at the bar is no longer watered down with gravy.

"We're a family pub," he said.

PARTY

So raise a glass to The Warm Zippy, and celebrate over 400 years of The Doig! Fry Up's new single *Oooh Oh!* is out on Skillet Records in time for the 2006 World Cup.

Back to the 70s with the great flavour of Sauce

FANS of the sensational 70ies should take their platform haircuts along to the Sockford Pork Exchange on Monday, where classic rock hitmakers Cranberry Sauce are reforming for one night only as part of their six week national tour.

Cranberry Sauce reached number 8 in the charts in January 1974 with their debut album *The Humble Emu In Orbit.* After their memorable headline performance at Tanglewood in 1975, the band's career took a chemical nosedive, and they split up during a car accident two years later. Monday will be the first time the group have played together since, so probably won't be very good. Tickets are too expensive.

Controversy for play

DAVID COLLAR'S shocking play *The Annoying Mr Socks* was commissioned by the BBC in 1971 but never written, because the writer found it "nauseating and distasteful".

But the author's qualms haven't deterred Stephen O'Mc of the Molford Stage Co-Op, who will be directing a two-week run of *Socks* at The Sewerside Leisure Centre from Sunday.

"It would probably have been about incest," Stephen told me, "or tractors. We'll do both to make sure."

This will be the first time that the Leisure Centre's swimming pool has been used to stage a play that doesn't exist, but Stephen hopes it won't be the last.

"The deep end is, I think, the perfect setting for the work. But it might not be. We'll just have to see what happens and hope there aren't any scenes involving people throwing hairdriers at one another."

Band unveil new material

CHART BAND The Vimtones have been added to the line-up for this year's Molford Spectacular. A perennial festival fixture, having played the second stage every year since 1991, the band will doubtless have a crop of fresh tunes culled from their new "The Greatest Hits of The Vimtones" album to add to all the old favourites this year.

"We're doing it again, yes," lead singer Carl Kite told The Examiner.

For you to enjoy this week at the
THE DOIG

WEDNESDAY 16th

THE LOOSE OWLS
Nu-Whoft Rock

FIRE ENGINE
Featuring members of The Bob Octopus Group and The Dullards

DAIDO
Welsh tribute act

THURSDAY 17th

DAVID VAN DAY'S DESMOND DEKKER
contains original member

LLED ZEPLLLYN
Welsh tribute band

GRAND CLOSING PARTY
FRIDAY 18th

Top local boy group
FRYU-P
with support from
RAR3BIT
Welsh FryUp tribute band

Plus all the best in 90s Mormon techno 'til 2am

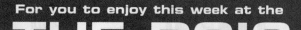
167 The Bizarres, Framley 01999 965543 www.doigg.co.uk

MODELS & EXTRA'S

WE ARE HOLDING INTERVIEWS AT THE
HONEYMOON MOTEL, MOLFORD

MAY13TH OCTOBER BETWEEN 9.00AM AND 500PM

FOR ONE DAY ONLY

NO EXPERIENCE NECESSARY DARLING

BRING YOUR OWN FLUFFER

For further information text PORN to 99909

without any furniture. The bastard. Codge 986542.

RANDY NEWMAN personalised birthday card, including specially composed song. "I Guess That's Why They Call It 49," "Once A Year We Talk," "Your Cake, My Cake, Everybody's Cake" etc. £4.99 up. 01999 491291 on or before weekdays after 6pm.

POTTY, £2 or £3.50 empty. 01999 203271 NC.

HAT, blue, size 5 3/4. It's nice, and I like it, but this bit on the rim is a bit, you know, sort of flashy or whatever. Oh, about £40 I think. Yes, it's 01999 42 – no, hang on, that's the office number – 418767.

GINGER NUTS

MEN'S bras, sizes 40AAA-48A. Gentle Men, 16 Market Parade, Godley.

MACLAREN F1 pram, navy blue check, vgc, with rain nappy, cosynose and Fat Teddy Pudding® headbag. Powered by quad cam 48-valve 6.1-litre BMW V12 nanny. The fastest production pram in the world. Some stains, hence £40. 01999 264267 eves.

MIRACLE HEADACHE PILLS!

Give the one you love a blistering headache and watch them sleep afterwards for up to 72 hours.

Llywylls Pharmacy
01999 346693

Private callers only. No canvassers or police.

A YEAR at a popular local girls' boarding school. Unwanted gift. 07999 356914 before Sep and ask for Jemma (year 10).

TINY TRONS™ digital christening outfit. Neon blue and white. £10. 01999 643233 after 1981.

POTHOLE available for hire. Stunning location on bleak Gloveswold hillside, running water everywhere, ideal for advanced hide-and-seek or keeping drinks cool in. £120/ week neg. Aretha or Jiggs 01999 781252.

PAIR OF STAG'S ANTLERS. Anyone know a decent plastic surgeon? Call me Molford 878892

SWEETCORN flavour baseball cap. Possibly unique. £5ono, 07999 761838.

ROWING MACHINE. Automatically starts domestic or public rows. With refills and four drums of argument fuel. £45ono. Chutney Le Basil 64315.

SONNY & CHER matching songlasses and deckchair. Unwelcome gift (frightened of Cher since I was a child) hence £1. Box FE8480.

SMOKING SERIOUSLY harms you and others around you. But not me. I feel invincible. FRAmley 6600

CIGARETTE CARDS, dozens of tins of tapioca, 23ft oil painting of Meg Ryan, many sound effects LPs, giant spoon made of KitKat foil, Evel Knievel memorabilia, two labradors (Getty and Britney), correspondence with the bassoonists in the Berlin Symphony Orchestra 1966-1989, matching his-n-hers caravan awnings, flight manuals for Reliant Robin and Reliant Rodney, much much much more. 01999 379013 and NO QUESTIONS.

Last year over
1,600
tons of adjustable spanners and marmalade were sold through
The Framley Examiner
classifieds.

DOUBLE BED with 1970 Double Diamond 'Double Top!' double duvet and built-in double oven, £210. 01999 541096.

DALEK, full size, great talking point and commanding babysitter. £250 after 6pm. 01999 487555 or nearest number.

BEATLES cigarette rolling papers. Each finest quality gummed sheet decorated with a photo of the fab four to be smoked in the order in which they died – Paul (1967), John (1980), George (2002) and The Drummer (2085). Pascal's Collectibles, Framley 468990 during office hours.

E-MAIL SHAPED food processor with many attachments. £35 hence 01999 259877 before long.

WEDGEWOOD TEAPOT with hand-sprayed naked lady design on side. £20. Box FE8521. WLTM friends.

WINMAU B.D.O.-standard tournament dartboard. Ear straps and eye-shield. £14. 01999 957381

JACK STRAW-SHAPED plastic turd. Brightens any family occasion or cabinet meeting. £4.50 Adrian Butterfly Collectables 01999 459868.

GIRL'S cupboard, £20. Contains the usual. Mr Hollyhock on 01999 623855.

RIDE-ON Brian Sewell on wheels. Handle on back to encourage walking. £10. 01999 4767178

RARE BIRDS EGGS available for private purchase. Muckhen, Spider Puffin, Grey Shrigg, Nutpecker, Loftcock, Big Tit, Yaffle, Gherkintail, Giant Auk (very big egg). Box FE8923 serious collectors please only.

FRED THE FLOURMAN shower cubicle. Three taps: hot, cold and self-raising. Sticky but quite nice. £85 buyer to collect. I have no phone.

BILL & BETJEMAN battery-operated talking salt and pepper set style alarm clock. "Come flubbalubs, and flub on Slough" and other memorable wake-up calls. Little Weed cup missing, hence £1.73. 01999 354205 no offers.

DAVID DICKINSON curtains. Make the twins dream the walls are being sick, hence £10 for quick sale. Maureen 01999 242458.

PLEASE BUY MY DOORBELL because it plays the whole of Tubular Bells when anyone presses the button and removing the batteries doesn't seem to change things. £275 or offers or anything or I'll pay you just take it away 01999 240947.

ANTWERP, 1923

COMPUTERS custom built. Entire systems from £4. Really good. Promise. How hard can it be? It's only wires. 01999 379 733

THIRTY FIVE MILLION air miles for only £700. Reluctant sale, but banned from flying after getting drunk and threatening to glass an air hostess while I was supposed to be landing the plane or something. 01999 358699.

SLIGHT FART SMELL yours for nothing if you can find and remove it from my kitchen. Paul mob 07999 597803.

McCLOUD

LARGE PICKLED ONION display cabinet good condition. With removable tweed jacket and certificate of authenticity. £110. Whoft 233432

NEST OF TABLES containing three mahogany Queen Anne eggs. Quick sale before they hatch. £280. Codge 323345

CHILD'S WOODEN BUILDING bollocks. Set of four. Help your child to spell the word – 'NUTS'. £2 Fram 789989

TOMORROW'S WORLD Award for Innovation. Full patent for E-Z Sting Wasp Attracting Carpets. 3-bed self-built house with constant buzzing noise. Will not separate. £offers. 01999 639 876

KARATE SUIT. Pinstripe. Double breasted. With tie and nunchuk cufflinks. Perfect for job interviews. £35. 01999 954522

HITACHI 25" colour. Good working order. Lavender. £140. 01999 880 900

"THE FELLOWSHIP OF The Sealed Skateboard". Molford Freaky Friday re-enactment society. Meets every Thursday (1976 Chapter) and Friday (2003 Chapter) in the Peterson Centre, Molford. All ages welcome. Tel 01999 744 325 for details.

GREENHOUSE. 8" x 2" x 8" x 2". Height: 2". £600. Buyer to be drunk, blind or really tiny. 01999 821 721

NAZI FRUIT, season's best, including Gruppenfruit, Blitzkurrants, Messerschmelons, Swatsumas. Call Sturmer and Sons Greengrocers, Little Godley. Tel 01999 499712

IF JANE from Classifieds spent less time boring the face off the girl next to her and playing pricktickler with the delivery drivers, she might find time to CHECK HER COPY once in a F=fcking while.

ARSEHOLE MAKE-UP. Cheek blushers, furry foundation, crab ladder wax. Bollingley's 01999 787834.

NEW TO THE BEAT?

Try the best in the area.

We offer the ultimate in police stress relief. Discreet massage. Ello Ello Ello, what's all this then? 01999 650010.

GOOD QUALITY armchair with two scatter cushions and great big boring husband, £60. 07999 784924.

MICROWAVE for sale, 23.6GHz. Looks lovely at night. £22 per metre. 01999 237912.

DINNER, steak and mushroom pie, frozen peas, boiled potatoes, gravy, salt, pepper, £4.50. First to see will tuck in. 01999 671483 6pm-7pm before next Friday (Best Before date of pie).

WEST HAM United memorabilia. Centre circle, back four and matchwinning save (all from 1994-5 season). £offers. Jerry on 01999 440 951

ROXY MUSIC'S EARS

YELLOW PAGES. Penguin edition of David Copperfield painstakingly coloured in with felt pen. 50p.

HISTORIC TURF. Mounted squares of turf, all certified authentic. Wembley, Wimbledon, Hanging Gardens of Babylon, The Lawn Where 25 Cromwell Street Used To Be. Pascal's Collectibles, Framley 468990.

CHILD'S EASEL. One side magnetic, with 7-year-old child attached firmly by orthodontic brace; other side blackboard, still usable. £15. 01999 852521

DOG KENNEL. Approx 85' long x 40' tall. Suit medium sized dog. £60. 01999 749 844. If dog answers, hang up.

COLLECTOR seeks Star Wars, Planet of The Apes, Action Men pre 1990, and Pokemon figures all based on himself. Best prices paid, using money with my face on. 01999 533 877

JACK-IN-THE-BOX Jack-on-the-Box. Your very own smiling clown on a spring who'll burst through the screen during Tonight With Trevor McDonald. £25. 01999 663 741

FORGET IT. It doesn't matter. 01999 530924.

NORDIC LEG SHAPER and instructional tapes. Two shapes (banana and triangle). Immaculate condition. Buyer to collect. Seller now housebound. £40. 01999 619874.

AMAZING
!

Upgrade your free as to a display ad

For ad little as

£1

NINTENDO GAMES

many to clear at top prices, incl

Snap · My Dad's Bigger Than Your Dad · Songs of Praise (Harry Secombe edition) · Counting Sheep · Germaine Greer's WWF Slamdown · KnitQuick II · Teach Your Parrot To Speak · Modern Problems · Lonely Planet (Italy) · Currency Converter Vice City · Laurel & Hardy

DUNN'S

Denegate, Framley. 01999 654122
Open 24 hours for second hand toys and shoes from Feb 1.

PASTA MAKER, with cutting attachments for spaghetti, linguine, tagliatelle and Nitin Sawnhey novelty shapes. £22. 01999 749 790

MAKE YOUR birthday go with a swing with a Hog Roast! We'll supply a whole pig and an automatic roasting machine. We also do weddings and children and midgets. Call the Blowout Party Company on 01999 562 319 for a brochure.

BAKED BEAN BAG. With removable cover. Although I wouldn't remove the cover going by the smell of it. £1. 01999 878799

MRS THATCHER The Board Game, £25. Board and counters complete, but Poll Tax riot gear and some Wets missing. 01999 571382.

AHOY THERE! Bathtime Beeper satellite navigation system for rubber ducks, soap and plug. £40. 01999 375 933

BILLY OCEAN'S "Devotional Emotion Potion" Body Lotion and tongue-shaped applicator. Unwanted gift £25. Also unwanted friend. £25. Yopney 737662.

SOFTWARE for sale, Norton AuntieVirus £10, Microsoft No £30, Adobe ChipShop £35, Gareth Gates XP £55. All boxed. 01999 204130.

VAGINAL MONOLOGUES. Alistair Cooke, Alan Bennett or Stanley Holloway. I will murmur them gently into your bits. Call Vince on 07999 764421.

PROCOM RIDING HAT with propellor and stablising fins. £8. Aerial showjumping video. £3. Quick sale due to imprisonment 01999 622 810.

ORBIT GUM

CALLAFORD Bantings. Obsley and Duff. 4 x 11. Jepsard armbells, gabs, and powls. Bristly nards, hence £14. 01999 359433

KETTNER EXERCISE MOTORBIKE. 0-60 in 12 secs. Minimal health benefits. £230. 01999 411231

PUNS, 3p each. Large, medium and pun-size! They're punderful! Punder and lightning! Hot crossed puns! Punnies from heaven! They're a pun in a million! You're the pun that I want! Pun nil to the Arsepunal! You're staring down the barrel of a pun! Feeling lucky, pun? 01999 987654 (no pun intended!!!)

VINEGAR

MINI WEIGHTLIFTING course. Build up muscle tone over the short distance between my front door and the boot of my car using two carefully calibrated Samsonite weights plus hand luggage. Course runs from 7.15 to 7.16am on 12 Aug 2004 followed by me going to Corfu. 01999 411699 for details.

HOT AIR BALLOON shaped like the lead singer from The Frank and Walters. Basket and anchors. Unwanted retirement gift. £offers. 01999 643774.

THE MOST DIFFICULT JIGSAW IN THE WORLD

is available for a limited time only from Blainhough Jigsaws of Thoxtoxeter.

This impressive handmade piece, a 58,000-piece puzzle made up of single pieces from 58,000 different jigsaws to which there is only ONE POSSIBLE SOLUTION makes an ideal pastime for anyone with up to 45 years to live, especially since it comes without an illustration of the finished thing.

POA. 01999 385553 at the usual time.

BLAINHOUGH JIGSAWS

At last missing boy is found again at last

by TAUNTON MISHAP

A SOCKFORD CHILD who sparked a Nationwide search when he disappeared in August 2001 has finally been discovered in an overgrown garden in Goa Way, just three streets away from where he was last seen, having lived wild for two years with a family of spacehoppers

5-year old Aaron Muecyth had gone missing in July 2001 during a barbecue party held at a neighbour's house. Explainers at the time explained that Aaron had been upset at his mother after she smacked the back of his legs for hiding minted lamb burgers and a bowl of tossed salad in a goldfish pond. The boy hadn't been seen since.

Framley Social Services Commandant Helen Fresh, who is caring for the boy while his mother calms down about the burgers, believes he had been living under his family's very, very, very noses all the time.

ADOPTED BY FREAKS

"It now seems that Aaron had been adopted by spacehoppers," she told

The missing boy (here with carer Helen Fresh) had been brought up by animals like a Mowgli. **PHOTO BY WOMBLES MINUET**

me. "He had been running wild with them in the local area, scavenging for scraps of food and scaring foxes or badgers. What are the ones with the stripes?"

Owner of the Goa Way property, Mr Nigel Reader, was shocked to find the filthy and underdeveloped boy bouncing ineffectively up and down the length of his back garden when he returned from having an affair with his secretary in North Wales. He immediately called the social surfaces.

DOCTORS ARE HOPEFUL THAT

Aaron is currently under observation at Framley General Hospital but doctors are hopeful that he might reach a fit state to return home at some point over the next fortnight.

During an entertaining operation to remove two callused growths from the child's forehead, Dr Torben Bumhammer warned watching reporters that Aaron might possibly never lose his residual orange glow. The surgeon also revealed that he was still displaying signs of feral aggression and that six nurses have already been bitten for refusing to ride him round and round the children's ward.

ARNHEM CENTRE IS RE-OPEN FOR THE BUSINESS

Customers are allowed to enjoy the Arnhem Centre once again. (Inset) A nervous Steeplecocque.
PHOTO BY SLACKJAW MUTTON

By BEAKY COXSWAIN

MP FOR FRAMLEY North East, Ianbeale Steeplecocque, re-opened the Arnhem Shopping Centre last Friday at the end of its enforced 3-week closure due to the sad murder of asking-for-it Curry's manager Alton Towels.

Mr Steeplecocque cut the "Police – Keep Clear" tape in an official ceremony attended by local dignitaries and schoolchildren.

Shoppers and shopkeepers alike were delighted by the re-opening if the ensuing mess in Poundmaster where I bought my lunch was anything to go by. Fears previously voiced by the MP that the date inside the sealed shopping centre might now be 21 days behind the rest of the town appear to be unfounded.

On other pages

Village plans accident black spot (p12)

Bus route outrage

Protesters protest their protest at the new bus route   **PHOTOGRAPH BY EWAN MEE**

By BOWERY TARPAULIN

BUS PASSENGERS FROM MOLFORD are up in their arms about changes to their beloved 77 bus route.

The 77, which starts at New Village Square and terminates at Framley Bus Station, is to be renumbered as the 77A from January, a decision which has caused outrage in Molford.

"I've been using the 77 for twenty years and it doesn't need changing," exploded a furious Harry Price, 77A. "We're going to fight this every step of the rest of the way."

"It's political correctness gone bad," said another angry resident wearing a YOU CAN KEEP YOUR 'A' t-shirt "and this is just the beginning – after all, 'A' is the first letter of Adolf Hitler. And we know

what he went and done."

CHILDREN'S

A statement from Local National, which operates the 77, said that the change was "moving forward to bring the route in line with current company enumeration policy" and represented "a fairer deal for customer choice and for our children's futures."

The company also stressed that the alteration to the 77 was only taken after wide consultation with focus groups, theatre workshops and the MoD.

Protesters have threatened to lay in the road or beat up a bus if Local National's controversial plan goes ahead. Community leaders are appealing for calm, and fifteen people last night held a candlelit vigil at the stop opposite the shops.

News In Brief

CIGARETTE OFFER

A Molford newsagent who was recently diagnosed with terminal lung cancer is offering free cigarettes to the first hundred customers to come through his door this week. Harry Accident, 53, told our reporter, "Everyone goes on about how cigarettes can give people cancer, I just thought it would make a nice change for someone with cancer to give people cigarettes."

PEDESTRIAN CAKE RABBIT

Framley's third annual Pedestrian Cake Rabbit will take place on the corner of Wig Street and the High Street on March 3rd. Last year's Rabbit made over £30,000 for local charities and created at least 10,000 permanent employment opportunities for passing pedestrians.

OLDEST RESIDENT

Molford's oldest resident, Huntley Teeth, died last week of the age of 103.

PUB CASH THEFT

Burglars intend to steal £3,500 cash from the Jolly Pocket Postman public house in Framley during the early hours of next Sunday morning.

because it's often left out of the fridge overnight and wanders over to the stove of its own accord". After his speech the councillor sat down on a rapturous applause and a vote of 'no confidence' was taken and confiscated.

Framley

Piano Cookery

WEST FRAMLEY BROWN TABLE. – More than 70 members and guests gathered to enjoy a delicious, home-cooked, two course piano recital by Winifred Harris-Hospital. The Rev. Karl Afternoon belched his rendition of John Farnham's hit single *'You're the Voice'* to a rousing reception and came fifth in the raffle. A DVD of the event is available for a limited period and contains a hidden extra feature, *"Informal and Friendly: A history of West Framley Brown Table in song."*

Snap, Flashbulb and Pop

FRAMLEY CAMERA CLUB. – Last week member's held a members colour slide competition. The invited judge was Sir Thomas Good, managing director of JJM Ltd. David Chang scored a perfect 10.0 for *Steaming Away*, a steam locomotive hauling the Andes mountain range through Latin America. 9.5 marks went to two slides from Melvyn Sshed, *Tuscany* and *I'm Bored*. Linda Minting was a privet hawk moth before being captured with an enormous piece of card and a pint glass. Third place went to Bernard Knibbs, with *It'll Never Happen*, his photograph of himself winning the competition, gaining 9.0 points. Mr Knibbs also proposed a picture of a vote of thanks and a round of applause for club chairman, Cliff Charman.

Minute is silence

ROYAL FRAMLEY REMARKABLES.– The RFR's annual Holly and Robin Roast was held last week. The chairman, Mr. Bert Levet opened proceedings by excusing himself and then asking the floor for a minute's silence while he sat down. A bottle of sherry was hidden and a straw hat was consumed. The following dates have been agreed for next year: May 10th.

TIDY UP AFTER YOUR PET

A NEW INITIATIVE to cut down on rubbish and general messiness is being implemented in parks around the Framley area. As well as the familiar brown-coloured chod bins for dog fouls, dark blue wastebins are being introduced to cope with the ever-growing amounts of dog litter, such as chewed slippers, broken frisbees and old bones found in the town centre. The public are advised that there is a fixed £50 penalty for any dog found not using the new bins.

PHOTO BY MAN LOW

Back In Time

FRAMLEY LADIES CLUB – In the absence of two regulars, Rhoda Finger and Enid Charmless, whom we hope are still alive, their place was taken by Mary List and the big bear from the raffle. Business being have been concluded, she introduced a very impressive guest speaker, Lyyn Spales, who gave a talk on "The Life Of A Typical Woman In Medeaval Framley", a subject of which many members and she herself appeared lamentably ignorant. Biscuits and coffee with skin on it.

Birthday Card

FRIENDSHIP CLUB. – The recent meeting was opened by Mr Couples and birthday greetings were sung to new member Mrs Pritchard in the mistaken belief that she wasn't made entirely from cardboard. Apologies for not being absent were offered by Mrs Windermere, whose irritable bowel it was agreed added to the distinct flavour of the evening. A single raffle ticket was sold to Mr Judason, who won the first prize of a dog's nose in a teapot.

Waste Collection

LEAF STREET – The 10-member 'D' Team from Framley Refuse Collection Services met in Leaf Street on Friday. The meeting was chaired by Don Mullally. The first item on the agenda was the emptying of the bins at 2, Leaf Street. Jack Wales proposed that the bins be emptied with immediate effect, and the chairman seconded the proposal. The motion was put to a vote, and carried

unanimously (with one abstention). A sub-committee of Deric Treadles, Roy Pepper and Gordon Surrowford was proposed to carry out the agreed work, seconded by Keith Bones, Barry McAllister and Bob "Slob" Hawkshaw. The sub-committee duly elected, they were despatched to carry out the work. Tea and beans were served, and the meeting was re-convened to discuss the second item on the agenda, emptying the bins at 4, Leaf Street.

St Eyots

75 Years Of

ST EYOTS ROTARY FELLOWS. – St. Eyots Rotary Fellows celebrated 75 years of getting on Mr. Cecil Finch's nerves this week with their annual charter dinner. A record attendance of over 50 members attended the event, which this year was held at a quarter to two in the morning in the back of Mr. Finch's Vauxhall Astra. Guests of honour were a crate of horse manure and an air raid siren. Tickets are still available.

Congratulations

D'ARBY & JOSIE. – Mrs Bonk presided at the meeting. Birthday wishes were extended to forty-five minutes and Jean's sponge was won by Mrs Toomey, who said she didn't normally have one in but she'd give it a go and see whether

her Eric got on with it. Meeting adjourned after collapse of human pyramid. Tizer and face paints.

Yearly Evening

WOMEN'S INSTITUTE. – Friends and relatives were invited to an annual soiree last week. A short talk on the work of the WI was delivered by Mrs WIcker while the audience chose to enjoy light refreshments instead. The guess the weight of the Mrs Lanford competition was won by a 16.5oz chocolate cake with icing and hundreds and thousands. An indoor firework was lit which met with an "oh" from Mrs Radcliffe's 13-year-old son Darren. It was suggested that if the guests had enjoyed their evening then they might like to stop taking the piss out of the WI members quite so much of the time.

Codge

20p Raised

CODGE MINORS. – The Codge Minors' Christmas Xmas Yuletide bazaar raised a record amount of money this week as regulars and new members bid for Ms. Audrey Flannelwash's traditional, clingfilm-wrapped orange squash cake. The cake, once again too wide for the main entrance, was this year manouevred into Codge School hall via an ingenious musical pulley system devised by me. The money raised is being put towards the cost of replacing the chairman's Doctor Who shoelaces.

Fun for All

COUNTRY FAYRE. – The main event of the calendar year of the Codge Infant School Association's calendar will take place tomorrow (tomorrow) between 2pm and the playing field and the school hall and 5pm. Events will include displays of country dancing (Nicaragua and Oman), as well as a performance by the under-7's motorcycle display squad followed by the under-7's paramedic team. The Junior School choir will be singing a barbecue, crockery smash, and beat the goalie. The Junior School choir will be singing. The Junior School choir will be more attractions for adults as well as for children.

Little Godley

Dates are Changed

VILLAGE OUTINGS – As many people are away on the proposed date, the trip to St Eyot's Castle on Tuesday, 16th April has been changed to Thursday, 16th April. It is hoped that this may enable more villagers to attend. The visit to Chessington Worlds of Adventure on Wednesday, 15th May has been cancelled and replaced by a mystery coach tour (for those that don't like mysteries – look away now! The coach will be driven by the Irish singer, Enya).

Sockford

Mediaeval Quiz Night

SOCKFORD. – On Monday evening December 3rd, teams filling the Pond & Sod pub took part in the annual Medeavial Quiz Night. First prize was a set of turnips, and runners-up got a go on the barmaid.

Toilet Disabled

ST ZORRO'S CHURCH. – The 12th century church is to complete the construction of a disabled toilet without getting into hot water thanks to a recent money-spinning raffle. Prizes included a chauffeur-driven dinner for two, a good night's sleep, a West Ham United shirt signed by a team, with a mildly libellous cartoon of Wendy Richards inside the left cuff and a disabled toilet. A new fund manager is due to be appointed before the next meeting.

Merger Decision

SOCKFORD CHEESE EVENINGS – The Sockford Cheese Evenings committee voted by a majority of 14-5 in favour of a merger with the nearby Sockford Wine Evenings society. It was proposed that the first joint venture be a one-off experimental "Cheese & Wine Evening," combining the best of both societies' expertise. Although dissenting members called the idea "a laughable combination" and walked out

Terrible twins are two good to be true!

STORY BY TAUNTON MISHAP
PHOTOGRAPH BY CONKERS McBONKERS

Three St Eyot's schoolfriends, known to their teachers as "The Terrible Twins" because of their cheeky classroom antics have raised over £100 for charity by being as good as gold for a whole week. The tearaway twosome (*left to right;* Jennifer Lagoon, Helen Off and Mandy Westlife) were on their best behaviour for five days in aid of BBC *Celebrities In Need* but promised they would be back to their old selves this week. Police say the tongue sent to them in the post on Monday has now been identified as that of missing Head of Biology Mary Joules but negotiations with the wayward schoolgirl duo are going well.

Your festive queries answered by syndicated columnist Father Christmas

Dear Father Christmas,

For Xmas last year, I got two pickled onions and a fork. This year, I want the other fork. What do they take me for? I'm not an animal, I'm just a man trying to finish his other pickled onion.

Harry Bland, Whoft.

Father Christmas writes:

Ho ho ho! If you're a very good boy, I'll bring you the other fork and some brand new pickled onions this year!

Dear Father Christmas,

I normally spend Xmas with my family, but this year I want to stay upstairs. Is there any way I could stay up here and still get my fair share of presents and bread sauce?

Tony, St Eyots!

Father Christmas writes:

Ho ho whoah there, Tony! There are easier ways to spend Xmas on your own! Try faking your own death – but wait until you've got your presents first.

Dear Father Christmas,

Is it true that you're not a traditional Christmas figure at all, but were originally a character designed for a Lucozade advert, with your distinctive orange fizzy coat?

Jim L Fix, Itley

Father Christmas writes:

No no no! That's Father Fizzmas, the lead character from the 1978 Lucozade TV ad campaign.

Dear Father Christmas,

What are the names of your seven reindeer actually?

(Name and address supplied.)

Father Christmas writes:

Ho ho ho! My trusty reindeer are called: Rudolph, Donner, Blitzen, Sonny, Cher and two other names.

Dear Father Christmas,

What is the best way to get red wine stains out of a photograph of The Beatles having sex with an ostrich?

Kelly, Sockford

Father Christmas writes:

Ho ho ho! If you're a very good girl, I'll bring you an Action Man make-up kit this year!

Dear Father Christmas,

Last xmas I gave my girlfriend the gift of finding me in bed with her brother. I'm worried it's raised her expectations, and she's going to expect me to splash out the same way this year. How do I top it?

Malcolm, Molford St Malcolm.

Father Christmas writes:

Buttons.

Dear Father Christmas,

Dean Bateson in 5G says you're just regular Framley Examiner advice columnist Captain Mitchell in a cotton wool beard.

Kevin, aged 5.

Father Christmas writes:

Phew, Kevin! I hadn't thought about it that way. Bye!

Strong view on Framlies library's

Star Letter

MISS – I have not written to your publication before, but this week my strong view became so strong that I felt compelled to put pen to paper.

Whenever I want to read a book,
I go to the library and have a very good look.
With so many books on so many shelves it's
Easy to find books about pigs and on Elvis.

There's novels and dictionaries. This week Oh dear!
I missed the overdue date (even though it was quite late!)
And got myself fined to the tune of 8p
But don't the firemen do a marvellous job?
Or so I thought until I phoned to complain that my wheeliebin had been set on fire again. I was kept on hold for twenty-five minutes before anyone answered. I worked for fourteen years in the retail catering industry, and had I treated any of our customers in this shoddy fashion
 My boss would have cautioned me, or let me go

EDGAR ALLAN POETRY
Yopney St Oh!

Framley Library casues opinion.
PHOTO BY MOCKNEY TOSSPOT

Show of supporters

I would like to express my gratitude towards Framley Borough Council for their flexibility in arranging a temporary ground for Framley Zabadak FC, following the shock discovery last week that our 94-year-old Embankment Way stadium had been turned upside down and buried during the night.

Thanks are also due to all those who turned out to try and help. Our thoughts are with the families of the three ground staff who are still missing, presumed upside down.

Fans will be glad to hear that, just for the meanwhile, local councillors have rushed through strict new Saturday Trading laws that allow us to play our forthcoming Division One matches inside the Tesco superstore on the Whoft Road. Could supporters please try to arrive six hours before the 3pm kick-off this weekend in order to help move the goods, shelves, tills and customer service desk temporarily out into the car park?

WILLY BREMNER
General Manager
Framley Zabadak FC

Idea is a good idea

MISS – The council's new idea is a good idea.

LAURA GLADIATOR
Ogley-St-Nicholas

Food for thought

MISS – I was amused to read that Framley General Hospital has won an award for its food.

I spent some time there last December, during a routine operation to unclench my fist, and I was so unimpressed that, since I was discharged, I have not been back for a meal once.

Maybe they should try encouraging more return custom before they waste their time cooking up any more awards!

ROSIE PLIMSOLL
The Dippy Soldier Cafe, Codge

Bad deterrent is badly needed

MISS – You reported (Examiner, Ovtover 21st) that teenage pregnancy on the Dungeon estate is three times the national average.

The UK once had the lowest number of unmarried fathers in Europe. Now it is the highest. Oh dear.

In pre-war Britain it was a rare event for a teenager to become pregnant. There was no sex-education because sex was not required.

Unmarried fathers did not exist and were held in contempt, also, probably, there was no council housing or state handouts, or a national average.

"Do-gooders" and politicals changed all that. Oh dear again. And then they abolished school canings, whoever "they" are!?

Is it any surprise that all children are expelled and murdering a pensioner on a daily basis before robbing? And then they abolished the capital P in 1965 when they murdered Ruth Ellis for using one so now there is no deterrent whatsoever.

As ye sew, so shall ye reap, take us as ye find us. Oh dear.

REV JOLIFFE BOOMBOX
The Old Rectory,
Batley

Endangered birds

MISS – When oh when will the Home Secretary stop turning a blind eye to the killing of penguins as constituted illegal by the Penguins Act 1956?

The I Heart Penguins penguin protection organisation estimates that up to 10,000 penguins are killed illegally throughout the county each year for their amusing waddles, even though the waddles themselves are utterly useless once they have been removed from the dead birds.

When?

MRS MARGARET HELFPUL
Millbury Mollymandeigh

Successful event

MISS – I would like to thank all the members of the "Imaginairy Hhaaaaarddd Kruw" who attended our very enjoyable JCB ride along Embankment Way last week, particularly those who brought their own spades. Information about further Framley Imaginaire FC events (alongside all our Newby's Conference League fixtures) will be posted on the website messageboard as usual.

GORDON MORON
General Manager
Framley Imaginaire FC

Quotes of the Week

"I know many patients are unhappy with the situation, but while these shortages continue we have no choice but to resort to drawings of doctors."

"On the contrary. Our figures show that old people like being cold."

"People buy lollipop men as presents but the novelty soon wears off and we're left to pick up the pieces here at the Home."

"Traders were expecting either to make lots of money this year, or none at all. In fact we made both."

"This so-called 'hole in the sky' is just the moon, as usual."

"Knowing you've helped to save someone's life is the best feeling in the world. No. Hang on. I mean worst feeling. And stepping in dogshit in socks. Yes. That's it. Stepping in dogshit in socks is the worst feeling in the world. No. I'm not a real fireman. Why do you ask?"

In Court

JANE Whift, 31, of Barleymow Crescent, Codge, was fined £30 with £30 costs for urinating in the High Street on January 21st.

ROBIN McRockaby, 29, of Dogsmuck Alley, Wripple, was fined £50 with £50 costs for urinating in Drive Lane, Framley on January 28th.

ADRIAN Hugme, 52, of Aston Villas, Nyth, was fined £2000 with £2000 costs for urinating in Framley Magistrates Court before Justice Constant Waxy.

MARTIN Balaclavine, 24, of North Promenade, Clinton, was fined £300 with £3000 costs for treading on the cracks beneath the pavement.

FLEXIBLE Mexican, 65, of Guadalajara Wobble, Rubmy, was found guilty of being constructed in Germany by thieves on May 19.

REBECCA Clipshow, 21, of Cod Row, Whoft was fined £100 with £50 costs for stealing a £2 chew from Bovis Newsagents.

FESTIVAL Boyd, 42, of Terrapin Chase, Whoft, was ordered to keep his dog, Swee'corn Niblet, muzzled and on a lead after a public complaint that the dog had run after and inhaled a moving vehicle on April 3rd. Costs were lots and lots.

"I saw useless UFO"

by Adam Wrent

A CODGE RESIDENT who claims to have seen a UFO was 'seriously unimpressed' by his experience.

35 year-old Brucie Bonus had been watching the moon 'to see what it actually did' from the back garden of his house in New Roman Way, when he saw what looked to be a silver disc flying across the night sky.

"The first thing I remember registering was disappointment," he yawned to us. "It wasn't travelling as fast as UFOs should. In fact it looked more like a tortoise. Or a plate. Something that could be thrown across a garden."

"It was at this time that I remember looking at my watch to make sure I wasn't missing *The World's Strangest Man* competition on the telly, because this year it's being presented by either Geoff Capes or Emu. When I looked up again however the silver disc had gone."

He then explained in great detail how he walked back indoors to get his camera, "I thought I might be able to get some good shots of the moon now that the UFO had gone."

Back outside, however, Mr Bonus was dismayed to find that the spaceship had landed at the foot of his garden crushing his pansies.

"I couldn't believe it," he told us, "It was possibly the worst thing I've ever seen. The ship looked terrible in the air, but that was as nothing compared to how diabolical it looked sitting on my floral border."

CODGE MAN

At this point a door creaked open in the large metal shape and two green men fell out. "They weren't like the ones you see on the *X Men*, they were rubbish. It looked like someone had hurriedly cobbled them together from some toilet rolls and roly poly paste."

"They stumbled across the garden, took a piss, bumped into each other and took off again. I was glad I didn't waste the last three shots in my camera on it," Mr Bonus winked as he proudly displayed two blurred photos of him posing in front of a mirror and one of the underside of the counter at Codge Smashing Snaps developers.

MOLFORD FARMER

This isn't the first time that aliens have been sighted in the Framley area. In fact, there are over 300 separate, confirmed sightings every year, with thousands of witnesses to bear testimony.

In 1945, after the World War II had ended, a large metal object fell into a farmer's field near Molford that was later famously identified as an Unidentified Flying Saucer.

The farmer, seizing the fantastic financial opportunity that had arisen, opened his hedges to the world's media and immediately sold the story to *The Molford and District Messenger*.

The craft contained two dead blue alien lifeforms which scientists immediately moved to Framley General Hospital where they are still awaiting an autopsy.

Man causes over £25,000 of damage to own hair

A WRIPPLE MAN is today recovering in Framley General Hairdressers after attemtping to cut his own hair with a knife and fork.

Keith Undertones, of Jambalaya Avenue, attempted the feat whilst under the influence of burnt toast fumes, caused from careless mid-afternoon breakfast preparations.

"I was just about to get the marmalade out of the cupboard when my thoughts suddenly turned to cutting my own hair." he told us, as a trainee hairdresser adjusted his conditioner drip. "It all seemed so simple. I'd get something sharp to cut it with, something to hold it in place and save myself five pounds fifty at the barbers."

Unfortunately, the haircut went disastrously wrong leaving Mr Undertones to foot a £25,000 bill for private emergency reconstructive hair surgery. "It's been an expensive lesson, but one that I had to learn." he croaked as he coughed up a hairball quiff.

Capture the moment YOU made the news!

Back copies of the Framley Examiner are available from our offices at special discount prices so you can remember the special day that you made the news.

01999 642344

Just phone the number above and tell us which edition you require and how many copies you would like. We'll do the rest. At only £5 a copy, you would be dangerously insane to miss out on this deal.

EDITIONS STILL AVAILABLE: #1316, #1319, #1325-#1330

Framley Examiner Promotions, Unit 149b, East Cosset Industrial Estate, Parkfields Bypass, Framley FR1 6LH

The Framley Examiner

MOLFORD PERVERT - THE HUNT GOES ON

lose up to 50% of your total body weight in just ½ hour

RING NOW FOR OUR OPEN WEEKEND DETAILS

fighting**fit**   stress**relief**   get**inshape**   meet**newpeople**   maximum**burn**

Lose weight the losing weight way!

At Nauyokas Gym we can provide you with everything you need to get fit. From baked bean baths to exercise wheels. From windypop machines to indoor heated swimming pans.

Special introductory price £30 this weekend.

Phone us for more details.

Try our new "Stretch Armstrong" machine!

103 Nyth Lane, Framley FR1 8GH
01999 234425

Nauyokas Gym

The management regret that they cannot return weight once lost. Weight is the property of the gym member and must be looked after at all times. Sorry about that.

Looking for love

getting people together over a dinner or maybe rough sex... The Framley Examiner!   **01999 94 76 94**

Women seeking Men

LADY
F, 30, WLTM three men digging a hole 3m x 1m x 3m at the same rate as one man digging the same three holes. When will I meet them/him? Show your working. Use both sides of the paper if necessary. Box FE6781

DAYS OF WINE AND FOOLS AND HORSES
Attractive F, 43, wltm man (looks/height/age unimportant) with at least 250,000 Tesco ClubCard points for shopping, maybe more than once. Box FE8561

PAY A TENSION
Retired teacher seeks young female who will stand up when I enter the room and share in with the rest of the class if it's so funny. There's always one. See me afterwards. Box FE6571

BE MY BUM!
06 Riding a bike
07 At the theatre
08 Morning after casserole
07999 9309XX

HELLZAPUFFIN
Unusual Molford woman, early 40s, shaped like a keyhole, seeks genuine man with big round head and narrow body that widens in a triangle towards his huge flat feet. Resemblance to keyhole unimportant. Box 9781

BULLSEYE!
Petite, slim Molford woman, 29, blonde hair, green eyes, mouth full of hazelnuts, seeks understanding male, 22-35 in Molford area for target practice. Box FE8711

HANDY MAN
Tall, slim Codge woman seeks quiet, petite, portable man with carrying handles and little wheels. Box FE7120

AS GOOD AS IT GETS
Divorced Chutney F, 45, no personality, seeks ghastly insipid cardboard cutout of a man with no opinions and someone else's hair. Box FE5122

INTERESTED?
Interested? NO! Box FE4242

NOT SURE
Vivacious / vacuous (never known which one was which) Framley woman WLTM local man with no fear of commitment / The Communards (never known which one was which). Box FE6451

HAIR RAISING!
Grim Personality, Sockford female, 33 blue eyes, likes eating brown hair, for fun nights in possibly baldness. Box FE1871

I'VE GOT JON BON JOVI'S HAIRCUT!
How old is this photograph? There's a Garfield mug in the background.
07999 790091

LOOKS UNIMPORTANT
Quiet, shy, Urling lady, 42, looks unimportant, actually very important. So pay attention. To me you are as a mote of dust on the collar of God. Mountains quake at my approach. Likes eating out and historical novels. Box FE4106

IN A BIT
Fun seeking F, own parrot, WLTM treasure-seeking pirate. Likes cinema, map-reading and long romantic walks up the plank. Yarl won't be sorry (you'll won't be sorry). Box FE3451

ROMANTIC EVENING
Lovely night out seeks young couple for lovely night out. Box FE6717

GAY DIVORCEE
Divorced Molford woman, 40-ish (63), curvy 36-24-38 (48-32-60), two legs (one leg) seeks caring, attractive, sensitive man with no head for figures. Box FE1998

F*CK MY OPINIONS
...and CUM some sense into them!
07999 3733XX
30 French people can't spell
31 All politicians are homeless
32 Toast always lands inside-out
33 They've got an alien in the reference library
34 Play it again, you stupid Sam
35 Kym (no), Suzanne (yes), Myleene (maybe)
36 This is not The Bee Gees
37 The more I clean the windows, the dirtier they get

THAT'S WHAT THE SMELL WAS!
There's a dead one of me in your water tank. 3 week-old action. Call the council. Three lines. Box FE8721

BEAR FACED CHARM
F, 41, blue eyes, brown hair, dressed as a bear, seeks two open-minded men dressed as a tiger for nights out WITHOUT the costumes. Box FE8791

GRACE SLICK
Very oily lady wishes to slip into your life. Box FE8633

TEXT SEX
You've tried the best...
... now try the TEXT!
SEND 'HOT' to 81Q37... or
SEND 'HOT' to 81Q36
To unsubscribe, send SUBSCRIBE to 81Q35
Each text costs £3 except unsubscribe which costs £3 per min from the time of sending

PRETTY WOMAN
Attractive Molford St Malcolm girl. Pretty. Blonde hair, green eyes, mouth. 29. Bubbly personality. Interested in outdoor sports, folk rock and Spanish cinema. Seeks prick. Box FE5498

Men seeking Women

UP "UP" AND A DOWN!
Reflective M, 38, seeks loving, genuine F who will look me in the eyes once in a while instead of checking her hair and make-up in me. I am not a mirror. I just look like one. Box FE2251

LOOK NO FURTHER
I have Sockford's biggest collection of glass eyes. Sockford man, 5' 11", interested in cinema, reading and glass eyes WLTM enthusiastic, loving female 20+, interested in glass eyes. Eye colour unimportant. Box FE4881

DREAM LOVER
Are YOU the girl of my dreams? Remember the time I saved you from those giant dream scissors? Show some imaginary gratitude you make-believe madam. Box FE5411

YULE LOVE IT
Messy man, 65, looking for woman. She's not in the huge pile of rotting clothes upstairs or out by the bins that haven't been emptied since she went missing. I think her name was Edith and she hated me. Box FE9891

CHEST A MINUTE
One-legged man, 51, seeks one-legged woman for two-legged race, perhaps more-legged race if she brings a friend or is a one-legged woman with two legs. Box FE6561

MY HUSBAND'S ANSWERING QUESTIONS IN THE HOUSE
Let's play!
01 Mrs Wilson
02 Mrs Callaghan
03 Mrs Ramsay MacDonald
04 Dennis Thatcher
07999 14546 X

CONSIDER ME
Whoft man, 27, seeks slim, pretty, blonde, blue-eyed, oval-faced, full-mouthed, small-nosed female, 5' 7" – 5' 8" tall, hair in symmetrical bangs, about three inches below the ear, looks unimportant. Box FE5190

DEAD WIFE
Tall, well-built, romantic Wripple widower, 46, no ties, WLTM pleasant older lady 45+. If forced to wear a tie, I will poke the fat end down inside my shirt and let the little thin bit stick out a couple of inches below the knot, and, at the first opportunity, will take it off and roll it into my blazer pocket. Box FE3922

CUM IN MY 38DD FACE
I've got a head like a BIG PINK PEA
- NO IMPLANTS! -
07999 979797

TRY SOMETHING NEW
Straight-curious Codge man seeks straight Codge man for straight gay relationship. No funny stuff. None of that. You people make me sick. Box FE9804

PRIVATE DANCER
Private Dancer, dancer for money, WLTM any other squaddies from the 24th Framley Fusiliers for fun, friendship, maybe war. Box FE9891

LETS GET TOGETHER!
M, 32, own house/car, seeks big affectionate breasts for fun and friendship. Woman attached to breasts need not be anything special. Box FE7891

I'M TOO SEXY
Whoft male, Take That look-a-like (doesn't matter which), 34, seeks Spice Girls look-a-like. I wanna ha I wanna ha I wanna ha I wanna ha I don't wanna no Melbs or Melcs. Box FE9008

LOOKING FOR LOVE
Inquisitive Framley male, 51, into golf, dining, and Rugby Union, just knows there's a slim, brunette, Framley female, 40-55 hiding somewhere in his kitchen. I know you're there. I saw something moving under the breakfast bar. I'm in no hurry. I've got enough food in this fridge to last me months. You'll have to come out soon. Box FE6100.

COULD U BE THE 1?
M, 28, likes eggs, bacon, beans, tomato, bubble and a fried slice, WLTM slim professional woman with GSOH, eggs, bacon, beans, tomato, bubble and a fried slice. Box FE3372

SEX PEST
Retired Catholic priest, 62, seeks forgiveness for fun. Box FE8962

INDOOR TYPE
Man, 45, behind wallpaper again, seeks non-smoking F for limited companionship, maybe rescue. Box FE8989

MAGNETIC PERSONALITY
M, 39, positively charged magnetically, seeks negatively charged woman without fillings, jewellery, pacemaker or own car for nights in stuck to fridge door. Box FE4981

EVER DONE IT AL-QAEDA?
I'll hide in my hole while you send in the troops!
07999 61 2424

TAKE ME
Are you guided by a signal in the heavens and/or the beauty of your weapons? If you have a birthmark on your skin and have practised every night with your monkey and plywood violin, you may be ready. Meet me in Manhattan on Sunday, or Berlin next week, to find out more. Box FE8681

SPORTS AHOY!
Now, in a moment I'm going to bang my clipboard on the dashboard, and when I do, I want to meet a warm, friendly, woman with a stopping distance of 38m (dry) and 42m (wet). I am not a driving instructor. Box FE9719

Men pretending to be Women seeking Women

SEIZE THE DAY
Genuine lesbian, usual description, seeks two other lesbians with long blonde hair to do things in front of me. Honestly, I am a real lesbian. Call Dave or Malcolm on 01999 742542

Men seeking Men

NEW BOY IN TOWN
Bi-curious Sockford man, new to scene, seeks experienced gay man to show him the ropes. Box FE1761

I'LL PUT ON MY WIFE'S ARMS AND LEGS AND DO THE MAGIC "MRS ME" DANCE
07999 430141
all calls charged at 50p per calendar minute. Please check with bill payer before calling. Registered as a charity by the RSPB

ANCHORS AWAY!
Bi-curious Fracton sailor, needs to moor boat but cannot find requisite equipment on board, seeks experienced gay man to show him the ropes. Box FE1981

LORD OF THE RING.
Bi-curious Sockford man, lost in middle of boxing ring and unable to find way out, seeks experienced gay man to show him the ropes. Box FE1676

HEAVE HO!
Bi-curious tug-of war organiser, standing in sports shed wondering what he came in there for, seeks well-equipped gay man to show him the ropes. Box FE1156

KETCH ME IF YOU CAN!
Bi-curious first-time gallows maker, almost at end of first two projects but lacking all-important final piece for both, seeks experienced gay man to show him the ropes. Box FE1338

RING THE CHANGES
Bi-curious trainee bellringer, until now convinced that bells are rung by trampolining into the belfry and nutting them with his forehead, but beginning to suspect there may be a means of sounding a peal of bells from the floor of the church using some kind of pulley system seeks huge black man to fuck him up the bum. Box FE1530

Unattached? **ACROSS THE ROOM**
For unattached business and professional people!
We hold fabulous party nights and sparkling dinners where we fire you across the room from a cannon at your prospective partner.
ACROSS THE ROOM – It's the great new way to get together!
01999 654241
cannondating.co.uk

BE SENSIBLE: We suggest that the first meeting always be held in a public place such as the centre circle of a football pitch during a cup tie, or on top of a speeding train in full view of a pair of men having a fistfight. Do not reveal your full name, address or face until you are comfortable doing so. Always dial 141 before calling a contact number to ensure confidentiality, and speak in either a very high or a very low voice to disguise your sex. Always meet in daylight, and carry a gun and mints.

It is a truth universally acknowledged that it was the best of times, it was the

The day I spent a night with a man!

by Katie Blirdsnest

BEING A SINGLE GIRL has never been harder or more popular than it is at the moment. With books like *Bridget Jone's Diary* and programmes like *Sex Of The City* riding high in the charts, it's hip to be a single girl. And being a single girl myself, I thought it was about time I tried the life of a single girl! So here's what happened when I tried a dating service. Here it is.

Monday, 11.00 am

I ring Ring-A-Singleton and place my advert. It says "Katy Blirdsnest WLTM a man." And at £1/word, it's a bargain!

11.30 am I check my message box: no-one there yet, but I'm hopeful!

12.00 pm Nothing yet.

12.30 pm Still hopeful!

1.00 pm Nothing yet!

1.30 pm Still hopeful!!

2.00 pm Nothing yet?! Ring three more times just to make sure.

3.00 pm Whoops! Get a verbal warning from the editor for making eleven calls to a premium rate phone line. Will have to try again when I get home.

Tuesday, 10.00 am

I've got two replies! One, it turns out, is a wind-up (you know who you are, Damiun Clavalier!) but the other is Greg, a nice-voiced man from Molford. He says he's 33 and looking for fun and perhaps more. Who knows, perhaps he'll get his fun............... and perhaps more!

Wednesday, 3.00 am

I ring Greg, who's asleep, and we agree to meet on Friday at a wine bar called Fingers.

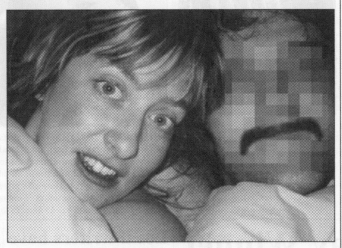

More and more single people are employing dating services or sedatives.
PHOTOGRAPH BY GINGERBREAD ROLLINGS

Thursday, 1.00 pm

Thinking about Greg. I wonder if he's what's he like? I bet I know!

Friday, 7.00 pm

It's the big occasion! I've got my best black trousers on and a glitzy new t-shirt with 'Myleene' written across it, and I'm quite the belle of the bar! I'm holding a copy of *How To Make Love To The Same Man For The Rest Of Your Life Without Ever Really Enjoying It*, so Greg'll know it's me.

7.30 pm No sign of Greg.

8.00 pm No Greg.

8.30 pm Blimey still no Greg!

9.00 pm Six glasses of Chardonné later, and it doesn't look like Greg can make it, but I'm being chatted up by Colin, a rep. He buys me another bottle of wine, and we talk about hairstyles and the zoo.

9.30 pm (Maybe it's just the wine!) but Colin's looking more and more dashing by the minute! He's got a Vauxhall Bombardier with heated front seats and a digital watch.

In fact, he's quite the Casablanca!

10.00 pm Who needs a dating agency when you can go to a bar and meet real people? Colin and I have so much in common: we're both right-handed, we both eat meat, and neither of us has a middle name! We're on our third packet of pork scrunchings and we've started on the cocktails. I've got a thing with a Spanish name and Colin's got a Harvey Wallpaper. Friday night is turning out to be a blast!

11.00 pm Club.

Saturday, 8.30 am

Whoops! I wasn't expecting the photographer to turn up so early and by the volume of his shouting Colin wasn't expecting him at all! He pushes the photographer down the stairs and leaves in a bit of a puff, but I've still got his mobile phone number 07999 739750 so it won't be long before I'll be hearing from him! Go Katy! Go Katy! Go Katie! (Like the Ricki Lake song.)

Next week: Line Dancing

THE BLIRDSNEST REPORT

News In Brief

SCHOOL WELCOMES NEW HEAD

Pupils and staff at St Oblong's School For Some Girls are celebrating the news that caretaker Colin Townsend has been successfully fitted with a new head. Mr Townsend has been on sick leave since a floor polisher ran out of control last June, but hopes now to return to work

MORE PUB CASH THEFT

The Jolly Pocket Postman public house in Framley was broken into last Sunday morning. The thieves removed a pane of glass from the conservatory to gain entry and stole £3,500 in cash and some other thieves who had broken into the pub moments before.

BABY SURVIVES ACCIDENT

A 12-week-old baby escaped serious injury in a road traffic accident on the FR404. The infant was strapped into the front seat when the car left the road near Whoft last Saturday afternoon. The driver had swerved to look at a hedgehog. The car landed on its side for 5 hours, blocking the eastbound carriageway until it could be removed. The baby was airlifted to hospital for checks after a breath test proved inconclusive.

SUN GOES DOWN AGAIN

The sun went down again on Tuesday at sunset. Crowds who stayed up to witness the event were said to be "satisfied".

ARE YOUR WINDOWS COCK-A-DOODLE-DRAB?

Misted, sealed units, patio doors. All glazing and repairs undertaken in cockerel-quick time! Hen-tastic!

DAPLEY'S GLAZING AND REPAIRS

01999 727472

UNDERCRANK & SONS
"Fast" Builders

It's as easy as A, B, C...

1 We will erect a new house for you and your family in less than ten minutes... GUARANTEED!

2 Then, at no extra cost, we will come round the next day and erect it again.

· Free estimates · Full technical and design support · Four sugars and just a splash · We're fairly sure we can probably do it!

UNIT 6, DOOZER YARD, SOCKFORD. 01999 664101 email myhousehasfallendown@undercrank_sons.co.uk

Weddings
Birthdays
Lunchboxes
Jaffa

collapse-a-cake

01999 422320

advertisement designed by Whoft Graphics
111 Granville Walk, Whoft
Open 10am – 6pm except Sun and Wed
Tel: 01999 616161
Fax: 01999 616162
email: steve@whoftgraphics.com
competitive rates. professional quality.
full design, artwork and reproduction service.

WRIPPLE BIDS FAREWELL TO FAITHFUL VILLAGE POSTIE

Mr Grinning bids farewell to the community he has served for over five sixteenths of a century.
PHOTO BY HIGGLEDYPIGGLEDY WELCH

WRIPPLE postie Trevor Grinning has retired after 40 years – 32 of them serving the village, and 6 of them enjoyable.

Blacksmith Roger Tube made and presented Trevor with a letter rack made of horseshoes and featuring a nice-cup-of-tea-and-a-sit-down design at a ceremony on the village green before Mr Grinning's body was surrendered to the flames in accordance with his wishes.

As Mr Grinning's remains were scattered into the flow of the River Sock, senior postmistress Marjorie Harth, who introduced him to his round in 1964, expressed the Post Office's wish that Trevor's unmarried soul would sup mead with other fallen "dawn warriors" in Mailhalla, the mythic hall of the postmen until Ragnarok, when, postmen believe a particularly heavy Christmas rush will summon the immortals to battle alongside their living comrades in a sorting office at the foot of Ygdrasil, the Tree At The End Of The World.

ALL THIS WEEK AT THE
WRIPPLE MASTODON

COLLANDER GIRLS (PG)
1.20, 4.00, 6.30, THU LATE 4.25am

QUEST FOR PIPS (U)
12.10, 2.15, 5.45, 7.30, MAT SUN 6am

GCSE SPANISH (15)
LUN 2.30, MAR 1.00, JUE 3.25

CALL OUR 24-HOUR BOOKING LINE
ON 08999 764541 DURING OFFICE HOURS

Geoff, are you sure about this headline?

FRAMLEY'S OUTSPOKEN MAYOR, William D'Ainty, has demanded that two Maine Coon cats be sent back to where they came from.

The two kittens, which were delivered to the Town Hall, were an unsolicited gift from an American pressure group.

Paying too much for your contact lenses?

At ClearBright, you can have hourly disposable lenses from as little as 32p/month.

ClearBright

120 Derngate, Framley 01999 etc

Prison breakout alert

POLICE are investigating an incident in which a canvas bag containing a 38' racing yacht and a tunnel were thrown over the wall at Chutney Prison.

The prison is on high alert following several escape attempts. Last month guards discovered a hot air balloon made out of bunkbeds under a crash mat in the gym, and in May a prisoner was captured after baking himself into a cake shaped like his wife and leaving the compound as part of a group of visitors.

A touch of Tinseltown as Framleys 'Walk of Fame's unveiled

The concrete contributions of two of Framley's best-known faces.
PHOTO BY OXBOW LAKE

by JESUS CHIGLEY

THE TITLE OF FRAMLEY's top tourist attraction may soon be snatched from the Ornamental Dog Bins outside the swimming baths if a new Hollywood-style landmark is taken to visitors' hearts.

On Thursday, the Framley Chamber Of Commerce finally opened its long-threatened tourist attractor, the Framley Walk Down The High Street On Top of Some Locally Famous Local Personalities.

A 200 yard section of the pavement between Empire of the Kite and the Zephyr AM gid=ft shop now features the faces of local notables impressed into the cement, and organisers hope the stretch of pavement will soon be designated an area of outstanding natural beauty.

CONCRETE FACES

Bystanders gawped while eating free cake and party poppers as Mayor D'Ainty and MP Ianbeale Steeplecocque left imprints of their faces in opposite ends of the wet

concrete (pictured). As an exclusion order still prevents bronze plaques from being used in the town centre, the includees have recorded an "ouch!" each that will be digitally replayed to help pedestrians recognise exactly whose face it is they're treading on.

The idea behind the walkway is a chance for those who had contributed to the community for the chance to leave behind a permanent reminder of the chance of community and pavements.

CONCRETE

Whilst wiping the rapidly drying grey sludge from his eyes and throat, Mr Steeplecocque made an emotional speech in which he expressed his hope that the concrete impression of his face would age at the same rate as his real face. The Mayor, by contrast, chose to nip into the snug of the Warm Zippy for a leisurely pint and a quick cryptic crossword.

Hernold Plath, the designer of the cement Walk of Face (for short) was yesterday still buried up to the neck in his prototype.

Charity Domino Rally

RUBMY – On Monday evening the Rubmy 2nd Scouts took part in a sponsored domino rally. A grand total of 5,000,056 dominos were toppled thanks to the scouts' final 56th domino striking the first domino in Carl Underfelt's world record attempt taking place in the hall next door. £8.42 was raised for sweets.

Molford

Celebrated Luncheon

PARISH COUNCIL. – The Council hosted a luncheon for the senior citizens of Molford last Thursday. More than 30 senior citizens attended the ten-course meal, prepared and served by parish councillors. Mr Graheme Kentwell, the newly elected chairman of the Parish Council called the event a "marvellous failure."

"Everyone enjoyed the first course but most of them were full after the tomato soup and bread rolls, so we binned the rest. Mr Bennett won the best designed party hat competition with a trilby he wears every day anyway, and Mrs Eldon's runner-up turned out to be just the shape of the top of her head, poor soul. We let him have a sing song. 'Bat Out Of Hell'. Every track. Some idiot left the lyric sheet on the book trolley at the day care centre, apparently. Unbearable."

Mrs Jessie Lovage – at 92, the oldest luncheon guest – requested one of the lovely red balloons for her great-great-grandson Toby before filling her wheeled shopping basket with the leftover gravy and heading for the FR404 where she was apprehended.

Annual Fit-Up

MOLFORD POLICE. – This year's annual fit-up was held on December 3rd, when officers from SO19, Framley's armed response unit, raided the house of William Turbot, an unemployed retail manager from Molford. Improvised explosives, Class 'A' drugs and child pornography were "found," as well as Nazi insignia and flight manuals printed in Arabic. Mr Turbot was released after 72 hours of questioning, and presented with a bottle of champagne and a polyester alarm clock necktie by Ch Insp John Stone. Over £6000 was raised in bail.

Whoft

Treasurer's Report

ROYAL ARTILLERY ASSOCIATION. – Members held their monthly meeting at Whoft Gun Club. All committee members were present except for Mr O'Neill who had that afternoon been shot in the elbow by his wife during an argument over how much time he thought was reasonable to spend at the Gun Club. After the treasurer's report, a letter was read out from the vicar of St Zorro's concerning the annual Gun Club dinner recently held in the church hall. The vicar wrote that his after-dinner speech – "The Meadow Walk" – had been delivered without incident many times in the past and never before had his grouse impression been met with the cry, "Bloody hell, boys! It must be August the Twelfth!" and 28 rounds of cartridge ammunition. The mention of legal action in the letter was unanimously discounted if the vicar knew what was bloody good for him.

Fracton

Full Attendance

PARISH FELLOWSHIP – Full attendance, with no absentees. Chairman Ken McJarawelski called the meeting to order shortly after six and scones. Under matters arising and the lack of electricity supply, it was agreed to take no further action. On the subject of the disconnection of the water, a motion of "no action" was passed. Members voted unanimously not to try and open the doors. A flare was let off to attract attention and more scones. Next meeting: 2008.

Teddy Bears Charity

BELLAIRE. – A gala fundraising night was held to raise money for Teddy Bears, a charity worker who has dedicated his life to rescuing abused bears in China and the Far East. The highlight of the well-attended evening was when Mr Bears introduced Senor Bongo, his marvellously entertaining dancing Peruvian bear which delighted the audience by jumping up and down on top of a red hot metal plate to the tune of La Cucaracha. Over £1800 was raised, which Teddy hopes to put towards buying an even bigger dancing bear.

Bellaire

Where Will It All End?

UNITED RECLAIMED CHURCH. – The departing minister the Rev James Spartacus led his final service, opening with the hymn "Toby The Pilgrim" and then readings from the Revelation To St John and it will all be over by Christmas they said of the First World War and soon it will all be over for me too. Rev Spartacus took communion but declined the antidote.

Deep-in-the-Greedy

Blazing row

AMATEUR RADIO CLUB. – Members had a very successful day recently when they took part in International Radio Day, a celebration of the work and achievements of radio enthusiasts worldwide. The whole day was rather marred, sadly, by two members, Smudge Cottee and Adrian Beatles, arguing about whether the club radio ought to be tuned into Radio Free Everywhere or the local minicab firm. The argument lasted nearly ten hours, and remains unresolved. Interested parties should call Nephew Betjeman on 01999 238446 or log all over www.internationalradoiday.com.

Correction

FRAMLEY EXAMINER. – Staff at local newspaper The Framley Examiner were treated to a complaint from the Deep-In-The-Greedy coven of the Amateur Radio Club. Apparently, the popular publication printed their website address wrongly this week. Staff voted by 55-14 to print a correction, and the motion was passed. We are happy to correct this.

Well Received Speech

CHUTNEY KANGAROOS. – The annual meeting was held in the Horace Andy Centre at St Barnaby's. A well-received speech was given by the chairman Peter Springs, which ranged over the events of the year, the chairs, the tables, out of the window and into the river. The branch has provided support to numerous events during the year including cattle rustling and a tombola. Election of officers is as follows: President; Marion Springs. Chairman; Bill Fitzgarden. Hon. Treasurer; Pphillipp Bristol. Rhythm Guitarist; Keith Marina. Class Clown; Andy Tortoise.

Chutney

Dead Chairman

CHUTNEY CONTORTIONISTS. – The many performers and several obsessives of the Chutney Contortionists met on Thursday at St Fleet's Chapel to celebrate the life of Roger Brough. Rubbery Roger had been an active member of the group since his early teens, but had been less active since tying himself in an irreversible knot in 1996. Acting chair Jessica Sparkle paid tribute to Roger's tireless efforts to untie himself, and recalled his failing health after several years of near-permanent straining. Treasurer Wayne Love gave a moving account of the last time he saw Roger, recounting how one of Roger's toenails had grown so far down his throat that he could no longer speak, and could only communicate by tapping the small of his back with his nose. By this time, Roger was in almost permanent pain, since he had to sleep on his own balls and could only manage ten to fifteen minutes rest a week, but Wayne said that his old friend did acknowledge his presence, once the mirrors had been rigged to allow Roger to see through the gap between his popped shoulder blade and the doubled back right knee wrapped around his neck.

Wripple

Club Outing

WRIPPLE OCTOGENARIANS – Forty-five lucky pensioners from residential homes in Wripple were treated to a minibus outing to a club in London this week. Jez, their guide, provided the daytrippers with three ecstasy tablets and two bottles of water each. The pensioners then paid their £22 to get into Slugz, a top hardcore night in a railway arch in K'ings Cross, for a cabaret evening by the Squarepushers. The music started at 2am, by which time most of the party were back on the minibuses and already asleep. Kebabs and lager were served, but there were no takers. A further outing to a two-night rave in Essex has been postponed due to legal conditions.

Delightful Evening

LAMELY CROSSFORD WI. – The 839th meeting of the Lamely Crossford WI was held on Tuesday in the Dustin Gee Memorial Hall. The well-attended gathering listened intently to guest speaker Oliver Clams, from Molford, speaking on the subject of sweating. With a variety of interesting slides and specimens, Oliver spoke for just under five and three quarter hours on the history of sweating from Jesus Christ to Tony Blair. Members were invited to sniff any of Oliver's 300 samples of famous sweat, including his signed Chas & Dave pants and shirts, which make up over two thirds of the collection. A light refreshment of salt water was served, after which Oliver complained that much of his collection seemed to have gone missing. Toileting was brisk.

Sockfrod

Yeasty Treat

1ST SOCKFORD SCOUTS. – A once-in-a-lifetime trip to a windmill to see how bread is eaten was organised by Timothy

Damiun's CELEBRITY CHALLENGE

Can you guess the identity of the celebrity pictured on the left?

No-one identified our mystery star last week, so the prize money rolls over, increasing to £500,000.

And this week, to make it easier, we've added a triangle of photo. If no-one gets it this time round, we'll reveal the answer in next week's issue. Usual competition rules apply.

Answers on a £10 note to Damiun Clavalier, c/o The Framley Examiner, Unit 149b, East Cosset Industrial Park, Parkfields Bypass, Framley FR1 6LH.

Chuck Le Corner's CHUCKLE CORNER

More big laughs this week kids as I get my hands on the cream of your chuckle muscles

Why were our teachers like a tortoise?
YES, BECAUSE THEY WERE SLOW TO TEACH OISE (US)?
from Kimberly Berlybutter, Chutney, aged 10

What do you call a man who a cliff on his head!
DOUG RICHARD?
Reginalt Behaviour, Whoft Borders, aged 8

Waiter waiter waiter, there's a fly in my soup waiter!
BE QUIET NOW THAT I THANK YOU VERY MUCH JERRY!
from Yessica Rentals, Framley, aged 9

Knock knock!
NOT YET?
Sorry. Doctor doctor, who's there!
DOCTOR WHO?
Reginalt Behaviour, Whoft Borders, aged 8

Who lives at 999 Irish Stew!
ELLO HELLO HELLO! I LIVE HERE?
Robin Wriggler, Codge, aged 8

What did a Pink Panther say to his ants!
DINNER DINNER DINNER DINNER DINNER DINNER DINNER DINNER, RAT FANS?
from Arty F. Leaf, Thoxtoxeter, aged 14

Did you see the one about the Irishman who heard that accidents happen a mile from an Englishman and Scotland!
HOW MOVING?
from 'Charles', address supplied, aged 29

Can you tell how old the Beatles is!
CUT THEM OPEN AND COUNT THE DRUMMERS?
from Susan Valve, Codge, aged 12

What's come dancing across the dancefloor!
WHITE PEOPLE INTRODUCED BY DAVID JACOBS?
from Solomon Yezyez, Wripple, aged 5 and a half

Which cheese is cheddar backwards!
E-S-E-E-H-C?
Barry Bally, Boxinglove Mt. Bellround, aged 12

How many does it change a lightbulb!
YOU CAN NEVER CHANGE A LIGHTBULB?
Ffiffiffer Fforbes-Smiff, Molford St. Malcolm, aged 8

Doctor doctor, here's my curtains!
PATIENT PATIENT, I'D LIKE A PAIR?
from Grahaeme Time, Bille, aged 8

When do elephants paint the town red!
BECAUSE OF WHEN YOUR NOSE TOUCHES THE CEILING?
from Sally Lady, West Jism, aged 7

Big Tit Lady Marmalade goes into a bar!
BECAUSE THE JAM'S CHEST RIGHT?
from Wendy Butterdolly, St Eyots, aged 10

SEND YOUR JOKES TO: Chuck le Corner's Chuckly Corner Corner, The Framley Examiner, Unit 149b, East Cosset Industrial Park, Parkfields Bypass, Framley FR1 6LH. Please try to keep your jokes clean and concise.

Contributors must, by now, be aware that some editing or rephrasing of jokes may be undertaken by the editor of this column. The Framley Examiner Group will never again enter into heated correspondence with children or parents regarding this practice. Any jokes not used are returned in an envelope marked 'Unwanted joke'.

ROGER THE HORRID BEAR

10733 "Roger's Records Riddle"

Roger needs to torch the shed on his allotment where he keeps his financial records, cheque book stubs, and receipts to get the Inland Revenue off his back. Which trail of petrol should he light?

Last week's solution: Plug 4 gets Roger access to next door's cable TV.

Chess, thank you!

Here is the news from the world of chess. This move was first attempted at the 1936 Munich Olympics by the grandmaster, Melle Melovich. He pulled out with a sprained brain and it was my grandfather who took his place in the German team, but he couldn't play because it was on a Tuesday for religious reasons. He didn't win either. Did I?

Well, Black to play first and split White's bishop in twain. This one may require a little less thought than usual.

CHIP'S TOO FLIP   by Glaucewicz

Plum is on holiday. "The Gypsies" will return next week.

Where's Framley Fred?

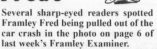

Several sharp-eyed readers spotted Framley Fred being pulled out of the car crash in the photo on page 6 of last week's Framley Examiner.

Prizes of a Framley Fred mug, shoe tree and badges go to Hong Kong Johnson of The Spines, Chutney.

This week's clue:
Football shaped, not flavoured.

Chuck le Corner's Corner Crossword
No. 2321 Set by Charlecornius

DOWN

3 Are these ready for picking from the skirting board tree? (4,4)
4 The saucy Dutchman done a football (4)
5 This doesn't taste like water! (5,5)
6 Ruler of the Ottoman Empire 1685-1710 and usurper of the throne of King Popeye (6)
7 I don't know about you three, but I can't stop thinking about sex (3)
8 Five ----- rings (5)
13 Play by William Omelette (5)
16 HQ for the Admiralty, perhaps (4)
17 I don't know about you three, but I can't stop thinking about sex (3)
19 It's the opposite of B, of course! (1)

ACROSS

4 My football game's got no ball. How do I start it again? (9)
9 TV's Ferkin, Fosey or Footle? (5)
10, 11, 12 Where Napoleon kept his sleevies? (5,2,8)
14 The insects that stop words arguing, perhaps (6)
15 I'm sorry, but no (anag) (4)
18 Our Loooooord (10)
19 A, B, C, D, E, F, G, H, I, J, K, L, M, N, O, P, Q, R, S, T, U, V, W, X, Y, Z, ? (1)

FRANKIE SAYS PRESERVE BRITAIN'S HISTORIC BUILDINGS

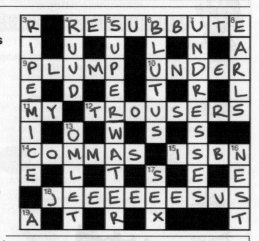

EVERY CORRECT ENTRY TO THE CORNER CROSSWORD COMPETITION WILL WIN ONE OF THESE HI-FASHION T-SHIRTS!
Entries to the usual Framley Examiner address. Please finish the crossword before sealing the envelope.

NAME: .... ADDRESS: ....
....
.... POSTCODE: .... SIZE: M ☐ L ☐ XL ☐ F ☐

The Framley Examiner

Framley's Traditional Favourite since 1978

FRIDAY CHRISTMAS 23rd, 2004   PRICE 45p IF SOLD

THINKING OF TALKING TO THE EXPERTS? TALK TO THE EXPERTS!

Mullings
THE EXPERT PEOPLE

WIN!
Your chance to feed Terry Wogan to a bear!

HEALTH
Could your children be downloading cigarettes?

BUSINESS
Record profits for region's fastest Morris dancers

After year of misery, shopkeepers have a reason to smile

FRAMLEY TRADERS ENJOY "YEAR'S BEST CHRISTMA'S"

by Jesus Chigley

FRAMLEY SHOPS are in buoyant mood at their latest sales figures, because this December is shaping up to be the best Christmas in almost twelve months.

Low Christmas sales all through August had led to fears that shoppers might be staying away from the high street, preferring to shop virtually, using the eBaynet, Ceefax or the wireless. But the good news is putting a smile back on the windows of shops and businesses.

"It's quite a surprise," says 007 Purvis, manager of Denegate Shopping Centre, with a chuckle. "We'd expected the cold weather to be quite a deterrent, but since the first week of December we've served more people than ever however."

TO SHIFT ANY

Mr Purvis hopes the excellent figures are a turn for the better. "We were struggling to shift any holly wreaths or brandy butter all through July, and a lot of our calendars were going off. Thank Anubis things have picked up."

If the current boom continues all next year, the shopping centre can dig itself out of a financial crisis. "We only need to keep this up til next May to pay off all the debts we've run up this year," says Purvis, bowing to a jade statue of Osiris for good luck.

The high street has seen a marked increase in "customember throughfoot" in the last month.
LIBRARY PHOTOGRAPH BY THE BEAUTIFUL QUISLING ROBERTS

Firemen act quickly

FRAMLEY Firefighters used special cutting equipment to slice open a birthday cake belonging to a Mr Chicomarx Hopkins of 32, The Startles, Rockney on Tuesday.

Mr Hopkins is currently trapped in his Vauxhall Astra near the Whoft turning of the FR404 with a steering wheel crushing his ribcage. His family celebrated in his absence with drinks and a chocolate finger buffet.

The firemen later went to the pictures.

Hunt for local oddball goes on

POLICE ARE still looking for a suicidal conman who has been impersonating Terry Wogan in order to gain people's trust.

The man, who is three picnics short of a basket, escaped from Sweet Valley High Security Psychiatric Hospital on Thursday. He was incarcerated for his own safety in 1998 after attempting to climb into the bear enclosure at Framley Zoo covered in marmalade.

DOUBLE MURDER APPEAL
Win a fridge
p33

CHRISTMAS AT NEWBY'S 2004!

¡Grand Sombrero Sale!

Due to a record-breaking error in our ordering department, we have 1000s of sombreros at El Knockdown Prices!

*Perfect for Juan's funeral: 'El Sombrero Negro'

*Sombrero Xmas Trees

*Give your phone a Mexican hat flavour with this snug-fitting sombrero phone case

Santa Cruz says...
"Leave me a tequila and a minced paella!"*

*Going to a fancy dress party dressed as a Mexican Tommy Cooper and don't know what to wear? This Fezbrero should do the trick!

The GRAND SOMBRERO SALE runs at Newby's of Molford throughout December. Customers wishing to purchase turkeys, Xmas decorations and food should contact El Magasin Colombino, Calle Señor Brian Robinson 46-48, Guadalajara.

* Minced paella available in startling quantities from NEWBY'S Foodhall

NEWBY'S of Molford

XMAS TELEVISION P71   XMAS HOOVER P40   UNCONVINCING WOMEN WITH BEARDS P12

with Ursula Cloybeam

Top comic to tell life story

LOCAL FANS will have a chance to hear a life story when Ball, one half of TV comedy act Bobby Ball reveals his amazing life and talking about his faith later this month.

Ball will be appearing at the Dean Tollett Memorial Scout Hut opposite Denegate boat pond from December 29th to September 12th.

No need to book.

WHAT'S ON!

CODGE PLAYHOUSE
'Some Upsetting Evening' (All week) Sophisticated entertainment with local singers giving Cole Porter a sound kicking-in.

GHASTLEY PARK
Jazz Dance on Skis (Thurs)
Boys and girls aged 6-10. All abilities. Parents to drop off children at top of slope at 11am. Collect from bottom at 11.05am. Free. Refreshments served halfway down,

ST FISTULA'S, DURBITON
Organ Recital: 'Toccata and Hall & Oates in Dm' (Saturday)
In aid of organ restoration fund. No high C or D notes if not enough raised by that point in the performance.

SOCKFORD HAIR BEAR CENTRE
The Lucy Nollings Cello Ensemble (Thurs) An evening of filth.

WHOFT BLUES PYRAMID
'Wednesday Jam' (Thurs)
Refreshments provided. Bring your own music. Please do not disturb other customers.

SOAP EXPRESS LAUNDROMAT
Soap Express Laundromat Gilbert & Sullivan Society Perform 'The Pirates of Penzance' in Washing Machines (All week, extra perfs on washdays)
40°, light soiling, colourfast (2pm).
90°, whites (7pm). Bring a book.

MOLFORD ST MALCOLM A.D.S.
'Igloo Victrix' (Tue-Fri)
Amateur Dramatic Society present the usual salsa musical comedy about desert rats trapped in a filing cabinet.

Four unbearable hours of local talent

IF THERE'S ONE THING as sure as Christmas, it's the Molford Drama Festival. And if there's one thing more sure than that, it's that the festival is going from worse to worst!

In the two years since new festival controller Penny Crayon took over, performances have become slack, set design shoddy and the interval lemon squash weaker than ever.

Perhaps a new face on the judging panel would make poor material like Ron Octopusson's self-penned comic monologue *The Creeping Shadow: My Struggle With Non-Hodgkin's Lymphoma* seem a little livelier. Once again, the absence of any panel member with solid journalistic expertise compromised the panel's objectivity, and consequently the entertainment on offer was dull and wearying for almost everyone – particularly my husband Dennis.

Compare this year's dreary fare with previous festivals under the steady hand of the eye of the late Norris Roman. Norris was a great friend of the local arts and always picked the judging panel with care and discretion and never gave us those cheap biscuits with raisins in.

Sophie Bread was also shit as *Chicago* and shouldn't wear stockings with legs like hers and the Alan Benet play by Durbiton Strollers should have been written by someone else. My judgment? Not that I was asked, thank you very much, but: Shit.

THE *Framley Pagoda* PRODLY PRESENTS A CHRISTMAS TREAT FOR ALL TH

THE ELECTRIC NATIVITY

ON-STAGE FOR THE FIRST TIME SINCE DECIMALISATION!

THE TWELVE DAYS OF CHRISTMAS

Darren Day   Sir Robin Day   The Green Days

Leonard "Good Old" Sachs "Days"   The Happy Mondays

LIVE ROCK CONCEPT

IF WET: Sir Robin Day and Sheffield Wednesday

A TRIP INTO THE 7th DIMENSION

also starring ORVILLE and "KEITH HARRIS THE MAN" as THE HIGH-VOLTAGE SHEPHERD

"BLOW YOUR FACE, GRAMPA!"
- Pressure Cooker Review 1971

Book & Lyrics by RICK WAKEMAN
Music by ZAP FLETCHER & CONSORTIUM

GET CLOSE TO THE GINGERBREAD AUTHORITY

AT THE FRAMLEY PAGODA THIS CHRISTMAS

THE DOIG
Enjoig the Doig this Christmas

MONDAY 6th Dec
BANNED DAVE
Framley's foremost Band Aid 2 impersonator (does all the voices)
£3/£4.09

TUESDAY 7th Dec
BRYN CRWSBY & DAFYDD BWYWY
Welsh tribute act. 'Llytl Drwmr Bwy' and all their greatest duets! All the hits!
£22 / £105

SATURDAY 11th Dec
ULED JONČ
The Czech Republic's foremost 'The Snowman' tribute act!
"He walks inside the sky (all snowballs)"
– The Karlovy Vary Gazette
£1/£offers
HURRY UP AND BUY!

XMAS EVE JUNIOR MATINEE
ROD, JANE AND BUSBY
Rainbow / GPO crossover act
(Folk puppet techno)
£4.50/£4.45

CHRISTXMAS DAY
CHARITY MESSIAH
A scratch performance of Handel's chart-topping oratorio by people who came in for the free soup
FREE SOUP ALL DAY

TUESDAY 28th DEC
72 HOUR PARTY!!!
Nearly see in the New Year from 11pm
Ends 11pm on 31 Dec
Attendance compulsory
£72 (£1/hour)

167 The Bizarres, Framley 01999 965543

especially when she's nervous. 01999 928928 but hurry.

MY LIFE IS exactly like a box of chocolates. Please help me. Box FE8261

INVISIBLE Jack Russell puppies. Both parents can be seen. 01999 358080

HANG ON, what was it again? Oh. God it's completely gone. I've got something to sell. What was it? Oh, I'll call you back. 01999 660072

PLAYSTATION, 32 games and man in gorilla suit. Very exciting. £16 01999 829387

GIVE MY REGARDS to Broad Bean. After 6pm. £12

POCKET THERMOMETER £15. Find out how hot your pockets are in seconds. 01999 749957

CAT toilet. Never used (by cat). £10. Box FE8952

YOU CAN DO THE TOMATO

COMPLETE BEN ELTON KIT for sale, including many pairs of spectacles, double seat, short-lived beard and very thin blue line. 01999 758085 after 6am

LADIES' BUTTOCKS, all shapes and sizes considered. No call-out charge for inspection. Ring Vince on 09999 535978

CHAS & DAVE special edition DVD with director's rabbit, deleted owsyerfather etc. Rated 18 for lip. £10. 01999 284508

CONTORTIONISTS' GUILD. Meets every Weds between members' toes. Guests admitted partially upside-down. 01999 390845 for details or more details

HAD AN ACCIDENT at work, home or in the car WHEN YOU WEREN'T EVEN THERE? Ring now to find out how to make a no-win claim. 09999 990990

HMM

COMPLETE WEDDING including service, reception, honeymoon and bride who's still sleeping with her ex. OIRO £14,000. Call David on 07999 270343

SEPTIC TANKS EMPTIED over the person of your choice. ROY THE TANK 07999 724599

AUCTIONEER'S GAVEL. Do I hear £5? 01999 593382

BABY BOY two days old. Unwanted gift. Laetitia 07999 978410 txt msg ONLY after 3.45pm

PAIR OF beautiful black and gold "Beardsley Boy" football boots. Black boot £10. Gold boot £35,000. Box FE8236

PLASTERING

NO JOB TOO SMALL (no small jobs)

Phone Norman on 07999 814411

PISS OFF TERRY!

GAS COOKER in tiny test tube. No-one wants it. 01999 823989

64GB POPIPAD. Spinach wheel of death. Bluetoothsk capability untested. Well, whaddya knowsk? 01999 738724

CHIPPENDALE sideboard furniture jigsaw. Corner piece missing. It was really cold, I'd run out of firewood and I had no idea how much it was worth. Hence £3500 the lot. Codge 87798

PROJECTION SCREEN with indelible image of Jenny in the coypu house in Jersey wildlife parc 1963. Also broken slide projector. £3 both. Frank and Jenny, 01999 859434

A EGG. £1. Framley 01999 1.

RADIO CONTROLLED dining table on wheels. As seen on TV's "Dinner Race" and "Did I Build That?". £250. Molford 366289

BIG GIRL'S BLOUSE £10, smartie pants £15, clever clogs £20. 01999 234780

USED TISSUE 5p. Real alive dolphin too big for jacuzzi £offers. Will not separate. BOX FE8052

DRAGONSBELT lead figurines in perfect condition, I think you'll find. Wizards' Wagon £6, Bradford and Bingley's War Chariot £7, a bag of tiny lead spells £40 and collection of colourful and unique 1-sided dice £5. Still boxed, with receipt in Forbidden Hobby carrier bag. Unwanted gift because I own the set in its entirety twice over, of course – one painted by my own fair hand, one for best. Correspondence on the subject should be carried out with a certain Mr. V. Balrog (that's me, for those of you who didn't guess, ho ho), 38 years old, 9 Beetroot Promenade, Fracton FR2 8BT. Phone for perhaps more. 01999 467889.

SONY MILKMAN with headphones. Holds up to 4000 cheery whistles. £30 Box FE8349

LOFT CONVERSIONS

Make the most of your roof space

Turn it into a cellar or a stable or a secret base

Ring for a no free quote 09999 920639

MICROSOFT OFFICE XP. Will convert to Microsoft Baby's Bedroom XP. £15 please 01999 234098

HAIRDRYING action game kit. "All the fun of hair-to-hair combat." With tongs, nets and two semi-automatic hairdryers. £15. 01999 887235

IT WAS ONLY A LITTLE ONE

MATERNITY LADDER extends to 35ft. British Midwife Association disapproved. £15. 01999 248708

THE GOOD, THE EBONY & THE IVOR THE ENGINEY. Eastwood/Wonder/Postgate concept album. I WILL PAY YOU to take this away. 07999 284800 (24-hours)

CORNER OF ROOM with assembly instructions. In original packaging. £35 01999 490692

RABBITS, PARROTS, snakes, lizards, tortoises, chinchillas. Guaranteed 30-minute delivery. Free garlic bread. 01999 779238

TOASTER, Russell Hobbs, stainless steel, used once. Some bathwater damage, hence £10. 01999 753943

PAIR OF wrought iron trousers with entryphone £80. Leonard after 01999 6pm.

LARGE 4-WHEEL roadgoing electric Jamie Oliver. Bound to come in handy all the time £350. 01999 293369

BOBBINS

YES PLEASE £15. 01999 793604

VINTAGE QUIZ MACHINE. Based on DLT's classic Radio One resignation speech. Generally good condition but in need of some restoration (broken quack quack oops). OIRO £200 incl. delivery if local. 01999 487686

CANON Pachelbel camera. Takes all photographs in D major and made of wool, otherwise in perfect working order. £375. 07999 737228

The Framley Examiner

Framley's Traditional Favourite Since 1839

Your obituary here could be reaching

15,000 readers

"I sold my deceased father within minutes. An intriguing and mysterious service. Many thanks."

Mr C. Myfanwy, Mountain Road, Waleshire.

LAURA ASTLEY wallpaper. Ten rolls with repeating sheet music for the late designer's hit single, "Never Going to Hang You Up" £5 each 01999 834377

MEN'S BEIGE TROUSERS. 36in waist, 32in leg, 28in piss stain. 50p. 01999 943577

MDF-EFFECT mahogany dining table. £25. 01999 350950

BRIAN JACKS reviews the 1984 computer game Juggles' Rainbow. This is not a joke. We have the proof. Spread the good word. Hallelujah. Box FE8390

WOMAN'S MOUNTAIN BIKE for sale. Pink. Hardly used due to pregnancy. VGC. £35. Also litter of baby woman's mountain bikes, mainly tabby, some ginger. Box FE8377

HELLO, THIS IS a message for Adrian in the classifieds department. Adrian, it's your mum. Can you bring a packet of fish fingers home for your tea? Haddock, not cod, you know how it upsets your father. Ring me before you leave 01999 262903

FACIAL EXERCISER as used by the stars. Sealed/still in box. This particular one hasn't actually been used by the stars, to be honest. Never mind. Box FE840468:)75

EIGHTEEN HOLE golf shoes. 01999 724920

WW2 GASMASK. Vintage. Ideal for chemical attack. Not tested for working. Still contains bits of Grandad's nose. £30. 07999 638374

SCRABBLE patio paving slabs. 50. (58 on double word score). BOX FE8223

AUDIOBOOKS, many titles including Framley & Wripple phone directory 1996, Renault Tic-Tac owners manual, Teach Yourself Sign Language, all read by me. I do requests in the accent of your choice (Welsh/ Pakistani or Elmer Fudd). Nigel 07999 230979

SEAT for bike for sale for £4. For details call Fforbes on 444444 after 4.40pm.

STRETCH ARMSTRONG. With worsening hernia, hence offers 07999 384798

FLAMPARDS. Set of 1970s TV tie-in novels by MK Peyton. Edwardian teenage girl plays soccer for Chelsea and England. Very rare. £80 the set. Box FE8510

CHILD'S RED PLASTIC Parliamentary Democracy playset, with 650 MPs and 300,000 civil servants. Oona King missing, hence £20. "*****" – Hansard. 01999 465530

1960s COLLECTOR'S ITEM. Original hand-drawn cel from Monty Python's Yellow Submarine. From 'All You Need Is The Bright Side Of Life' sequence. Features all four Pythons and Norwegian Blue Meanie. £offers Box FE8603.

ABSOLUTE BALLS

BIBLE, rare David Bowie translation. £offers BOX FE8255

BLACK & DECKER BustDuster. Hand operated service in the privacy of your own home. Call Vince on 07999 914663

AU PAIR wanted. Must have pierced tongue. BOX FE8980

A PICTURE of your child! 1000's available. Hi-resolution. Salvaged hard-drives. Call Framley Vice Squad for availability. 999 after 999pm

DIGGER HIRE. Driveways. Trenching. Landscaping. Turning up at work in a great big fuck off digger and screwing with their tiny fucking heads. Ha ha! BOX WITHHELD

DEAR Mrs Thatcher. My balls smell. Please come and live with me. I mean you no harm. Box FE8236.

COOKBOOK. Cooking with Renault Espace Airbags. They're a bit like dumplings. Quite nice but not nice enough, hence £2. 01999 845300

CLEAN ME CLEAN ME CLEAN ME. I am, after all, your hair. BOX FE8409

TEENAGE GIRL'S writing desk with big hearts over the i's and kisses at the bottom. 01999

PAIR OF chocolate brown draylon 'Armchair Gloves'. Let people sit in your big, comfortable hands. Make guests feel like a right pair of idiots. 01999 410923

FOOT SPAR convenience store. Soothes, relaxes & half-price luncheon meat. 01999 521911

CURTAINS. 67" by 126". With my bare bum printed on them. Bound to be an unwanted gift. £55 BOX FE8209

6 CUPS with matching saucers, coasters and people drinking from them. Will not separate. £5 and 01999 859023

KEEN RECORD COLLECTOR seeks 16s, 33s, 45s and 78s for fun nights out perhaps more? Box FE67738

DOG training in the privacy of your own home. Adobe Illustrator and Billy Crystal impressions. Reduced rates if both booked. 07999 238849

CRACK PIPE. With colourful logo 'World's Number One Mum'. £15 01999 823409

FISHMONGER'S SWEATER. Distinctively aromatic. £anything 01999 823356

LIGHTWEIGHT folding grandmother. Ideal for business travel, family functions etc. 01999 838378 for detail's

A MAN and a man require a van and another van to start two businesses. 07999 234888

MOTORWAY FOOTBALL SET. Ideal for tailbacks (during or causing). Some 'minor' damage to one set of goalposts and only six 'Careful! I'm playing motorway football!' stickers left hence £15ono. 07999 384758

LEONARDO DICAPRIO. Collection of one video and one book. In fair condition. Would suit fan. £8.29 in all. 01999 what am I saying I haven't got a phone

UNWANTED GIFTS wanted. 01999 209739

Z.Z.A.A.A.A.A.A.A.A.1.A REMOVALS

We're last in the phone book but first in the trade

07999 ZZAAAA

VERY OLD 1920s picture mirror depicting a jolly sailor wanking into a bin. Classic advertisement for Player's Navy Cut. Serious offers only. 01999 735030

MC Hammer's Nursery & Babycare. Childminding in the style of MC Hammer by qualified childcare professional with 28 years' experience (3 years' experience as MC Hammer). Stop! Bedtime! 01999! 859298!

COMPUTER DISK. Pine. £35. 01999 480393

BOOK. 100 Great Bedtime Stories About The Nokia 7880 Mobile Phone. Sends them straight to sleep. £1,875 ono BOX FE8345

PAIR OF oh what are they called? Oh no, I remembered just now. Now it's gone again. Ah. Oh bugger. I'll call you back. 01999 660072

RACIST? But racist in a nice way? We meet every week at the Village Hall in Chutney Percy. Chutney Percy Nice Nazis Guild. Almost all welcome.

SINGING CRAB. With display rug. Packs flat for transport. 01999 244951

BLACK LEATHER Footstool. Factory sealed, never used. First person shooter, team tactics, realistic graphics. Xbox I think. 07999 947437

FLYING LESSONS. The secret men have craved for centuries, revealed. If you're scared enough, you can fly! I will scare you into the air. Discreet, frightening service. BOX FE8458

BUM MASTER Bathtub. Soothing then surprising. Spring loaded mechanism. £135ono. 01999 534009

HIGH QUALITY print of low quality painting. £whatever 01999 734943

EBAY for sale. There's one in my computer. It can be yours for just £25. Buyer to collect the lot. 01999 359490

KIDNEY SHAPED pond and pair of pond-shaped kidneys (human). £01999 923409

STUFFED STAG. Roll of barbed wire. Assorted Thompson Twins singles. Jar of pickled onions. Nailgun. Used once. Can't remember what on earth for. £30 the lot. Altogether now, 0-1-9-9-9, 9-5-9-double-5-0

PAUL LUMB PLUMBING

24 hour service

No call out charge too large

01999 42974

LIL' UMPIRE'S 5ft tall Tennis Pushchair. With two bottles of Robinson's Gripe Water. £15 BOX FE8345

DIDDLE-dee-di-de-dee two ladies' suede jackets. Diddle-dee-di-de-dee £2. 01999 375850

JOHN GRISHAM NOVELS. Full set. Some hardback. Some paperback. Some not by John Grisham. Some not books. Load of old stuff in a bag. Ring me.

SWALLOW PRAM. I swallow pram for you. I swallow real good. Real fast. Real hungry. Spit out baby if asked. BOX FE8155

ZIPPY-TO-ZIPPY COMBAT

COLLECTORS PLATE. Showing cast of 1960s ATV series 'The Collectors'. Peter McCorkney, The Organiser, Mrs O'Lady. Very rare. £offers 01999 723020

PAYING too much tax? It's easy. I will show you how. Call Vince on 07999 923023

MARSHALL 100 watt sandwich amplifier. Best results with toasted. Buyer to collect £85. 01999 734599

The Framley Examiner

Framley's Traditional Favourite Since 1839

SENSATIONAL!

Your ad may look sensational in a box for only £8.45

SENSATION AL

I offer all sensations apart from queasiness and sexyal joy.

Phone Alan now on 01999 838200 for free sample

CAR, HOUSE AND various expensive electrical consumer goods. £3. Call now while I'm drunk. 01999 we got cut off

WOODEN rabbit hutch with mesh to prevent those bloody mice breaking in and riding the rabbits round and round in a little race again. £55ono 01999 609292

WELL ESTABLISHED BUSINESS FOR SALE

SUCCESSFUL and thriving Borough Council, Framley town centre area. £244.8m to you.

All enquiries to Mr Mayor on 01999 850594

Mayor has balls done

by Challenger Putney

BEAUTY IS SAID to be only skin deep and Framley mayor William D'Ainty found out how true that is when he had his balls done (see picture).

The Mayor was visiting Framley Community College's newly refurbished Department of Therapeutic Beauty. "It's been ages since I've had my balls done," he purred whilst partaking of the executive service provided by 17-year-old trainee Julian Boscography, who is currently studying for a BTEC National Diploma in Balls Science.

PUBIC HEALTH

The refurbishment caused the temporary closure of the department last October and Mr D'Ainty's balls have needed doing since the week after that. He was recently forced to travel to and from work in a motorised

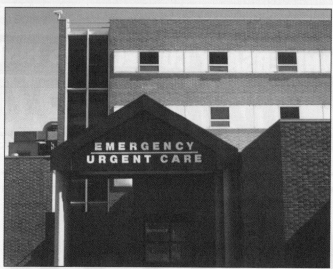

The capable hands of Framley Community College.   PHOTO BY RAISIN D'ETRE

pram following concerns from other bus passengers.

A narrow range of training courses is available at the college and the salon is open Mon-Fri 9pm-5pm

during term-time for any member of the public wishing to have their balls done. For further information or to book an appointment ring 01999 827462.

CHUCK LE CORNER's

Wonderful World of Our Wonderful, Wonderful World

Here are some more facts about our world. If you know anything, do send it in! Some of these are from Mrs E. Gosling of Whoft, and the rest are from other readers (do write in to me if you spot one of yours of course!) All copyright Chuck Le Corner!

If you have difficulty remembering the RAINBOW and how to spell then try this simple trick...
Red, **A**mber, **I**ndigo, (**N**o colour), **B**lack, **O**live, **W**hite.

The easiest way to remove salt from your carpet is to pour red wine over the affected area if superstition dictates that when you spill the salt you should throw some over my left shoulder.

To tell how far away you can run from an approaching storm, try drinking a fizzy drink and count the time between the lightning and your eventual burp.

Ostriches can run at over 100 miles per hour, but they can't hide.

If it rains for a year and a day on St. Swithin's Day, then Our Lord Jesus Christ will rise from His watery grave to judge us all!

Here's some more of my popular cow facts! (I'm running out, of course!)

If the cows in the field are upside down, we'll never hear the last of it.

A sheep has three stomachs; skimmed, semi-skimmed and fat cow.

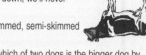

You can tell which of two dogs is the bigger dog by measuring them both and taking away the smaller of the two dogs.

Wind is caused by clouds clapping. I think this is where we get the phrase 'cloud pleasing'.

Well, can you hear the sound of the sea in daylight from the bottom of the well?

The first cuckoo in space is always the first sign of spring.

If you laid all the clocks in the world end to end they would reach to the end of time.

The Apple Moth is so named.

Oh! I've found another cow fact.

YOUR LAST CHANCE TO ENTER MISS FRAMLEY!

SEE PAGE 31

30th April 1981

Drunken revellers at a Sockford fancy dress party left a man with a broken collarbone and a green face after solving his Rubik's cube costume in less than three minutes.

18th June 1997

Food & Drink star Anthony Worral-Thompson opened St Icklebrick School's summer fete and was the first to take his shoes off to have a go on the bouncy Caesar salad.

Recall of soldiers

FRAMLEY COUNCIL HAS warned residents of a recall of tinned soldiers.

The recall is of tins of Newby's Premium Bread & Butter Dipping Soldiers in Brine with best before dates of March and April 2004.

Last week Newby's of Molford received complaints that the contents were foul smelling as well as reports of exploding cans and fizzing bread.

Anyone who has bought one of the affected tins should bury it six feet down in their back garden and call the council Bomb Disposal Unit as a matter of utmost urgency. Anyone who has eaten any of the affected contents should be evacuated as soon as possible.

LE MANOIR AUX QUAT'STEVENS

Framley's only Michelin-starred restaurant invite you to enjoy an exciting new menu of dishes created by our new commis chef

HE SAYS HIS NAME IS BERT

with a special introductory offer of
10% off
tous les plats de Bert

LE MANOIR AUX QUAT'STEVENS, 14 MONA BONE JAKON STREET, FRAMLEY
BOOKINGS ON 01999 65 63 60

News In Brief

NEW VIEW OF TREE

Molford tourist information centre has commissioned a calendar of Moldford's oldest oak tree for next year. There are nine different views of the tree including one or two from above, and three of significant leaves. More than 1000 calendars have been printed at an overall cost of £10, on recycled paper aeroplanes.

POLICE WEAPONS IDEA

More weapons have been handed out at Framley police station that at any other station in the Framley area over the last 5 weeks. Police say that they believe that the public will only use them for lawful purposes. A total of 425 knives, 30 forks and a 10ft nutcracker have been put back on the streets "where they belong". "It could easily save a crime" says Top Copper Rupert Bone. "People can come and collect weapons from me at the front desk anonymously," he added in a different voice.

Secrets

Framley's residents-only fish and chip shop

INVISIBLE TO OUTSIDERS

When you've lived here for five years, you'll see it!

EXCLUSIVE: Invisible pickled egg 50p

WRIPPLE MASTODON

BRIEF ENCOUNTER: RELOADED
Daily 1.00, 3.20, 5.00, 7.25

L'ANNÉE DERNIÈRE À MARIENBAD 2 THE LEGEND OF CURLY'S GOLD
Daily 1.00, 5.20, 8.00, 10.25

BENEATH THE PLANET OF THE MANON DES SOURCES
Daily 4.00, 6.20, 6.25, 9.45

THE UNBEARABLE LIGHTNESS OF BEING, FOLLOW THAT CAMEL
Mon – Thu 3.00, 6.10, 11.45

Telegram bookings. Luncheon vouchers accepted.
103 Wagon Wheel, Wripple 01999 900 167

Turn over a new leaf (page) this Christmas at TWEBBINS with these Bestsellers (books)!

The Best Selling book in the history of the Universe

DAN BLAND THE ROLF HARRIS WORDSEARCH

DAN BLAND THE ROLF HARRIS WORDSEARCH
The 'Run Away!' bestseller. Renowned binman Jacques Oblong is found dead alongside a wordsearch alluding to the paintings of Rolf Harris. Can completely original hero Montana Jones solve a series of crosswords, *Call My Bluff* rounds and which-child-has-caught-the-fish puzzles and unravel the mystery? Comes with a free set of Boggle dice and a proper book.
"Answers on page 68" – JUMBO PUZZLER

LEVIATHAN BENZ THE SODDING BIG BOOK

PLEASE CONSULT A STRUCTURAL ENGINEER BEFORE PLACING ON YOUR BOOKSHELF

LEVIATHAN BENZ THE SODDING BIG BOOK
"Compelling epic sci-fi fantasy that almost broke both my arms" - ORBITOID
Bound in lead with an articulated iron bookmark and endpaper maps etched onto solid bronze.

TOBY SPITFIRE THE MOUSTACHE
In 1942, the Allies have only one thing in their sights... A tale of sabotage based on a true moustache.
"The book his publisher made him write".

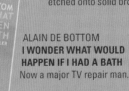

ALAIN DE BOTTOM I WONDER WHAT WOULD HAPPEN IF I HAD A BATH
Now a major TV repair man.

GWYNETH BILLIONS DANNY PUDDING AND THE PICTURE OF A DRAGON ON THE FRONT
"...another one."
- THE BOOKSTACKER

MELISMA HOITY-PLANK & TRILBY FATZDREADFUL HOW TO LOOK LIKE AN EGG
Must-have makeover bible from the authors of WHAT NOT TO PUBLISH and HOW OLD IS YOUR ROPE?

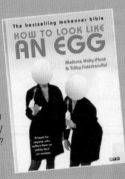

The bestselling makeover bible
HOW TO LOOK LIKE AN EGG
Melisma Hoity-Plank & Trilby Fatzdreadful

ANNE RUBBISH THE COERCIVE LESTRADE
"Erotic vampire fantasy that doesn't help" – PSYCHOLOGY TODAY

HISTORIC PLASTIC BAGS OF OLD FRAMLEY – IN POSTCARDS
with a forward by Martin Spar
"... the only book you'll ever need" – FRANLEY EXAMINER

Having a happy Christmas from Twebbins of Newby's of Molford

TWEBBINS

THE BOOKSHOP WITH NO IMMEDIATELY DISCERNIBLE DIFFERENCE

Road safety week gets off to a smashing start

by Adam Wrent

A NEW BID has been launched to cut the number of road traffic accident's on Framley's roads.

Each year nearly 200 people are killed on the town's roads, a statistic which remains the only one I could find on the subject. >wheres my desk gone everyone ha ha very funny AW>system:

Launching Road Safety Week, Chief Constable Rupert Bone said that 317 people were injured or injured and killed on the area's roads last year.

SMILEY FACE

He also unveiled portable electronic indicators which will be installed at blackspots around Framley. These display a smiley face if a vehicle passes them safely and a sad face if the car is involved in an accident.

Ch Con Bone went on to explain that of the road crash statistics, nearly 20% were children, about half of whom were little boys.

"For this reason, we will also be launching our True Driving Waits campaign, to encourage the under sixteens not to drive until they're sixteen," he said.

One of the white lines on the new Pelican Crossing near Denegate bursts into flames, showing the dangers of road safety more clearly than a million words.

PHOTOGRAPH BY CHRISTMAS TANGERINE

Among other ideas being tried out is a new scheme to encourage more lollipop ladies to come forward. Next month, a new One-Stop Lollipop Shop will open in Denegate, where anyone can buy a £3 daily licence to lolly people across the town's roads whether they want it or not

House theft horror

Property worth £960,000 was stolen from an address in Chutney-le-Basil last Thursday. Thieves made off with a house, double garage and over 4 acres of grounds.

Molford Spectacular

The waiting is over for those of you who have been reading about "the summer's biggest family day out" to be staged at the Molford Showground in August! This year's Molford Spectacular has been cancelled after Molford Borough Council refused to grant the organisers an entertainment licence.

Councillor's "worst nightmare" comes true

A Framley councillor says that his "worst nightmare" has come true after a car collided with a milk float driven by the Devil and hundreds of six-foot tall heavy metal rabbits wearing Russell Grant masks on Tuesday.

Fears that other nightmare scenarios from the tired mind of Councillor Henry Armour may come true were fuelled by the appearance of his old Economics teacher, the late Mr Porling, in the nude, waving some unfinished homework at the corner of Bilham Court and Denegate.

Traffic calming measures and a nice mug of Horlicks are likely to remain in place in the area and on Councillor Armour's bedside table until the matter can be resolved.

In Court

MARTIN Eeyore of 11, Edd The Duck Terrace, Glibley was convicted of an act of gross confusion involving a half-empty glass at the Molford Optimists' Association on Feb 18th 2004. He was screwed to a silver cloud and hoisted into the sky as an example to us all.

PIOTR Pumpkinytr, a Ukrainian immigrant, of Mandy Robot House, Dungeon Estate, Batley, was sentenced to 24 years wrongful imprisonment for keeping himself to himself with intent. A substantial ledger of binocular observations from his neighbours was taken into consideration.

SNOOP Deputy Dogg of Asphalt Reach, Effing Sodbury was fined £350 with £120 costs for erecting a Michelmas Noggin on St Hector's Field in Wripple after Cockcrow on All-Bottom's-Eve. He will be forced to be Queen Of The May and live on a carnival float until 2005, when he will be invited to defend his title, as is traditional, against all-comers and His Worship The Mayor.

HERMIS Bougalou was fined £110 and £30 costs for driving a table football table without due care and attention, in the fast lane near Junction 14 of the FR404. He was also asked to surrender the table for examination by a team of postgraduate Engineering students from the Sockford Academy, and never speak of it again.

WEATHER WATCH

CORRECTION

In our weather report last week, we suggested that the Tuesday would be warm, with a light SE wind. In fact, it was -14C with 280mph winds from the N and structural damage from the S. In addition, it was no warmer on Wednesday, and brimstone and wormwood did not rain down hot from the heavens, as we also predicted. We apologise for this minor oversight.

PICTURE OF THE WEEK

Battery Flatford's new European signing, Olirehndinho, lines up to take a rare elevated penalty against Durbiton Wonderful after a mid-air clash above the six-yard box with Wonderful's defender Colin Pipe left the Flatford winger shoelaceless. This remarkable picture was taken by Durbiton's goalkeeper George Wanderers on his trusty Pentax K-series, just before his timely substitution.

FRAMLEY'S OLDEST BODYGUARD SERVICE

GENTS

At Gents we know all about looking after our customers. After all, we've been doing exactly that since Mr. Gents started his exclusive personal protection business from the back of his father's famous Clocks and Mussels stall in Fracton way back in 1843. Time moves quickly, but we don't. Mr. Gents still runs the firm in the same way that he always has, just as his father still runs his.

Call us today for instant* peace of mind.

09-5342

*may take a little while to respond. Our ears and legs aren't what they once were.

PUTTING THE CUSTOMER FIRST SINCE 1843
WE'RE BEHIND YOU ALL THE WAY!

A CHANGE IS AS GOOD AS

Ccommittee treasurer Michael D'Ordinaire proudly displays the historic 1992 poster for the historic concert. **PHOTO BY RYAN CHAMPAGNE**

DOODLE MAGNA, a village on the outskirts of Whoft, has voted by three to one in favour of changing its name to Chrisdeburghborough, commemorating a pop concert that was cancelled at the last minute in September 1992. "It's the second most exciting thing that's ever happened here, and what better way to mark the occasion," according to the village committee.

Hard to shift

MISS – Every day on my journey to work I take the path between Blandings Avenue and Collaborator Crescent and every day (on my journey to work) I am shocked by the dog mess that is there.

According to my records, this particular turd was laid in the alley sometime in the summer of 1998. Since the entire alleyway is blocked by the offending chod and the council have refused to answer their CB radio hotline since 1981, I took it upon myself to take the dimensions of the dirt to see if it constitutes an obstruction under the highways act.

Unfortunately it doesn't, even though it's now home to three abandoned shopping trolleys and a double mattress. 83% of Framley's homes now have lots of it trodden into their carpets (according to this independent survey).

If the council are refusing to deal with the ploppe then at the very least they should remove the grafitti from it – it's a real eyesore. Children pass by it every day – some as young as

an half. I was once very happy to live on this estate. Now I'm not very happy to be writing to you in this way.

EBITH RODINSON
Psmith Pstreet
Codge

Parent is concerned

MISS – In my day, if a child was different in any way whatsoever, then they would have been relieved of their dinner money before they had got halfway across the school playground.

Nowadays it seems that a shy, 4'8" 13-year-old with a speech impediment can go a whole term without being picked on once.

I've tried everything. I've bought him a pair of £5 market shoes and I always cut his hair for him with nail scissors. I've even tried sending him to school on a girl's bike but to no avail. I've even been round to have a word with the bully's parents and they gave me a Chinese burn, so it's not a problem with the family.

Why is my son unbullyable?

PROF MARTIN LITTLENOSE
Gaylord Avenue
Whoft

A racist remark worth remembering

MISS – Last week, while riding the Whoft to Molford bus, I overheard a new abusive term.

A Swiss-looking gentleman was fiddling with his change while getting on board, holding up the whole queue.

The driver referred to the obstructive passenger as a "bungling clockhead". I thought your readers might find this term useful.

NAME AND ADDRESS SUPPLIED

Very helpful aun't they?

MISS – Are record shop staff actually no better than trained monkeys eating a banana each?

When I went into the Whoft branch of an anonymous national entertainment retail chain (with a man up a balloon) (which I shall remain anonymous) none of them had even heard of the brand new Jimmy Edwards single. I bought it from Woolworth's where they were also very helpful. Please pass on to their thanks.

MR STEPHEN FRANKLYN PINVIN
6 Malvern Walk
Whoft

A local hero to be proud of

MISS – With reference to your story (Examiner, July 10) headed "A local hero to be prod of", I feel there is another surefire contender for the crown.

You need not look any further than this letter, in which I am about to divulge whom I believe I am talking about.

Granary Belborough, a former mayor, schoolmaster, driving instructor, leading rotarian, explorer, undercover milkman and cold air balloonist, was a pillar of the local community

and an example to us all.

Mr Belborough lived a full life until he and his family were killed in 1940 when their street received a direct hit from a particularly well-struck cricket ball.

The ball in question was delivered by my grandfather, Roger Opiate, then leading bowler for the county cricket team, on his way to an unbeaten 729 for 0.

This scoreline alone should have guaranteed his immortality at the expense of Mr. Belborough's.

POPPY O'PÂTÉ
Flat B
The Old A-Team Van
Railway Arches
Sockford

358 Short Road Wripple

MISS – Call me old-fashioned but it's political correctness gone mad! You can't even call me old-fashioned any more! Apparently I'm now "Mr Dawson".

MR J. DAWSON
358 Short Road
Wripple

And penultimately...

MISS – Regarding the letters of complaint regarding the new wind farm, I must add a single voice of approval.

Since its opening I have managed to convert my entire fleet of miniature animatronic dustmen to wind-power with relatively few union issues needing to be resolved.

Iamthedirectorof@tinylittle-littermen.co.uk
Slovenly

Help requested

MISS – At the recent Zephyr 1375AM roadshow held upon the seafront at Clinton, my co-presenter The Colonel got rather carried away. In a minute of madness during the Swap-a-Doodle-Doo section of the show, The Colonel somehow managed to exchange our three-

year-old pedigree poodle, Maniche, for a signed Polaroid of the late Formula One racing champion, James Hunt.

Following the show, he admitted that in the heat of the moment he may have become somewhat overexcited. Unfortunately by this time the pre-pubescent young lady with whom he had entered into the barter, had already departed. Chien à complêt!

We would very much appreciate it if the girl, who was wearing toffee-coloured flip-flops and a fake Blue Peter badge, could get in touch with us to negotiate the return of Maniche.

Adequate compensation will of course be offered, although due to unforeseen circumstances, we have now lost the singed Polaroid of James Hunt.

TENBY AND THE COLONEL
c/o Zephyr 1375 AM
Peking Duck Street
Framley

Quotes of the Week

"I can't say that I'm pleased with the outcome, but it's certainly a start. And they can start by sticking it up their arses."

"No, I'm not bald. You're bald."

"This initiative could provide every family in Framley with seventeen years' worth of my breast milk if all goes to plan."

"She said 'it was raining and you'd best wear that balaclava'. I think."

"It's all too easy to say that conscription is the answer. But that would mean 17 Across is wrong."

"Blimey! You're right, I'm bald. As you were."

This week's apology

The Framley Examiner would like to apologise to the family of Anthony Tonibell, whose sad death on November 11th was announced on the obituary page of the November 4th edition of the paper.

This was due to space restrictions.

SOLICITORS ADVICE with Captain Mitchell

We've all been there. It's two in the morning, you have finally drifted off to sleep and then out of nowhere comes the blast of a flugelhorn. In 9 out of 10 cases, this sound can be attributed to anti-social nocturnal trumpollution caused by your next door neighbours. Sometimes the noise made by these thoughtless people is so loud that you end up in the same room as them.

So, if you're suffering from sleepless nights due to neighbours who create unwanted noise by:

• growing wooden beards
• going through your dustbin looking for clues
• riding a drumkit up and down the stairs
• hosting late-night strongman competitions
• posting their baby repeatedly through your letterbox

then don't panic, because help is at hand.

Framley Environmental Health Department have published a leaflet entitled *Shut Up! – 10 easy ways to make your neighbours shut up.*

It describes in a simple, easy-to-learn language how to approach the problem and includes useful advice from solicitors, counselors and a fishmonger.

The Health Department have also issued the following short-term advice to help deal with any issues arising from noise pollution.

No one wants to upset their neighbours, so the first step you should take is to go around their house and quietly pin them to the wall. If this has no effect then stay indoors making a similar sound but facing the opposite direction and see if it cancels out the offending noise. If all else fails the easiest way to deal with unwanted noise is to go deaf.

TURN YOUR SPARE CASH INTO COL£SLAW

MORE ONION!

SECRET EUROPEAN PROCESS

THE ALL NEW ORIGINAL CABBAGE & CARROT COMPANY

40, Diddyman Parade, Framley

Wallace Umbodsman

Solicitors, Estate Agents and Circus Strongmen   01999 712223

BRADLEY MILTON

We are pleased to offer accomodation in this much-sought-after wooden tower. Living space is well-situated on the strong side of the tower with good prospects of not falling over for at least three more moves. Planning permission to remove bottom of tower pending.

£420pcm

PLEASE DON'T ASK WHERE

Deceptively habitable coal bunker conversion on the border of civilisation. Look at the kitten. Keep looking at the kitten and give us

£182,000

GHASTLEY ST MATTHEW

Desirable Money-For-Nothing-style property near local services and main road.

£210,000

NEWBURY HOBGOBLIN

Rare opportunity to own this attractive period property set in the middle of a

£276,950

POTTYMOUTH

Unique character cottage with horn section in every room. Bathroom (Kick Horns), 2 beds (Nelson Riddle Orch), 1 Recep (Elmer Bernstein). Must be heard.

£276,950

THOXTOXETER BASIN

Increasingly detached house. South facing when approached from North. North facing when approached from south. Boiler blows hot and cold. Separate bedrooms. Imminent-Split-Level sulking room. Quick sale preferred before it goes back to live with mother.

OIRO £240,000

HAVING A BIT OF TROUBLE FINDING A PROPERTY?

FRANK O'BETTYS

BEEFBURGER HILLS. Two bedroom end of terrace house within easy walking distance of Framley Rail station (although impossible to reach the southbound platform except by leaving via the small bathroom window). Available now £705pcm

XXX-RATED HOUSE. Pool constantly needs cleaning. Beautiful red hot views. Double chimney breasts. Rear entry. Back garden with beautiful Brazilian shaved bushes. £POA

OLD FRAMLEY. Stupid bungalow specially adapted for idiots. Many moronic features. South-facing garden for south-facing cretins. £15pcm

FULLY FURNISHED ground flr flat. Lounge, bedroom, kitchen (with white goods), dead horse dressed up as a weatherman, new bathroom. £475pcm

SPACE TO RENT on lap or knee. Call Grandpa Jilly on Tiswas 239887

DETACHED house with detached roof attached. Or without, I don't mind. £?

STAR PROPERTY

THIS UNIQUE listed property is here listed alongside other properties. **£850pcm**

A SUPERIOR DEVELOPMENT of nine luxury flats and four shithouses. Prices range from £2pcm to £350,000pcm.

SPECIAL EDITION HOUSE with builder's commentary, deleted rooms, French windows with subtitles. £1,895pcm

SPENCER ROAD   CLIFF EDGE   FRAMLEY

01999   OOOOOO

Sampson & Simpson

PROPERTY CONSULTANTS SINCE 23AD

48, WALKERS WALK, FRAMLEY

01999 624090

**OPEN 7 DAYS A WEEK
SELLING 3 DAYS A WEEK**

STREPSILHAM

A three-bedroom bungalow with off-road bathroom, open plan front door, double-glazed central heating and walk-in boiler.

Guide price: £215,085

EFFING SODBURY

A beautifully presented but very very very small house. One brightly lit room, approx 3 ft high. Weighs less than 300g. Ideal second home for child (2-4yrs).

Guide price: £257,500

CHIPNEY

An extended two-bedroom terraced house with Shakin' Stevens-style kitchen. Excellent bathrooms throughout.

Guide price: £199,999

MOLFORD

This 10-bedroom, semi-detached property in a popular area. 3 spacious bedrooms, plus 1 bedroom with bath / sink / wc, 1 bedroom with cooker / fridge / sink, 1 bedroom with fireplace / TV point, 1 bedroom with french windows / serving hatch, 1 bedroom with bottom of stairs and front door, 1 bedroom with top of stairs and commanding view of front door, and master bedroom with cold water tank, fibreglass carpeting and little pets. Also greenhouse with planning permission for conversion to bedroom.

Guide price: £295,000

MOLFORD ST MALCOLM

An immaculately presented cottage pie in the heart of a charming village kitchen. Serves four (two en suite). Still warm at time of going to press.

Guide price: £3.99

CUBBING BROCCOLI

A classic Bond house. Lounge with fish tank and casino, bow-tie shped swimming pool, double '0' garage with car chase, secret passages, mad scientists, tiny manservant, octopussy galore. Leasehold explodes in 69 years.

Guide price: £CLASSIFIED

DURBITON

A beautifully refurbished one-bedroom, five-storey town house. Lounge with open fireplace, kitchen with open door, four-storey bedroom with ample space for human pyramid.

Guide price: £159,950

The Framley Examiner

The Everglade H(M)OTEL
Come again!
Lightning rarely strikes twice!
01999 765 761

Framley's Traditional Favourite since 1978

FRIDAY MAY 8th, 2007   PRICE 45p IF THAT

PRIZES

Why not try our impossible crossword again?

FASHION

Waiting lists slashed for NHS haircuts

INSIDE

Free DVD of every reader!

Mayors hocked by the morning discovery about the new library

NEW LIBRARY: 'THE DREAM IS 'IT IS OVER"

by Jesus Chigley

THE GRAND OPENING of Framley's new County Library building has been cancelled after Mayor D'Ainty woke up and found it was all a dream.

Though the demolition of the old Framley Library in 2004 did apparently definitely happen, leaving Framley residents without librarying facilities for the last three years, the construction of the new £11m library centre was nothing more that a series of lively night-time fantasies enjoyed by Framley's ebullient mayor, according to Framley's ebullient mayor.

IT WON AN

'I dreamed it all,' Mayor D'Ainty apologised over a heavy cheese supper to reporters last night. 'But then so did the builders and architects. It's been a monstrous waste of all our time.'

< REPLACE WITH PHOTO TAG FE67785 >

The historic botting dunes which face closure and the sea.

PHOTO BY JOGALONG DOG

The muddy site, on the corner of Nesmith Avenue and Denegate, has remained untouched behind hoardings for thirty-six months while a state-of-the-art library, IT centre and adult learning facility took shape in D'Ainty's sleeping mind. He also dreamt it won an award, which, due to pressing work commitments, he

dreamt was accepted on his behalf by Dame Helen Mirren dressed as a sexy tiger lady with no pants.

SO IT GETS

Framley North MP Ianbeale Steeplecocque, who recently married Soul II Soul star Jazzy B, was not available to comment properly.

'I wholeheartedly condemn the actions of these time-terrorists,' he insisted from his bath. 'To propel a major civic building through a wormhole in the structure of reality so it gets bombed in the Blitz before it was even born is an act of extreme cowardice.'

Vince Previous Contractors, the Belize-based construction firm who won the non-existent project, have got a very complicated touchtone menu on their phone and the Hamlet cigar tune.

Mystery death of scientist solves scientific mystery

WHEN BELLAMY BOGLE went for a walk in the woods alone with a dictaphone, he hoped to return with the answer to a long-standing scientific theory.

But when the botanist and father of three failed to return home that evening, his wife raised the alarm. Twelve hours later, his body was found under a fallen tree by officers from Molford police.

Bogle, then 48, now still 48 but getting no older, had long been fascinated by the possibility that a tree falling in the woods with no-one to hear it would make no sound.

BOGLE BOOGALOO

Armed only with an axe and a borrowed dictaphone, he set off on a crisp Wednesday morning through Pollard's Wood to chop down, run away from and record a falling tree.

Police who found his body say that the tree crushed him to death instantly, but added that a thorough investigation of his dictaphone tape revealed no sound at all, proving the old wives' theory.

Bogle will be buried at St Benny's-on-the-Hill next month. The tree is still being questioned by police, but has so far remained silent.

EVER WISHED YOU COULD

RIDE A PLUM?

WELL, OF COURSE YOU CAN FOR F***CK SAKE!

AT

Molford St Malcolm

'MAGICAL' PLUM SANCTAURY

The worlds largest jam Plums from around the county

Avant Garde 'FLINTLOCK' (Police aware)

The biggest pile of dogs you'll ever see

Open all day. No kids.

Geoff's Capes

Framley's first stop for strongman fashion

LEOPARDSKIN / SEQUINS / CHAIN MAIL
PARKING FOR 120 UPSIDE-DOWN CARS
FIND US IN THE YELLOW PAGES (DO NOT TEAR IT UP)

19 Sigmarsson Street, Sockford, FM8 7GT

ATTENTION HEADMASTERS!
HAVE WE GOT ANGLE GRINDERS FOR YOU...!

WAS...
A5 Exercise books – £2.99 a dozen
...NOW G490 Angle Grinder – £199.99

WAS...
Box of 50 x HB pencils – £3.49
...NOW BD 'Falcon' Angle Grinder – £89.99

WAS...
Ringbound notebooks – £0.89 each
...NOW JT1000 Angle Grinder – £399.99

KDL IF WE HAVEN'T GOT WHAT YOU WANT, WE HAVE GOT LOTS OF ANGLE GRINDERS

SOCKFORD 'FUNKY NEWSAGENT' 2007 FINALISTS p42   GOBLIN FORECAST p81

Picture Perfect

The Mayoral portrait in place in the foyer of the Civic Centre and (inset) an artist's impression of the conroversial painting.

PHOTOGRAPH BY OAK NONION

by Challenger Putney

A challenging new portrait of this is the Mayor William D'Ainty was unveiled at a ceremony held in the foyer at Framley Civic Centre last week.

The painting, local artist Fabien Giraffe, and the Mayor himself were all present at the occasion which was timed to coincide with the twentieth anniversary of June 3rd, 1987.

Senior council members registered some concern and no surprise that the picture depicted His Worship the Mayor in his vest and pants rather than his official robes.

"He forgot his kit and I only noticed halfway through the third sitting," said Mr Giraffe. "It was too late to do anything about it by then."

The artist usually spends most of his time on the head, trying to get the eyes aligned.

LICKING

A dirty protest made by Mayor D'Ainty during the initial sketches was also caught on canvas by Mr Giraffe, who cleverly managed to transform it into a King Charles spaniel licking at the mayoral feet.

"What?" shrugged D'Ainty in a short speech to those attending the unveiliture. Wearing his trademark vest and pants, he named the portrait The One with Chandler in a Box, and declared it open by cutting it with a pair of council scissors.

"It's perfect, exactly as I intended, Challenger. Leave it. Have you put the milk on?" he told one journalist.

Giraffe's painting replaces the gap on the Civic Centre wall that replaced the depiction of the late Malcolm Butterfly's unaided flight around Sockford in 80 days (later disproved).

Council tax-payers will only be able to see the portrait at specific times; three-minute slots in the special viewing deckchair will be available between 2pm and 4am on weekdays and must be pre-booked. The deckchair, a childhood favourite of D'Ainty's, is to be occupied by a waving mechanical mannequin of the Mayor at all other times.

News in Brief

NEW WAVES

Fracton district councillors have agreed to subsidise much needed improvements to the sea. The council agreed to pay for the overdue replacement of the current 'tatty' waves which have been washing ashore at the town since they last received any significant investment in 1951.

FRAMLEY SALUTES GR8 VICTORIANS!

A competition to send a humorous pornographic text message to Benjamin Disraeli has been organised by Framley's Victorian Society. Entries must be accompanied by a moustache.

SPORT-U-LIKE

Everyone at St Gahan's School for Boys in Framley enjoyed a sports day last week, apart from Nathan Fisher who broke both ankles while measuring the long jump. And his sister Bossanova who sprained her guts during an arrogant display of vertical limbotics. The event raised 24 Bulgarian Lev for the new school beehive.

THIS IS THE POLICE

Framley Police are appealing for volunteers to take part in an ID parade. Volunteers need to be male, white, aged 30-40, about 5'10", wearing thermal dungarees and have murdered a 55-year-old man in the Codge area on 3rd June 2005, but not Leonard Ayling.

CHARLES BUSINESSPLAN & RECEIVERS

"What on earth could possibly go wrong?"

GRAND OPENING SALE

100% OFF EVERYTHING

WHILE SHOP LASTS!

C. Businessplan & Receivers, 52 High St, Thoxtoxeter

Noisy, nosey, nasty next-door neighbours?

CLOSE THAT WINDOW! It's

Mr Sewage

£1/foot. £3.50/yard. Bulk discounts. Sundays half price.

We also fail to provide a carpet cleaning service.

YOUR BUSINESS IS OUR BUSINESS

01999 908070

Est 1967. Celebrating 30 years of indiscriminate effluent redistrribution

Fluff vaccine in short supply

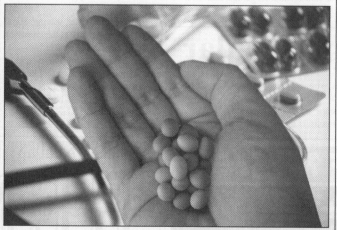

A generous helping of Hmoxydoxylix tablets which look, and taste, like little eggs.

PHOTOGRAPH BY DAVE-BRIAN BONEO

by Dave-Brian Boneo

Extra supplies of the fluff vaccine will need to be shipped in from the United States to meet local demand.

Framley's current outbreak of fluff is now classified as having reached epidemic status, and the vaccine has proved extremely popular and highly addictive.

A spokesman for Framley's Health Department revealed that the vaccine had been "selling like boiling hot cakes" and that their chosen dealer was unable to meet the outrageously high demand.

If vital stocks of the naturally occurring phials are not replenished soon then the police may have to re-resume turning a blind eye to their own brisk underground trade in the deliciously unpredictable hallucinogen.

Even your outspoken Examiner weatherman Dave-Brian Boneo is not in the least bit surprised.

"I've been off my hopscotch on Hmoxydoxylix since 1983, and even I could see that they were going to run out by Whit Monday. If if erm if the supplies if or yes. This is my message to you all."

On other pages

"Let's party," demands clockwork rapscallion (p20)

Looking for love...

getting people together for some small talk and dinner perhaps more... or less! 01999 94 76 94

Women seeking Men

SATURDAY NIGHT FEVER
I love dancing and have no legs. Maybe you have legs and hate dancing. Together I could ride you to happiness (mine). Box FE4388

LANK HAIRED LOVER
Attractive, 29yo female with long, dark hair sprouting from pupils of eyes, otherwise bald, WLTM Griff Rhys-Jones smellalike for traditional country dancing and long walks into the sea. Box FE2719

SOULMATE
Dark-eyed, lively brunette, 5'9", seeks a single man who likes spending time with my mates. I have absolutely no interest in you whatsoever. Box FE7631

SPLASHING OUT
I look like that one from Girls Aloud. No, not that one. The one with the big legs that stands next to the fit one. Fancy a crazy, crazy, crazy, crazy night? Or was that Whitesnake... Box FE9290

DON'T CALL US...
WE'LL CALL YOU!
YOU CAN EARN UP TO £1.50/MIN BY TALKING TO OUR GIRLS
THEY'RE HORNY AND BORING!
08999 997971

BUSINESS ARRANGEMENT
Young-looking 40yo professional woman, 5'4", blonde, with own car and interior decoration business, seeks committed, genuine gentleman 35-45, with a yo ho ho and a hey nonny no, sing ho for the highwayman king! Now gather ye round and contact box FE2778 for the rest of my tale.

LIVELY LADY
Vibrant, lively, 41 year old, single-minded female, interested in that song about the mouse in the windmill and nothing else. Do not attempt to talk to me about anything else. I will not be distracted. Want to meet up? It could (won't) be fun. Box FE5422

PET LOVER
Friendly Framley F, 42, recently widowed, seeks lively, fit, alert M, 35-45 with no fear of commitment or lions. Box FE4188

CALL ME!
I'M ALL STRETCHY!
08999 554341

THREE BREAKFASTS
Caring, slim, petite, attractive F, 27, blue eyes, brown fur, seeks understanding. Box FE9981

OFF AND AWAY!
I'm away for the week. Call my number and hear my sexy answerphone. I will delete your message! Box FE7881

ROBINSON'S BARLEY WATER
Sophisticated, beautiful female, 16-35, sought by optimistic Sockford male, 12. Box FE1635

LITTLE BIT MAYBE YEZYEZ
Attractive mum, St Eyot's, late 30s, sparkling blue personality and long blonde sense of humour seeks toyboy for discreet cuddles that are so discreet my husband won't notice what's going on and neither will I. Box FE8772

HOT LOLLYSTICK JOKE ACTION
08999 5403+
01 Footprints in the butter
02 Doctor Who!
03 Pull Yourself Together
04 Doing the breaststroke, Sir
05 To get to the other side
06 That's what I said, diddle-I?
ADULTS ONLY!

HEAVENS ARE TELLING
Early 40s Whotten Plodney female, Scorpion, seeks lasting relationship with Cancerous man, age irrelevant. Keen interest in astronomy a must. Box FE6110

AAAH! ERIC BRISTO
Hate tall good-looking athletic 32-year-old men? Then read the next advert, I probably shouldn't have mentioned them. Shy redheaded female, 40, looking for tips on how to meet new people. Box FE9383

SQUEEZE ME
Fracton female with real zest for life seeks understanding man made of lemons for citrus-based romance. Box FE1099

HER MAJESTY QUEEN ELIZABETH THE QUEEN
My husband and I WLTM couples for garden parties, overseas tours and state openings. Arise Sir Suitable. And what do you do? Box FE1099

I LOVE THE WAY MY BIG JUICY BUMS SWING
WHILE YOU BANG ME UP THE LEGS!
08999 101033

GOODBYE I'M HELLO LESLEY
Lovelie Lesley, 510, 2'3", with filthy hair and blonde hands, lazy cow and own eye. Why don't you see if you can come up me some time? Box FE8412

LOOK ME UP
Enormous-breasted woman WLTM a man who'll be able to tell me what colour my sodding eyes are after dinner for a change. Information on my shoes also welcome. Box FE9671

JUICY JUDAS
I am the physical manifestation of a wolf-whistle. Imagine that! Ph-wit-ph-woo! Oh. Actually, there's nothing attractive about that. How very disappointing. Sorry about that. Box FE4511

SOME ISOLATED SQUALLY SHOWERS
Pretty tall lady, ugly, likes antiques, dining out and travelling in style seeks relatively wealthy man (must be over 6'2" with a brother worth over £2m). Box FE4739

JOGGING ACCIDENT
You make me feel. You make me feel. You make me feel like a natural yoghurt. New to area 07999 235437

MAINE ATTRACTION
Stephen King fan, gothic female, 38, brown / blonde / blonde, into cinema, reading seeks nice, gentle guy for tying to bed and breaking his fucking ankles, maybe more. Box FE1276

LOOKING FOR LOVE
Single mum, 32, enjoys being single. Fuck off. Box FE8778

OPEN UP, IT'S ONLY THE LAW
Caring F would like to meet considerate M for capital fun. In the armpit if compatible. Box FE8393

REFERENCE LIBRARY
Ho, M, o'sexual. Confused? Far from it. Ring me.

HUGE GAINS ON THE LEFT
European lady, 40, single, likes cooking, seeking tender gentleman, 40-50, for cooking. Box FE1090

HARRYHAUSEN'S HAIR
Not young/beautiful, not old/ugly, not middle-aged/ moderately attractive. Literally no idea Box FE5444

CELEBRITY GOLF
Professional female, 37, WLTM amateur male, age / looks unimportant. FE8381

PLINY THE ELDER
Shy lady seeks warm gentleman with a teaspoon. Oh, and a hat. Box FE8323

Men seeking Women

NO WAY HOME
Cruet-shaped 38yo Framley man, 6'9", twin vertical moustaches, blue hair, enjoys Chinese cinema, yachts and lying about my appearance, WLTM curvaceous & credulous blind woman 25-45. Box FE7384

DIRTY
Well-built male, 39, award-winning Norman Foster design, WLTM statuesque female – no Henry Moores / Rodins. Box FE2577

HOH-HE-HOH-HE-HOH
Hardcore Francophile seeks French-made French maid for French kissing, French dressing and French horn, peut-être plus. Box FE8118

ON THE ROCKS
Male, 27, lifeguard, enjoys pubs, drinking and off licences seeks bottle of Smirnoff. Not usually a violent man. Box FE4923

100% GENUINE
Tall male, 33, sporty, romantic, happily married, seeks extra wife to take over some of current wife's duties, including horseriding and the good things in life. Box FE4090

CONSIDER ME
Oi! Katie Barratt! When I meet you, I will marry you. And marry you HARD. Oh yes. You'll bleeding know it. Get used to the idea. Listen to what I say. Hoping this finds you and your family in good health. With every best wish. Your obedient servant, Sir Triumph Hamstrong CBE. Box FE6541.

WRITE IT DOWN
Yopney St Oh! male, 46, enjoys most things in life except series 3 of Man About the House and untreated wood WLTM Henry Kissinger and / or Richard and / or Judy for autograph-related fun. Box FE2065

Private Fantasies
VERY DISCREET
Coach parties welcome
08999 651175

FREE AND SINGLE?
Framley man, looks 38, own home/business/hair, seeks fun-loving half-French half-Chinese woman, 5'1", who likes 12-bar blues and extra anchovies, dislikes 475m greyhound racing and late morning Radio Four, and is indifferent towards bright colours and the number eight. I'm sure we could be fairly happy. No QPR fans. Box FE7671

TURN BACK TIME
Attractive, professional M, 40, own house, seeks fun woman for fun in May 1973. It may seem a long time ago, but I'm optimistic. Box FE1992

THREE MORE BREAKFASTS
Deaf Stevie Wonder impersonator, 55, seeks blind Evelyn Glennie impersonator for musical evenings, novelty duos, that kind of thing. Box FE7671

I'VE NODDED OFF
BUT YOU PROBABLY WON'T NOTICE!
08999 515160

DEREK GROGAN
Late 1946 model in poor condition thanks to one reckless female owner would like to meet flashy E-type. Rusty bodywork in need of repair, unable to get going on cold mornings, just failed MOT test as not officially a car. Pre-op. Box FE5976

FIVE STAR TREATMENT
I will spend all of your money on flash cars and send you a picture of me masturbating in the toilets at Romford bus station 01999 555555

GONE FOR A BURTON
Outgoing, easygoing, oceangoing go-getter, likes going out, going steady and go-go dancing. Go away. Box FE2319

PASSION FOR PASSION
Androgynous Wripple male, 40, medium height, average build, normal hair, 2.4 children, seeks mean woman for nights out in the middle of the road. Box FE1334.

PARTY ANIMAL
Single dad, 36, 6ft, GSOH, works for council. Interests include model railways, country walking, and drinking so much I get a bit handy WLTM either understanding woman who will love me for who I am, or stubborn woman who doesn't mind having some sense knocked into her. Box FE6416

HELP ME LOSE MY L-PLATES
25-year-old virgin wants to wait until after marriage. I've been seeing her for a couple of months now and I don't think I can wait until after lunch. Box FE7205

NOWHERE TO SLEEP?
That's because I ate your bed. Fill me with your duvet. I'm hungry and hiding. Box FE9098

CANDLELIGHT NITS
Sociable male, 40, 40-slices-of-toast-a-day habit seeks lively woman with a toaster instead of a head for toast fun and possibly more toast. Box FE3195

GOOD SPORT
Attractive, separated, sporty 47-year-old male. Very sporty sport sport and I am sport. Looking for sport sport sport. How many words am I allowed? Thirty? Oh alright. Sport. Box FE6660

I'M READY & WAITING
FOR EASTENDERS TO START AND EARNING A BIT EXTRA IN THE EVENINGS
08999 656 510

FRENCH FROSTIES
What do you look like with your clothes off? Here's what I look like with my clothes off: happy, grumpy, bashful, dopey, beaky, mick and titch all rolled into one nude bundle of man. Get in! Box FE1091

LET'S GO FOR A DRINK
Blue-eyed male, 39, medium hair, own stool in the snug bar of The Crown & Cuttlefish, seeks caring, loyal, genuine pint of weak lager top and packet of cheese and onion peanuts. Box FE9891

CHAIRMAN OF THE BOARD
Alarmed backgammon player seeks less alarmed backgammon player for gentle chess with plenty of warning. Box FE8343

HOTPOINT
WASHING MACHINE
Good condition
New filter
BUYER TO COLLECT
£75 ono
07999 254680

OPERA LOVER
Caring, sensitive, 46 year old divorced man, likes reading, opera and show me your boobs. Box FE8286

CRAZY GUY
Mad individual, crazy hair, real wild card, seeks quiet, shy F 24-34 who I can be hilarious at. Box FE6286

I saw you...

SOCKFORD POLYHEDRON FILM CLUB. April 2nd. You were sitting in front of me facing the wrong way during Batman Returns, muttering into my popcorn and gnawing my chair. Sorry I got you thrown out. Will I ever get to tell you how it finished? Box FE6989

BOTTOM OF THOXTOXETER CANAL. You were drowning, I was trying to retrieve my shopping trolley hence I was a bit pre-occupied. Still want to be rescued? Box FE1717

I WAS ON THE TRAIN, you were on the train, he/she was on the train, we were on the train, you (with your friend) were on the train, they were on the train 23/3/04. Did any of you spot my umbrella? I think I must have left it on the seat. Box FE4240

YOU SHOW ME YOURS
AND I'LL DESCRIBE HOW MINE USED TO BE BEFORE I HAD THREE KIDS
08999 904406

I SOLD YOU BREAD. Want to meet? Box FE5502

I LIKE THE WAY YOU MOVED 10th of June 2002. Semi to detached, wide wheel base Transit in one go with late-night take-away curry. Textbook. Box FE1223

I SAW ME but it wasn't me, it was the woman version of me. At least that's who I think I was. It might not have been me at all. Can you clear this up for me? Box FE7888

I'M A DIFFERENT GIRL
THAN I WAS IN THAT AD UP THERE JUST NOW
08999 656 511

LIFT TO FOURTH FLOOR OF COUNCIL OFFICES. You farted so hard the lift broke down. It was the most magical day of my life. Want to try again? Box FE9879

YOU WERE IN THE BUS QUEUE in November '76, I was there in October '93. Ah! Buses! Box FE1212

REMEMBER ME FROM SCHOOL? You grew a full beard during playtime and somehow got me expelled. It was never meant to end like this. See me. Box FE4533

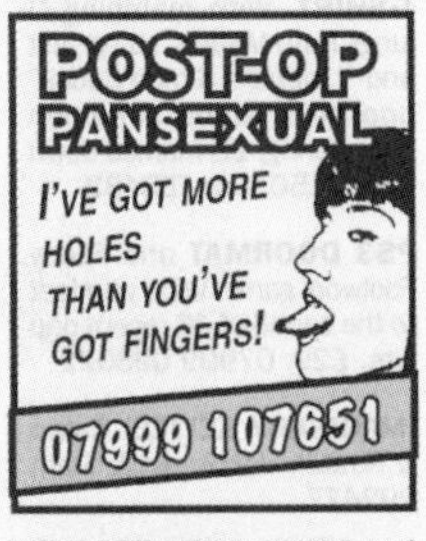
POST-OP PANSEXUAL
I'VE GOT MORE HOLES THAN YOU'VE GOT FINGERS!
07999 107651

I DIALLED 07999 242526 and brought myself to climax while you told me you were hiding in my wardrobe. Now I've lost your number. Please ring me again. Box FE4239

YOU REVERSED OVER MY FATHER whilst attempting to

DOGS AND THINGS
Created and written by Dhebora McLeopard

PAMPERED POOCH WEEK 54: You top dogs

PETS WIN THE PRIZES

This year's Pampered Pooch competition has received a record number of entries and there's still a week to go.

The Examiner would once again like to remind readers that cats and budgerigars are not eligible for the competition, however in the absence of valid photographs we are happy to print all pictures entered. The first reader to submit a picture of a dog bags a lifetime's supply of Duchess tinned dog owner's food – so get snapping!

CATS SLEEP ANYWHERE?
Submitted by Jessica Wyles, Framley

YOU RANG, M'MA'AM?
Submitted by Lady Caroline Mnenmimmenn, Codge

EGGORY PECK?
Name and address supplied

MIAOW'S A PRETTY BOY THEN!
Submitted by Damiun Clavalier, Sockford

Filling Lazenby's Boots

by DHEBORA McLEOPARD

Holness, oldest son of Lazenby who was until recently Framely's biggest hedgehog, has finally been crowned Framley's newest biggest hedgehog.

Following years of legal wrangles over the estate of the late 10lb hog, the title was passed to his 9lb 6oz male heir.

Despite a weigh-off ordered by solicitors representing Medford's non-identical twin brother, Dinkle (12lb 2oz), the umpire declared that the title of biggest hedgehog was hereditary rather than a 'vulgar matter of weight'.

Together with the title, Medford receives a pair of Nandrolone tablets

PHOTO BY WINDREW MILLER

and a year's supply of theatre tickets for the West End musical of his choice.

Holness's personal trainer, Mrs Margaret Helfpul, who managed the business affairs of Lazenby in the years preceding his untimely death from prickleworm said that had he still been alive and able to talk, he would have been very proud.

Pet of the week

Say hello to Ormerod the tortoise, who sadly lost his shell after a shoehorn accident in Newby's ShoeWorld. Luckily he was saved by the helpful staff, who fitted him with this fine boot. He is expected to live another week.   PHOTO BY ARTY QUMSCHOTT

Hopeless Dogs

We are seeking homes for these abandoned pets before we abandon them altogether. Our dogs:

- Chase themselves upside down
- Get bones jammed up their noses
- Lick burglars' faces and lead them straight to the jewellery box
- Have rubbish tails

We're their penultimate chance... you're their last

All of them are absolute doughnuts – guaranteed!

Unregisterable Charity no. 2377689

YOUR PET QUESTIONS ANSWERED
BY FRAMLEY EXAMINER DARTS CORRESPONDENT STAN RUBBISH

DEAR STAN... Where's my owl?

STAN SAYS: On my head. Please pop round the office any time and pick it up.

DEAR STAN... I want to teach my dog some simple tricks such as endos, bunnyhops and loop-de-loops. Any tips?

STAN SAYS: Can I make another appeal to the owner of the owl on my head – can he please collect it as soon as possible?

DEAR STAN... Is it safe to keep goldfish in a harpsichord? I am about to play a very fast bit of Scarlatti – should I take them out?

STAN SAYS: Yes. Can someone get me a tissue? The owl on my head is starting to draw blood now.

DEAR STAN... My Canary doesn't understand me. What is the Spanish word for 'seed'?

STAN SAYS: Ow.

HAVE YOUR PHOTO TAKEN BY YOUR PET

A life changing experience and a photo that you and your loved ones will cherish for eternity. Allow at least 24 hours for each exposure required (patience needed).

CODGE SNAPS
The choice of a lot of Codge photographers
01999 433298

GUINEA PIG SHOW
21/22 August · Framley County Showground

Tower of Guineas · Saxophone Guinea Pig Archery · Guess The Taste Of The Guinea Pig · Guinea Gang Show (some audience participation) · Dave Wimbush's Complete Sexual Satisfaction Or Your Guinea Pig Back

Please bring your own food & sausages Guinea pigs will be provided. **NO REAL PIGS**

DOG IN A CARDBOARD BOX LTD
a discrete and personal service

Is your dog annoying, demanding, smelly, noisy or plain boring?

Keeping them alive doesn't have to be the right answer. Don't compromise the quality of your life just because your kids keep pleading with you not to put Rover down. We've got all the latest lethal injections and some top quality permeable sacks weighed down with beautiful reclaimed Victorian sandstone bricks.

DICB Ltd, 76 Trombonesinthebig Parade, Whoft Tel. 01999 325455 (evenings)

A DOG ISN'T JUST FOR CHRISTMAS. IT'S ALSO FOR NEW YEAR'S EVE.

The Framley Examiner

STOP! Don't forget that from 1am tonight, Framley switches back to British HAMMERTIME!

Framley's Traditional Favourite since 1978

FRIDAY SEPTEMBER 15th, 2005   PRICE 45p IF SOLD FOR 45p

TRAVEL

Escape to exotic Holland on stilts!

WIN!

A lifetime's pair of gardening dentures

FOOD

Restaurant introduces pepper and salt

Amenity cutbacks set to delivers another serious blow to local region's amenities in area

SODHAM BOTTING DUNES TO CLOSE

by Adam Wrent

THE THREAT TO FRAMLEY'S regional amenities received another boost yesterday when it was announced that a shortfall in the 2006 budget will mean the closure of the botting dunes by the sea front at Sodham.

The dunes have been used since the 1700th Century, but soon botters will have to travel to Fracton to use the facilities there, which will possibly.

WITCH TO SOD

With the closure of Sodham, the nearest similar leisure amenities are in distant Molford, where enthusiasts can make use of small areas of botting scrub in the Fram valley. The popular botting reeds in Doggingley were sold to developers in 1989, leading many botters to switch to Sodham's ancient dunes. Now there are fears of overcrowding at the remaining sites.

The historic botting dunes which face closure and the sea.   **PHOTO BY JOGALONG DOG**

Botters and representatives of botters' groups plan to protest the plan. Dunstan Brigloo of the Sockford and District Botters' League and Alan Porknoy of the Honourable Company of Botters have both written strongly worded letters to the mayor, but about something else entirely.

What do YOU think about the plan? Write to us from your usual address.

Worst thing happens at sea

COASTGUARDS stationed at the mouth of the Urling estuary reported yesterday that the worst possible thing had happened at sea.

Details are being kept under close wraps for fear of causing public distress, but the incident is said to have involved sweet grey-haired war widows, a malfunctioning thresher, smiling schoolchildren, a lake of scalding flame, non-consensual kite-flying, throat cancer, and the Loch Ness Minister.

Anyone worried that they may be able to visualise the event from those elements is being asked to contact a special telephone where they will be offered councilling and a cup of tea.

The number, which is believed to contain a 7, cannot be revealed for legal reasons, and is open from 8am to 8pm every day except birthdays.

CHATTELS WAREHOUSE

FORMERLY GOODS & CHATTELS WAREHOUSE*

JUST LOOK AT OUR PRICES!

CHATTELS FROM £3.99

IN SIZES 4 – 14 AND OTHERS!

BUY TWO CHATTELS GET ONE FREE!

15% OFF ALL CHATTELS

CHATTEL WAREHOUSE
128 THE INDUSTRIAL ESTATE
RETAIL PARK, FRAMLEY FM4 1PE

*Please note: We no longer sell goods, ONLY chattels.

FRAMLEY COUNCIL

Because making matters better matters...!

SOCKFORD NEIGHBOURHOOD FORUM

PUBLIC MEETING

Tuesday 24th September at 7.30pm
Methodist Hall, High Street, Sockford

TO DISCUSS THE FUTURE OF
JANET FORSYTH
of 48 Vicarage Lane, Sockford

More information from Framley Borough Council or Angela Wirral, 49 Vicarage Lane, Sockford

EXPRESS TYRE SERVICE WHILE-YOU-WAIT!

WE WILL CHANGE ALL THE TYRES ON YOUR VEHICLE WHILE HOLDING OUR BREATH!

WE WILL NOT BREATHE UNTIL THE JOB HAS BEEN COMPLETED TO YOUR SATISFACTION

DON'T WORRY! WE ARE INSURED!

ALAN PUFFY & SONS   WHOFT
01999 482348

LETTERS p48   'OGILVY' p61   JUDO PUZZLE p81   FRANKLY ALARMING CHILD p9

'Coffee shop' row reaches boiling point

by JESUS CHIGLEY

RESIDENTS AND COUNCILLORS from the Dungeon Estate took to the streets last Friday in a show of opposition to the opening of a European-style coffee shop.

High Tea, the first drug café of its type in the area, is due to start trading on 23nd of 23nd of March, although ironicly, protesters hope its doors will never ever open.

Planning permission for the shop was refused 38 times, but was finally approved after an extraordinary intervention by a giggling mayor, William D'Ainty.

"This is the last thing this area neeeds,' said Cllr Martin Royal, Batley (East by East West). 'We're already up to our forelocks in crime'.

After an EU ruling, the Dungeon Estate in Batley is now described as "horrible" on road signs. The decline seems irreversible since Mustardwell's biscuit factory, the area's only remaining employer, was closed last year by new owners Ventrica (a Belgian conglomerate who manufacture abject social misery for the European documentary film market) sacking both its staff.

FUSS

But the proprietor of High Tea,

Jesmond Purvles, is confident.

PHOTO BY TORTOISE VINDALOO

Jesmond Purvles, is confident and has a pleasant telephone manner.

"This is a lot of fuss about a few rocks," he told me from a secret location. ""The hit from crack only lasts about ten minutes, and the worst that can happen is that you can have a brain seizure at the same time as a

fatal heart attack.

"Most of our customers know what they're doing. And we will be offering sedatives, in case anyone gets a bit busy behind the eyebrows," he also.

Mr Purvles says the café will offer over 300 types of crack, including Plain, Butterscotch and Belushi.

News In Brief

NOTHING

Police called to investigate something that was reported to be happening in Framley town centre last Friday lunchtime were relieved to find that nothing was happening.

PRAISE BE BAD

Churches are being warned that a bogus Songs of Praise is operating in the area. A TV crew and congregation of 250 pretended to record an episode of the hit show at St Stammer's, Whoft, before stealing the font and a stained glass. The suspects are between 5'0" and singing The Old Rugged Cross.

SHRINE CLOSEd

A shrine once visited by the Pope has been shut down by police after a tip-off. Milky Mary, a lactating statue of Jesus's mum that cried milk from its ears, was found to be attached by tubing to a cow in a cupboard. The proprietor, Jean-Paul Gluf, done a runner.

NEW CARNIVAL QUEEN

Wripple's carnival queen, Katherine Peck, has died at the grand old age of 92. The title, which is hereditary, will now be passed to her daughter, Molly Mister-Jones (knée Peck). Molly, 69, says that before she retired she liked working with children and animals.

APOLOGY

We would like to apologise to Jennifer Kunz, 56, and her daughter Emily, 19, for references to them ('Straight from the horse's mouth,' Framley Examiner last week) as "a clunky yellow-toothed mare bound for the knacker's yard" and "a smashing young chesnut-haired filly, ripe for a good cropping" respectively. This was a spelling mistakes.

Increasing numbers they are 'on the rise'

by ADAM WRENT

THERE HAS BEEN an alarming rise in the number of people in the area who

Last year, there were only 4,912 known in the area. But since then, that figure has risen by 6,851 – a increase of almost 39.47 and a half per cent.

INCREASE

One anonymous source said that the statistics point to "a worrying trend." He added, "If the number keeps rising, we may have to take some very serious action Adam."

"As long as the numbers are rising, none of us is truly safe. And if the authorities won't do anything about it, then someone else will – and that c o u l d t u r n ugly."

But this veiled threat has angered

the Fire Brigade. "We're not trained to deal with a problem on this sort of scale," said one serving firefighter at a hastily assembled emergency basketball tournament last Tuesday.

OH THE WORRY

"To be properly equipped, we'll need thousands of pounds of extra resources, as will dentists, IT experts, parking attendants, restaurant proprietors, voice over artists, newsagents, bus drivers, care workers, people who live in trees – the list is almost endless."

Community leaders have appealed for a calm.

• *Do you know someone who might be affected? Oh good, because a confidential helpline can be found at the other end of a phone line if you type the address 07999 313131 into your handset and talk to the machine at the other end pretending to be a person listening.*

Unplug it!

The amount of water wasted by leaving baths and sinks plugged in is enough to drown a town full of dwarves or a village full of normal people every day

Unplug baths and sinks before you go to bed

Framley Energy Council
Saving energy by coming up with bright ideas 24 hours a day

Gr@ve must go

by Jesus Chigley

A FRAMLEY widower has been forced asked told ordered to remove the headstone from his wife's grave by cemetery officials who claim the memorial is "inappropriate".

The headstone, which is in the form of a fruit machine, marks the last resting place of Nary Grandreams, who died of complications arising from a bus in April 2005. Her husband Nichael Grandreams is planning to appeal against the removal order.

Framley cemetery is furious.

PHOTO BY MARCUS UNREAD

PUBIC HEALTH

"My fruit machine is respectful, appropriate and fun," Nichael says. "What better incentive could there be to come and mourn the loss of my dear wife than the possibility of a big cash jackpot?"

forced asked told ordered requested subpoenaed instructed made

QUEEN'S CARNIVAL JOY

THE SOCKFORD CARNIVAL was its usual success as usual this year, with over six floats taking part from local organisations and groups and only two inches of rain falling from the minute the procession set off. But spirits couldn't be dampened and traffic should soon be running normally.

Pictured above is Whoft Hospice's prizewinning Hawaiiian-themed floar at the start of the two hour procession. Smiling from her Carnival Princess' throne, is Diane Baddersley, who has 45 minutes to live.

Fathers Day Winner

The winner of the Framley Examiner Father's Day drawing competition is **JOSIE HOLLYHOCK** from Molford St Malcolm with this charming picture of her dad, Mr Hollyhock. Josie has called her picture, here reproduced in full colour, *I Love My Daddy*.

Josie wins a box of Newby's colouring paints as well as a personal drawing lesson from much-loved children's television personality Councillor Geoffery Cauchaugh.

The contest is now closed. Any further entries received will be treated as 'Letters To The Editor'.

Local writers have the write stuff!

TWO FRAMLEY authors have had their short stories included in a bin at top publishers Haddon & Whateley.

Hopeful authors Polly Robinsons and Toby DePipe met at the Molford Writer's Fellowship and regularly send samples of their work to publishers, but this is the first time they have put the right stamps on.

The pair of tales will be available soon as hamster bedding from selected pet shops in the Framley area.

IF WE'RE NOT FRAMLEY'S HUNGRIEST PLUMBERS...

We'll eat your hat!

Twelve sugars, please. And biscuits.

McCARR-O'DISNEY PLUMBING 01999 656541

N + FRAMLEY EXAMINER COMPETITION + FRAMLEY EXAMINER COMPETITION + FRA

WIN £1m!

THE FRAMLEY EXAMINER, in association with NEWBY'S OF MOLFORD, is/are giving YOU the chance to win £1m.

YES, THAT'S RIGHT – A METRE OF MONEY!!

All you have to do is to send your name and address to the name and address below, and we'll do the rest!

Just think what you would do with a metre of money!

NAME.............................. ADDRESS................................
POSTCODE...
TIEBREAKER: *"I think money is.....................because.....................got any."*
(no more than 10 words)

Send your entries to FRAMLEY EXAMINER IN ASSOCIATION WITH NEWBY'S OF MOLFORD WIN £1m COMPETITION, The Framley Examiner, Unit 149b, East Cossett Industrial Estate, Parkfields Bypass, Framley, FM1 6LH, Tel 01999 947694, marking your envelope 'FRAMLEY EXAMINER IN ASSOCIATION WITH NEWBY'S OF MOLFORD WIN £1m COMPETITION, The Framley Examiner, Unit 149b, East Cossett Industrial Estate, Parkfields Bypass, Framley, FM1 6LH, Tel 01999 947694.'

* £1m is a metre (1000mm) of 2p coins laid edge-to-edge. One 2p coin is 25.91mm in diameter, so the prize is 38 coins, redeemable to a value of 76p. The judges are final and cannot be entered into. NEWBY'S OF MOLFORD was correct at the time of going to press but may have since gone wrong.

Molford & District Denis Norden Club

are looking for new members to help with their annual fete. **IF YOU'RE ONE OF THOSE PEOPLE** who think they can help out with face painting, motorcycle display teams, costumed re-enactments, etc., give us a ring.

Rides on the mighty Autocue

Pin the script on the clipboard

Sadly, we won't have time to show you the coconut shy that turned out to be less shy than expected, but before we go, here's a few numbers we've put in the file marked 'phone number'.

01999 651075

We're also looking for someone to man our office and answer the phone while smacking themselves in the forehead with it.

(Formerly Molford & District Steve Penk Club)

New Arrivals

BRIDGEMAN

To Josh and Sarah, a beautiful baby boy, Benedict Like Beckham, a wonderful brother for Ernest Is East, Leighanne Good Friday and Snatch.

It's a Girl!s bike

It's pink.
Your Gay
Best wishes
All the nurses and staff at St A Million's Hospital

The Framley Examiner

Everyone has to have a BABY sometime!

And what better excuse to have a baby than to see yourself in the Framley Examiner classifieds? All it takes is a few sweaty minutes and nine months later, you're famous! And we are pleased to announce that for every birth announcement placed, we will open an account at Newby's Bank, with £4.75 deposited for the baby.

Standard Ad £6.50
Newby's Offer Ad £11.50

It's a Shame!

Wylie. On March 13, to Kerry & Michael, a son, Alice, which was supposed to be a beautiful baby daughter. 01999 428096. Genuine offers only

It's A Train!

Celebrating the safe arrival of the 07.15 from Chigfield. From all at Framley Station.

Sadly We Missed

Roy Dibnah

Peacefully, in his sleep machine.

3rd October 2005

In loving memory
Barry Goodman

A much loved Mum and Dad You will always be in our thoughts.

Love, Eric the twins xxx

In loving memory
Angela Bleakley

Today is filled with memories,
And loving thoughts of you,
Di dum di dum di something,
Di dum and things you do,
Forever something ever,
And something dum di dum,
As long as something something,
Something haircuts dum di dum.

Tom and Geraldine

Utterly Conkers!
Milton Prentock

FRAMLEY JUNIOR CONKER CHAMPION
1999-2007

So sorry. You were allergic after all. In accordance with your wishes there will be a short ceremony on 15th April, where we will boil you in vinegar, bake you in a 220 degree oven and throw you, full whack, at Octavius Knutt, Stuttgart Young Conker Player of the Year and runner up in the World Conker Championships 2006. Forever victorious. Love mum, dad and Putter Smith, The Conker Pianist.

In loving memory
Alice Glengould Wantage

who died after a brave, long battle with illness that, all things considered, now seems a waste of time and effort.

In loving memory
That Man With The Grey Hair

You will forever be in our hearts, but none of us can remember your name. Love Victor, Dorothy, Patricia, Alfred, Joan, Gerald, Diana, Dennis, Robert, Winifred, Arthur, Mary, Isabella, Edna, Rose and literally everyone at the home.

Leg

I got a dead leg the other night but it was alright in the morning.

Jim xxx

Basil Adams

1758-2003

"Old, old, you were very, very old –
Oh, old, old, you were just too old,
You were just too very, very old."

A blessed relief.
Cosmolina and Sebastiessiettienne

R G BARGY

DISPOSALS

Satisfaction guaranteed ~
Cash only –
No questions mate

See Trevor in the saloon bar of the Horse Or Groom Keep it down

---

Winifred Pips

Passed away aged 86, peacefully after twelve years in hospital following an unexpected complication during a human cannonball act.

In Anticipation

Uncle Snouts

Hurry up

Auntie Woodbine

In Memoriam

THE FAMILY AND FRIENDS of Framley gravedigger Dan Jarvis would like to thank the family and friends of Ethel Tenniel for agreeing to postpone her funeral so Mr Jarvis could be buried in the grave he was digging her when he died.

In memory of
DAVID McMAMMERLY POOLE

Inventor of the bicycle scissors.
"We told you so"
Louise and Barnaby.

ANNETTE LONELY
The mortician and undertakers of Annette Lonely would like to thank someone, but apart from the ambulance crew, no-one else was involved. She had been dead for 22 years, and her milk hadn't been taken in for just as long. Her neighbours met her once, in 1987. She leaves a tissue and half a slipper.

"Who?"

FONZLY REMEMBERED
OK Grandad, as requested in your will, we remember you in the style of the Fonz. Heyyy... sadly missed!

DAVIDSON
Treasured memories of my dearest wife Elsie, who died, April 19th, 2002. You will always be in my heart. Only joking, darling. You will, of course, always be in your coffin – Robert.

JACKSON
Rose Louise

Died in Framley Hospital on 7th May, 2004. Sadly missed by your husband "My Len" – He's all mine now, Rosie, love Doris :-p

BABY MARK CORBETT
3 May 1974

We will never forget you or where we left you ever again. Hope that you're O.K., wherever you are! Love Mummy & Daddy.

Look!

Look Who's Gay!

GARY POLLARD.
We're so proud of you.
Love Mum and Dad

LOOK WHO'S 50 !

ANDY BINATONE
And you still look like this!

Look! I'm not gay!

Mum and Dad, it's nice you're so good about it, but I've got a wife and two kids. Why don't you ask Helen? She might be.
Gary.

LOOK WHO'S 10!

Love Daddy Puppet, Mummy Puppet and Girl The Girl

LOOK WHO'S driving me to bloody distraction!

Neville, this conversation about bindweed was sort of interesting at first, but it isn't half going on a bit. I've got to pick the kids up in a minute and you're blocking the porch. Lesley

LOOK WHO'S 40

STONE!

LIAM SPENCER
Have a great day Wobbly From all your friends at The Ark

Happy 18th Matthew!

Congratulations Henry & Veronica Chadwick. Another brother for Matthew, Matthew, Matthew, Matthew, Matthew, Matthew, Matthew, Matthew, Matthew, Matthew, Matthew, Matthew, Matthilda, Matthew, Matthew, and Matthew.

LOOK WHAT YOU'VE DONE TO YOUR LOVELY HAIR

Gail, that's it. I'm leaving you. You look like a bag of springs.
Mike

READ WHO'S 7!

JOSIE HOLLYHOCK

Doesn't merit a picture, the 7th birthday GROW UP Perhaps if you save up all your pocket money then you might be able to afford one for your 10th Where's my present? Dad (Mr Hollyhock to you)

PATRICK'S MEMORIAL PANTRY
FUNERAL DIRECTORS

Let us bake you into a lovely pie with a smashing pastry coffin

"His meat just fell straight off the bone – I was delighted" – Mrs Eric Kennedy

Your delicious body will be born aloft by our master bakers wearing black chef's hats, their solemn faces darkened with cinders. Each is trained in the art of holding a hot pastry coffin by its crinkly crust.

• *Special offer on puff pastry headstones* •

FREEFONE 08999 910910

Calls charged at £1.50/min. Please aks permission.

Pimp My Final Ride

Ol' Skool Funerals

Trick Out Da Hearse
Chrome rims • Raised rear end • Shoe rack full of Nikes • Karaoke machine • DVD player • Cristal cooler • Massage seats • Fire shooting exhaust pipes (not strictly legal)

Ka-Ching Yo Coffin
DEAD HOT cherry red paintwork • Ripspeed chrome handles • Supercrunk air inlet • Under-casket UV • Rude lid spoiler • 8-colour neon waterfall lights • Green suede lining • Bling wings

Free gold tooth for da loved 1

MC BONEYARD & THUGZ
Brown Bread Towers, 24 Thrubnalls Walk, Framley FM1 4AH 07999 324879

Books are signed at book signing

Susan sings some of the books at the Twebbins booksinging last Wednesday

PHOTO BY KIP STILTON

by Taunton Mishap

The rain didn't dampen the spirits of hundreds of Framley fantasy fans who queued in the rain to get the latest Danny Pudding book, 'Danny Pudding And The Finger In A Matchbox Full Of Cotton Wool', even though it was raining.

Framley bookshop 'Twebbins' opened especially on a rainy Monday to cater for the crowds who thronged the Denegate Centre, eager for the chance to have the chance to have their books signed by Framley's very own Susan Humble, who once shared a railway carriage with bestselling Danny Pudding author Gwyneth Billions.

PUDDING

'It's really exciting to meet her,' said pudding-crazy Pudding fan Kathurine Goole, finishing a pavlova in the queue. 'I want her to sign all my other books, too,' she added, pointing to a tea chest containing washing machine repair manuals.

Humble has been swept to local fame after having been in the fateful railway carriage in 2004, and said her life had been a 'dream-cum-true' since that day, with people stopping her in the street to take her photograph and purse, sadly, in August 2005, with police baffled and a black eye, but has bounced back.

PUDDING

'No,' Humble told every single fan in the queue, one at a time, over the eight hour signing session, 'the railway carriage didn't leave from platform 11 and a half!'

The Danny Pudding books are being made into some films, starring glamorous US star Calista Flockhart from hit TV series 'Ian McBeale' and Kenny Baker as Danny Pudding, which Humble plans to see because they're quicker than the books.

The floodwaters, which swept in from Twebbin's storeroom as usual following the unseasonally heavy rain, destroyed over £400,000 of stock.

TWEBBINS
Bookshop
EVENTS

LAST WEDNESDAY

BOOK SIGNING
THE NEW DANNY PUDDING BOOK

Signing by local travelling companion of best selling author.

This signing took place last week, so please arrive earlier than that to avoid disappointment.

EVERY WEEKNIGHT

BOOK BURNING
FAR FROM THE SODDING CROWD

Sequel to travel guide snubs Framley area a second time again.

Join a lively local crowd for burning of stock as it arrives from wholesalers nightly.

UNIT 98, DENEGATE, FRAMLEY

REMEMBER: Because we don't have it in stock, we can order any book for you from the internet!

Residents fed up of vandalism

Residents on the Dungeon Estate in Batley are "fed up of vandalism and sick with bad behaviour", according to Residents' Association spokesmouth Mary De La Dairy.

Mrs De La Dairy has asked the council to "take responsibility of the problem and lay some of the blame from their own shoulders" following a hundred percent increase in criminal damage on the estate since Tuesday.

Dungeon's people are so "concerned of vandalism" according to Mrs De la Dairy that on Tuesday, a group of thirty locals, led by herself, sprayed the words "Why Vandalism?" along the boundary wall of Catacomb House, and smashed all the windows of the Cameron Stout Community Centre to draw attention to the crisis.

"We're totally fed up of all this," Mrs De La Dairy said again, shouldering her mallet. "Fed up of it," she said again. "Look at the state of the Community Centre. It's a disgrace. We must find these people and make them accountable from the consequences with their actions."

Drunk mars bar

A man went on the rompage in a Framley bar after drinking 52 pints of Wripple St George, a court heard last week.

Rex Tremendae, 35, caused £16,500 of damage went he went berserk and ran amok in Humpty's Wine Bar and Barsserie with a clothes iron in either hand.

Sentencing Mr Tremendae to death by chocolate, the judge, Justice Confutatis Maledictis, called him 'a cunk' before playing his theme tune.

Costs were awarded to the owner of Humpty's, BBW Caroline Humpty.

TURN YOUR
DRIVING THEORY TEST
INTO CRISPS

Pass or fail – capture the moment for all time in potato snack form.
Smoky Plain or Cheese 'n' Plain

01999 977 451

Don't forget!
FLAMERS

... is the new name for the Framley Fire Service!

So, when YOU dial 999, don't forget...

"Which service do you require?"

"FLAMERS!"

FRAMLEY DISTRICT COUNCIL
making things happen... and beyond!

All this week at the
SOCKFORD
POLYHEDRON

THE LION, THE WITCH AND THE ADANDONED CHEST FREEZER

Mon – Thu: 11.00, 13.45, 16.20, 19.15
Fri – Sun: 9.00, 13.00, 13.05, 23.30

The enchanting story of four children who enter a magical land by shutting themselves into an abandoned chest freezer on a rubbish tip.

CERT: PG (Warning: Quite persuasive)

LEONARD CLOCK
EXCLUSIVE NO-POINT SERVICE
There is no point in having your car serviced by us!

Why not pay us a visit?
Here's why not:
"slovenly service" "inefficient"
"too expensive" "underqualified"
"rude man" "the smells"

Leonard Clock, 9 Borrowmywheelbarrow Street, Chutney. 01999 522 980

THE CODGE TARGETEER

Classifertisements

PEACHES N' PLUMS

FIVE-PIECE VARIETY PACK of cereal. One junior-sized box each of Uf-Os, Jet Flakes, Bikini Atoll Pops, Closet Puffs and Kellogg's Atomicles. 3/-. FRAmley 1167

HAVE YOU NOW or ever been a member of the communist party? Pub Quiz. American Embassy, every Friday. Big career-destroying prizes! Call Joe on FRA8431

TURN YOUR war memoirs into crisps! Good per-word rates. Little Blue Battlefield Anecdote Bags for no extra cost. Call FRAmley 6344 for details.

PROPSHAFT, engine cowling, aileron and wheels from single-seater aircraft. Loft clearance. Also Amelia Earhart. Offers. WHOft 6888

TELEVISION ARIEL. Also gramophone prospero and shortwave caliban. 2 guineas the lot. FRA7110

WILDLIFE BOOK. "The Colourful World Of Penguins". Enormously disappointing. 4/6. SOCkford 588.

STICK of Stanley Matthews Blackpool Rock. Causes excessive dribbling and my teeth have been capped over 100 times. 1/-. FRAmley 7009

ACTION STATIONS

BLONDE bombshells. Army surplus. Assorted ordnance dressed crudely in yellow wigs. Strangely alluring yet incredibly dangerous. Call Col. Colin Callard at RAF Harmonium (xt 2508) btwn 6 and 8am. Details on application.

RUBBLE without a cause. I've just smashed up my fireplace for no real reason. £1. FRA0664

WURLITZER DUKEBOX. Ideal for coffee shops. Delivers all John Wayne's classic lines at the push of a button, and dispenses milk from a horse-shaped siphon. £8. WHOft 763.

LATEST SCORES, news headlines and Suez updates delivered hourly to your hall telephone! Newest ringtones and logos. FRAmley 8633

CUSHION'S Imperial Lather Toilet Soap. Ideal for the sort of people who wash their hands in the toilet. Box of 40. £2. FRAmley 6311

DUNLOP "Wet Weather" vulcanised rubber raindrops. Pack of seven. 18/-. SOCkford 6417

PAIR OF haute couture Givenchy gumboots, as worn by Audrey Hepburn in Prestatyn Holiday. £1 5/6. MOLford 4599.

BED-SITTING room to rent £10 per calendar month. Also toilet-garage and bath-garden. Will not split. FRA1673

VARIETY RICHARD

CONFIDENTIAL information for single people leading to happiness - romance - maybe even death. Write today! Emberly Whunt, Ph.D. Director Personal Services

N-BAG service. I will

HALF a hundredweight of Coalex Smokeless Flameless Heatless Coal. Useless bag of black lumps. Doesn't even taste very nice. £offers. FRA6310

"COOL IT, DADDIO!" paternal refrigerator. Keeps Pops on ice whatever the weather! £5. FRAmley 7100

KITCHEN BENDY

PAIR OF absurdly high-waisted trousers with wing collar and epaulettes. Offers. FRAmley 6898

BEATNIK traps. 10/6 ea. Twelve bags of freeform poetry bait. 4/-. MOL9077

STRING of Capstan medium strength Navy Cut sausages. Filterless. "You're Never Alone With A Sausage". 1/6. FRA8663

WHAM BAM-BAMS

COMRADE Stalin's Little Red Book. The Tale of Jeremy Fisher. It's his favourite. 8½d. FRAframley 4555

DELIGHTFUL framed photographs of your children. Framley Zoo, June '55. Blackpool Pleasure Beach, September '57. Paddling pool in your back garden, August '51. Offers. FRA9848

THE SECRET of Successful After Dinner Speaking. 1000s of sure-fire jokes. All hilarious, all in Portugese. "Had them rolling in the aisles" - Lisbon Advertiser. "If I had been Portugese then I'm sure that the evening would have been a great deal more enjoyable" - British Poultry Breeders' Gazette. Call Speechmakers di Porto on WHOft 451.

HOME-MADE chutneys & preserves. Sock jam, shirt pickle, duffelcoat conserve and shoe marmalade. Witness! For now I am wiser. And nude. Prices on application. Dennis. FRAmley 5051

PARPTICUS THE LEOPARD

TWO TICKETS for maiden flight of the "Spirit of St Bernard", experimental subsonic airliner. "An inaudible journey of discovery" - Practical Mechanics Magazine. Offers please to Delores or Branston on FRAmley 3998

COFFEE TABLE, kidney-shaped. Heart-shaped box with restricted left ventricle. Appendix-shaped desk requiring urgent removal before it bursts. £8 the lot. Tel: FRAmley 7339

"MATHS Made Simple" book. 2+6. 2+5. All these and dozens more. £1. FRAmley 9401.

MINI-MITTENS safe cracking gloves. Make your hands as small as keys. Open all doors, safes and bubblegum machines. Great for sexy stuff. 3/- a pair. FRA4019

CHILDREN'S HARDBACK treasury including The Wind-up Willows, Chitty Chitty Kissy Kissy Bond Bond Bang Bang and Charlie & The Chocolate Charlie. Only read four times. 10/6 the lot. FRA7411

BROWNIE UNIFORM, pristine, accessories - hair lice, parachute and spit roast. Also Brownie with 26 badges sewn onto face. Very collectable. Offers. FRA8191

SEWING MACHINE, SINGER, Maria Callas style, once performed Tosca at Covent Garden, some damage from final parapet fall. Offers. FRA6063

THE AMBRIDGE PLAYBARN including screaming Grace Archer costume, inflatable stampeding animals and one book of matches. £2. FRAmley 9599.

GHOSTIES

INDOOR FAIRGROUND. All the miniature fun of the miniature fair in miniature form. Tabletop rollercoaster, Waltzer in your lap, pin three darts in the goldfish and win a dead goldfish. 3 Guineas. WRIpple 725.

AIR VENTS. Massive hit at the Edinburgh Festival. Imagine Marilyn Monroe in the Seven Year Itch wearing a kilt with her meat and two veg out for everyone to see. Now you want one! Call for details. SOCkford 336.

DISPOSABLE CANOE. Use once, then throw away. Used once, hence bargain. 11/3. Framley 5419.

VERY SMALL oval record collection. Rare and unpopular. £10. FRAmley 934.

CAN YOU TELL THE TIME? I can't tell the time! Why can you tell the time? You say half past six! I say flowerpot Keith! Now who's missed this bus? Me. Sockford 688, after 5pm.

BE YOUR OWN BOSS! In just 5 weeks we will teach you how to do a perfect impersonation of your current employer. Box 6541 Whoft.

JAPANESE FIGHTING MICE rare

---

unusual pets. £

DETECTIVE suprise you never again!

LEV

LIVING MIN as large of because of but as long

ROACH KI bomber. One or your money FRA9445

AROMATIC BEL as far as you can then tighten for i because you can! three delightful FRA2433

16MM CAMERA 12mm bottle! I sounds crazy next week treatment. WHO

BINGO MELVIN

HYPNOTISM for men and women. You will write to us for free details. Box 7655 Framley.

AMAZING new electric Roto-Moto Roto-Motorotometer-Oto Motorotono-Onomo-Momotonic-Oto Otometer. Startling new principle for spinning action. Can you work out why it rotates? WHOft 768

MAKE Money by forging bank notes! As easy as 1 million, 2 million, 3 million. Our information reveals how. FRA6577

PIECES OF EIGHT, slices of nine, cutlas cutlets. me hearties FRAmley8755

AUTOMATIC washing machine. Knows exactly when it's time to clean your families clothes. Sale due to being far too clean, far too often. Being washed as I write. Not entirely unpleasant. WHOft 765

MUSCLES

PREVENT thieves from stealing yo wallet by disguising it as a bran one pound note. Now your wa look just like cash! Unbeli unbelievable. WHOft

ODOUR removi by number like

THE CODGE TARGETEER, a mid-century periodical for Codge is fondly remembered for its regular Classifertisements section, where readers could pick up anything from a 'Walk-Me-Up' sock radio to a tartan-plated unhip flask. Unfortunately its readability was severely hindered by its unorthodox shape *(above)*.

A New Yesterday Cometh

Internet Updates (2012–20)

The Framley Examiner

Framley's Traditional Favourite since 1978

FRIDAY JANUARY 2010th, 18

PRICE 45p IF SOLID

RECYCLED NEWSPAPER

made up 65.1% of the raw material for making new trees in 2009

WIN!

A lifetime's supply of funerals

ENVIRONM!

Pond soaked up by duck bread

CULTURE!

Strong, strong cider is back!

Troublemakers sent packing by residents this needs to be longer

DISASTER VERTED AT LOCAL HALL

by Taunton Mishap

Police acted swiftly on Thursday when undesirables threatened to disrupt a meeting at a local hall on Tuesday.

A gang of unusuals was spotted 'behaving oddly' near Molford St Malcolm's C18th C18ury Atheist meeting house, where a regimental reunion was taking place.

COMRADES

Old comrades from the Fifth Royal Framley Ghostbusters watched in horror as the troublemakers unlashed a torrent of antisocial behaviours, selling foreign food to customers and using a bad language.

"If there hadn't of been walls round their restaurant, and if it hadn't of been on the opposite side of the village green," said one veteran, "it could all of kicked of."

Another explained that it's not like Chinese food, that's all right, he doesn't mind that. This stuff smells.

"They do takeaway. That attracts all sorts. And them ones get p*issed and leave theirs on the wall."

DETACHMENT

With the meeting in uproar, the police were called, but declined to attend, saying they were washing someone's hair. A detachment of reunioners then took matters into their own right, explaining to the undesirables to go away, using dog mess.

As they say, old soldiers never learn, and soon a WWIV-style watchpost was set up in the hall with binoculars and biscuits.

Two hours later, police were alerted to the arrival outside the takeaway of

KERALA OBLONG TANDOORI

A great selection of authentic regional dishes to suit all pallets   **PHOTO BY RAISIN D'ETRE**

a black people carrier, containing four. Officers acted immediately.

Five-armed fire arms officers surrounded the restaurant, a new venture from local businessman Panjit Nanduvet, offering the very finest in Keralan and North Indian cuisine, with the accent on spice, and opened fire.

MAKE CLEAR

Manager Manish Alhambra emerged from the restaurant with his hands up (UP WHAT? >MAKE CLEAR – GARY<). Police shot him to safety, where he later died.

Victims have described Framley police's new stop-and-shoot policy as 'too policey'. Turmeric = yellow. £3.25 or £4.95 as a main dish.

At Wednesday's presconference, DCI Picken McScounter told reporters, "Violence is not the answer. Unless

the question is, 'What is not the answer?', in which case the answer is, of course, violence."

The atmosphere is welcoming but the orange one is too hot. I made my excuses and left mine on the wall. Sick in hand (twice). Four stars!

CD man held by police

A MAN WHO was once bought two copies of Fleetwood Mac's 'Tango In The Night' was yesterday arrested for raping and murdering 44 horses in the Sockford area over the last decade.

The man who cannot be named Paul Eagle-Reasons, is expected to plead.

INSIDE

Woman driven to seaside driven to suicide (p9!)

COME AND SEE WHAT'S ON OFTER AT THE

The King's Ars
AT WHOTTEN PLODNEY

HOME COCKED FOOD
REAL ALEX
FULL-SIZED POOH TABLE
ENJOY OUR NEW BEEF GARDEN!

MOLFORD PERSON RESCUE
Registered charity No. 98100107   VOLUNTEERS WELCOME

Could you help a person like Leonard?

We always have people waiting for loving homes...

LOST IN SHOPS
GONE INTO GARDEN AND CAN'T REMEMBER WHAT FOR
UNABLE TO FIND PARKING SPACE
STILL IN THE MAZE WHEN IT SHUT FOR THE DAY
UNWANTED GIFT

A PERSON IS FOR LIFE, NOT JUST FOR XMAS

Tel: 01999 340988

LOTTERY: WE PREDICT YOU'RE BALLS p20   BINS p31   WEDDING REVIEWS p4   RUDE-O-KU (NSFW) p71

188

Parrot helps find missing medium

Joan St Joan (centre), demonstrates her amazing powers of the mind (not pictured).

PHOTO BY ALTON VIABLES

by Adam Wrent

A PSYCHIC MEDIUM has been found after she went missing after falling in a hole after getting lost after a trip to the dentist's after a toothache after eating too many sweets for three days.

Joan St 'Mystic' Joan, whom's uncanny powers have been used in the past by the Police to find missing people, was trapped for three days in a hole with a broken ankle and grass over the top. She called for help using only the power of her mind for three days.

'I psychically yelled and yelled, but nobody heard. It must of been a disturbance in the force,' she says.

'It was the last thing I expected,' she says. Psychic waves can travel through walls, and bread, and dowsing is also used to detect kinks in the flow of Chi, she says, but soon she found she feared she would never be found.

'I can find missing people, but the energy flow is one-way, so I couldn't be found,' she found.

X

'It is like something from the X Factor,' said the Police. 'I suppose there are some things we just aren't meant to understand. Like French.'

Mystic Joan, who has a popular column in her garden supporting a bird bath, has solved four crimes, including impersonating a police officer and A Touch of Frost.

'I align my mind with the waves of the Universe and let my essence flow along them,' she says.

The clairvoyant was eventually rescued by a parrot.

Memories of Yesterdays

'A COUNTRY GIRLHOOD', submitted by Briony Kimple, aged 14, of Molford St Malcolm, showing Denegate shopping centre in early 2003 and taken on an Ericsson 3-megapixel phone. Please send your pictures of bygone Framley to the usual address. There is a £10 photo for any prize used. Any submissions from before the fall of the Major government much appreciated.

Mayor found in box of cereal

A woman from Bootington Wells has received £20 in compensation from Wand Supermarkets after she found the Mayor of Framley William D'Ainty in a king-size box of Wand Egg-n-Breakfast morning puffs. The blunder, described as a 'health and safety error by Wand management' by Wand management is the third such incident since February. The Mayor claims the incidents are part of a 'community outreach programme'.

Framley Examiner
READER OFFER
WIN A WEEK'S HOLIDAY
WITH MRS EDMONSON
READER CLUB SEE PAGE 48

News In Brief

BURGALRY EPIMEDIC

Three more homes have been broken into on the Dungeon Estate in Batley. Goods worth a total of £5,500 in total have been taken from a total of eight homes over a total of the last fortnight. Police believe the crimes are the work of a single burglar, or 112 well-organised rabbits. Anyone who has seen anything, particularly the rabbits, should contact the police via Youtube.

MENTAL HOME FUSS

The row over the budget for Molford St Malcolm's new home for the mentally ill has split the local council in a situation that Whig councillor Peter Yesminister calls 'correctional madness gone political'. If councilmembers remain deadlocked, patients may have to be moved to the Big Purple Self Storage in Urling.

VERY VERY ORGANIC
the lamb man
★ LOCALLY SOURCED ★
★ FREE RANGE ★
★ QUITE FRIGHTENING ★

Local farmer comes direct to your home and slaughters an organic sheep on your doorstep!

NOTE: Farmer may need to scream. Please keep children upstairs in a dry, tin box when The Lamb Man calls.

01999 654 377

YOU'VE
got a great business idea!
WE'LL
turn it into crisps!

NOW WITH 35% LESS FAT!

01999 710 711

Rock and Roll ALL NITE
with the ama'zing'!
CHUCK BERESFORD
Chuck Berry Impersonator

'hear's what they've said!

"... name slightly ... value"
- WHOFT SENTINEL
"... almost ... but"
- MOLFORD COURIER

BONGALOW!
4pm-6pm

BOOGALOO!

WEDNESDAY NIGHTS @ THE DOIG

People stunned by the events that happened there in that place as

MAINAC BEGINS BOTCHED KILLING SPREE BY TURNING GUN ON SELF

by Taunton Mishap

A TOWN WAS reeling yesterday, as the silent quiet and peace of market day was torn up by a manaic.

Today it was that everyone in the town, whether a policeman or residents was counting the cost of a multiple homicide that left one dead.

The town wasn't expecting to be counting the cost, and, tragically, that's exactly what happened as Whoft's ccoolteacher Justin Booon ran amok in the streets, firing indiscrintimately.

MERCIFULEND

Mr Booon began his trigger happy rampage at home in his garage at 4am, taking his own life with the James Bond-style pistol, bringing the carnage to a merciful end.

One local of the town said, 'We were lucky. It could'of been so much more worse.'

WHO WAS ON

PC Jonathohn Bell, who was on duty at the shops when the spree was cut short told me, 'No-one likes a killing spree, but if a town has to have one,

Town: the scars will take years to heal, the scars even longer. **PHOTO BY PURCELL ROOM**

as seems to be the case here, a botched one is the best.' And then he gave some thumbs.

Mr Justin Booon, 41, left a note simply reading 'So sad. Goodbye, Mel :-(' sparse words that barely scratch the surface of what nearly couldve turned a normal man to become a relentless killing machine, mowing a swathe through a town in a clattering fountain of spent cartridges, hooting like a tug, naked as nature intended.

THAT'S ROADKILL STAN RUBBISH
100% ANONYMOUS ADVICE FROM OUR DARTS CORRESPONDENT

DEAR STAN,
I reversed into a sweep in my van yesterday. Not a chimney sweep, the puppet. I am orthodox Jewish. Are sweeps kosher?

STAN SAYS:
If I remember correctly, sweeps have cloven hooves (is that sweeps?), so aren't really kosher. Pop it in a stamped addressed envelope and I'll sort it out.

DEAR STAN,
A herd of pedestrians ran into the path of my van. I am the same bloke as above and below. One of them died on my windscreen. How long should I hang it to get the flavour? And if not, now much would I get for it down the you-know-what?

STAN SAYS:
£45. Caravan on the left.

DEAR STAN,
And a shire horse.

STAN SAYS:
Call it £100 the lot.

Manaic begins botched killing spree by turning gun on self

by KATY BLIRDSNEST

IT WAS AN ORDINARY day in Framley except for the fact that a maniac went loose with a gun... So far from ordinary in fact!

Justin Boon a schoolteacher from Whoft terrified the town in a rain of terror. As soon as the news broke, I went down to the town to find out what it felt like to be terrified, and I

couldn't believe my eyes!

It was a heavy feeling in the stomach, like a big breakfast or The Big Breakfast. I bought some dry shampoo then came back to my desk to share my story. It's just one woman's view, but you have to agree.

You can read more about my lucky excape on my blog at blog.twitter.com/singleshoes. I was one of the lucky ones. I lived. Maybe you will too.

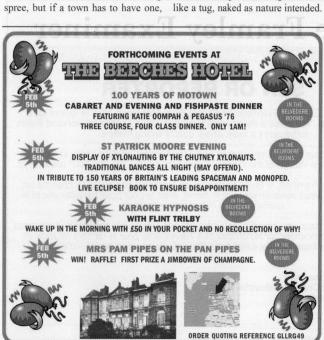
FORTHCOMING EVENTS AT THE BEECHES HOTEL

FEB 5th
100 YEARS OF MOTOWN
CABARET AND EVENING AND FISHPASTE DINNER
FEATURING KATIE OOMPAH & PEGASUS '76
THREE COURSE, FOUR CLASS DINNER. ONLY 1AM!
IN THE BELVEDERE ROOMS

FEB 5th
ST PATRICK MOORE EVENING
DISPLAY OF XYLONAUTING BY THE CHUTNEY XYLONAUTS.
TRADITIONAL DANCES ALL NIGHT (MAY OFFEND).
IN TRIBUTE TO 150 YEARS OF BRITAIN'S LEADING SPACEMAN AND MONOPED.
LIVE ECLIPSE! BOOK TO ENSURE DISAPPOINTMENT!
IN THE BELVEDERE ROOMS

FEB 5th
KARAOKE HYPNOSIS
WITH FLINT TRILBY
WAKE UP IN THE MORNING WITH £50 IN YOUR POCKET AND NO RECOLLECTION OF WHY!
IN THE BELVEDERE ROOMS

FEB 5th
MRS PAM PIPES ON THE PAN PIPES
WIN! RAFFLE! FIRST PRIZE A JIMBOWEN OF CHAMPAGNE.
IN THE BELVEDERE ROOMS

ORDER QUOTING REFERENCE GLLRG49

BELMAN'S OF DURBITON
ALL YOU CAN EAT **FURNITURE SHOWROOM**
UNIT 49H, MILLBROOK IND. ESTATE

The Warm Zippy
TRADITIONAL FREE HOUSE
PUB SEX QUIZ
EVERY MONDAY
with Quizmasters Framley CID
VINTAGE CASK PIES
HOME-MADE ALES
BEER IS FOR CUSTOMERS ONLY
THE WARM ZIPPY, FROTH STREET, FRAMLEY

travel case & 6 x refills. Allso works on Italians / spiders. £20ono. 01999 656177

HUNGRY HUNGRY HITCHCOCKS. The game of terror, complete with four brightly coloured Hitchcocks! Gobble up marbles just like the real master of suspense! (Please don't give away who wins the game.) £10. Framley 611872

GARDEN CHANDELIER with infinitely long "sky chain" . Buyer to unhook chain. 01999 454344

CAPTAIN'S TRUNK. Inherited from grandfather. 25" x 30". Filled with old fish fingers. £10. 01999 768165

FIGHT, £30. I don't mind losing. Box FE8722

DEHUMIDFIER. Very efficient. £90. Assorted powdered relatives. £20. 01999 865271

CHICKEN ON TOAST

DINING TABLE with inflatable Denis Norden. Detects real-life 'cockups' / 'bloopers' and springs into action. With clipboard. Switchable to ON / OFF / AUTONORDEN. £120 01999 464438

ALUMINIUM WINDOWS x 2. Lovely view. £20. 01999 617765

JEHOVAH'S WITNESS OPERATION GAME. Can you remove the funnybone? No you can't. £8. Framley 606614

BEDSIDE STOMACH CLOCK. 'Burping' alarm with 144 distinctive late night smells (bhaji / spicy wings / taxi sick). Ideal for deaf-blind shift worker. £12. Framley 634610

COMPLETE LEATHERBOUND SET of everything. No more cows left. £OFFERS

SMALL FREESTANDING handstand. £15ono. 01999 988769

MIGHTY KING GRAPEFRUIT. Monarch of all breakfasts. Herediitary title and padded suit. £125. 01999 337315

OVERWHELMING

HEART-STOPPING BRILLIANCE at the violin. Unwanted gift. Buyer to collect. £9. Ring Nigel's Plumbing Supplies on 01999 766808

MOST OF THIS MORNING. Unused. £25. 01999 657177

BABYBELLING COOKER. Cooks food by covering it in red wax and making it taste of cheese. £200ono. Framley 277561

MDF-EFFECT mahogany dining table. £25. 01999 350950

The Framley Examiner

"There are more things in heaven and earth than there are in the Framley Examiner classifieds!"

- Mr Ian Shakespeare

BLUE WOODEN COAT. Impervious to fencing blades / rapiers / cutlasses etc. No longer required (nemesis vanquished). Framley 559868

KING SIZED QUEEN bedspread. £15. Framley 845611

SEXY THIGH-LENGTH DESK. Saucy office fun. £95. Framley 828819

SHARP MICROWAVE oven. Nearly had my bleeding eye out. £20. 01999 797162

VICTORIAN TOURIST memorabilia, incl. "My betrothed went on 'The Grand Tour' and all I got was this infernal top hat" top hat. £20. Framley 611462

TRAMPOLINE. £50. Assorted children's shoes. £10. No questions. Framley 533172

CORRS & FX. Experimental cassette of Best of Corrs remixed with horror sound effects. What Can I Do To Make You Love zombies feasting on human flesh, Women screaming Breathless and many more. £01999388109

BOB PLUMBING

Anything from a tap washer to full-frontal nudity. Sealing baths, draining radiators, nothing left to the imagination. I may need to borrow a spanner.

01999 211506

BABY GRAND PIANO. Fits concert-sized cot. £125. 01999 232341

SET OF PROFESSIONAL level tungsten snooker clubs. "The Curse of the Crucible". Includes putter, sand wedge and driver. £Offers above £200. Whoft 36678

1400 x 2 SEATER SOFAS. Unwanted Christening gift. £24,000 ono. Framley 436119

COW-KILLING GUN. Hours of fun. Also probably works on people, cats etc. £15. Framley 657199

COLLECTOR'S BUS MAGAZINES. Collection of magazines found on the bus. £1. Also collector's bus food. £2. Framley 548109

FORNICATION

SET OF 8 x life-sized gilt-framed oil paintings of the men from Dire Straits' 'Money For Nothing' video in the nude and doing it and doing it and doing it. Best thing in the world. I done these. £2. 01999 664180. Ask for Vestry extension. Hang up if wife or verger answers.

HITACHI 28" TV with picture of man driving a car round a mountain on it, no a lady on a beach, no a load of clouds, hang on here's the man in the car again. £120. 01999 299281

BISCUIT. Half-eaten. Don't really like coconut. 5p. Box FE3025

CAST IRON. 2 steam settings. Plays 'Fine Time' and 1 other Britpop hits. £8. Box FE9011

'THE MIRACLE OF LIFE' DVD. Explains how all 6,678,873,050 of us came to be here, in alphabetical order. £1. Framley 324888.

TROLLFLOUR

ELEGANT LADIES' high heels, backless evening gown, trampoline and crash helmet. Make a big entrance. £95. Framley 878199

MAUVE LIPSTICK. Half-eaten. Don't really like lipstick. 50p. Box FE3025

FITTED CARPET. Unused.

Because I hover 3 inches above the ground. Experiment successful! Call Prof Arthur Bostrom on 01999 499100

BOOBS WANTED. Collector pays top prices for good quality boobs. Particularly interested in Franz Bafba, Jerome B Jerome, J.B. Rowling. 01999 562619

THAT'S COMPUTERISATION

WELSH CROSSDRESSER. With 3 pairs of drawers. £90. 01999 972691

FULL SET of vintage theories about Jimmy Savile. Some beer stains and wear. £5. 01999 518955

MOUNTAIN BIKE. £30. Mountain. £145,000. Box FE8029

DIVORCE MADE EASY! With this fig-roll-and-tinned-potato-smoothie maker. "What have you been eating darling?" £12. 01999 452700

40 GALLON drum of owls. Cost £35 (hand written receipt). Will accept £10. 458281

TABLE LAMP floor chair stool cupboard and other simple English words for things you might find in a room. I will teach you them all. Call Don at the Very Basic Language School. 01999 819910

The Framley Examiner

Your obituary here could be reaching

32,000

readers!

"I sold my deceased father within minutes. An intriguing and mysterious service. Many thanks."

Mr.C. Myfanwy Mountain Road, PR0 9EN.

FULL LENGTH CURTAINS. Decorator's cut. With deleted seams. £35. 01999 678659

RECLAIMED MATERIALS. Bogeys. Kitchen bin scraps. Comb jam. No trade enquiries. 01999 467508

BRIDESMAIDS' wetsuits x 3. Apricot. Size 12-16. £30 ea. 01999 255162

1965 DR WHO Annual. Cover good but all pages missing and cover missing and not the 1965 Dr Who Annual. Suit really obsessive Dr Who collector. £40. Framley 856156

CROTCH HOOVER. Full. £10. Framley 657198

LUDWIG COSTUME. Full-sized. Will swap for key for Ludwig Costume. Very hot under all this glass. Framley 986488

RICHARD DAWKINS' Face-Your-Genetic-Legacy Girls' World. Make up and beauty set for girls ages 6-10. Unflattering mirror, harsh lightbulb and no make up. £10. Box FE8901

BED BUG infested settee. Probably best not to mention bedbugs in the ad, Dan. Oh, okay. Settee. £59. 01999 748992

MASSIVE BATTERY made by melting down all the batteries in my house and cooking them in a pot to make one big battery. Stuns dogs, bursts lightbulbs, hair always on end. £45. Framley 910402

SIMPSON DUVET COVER

showing popular BBC character being smuggled into Afghanistan in a burqa. £8. 01999 665700

JCB INDUSTRIAL Piano Capo. 4000 Brake Horsepower. 1100 Newtons of Torque. Changes the key of any piano via enormous pressure on the casing and strings. Ideal for buskers. £250ono. Framley 520988

JAPANESE EDUCATIONAL 'Monsters of World War II' vintage toys. Churchilla and Churchzooky. £6. Framley 01999 672122

HECKLING CLOCKWORK GOAT-O-NAUT. Plastic goat demeans you, while dressed as an astronaut. Soviet-era technology. Cures high self esteem. Requires car battery. 'You're hopeless and will never amount to anything. I've been to the fucking moon. Where have you fucking been?' and one other phrases. Offers. Box FE8719

TINY TONY

IN-SHOWER SHOE RACK. Keeps your shoes clean but wet. £5. Framley 871002

THIS BELONGS TO WARREN ELLIS interior designs. Modern decoration using Dymotape dispenser. Furniture, walls, windows finished to a professional standard. One message only. Call Warren Ellis on 01999 744 542

JENNER BABY SWING. With roof mount for Renault Clio. £25. 01999 7444719

FOOT SPAR convenience store. A tiny supermarket that balances on your foot. Soothes, relaxes & half-price luncheon meat. 01999 521911

ORANGATRON MONKEY MAGNET. Attracts bananas, tea parties and biplanes. £4. Framley 978118

MR CRBEEBIES children's entertainment and discipline. 01999 723243

NEWBY'S

of Molford

WIN! WIN! WIN! W!N

Over 100 socks and up to a pair of trousers!

See our ad on p47

POCKET GAME 'Travel Swimming'. Perfect for long car journeys. £8. Framley 454906

HENRY KISSINGER Negotiating Furby. Place between any two other furbies and Henry forces them to come to an agreement! With new hair. £12. 01999 761170

LYONS CHER. Vintage 1968 ice lolly. £2. 01999 252390

BARBIE SHELTERED DOLLHOUSING Includes working stairlift, 3 sachets of magic blue rinse and Forgetful Ken. £25. Box FE4330.

DVDs. Stephen Merchant's friend doing standup. £5. American films with Stephen Merchant's friend. £2. Box FE7681

CAR BOOT LOT. £50. Framley 764001. Includes 4,000 pcs china, pottery and statues, stuffed animals, flint arrowheads, diorama of Victorian family, jars, farm machinery through the ages, guidebooks, pencils, staff and museum. Offers. 01999 687281

HOTPOINT harmonica / fridge. With neck brace and songbook. £25. Framley 01999 767819

SCALEXTRIC 'WARM WHEELS' carbon-neutral race set w/ two dozen potted plants and recycled cars (tins). £25. Framley 244310

LOVELY UNUSUAL wine cabinet full of lovely unusual wine. £30. 01999 902771

20 VHS VIDEO TAPES including 'Josie's 2nd birthday', 'Grandad's Last Christmas' and 'Woolacombe Jun 03'. With roll of sellotape. £2 the lot. Call 01999 644572 and ask for Mr. Hollyhock.

LEFT ARM CHAIR. Washable def leopardskin cover. I suppose £150's out of the question. Wripple 299509

50" FLATSCREEN TV COSY shaped like a Spanish lady. Discreet, enormous and classy. Call Sarah on 01999 786810

Leonard's

of Yopney

EXCLUSIVE SUPPLIERS OF

'YOUR CHOICE'

CIGARETTES

Every cigarette shortens your lifespan by 4 minutes...

But now you get to choose WHICH four minutes!

Ad breaks

Phone calls from your mum

Angels by Robbie Williams

Waiting for egg (soft)

ANTIQUES ROAD SHOW, Anti-Corrode Shoes, Auntie Crow's Chose. Not clear. Vendor has loud Austrain / Americain (?) voice. Email correct details to kelly@framleyexaminer.com. Do NOT phone again. Loud voice. £15.

UPTIGHT PIANO. Very highly strung. £225. 01999 808190

SET OF VERTICAL DINNER PLATES. Wedding gift. Used once, briefly. £15. Mop. £3. Framley 320287

5 PIECE chicken drumkit, with egg-shaped bass drum. Egg drum features door, windows and seat (planning permission granted for leg holes) BOX FE5576

MONOPOLY 'CLUEDO' EDITION. Game unfinished with hotels on lead piping and all suspects in prison. £8. 01999 653651

'YOU MANX TWATS'. 'Why Skye is Shit'. Assorted other Wight-supremacist publications. £2.50 each or £2.50 for one. FE6810

VICTORIAN EFFECT CELERY GRINDERS. Pair of three. £2 01999 722912

MIDDLE LANE of UK motorway network. 99 year lease. Convenient for everywhere. £offers. Vince on 01999 675857.

COMPUTER GAME. 'Anthony Eden's Jet Force – Assignment: Suez' for Bletchley Park Colossus II prototype valve computer. Four exciting levels on 3.25 million punch cards. £800ono. Framley 644511

BIG STING. Would suit big Sting fan. £90ono. 01999 288312

HAIR CLEANING TRUCK. Little roadsweeper that cleans your hair. 24/7. Warning: little man who drives little truck is ALIVE and under ENCHANTMENT. He only speaks Palatu. NOT A TOY. For details, apply Loa Simbe, after midnight, on Framley 977653

ESTELLE FOLDING CARAVAN. 4 berth / fridge / cooker / bath. In handy pocket wallet. Stand well back. £1100. Framley 690902

WIND UP gramophone advert. Call 01999 878441 and ask for Ivan Embarrassing-Knobrash. No. Hang on. Mike Ockhurts.

BIG NIPPER horse traps. £50 per dozen. 01999 761181

BOX SET OF BOND DVDS. Only dropped once. Titles seem to include 'Gunfinger', 'No Ball', 'You Only Eyes Only', 'Live Twice And Let Die Another Daylights Forever Never Dies To Kill A Kill' and 'On Her Majesty's Giant Peach'. Buyer to bring own bag and spade. £5. BOX FE8626

DROSSELMEYER

I DONE BUM PUDDING in Uncle Dave's hat. I can't. You tell him. OK. Put me through to Announcements. 01999 551909.

DYSON PLASTIC OVEN. Some ideas are best left on the drawing board. £10. Box FE8711

RUDE SOOTY glove puppet. Whispers swear-words, fires 'water' pistol and breaks vases. 9-year-old operator included. £4. Box FE8484

The Framley Examiner

Make your ad STRAWBERRY FLAVOURED for just

£15

Stand out from the crowd with the great taste of strawberries.

The Framley Examiner is licked by over 30,000 readers every week.

CHAMPIONSHIP BELT. 'Terryweight Championship Of The World'. Attached to radiator. £offers. Framley 477900

SHED PUPS. 6wk litter of baby garden sheds. Mother good temperament and felt roof. Dad pedigree T & G shiplap. SC reg. 01999 296 566

BRAS RUBBING sessions. Discrete and sudden. Call Vince for more graphic details. 07909 315345

JUDO skis. £7. Brian Jacks' Off Piste Grappledown VHS. £2. 01999 441565

BADMINTON TROPHIES, Olympic bronze medals etc. What was I thinking? £6 or will swap for proper job. 01999 654739

POLLY POCKET. Annoyed parrot trapped in inside pocket of otherwise immaculate Savile Row suit. No idea how this happened. £40ono. Box FE4775

INCREDIBLE LESLEY. Limited edition. Quite, quite incredible

The Framley Examiner

Framley's Traditional Favourite since 1978

JUNE, FRIDAY 21st, 2013   PRICE 65p

BACK UP YOUR HARD DRIVE ONTO CRISPS

Peace of mind in three tongue-tingling flavours

www.crispcloud.co.uk

OFFER!
A photo of your dog printed on your cat

WIN!
A circle!

INSIDE!
Can ye do the Tudor Boogaloo?

Town could be new Tinse1town as movie gets "green-light" from Mayor!

A TOUCH OF HOLLYWOD!

A touch of Hollywod came on Friday to Framley because of the fact that a film crew is going to plan to come to Framley to shoot some film in Framley for a film.

The film "Manhole Covers Britannia" is being made for the television channel BBC Radio 4, and Framley is going to be the star, after a television van was seen and a woman with a personal telephone got out and looked at a manhole outside Newby's Gloveworld and then wrote it down.

According to the internet, in fact, the programme will be showed at 9pm and again that night in the morning. "It will also be 55 minutes long," the internet said.

Mayor D'Ainty confirmed that he had signed a form and that filming was going to take place in the town. The Mayor told the Framley Examiner, "this will really put Framley on the map," and to get more toilet paper.

It's certainly that the silver screen will be good for business, with tourists and international companies getting to see the region in a new light, rather than despair, which is often the case in fact, with boarded up High Street shops becasue of the internet and fuss about the new bins..

A local journalist's friend Polly said the film could make Framley, "could become as famous as Midsomer or Summerwine, where they film Last Of The Summer Wine is filmed," and it's hard to argue, with places like New Zealand becoming famous because of the Jacksons and New York (Sex In The City Notting Hill where did they do hogwarts ask twitter for more films)

But there were signs that the protestor

by Katie Blirdsnest & Ch&llenger Putney

community were angry about the film, making angry signs about parking restrictions, think of our children and gay weddings.

"What if their cameras steal our souls?" asks local builder Wojtek Vzszlzavzkzszvwrzcz. And market trader Cathy Pacific, who runs the flour stall in the market, was disimpressed.

"I can't afford a new cardigan for the red carpet if I win an Oscar. I'll just say no like Marlon Zammo and send an Indian."

The Framley area has more manholes per square mile than Frankfurts.

The film crew, who cancelled, were not available for comment.

Could this manhole be the star of the next James Bomb or Batman's film?
PHOTO BY EWAN PUSSYCLART-NOSE

FRAMLEY-ON-SCREEN

Despite the exciting, it's not the first time that Framley has been on the big screen! Here's some places you may have seen the places of the Framley district...

The Story Of Pipes (1961)
- People driving past

Mind That Spare Wheel (1963)
- Hedge

Clap Hands, Here Comes Concrete! (1964)
- Van passes exit for Molford

The Town That Hope Forgot (1978)
- Various scenes

Crimewatch (1988)
- Mayor's office used as murderer's caravan

Apollo 13 (1996)
- Area glimpsed as capsule orbits Earth

Fine for driving with faulty tyre

A Molford St Malcolm man was told it was 'fine' for him to be driving a car with a faulty tyre by a man impersonating a plainclothesed policewoman.

An appeal for real witnesses has been made by police after the same man was arrested yesterday for impersonating a witness.

The tyre has been cautioned.

KEEMA KORMA AND CURRY ON! ON BHAJI

at *Quantifiably Balti*

New premises closed due to split sides. Takeaway only.

01999 564 888

LETTERS & PARCELS p32   BONNIEST LINE MANAGER CONTEST p44 YOUR RACIST PUNS p19

Stuntman is hurt as his stunt goes wron

A promotional image of Terry Allgold, with some of the fingers he will sadly miss.
PHOTOGRAPH BY GINGER BREADMAN

By Jesus Chigley

Stuntman and local national treasure Terry Allgold was recovering at hospital on Monday, according to events.

Mr Allgold became injured after a sensational daredevilled 'sword-swallowing' act at St Icklebrick's School Fete went badly badly in front of a crowd of children some of who'm are now all right.

The much-loved hard-guy who rose to fame as Heavy Four (uncredited) in the 1988 action film *The Thumping Man* cut eight of his popular fingers off while attempting to remove a sword he'd accidentally swallowed hilt-first.

Doctors say, "his condition is stable", but none were available to comment.

CARNIVAL HOPE

Organisers of the Molford Carnival say that they say that they hope that an operation to reattach the fingers will not be a mess, and Terry will still be able to perform his scheduled bareknuckled tug-of-war with a telephone directory on the Amaze-o-glaze Windows cagefighting float next Saturday.

According to Allgold's website, his trademark 'IM NOT GREAT IM BRILLAINT' singed promotional teatowel is now available from the hospital shop, with all proceeds going towards the till.

On other pages

Mayor Worn Down By British Emery Board (p23)

Uninvited Rugby Star Drops Guts At Fete **p7**

New market sign "Too colourful" say epileptics **p15**

Planning permission granted for controversial tortoise **p10**

Organic dinner ladies lay own eggs **p20**

Mayor forced to replace £8m bus shelter **p42**

Tragic jumble sale seeks right to die **p22**

Boycott Boy Caught By Quad Bike Ought Be Called By Court Beak Orders **p18**

THE
Framley Examiner

US ON CEEFAX

PAGE 876 and PRESS 'REVEAL' to find out how!

News in Brief

TEAM FOLLOW THROUGH TO THE FINALS

The Sockford Pretending To Have Hiccups League were on Wednesday night celebrating on Wednesday night the triumph of table toppers Urling Exhaust Centre Second V on Thursday night. The team's eleven point lead takes them through to the national finals at the Millennium Stadium Metro in Newton-Le-Willows on August 23rd, where they will meet Bill Oddie.

HIGH-SPEED CHAS STOPPED

A Saturday night 90 mph high speed police chase ended outside Robot Oak on Tuesday. A 56-year old Whoft man was charged with being drunk, but not in possession of a vehicle. "I feel invincible.", he, told officers.

ONION FACTORY WIN

Five lucky pupils at St Ulf's School went on a magical Willy Wonka-style day out to Glossop's Pickled Onion Works in Whoft. During their visit, four of the excited children on the greatest day of their life were victimised for minor character defects and thrown into the car park, broken. Clarence Mopp, a Year 6 pupil, inherits the factory and will never need for pickled onions again so long as he lives.

TRAIN JUMP

Rail services between Framley and Urling were suspended for six hours after a passenger jumped over a train. Relatives of the man, a Sockford plum-monger, say he had been incredibly happy for some time. The man cannot be named Damiun Clavalier, because that's my name.

Hilarious death was hate crime

Mayor D'Ainty has told Framley reporter Challenger Putney that now that full facts have come to light, he can only "express regret" at his public reaction to the hilarious death of Whoft clown Paul PacMahon.

"Framley is a safe place for all races and cultures," the Mayorsaidsaidsaid, "and I have asked my secretary to send a letter to all Youtube users, withdrawing my comments. Do you want the rest of that egg?"

EVERYONE'S* A WINNER AT

The Warm Zippy
ALEHOUSE AND TIE RESTAURANT

You won't believe the prizes we've got in our

AMAZING PRIZE DRAWER

MEAT
CUFFLINKS
COUPONS
A-LEVELS
PROPELLANT

Pop your business card in our shredder. The lucky phone number we assemble wins the shredder and all this hamster bedding!

THE WARM ZIPPY, Froth Street, Framley

*Not everyone is a winner.

WRIPPLE MASTODON

CLASSIC FILMS NOW IN ★ 3-D ★

Snow White And The 21 Dwarves
CERT U 8.15, 13.00, 16.20

Jaws 9-D
CERT AA 15.15, 17.10, 17.20

303D-almatians
CERT U 6.15

3 Of Our 3D-inosaurs Is Missing
CERT U 11.20, 16.00, 23.45

9 Colours Red
CERT PG SUNDAY ONLY 4.15

Where film comes a life!

Chez Maximillian
ROBOT HAIRDRESSING

Wash and blowtorch £8.50
We do not do humans.
No Metal Mickeys.

32 Producedbysteven St, Glibney

THE PRINCE 12" REMIX'S ARMS

A great family pub
BUT
Nightly Karaoke!

CAMRA WORST PUB 2003

Iranian Embassy Parade, Dungeon Estate, Batley

Erybody & Rybody

We know where you live

Moving people from one place to another is that's what we do!

- Ex-Shower home
- Two showers
- Shower room
- 70ft rear shower
- Front shower

- Double shower (w. en-suite shower)
- Dining room/Dining shower
- Off-street showering
- Three showers
- Planning permission granted for shower

Apply Whoft (01999) 526826

Paddington Hardstairs £335,000

SOLID STC

Clifton-on-Ostrich £235,500
- Hollywood-style property with Walken wardrobe.
- Feature 'Happy Day Fonzie' fireplace.
- The Whitepube area, which is hugely popular with arseholes, is well situated for many leisure activities, like golf.

Apply Whoft (01999) 526826

Foodhall £415,000 ono
- Traditional public house.
- Wealth of Pernod features.
- Two Norman Cliffy designer bar stools.
- Extended lock-in with all features/ fittings/customers included in sale.
- Best before end May 2007.

Apply Framley (01999) 562222

Mesgetty Lane Whoft

Piss Artist's Impression

An exciting new development of two 3 bedroom houses with absolutely nothing wrong with them whatsoever

PRICES FROM £2
(plot 2)

Whoft
(01999) 354322

Erybody & Rybody NEW HOMES

Sploshey £195,000
- Surprisingly intolerant property with narrow outlook over Native American burial ground.
- Unacceptable views.
- Cavity wall insularity.
- Permanently closed doors.
- 50ft not in my back yard.

Apply Framley (01999) 562222

Middle Eyot £235,500
- Architect designed but builder ignored shady private property with plenty of room for improvement and windows.
- Needs some modernizing and all windows.
- Viewing is highly recommended but impossible from the inside..

Apply Framley (01999) 562222

SOLD!
THE SAME PROPERTY REQUIRED AGAIN

Investment Opportunity £48m
- House in the recently renamed village of Investment Opportunity.
- Charming 1980s property with deeley boppers, rotating coloured sides, flashdance room and red-framed windows.
- Offers over £48m. Greed Is Good.

Apply Framley (01999) 562222

Sicdup £325,000
- House of Fun in the middle of the street.
- Access to mainline Nutty train with its frequent nightly boat link to Cairo
- Features castle and keep.
- Catchment for local nasty schools.
- Close to chemist and jokers' shop.

Apply Framley (01999) 562222

NEED TO SELL QUICKLY?

We can sell your house in under 30 seconds, whatever the reason.

Monster attack / Sink hole / Ancient Indian Burial Ground

CALL NOW!

WE MAY ALREADY HAVE SOLD YOUR PROPERTY!

FANTASTIC DAY

Internal inspection of this 5 bedroom executive house is highly recommended. Constructed to a high specification by Galvedere Burnwig Homes, the property benefits from a 50 ft bronze bust of Nick Heyward in the rear garden and detached garage..

£195,000

MNOTGOMERY HERB & CO

52 OLD DENEGATE WAY, FRAMLEY FM1 2BQ
PHONE: 01999 866423 FAX 01999 866424

LARGE SEMI

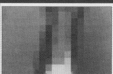

Recently erected, deceptively large semi in a conveniently central, yet rural location. Front elevation boasts prominent belltower with water feature and capacious downstairs ballroom. Firm offers only.

£195,000

VIEWS TO DIE FOR

LOOK OUT! LOOK OUT OF THE HOUSE.
Through the window. Don't look in. At the house. Don't look in the cupboards or the cellar. Look out. At the view. Not at the house.

£195,000

MUST BE SMELLED

Remarkable smelling property. It's a bit like a cross between off-mutton and cooked swede. Although not as nice. You don't have to buy it. Just come round and smell it and confirm it's not just me. It reeks.

£195,000

TURKISH DELIGHT!

Brown-clad property with distinctive pink jelly interior.
Southern-facing, but full of Eastern promise. Possibly subsidence. Possible melting.

£195,000

NO IDEA WHAT THIS IS

Refitted room? Good-sized room? Outside? Is it part of a house? I can't make it out from this angle. It might be a roof. Is it a roof? I think it's the roof. Book early to avoid missing the opportunity to see this roof.

£195,000

GOORAY FOR GOLLEYWOOG!

Exclusive property in sought after, recently renamed hamlet of Golleywoog with its bygone age charm and attitudes, it's the perfect retirement spot for a certain type of person (residents' association vetting).

£195,000

CONVENIENT FOR PRISON

Situated in B-Wing of Framley Prison (where the film 'Podge' with Ron Baker was filmed). This couldn't be closer to local amenities and some of the region's liveliest characters. Full cavity search before viewing.

£45k with good behaviour

ENJOY THE HIGH LIFE

This magnificent contemporary, 19 bedroom, brutallist thatched underwater terraced hotel conversion has been built to exceed all human requirements. Features Tudor atomic kitchen, robo-concierged Elevodium, discrete washbots, prismic glazing and off-street parking. Would suit sentient gas or multi-dimensional entity. Must be seen; cannot be seen; cannot not be unseen.

07999 328464

OM-POM-PUSH

Badly presented, 2 storey ex-council marionette within sprinting distance of all local amenities and schools. Some strings visible, but no onward chain. Grotesque. Absolutely grotesque.

£95,000

Parker & Milady

WHOFT One / Five Beds. Impressive one bed or unbearable five bed property. £125,000

ROBOT OAK Pan-fried semi-detached property in a redcurrant and popular area, with 1.5 acres of creamed grounds and chips (or jacket potato) £57,800.

SOCKFORD Small, charming, detached property near local house with own lid and wheels. Collected weekly. No onward chain, hardcore or hot ashes. £2,000

FIDO ST. DIDO House. Energy rating A. Highly sought-after Earth-centre location with good links to core, mantle, crust and shops. Central heating. Parking for one mole machine. £235,000

STABBING Recently demolished 5 bedroom house conveniently arranged in a skip. Excellent off-road parking. Requires some modernisation. £20

KING'S MUSTARD On the popular Dan Brown estate this newbuild property fulfils all energy rating requirements and, amazingly, weighs less than a bag of flour. The secret is this: This tiny microprocessor concealed within ifs roof felt. And, who knows, maybe we'll all be living in a home like this by the year 2000. Judith.

56 Poldance Crescent, Whoft FM3
01999 523533

CLASSIFIED ADS FOR SALE

Sell everything you own for **FREE** and buy it back for next to nothing. Then sell it again!
Call our friendly answering service online on **01999 947 694**

In this area where you live, here are the items that you sell!

SIR BOWLEO

VHS TAPE. "The Cannibal Run". Upsetting goofball video nasty with Burp Reynolds and Dom DeLicious. Serious offers only. Fram 884948

MB 'BIG TRAKTOR'. 1:1 scale programmable agricultural vehicle. Causes chaos and blind fury on narrow country lanes. Comes with trailer of 2:1 scale manure. £45,000 01999 122589

LITTLE FURRY TRIANGLES I done cut off to make the heads smoother. Assorted. Black, brown, tabby, tortoiseshell, ginger. £1 each 01999 710052

MYSTERY COLESLAW. one large, man-sized tub of cabbage, carrot, onion and secret ingredient in a creamy sauce of its own devising. Please text to 07900 900343 as reception not great in tub.

DVD BOX SET OF BORN TRILOGY (Born Free, A Star Is Born, Born Bjorg v John McEnroe Wimbledon 1980) £9.99 ono Framley 262834

ROWING MACHINE. Takes effort out of domestic disputes. Will squabble with spouse / neighbour / teenage child while you get on with hobbies, paperwork etc. £99. Framley 657107

WEATHERHOUSE. Man and woman figures battle to the death with umbrella and parasol if overcast. Also has a dozen confused Inuit figures for different types of snow. £38. Framley 292948

NIKE AIRFIX KIT. Unused. Makes one uncomfortable size 9 grey plastic trainer with fragile air cushion heel and invisible thin string laces. 50p. Box FE8666

MISTER MEN BOOKS. Mr Howard Tickle, Mr John Silly & Air Vice Marshal Sir Brian Bump KCBE. 30p each. Framley 790002

I HEART SU POLLARD T-SHIRT. With matching "I lungs Ruth Madoc" string vest and "I toenails Simon Cadell" popsocks. Good condition considering. £8 marked down from £150. Box FE8482

PS3 DOORMAT and Fancy Footwork game. Wipe your feet to the sound of 48 recent pop hits. £29. 07999 098022

IMAGINARY KETTLE. Calvin & Russell Hobbs. £10. Fram 292477

CORPORAL TOOT'S FLUTE BOOTCAMP DVD. Rapidly teaches your child the flute to Grade 8 standard with beatings for lacklustre performances. Three course ferocities – 6 months (hard)/ 3 months (harder)/5 minutes (hardest). £10 Fram 764282

ASSORTED THOMAS THE TRAIN SET, 1 train (angry face), 75 pieces, all straight. Suit inflexble enraged toddler. 01999 710861

BIG CEILING FAN. Top prices paid for your ceiling. NO FLOORS. BOX FE4042

HOZELOCK

HOZELOCK HOZELOCK. Hozelock? Hoze? Lock? No! Hozelock hozelock. Sorry. Wrong number. Hozelock.

IN SAUCEPANS

PETROL MOWER with AutoChord and rhythm unit. £35 01999 674805

CHILD'S CUSTOMIZED BUNK BED with luminous spring-loaded whispering fish-witch and hidden shrimp-and-brine heated stinkpockets. Call Mr Hollyhock on 01999 644572

RABBIT HUTCH. Seventies pet fancy dress costume. Also Hamstarsky and Guinea Piggy Bear. Worn once. £10 BOX FE4628

APIDAS BLACK/YELLOW FOOTBALL BEES. Size 10½. As new. Classic three stripes with screw-in stings and hand-stitched 'Nectar' logo on synthetic leather tongue. £20 Fram 614517

HENRY VACUUM COOPER with 3 unused punchbags, one black eye and knighthood for services to skirting boards. £10 01999 541473

BOSCH CORDLESS HEDGEHOG TRIMMER. Cuts hedgehog spines, eyelashes and pubes. Needs sharpening.£15 01999 310028

LITTLE TYKES Magic Sounds Play Arse. £6. BOX FE3568

ANTHONY WORRAL THOMSPON PROCESSOR with pulse/no pulse setting and handy mute button. One touch beard removal. Extracts all juice in a jiffy! £40 01999 656601

ITALIA 90 PANINI STICKER ALBUM. Mozarella & Parma Ham sticker missing otherwise complete. Pages stuck together with cheese. £5 Fram 136155

ANTIQUE 1999 DANCING HAMSTER. Unwanted GIF. £2 BOX FE5271

CHILD'S CHEVY CHASE 'YOU CAN CALL ME AL' COSTUME with sheriff's badge and wigwam. Constantly worn, in fact you'll have to prise it from her cold, dead fingers. £8. Framley 491057

SUEDE JACKET. Denim trousers. Corduroy waistcoat. And other unwanted 90s memorabilia. 01999 901153

The Framley Examiner

ELEVEN GLORIOUS YEARS OF NOT BEING ABLE TO SELL...

PARROT CAGE with Ceefax. No offers. No questions. (No answers) Fram 695892

THEY ALL LOOK THE SAME WHEN THEY'RE BORN and that's how mistakes get made in hospital. I should know. 01999 975896

LAMP, provisions, the gold key, spade, the red key, bag of carrots, rope. £50. You can not SELL INVENTORY. SELL ROPE. Rope £5. BOX FE2823

HORNBY 007 GAUGE TRAIN SET with laughing Baron Samedi sat on back carriage. Fram 960784 This classified will return in Goldenexaminer.

COMPLETE SET of hand-painted commemorative collector's plates on neat little shelves showing views from the CCTV at Clifton Cards in the Arnhem Centre, Framley. Mainly 1998. Now you can be the security guard! £185. Framley 773987

WORLD OF NEEDLECRAFT. Online PC Game, sampler downloads, and cross-stitch upgrade. £15. Framley 874092

4 BRIDESMAIDS' DRESSES Suitable for Transformers-themed wedding. Apricot silk edged with pearls and wheels. £200. Framley 200876

SNOOKER QUEUE. Waiting for Dennis Taylor's autograph outside the crucible in 1987. Stuffed and mounted. Highly collectible. Offers. Box FRA8708

FUNDING SOUGHT FOR FILM about two scientists who invent a time machine and go back in time to stop themselves from inventing a time machine. My head has caught fire. Help. Framley 494967

COLOR ME BREADD

ANTIQUE ROYAL DOULTON LOUIS MOUNTBATTEN signature breakfast stilts. Ivory / bone china. Recently resprung. A touch of class. £offers. Framley 272810

VIDEO COLLECTION. Jean Claude Van Dyke films. Timesweep. Universal Cockney. Kicky Kicky Box Box etc £15 the lot. 768190

J-LO THE MUSICAL. Based on the songs of J-Lo. Abandoned project. Book and libretto written. Needs tunes. £3.99. Fram 395852

FERGUSON Video Frog Mk1. £20 Fram 728653

4 DOWN-FILLED PILLOWS (6,3). 26 across – Man talking about dinner last night perhaps (10). Answers please. 01999 406222

ELEVEN PHOTO ALBUMS containing numerous photos of me masturbating into Newhaven Harbour. £2. Will not separate (even when steamed.) BOX FE2633

10 X RECLAIMED 3 PANEL 1930S INTERNAL DOORS. All hinged at top like a bleeding catflap. My shins hurt. Fram 694671

WALMART WALNUT WALLUNIT. Wal not separunit. £20. 01999 682922

SOLID PINE WARDROBE signed by Rachel Whiteread. £450,000. BOX FE4629

ATOMIC SKIS. Used once (experiment successful), but where is my beautiful wife? Call Professor Arthur. Bostrom £150 01999 499100

MI CASA, SU CASA, MI CASA I move out of my house, you move into my house, I move back into my house, I eat your furniture. Me real hungry. Will stop at nothing, ono. Call Wild Bill McO'McKeith 07900 900297 and ask for Gordon. I always leave crumbs.

BOSCH TUMBLE FREEZER. Freezes your clothes and keeps them fresh for decades. 01999 247528

COMPUTER GAMES. Range of WWII wii games and non-PC PC games. Call for list. £30. Framley 940981

JARS OF TOM BAKER'S UNWANTED DRIED SKIN. Collection from convention chairs across the known galaxy. Also one pair ladies'; knickers. For viewing only – not for sale. Call 01999 375549 and ask my mother for Alan.

RUBBISH REMOVAL. Two blokes built like Charles Hawtrey will drop your furniture down the stairs and bash it all in. No van. No jobs too. Small. Eugene 07900 900672

DVD of Triumph of The Will, with Dictator's Commentary. Framley 879188

VINTAGE 1978 PACKET OF QUINCYPOPS. Jack Klugman tie-in 'detective cereal'. Find the clue. Still two months to win. £9. Framley 967190

GLASS TABL. Small tabl, 30" square. Silver ornate stand plus two fold-up stols on silver frames. This is not a table. These are not stools. This was not my idea. BOX FE2397

CHILD'S 'LIL' PRIME MINISTER' SET with Tiny Blair, John Minor and Benjamini Disraeli. Comes in Wendy Houses of Parliament. £offers BOX FE2909

WALLPAPER WITH "HIDDEN FACES" DESIGN. Great for nervous kids. 07900 900428

G-PLAN 1960S VERY RARE WINGED BACK LEATHER OZZY OSBOURNE. Swivel rosewood base. Would look fantastic in a mahogany Black Sabbath. £140 01999 749588

MILD AMERICAN MUSTARD GAS canisters. Great for dispersing rowdy BBQs. In 5ml, 10ml, 2l sizes. Call for prices. 01999 687973

ITCH-A-SCRATCH. Draw an infinite number of skin complaints with a series of 90 degree angles. Scratch screen to enflame like magic! £10 BOX FE4673

GOBLIN TEASMADE. Also Goblin kettle. Goblin hat and goblin shoes. I am a goblin and I am selling my goblin things. BOX FE9124

HIGH PITCHED SQUEALING WARDROBE. £45. Complete Narnia hardback box set. £6. Assorted child's clothes and toys. £60. Framley 453655.

PAIR OF EXORCISSORS. Trim that devil right out of your hair. £5 ono. Framley 902711

NORTEX FULL-BODY EXERCISE WELLINGTONS. Every muscle given a full workout on rainy days. Perfect for puddle starjumps. £35 01999 768192

HAND VACUUM CLEANER. Removes fluff and dust from between fingers. £8. 01999 719180

ANAL SEX. Unwanted wedding night present. Also 50% share of wedding presents. Bastard. Offers. Box FE3950

NAVY BLUE. Excellent condition. Very comfortable. Flame-retardant. Don't actually know what it is but it goes like a rocket. £100. Box FE 8409

REPRODUCTION DISPLAY CABINET. Proudly displays images of you and your partner conceiving and bearing your children. Embarrassing and intrusive. 01999 768268

TRACY ISLAND. Helipad. rock-face aircraft hangar, retractable swimming pool. Rocket launch silos. Also includes Tracy Mansion and four rescue ships. £345m with freehold.

RECORDS WANTED. 45s, 78s, 50s, 60s or 70s. Call Fram 33.3333

SHERLOCK COMBS. Solve the mystery of hair. Comes with year's supply of opium-flavoured brylcreem. £5 or murder my husband for me. Framley 292710

ELBOW DOILIES. Keeps cake plates and fruit bowls perfectly balanced. Framley 686972

KEBABY. With pitta nappy, chilli dummy and salad rattle. Also frozen sperm doner and turkey baster (used). 01999 903595

MESGET

3-PANEL ROOM DIVIDER. Printed with contentious and argumentative opinions on religion, politics and best Beatle. Ideal for parties. Box FE8671

OBJECT. £10. Framley 979962

TOPSOIL, loose or bagged, free to collector. Bottomsoil, very loose, proving impossible to bag. I will pay you to take this away. 01999 774902

'TUCKER'S TICKER' GAME by Action GT. Wind up the clockwork Todd Carty. Can you solve the puzzle before he pops up and vomits? With refills. £8. Framley 973431

CARPET 80% wool, 20% ground in cat hair. Burgundy/ tabby. Started off 100% cat hair. This isn't what I ordered. £30. 01999 635422

REGGIE REGGIE PERRIN SAUCE. 256 crates of ill-advised third series spin-off condiment. Authentic Leonard Rossiter flavour. Might have gone off. £2 each. BOX FE4254

MAHOGANY EFFECT Framley Examiner sports desk. With oak effect Pigshit Nelson. Subs missing and handy bottom drawer. 01999 975585

DON'T LET YOUR WEDDING TURN INTO A

DISASTER!!!

Don't leave anything to chance. Arrive in style on your big day in luxury, chauffeur-driven, His n' Hers Hindenberg-class wedding zeppelins

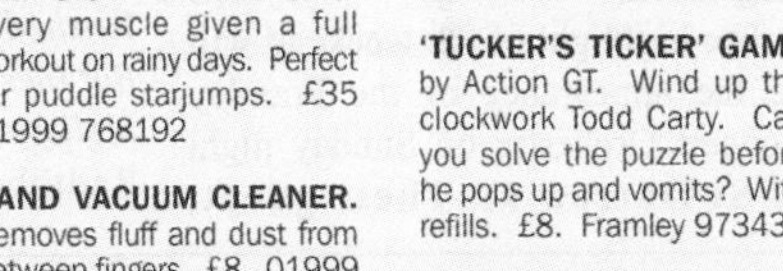

One way £500 • Private hire only

Involuntary Trips Limited 01999 344675

The Framley Examiner

Framley's Traditional Favourite since 1978

FRIDAY AUGUST 11th, 2019 — PRICE 45p, AS USUAL

THIS WEEKEND ONLY AT
Ree Severs
SHOPPING CENTRE
Register you and your family with the Earwig Police for FREE at *Bum Tektonix*
Come and have your cagoule sandblasted while-you-wait at *My Virtual Gnome*
If you're in the Atrium at midday, get approved by sea lions at *Helium Handbag*.
Find us on the High Street between The Precinct and Newby's Mall.

KIDS

He's the greatest dancer!

STYLE

How to find your perfect hairs

SPORT

Liver 3 Onions 2 Full match report

'Weeping' statue is no miracle says 'woman' as miracle mayor statu

MIRACLE MAYOR STATUE UNMASKED

by Adam Wrent

A statue of Framley's Mayor which has been attracting pilgrims from all over of the area because of the fact of its miraculous properties has been exposed as not at all.

The eight-foot-tall bronze statue was presented as a gift to the town by Claus Freneddt, Mayor of Framley's twin town Baden Schleissgarten in Germany. The German mayor drove to Framley a month ago with the statue aboard his mayoral dropside flatbed VW Transporter van, and waved (his hand) to crowds.

But only days later, the gift statue began to weep real salty tears, from its groin. The miraculous miracle of the tears was declared a "miracle" by the Bishop of Framley, and pilgrims began too, gather from all around, paying worships at its plinth in historic Bostrom Square.

WEEPING GROIN

A week later the miraculous flow became stronger, producing a forceful arc, and a makeshift pond was constructed at the base of the plinth, where children have become to like to play. The healing properties of the sacred Mayoral water have become famous, selling for £15 a bottle. Mayor D'Ainty himselfth has visited his statue on several occasions to play in the fountains, explaining to reporters that he felt "invincible".

But Karenanne Woob, an investigator from local website d-bunkers dot co dot U.K. says she has explosed the myth.

PIPE FOUND

"Closer examination has revealed a pipe coming from the statue and leading into the ground," she revealed, "and closer examination of that has revealed that we can hear alpine horns coming down it, the sound of slapped lederhosen, and the tell-tale smell of bratwurst."

"The water is not water," she says next, "but urine. And closer examination has revealed that it is German urine."

The D'Ainty statue (left) and the Mayor Freneddt actual person (right)
PHOTOS: (LEFT) PAT ONION-FAMILY (RIGHT) IPPY QUESNELL

When asked for a comment, a spokesmayor for Baden Schleissgarten council replied, "Now your town stinks. Never forget." And waved his finger and smiled using some emojis.

Forty-six children and a Mayor are recovering in hospital.

What would YOU do if the Framley Examiner Easter Bunny 2003 visited YOUR school?

He is Risen!

Call
01999 484748
for current prices* **

*Price includes The Framley Examiner Easter Bunny (2003) and 1½ Newby Crème 'Eggs'.

**Price also includes guaranteed appreance from The Framley Examiner Easter Bunny (2003)'s sworn nemesis, The Whoft Sentinel March Hare 2004.

Archer kills seven before turning bow on self

THERE WAS SCENES in central Framley this week after a rogue archer went on an fatal bow-and-arrowing spree.

The assailant, Gordon Archer, 46, of 46 Gordon Archer Way, was said to have been driven "to the point of mass murder" in a minicab booked from Pimpmy Newby's Rides of Molford.

The archer first took aim at a passing ventriloquist, Gobby Gaskerville, striking him fatally in the mind.

ARCHER

Archer's next kill was much-known fruiterer Sandra Arreau, and after that he picked off local bookseller Miguel 'El' Beau.

Beau and Arreau were pronounced dead at the scene of the archering, as were Gaskerville, four others whose identities I'll get before filing this copy, and Archer, the main man himselve.

Archer was named by locals as Gordon Archer and his Facebook page immediately looked at by journalists to see if he had left a manifesto. It was found to contain only three posts, most of which were about bins.

Forensics have retrieved the lethal weapon from the scene (Archer's dead hand) and are searching the area with a five-toothed comb for clues.

ANYONE

Anyone with any useful information is asked to contact Framley Po *(cont on p.130)*

The scene where the crime
PHOTO BY OCTOR DOCTOPUS

196

Picture-By-The-Sign to get sign

By Jesus Chigley

After a successful two-year campaign, the village of Picture-By-The-Sign is to get its own village sign.

For a number of years (see above) residents of the chocolate box village have campaigned to get a sign for their village, and now it looks as if they've succeeded.

"We've never had a village sign, and people driving through often park up by the green and ask why we haven't got one. Especially with the name of our village, which is probably why people drive here and look for it. So they can take one by it, you see," said local campaigner Margaret Helpful, who moved to the area last year to get involved and is now

planning on moving back to her original house in near-by Millbury Mollymandeigh.

"A village sign is as much a quintissential part of the English countryside as a fat hen or clotted tea. And now we've got our wonderful sign, made for us by talented local artist, Paul Something-Orother, we can well-and-truly let passers-by know that Picture-By-The-Sign's name lives up to its name!", she continued while our photographer lined up a photo.

Helpful then continued pointing at the bottom of the sign while going redder and redder until we put our equipment away and left. The sign, which is situated in the middle of the village green, is expected to draw crowds of ten or so people a year.

Picture-By-The-Sign's new village sign is up there ^

PHOTOGRAPH BY RIVERSIDE HUMPTY

Man fired from cannon died of "natural causes"

A 76-year-old man died of "natural causes" after being fired from a cannon at the Codge Age Concern fete, in March, a month earlier this year.

Corky Monster, 76, won the trip-of-a-lifetime across the green as a prize on the Hook-a-Goldfish stall. "He'd only been trying to win a duck in a plastic bag of water," said his daughter, Honey, 48. "But the man on the stall insisted the ducks were for display purposes only."

The coroner's report said that it was entirely natural for a man of Mr Monster's advanced years with several underlying health conditions to die after being launched 40 feet in the air from a compressed air cannon, in a blaze of fireworks.

"It is nice to know his death was entirely natural," said Ms Monster, who has dropped all charges. The fete organisers have agreed for a duck in a bag of water to be buried with the late Mr Monster, as a "gesture of healing."

Mayor carpeted

On Saturday afternoon, the Mayor of Framley laid a square of carpet over the last remaining section of the town's historic, four-hundred year-old cobbles.

The carpet tile, featuring the Framley crest drawn on it with a red magic marker pen, was the first to be laid as part of Mayor D'Ainty's "Keep Britain Carpeted" campaign, started in order to allow senior council dignitaries to wear their slippers whilst on official business.

READER'S OFFER

Luxury Segway Experience *for Two*

Simply collect the tokens given away over the next few weeks in the Framley Examiner, then then choose your Luxury Segway Experience from either 'GOOD' (50 tokens) or 'BAD' (2 tokens)

The Framley Examiner
Framley's Traditional Favourite Since 1978

Rick Wakeman's

ONLY £299.99

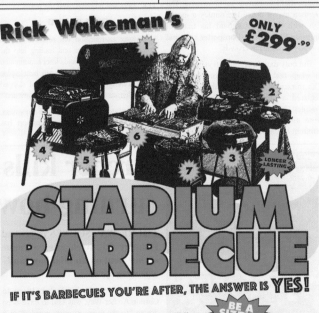

LONGER LASTING

STADIUM BARBECUE

IF IT'S BARBECUES YOU'RE AFTER, THE ANSWER IS YES!

BE A SIZZLE WIZARD!

TONY PARSONS says "I can't wait for punk"

I'm a busy musician, but I won't go on stage until I've had my tea. And my favourite tea is the great outdoor taste of a **BARBECUE**. But with my concerts lasting up to three hours sometimes that means having **SEVEN** barbecues on the go.

My **STADIUM BARBECUE** set is inspired by my music, offering one big barbecue, and its six wives. Allowing you to do **CHOPS. BURGERS. KEBABS. DRUMSTICKS. CORN-ON-YE-COB.** And a **VEGETARIAN OPTION (FISH).**

Now you can perform **SIZZLING** 15-minute sausage solos that will make your family cheer for more! It really is a **JOURNEY** to the centre of the barbecue-niverse!

Back in stock at...
NEWBY'S
of Molford

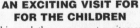

Man dies peacefully in panther's arms (p23)

"Totally appalling" clifftop fall man overly-critical **p15**

24-hour pedestrian crossing given green light - latest casualties! **p21**

Tiny robin hops into Mayor's open mouth **p24**

Framley octogenerian receives fresh lick of paint **p25**

Annoying truth gets in way of great story **p12-13**

Local bobby given hero's ride home in own helmet **p27**

News in Brief

AN EXCITING VISIT FOR FOR THE CHILDREN

This week there was great excitement for St Icklebrick's year 2 children when they had a visit from Framley Fire Brigade, complete with fire engine. The children climbed in the fire engine, used the hose and even dressed up in the firefighters' uniforms. Unfortunately due to complications, the fire brigade were unable to save the Grade II listed gym block from the flames, but a great time was had by all.

LADIES TOILETS RE-OPEN

The ladies' toilets next to Framley's Church of the Wholly Family have finally re-opened after a three-year battle against remaning closed. The toilets were shut in 2005 after the council deemed them too expensive to run. Of the four ladies who were inside when they closed, two survived. They are believed to have lived on soap and toilet paper for the duration of the lock-in. A cathedral spokesparson described their condition as near-mint.

When is a pub not a pub? This one is!

By LaVimto Blirdsnest-Clavalier, GCSE

"What's for tea, Mum?" I ask every single evening but not on this evening because it was a very special evening – an evening when my mother was not cooking our tea! She had actually booked us a table, two chairs and even some cutlery at a newly refurbished gastropub! What a relief!

THE SKY SPORTS & HORSES on Whoft High Road, beformerly The Just Horses, only reopened last month in a tape-cutting ceremony scissored by local celebrity Mad "Lizzie" Webb, but they are already serving food!

ALREADY EXCITED

I was so excited when we arrived that my mother said that perhaps we should simply go home again! Once I'd put all the ketchup sachets back where they belonged, we both agreed that I could stay after all and a waiter showed us to our table. Luckily there was a lovelier aroma coming from the kitchen so we had already decided that our meal would be delicious!

Our first course came very quickly, which was fantastic because neither of us had eaten a thing since we'd shared a packet of **wine gums** in the taxi on the way there. I had a starter called **tuna salad** (£7), which was literally amazing to me, while my dining componion had a **chicken salad** (£8.50), which was nothing like the chicken we have at home that you can dip (£2.49).

Between courses we took in our

Food is available (Artist's impression)

surroundings. This is a true spit and spacedust pub, which is also one of the pudding options. There were so many people there that it was hard to hear ourselves eat at times, but it was a very relaxing atmosphere if you like watching people watching football.

TUBES

We had the same mains so that we could compare them: **posh liver and onions** with a **potatoey mash** (£11.50), which my mother said to the waiter was very tasty, thank you. I smiled politely and left it all because **tubes** (£11.50).

While we waited for our puddings to come, whisky-loving pub owner Gwen "Eight Bells" Toll asked us if

we would like a free bottle of Prosecco in exchange for a five star review. On hearing that we were actually eating anonymously and anyway our ratings are sausages not stars, she apologised professionally and brought us a pint of tomato gin with **two straws** instead (free).

Although the kitchen forgot to send our puddings – a **selection of ice creams** (£5) and a **selection of nice creams** (£14.50) – the menu photographs looked good enough to eat but weren't. It didn't matter how many times we asked for them, the desserts never came, which all added to the fun of the evening! We could also have not had profit rolls, Hot Chocolate's fudge cake or sticky pudding. Yum!

HER BOTTOM

Mummy said it didn't really matter because there was still a mint Viennetta in the freezer at home. I didn't want to remind her that she'd actually eaten the whole thing the night Dad popped over very drunk and told her he still loved her bottom.

All in all, we had a wonderful evening at this wonderful gastropube, which landlady Gwen says still sticks in the back of her throat, but the brewery insists on calling it that so what can you do? Pay for your meal and go home again, that's what.

Meal including drinks: **£48, I think,** plus service charge.

Five sausages.

⟨⟨⟨⟨⟨

OUR LANDLORD **Tony Corkscrews** SAYS!

Behave!

I LOVE MICK MOUS

● STEEL SHUTTERS DON'T MEAN WE'RE CLOSED!
● NEW WINDOWS EVERY TUESDAY!
● NO FAST MOVES!
● BRING OWN DARTS! (NO BOARD!)

THE NAILGUN & GUN

133 Binjuice Parade, Dungeon, Batley FM17

Framley's newest "g'astro-pub"

The Royal Oaf

JUST LOOOK AT OUR MENU!

Peanuts in the dry roast style
Peanuts a la salt
Yeast-seared wheat twigs
Whole roast beef Monster Munch
(SUNDAYS ONLY)
Extensive mini-Cheddar board

80 Foresters Link, FM3 01999 335166

"How YOU doin'...?"

Have a Central Perk coffee at at...

F.R.A.S.I.E.R.S

Traditional

90's coffee-pub

(formerly The Old Wheatsheaf)

"We were ON A BREAK!!!!"

34 Old Forge Lane, Wripple

The **Goose & Maverick**

Home of Framley's longest running hen party

Since 1988

POLICE AWARE

16 Allgold Terrace, Framley 01999 778119

Why 'not' try?
FINE DINING at .....?

WORZEL'S

MOLFORD'S NUMBER ONE
HAY 'N' RAW TURNIP
THEME RESTAURANT

Lose yourself in a magical world of hay and raw turnip at 'WORZEL'S

Please note that ALL dishes are served with hay and raw turnip. No substitutions.

130 Dafthead Terrace
Molford-St-Gavin
01999 676199

★ The Man Of The Voices Of The Stars ★

BENEDICT BENDERSON

Still plenty of tickets left!

He's been the "best in the business" for 30 years, and fresh from his briefly remarkable appearance on the Zephyr AM Roadshow, Framley's top mimic brings his wide* range of unmistakeable famous voices to the snug of *The Warm Zippy* every THURSDAY.

Ben's celebrity impressions are:

☆ "Northern charity runner"

"Australian cartoonist" ☆

The Warm Zippy

THE WARM ZIPPY, Froth Street, Framley

*'wide' is used here in the sense of 'broader than is tall'. The range of impression characters, if stood alongside one another, one metre apart, would occupy more horizontal space than vertical. This definition is legally applicable and will be employed in any case of misleading advertising or false claim.

Ye Olde Pub-by-the-Sewage-Works

UNDER NEW MANAGEMENT AGAIN!

★ RIVERSIDE VIEWS!

★ NEW CHEF!

★ NEW MENU!

★ FREE WINE!

WE ARE LOOKING FOR STAFF

Established: 1846
Sewage Works Est'd: 1848

01999 667111 Follow us on ITV Oracle

Tony and Diane (names correct at time of going to press) welcome you to Sockford's premier "river"side dining experience, with fine wines (free) and aromatic dishes.

"Ye get used to it!"

Carnival memories

MISS – I am writing in to see if any of your readers might have any photographs of memories from Framley Carnival in the late 70's / 80s?

I was just a young girl at the time, but I remember being very excited as we drove down the high street – I was one of the shoelaces on the giant Joe Longthorne's shoe on the Framley 4th Guides float.

I vividly recall crowds of people waving and throwing money and insults at us as our jolly float gently ploughed into the back of the Mayoral cortege. How we laughed as the inflatable Mayor came loose from its tethers on top of the Mayor's Rolls Royce, sending it tumbling into the back changing rooms of Newby's Electricals, crushing passers-by. The look on its face was a picture!

BARBARA LICIOUS
Sowthistle Street
Whoft

Star gazing?

MISS – I cannot help but be the only one who has noticed that The Seven Stars pub now has eight stars on its sign. Where will it end? Nine stars? I hope not to live to see the day.

I may not be as young as I was but I still count. What are they after? What is their game? Trying to make the so-call Europe flag? They won't make me see it. I was in the Wrens.

It's not been the same since that "mobile" telephone mast went up in Durbiton. Seven Stars? More stars more like. And I don't like! Not one bit.

MR M.S. WINDOWS
Cilla Villas
Urling

Boyd Racers

MISS – I am sick and tired of these so-called 'beer lags' and 'lazy lots' with their souped-up vehicles, tearing around the Fracton ring road like they're Lewis Hamilton III.

With their modified exhaust tubes pumping out deafening petrol pop-pops at six-of-one-two-a-penn'orth, I've often entertained the thought of building a hydraulic exo-skeleton with a modified mechanical arm so that I can catch them as they come round the Clinton gyratory and hurl them into the mighty ocean!

The authorities seem to turn a 'blind-eye', as they say, to this anti-social behaviour so, if any of your readers were interested in helping me build my skeleton, I'd appreciate any help since my knowledge of mechanics is patchy, at best.

TOBY C'AVERY
Mintybitstronger Crescent
Fracton

Could of done better

MISS – I of'nt written to you for a while, but I was so incensed by your story, "Trying Their Hardest!" (Framley Examiner 03/06/2008) that I felt that I needed to say something.

They could of done better.

DR ALCOCK BROWN
Roy Newby Villas
Molford

Some Neighbourly Advice

MISS – this is a poem I wrote some years ago, but I still stick to this philosophy today.

"When my dog turds
My neighbour has words
With me over t'fence
Because of the stench.

I say that it's normal
And to keep things quite formal
I now post through his letterbox
The turds of my better dogs.

But poor old Nathaniel
My Welsh springer spaniel
Has bowels that are loose
And can only make juice.

So this I do keep
In a bowl good and deep
And in darkness of night
Tip it o'er his car white.

Now his Lexus is brown
Which is getting him down
But he should've kept quiet
The fucking old twat."

I hope that this ditty may help some of your readers to remember to be kinder to animals.

REV UNITY MEDFORD
The Old Vicarage
Sockford

Reader noticed

MISS – I cannot be the only one who has noticed.
Yours,

HERMES FEEDBACK
Horns Lock
Plinth

More mess

MISS – My wife and I have been disappointed by the standard of dog mess in the alleyway between Wripple library and the shops.

In my day, 'Dog's Muck Alley' as we called it, was crawling in firm hound chod. Now we can barely get our fingers under it to pick it up and photograph to complain. What? Is the world coming, too?

MAUNSELL C FORT
Zippy's Granary
Wripple

Social days

MISS – do any of your readers have any memories of Chutney Meadows Sports Ground Social Club in days gone by?

In particular do any of them remember where I left my car keys? It would be lovely to share some recollections of times past, particularly since I can't get into my car now, and there's a pound of pork mince on the parcel shelf.

TERRY CLOTH
Speedwell Avenue
Chutney

Had to laugh

MISS – We had to laugh at church on Sunday as our vicar walked up the aisle to deliver his sermon carrying a egg timer.

We all thought it was because he wanted to keep the length of his always interminably boring sermon to a minimum, but it turned out it was because he wanted to boil a egg.

I had to laugh! God was watching.

VERA MISANTHORPE
21 The Green
Wripple

Last word

MISS – I notice with dismay that the council are thinking of closing down Clinton's historic Indoor Bowels Club.

I have been a member of the club for over forty years, taking part in league and championship events, for which I have many treasured trophies on my shelves.

When it closes, where will I go?

MR C. SHAMEN
Pat Roach Approach
Clinton

TENBY & THE COLONEL'S PIRATE RADIO AIRSHOW

FORMER *Zephyr* 1375 HOSTS – NOW *TOO BLUE FOR RADIO!*

BROADCAST **LIVE & UNLEASHED** FROM THEIR HOT-AIR BALLOON TETHERED 20M ABOVE THE CAR PARK OF THE WARM ZIPPY PUBLIC HOUSE

FREE to all attendees – the paper hats THEY don't want you to see!

With special in-balloon guests: Celebrity impressionist Benedict Benderson and musical duo Arnold and Maureen, who'll be performing *The Quasimodo Song* in full!

PC-FREE ZONE! *WARNING: some audience participation

GREATEST MEMORIES LATEST DEMANDS

IT'S BACK! ARE YOU A HORNY HONKER?

Saturday 20th August 12-3pm

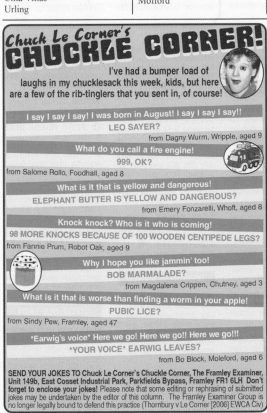

Chuck Le Corner's CHUCKLE CORNER!

I've had a bumper load of laughs in my chucklesack this week, kids, but here are a few of the rib-tinglers that you sent in, of course!

I say I say I say! I was born in August! I say I say I say!!
LEO SAYER?
from Dagny Wurm, Wripple, aged 9

What do you call a fire engine!
999, OK?
from Salome Rollo, Foodhall, aged 8

What is it that is yellow and dangerous!
ELEPHANT BUTTER IS YELLOW AND DANGEROUS?
from Emery Fonzarelli, Whoft, aged 8

Knock knock? Who is it who is coming!
98 MORE KNOCKS BECAUSE OF 100 WOODEN CENTIPEDE LEGS?
from Fannie Prum, Robot Oak, aged 9

Why I hope you like jammin' too!
BOB MARMALADE?
from Magdalena Crippen, Chutney, aged 3

What is it that is worse than finding a worm in your apple!
PUBIC LICE?
from Sindy Pew, Framley, aged 47

Earwig's voice Here we go! Here we go!! Here we go!!!
YOUR VOICE EARWIG LEAVES?
from Bo Block, Moleford, aged 6

SEND YOUR JOKES TO Chuck Le Corner's Chuckle Corner, The Framley Examiner, Unit 149b, East Cosset Industrial Park, Parkfields Bypass, Framley FR1 6LH Don't forget to enclose your jokes! Please note that some editing or rephrasing of submitted jokes may be undertaken by the editor of this column. The Framley Examiner Group is no longer legally bound to defend this practice (Thornbury v Le Corner [2006] EWCA Civ)

Chuck le Corner's Corner Crossword
No 4332 Set by Charlecornius

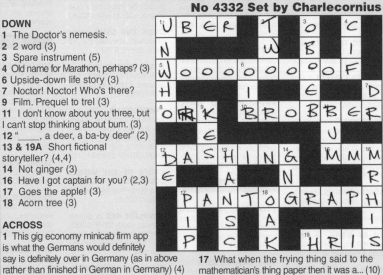

DOWN
1 The Doctor's nemesis.
2 2 word (3)
3 Spare instrument (5)
4 Old name for Marathon, perhaps? (3)
6 Upside-down life story (3)
7 Noctor! Noctor! Who's there?
9 Film. Prequel to trel (3)
11 I don't know about you three, but I can't stop thinking about bum. (3)
12 "____, a deer, a ba-by deer" (2)
13 & 19A Short fictional storyteller? (4,4)
14 Not ginger (3)
16 Have I got captain for you? (2,3)
17 Goes the apple! (3)
18 Acorn tree (3)

ACROSS
1 This gig economy minicab firm app is what the Germans would definitely say is definitely over in Germany (as in above rather than finished in German in Germany) (4)
5 Dog's biggest word (10)
8a (Cryptic) Horrible acorn tree (3)
8a (Quick) Broken pig (3)
8a (Kids) ____ & Indy - TV prog (3)
10 "Who stole your diamonds, b'ma'am?" (7)
12 ____ for a living (7)
15 These three American chocolates are delicious (1,1,1)
17 What when the frying thing said to the mathematician's thing paper then it was a... (10)
19 See 13 down!

Solution to Prize Corner Crossword No 4331
DOWN: 11. Teste. 17. Chokey. ACROSS: 3. Arthurask. All other answers, down and across: Artichonke.
1st prize winner (flying boat) Ms S. Mesgetti, Codge. 2nd prize winner (flying hat) Ms S. Mesgetti, Codge. Congratulations to both of you, again!

happily ever after. The end. Fram 810324

AREN'T PAT

COLLECTION OF MOUNTAIN BIKES. Divorce hence quick sale. £500 per 10 bikes, or £14,000 the lot. Call Steve on 01999 663642

SMART SNOWSHOES. Used once. Great for snowman weddings. £10 or £18 the pair. Call Sockford 657292

FORGOTTEN WHAT YOU CAME UP HERE FOR? Portable roof reminders fitted to all roovs. Gilbertson-Sullivan Roof Reminders. Molford St Malcolm. www.remindersforroovs.co.uk

FOR SALE: FOUR SAILS. £40. Oar (newer, rougher) £5. Or near offer. Buy all two correct. Buyer to collect. BOX FE8664

MORPHY RICHARDS American Style kettle. Boils 6ft of water in under 3 days. Boiled ice dispenser. £200 ono BOX FE8240

ADULT WET SUIT. Pissed myself after Best Man's speech. £20 ono 01999 755 421

DOLLS' HOUSE. 5 bedroom. Good access to local dolls' amenities/schools. Local dolls' authority building approval for extension above the garage. Plans available. £70 Wripple 529969

2-MAN POP-UP TENT. Used a couple of times, but men never popped up. Hence selling for spares. £35 01999 244561

BATH IN A BAG. Everything you need for a relaxing bath, including 75 litres of piping-hot water, in one unwieldy bag. Includes seasoning (look for the little blue Epsom salts bag!) Box FE81114

BROKEN ATM MACHINE. Selling due to constant money issues. £1 ONO 01999 740080

PORTABLE AIR PUTRIFIER. Putrifies any room. £1 or doesn't matter. BOX FE8090

FINGERS OF FUDGE, Gold, Dave Allen's. Any fingers possible. BOX FE8766

BACK AND FRONT massage chair. Happy/Unhappy ending settings. £110 BOX FE8003

BUYER TO COLLECT. Came into my shop a week ago, paid for stuff, but won't go home. £HELP 01999 913334

THE WICKER 3-Piece Suite: Two-seater settee and 2 armchairs. Settee has central hatch to fit one willing, king-like virgin fool. Fire safety labels slightly burnt. £85 Whoft 323235

PACKET OF POLOS. Found in washing machine filter. Mint condition: poor. £1. 01999 554588

POT OF BABY A UM POWDER. Needs a little TLC. £2 01999 600858

COMPILATION CD of 90s female hip hop with several obvious tracks missing. Also hip hop CD by someone called " one o ". Needs TLC. £3 01999 214300

BLACK AND WHITE singed photo of A an it hmarsh. In need of LTC. £2.50 ONO 01999 970677

ASSORTED HOSTAGES. Call for full details and demands. Will not negotiate. 01999 756283 and ask for Chris or Sheila.

GREY "TUNGLE" BULGARIA doll. Also full set of Jew Randoo Ranell Peas and original classic Roo-bick Scoob. Please call to check details and prices. Telesales ad person quite young. £25 ono. 01999 711409

15 x 12ft BURSTY CASTLE. Make your child's birthday party go with a bang. Used once. Call Mr Hollyhock on 01999 644572

BUNGLEBONCE

BRICKS AVAILABLE. Mixed. Will deliver through your windows. £50 Call Vince on the usual number. No funny business guaranteed.

The Framley Examiner

The Framley Examiner will celebrate its 1 m,ill,ion th classified ad by printing a copy of YOUR classified advert for you in 24-carat gold! For you to own!

Good luck to all Our readers!

Call or e-mail Damiun Clavalier on the usual FRMALEY CLASSIFIDS e-mail number

COLLAPSIBLE WHEELCHAIR. Also selling bendy crutches. £40. Fracton 844194

BETAMAX OF 1979 concert 'The 3 Degrees and the 3D Bee Gees LIVE in London'. Includes red and green cellophane glasses with cardboard lenses. £8 Bellenden 900455

FLYMO RIDE-ON QuimTrim and BikiniEdger with 5 replacement clippings bags (full) £24.

NAHTZEE Non-PC, possibly racist 1970s dice game. Inappropriate 'Colonial' box art. Highly collectible. No police please. POA BOX FE8741

SOFT SERVE ICE CREAM machine and toboggan. Great for parties. £180 Buyer to collect (Mail-on-Sunbury area) 01999 768585

FARROW AND BALL memorabilia. Much loved double act. Tour programmes, tickets, swatches, catalogues, signed VHS of Brush Boys, certificate of authenticity from Tommy Farrow & Bobby Ball. POA. 01999 566510

AWOPBOPALOOBOP

STOOLPIGEONS. Brown with sweetcorn beak. Also shitehawks. Distinctive garden ornaments. Call for catalogue. 01999 718525

400+ BACK ISSUES of Carp Fishing Magazine. Last week's issue. Unwanted ram-raiding gift. £12. 01999 466361

FOR SALE Diorama of Parisian river guano, entitled 'Bat Shit In Seine'. Can't remember what provoked me to make it, but it didn't bring her back like the man said it would. Box FE 9610. 01999 568180

NIKE TRACKSUIT BOTTOMS £10. Adidas tracksuit willies £5 each. 01999 653282

SET OF FAUX LEATHER dining chairs. £45. Need a clean, but can't be arsed. Buyer to collect. Chairs need cleaning. Awful state. Clean them, I'll buy them back off you. I'll give you £50. There's a fiver in it for you. Don't make me look at the chairs. Red leather. Clean my chairs. What is it? Don't know. Skidmarks. Don't ask. Easy to clean. £45. Dirty chairs. I've been a bad boy. £50 / £45. Chairs. 01999 643220

PIRATE DVD PLAYER. Yohoho 7C model. Parrot subtitles. Bosun's commentary. Black spot on screen. Wired for Spanish mains. £25. 01999 277511

YOU'VE TRIED THE BEST now try to rest. Framley 01999 000001

4 FUNCTION SLOW COOKER. Cook / cook / cook / cook. 1 function really. £20. 01999 925611

JESUS, JOSEPH AND MARY, MUNGO AND MIDGE bath towel. Not blasphemous (Methodist / CoE guarantee) £10 01999 907228

1 MILLIONTH! CLASSIFIED AD!

FOR SALE: SOLID GOLD CLASSIFIED ADVERT. OFFERS? D. CLAVALIER, BOX FE 8023

MATTRESS FOR SALE. Used once. Apply S. Beauty, VOAPs' home, Whoft. £0.01 ono. 01999 744344

TINY MICHAELS

MAHOGANY TV UNIT / SIDEBURNS. Face mounted. Don't miss your favourite shows. £25 01999 768181

VINTAGE 'SHABBY CHIC' fish-and-chip supper. In original paper. Peas all gone, but perfect for upcycling / craft project. £35 01999 442287

DUCK EGG BLUE movie collection. Very tasteful. £5 each. Box FE 8767

BRAND NEW HACKSAW, plus work gloves and fingers. Can separate. £18 the lot or offers. BOX FE8998

LAWN FOR SALE. 200 sqm. I don't want it any more. I want lots and lots of mud. None of this horrible green land fur. It's revolting. Buy if you agree. £400. 01999 251444

KNOTS OF THE WORLD COLLECTION. Needs expert untangling. Probably worth £3 Codge 700120

COMPLETE SET of British birthday cards 1976-1985. Will not separate. Make me an offer! Tony on 01999 767691 after 2am.

BLACK LACY UNDERWEAR. Y-fronts with Superman logo. Ideal for gangbangs. Peekaboo Agadoo bra. £6 BOX FE76887

COLLECTION OF 50 Glam Rap albums including Biggie Stardust, Terminator Rex on the White Swan of Steel, De La Essex, Uzi Quatro, Roy Wood's WZA. £2 each. 01999 872910

MR MEH ICE CREAM MAKER. Makes 10 gallons of authentic Mr Meh ice cream with bits in. Complete with one unopened flavouring sachet (Vaseline?). £4 or offers. 01999 768361

PARTY VALVES

UNEATEN PACKED LUNCH. Chopped sausage and white chocolate mice. Owner to collect. £2. BOX FE8555

COLLECTION OF 1000 RADIO-CONTROLLED WASPS. Great for picnics or barbecues. Requires 1000 x AAAAAAAAAA batteries. £35 Durbiton 275108

BREEDING PAIR of fighting fish, each with own tank (Sherman M4 with working water cannon). £30 or reasonable offer. 01999 244151

ADULT NEST FETISH KIT. Fecal sacs, kinky twigs and love eggshells. One previous owner, fully fledged. £45 Cloxted 867881

LIFE-SIZE 'Friendless Rhys Jones'. Unwanted Griff. Would make a lonely Christmas present. £12 01999 874441

LIKE NEW TROUSERS man. Like real new trousers. Blew my mind. £3 Like wow. 01999 672811

BABY WALKER. Choose from one design: Roy and Des. £5ono 01999 336334

TWO PACKS UNOPENED swim pants; Pull-Ups, 7-13kg £5. One pack opened swim pants; Fall-Downs, 80-95kg £10. BOX FE8199

VEGAN CEREAL variety packs. Incl. Meatabix, Streaky Baco Pops, Mice Krispies. May contain meat. £2. 01999 465777

KIDS' MARKET STALL Colourful, easy to wash, with 100 items of plastic fruit and veg to sell. With 5-year commercial lease agreement. Pitch 57. Contact Framley Borough Council. 08999 660661

MANY HAPPY RETURNS of the Saint novelisations. Covers improved with Ian Ogilvy Magic Marker smiles. Prices on application. 01999 822522

EGG PEG

CHILDREN'S ENTERTAINER Mister LaVey. Perfect for all ages (eternal). Balloon animals (serpent / satan). Face painting (satan). Black magic. 'Do what thou wilt shall be the whole of the party.' Party bag (satan). No church halls, please. I catch fire. Pricelist on application. 01999 665665

SLINKY STAIR SPRING. Up version. Caution: very high tension. £12 01999 367884

POLISHED OAK COMMA. Ideal for bespoke wooden sentence, including finely carved genitive. We've all been there. £35 01999 657100

OH IT WAS AN APOSTROPHE. Still £35. Actually, call it £40. I'm tired of this shit. 01999 657100

DYSON BALLS VACUUM CLEANER. Full, hence quick sale. £4. BOX FE8002

2LBS OF MIXED BATTERIES and a pillowcase with my face printed on it. Guaranteed unwanted gift. £15. 01999 836299

CHEESE PLAYSET. Based on the imaginary hit sitcom 'Cheese'. Figures include Ched Danson, Briea Perlman, Yarg Wendt, Applewoody Harrelson, Babybelsey Grammar and Curdsey Alley. Please call. I have made this. It is of cheese. Please call me. Do you want to talk about cheese? I do. Call me. Cheese is ripened before a live studio audience. 01999 879710.

HAPPY HARDCORE / crazy raving. Laid by qualified DJs. No fish too little. No fish too big. Cardboard box. 01999 811320

ONCE IN A LIFETIME OPPORTUNITY to buy my entire Angel Delight collection. Two butterscotch / one pink one. A Genuine enquiries only. £offers. 01999 404566

FENDER MUSICMAN FIVE STRING VEST with spare strings, underpants and amplifier. £185 01999 761979

"KEEP OUT" SIGN with koala wanking at top of eucalyptus tree. Ideal for child's bedroom door, apart from the koala. £8 01999 877811

JOBS EARCH!

SUPER POSITION available in our wonderful quantum physics lab alongside our fantastic team. Applicants will be informed either way by 6th August. 01999 994651

SOUS-CHEF WANTED full time, at Le Jardin Des Herbes, Sockford Basin. Professional outlook and neat approach are a must. No thyme-wasters. 01999 767501

ADMINISTRATIVE ASSISTANT required for administrative assistant's assistant. Some admin. Note: we are unequal opportunity employers. . Fram. 520900

AFTER-SCHOOL CLUB ASSISTANT for Dungeon School. Ex-special forces / WWE preferred. Competitive salary / exemption from prosecution. Firearms licence. 01999 390109

KITCHENER'S PICANIC BASKETS are looking for a picanic basket tester to work in our busy picanic basket factory. £12ph. Full benefits. No bears (or bears in disguise) www.picanicbaskets.com 08999 658890

THE ROYAL OAF PUB is looking for a doofus to replace our regular knucklehead Pete. Usual duties, plus some bar work and light duncery. £40pcm. Pub located on the B1004 near Old Molford Furniture Village. 01999 118111

NO JOB? TOO SMALL? If you're ambitious but unemployed because you are under 6cm tall, we specialise in placing people like you in senior management positions. Must supply own tiny boss chair. email tommymustardseed@nojob2small.co.uk or call 01999 652201

FUNKO POPS of 1980s shadow cabinet. Merlyn Rees, Eric Heffer, Roy Hattersley. Korean import. Not available in UK. £10 each. 01999 768255

2015 APPLE MACBOOK. System wOrking. MOst alphabet keys wOrking and sOme numbers. Otherwise fine. Easy to wOrk arOund. Battery dOesn't charge. Gets very hOt. But keybOard nOt prOblem. GOOd spare if dOn't really need spare. £210 OnO. 0215 215512 (nOt real number).

ROAD CONES. Approx. 27,000, used once. Will not separate. Perfect gift for student graduation / Highways Agency function. POA BOX FE8200

DAMIUN IS BORED

HERE IS A BOX. A musical box. Wound up and ready to play. But this box can hide a secret inside. Can you guess what is in it today? (Mostly stolen socks and half-sucked antidepressants.) £8 Urling 344543

ICE AGE DVD plus Paleolithic DVD player (multi-region). Experiment successful! Call Prof Arthur Bostrom on 01999 768111

GIRLS BIKE. Genuine vintage bullying kit. With own-brand supermarket trainers and home haircutting DVD. £26 01999 633009

WORMS. Can cut to length. Ideal gift. £2pm. BOXFE8141

LE PETIT TRICOU-BÉBÉ Wooden French clown-walrus baby activity toy. squeaks and dispenses soft mushroom omelette. Must-have! Babies hate it. As seen in Sunday Times / Guardian / Telegraph parenting supplements. Neighbours have seen, so no longer required. £23 Molford St Malcolm 640091

BOOK. 330 pages. Woman on cover. £1 01999 700981

FREE MOSES BASKET. rare follow up 7" single by the Special AKA, celebrating little-known civil rights figure. £25 01999 768155

LITTLE OLD LADY

GENTLEMAN THIEF'S WORK TROUSERS. Reinforced pockets for diamond necklaces. Guaranteed rustle-proof. £30 01999 444421

ASSORTED RESTAURANT CHAIRS. Various colours. I have a very big coat. £POA 01999 45115

THANKS to our sponsor"s!

Framley Golf Course

Welcomes New Members & Visitors & Will Co-Operate With The Police

No joining fee

No riff raff

 Framley Golf Course offers 17 normal holes and one crazy one. Professionals and amateurs alike will be delighted to discover that Hole 14 is a windmill with popular monkey King Kong on top.

○ **Have a drink from the 18th hole!** (Bar under construction. Straw hire available Mon-Thu)

○ **Golf Club Hire and Golf Club Hire.** Both the golf club and golf clubs are available to hire at reasonable rates. Call for a pricelist.

○ **Our resident professional Tidal Whoops gives lessons to handicapped standard.**

○ **NOTE:** Due to its geographical location, hole 12 can only be emptied once a week on Friday afternoon. Please call ahead to check there is room in the hole for your ball.

NEW! £1 coin-operated, M60 ball dispenser (the US Army's standard golf ball dispenser since 1950. Delivers 550 balls per minute cyclic, 100 bpm rapid fire, metallic link-belt fed ideal for ground operations and pitch and putt with a muzzle velocity of 2800 feet per second.) **PARENTS ARE WARNED TO KEEP CHILDREN AND PETS CLEAR WHEN USING THE BALL DISPENSER**

FOR BOOKINGS & FURTHER INFO

TEL: 01999 968 960

Only 2 miles from the Molford St Malcolm turning on the FR404. Good foot access and excellent rail links to the mayor's house.

Benedict-Templeton-Peck
ACCUMULATOR INSURANCE

Take the risk and reap the rewards!

Take out our comprehensive six-part cover insurance package and we will pay out if ALL SIX things happen to you at once.

FOR EXAMPLE:

For just **£48** a month, we will guarantee you a **LUMP SUM PAYMENT** should an aeroplane fly into the flooded basement of your burning home which a car has just driven through causing subsidence which could affect your ability to earn.

Call us now on 01999 788 788

or visit our offices on the corner of Amundsen Halt and Denegate

---

DOES HE TAKE
SUGAR?

NO, HE GETS TOO EXCITABLE

 Framley Social Services

Tel. Framley 01999 900 900

The Sprawling Gallery

Exhibitions of sculpture, pottery, fine art & craft and paintings of Drok. Also video work and installations. **ARTIST'S MATERIALS COFFEE SHOP** Open Mon - Sat 9.35-5pm 2, Market Street, Whoft TEL 01999 499 551

FRAMLEY IMAGINAIRE VILLAGE

A new leisure complex built surrounding Framley Imaginaire FC's stadium.

The Football Dream!

Conference centre, shopping village, 10 pin football alley, fully heated indoor staff, latest pay-per-view prostitutes offering continental and full English blowjobs, superb view of spectators and ball.

Marriage ceremonies conducted in the wall at home games if a free kick is awarded against us.

We advise you to book early to avoid our bankruptcy.

Air-conditioned rooms with en-suite football match and screen door giving out directly onto the pitch.

Call 01999 424242 or Email: hostipality@imaginaire.co.uk

"WITH GENERIOUS SUPPORT FROM.."..

CARDIGAN & SON
Canoeing Funerals

"It's what he might have wanted"
- Blade McAllister
Sockford Chapter
Hell's Kayaks

Full sendoff with dignity and a cagoule.

Choice of traditional burial, or the body of your loved one delivered into the mercy of the flames in a low brace roll.

CARDIGAN & SON
109 Michigan & Smiley Road,
Ghastley St Matthew, Framley
01999 76 76 90

Discretion, courtesy, canoes

Hotel Hydro

£12.99

SWIM LUNCH OFFER!!!!!!!!!!!

3-course meal followed immediately by extensive water leisure facilities and easy transport links to Framley General Hospital afterwards.

15-32 Blegvad Avenue, Chutney.
01999 648479
www.chutneyleisure.com/watersports.html

Sockford Cycles

Sockford's biggest selection of one- and three-wheeled bikes!

SORRY! 2 sold out!

Saloon and Hatchbikes
Stupid helmets

JUST IN!

Yamaha 6-String Racing Bike

73, Mechanical Idiot Avenue, Sockford (opposite Gindy's)

Tel: 01999 592212
Fax: 01999 592213
Bike: 41-65 00 (ext 771)
Teleport: A3- 14'3"N, 11-44

P.E.KITT

Licence Architect
Whoft 8677
Mobile: Orange
or email us for
instant building

24 HOUR
PLUMBING SERVICE

Flushing a toilet? Emptying a washing up bowl? Putting a plug on the end of a chain? Hiding a tap under your pillow?

Even if you only want a new washer on a tap, I GUARANTEE it will take me 24 hours.

NO JOB TOO BIG!*

01999 542542

(*unless it's bigger than these jobs)

NEW FROM
TAIWAN
JUST 18
VIP Bubble Bath Service
Hotel / B&B
Visits
Body to Body

LUXURY SURROUNDS

01999 235576
CALL ME!
MAKE ME SHOUT

SINGLES ONLY
GLASSBLOWING NIGHTS

Fascinating Pastime! We will blow you a wife/husband/? as you watch. Remember glass partners are easier to clean and shut up.

Durbiton Glass Works, 3 Grande Marchee, Durbiton FM7
www.durbitonglass.co.uk   email: info@durbitonglass.co.uk

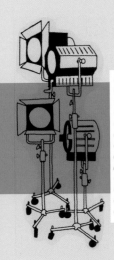

The
Framley Examiner

Behind the Magic

The Story of Framley (In Crisps)

The Framley Examiner

21st February 1994 · Framley's Top Seller since 1974! · No. 1276

Shock as -
Local Grocer Finds Tins of
Cling Peaches Stolen -

From his shelves.

Bradley Shopkeeper Norris Roman was subjected to a shock, when he returned from a trip to the Supermarket to find that two tins of cling peaches had been deliberately taken and put somewhere else by somebody, almost certainly, say police, not him. Mr Roman, 15, said he was both "horrified and delighted" by the theft. "I've been myself for over thirty years, and in more than two of them I have never seen anything like this" he bemoaned.

by SUE MORON

Chief Supt. Lomax Castellan IV, of Midford Special Weapons and Tactics Division, said "This is an extremely serious crime. We are treating it as murder.

Mr Roman has been put through a terrible psychological ordeal, particular by my officers by my officers by my officers by my officers by my officers by my officers."

Mr Roman, a professional set critic and fashion, is offering a reward of a tin of shredded pineapple for information leading to the arrest of his wife.

Professional footballer, Mr Roman Norris, puts a brave but ugly face on.

The twelve year old grocer had to be restrained by nurses when leaving the magistrates Court where he has been living for the past million years.

A hotline for anyone concerned that a relative may have been killed in the theft has been established, and will be manned by Roger DeCountey and Scotty Boor until yesterday.

Menace To Society
"menace to society"

Local pop group "Menace to Society" have been labelled a "menace to society" by two Framley pensioners. The two splinters, Janet Thanet and Mary Carey, complain that they have not been able to "sleep" since the band started shouting at them.

The pop group's noisy vigil began two years ago, and the pensioners are now starting to complain of difficulty sleeping.

The pop group's lead singer, Hutton Hutton, complains that, although he admits screaming at the women for the past twenty six months, no-one has heard their side of the story.

"They started it. Those two old ladies follow us round all day, shouting. It's just noise, really, no 'tuns'," complains Hutton. "We're just getting our own back," he added.

Menace - "Shouted"

Local bye-laws set to change

Arson, murder, rape and child abuse may all soon be illegal in Framley if a proposed review of local bye-laws goes ahead.

Councillor Honey Whitlow proposed the review at a meeting of the Honourable Guild of Gentlemen last Tuesday. He has not been seen since.

A spokesman for everyone declined to complain.

Mrs Thanet was 82. Donations can be sent to The Royal Northern Hospital for the Dead, Sceptry Road, Deeby Doo, Manchester. The case continues.

Bargain's!! Bargain's!! Bargain's!!
SALE NOW ON
Up to 50% off -

Doddery old fools · Pensioners on Wet patches · Miserable old cows moaning about their feet

NEWBY'S OF MOLFORD
off the A145 at Pool Corner

The firstermost Framley Examiner *from around 1994, leading with a story about cling peaches.*

Why Framley? Possibly echoes of childhood holidays near Framlingham in Suffolk. Possibly the spine of some Anthony Trollopes. It just appeared, fully formed. We'd seen mock local papers before (the Pythons had done a great one), but the more we thought about it, the more we realised the secret ingredient was going to be density. Not a joke. Not a page of jokes. A whole newspaper. All of it. And every bit of it – even the weather and the price banner and the planning permission reports – was going to be stupid.

Back in 2001, internet comedy was in its infancy, shackled to sluggish 56k modems. If a joke required an image to be downloaded, you'd go off and make a cup of tea, returning to find only the top half of it was there. We worked out that a 200kB image was about a kettle's worth of data, and we could just about squash a newspaper page to that size. We vowed that by the time a reader was binning the tea bag, there would be up to 100 jokes on their screen. That was the bargain.

The Tetbury Gazette

12th March 1992 · Tetbury's Top Seller since 1974! · No. 1276

SHOCK AS -
LOCAL GROCER FINDS TINS OF
Cling Peaches Stolen -

The Tetbury Gazette, an earlier test run from 1992. Note the focus, *as ever, firmly on missing tins of cling peaches.*

The Story of Framley (In Crisps)

WE MET at school (though the brothers had met earlier) and made each other laugh.

In 1991, having left school, we went on a very ill-advised holiday together in a tiny 1970s caravan in Holland-on-Sea, a gruesome, pickled-onion-saturated week of which this book can in many ways be said to be a direct consequence.

About a decade later, in 2001, we sent a batch of material to Charlie Brooker to see if he wanted any for his TV Go Home website. He sent us a nice four-lettered email telling us the material was "good, and you cunts know it is, so piss off and do your own website". We asked him how that was done, and he said it cost about £20, that this was what he'd done, and, most excitingly, nobody could stop you. He also showed us how to do a thing where you put an overlay of a horizontally flipped newspaper page at 5% opacity over the top of your layout and it looks like it's been scanned from newsprint. (He'd not done that for TV Go Home, but we'd noticed it on a Fred Basset spoof he'd drawn, and asked for the secret.) That was all we needed.

The idea for a spoof local newspaper had been buzzing around for a while. The name *The Framley Examiner* had existed since about 1994, when a dummy page was given to a college rag mag as a back-page filler *(left)*.

Joel and Rob being interviewed by BBC Radio 6 Music's Andrew Collins, presumably about cling peaches.

We designed eight pages, published them anonymously, and emailed twelve friends. Within 24 hours we were being sent the link back from all corners. "Have you seen this?" That seemed promising. Two weeks later, incredibly, we had a book deal. Which meant we had to work fast. We were new and there was no back catalogue, so that first book, *The Framley Examiner*, was written almost from scratch, in a slightly boozy frenzy of laughter. A second book, *Historic Framley*, followed a year later (from which the *Gazetteer* and endpaper adverts are taken here, because we can't imagine an *Incomplete Framley Examiner* without them).

Where is Framley? We used to say it was ten miles from wherever you lived. But it was certainly informed by the anonymous Essex towns and estates where we'd grown up. We had rough equivalents of the local towns, as shorthand, and an imaginary un-map, deliberately never drawn. Framley was intended to be dreamlike and nebulous. Reading the paper was meant to feel like flipping through a local rag while very sleepy.

The demands of coming up with so much material that fast meant we needed fresh injections of smalltown, and we started going on road trips to write, and welcoming donations from newspapers from all over the British Isles. Some of those papers and places – the stentorian *Westmoreland Gazette*, the tiny *Arran Banner* (lead story: "Big Dougie plans to lose some weight") – found their way into the DNA of Framley, broadening its voice. Framley was everywhere.

It's probably the happiest we've ever been writing. The TV series never happened, though we loved writing it, and the radio pilot is one of the most joyous things we've ever been attached to, but that never made it to air either. Framley exists on the page, here, and in your mind.

And at last it is all together. Thank you to everyone who made it possible.

In the words of Mayor D'Ainty, from the town hall steps as his jetpack explodes, "I feel invincible!"

"BEHIND THE MAGIC"

The Framley Examiner - The Magic Years - 2001 - 2003

UNBOUND IS **the world's first crowdfunding publisher, established in 2011.**
We believe that wonderful things can happen when you clear a path for people who share a passion. That's why we've built a platform that brings together readers and authors to crowdfund books they believe in – and give fresh ideas that don't fit the traditional mould the chance they deserve.

This book is in your hands because readers made it possible. Everyone who pledged their support is listed below. Join them by visiting unbound.com and supporting a book today.

Andrew Adams
Phil Agius
Jussi Alantie
Benjamin Alborough
Micky Alexander
Paul Aljabar
Moose Allain
Ashley Allen
Martin Allen-Smith
David Allison
John Allison
Gary Alltimes
Vinaya Almeida
Danny Amey
Jake Anders
Fran Anderson
Jared Anderson
Stuart Ansell
Stephanie Armitage
Alfred Armstrong
Dion Ashton
Adam Atack
Luke Atkins
Ryan Atkins
James Austin
James Bachman
Katie Badman
Geoff Bailie, Lord of Sealand
Ben Baker
Nicholas Baker
Paul Baker
Rob Baker
Jeff Balaz
Baldie
Gemma Ball
Simon Ballard
Justin Banyard
Alison Barber
Dominique & Suzanne Barcz
Bill Barksdale
Paul Barrett
Victoria Barry
John Bassett
Matthew Bate
Paul Batey
Will Beard
Brycen Beck

Alex Beckett
Richard Beckett
Andrew Beehag
Hannah Beety
Joseph Begley
Gaz Beirne
Kelly Bell
Gareth Bellamy
Chirstopher Bennet
Christopher Bennett
Katie Bennett
Simon Bennett
Julian Benton
Bernadette & Kate
CJ Betts
Stephen Biggs
Celine Bijleveld
Ian Billings
Alexander Bird
Steven Birks
Suman Biswas
Matt Blackler
Jon Blaine
Ashley Blaker
Joss Blamire
Yort Blumpkwist
Dave Blundell
Julian Boardman
Will Boase
Gavin Bollan
John Bone
Kat Booth
Ken Boswell
Paul Boswell
Jools Bourne
Nicola Bourne
Neil Bourque
Cheryl Bousfield
Paul Bovey
Dan Bowen
Mark Bower
Chris Bowers
Blair Bowman
Phil Bowman
Steve Bowring
Thomas Bowyer
Jon Boxall
Stuart Boyland
Brian Brady
Neil Brand
Hal Branson
Jeremy Bray
Lucy Brennan
Alastair Brent
David Brentnall
James Brew
Garry Bridle
Melanie Briggs
Kieran Brocklebank
Robert Broke
Charlie Brooker
Brad Brooks
Chris Brooks
Scott Brooks
Ant Brown

Dani Brown
Rick Brown
Sam Brown
Simon Brown
Brian Browne
James Browne
Paul Brunger
Michael Bryan
Simon Bryant
Steve Bryant
Barry Bryce
Paul Buckley
Robin Burgess
Tom Burgess
Hazel Burke
Ross Burman
Julian Burnell
Girvan Burnside
Simon Busby
Maria Bustillos
Christian Butler
Ian Calcutt
Alan Calder
Tim Callagan
Lucy Callaghan
Simon Cam
Chris Campbell
Douglas Campbell
Gordon Campbell
Iain Campbell
Jonathan Campbell
Mark Campbell
Victoria Cargill-James
Anthony Carpendale
Alan Carter
Dom Carter
Ande Case
Neal Casey
Paul Casey
Annie Cash
Christine Cash
Liam Casserly
Steven Cassidy
David Catley
Chris Cawte
CeriLD
Eileen Chan
Gordon Chapman-Fox
Paul Cherry
Robert Chilton
Randy Chins
Mahogany Christ
David Clark
Paul Clark
Simon Clark
Ciaran Clarke
Greg Clarke
Rosie Clarke
Tom Cleaver
Daniel C Cole
Chris17 Coleman
Frankie Coleman
Joe Coleman
Peter Coleman
Rebecca Coleman

Stevyn Colgan
Alex Collier
Ben Collier
Stephen Collins
Susannah Collison
Mark Collyer
Norberto Colono
Péter Connell
Blake Connolly
Isobel Conroy
David Constable
Alex Cook
Alex Cooke
Katie Cooke
Paul Cooke
Martin Cookson
Peter Coombe
Mark E Cooper
Darren Corcoran
Christopher Javier Corfield
Joseph Costello
Katy Costello
Matthew Costelloe
Shaun Coward
Simon Coward
Christopher Cox
Paul Coxon
Martin Coyle
John Crawford
Emily Crosby
John Crowther
Simon Cudlip
Graham Cumming
Aaron Cupboard
Mark Curran
Martin Curtis
Lindsay Cuthill
William D'Ainty and Ursula Cloybeam
Glen Dallas
Laurence Niall Dampier
James Darrall
Chris Davey
David Davies
James Davies
Paul Davies
Peter Davies
Alice Davis
E R Andrew Davis
Jon Davison
Lynwen Davison
James Dawes
Andrew Dawson
Andy Dawson
Simon de Winter
deadmanjones
Jo deBank
Chris Dee
Heather Deeming
Ian Delaney
Jay Denyer
Debbie Devall
Sarah Devine
Anthony Dhanendran
Ian Diley
Gareth Dimelow

Joel Dimmock
Simon Dixon
Anthony Doherty
Alex Donohoe
Tiernan Douieb
Chris Dowling
Kevin Dowling
Maria Doyle
Katy Driver
Neil Dube
Simon Duckworth
Eddie Duffy
Liam Duncan
Mark Dungworth
Aaron Dunn
Tim Dunn
Andrew Dunne
JJ Dunning
Al Duprés
David Durose
Paul Duxbury
Katy Dyer
John Earls
Barnaby Eaton-Jones
Andrew Eccles
Sarah Eden
David Edgar
Simon Edmond
Brian Edwards
David Edwards
Geraint Edwards
Martin Eggleston
Håvar Ellingsen
Joe Elliot
Martin Elliott
Dr James Ellison
Andy Elms
Stephen Elsden
Mark Elton
Louis Emmett
Daniel England
Dave Espley
Gareth Evans
George Evans
Ian Evans
Lloyd Evans
Mark Evans
Matthew Evans
Zack Evans
Ian Evenden
Guy Fabron
Greg Fahy
Tom Fardell
Ian Feather
Victoria Fendall
James Fidler
Paul Fillery
Matthew Finch
Stephen Finch
Alistair Findlay
Kevin Fingleton
Allan Finlay
John Finnemore
Caroline Firth
Nick Firth

Billy D Fish
Gwyn Fisher
Paul Fitzsimmons
Richard Flagg
Janet Fletcher
Jonathan Fletcher
Philip Flint
Sari Flowers
Helen Ford
Neil Forsdyke
Chris Fosten
Andrew Foxley
Ben Francis
Dave Francis
Matt Francis
Oliver Frankham
Alistair Fray
Alison Freebairn
Harry French
Rossfrom Frends
Bud Fudlacker
Thomas Futter
Marty Gabel
Suzi Gage
Steve Gale
Paco B. Garcia
Paul Gardiner
Martin Gardner
Neil Gardner
Ryan Gascoyne
Roderick Geddes
Rory Geoghegan
Lance Gerrard-Wright
Rufus Gerrard-Wright
Emma Gibbs
Andy Gibson
Julie Giles
Daniel Gillett
Jeremy Gillies
Michael Gipson
Robin P. Gissing Jnr (the 2nd)
Ged Gleeson
Sara Glover
Will Goatcher
Daniel Goddard
Ben Golding
Leo Goldsmith
Rob Goodchild
Chris Goode
George Goodfellow
Stuart Goodwin
Tom Gordon
Penny Gore
Harry Gorin
George Gough
Lucy Gough
Adam Gow
Adrian Graham
Dickie Graylin
Neil Green
Nick Green
Simon Greenwood
Spike Greenwood
Phil Gregg
Eamonn Griffin

Rhys Griffith
Dave Griffiths
Matthew Griffiths
Sarah Griffiths
David Griliopoulos
Laura Grimshaw
George Grimwood
A Gunning
Owen Guthrie-Jones
Alex Hacker
Lucy Hagg
Greg Haiste
Ben Hall
Duncan Hall
Gareth Hall
Nick Hall
Steve Hall
Chris Hallam
Timothy Hallam
Stuart Halliwell
Rob Halloway
Ian Ham
Gaz Haman
Chris Hamilton
John Hamilton
Jon Hancock
Matthew Hancock
Drew Hardy
Simon Harper
Ian Harris
Jamie Harris
Jim Harris
Lawrence Harris
Norman Harris
Paul Harris
Simon Harris
Paul Harrison
Jim Haryott
Julian Haslam
Chris Hatton
Stuart Hawker
Lee Hawkins
Stephanie Hawkins
Julian Hazeldine
Chris Hazell
Dave Healy
Stephen Hebditch
Joe Hegarty
Colin Heggie
Cathy Henderson
Stuart Heritage
Mark Herron
Melinda Hey
Adrian Hickford
Dave Higgins
John Higton
Dan Hill
Roger Hill
Rosie Hill
Symon Hill
Christopher Hind
Dan Hind
Ed Hind
Alan Hitchin
Tim Hodkinson

Stephen Holbrook
Jaime Holder
John Hollinrake
Andrew Holmes
Caroline Holmes
Matt Holt
Sam Hooper
Chris Hough
Stuart Houghton
Rufus Hound
Robert Howell
Lesley Hoyles
Chris Hudson
Bernard Hughes
Jonathan Hughes
Luke Hughes
Nic Hughes
Simon Hughes
Matt Hulme
Issac Hunt
Jon Hunter
Michael Hunter
Justin Huntley
Nancy Hutchings
John Hyde
Anthony Hynes
Dave Ingham
Linus Ingoldsby
Hazel Ireland
Andrew Irvine
Mark Irwin
Darren Izzard
Carl Jackson
George Jackson
Stephen Jackson
Dave James
Pete Christopher James
Richard James
Tracy Jeffrey
Michael Jemmeson
Dan Jenkins
Karl Jermyn
Dean Johnson
Georgie Johnson
Emmy Maddy Johnston
Phil Johnstone
Alun Jones
Davey Jones
Kevin Jones
Mick Jones
Paul Jones
Rufus Jones
Tristan Jones
Harriet Judson
Lucy Judson
Mo Kanneh
Philip Kaye
Robert Kealey
Guy Kelly
Jen Kelly
Al Kennedy
Matt Kennedy
Sarah Kennedy
Dylan Kenny
Nick Kent

Stephen Kent-Taylor
Stuart Kenworthy
Molly Ker Hawn
Rachel Kershaw
Jonathan Key
Adam Khan
Dan Kieran
Colin Kiernan
Alex King
Susan A King
Nick Kirk
Alan Kirton
Andy Kitching
Filip Klofczynski
Timothy Knapman
Alan Knight
Mattie Konig
James Kontargyris
Alexander Krause
Tom Krawec
Tessa Kulik
Brian Lace
Ralph Lachmann
John Laking
Simon Lamont
Roger Langridge
Michael Larcombe
Ali Larkin
Peter Laskie
Andrew Latham
Sarah K Lawson
Elisabeth Le Maistre
Emma Levin
Jonathan Light
Chris Lines
Judith Linn
Catherine Lister
John Lloyd
Jonathan Russell Lloyd
Basil Long
Gareth Long
Mark Longmuir
Stephen Longstaffe
Philip Lovell
Faraday Lovetrumpet
Joanne Lowe
Matt Lucas
Richard Lucas
Jose Miguel Vicente Luna
Stuart Lutes
Andrew Luther
David Lydon
MM Lyle
Alex Lynch
Ross MacFarlane
Richard Mackney
Iain R MacLeod
Stuart Maconie
Sean Macreavy
Dirk Maggs
Shauneen Magorrian
Bernadette Main
Ian Malcolm
Dr Joe Mallalieu
George Mansour

Rob "Subscribe to the B3ta newsletter" Manuel
Evelyn Marsh
Chris Marshall
Ian Marshall
Jonathan "4548" Marshall
Brian Martin
Ian Martin
Neil Martin
Rob Martindill
Sharon Martiny
Charlie Mason
Jon Mason
Justin Mason
Dom Matthews
Greville Matthews
John Matthews
@MattTheRhino
Chris May
Dr Peter May
Andy Mcananey
Kieran McCallum
Ian McCann
Trevor McCarthy
Brian McCloskey
Dan McDaid
Peter McDevitt
Tom McEnroe
Michael McEvoy
Daniel McGachey
Peter McGladdery
Paul McGrory
David McGuinness
Dave McKenzie
John McKenzie
Gareth McKibbin
Steven McKiernan
Simon Mclean
Jack McLellan
Peter McMinn
Adrian McMullan
Mr. P. R. McMullan
James McMurray-Cole
Joe McNally
David McNay
Kyle McNeill
Stuart McNeill
Richard McTighe
Barbara Joan Meier
Duncan Metcalfe
Ailie Miles
Jonathan Miles
Scott Millar
Darren Millburn
Rob Miller
Scott Miller
Martin Mills
Tony Milne
@MintyMat
Tom Mitchell
John Mitchinson
Gordon Moar
Duncan Moir
Neil Moir
Tom Monger
Alison Moore

John Moore
Kerry Moore
Pippa Moore
Anna Morgan
Conor Morgan
David Morgan
Scott Morgan
Joanne Morris
Phil Morris
Will Morris
Ed Morrish
Jim Mortleman
Iain Moss
Sarah Moss
Craig Munro
Adam Murphy
Claire Murphy
Joe Murphy
Liam Murphy
Owen Murphy-Evans
Nicholas Nada
Mick Nagle
Joshua Nall
Craig Naples
Carlo Navato
Andrew Nelson
Andrew Nettleton
Ron Nevett
Robert Newell
Christopher J Newman
Dave Nicholls
Scott Nichols
David Nicol
Stewart Nolan
Chris Norsworthy
Kirk Northrop
Brian O'Neill
Mark O'Neill
Paul O'Neill
Shannon O'Neill
Ros O'Sullivan
David O'Callaghan
Phil Oakes
Nathan Odenkirk
Robert Odenkirk
Richard Ogden
Chris Ollis
Bridget Orr
Mark Oswin
Pete Owen
Christopher Owens
Ian Painter
Lev Parikian
Dean Parker
Tom Parker
Giles Pattison
Anthony Payne
Jimmy Pea
Roger Peachey
Emily Penkett
Christopher Pennell
Mike Pennell
Simon Pennell
Matt Perdeaux
Andrew Perks

Richard Perrett
Claire Perry
Will Pethen
Sarah Phelps
David Philip
Derek Phillips
Hywel Phillips
Jeff Phillips
John Phillips
Mark Phillips
Trevor Phillips
Mark Phippen
Jon Phipps
Tim Pike
Ian Pleace
Justin Pollard
Chris Ponting
Matt Poole
Simon Poole
Robert Popper
Richard Porter
William Potter
Matt Powell
James Power
Guy Pratt
Richard Preddy
Geraint Preston
Richard Price
Vincent Prince
Tim Prollins
Stuart Prouton
Robert Purkis
James, Heidi, Harri & Tom Purnell
Simon Pursehouse
Ian Purser
David Quantick
Rob Quarterman
Thomas Quigley
Karen Quinn
Susi Quinn
Gareth Radford
Shaun Rafferty
Duncan Raggett
John Rain
Mike Rampton
Chris Rand
Robert Randolph
JP Rangaswami
Mark 'Buvreh' Raynham
Steven Raynham
Geoff Read
Joe Reaney
Peter Reay
Recluse52
Michael Reed
Chris Reeves
Stephen Reid
Charlotte Reid and Jonathan Cresswell
Sean Reynard
Dylan Rhodes
Thomas Ribbits
Andrew Richardson
John Rivers
John Luke Roberts
Jonathan Roberts

Wyn Roberts
Gordon Robertson
Andrew Robinson
John Robinson
Richard Robinson
Ian Robinson @ChorleyRobbie
Eddie Robson
Mark Robson
Keith Roche
Andy Roden
Matthew Rodgers
Toby Rodgers
Steve Roffey
Matt Rooke
Ros & Monty
John Roughton
Su Rowbotham
Ronnie Rowlands
James Rudd
James Russell
Patrick Ryan
Barnaby Salton
Christoph Sander
John Sanders
Sanjay Sanghani
Rob Sargant
Kevin Sargent
Cate Schofield
Michael Scott (Dr Death)
Jason Searle
David Shah
Johnnie Shannon
Emily Sharman
Dale Shaw
Robert Shaw
Mike Sheard
Mark Shepherdson
Lynette Sherburne
David Shipway
Dan Shires
Bartosz Siepracki
Christian Simcock
Lorna Simes
Stephen Simpson
Stuart Sims
Sis
Collaterlie Sisters
Charles Skinner
Murray Skinner
Ross Smail
Janet Small
Andrew V. Smith
Dan Smith
Darren Smith
David Smith
David J. Smith
Elliot Smith
Mark Smith
Matt Smith
Nick 'Shotgun' Smith
Patrick Smith
Phil Smith
Stu Smith
Paul Smyth
David Snape

Mark Snowden
Matt Soell
Parsifal Solomon
Nick Sommerlad
Michael Sonnenschein
Tony Southgate
Spelling Mistakes Cost Lives
Dave Spencer
Sinclair Spencer
Martin Spiers
Mr Spoon
David Standen
Maureen Standen
Jason B. Standing
Lloyd Stanton
Mark Stay
Jamie Stephen
Mark Stephens
Edward Stern
Rosalind Stern
Pete Stevens
Craig Stewart
Justin Still
Gerard Stilliard
Mitchell Stirling
Dan Stockley
David Stokes
Richard Stokes
Bill Stone
Christine Stones
Jon Stones
Alistair Storer
Dawn Storey
John Stovin
Louis Strong
Ben Strowger
Gillian Faulkner's son, Stuart
Julie Stumbaugh
Terri Sturman
Tobias Sturt
Andrew Sturtevant
Lee Stutt
Neal Sussman
Gavin Sutherland
Russell Swindle
Marc Sykes
Mark Symons
Jeau-juan Tailer
Adrian Tankard
Nathaniel Tapley
Richard Tarrant
Alexis Taylor
Phil Taylor
Diane Telford
Ben Thomas
Victoria Thomas
Alexis Thompson
Marc Thompson
Sarah Thompson
Douglas Thorp
Dave Tickner
Mick Tickner
Simon Tierney-Wigg
Jason Toews
Ian Tollett

Zoe Tomalin
Colan Tonkin
Chris Torney
Ross Tregaskis
Steve Tregidgo
Jonathan Treml
Sarah Trevarthen
Jason Trout
David Turnbull
Iain Turner
Martin Turner
Peter Tye
David Tyler
Rgovula Uncleshanks
Jo Unwin
Claudine Vant
Guy Veale
Jennifer Venn
Mark Vent
Angel Victorio
Paul Vincent
Sean Vrabel
Richard Vranch
Simon Wagstaff
Richard Wainman
Martyn Waites
Graham Wakley
James Wallin
Eleanor Walsh
Craig Ward
David Ward
Matt Warren
Daniel Wasserman
Tom Waterman
Steve Watts
Ryan Watts-Blirdsnest
Tony Way
Chris Webb
Josh Weinstein
Jim Wells
William Wells
Levin Wheller
Stuart Whitaker
Kris Whitmore
David Whittam
Jason Whyte
James Widden
Chris Wignall
Jennifer Wigzell
Natasha Wilding
Tom Wiles
Daniel Wilkin
James Wilkinson
Philip Wilkinson
Chris Williams
Danny Williams
Elric Williams
Gareth Williams
Glen Williams
Nik Williams
Si Williams
Paul Barry Willis
Gavin Wilson
Will Wivell
Lucy Wood

Adrian Woodfield
Paul Woodfield
Peter Woodman
Nick Wookey
Alex Wright
Chris Wright
Joe Wright
Katharine Wright
Tom Wright
Jamie Wyver and Paul Brown
Joel Young
Peter Young
Adrian Zak
Julie Zeraschi

Love and thanks to

Cariad,

Daisy,

Doddy,

Douglas,

Ivor,

Julia,

Nathalie,

Sue,

Stanley

and our parents.

xxxx